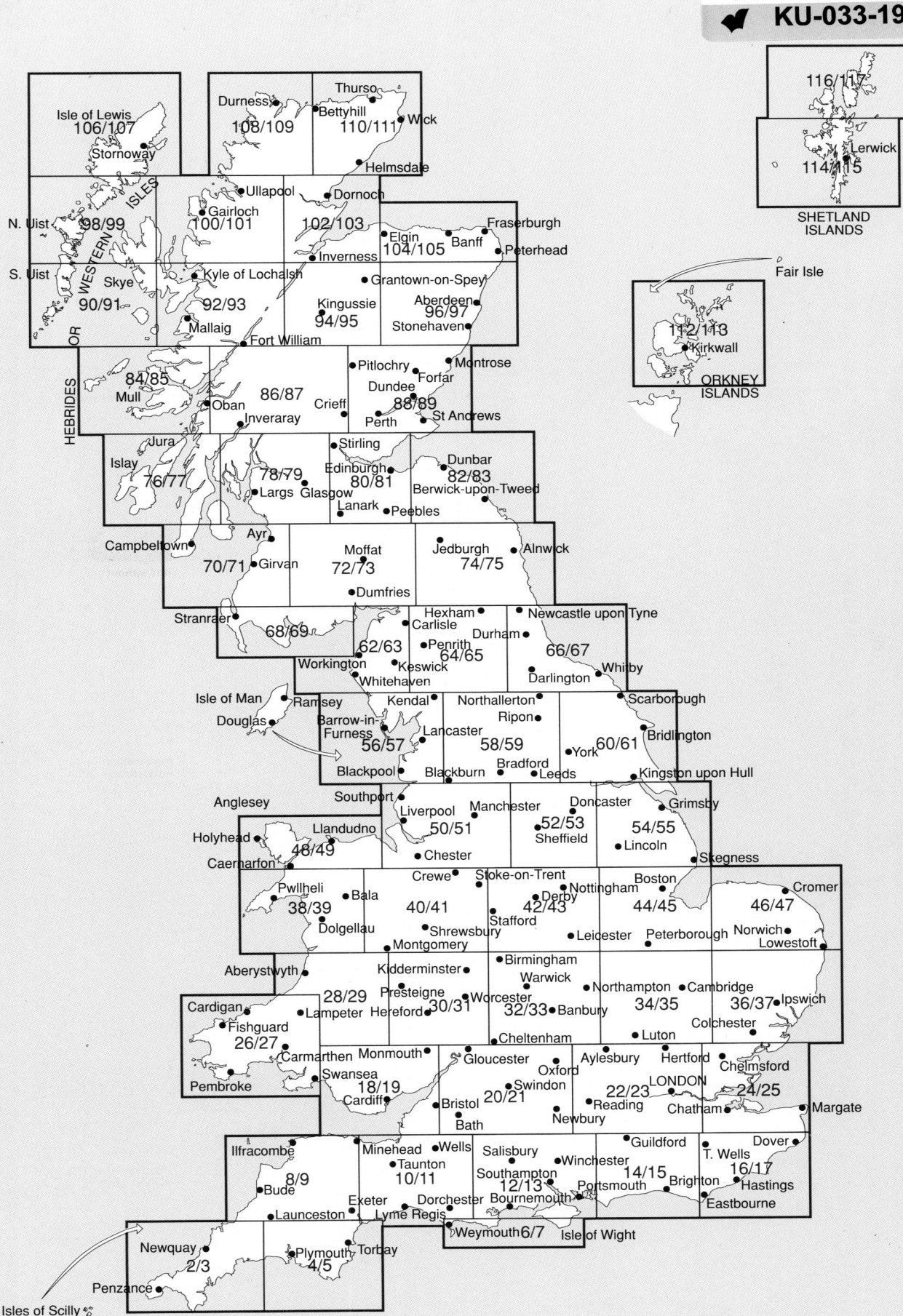

116/117

114/115

SHETLAND ISLANDS

Fair Isle

112/113
Kirkwall

ORKNEY ISLANDS

Isle of Lewis
106/107
Stornoway

Durness
Bettyhill
Thurso
Wick
108/109
110/111

Helmsdale

Ullapool
Dornoch
Gairloch
100/101
102/103

Fraserburgh
Elgin
Banff
Peterhead
Inverness
104/105

N. Uist
98/99

WESTERN ISLES

S. Uist

Skye
Kyle of Lochalsh
92/93

Grantown-on-Spey

90/91
94/95
Kingussie

Aberdeen
96/97
Stonehaven

Mallaig
Fort William

HEBRIDES

84/85
Mull
86/87
Oban
Inveraray
Crieff

Pitlochry
Forfar
Montrose
Dundee
88/89
Perth
St Andrews

Jura
Stirling
Islay
76/77
78/79
Largs
Edinburgh
80/81
Glasgow
Lanark
Dunbar
82/83
Berwick-upon-Tweed
Peebles

Campbeltown
Ayr
70/71
Girvan
Moffat
72/73
Dumfries
Jedburgh
74/75
Alnwick

Stranraer
68/69
Hexham
Carlisle
Newcastle upon Tyne
62/63
Penrith
Durham
Workington
64/65
66/67
Whitby
Keswick
Whitehaven
Darlington

Isle of Man
Ramsey
Kendal
Northallerton
Scarborough
Douglas
Barrow-in-Furness
Ripon
Lancaster
60/61
Bridlington
56/57
58/59
York
Blackpool
Blackburn
Bradford
Kingston upon Hull
Leeds

Anglesey
Southport
Doncaster
Grimsby
Liverpool
Manchester
Holyhead
Llandudno
50/51
52/53
54/55
48/49
Chester
Sheffield
Caernarfon
Lincoln
Skegness

Crewe
Stoke-on-Trent
Boston
Pwllheli
Bala
Nottingham
Cromer
38/39
40/41
Derby
44/45
46/47
Dolgellau
42/43
Stafford
Shrewsbury
Peterborough
Norwich
Montgomery
Leicester
Lowestoft

Birmingham
Aberystwyth
Warwick
Kidderminster
Northampton
Cambridge
Cardigan
28/29
Presteigne
34/35
36/37
Ipswich
Fishguard
Lampeter
Hereford
Worcester
32/33
Banbury
Colchester
26/27
30/31
Cheltenham
Luton

Carmarthen
Monmouth
Gloucester
Aylesbury
Hertford
Chelmsford
Swansea
Oxford
LONDON
18/19
Swindon
22/23
24/25
Pembroke
Cardiff
Bristol
20/21
Reading
Chatham
Margate
Bath
Newbury

Guildford
Dover
Ilfracombe
Minehead
Wells
Salisbury
Winchester
T. Wells
8/9
Taunton
Southampton
14/15
Brighton
16/17
Bude
10/11
12/13
Portsmouth
Hastings
Exeter
Dorchester
Bournemouth
Eastbourne
Launceston
Lyme Regis
Weymouth 6/7
Isle of Wight

Newquay
2/3
Plymouth
Torbay
4/5
Penzance

Isles of Scilly

ORDNANCE SURVEY

Road Atlas of

Britain

BCA

LONDON NEW YORK SYDNEY TORONTO

This edition published 1994
by BCA by arrangement with

Ordnance Survey and Hamlyn
Romsey Road   an imprint of
Maybush   Reed Consumer Books Ltd
Southampton   Michelin House, 81 Fulham Road
SO9 4DH   London SW3 6RB

CN 4112

First published 1983

Sixth edition 1994
First impression 1994

The representation in this atlas of a road is no evidence
of the existence of a right of way.

A catalogue record for this atlas is available from the British Library

Printed in Italy

CONTENTS

Front Endpaper: Legend, Key to map pages

IV Route planning

X Restricted motorway junctions

XI Motorways and major routes

XII Road signs

XIV Radio information and distances

XVI National Parks, Forest Parks and Long Distance Paths

1 Legend to 1:250 000 scale maps

2 Ordnance Survey 1:250 000 scale maps

118 Central London

125 Street index to Central London maps

130 Town plans

130 *Aberdeen, Bath, Birmingham*
131 *Blackpool, Bournemouth, Bradford, Brighton*
132 *Bristol, Cambridge, Canterbury*
133 *Cardiff, Cheltenham, Chester*
134 *Coventry, Croydon, Derby, Dundee*
135 *Durham, Edinburgh, Exeter*
136 *Glasgow, Gloucester, Hull*
137 *Leeds, Liverpool*
138 *Leicester, Manchester, Middlesbrough*
139 *Milton Keynes, Newcastle, Oxford*
140 *Norwich, Nottingham*
141 *Peterborough, Plymouth, Portsmouth, Reading*
142 *Salisbury, Sheffield, Shrewsbury*
143 *Southampton, Stratford, Swansea, York*

144 Airports

144 *Aberdeen, Birmingham International, East Midlands,*
    Edinburgh, Glasgow, Stansted
145 *Gatwick, Leeds and Bradford, London Luton,*
    Manchester, Prestwick
146 *Heathrow*

147 Channel Tunnel terminals

148 Urban areas

148 *London area*   158 *Leeds and Bradford area*
152 *Birmingham area*   160 *Liverpool area*
154 *Edinburgh area*   161 *Manchester area*
156 *Glasgow area*   162 *Newcastle area*

163 Index to 1:250 000 scale maps

Back Endpaper: M25 and routes into London
              Routes into Liverpool and Manchester

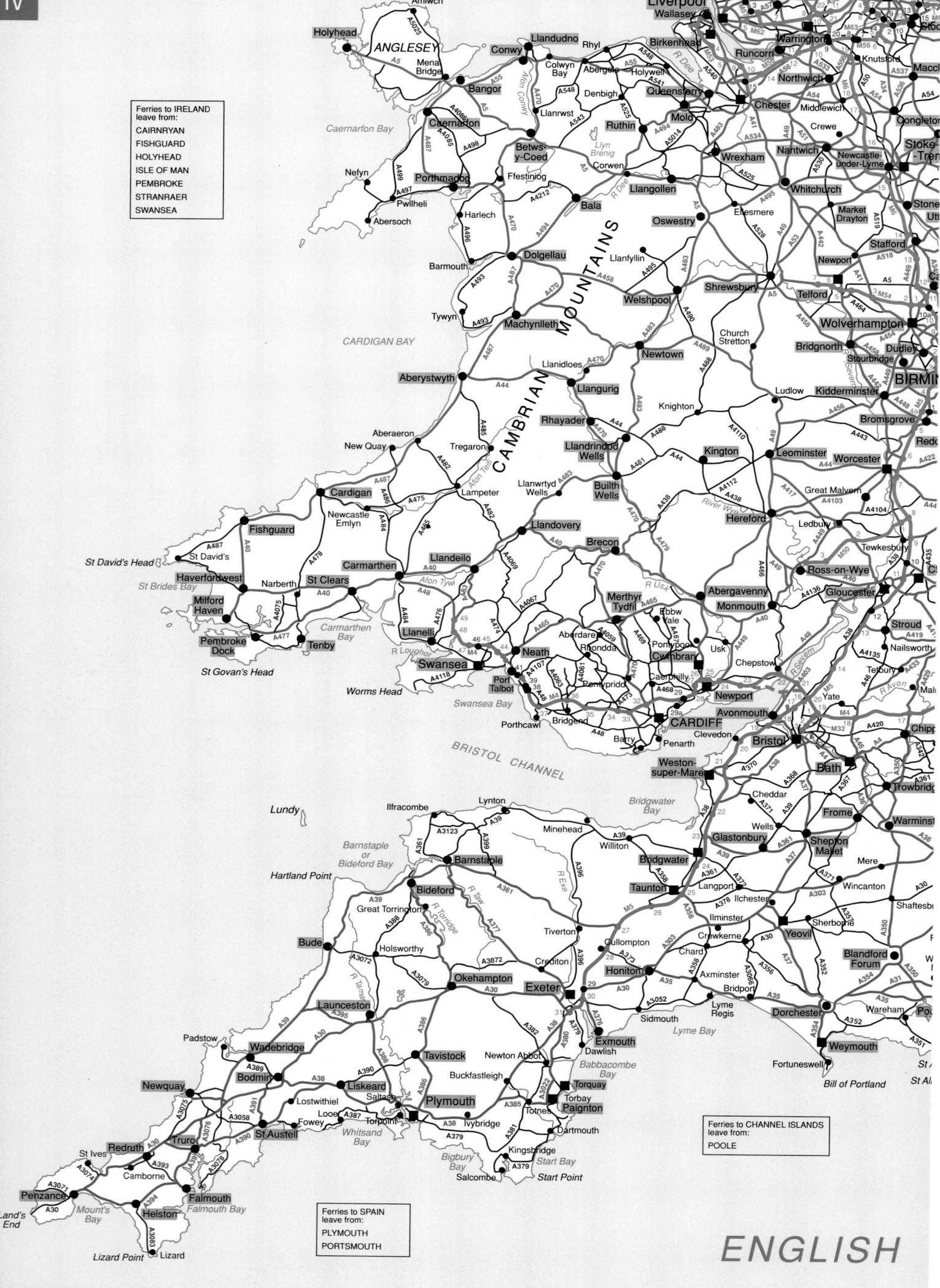

IV

ENGLISH

ROUTE PLANNING

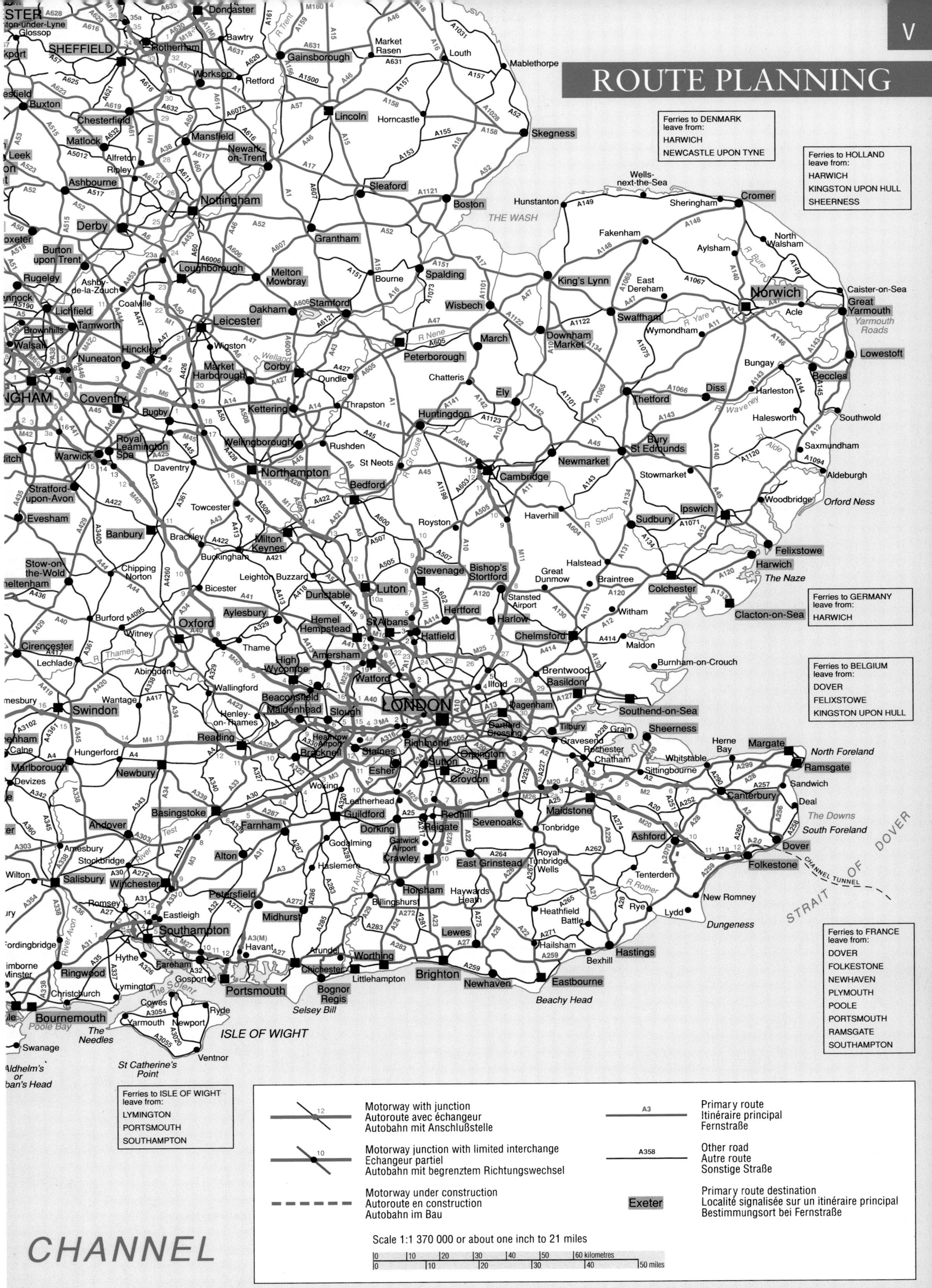

Ferries to DENMARK leave from:
HARWICH
NEWCASTLE UPON TYNE

Ferries to HOLLAND leave from:
HARWICH
KINGSTON UPON HULL
SHEERNESS

Ferries to GERMANY leave from:
HARWICH

Ferries to BELGIUM leave from:
DOVER
FELIXSTOWE
KINGSTON UPON HULL

Ferries to FRANCE leave from:
DOVER
FOLKESTONE
NEWHAVEN
PLYMOUTH
POOLE
PORTSMOUTH
RAMSGATE
SOUTHAMPTON

Ferries to ISLE OF WIGHT leave from:
LYMINGTON
PORTSMOUTH
SOUTHAMPTON

Legend

Motorway with junction
Autoroute avec échangeur
Autobahn mit Anschlußstelle

Motorway junction with limited interchange
Echangeur partiel
Autobahn mit begrenztem Richtungswechsel

Motorway under construction
Autoroute en construction
Autobahn im Bau

A3 — Primary route
Itinéraire principal
Fernstraße

A358 — Other road
Autre route
Sonstige Straße

Exeter — Primary route destination
Localité signalée sur un itinéraire principal
Bestimmungsort bei Fernstraße

Scale 1:1 370 000 or about one inch to 21 miles

0 10 20 30 40 50 60 kilometres
0 10 20 30 40 50 miles

CHANNEL

THE WASH

STRAIT OF DOVER

CHANNEL TUNNEL

ISLE OF WIGHT

The Needles

Poole Bay

The Solent

Yarmouth Roads

Orford Ness

The Naze

The Downs

South Foreland

North Foreland

Beachy Head

Dungeness

Selsey Bill

St Catherine's Point

St Aldhelm's or St Alban's Head

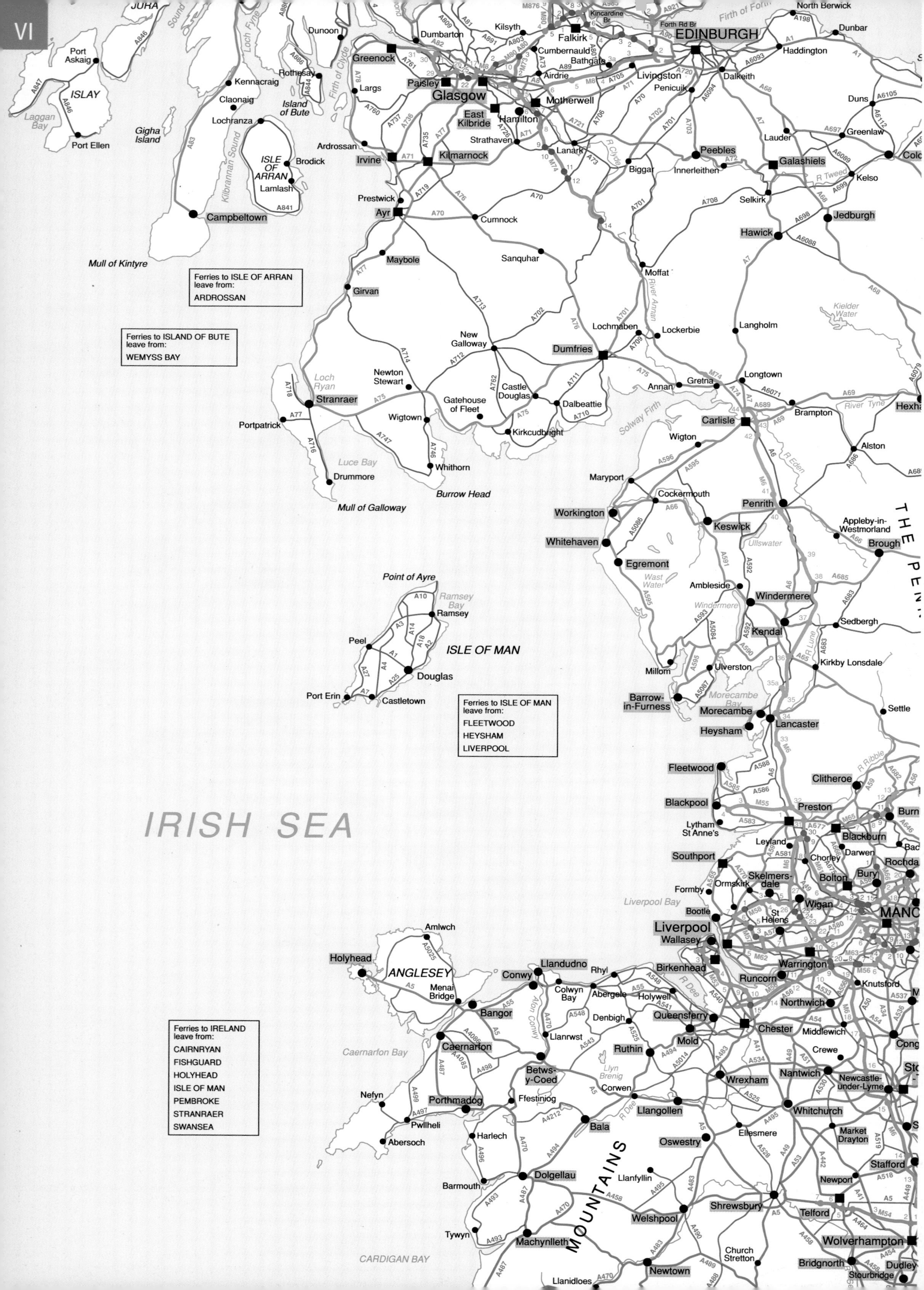

JURA
Port Askaig
ISLAY
Port Ellen
Laggan Bay
Kennacraig
Claonaig
Lochranza
Gigha Island
Kilbrannan Sound
ISLE OF ARRAN
Brodick
Lamlash
Campbeltown
Mull of Kintyre
Dunoon
Rothesay
Island of Bute
Loch Fyne
Firth of Clyde
Greenock
Largs
Ardrossan
Irvine
Kilmarnock
Prestwick
Ayr
Cumnock
Maybole
Girvan
Sanquhar
Dumbarton
Paisley
Glasgow
East Kilbride
Hamilton
Motherwell
Strathaven
Lanark
Kilsyth
Cumbernauld
Airdrie
Bathgate
Falkirk
Kincardine Br
Forth Rd Br
Firth of Forth
EDINBURGH
Livingston
Penicuik
Dalkeith
North Berwick
Dunbar
Haddington
Duns
Lauder
Greenlaw
Peebles
Innerleithen
Galashiels
Kelso
Selkirk
Hawick
Jedburgh
Biggar
R Clyde
Moffat
River Annan
Lochmaben
Lockerbie
Langholm
Kielder Water
Dumfries
Ferries to ISLE OF ARRAN leave from:
ARDROSSAN
Ferries to ISLAND OF BUTE leave from:
WEMYSS BAY
New Galloway
Newton Stewart
Loch Ryan
Stranraer
Portpatrick
Gatehouse of Fleet
Castle Douglas
Dalbeattie
Kirkcudbright
Wigtown
Whithorn
Burrow Head
Luce Bay
Drummore
Mull of Galloway
Solway Firth
Annan
Gretna
Longtown
Carlisle
Brampton
River Tyne
Hexham
Alston
Wigton
Maryport
Cockermouth
Workington
Whitehaven
Egremont
Keswick
Penrith
R Eden
Appleby-in-Westmorland
Brough
Ullswater
Wast Water
Ambleside
Windermere
Kendal
Sedbergh
Kirkby Lonsdale
Millom
Ulverston
Barrow-in-Furness
Morecambe Bay
Morecambe
Heysham
Lancaster
Settle
THE PENN
Point of Ayre
Ramsey Bay
Ramsey
Peel
ISLE OF MAN
Douglas
Port Erin
Castletown
Ferries to ISLE OF MAN leave from:
FLEETWOOD
HEYSHAM
LIVERPOOL
IRISH SEA
Fleetwood
Clitheroe
R Ribble
Blackpool
Preston
Lytham St Anne's
Blackburn
Burnley
Leyland
Chorley
Darwen
Southport
Ormskirk
Skelmersdale
Bolton
Bury
Rochdale
Formby
Wigan
Liverpool Bay
Bootle
St Helens
Liverpool
Wallasey
Birkenhead
Warrington
MANC
Runcorn
Knutsford
Northwich
Chester
Middlewich
Congleton
Crewe
Nantwich
Newcastle-under-Lyme
Stoke
Amlwch
Holyhead
ANGLESEY
Menai Bridge
Bangor
Conwy
Llandudno
Colwyn Bay
Rhyl
Abergele
Holywell
R Dee
Queensferry
Mold
Denbigh
Llanrwst
Ruthin
Wrexham
Afon Conwy
Caernarfon
Caernarfon Bay
Betws-y-Coed
Llyn Brenig
Corwen
Llangollen
Whitchurch
Market Drayton
Ferries to IRELAND leave from:
CAIRNRYAN
FISHGUARD
HOLYHEAD
ISLE OF MAN
PEMBROKE
STRANRAER
SWANSEA
Nefyn
Porthmadog
Ffestiniog
Pwllheli
Abersoch
Harlech
Bala
Oswestry
Ellesmere
Stafford
Newport
Llanfyllin
Barmouth
Dolgellau
Shrewsbury
Telford
Welshpool
Tywyn
Machynlleth
Wolverhampton
Church Stretton
Bridgnorth
Dudley
Stourbridge
Newtown
Llanidloes
MOUNTAINS
CARDIGAN BAY

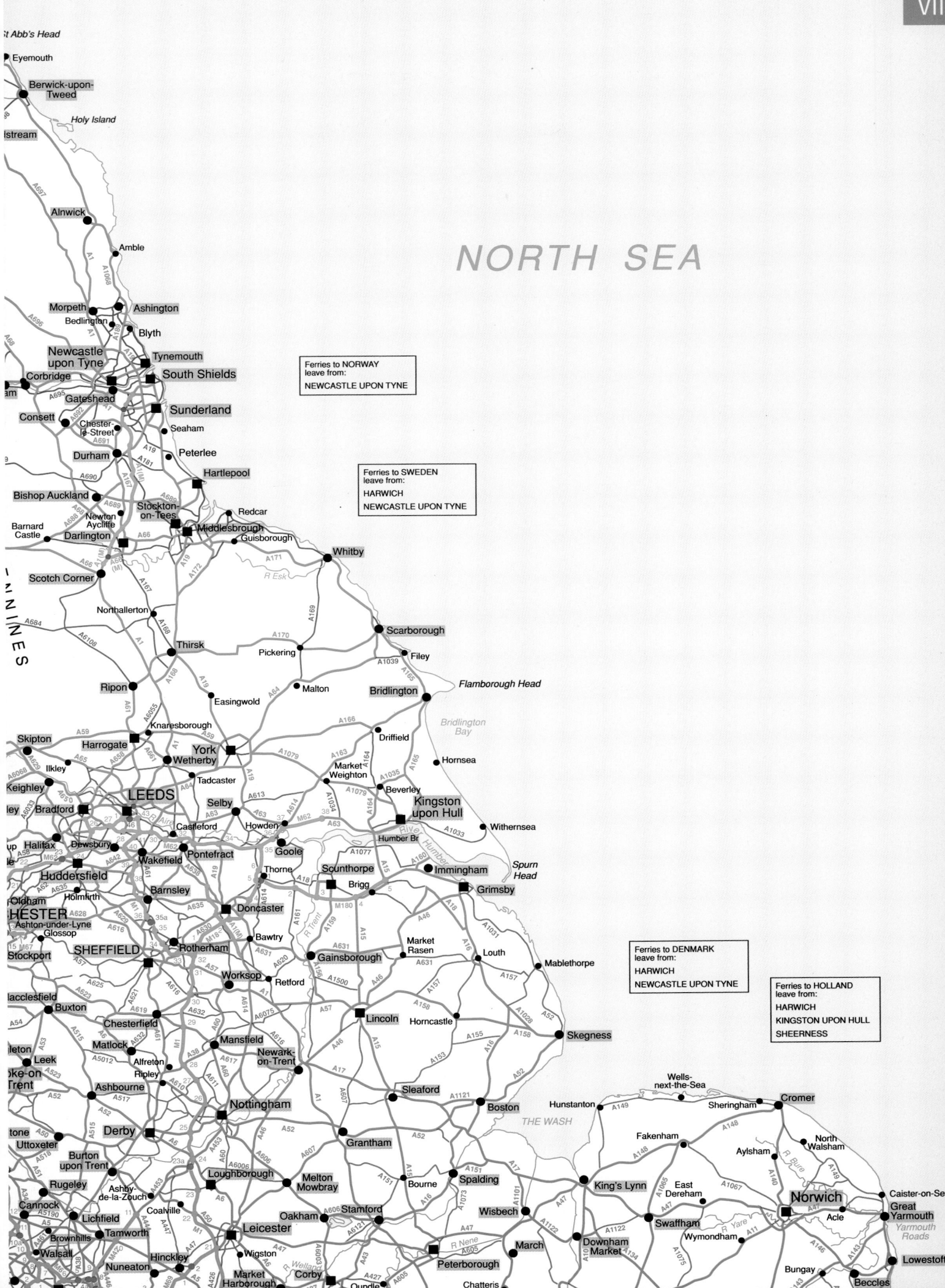

NORTH SEA

Ferries to NORWAY
leave from:
NEWCASTLE UPON TYNE

Ferries to SWEDEN
leave from:
HARWICH
NEWCASTLE UPON TYNE

Ferries to DENMARK
leave from:
HARWICH
NEWCASTLE UPON TYNE

Ferries to HOLLAND
leave from:
HARWICH
KINGSTON UPON HULL
SHEERNESS

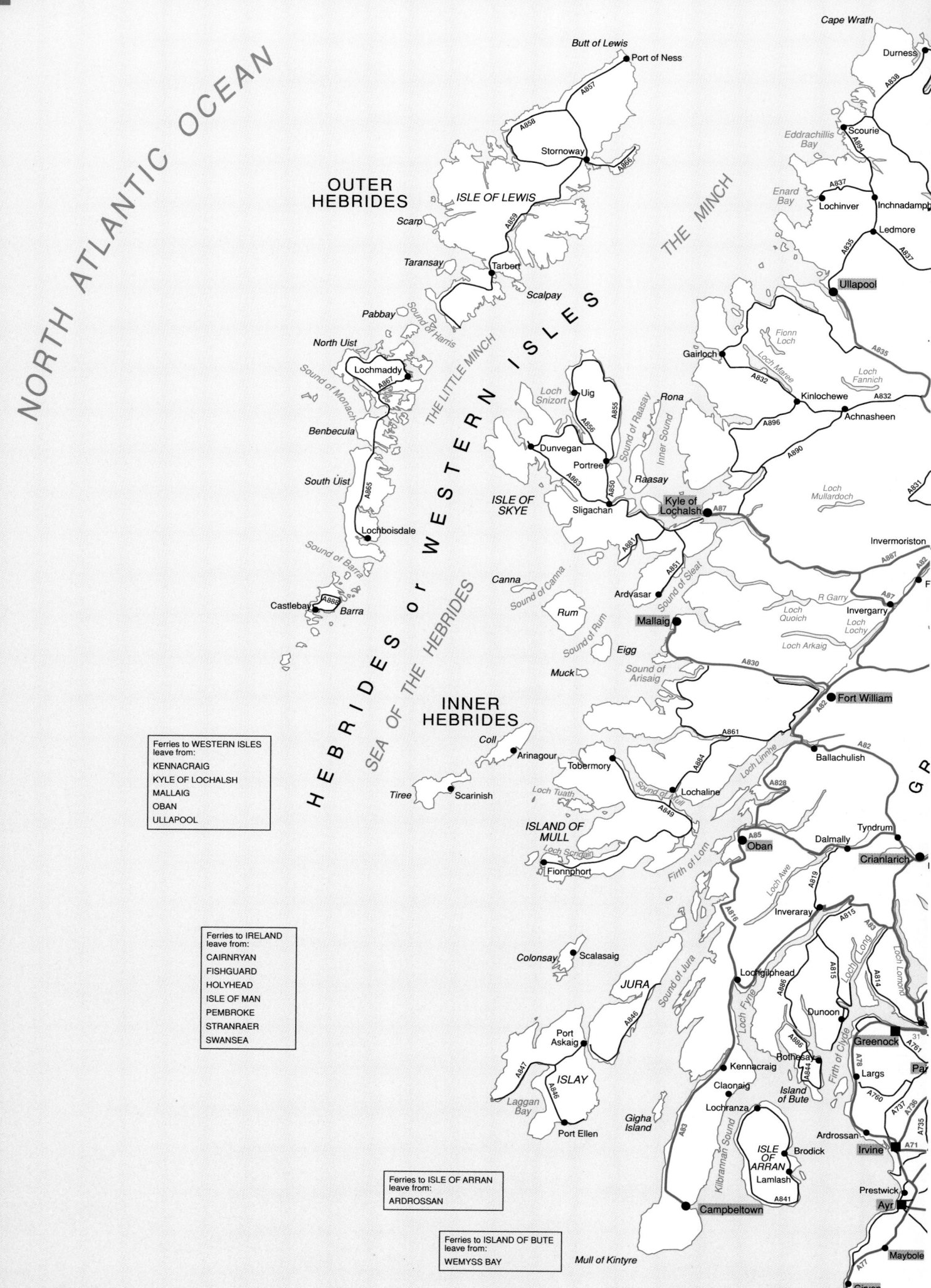

NORTH ATLANTIC OCEAN

Cape Wrath

Butt of Lewis
Port of Ness

A857

A858

OUTER
HEBRIDES

ISLE OF LEWIS
Stornoway

A866

Scarp

THE MINCH

Durness
A838
Scourie
A894
Eddrachillis Bay
A837
Lochinver
Inchnadamph
Ledmore
A835
A837

Enard Bay

Ullapool

A859

Taransay
Tarbert

A835

Scalpay

Gairloch
Fionn Loch
A832
Loch Maree
Loch Fannich
Kinlochewe
A832
A896
Achnasheen

HEBRIDES or WESTERN ISLES

Pabbay
Sound of Harris

North Uist
Lochmaddy
A867

THE LITTLE MINCH

Uig
Loch Snizort
A855
A856
Dunvegan
A863
Portree
A850
Sligachan

Rona
Sound of Raasay
Inner Sound
Raasay

A890

Loch Mullardoch
A831

Benbecula

Sound of Monach

A865

South Uist

ISLE OF
SKYE

Kyle of Lochalsh
A87

Invermoriston

A887
A82

Lochboisdale

A851
Ardvasar
Sound of Sleat

R Garry
Loch Quoich
Invergarry
Loch Lochy
A87
F

Sound of Barra

Mallaig

Canna
Sound of Canna
Rum
Sound of Rum
Eigg
Muck

Loch Arkaig

A830

Castlebay
A888
Barra

Sound of Arisaig

Fort William
A82

A861

Ballachulish
A82
A828

SEA OF THE HEBRIDES

INNER
HEBRIDES

Coll
Arinagour

Loch Tuath
Tobermory
A884
Lochaline
Sound of Mull
A849

Tyndrum

Tiree
Scarinish

ISLAND OF
MULL
Loch Scridain
Fionnphort

Oban
A85
Dalmally
Crianlarich

Firth of Lorn

Loch Awe
A819

Inveraray
A815
A83

A816

Colonsay
Scalasaig

JURA

Sound of Jura

Lochgilphead
A816
A815
Loch Long
A814
Loch Lomond

Dunoon
A885
Loch Fyne
A83

Greenock
A761
Pa

Rothesay
A844
Largs
Island of Bute
A78

Port
Askaig
A846

ISLAY
A847

Kennacraig
Claonaig
Lochranza
Kilbrannan Sound
Gigha Island
A83

ISLE
OF
ARRAN
Brodick
Lamlash
A841

A760
A737
A78
A735

Ardrossan
Irvine
A71

Laggan Bay

Port Ellen

Prestwick

Campbeltown

Mull of Kintyre

A77
Ayr

Maybole

Girvan

GR

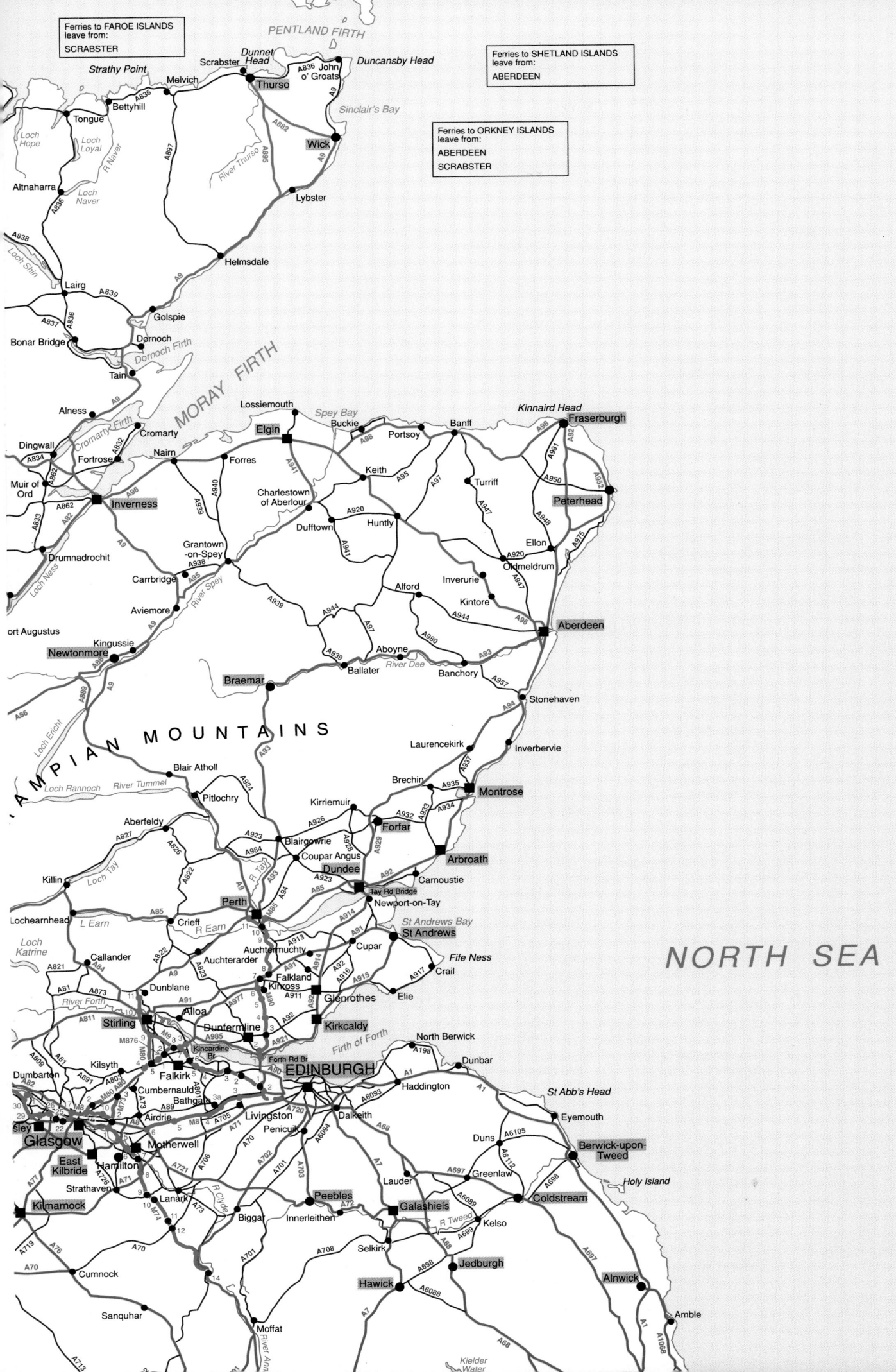

Ferries to FAROE ISLANDS
leave from:
SCRABSTER

Ferries to SHETLAND ISLANDS
leave from:
ABERDEEN

Ferries to ORKNEY ISLANDS
leave from:
ABERDEEN
SCRABSTER

PENTLAND FIRTH

NORTH SEA

GRAMPIAN MOUNTAINS

RESTRICTED MOTORWAY JUNCTIONS

M1	Southbound	Northbound
46	No access	
45	No exit	No access
44	No access	No exit
35A	No exit	No access
23A	No exit to A453	No access from A453
17	No exit	No access
7	No access	No exit
6A	No access from M25	No exit to M25
4	No access	No exit
2	No access	No exit

M2	Eastbound	Westbound
1	No access from A2 westbound	No exit to A2 eastbound

M3	Eastbound	Westbound
8	No exit; access from A303 only	Exit to A303 only; no access
10	No access	No exit
14	No exit	No access

M4	Eastbound	Westbound
46	No exit	No access
41	No access	No exit
39	No access; no exit	No exit
38		No access
29	No exit	No access from A48(M)
2	No exit or access from A4 westbound	No exit or access from A4 eastbound
1	No exit to A4 westbound	No access from A4 eastbound

M5	Southbound	Northbound
10	No access	No exit
12	No exit	No access
29	No exit	No access

M6	Southbound	Northbound
30	No access	No exit
25	No exit	No access
24	No access	No exit
20		No direct exit to M56 eastbound
10A	No exit	No access
5	No exit	No access
4A	No access; exit to M42 only	No exit; access from M42 southbound only

M8	Eastbound	Westbound
25	No access from A739 northbound	No access from A739 northbound
23	No exit	No access
22	No exit	No access
21	No access	No exit
20	No exit	No access
18		No access
16	No exit	No access
14	No access	No exit
9	No access	No exit
8		No access from A8 eastbound, A89 eastbound or M73 southbound

M9	Eastbound	Westbound
8	No exit	No access from M876 northbound
6	No access	No exit
3	No exit	No access
2	No access	No exit
1	No exit	No access

M11	Southbound	Northbound
14	No access from A1307 or A45 eastbound	No exit to A1307 or A45 westbound
13	No exit	No access
9	No exit	No access
5	No exit	No access
4	No access; no exit to A406 eastbound	No exit; no access from A406 westbound

M20	Eastbound	Westbound
2	No access	No exit
3	No exit	
11A	No access	No exit

M23	Southbound	Northbound
7	No access from A23 northbound	No exit to A23 southbound

M25	Eastbound	Westbound
5	No access to M26 from A21	No exit to A21 from M26 and no access to M26 from M25
9 (Central)	No access; no exit	
9 (North)		No access; no exit
19	No access	No exit
21	No exit to M1 southbound; no access from M1 northbound	No exit to M1 southbound; no access from M1 northbound

M27	Eastbound	Westbound
4 (West)	No access	No exit
4 (East)	No exit	No access
10	No exit	No access
12	No access	No exit

M40	Eastbound	Westbound
16	No access	No exit
14	No access	No exit
13	No exit	No access
8	No access	No exit
L	No exit	No access
7	No exit	No access
3	No exit	No access

M42	Southbound	Northbound
1	No access	No exit
7	Access from M6 only; no exit	Exit to M6 West only; no access
7A	No access; no exit	Exit to M6 East only; no access
8	Exit to M6 only; no access	Access to M6 only; no exit

M45	Eastbound	Westbound
L	No access	No exit

M53	Southbound	Northbound
11	No access	No exit

M56	Eastbound	Westbound
15	No exit	No access
9	No direct access	No direct exit to M6 southbound
8	No access; no exit	No exit
7		No access
4	No exit	No access
2	No exit	No access
1	No exit to A34 southbound or M63 westbound	No access from A34 southbound or M63 westbound; no exit to M63

M57	Southbound	Northbound
3	No access	No exit
5	No access	No exit

M58	Eastbound	Westbound
1	No exit	No access

M61	Southbound	Northbound
9	No exit	No access
3		No access
2		No access from A580 eastbound

M62	Eastbound	Westbound
14	No exit to A580; no access from A580 westbound	No exit to A580 eastbound; no access from A580
15	No exit	No access
23	No access	No exit

M63	Southbound	Northbound
7	No exit	
9	No exit to B5103 northbound; no access from A5103 northbound	
10	No exit to M56 or to A34 northbound	No exit to A34 northbound; no access from M56
11	No access	No exit
13	No exit	No access
14	No exit	No exit; no access
15	No access	

M65	Eastbound	Westbound
9	No access	No exit
11	No access	No access

M66	Southbound	Northbound
1	No exit	No access
12	No access	

M67	Eastbound	Westbound
1	No access	No exit
2	No exit	No access

M69	Southbound	Northbound
2	No access	No exit

M73	Southbound	Northbound
3	No access from A80 northbound	No exit to A80 southbound
2	No access from A89; no exit to M8 (Junction 8) or A89	No exit to A89; no access from M8 (Junction 8) or A89

M74	Southbound	Northbound
7	No access	No exit
9	No access	No exit; no access
10	No exit	
11	No access from B7078	No exit
12	No exit	No access from A70
14	No exit	

M80	Southbound	Northbound
5	No exit	No access

M90	Southbound	Northbound
10	No exit to A912	No access from A912
8	No exit	No access
7	No access	No exit

M180	Eastbound	Westbound
1	No access	No exit

M876	Eastbound	Westbound
2	No access	No exit

A1(M)	Southbound	Northbound
L	No exit to A1	No access from A1
L	Junction with A66(M), no access	Junction with A66(M), no access
5	No exit; no access	No exit
3	No access	
2	No exit	

A3(M)	Southbound	Northbound
L	Junction with unclassified road, no exit	Junction with unclassified road, no access

A40(M)	Southbound	Northbound
L	No access	No exit

MOTORWAYS AND MAJOR ROUTES

ROAD SIGNS

SIGNS GIVING ORDERS

These signs are mostly circular and those with red circles are mostly prohibitive

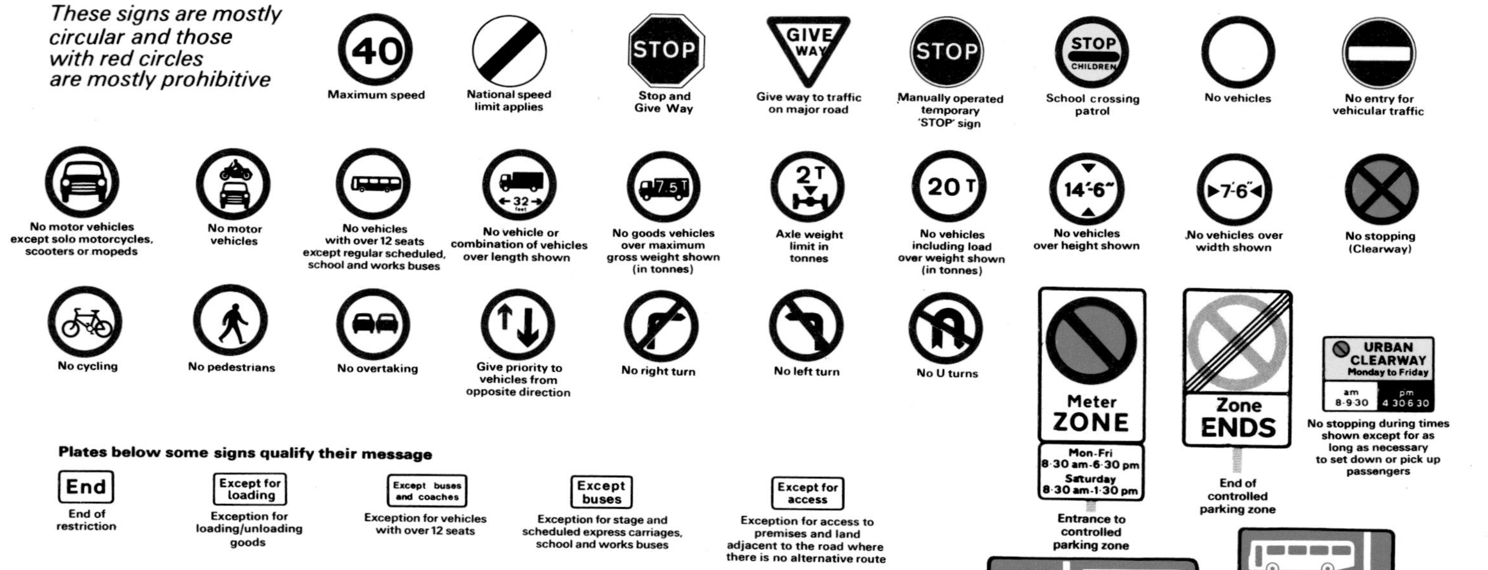
40
Maximum speed
National speed limit applies
STOP
Stop and Give Way
GIVE WAY
Give way to traffic on major road
STOP
Manually operated temporary 'STOP' sign
STOP
CHILDREN
School crossing patrol
No vehicles
No entry for vehicular traffic
No motor vehicles except solo motorcycles, scooters or mopeds
No motor vehicles
No vehicles with over 12 seats except regular scheduled, school and works buses
32 feet
No vehicle or combination of vehicles over length shown
7.5T
No goods vehicles over maximum gross weight shown (in tonnes)
2T
Axle weight limit in tonnes
20T
No vehicles including load over weight shown (in tonnes)
14'-6"
No vehicles over height shown
7'-6"
No vehicles over width shown
No stopping (Clearway)
No cycling
No pedestrians
No overtaking
Give priority to vehicles from opposite direction
No right turn
No left turn
No U turns
Meter ZONE
Mon-Fri 8·30 am-6·30 pm Saturday 8·30 am-1·30 pm
Entrance to controlled parking zone
Zone ENDS
End of controlled parking zone
URBAN CLEARWAY Monday to Friday
am 8·9·30 pm 4·30 6·30
No stopping during times shown except for as long as necessary to set down or pick up passengers
Plates below some signs qualify their message
End
End of restriction
Except for loading
Exception for loading/unloading goods
Except buses and coaches
Exception for vehicles with over 12 seats
Except buses
Exception for stage and scheduled express carriages, school and works buses
Except for access
Exception for access to premises and land adjacent to the road where there is no alternative route

Signs with blue circles but no red border mostly give positive instruction

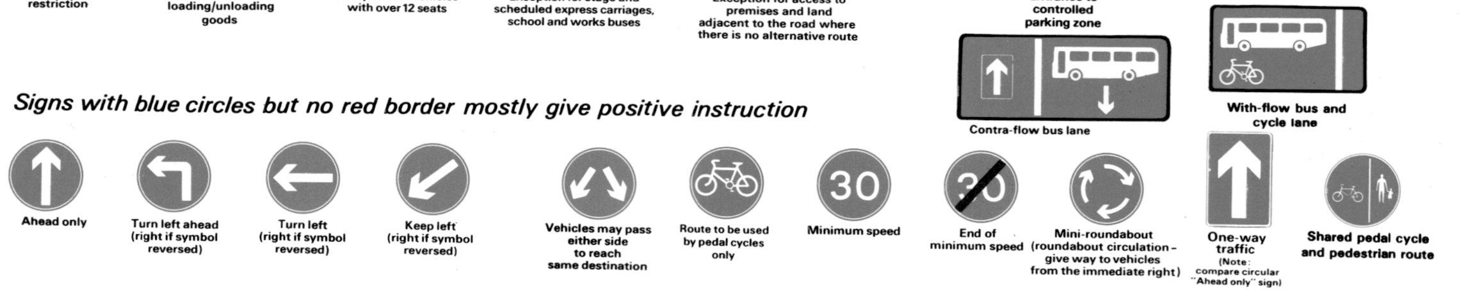
Contra-flow bus lane
With-flow bus and cycle lane
Ahead only
Turn left ahead (right if symbol reversed)
Turn left (right if symbol reversed)
Keep left (right if symbol reversed)
Vehicles may pass either side to reach same destination
Route to be used by pedal cycles only
30
Minimum speed
30
End of minimum speed
Mini-roundabout (roundabout circulation – give way to vehicles from the immediate right)
One-way traffic (Note: compare circular "Ahead only" sign)
Shared pedal cycle and pedestrian route

WARNING SIGNS

Mostly triangular

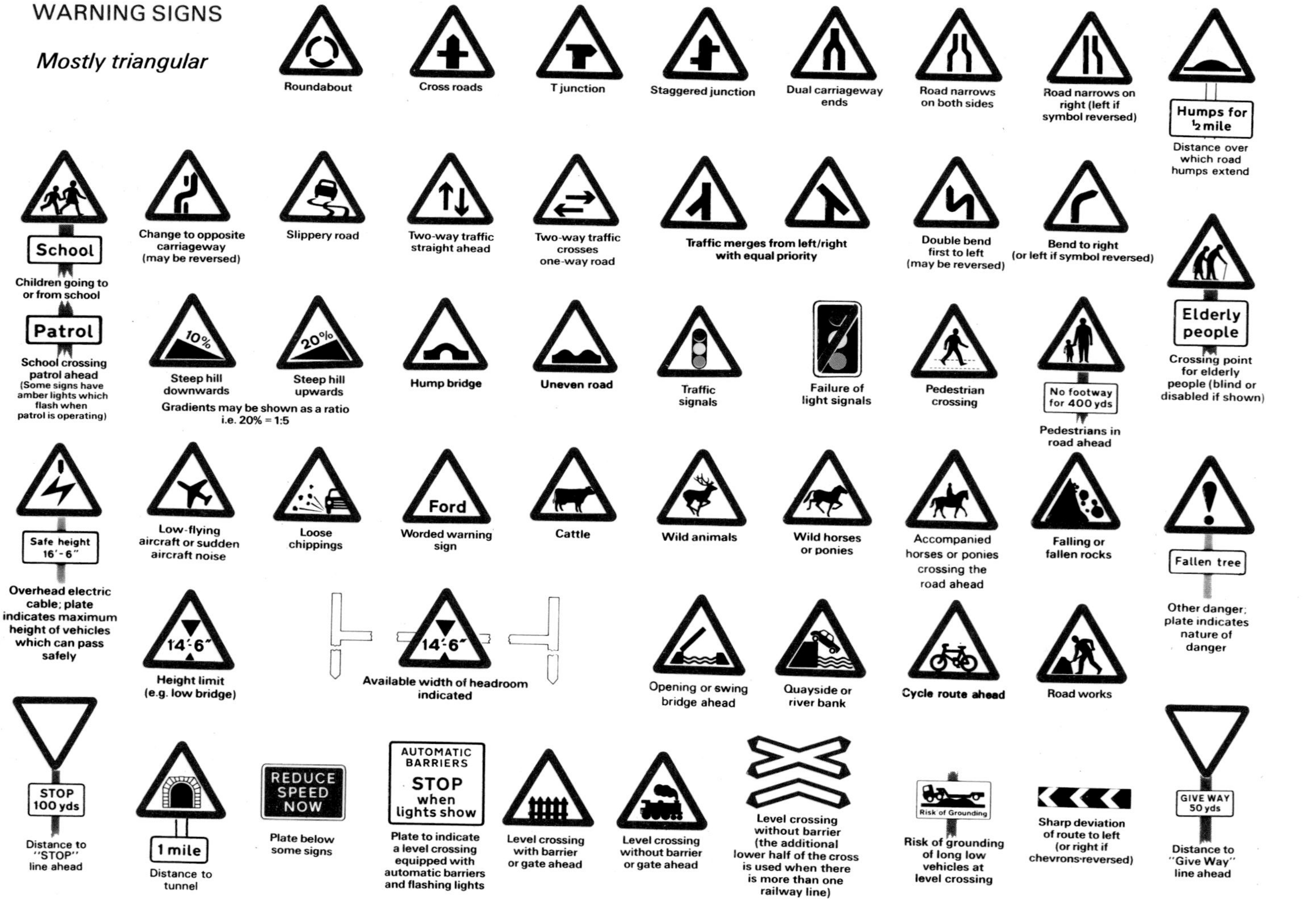
Roundabout
Cross roads
T junction
Staggered junction
Dual carriageway ends
Road narrows on both sides
Road narrows on right (left if symbol reversed)
Humps for ½ mile
Distance over which road humps extend
School
Children going to or from school
Change to opposite carriageway (may be reversed)
Slippery road
Two-way traffic straight ahead
Two-way traffic crosses one-way road
Traffic merges from left/right with equal priority
Double bend first to left (may be reversed)
Bend to right (or left if symbol reversed)
Patrol
School crossing patrol ahead (Some signs have amber lights which flash when patrol is operating)
10%
Steep hill downwards
20%
Steep hill upwards
Gradients may be shown as a ratio i.e. 20% = 1:5
Hump bridge
Uneven road
Traffic signals
Failure of light signals
Pedestrian crossing
No footway for 400 yds
Pedestrians in road ahead
Elderly people
Crossing point for elderly people (blind or disabled if shown)
Safe height 16'-6"
Overhead electric cable; plate indicates maximum height of vehicles which can pass safely
Low-flying aircraft or sudden aircraft noise
Loose chippings
Ford
Worded warning sign
Cattle
Wild animals
Wild horses or ponies
Accompanied horses or ponies crossing the road ahead
Falling or fallen rocks
Fallen tree
Other danger; plate indicates nature of danger
14'-6"
Height limit (e.g. low bridge)
14'-6"
Available width of headroom indicated
Opening or swing bridge ahead
Quayside or river bank
Cycle route ahead
Road works
STOP 100 yds
Distance to "STOP" line ahead
1 mile
Distance to tunnel
REDUCE SPEED NOW
Plate below some signs
AUTOMATIC BARRIERS STOP when lights show
Plate to indicate a level crossing equipped with automatic barriers and flashing lights
Level crossing with barrier or gate ahead
Level crossing without barrier or gate ahead
Level crossing without barrier (the additional lower half of the cross is used when there is more than one railway line)
Risk of Grounding
Risk of grounding of long low vehicles at level crossing
Sharp deviation of route to left (or right if chevrons reversed)
GIVE WAY 50 yds
Distance to "Give Way" line ahead

DIRECTION SIGNS *Mostly rectangular*
Signs on motorways *Blue backgrounds*

Start of motorway and point from which motorway regulations apply

"Count-down" markers at exit from motorway (each bar represents 100 yards to the exit). Green-backed markers may be used on primary routes and white-backed markers with red bars on the approaches to concealed level crossings

Distance to service area with fuel, parking and cafeteria facilities (The current petrol price may be shown in pence per gallon or litre, or may be omitted)

On approaches to junctions (junction number on black background)

Downward pointing arrows mean "Get in lane"

The panel with the sloping arrow indicates the destinations which can be reached by leaving the motorway at the next junction

At a junction leading directly into a motorway

Route confirmatory sign after junction

End of motorway

Signs on primary routes
Green backgrounds

At the junction

Ring road

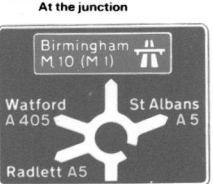

On approaches to junctions (The blue panel indicates that the motorway commences from the junction ahead. The motorway shown in brackets can also be reached by proceeding in that direction)

Route confirmatory sign after junction

On approaches to junctions

Route confirmatory sign after junction

Primary Routes

These form a national network of recommended through routes which complement the motorway system.
Selected places of major traffic importance are known as Primary Route Destinations and are shown on this map thus **EXETER** Distances and directions to such destinations are repeated on traffic signs which, on primary routes, have a green background or, on motorways, have a blue background.
To continue on a primary route through or past a place which has appeared as a destination on previous signs, follow the directions to the next primary destination shown on the green-backed signs.

Signs on non-primary routes
Black borders

On approaches to junctions (a symbol may sometimes be shown to indicate a warning of a hazard or prohibition on a road leading from a junction)

Ring road

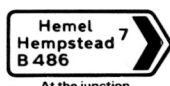

At the junction

Local direction signs
Blue borders

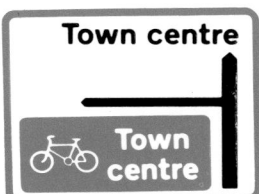

On approaches to junctions (where there is a different route for pedal cycles this may be shown in a blue panel)

On approaches to junctions

At the junction

Airport

Direction to toilets with access for the disabled

Picnic site

Direction to camping and caravan site

INFORMATION SIGNS *All rectangular*

Parking place for towed caravans

Parking restricted to use by people named on sign

One-way street

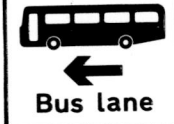

Bus lane on road at junction ahead

Appropriate traffic lanes at junction ahead

No through road

With-flow pedal cycle lane

Recommended route for pedal cycles

Tourist information point

Permanent reduction in available lanes, e.g. two-lane carriageway reducing to one

Temporary lane closure

The number and position of arrows and bars may be varied according to lanes open and closed

Hospital ahead

Weight limit 10 tonnes 3 miles ahead

Advance warning of restriction or prohibition ahead

Priority over vehicles from opposite direction

Other direction signs

Advisory route for lorries

Diversion route

Route for pedestrians

Holiday route

Tourist attraction

Ancient monument in the care of English Heritage

Recommended route for pedal cycles to place shown

Lane control signals

White arrow — lane available to traffic facing the sign. Red crosses — lane closed to traffic facing the sign.

RADIO INFORMATION AND DISTANCES

London

Distances are shown in miles and in *italics* kilometres

National Radio Information

BBC National Radio gives frequent road and weather information

The frequencies used are:

	kHz/metres	VHF(MHz)
Radio 1	1053/285	97.7 - 99.6
	1089/275	
Bournemouth	1485/202	
Merseyside	1107/271	
National FM coverage due in 1994		
Radio 2		88.1 - 90.2

	kHz/metres	VHF(MHz)
Radio 4	198/1515	92.5 - 95.8 / 103.5-105.0
Aberystwyth	198/1515	
Aberdeen	1449/207	
Carlisle	1485/202	
London	720/417	
Plymouth	774/388	
Redruth	756/397	
Tyneside	603/498	
Radio Scotland	810/370	92.5 - 94.7
W Scotland		97.7 - 99.4
Radio Aberdeen	990/303	92.7 - 94.5
Radio Highland		92.5 - 94.6 / 104.9
Radio Orkney		92.7 - 93.7
Radio Shetland		92.7
Radio Solway	585/513	93.1 - 94.7
Radio Tweed		92.8 - 93.9 / 103.6
Radio Wales	882/340	95.1-95.9
Mid Wales	1125/267	
Radio Clwyd	657/457	
Radio Cymru		92.5-94.5
Blaenavon		104.0
Wenvoe		96.8

Distance chart (miles, with *kilometres* in italics below each row):

```
Aberdeen                503
                        810

Aberystwyth             211 445
                        340 716

Ayr                     394 177 317
                        634 285 510

Berwick-upon-Tweed      338 182 311 134
                        544 293 501 216

Birmingham              105 420 114 289 264
                        169 676 183 465 425

Blackpool               226 308 153 180 193 123
                        364 496 246 290 311 198

Bournemouth             100 564 207 436 412 147 270
                        161 908 333 702 663 237 435

Braemar                 482  59 405 143 148 377 268 524
                        776  95 652 230 238 607 431 843

Brighton                 52 556 235 446 390 163 286  92 534
                         84 895 378 718 628 262 460 148 859

Bristol                 122 493 125 370 352  81 204  82 458 137
                        196 793 201 595 566 130 328 132 737 220

Cambridge                54 458 214 357 294 100 208 154 426 106 144
                         87 737 344 575 473 161 335 248 686 171 232

Cardiff                 157 490 105 382 368 103 209 117 470 182  45 179
                        253 789 169 615 592 166 336 188 756 293  72 288

Carlisle                301 221 224  93  87 196  87 343 181 353 277 264 289
                        484 356 360 150 140 315 140 552 291 568 446 425 465

Doncaster               159 344 176 235 198  94  94 235 310 211 175 116 197 142
                        256 554 283 378 319 151 151 378 499 340 282 187 317 229

Dover                    71 576 282 465 409 176 297 174 553  82 186 125 238 372 231
                        114 927 454 748 658 283 478 280 890 132 299 201 383 599 372

Dundee                  434  67 376 117 113 349 239 495  52 486 430 391 441 152 275 505
                        698 108 605 188 182 562 385 797  84 782 692 629 710 245 443 813

Edinburgh               378 125 320  73  57 292 183 439  91 430 373 335 385  96 219 449  56
                        608 201 515 117  92 470 295 707 146 692 600 539 620 154 352 723  90

Exeter                  172 569 201 456 428 157 282  82 534 166  76 220 121 353 251 248 506 450
                        277 916 323 734 689 253 454 132 859 267 122 354 195 568 404 399 814 724

Fishguard               260 491  56 373 393 170 209 234 461 291 154 270 112 280 331 331 432 376 230
                        418 790  90 600 632 274 336 377 742 468 248 435 180 451 375 533 695 605 370

Fort William            497 165 430 133 190 392 283 539 125 549 473 460 485 196 338 568 127 144 549 486
                        800 266 692 214 306 631 455 867 201 884 761 740 781 315 544 914 204 232 884 782

Glasgow                 397 145 320  33 101 292 183 439 110 449 373 360 385  96 238 468  83  44 449 376 101
                        639 233 515  53 163 470 295 707 177 723 600  58 620 154 383 753 134  71 723 605 163

Gloucester              109 468 102 330 318  56 174  99 419 133  35 123  56 237 150 180 390 334 111 153 433 333
                        175 753 164 531 512  90 280 159 674 214  56 198  90 381 241 290 628 538 179 246 697 536

Great Yarmouth          128 495 294 402 345 180 252 228 477 180 241  62 261 309 167 185 442 386 297 309 505 405 205
                        206 797 473 647 555 290 406 367 768 290 388 132 420 497 269 298 711 621 478 563 813 652 330

Harwich                  76 505 281 439 372 167 275 176 504 128 191  67 246 336 194 125 469 413 248 337 532 432 178  82
                        122 813 452 707 599 269 443 283 811 206 307 108 396 541 312 201 755 665 399 542 856 695 286 132

Holyhead                253 439 111 305 311 148 141 288 393 311 206 248 216 212 167 339 364 308 282 167 408 308 180 313 315
                        407 707 179 491 501 238 227 463 632 501 332 399 348 341 269 546 586 496 454 269 657 496 290 504 507

Inverness               536 105 486 199 215 458 348 597  75 588 539 493 549 262 351 607 132 158 618 542  66 166 504 518 545 474
                        863 169 782 320 346 737 560 961 121 946 867 793 884 422 565 977 212 254 995 872 106 267 811 834 877 763

John o'Groats           663 232 615 328 342 587 478 724 202 715 668 620 680 391 478 734 259 285 744 671 195 295 628 645 672 603 129
                       1067 373 990 528 550 945 769 1165 325 1151 1075 998 1094 629 769 1181 417 459 1197 1080 314 475 1011 1038 1081 970 208

Kingston upon Hull      206 364 223 251 185 152 127 282 307 258 233 163 244 158  47 277 272 216 309 280 354 254 198 169 232 214 374 501
                        332 586 359 404 298 245 204 454 494 415 375 262 393 254  76 446 438 348 497 451 570 409 272 333 373 344 602 806

Kyle of Lochalsh        576 189 499 212 243 471 362 618 159 628 552 539 564 275 447 467 186 216 628 555  79 179 512 584 611 487  84 189 433
                        927 304 803 341 391 758 583 995 256 1011 888 867 908 443 671 1041 299 348 1011 893 127 288 824 940 983 784 135 304 697

Land's End              297 692 325 570 552 281 405 289 665 200 334 245 477 374 366 630 574 123 353 672 573 235 420 371 405 741 868 421 752
                        478 1114 523 917 888 452 652 330 1070 465 320 322 538 394 768 602 589 1014 922 198 568 1081 922 378 676 597 1193 1397 678 1210

Leeds                   189 327 181 212 156 113  72 255 293 241 194 145 220 119  29 260 258 202 270 237 315 215 159 196 223 164 360 487  55 394 394
                        304 526 291 341 251 182 116 410 472 388 312 233 354 192  47 418 415 325 435 381 507 346 256 315 359 264 579 784  89 634 634

Leicester                97 414 153 299 252  39 140 158 378 149 126  68 142 206  74 168 349 283 196 209 402 302  83  85 140 349 461 588 140 360 95
                        156 666 246 481 406  63 225 254 608 240 203 109 229 332 119 270 562 455 315 336 647 486 137 225 217 562 742 947 195 774 153

Lincoln                 131 383 199 274 224  90 128 209 343 183 171  85 193 181  39 202 314 258 247 255 377 277 136 128 155 200 427 554  44 456 371  68  51
                        211 616 320 441 360 145 206 336 552 295 275 137 311 291  63 325 505 415 398 410 607 446 219 206 249 322 687 892  71 734 597 109  82

Liverpool               202 341 104 213 219  93  49 234 307 256 161 168 165 120  86 273 272 216 237 160 316 216 126 240 235  92 382 511 130 395 361  75 100 118
                        325 549 167 343 352 150  79 377 494 412 259 270 272 193 138 439 438 348 381 257 509 348 203 386 378 148 615 822 209 636 581 121 161 190

Manchester              185 340 141 212 196  80  48 227 306 237 151 172 119  51 172 119 315 259 243 277 357 192 125 271 251 172 373 500  95 394 361  40  92  84
                        298 547 227 341 315 129  77 365 492 381 259 243 277 192  82 412 436 346 380 317 507 346 203 203 303 385 200 600 805 153 634 581  64 148 135

Newcastle upon Tyne     274 235 273 149  64 207 129 347 201 326 288 230 304  57 114 345 166 110 364 329 253 148 253 281 308 247 268 395 121 318 488  92 187 159
                        441 378 439 240 103 333 208 558 323 525 463 370 489  92 183 555 267 177 586 529 407 238 407 452 496 398 431 636 195 512 785 148 301 256

Norwich                 114 475 276 382 328 166 232 214 457 163 221  62 241 289 147 174 422 366 289 280 330 385  20  73 293 186 625 149 664 421 176 119 105
                        183 764 444 615 528 267 373 344 735 262 356 100 388 465 237 280 679 589 454 531 781 620 299  32 117 472 801 1006 240 908 678 283 192 169

Nottingham             122 379 164 274 221  50 111 183 353 174 145  83 153 181  43 193 318 262 221 220 377 277 110 142 150 171 430 557  90 456 345  70  25  35
                        196 610 264 441 356  80 179 295 568 280 233 134 246 291  69 311 512 421 356 354 607 446 177 228 241 275 692 896 145 734 555 113  40  56

Oban                    489 178 412 125 180 384 275 530 141 541 465 452 477 188 330 560 117 123 533 468  49  92 424 497 524 400 134 244 346 128 665 307 393 368
                        787 286 663 201 290 618 443 853 227 871 748 727 768 303 531 901 188 108 858 753  79 148 682 800 843 644 185 393 557 206 1070 494 632 592

Oxford                   57 483 154 353 324  64 187  90 448  99  78 108 103 260 145 128 413 357 145 213 456 356 156 126 126 209 515 642 192 535 274 168  73 124
                         92 777 248 568 521 103 301 145 721 159 119 134 172 418 233 206 665 575 229 330 734 573  84 251 203 309 861 1033 309 861 441 270 117 200

Plymouth                218 615 247 492 474 203 328 128 587 122 263 167 399 297 289 552 496  46 276 595 495 157 343 294 328 664 790 355 674  89 316 242 293
                        351 990 398 792 763 327 528 206 945 341 196 423 269 642 478 465 888 798  74 444 958 797 253 552 473 528 1069 1271 571 1085 143 509 389 472

Portsmouth               70 560 222 430 401 141 264  52 526  48  97 124 142 337 222 130 491 435 176 186 198 146 269 241 150 201 589 146 592 719 269 612 241 150 201
                        113 901 357 692 645 227 425  84 847  77 156 200 229 542 357 209 700 190 404 858 697 174 319 235 463 953 1157 433 985 388 393 241 323

Sheffield               159 360 159 245 190  76  86 216 320 211 161 120 179 152  18 230 291 235 237 215 348 248 126 166 187 149 393 520  65 427 361  33  62  46
                        256 579 256 394 306 122 138 348 515 340 259 193 288 245  29 370 468 378 381 346 560 399 203 267 301 240 632 892 105 687 581  53 100  74

Shrewsbury              150 399  77 269 265  45  98 185 357 208 103 145 111 175  99 221 330 274 179 133 372 272  77 225 220 103 438 567 146 451 303 109  84 117
                        241 642 140 433 426  72 158 298 575 335 166 233 179 283 159 356 531 441 288 214 599 438 124 362 354 166 705 912 235 726 488 175 135 188

Southampton              77 547 201 417 388 128 212  52 561  61  76 131 124 324 209 143 477 421 105 176 504 404  66 150 153 275 506 706 256 599 228 232 137 188
                        124 880 323 671 624 206 404  50 824  98 122 211 195 521 336 230 768 678 169 375 837 676 150 330 246 439 932 1136 412 964 367 373 220 303

Stranraer               402 228 325  51 158 297 188 444 194 473 167 124 454 381 184  84 343 410 435 313 250 379 259 263 578 230 307 282
                        647 367 523  82 254 478 303 715 312 731 608 587 628 163 391 565 426 200 731 613 296 135 552 660 700 504 402 610 417 423 930 354 494 454

Swansea                 194 494  73 366 383 119 216 167 483 222  85 217  41 273 274 269 392 361 167 469 369  57 349  66 217  41 273 274 184 535 664 264 548 285 227 158 209
                        312 795 117 589 616 192 348 269 777 357 137 349  66 439 349 441 721 631 259 108 755 594 143 473 430 296 861 1069 425 882 459 365 254 336

York                    193 319 205 214 148 130  96 269 285 245 211 150 244 121  34 264 250 194 287 261 317 217 176 201 228 188 352 479  37 396 411  24 108  75
                        311 513 330 344 238 209 154 433 459 394 340 241 393 195  55 425 402 312 462 420 510 349 283 323 367 303 566 771  60 637 661  39 174 121
```

Local Radio

Local radio stations giving road and weather reports. BBC stations are listed in red, Independent Local Radio stations in blue.

	MW (kHz/metres)	VHF (MHz)

1 BBC CWR
	94.8
	103.7
	104.0

Mercia Sound
| 1359/220 | 97.0 |
| | 102.9 |

2 BBC Essex
729/412	95.3
765/392	103.5
1530/196	

Essex Radio
| 1359/220 | 96.3 |
| 1431/210 | 102.6 |

3 BBC Hereford & Worcester
738/406	94.7
	104.0
	104.6

Radio Wyvern
| 954/314 | 97.6 |
| 1530/196 | 102.8 |

4 BBC Three Counties Radio
630/476	95.5
1161/258	103.8
	104.5

Chiltern Radio
| 792/378 | 96.9 |
| 828/362 | 97.6 |

Horizon Radio
| | 103.3 |

5 BBC Wiltshire Sound
1332/225	103.5
1368/219	103.6
	104.3

6 Greater London Radio
| 1458/206 | 94.9 |

Capital Radio
| 1548/194 | 95.8 |

LBC London Broadcasting Company
| 1152/261 | 97.3 |

7 Greater Manchester Radio
| 1458/206 | 95.1 |

Piccadilly Radio
| 1152/261 | 103.0 |

8 Radio Berkshire
	94.6
	95.4
	104.1
	104.4

9 Radio Bristol
1323/227	94.9
1548/194	95.5
	104.6

GWR
936/321	96.3
1161/258	96.5
1260/238	97.2
	102.2
	103.0

10 Radio Cambridgeshire & Peterborough
| 1026/292 | 95.7 |
| 1449/207 | 96.0 |

CN FM
| | 97.4 |
| | 103.0 |

11 Radio Cleveland
| | 95.0 |
| | 95.8 |

TFM Radio
| 1170/257 | 96.6 |

12 Radio Cornwall
630/476	95.2
657/457	96.0
	103.9

13 Radio Cumbria
756/397	95.2
1458/206	95.6
	96.1
	104.2

14 Radio Derby
1116/269	94.2
	95.3
	104.5

15 Radio Devon
801/376	94.8
855/351	95.8
990/303	96.0
1458/206	103.4

16 Radio Furness
837/358	95.2
	96.1
	104.2

17 Radio Gloucestershire
	95.0
	95.8
	104.7

Severn Sound
| 774/388 | 102.4 |
| | 103.0 |

18 Radio Humberside
| 1485/202 | 95.9 |

Viking Radio
| 1161/258 | 96.9 |

19 Radio Kent
774/388	96.7
1035/290	97.6
1602/187	104.2

20 Radio Lancashire
855/351	95.5
1557/193	103.9
	104.5

21 Radio Leeds
774/388	92.4
	95.3
	103.9

Radio Aire
| 828/362 | 96.3 |

22 Radio Leicester
| 837/358 | 104.9 |

Leicester Sound
| 1260/238 | 103.2 |

23 Radio Lincolnshire
| 1368/219 | 94.9 |

24 Radio Merseyside
| 1485/202 | 95.8 |

Radio City
| 1548/194 | 96.7 |

25 Radio Newcastle
1458/206	95.4
	96.0
	104.4

Metro Radio
| 1152/261 | 97.1 |
| | 103.0 |

26 Radio Norfolk
| 855/351 | 95.1 |
| 873/344 | 104.4 |

Radio Broadland
| 1152/261 | 102.4 |

27 Radio Northampton
| | 103.6 |
| | 104.2 |

Northants 96
| 1557/193 | 96.6 |

28 Radio Nottingham
| 1584/189 | 95.5 |
| | 103.8 |

Radio Trent
945/317	96.2
999/301	96.5
	102.8

29 Radio Oxford
| | 95.2 |

30 Radio Sheffield
1035/290	88.6
	94.7
	104.1

Radio Hallam
990/303	96.1
1305/230	97.4
1548/194	102.9
	103.4

31 Radio Shropshire
| 1584/189 | 95.0 |
| | 96.0 |

32 Radio Solent
| 999/300 | 96.1 |
| 1359/221 | |

33 Radio Stoke
| 1503/200 | 94.6 |
| | 96.8 |

Signal Radio
| 1170/257 | 96.9 |
| | 102.6 |

34 Radio Suffolk
	95.5
	103.5
	104.6

35 Radio Surrey
| | 104.6 |

36 Radio Sussex
1161/258	95.0
1485/202	95.1
1368/219	95.3
	104.0
	104.5
	104.8

Southern Sound
1323/227	96.9
	97.5
	102.0
	103.5

37 Radio WM
| 828/362 | 95.6 |
| 1458/206 | |

Beacon Radio/ WABC
| 990/303 | 97.2 |
| 1017/295 | 103.1 |

38 Radio York
666/450	95.5
1260/238	103.7
	104.3

39 BRMB Radio
| 1152/261 | 96.4 |

40 Devonair Radio
666/450	96.4
954/314	97.0
	103.0

41 Fox FM
| | 97.4 |
| | 102.6 |

42 Hereward Radio
| 1332/225 | 102.7 |

43 Invicta Radio
603/497	95.9
1242/242	96.1
	97.0
	102.8
	103.1

44 Manx Radio
1368/219	89.0
	97.2
	103.7

45 Marcher Sound
| 1260/238 | 103.4 |

46 Moray Firth Radio
| 1107/271 | 97.4 |

47 North Sound Radio
| 1035/290 | 96.9 |

48 Ocean Sound
| | 96.7 |
| | 97.5 |

Power FM
| | 103.2 |

South Coast Radio
1170/257	
1557/193	
1323/227	

49 Orchard
| | 97.1 |
| | 102.6 |

50 Plymouth Sound
| 1152/261 | 97.0 |

51 Radio Borders
	96.8
	97.5
	103.1
	103.4

52 Radio Clyde
| 1152/261 | 102.5 |

53 Radio Forth
| 1548/194 | 97.3 |
| | 97.6 |

54 Radio Mercury
1521/197	96.4
	97.1
	102.7

55 Radio Tay
| 1161/258 | 96.4 |
| 1584/189 | 102.8 |

56 Radio 210
| 1431/210 | 97.0 |
| | 102.9 |

57 Red Dragon Radio
| 1305/230 | 97.4 |
| 1359/221 | 103.2 |

58 Red Rose Radio
| 999/301 | 97.4 |

59 SGR
1170/257	96.4
1251/240	97.1
	102.4

60 Swansea Sound
| 1170/257 | 96.4 |

61 Two Counties Radio
| 828/362 | 102.3 |

62 West Sound
| 1035/290 | 96.7 |

63 Isle of Wight Radio
| 1242/242 | |

64 Buzz FM
| | 102.4 |

65 Lincs FM
| | 102.2 |

66 Minster FM
| | 104.7 |

67 Great Yorkshire Radio
990/303	
1161/258	
1278/235	
1305/230	
1530/196	
1548/194	

Liverpool
| 35 | |
| 56 | |

Manchester
| 155 | 132 |
| 249 | 212 |

Newcastle upon Tyne
| 220 | 185 | 264 |
| 354 | 298 | 425 |

Norwich
| 98 | 63 | 157 | 122 |
| 158 | 101 | 253 | 196 |

Nottingham
| 308 | 307 | 233 | 477 | 369 |
| 496 | 494 | 375 | 768 | 594 |

Oban
| 157 | 144 | 260 | 145 | 98 | 448 |
| 253 | 232 | 418 | 233 | 158 | 721 |

Oxford
| 283 | 283 | 410 | 343 | 267 | 587 | 185 |
| 455 | 455 | 660 | 552 | 430 | 945 | 298 |

Plymouth
| 234 | 221 | 337 | 186 | 175 | 525 | 77 | 164 |
| 377 | 356 | 542 | 299 | 282 | 845 | 124 | 264 |

Portsmouth
| 72 | 38 | 125 | 146 | 37 | 339 | 135 | 283 | 212 |
| 116 | 61 | 201 | 235 | 60 | 546 | 217 | 455 | 341 |

Sheffield
| 58 | 69 | 201 | 205 | 82 | 364 | 106 | 225 | 185 | 82 |
| 93 | 111 | 323 | 330 | 132 | 586 | 171 | 362 | 298 | 132 |

Shrewsbury
| 221 | 208 | 324 | 193 | 162 | 512 | 64 | 151 | 21 | 199 | 170 |
| 356 | 335 | 521 | 311 | 261 | 824 | 103 | 243 | 34 | 320 | 274 |

Southampton
| 221 | 220 | 158 | 390 | 290 | 176 | 362 | 500 | 438 | 263 | 277 | 425 |
| 356 | 354 | 254 | 628 | 467 | 283 | 583 | 805 | 705 | 423 | 446 | 684 |

Stranraer
| 153 | 187 | 319 | 274 | 169 | 461 | 141 | 206 | 182 | 200 | 118 | 161 | 374 |
| 246 | 301 | 513 | 441 | 272 | 742 | 227 | 332 | 293 | 322 | 190 | 259 | 602 |

Swansea
| 99 | 64 | 84 | 181 | 77 | 309 | 181 | 333 | 258 | 52 | 133 | 245 | 222 | 251 |
| 159 | 103 | 135 | 291 | 124 | 497 | 291 | 536 | 415 | 84 | 214 | 394 | 357 | 404 |

York

NATIONAL PARKS, FOREST PARKS AND LONG DISTANCE PATHS

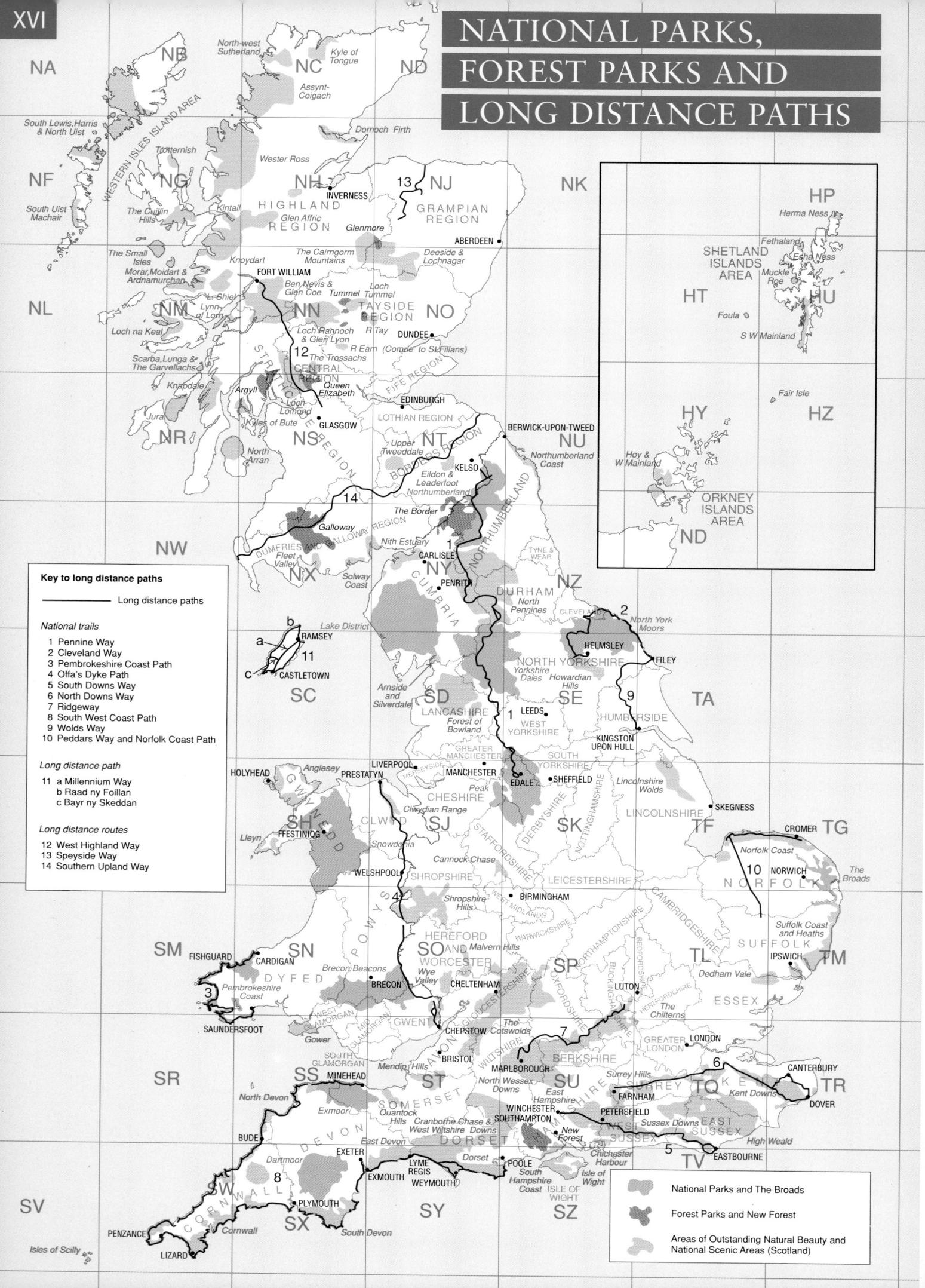

Key to long distance paths

——— Long distance paths

National trails

1 Pennine Way
2 Cleveland Way
3 Pembrokeshire Coast Path
4 Offa's Dyke Path
5 South Downs Way
6 North Downs Way
7 Ridgeway
8 South West Coast Path
9 Wolds Way
10 Peddars Way and Norfolk Coast Path

Long distance path

11 a Millennium Way
   b Raad ny Foillan
   c Bayr ny Skeddan

Long distance routes

12 West Highland Way
13 Speyside Way
14 Southern Upland Way

National Parks and The Broads

Forest Parks and New Forest

Areas of Outstanding Natural Beauty and National Scenic Areas (Scotland)

LEGEND TO 4-MILE MAPPING

Straßen

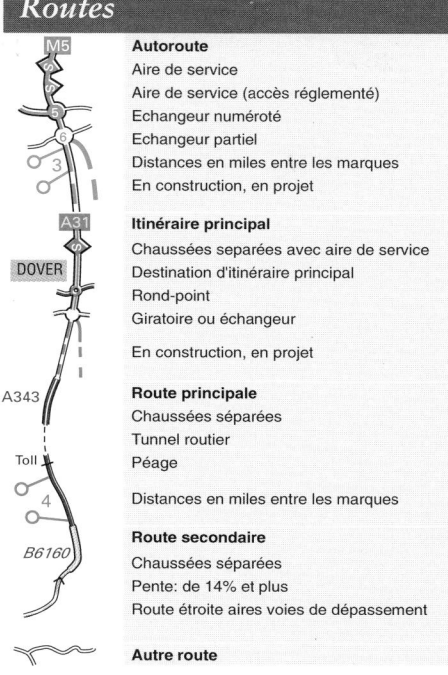

Autobahn
Servicestation
Servicestation (mit begrenztem Zugang)
Anschlußstelle mit Nummer
Teilanschlußstelle
Entfernung in Meilen
Im Bau, Geplant

Fernverkehrsstraße
Zweibahnige Straße mit Servicestation
Bestimmungsort bei Fernverkehrsstraße
Kreisverkehr
Anschlußstelle

Im Bau, Geplant

Hauptstraße
Zweibahnige Straße
Straßentunnel
Straßenbenutzungsgebühr

Entfernung in Meilen

Nebenstraße
Zweibahnige Straße
Steigungen: 14% und meh
Enge Straße mit Ausweichstelle

Sonstige Straße

Routes

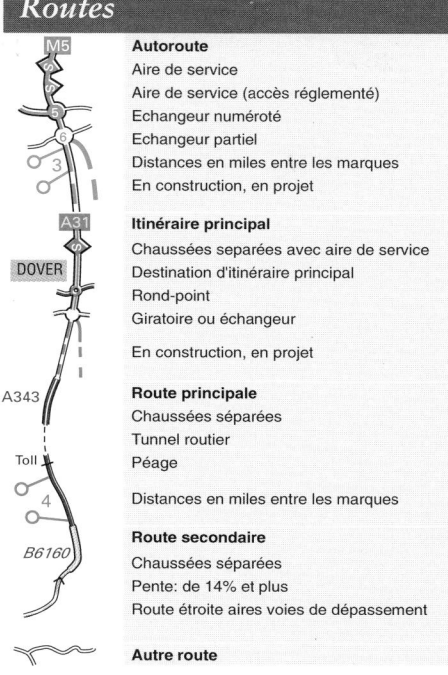

Autoroute
Aire de service
Aire de service (accès réglementé)
Echangeur numéroté
Echangeur partiel
Distances en miles entre les marques
En construction, en projet

Itinéraire principal
Chaussées separées avec aire de service
Destination d'itinéraire principal
Rond-point
Giratoire ou échangeur

En construction, en projet

Route principale
Chaussées séparées
Tunnel routier
Péage

Distances en miles entre les marques

Route secondaire
Chaussées séparées
Pente: de 14% et plus
Route étroite aires voies de dépassement

Autre route

Roads

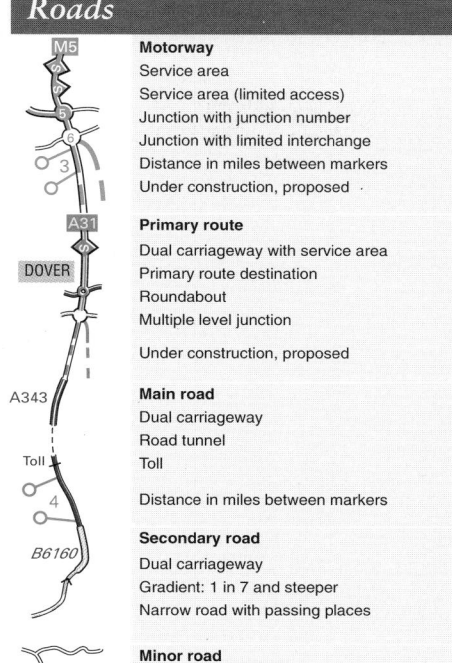

Motorway
Service area
Service area (limited access)
Junction with junction number
Junction with limited interchange
Distance in miles between markers
Under construction, proposed ·

Primary route
Dual carriageway with service area
Primary route destination
Roundabout
Multiple level junction

Under construction, proposed

Main road
Dual carriageway
Road tunnel
Toll

Distance in miles between markers

Secondary road
Dual carriageway
Gradient: 1 in 7 and steeper
Narrow road with passing places

Minor road

Tourist Information Renseignements Touristiques Touristeninformation

Abbey, Cathedral, Priory
Abbaye, Cathédrale, Prieuré
Abtei, Kathedrale, Priorei

Aquarium
Aquarium
Aquarium

Camp site
Terrain de camping
Campingplatz

Caravan site
Terrain pour caravanes
Wohnwagenplatz

Castle
Château
Schloß, Burg

Cave
Caverne
Höhle

Country park
Parc naturel
Landschaftspark

Craft centre
Centre artisanal
Zentrum für Kunsthandwerk

Garden
Jardin
Garten

Golf course or links
Terrain de golf
Golfplatz

Historic house
Manoir, Palais
Historisches Gebäude

Information centre
Office de tourisme
Informationsbüro

Motor racing
Courses automobiles
Autorennen

Museum
Musée
Museum

Nature reserve
Sentier de grande randonnée
Naturschutzgebiet

Other tourist features
Autre site intéressant
Sonstige Sehenswürdigkeit

Picnic site
Emplacement de pique-nique
Picknickplatz

Preserved railway
Chemin de fer touristique
Museumseisenbahn

Racecourse
Hippodrome
Pferderennbahn

Skiing
Piste de ski
Skilaufen

Viewpoint
Point de vue
Aussichtspunkt

Wildlife park
Parc animalier
Wildpark

Zoo
Zoo
Tiergarten

Wolds **National trail Long Distance Route**
Way Sentier de grande randonnée -
Itinéraire de grande randonnée
Nationaler Wanderweg-
Fernverkehrsstraße

General Features Aspects généraux Allgemeine Merkmale

Airfield with / without customs facilities
Aérodrome avec / sans poste de douane
Flugplatz mit / ohne Zollabfertigung

Buildings
Bâtiments
Gebäude

Heliport
Héliport
HubschrauberLandeplatz

Lighthouse in use / disused
Phare en usage / désaffecté
Leuchtturm in Betrieb / außer Betrieb

Motoring organisation telephone
Téléphone d'associations automobiles
Automobilklub - Telefon

Public telephone
Téléphone public
Öffentliches Telefon

Radio or TV mast
Pylône de radio / TV
Radio oder Fernseh - Antennemast

Windmill
Moulin à vent
Windmühle

Wood
Bois
Wald

Youth hostel
Auberge de jeunesse
Jugendherberge

Antiquities Antiquités Historische Sehenswürdigkeiten

Ancient monument open to the public
Monument historique ouvert au public
Kulturdenkmal, der Öffentlichkeit
zugänig

Native fortress
Forteresse pré-romaine
Einheimische Festung

Castle **Other antiquities**
Autres antiquités
Schloß / andere historische
Andere historische Sehenswürdigkeit

ROMAN CAMP. **Roman antiquity**
Antiquité romaine
Altertum römisch

Roman road (course of)
Route romaine (cours de)
Römerstraße (Verlauf)

Site of battle (with date)
1066 Champ de bataille historique (avec date)
Schlachtfeld (mit Datum)

Boundaries Limites Grenzen

National
National
National

County, Region or Island Area
Comté, Région ou île
Grafschaft, Region
oder Inselgruppe

Railways Chemins de Fer Eisenbahnen

Standard gauge track and station
Voie normale et gare
Normalspurgleis und Bahnhof

Road under, road over
Voie en passage inférieur, voie en passage
supérieur
Straße unten, Straße oben

Tunnel, level crossing
Tunnel, passage à niveau
Tunnel, Höhengleicher Übergang

Narrow gauge track
Voie étroite
Schmalspurgleis

Water features Aspects hydrologiques Gewässer

Ferry routes for vehicles (Boat/Hovercraft)
liaisons maritimes (par bateau / par aéroglisseur)
Fähre für Fahrzeuge (Schiff/Luftkissenfahrzeug)

Foreshore
Estran
Vorland

Light-vessel
Bateau-feu
Leuchtschif

Canal
canal
Kanal

Bridge
pont
Brücke

Ferry route for vehicles
bac pour véhicules
Kurzer Fährweg für Fahrzeuge

Lake
lac
See

Sand
sable
Sand

Relief Topographie

Heights in feet above mean sea level

2000	610	Altitude en pieds Höhe in Fuss über dem mittleren Meeresspiege
1400	427	
1000	305	
600	183	
0 feet	pieds fuß	
0 metres/mètres		

Scale

1:250 000 or about 4 miles to 1 inch

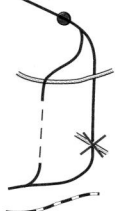

| 0 Kilometres | 5 | 10 | 15 |
| 0 Miles | | 5 | 10 |

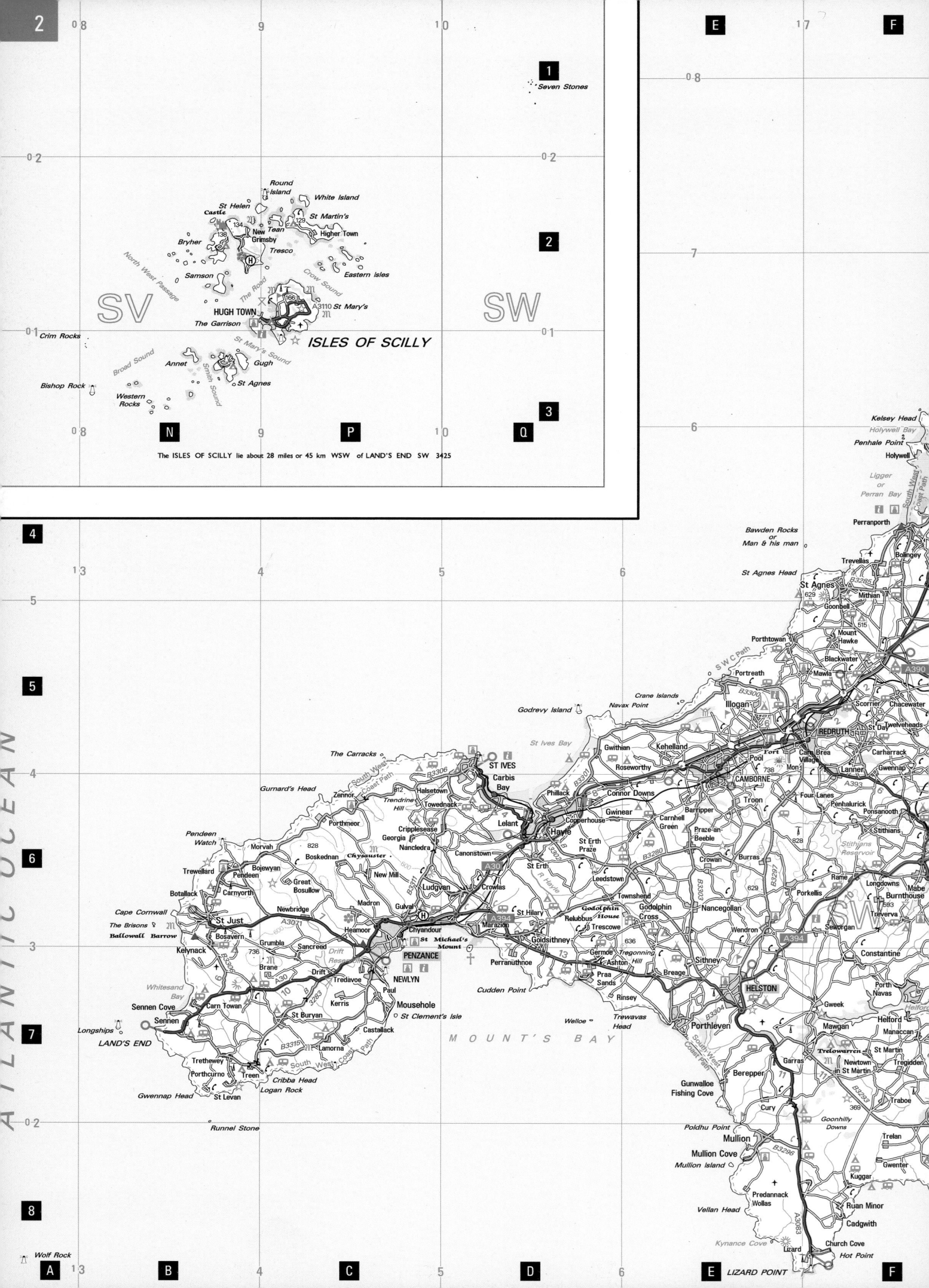

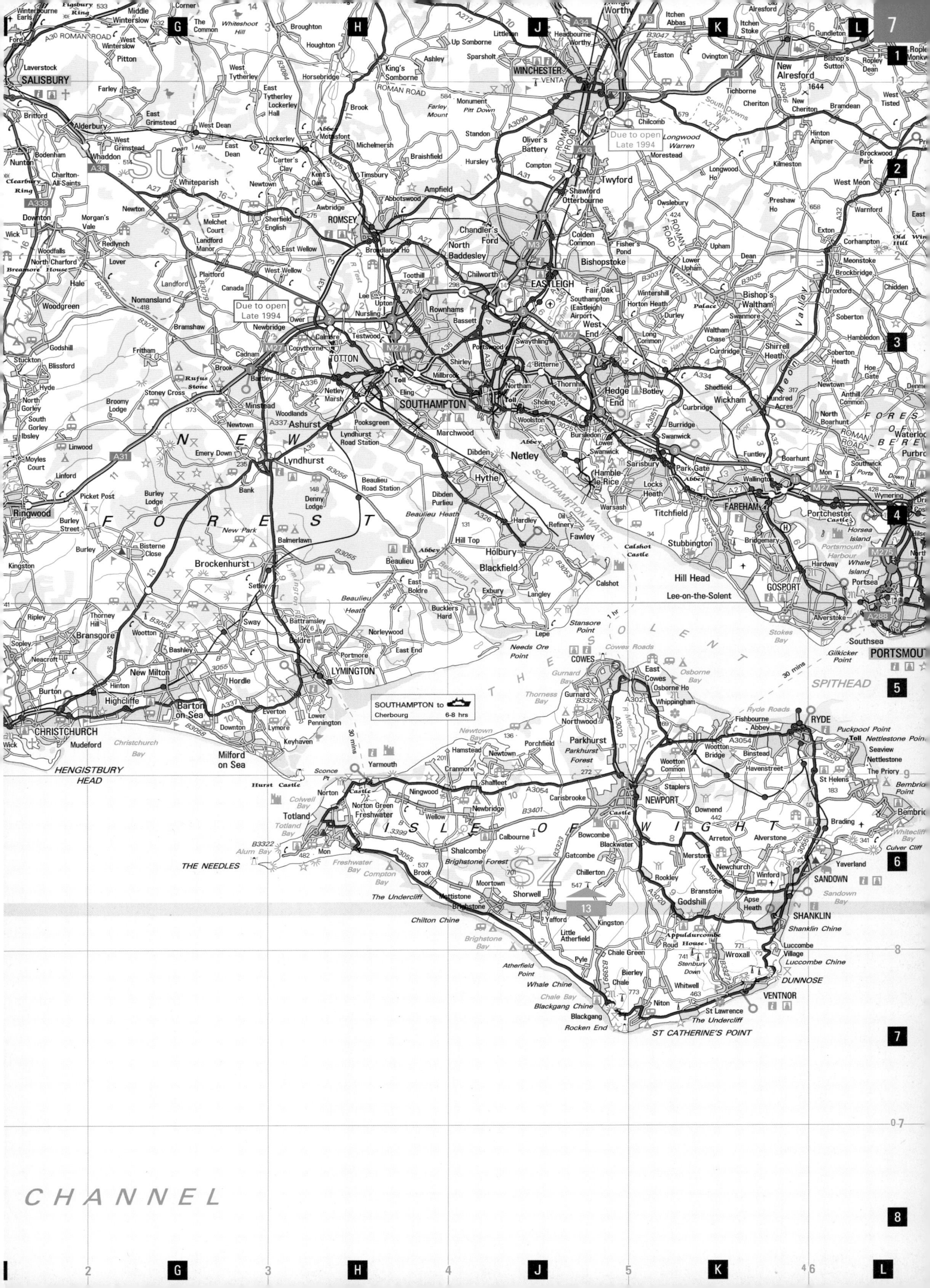

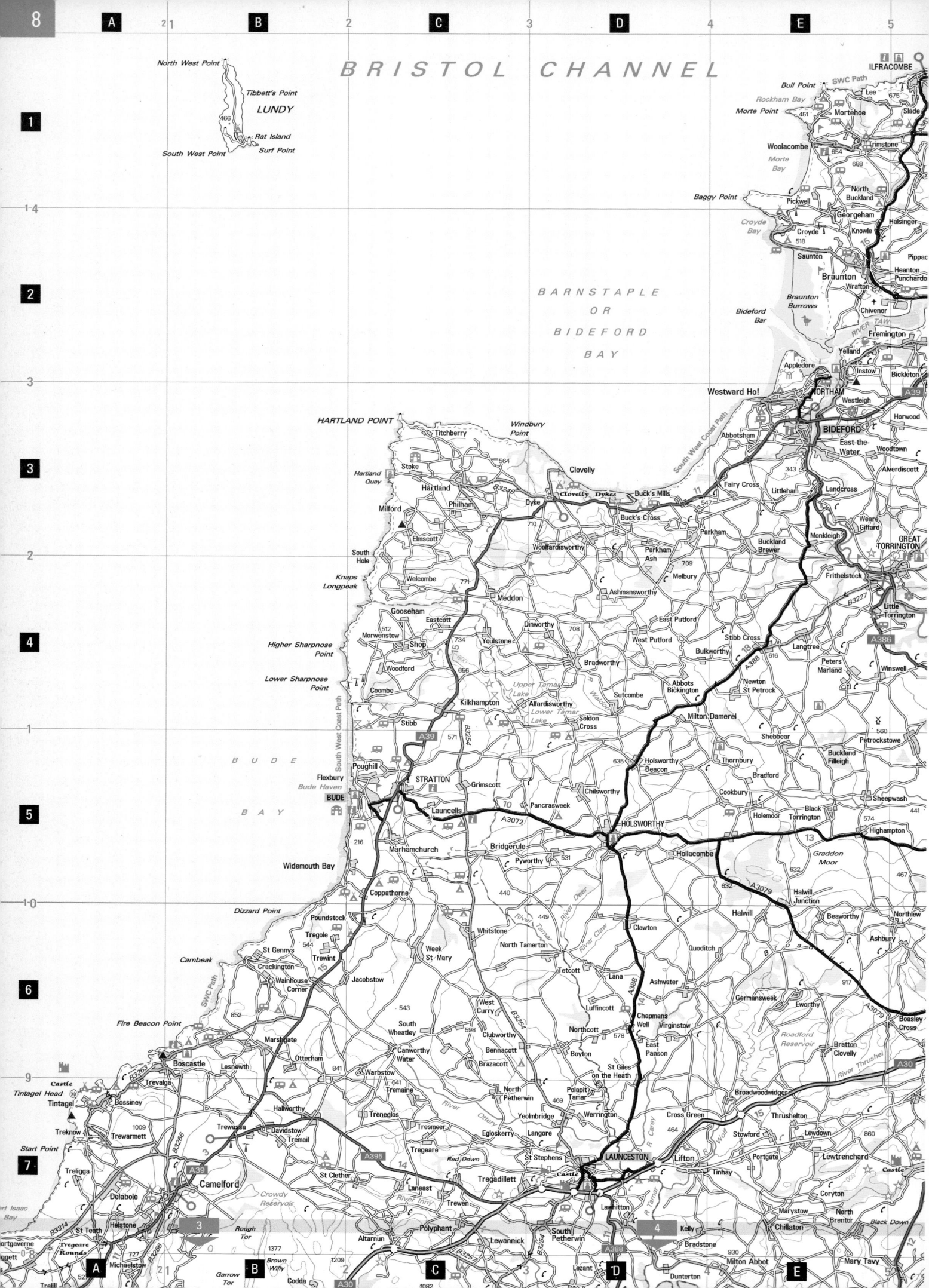

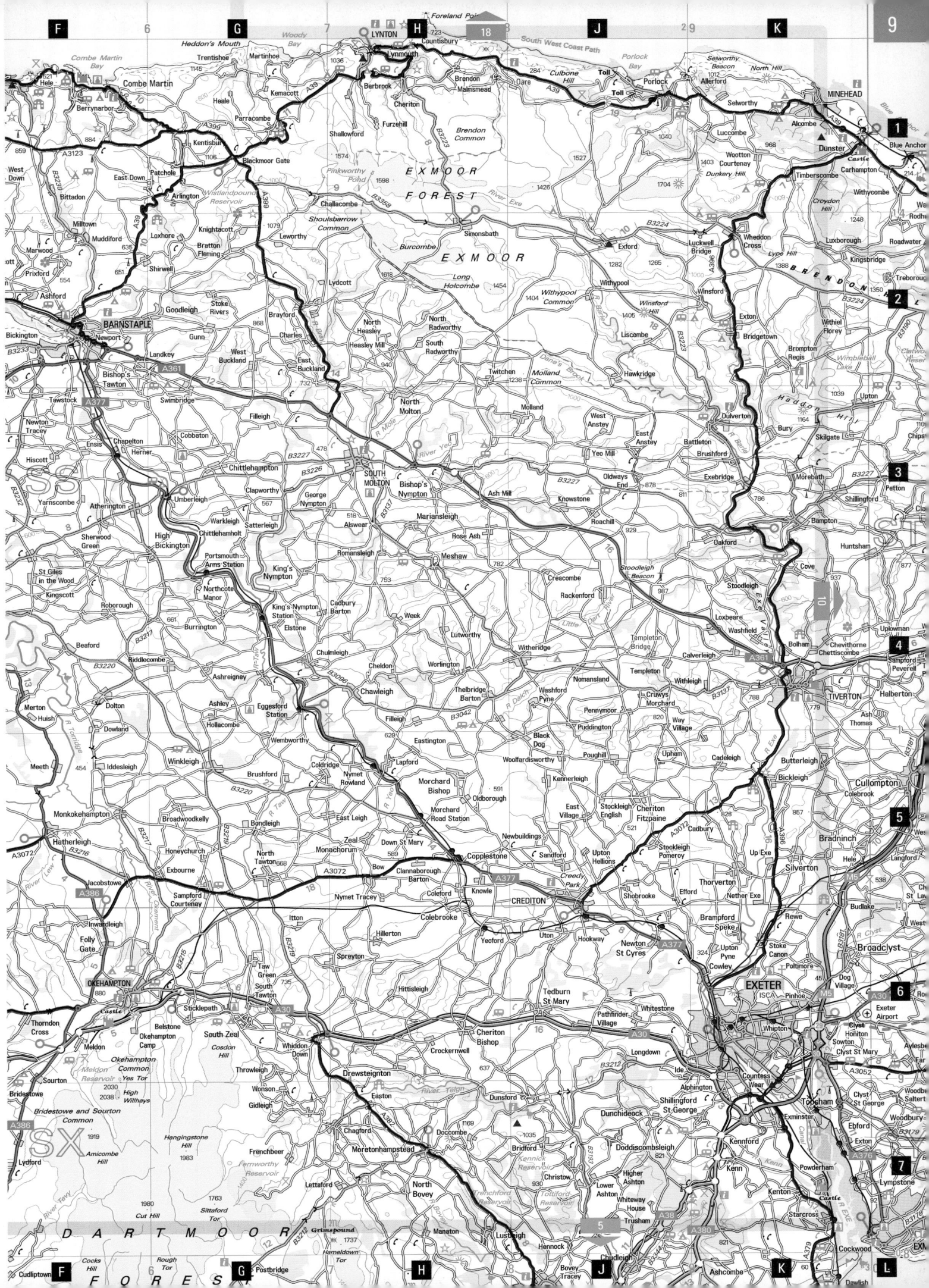

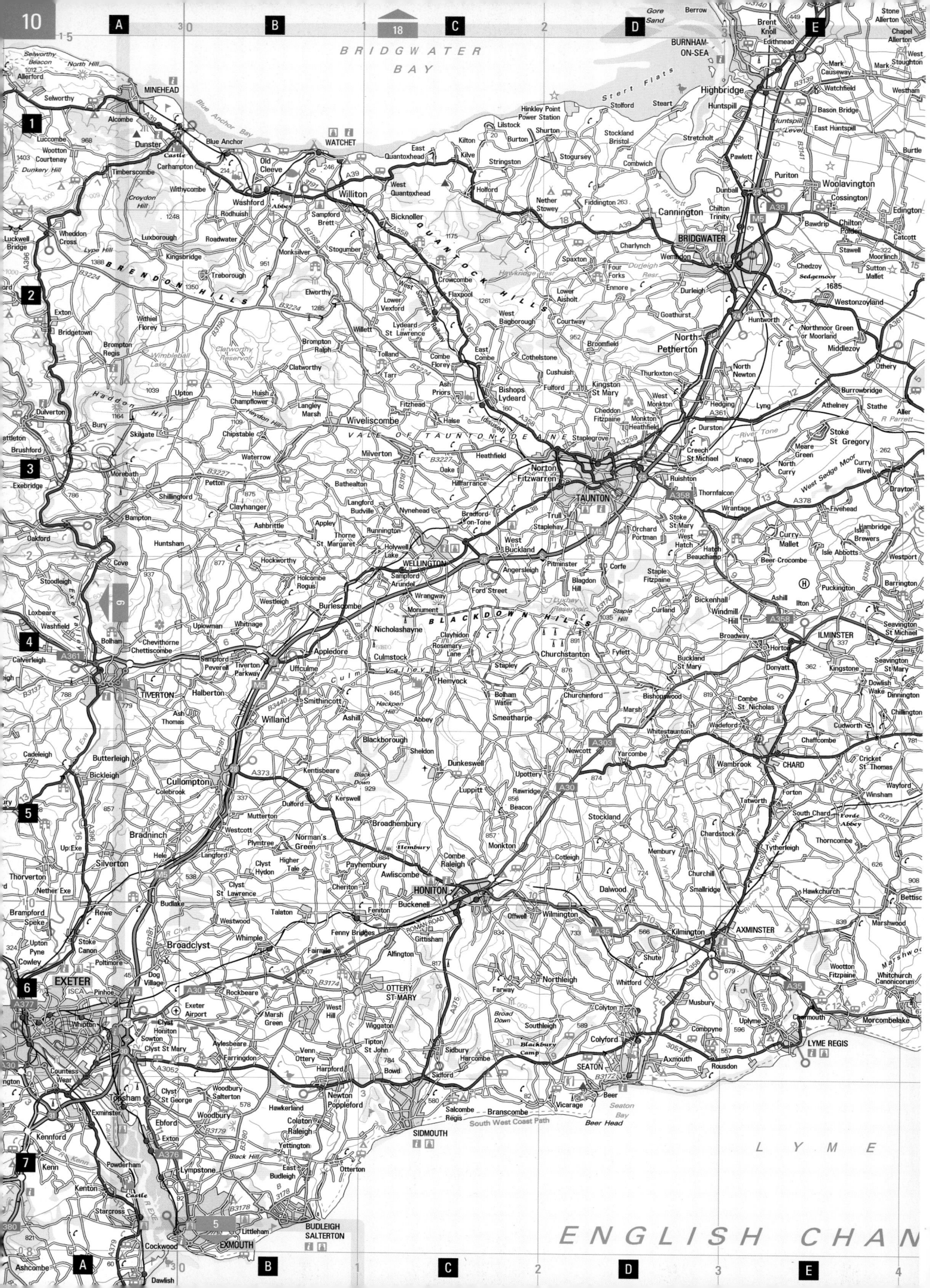

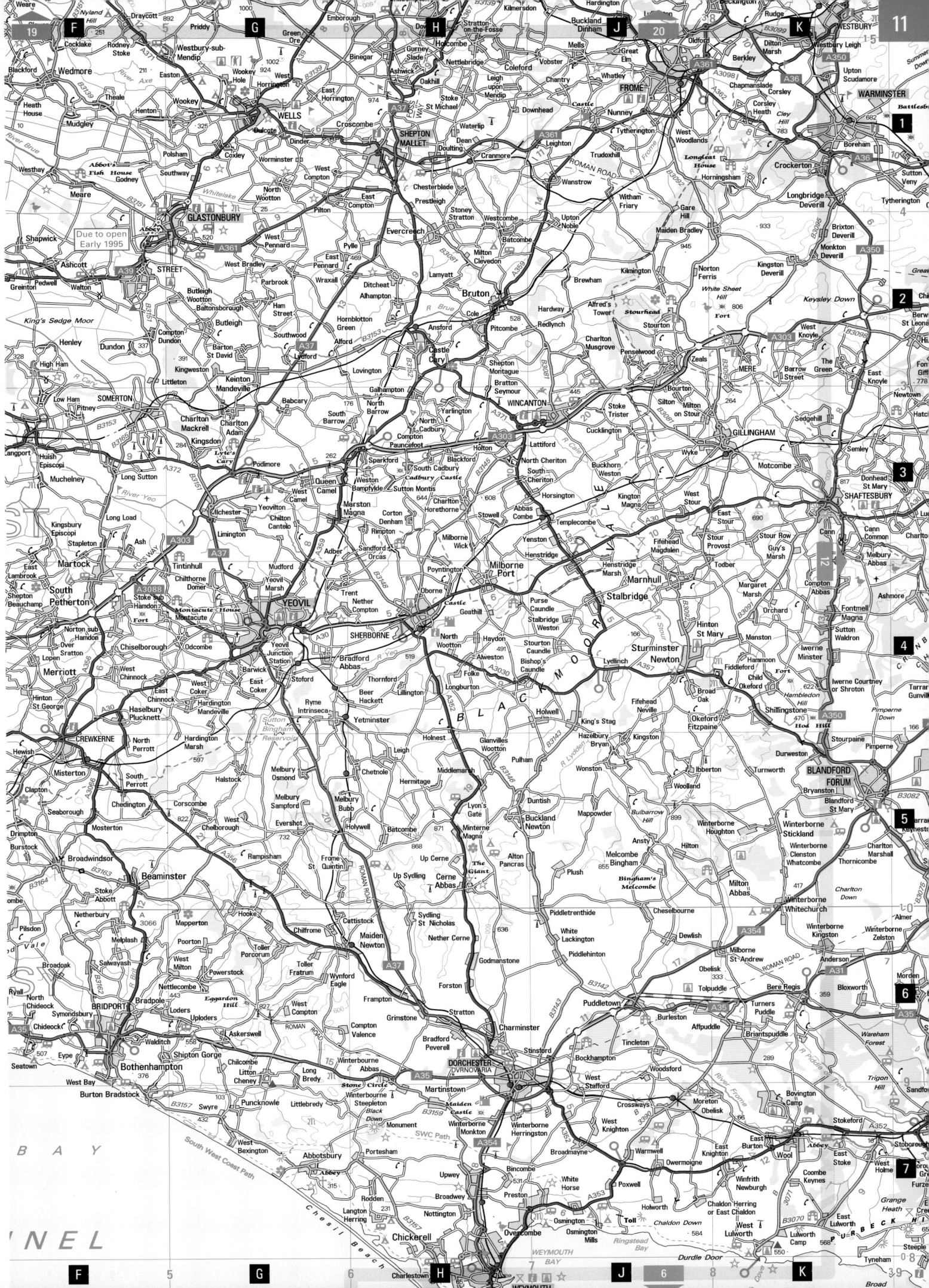

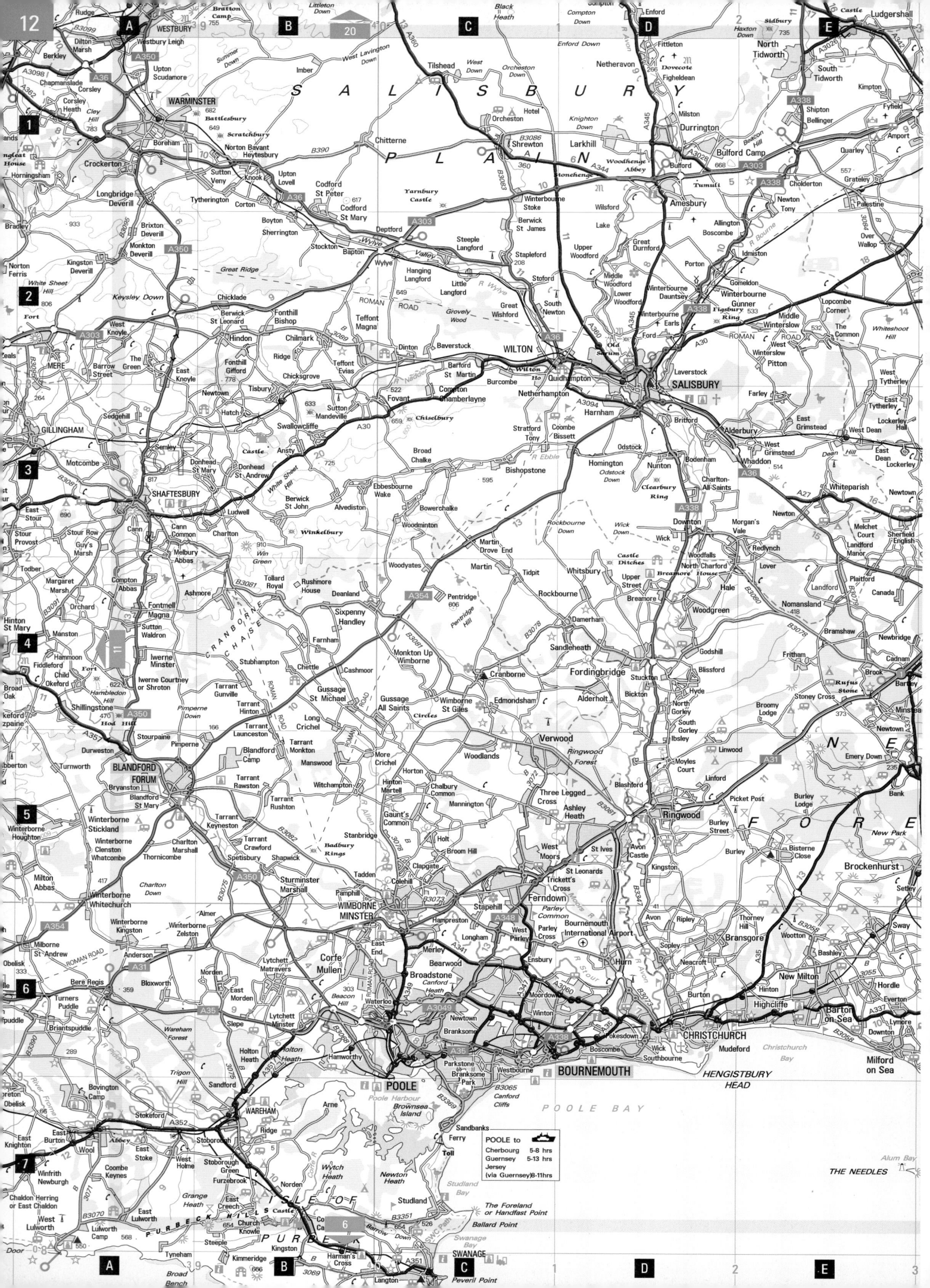

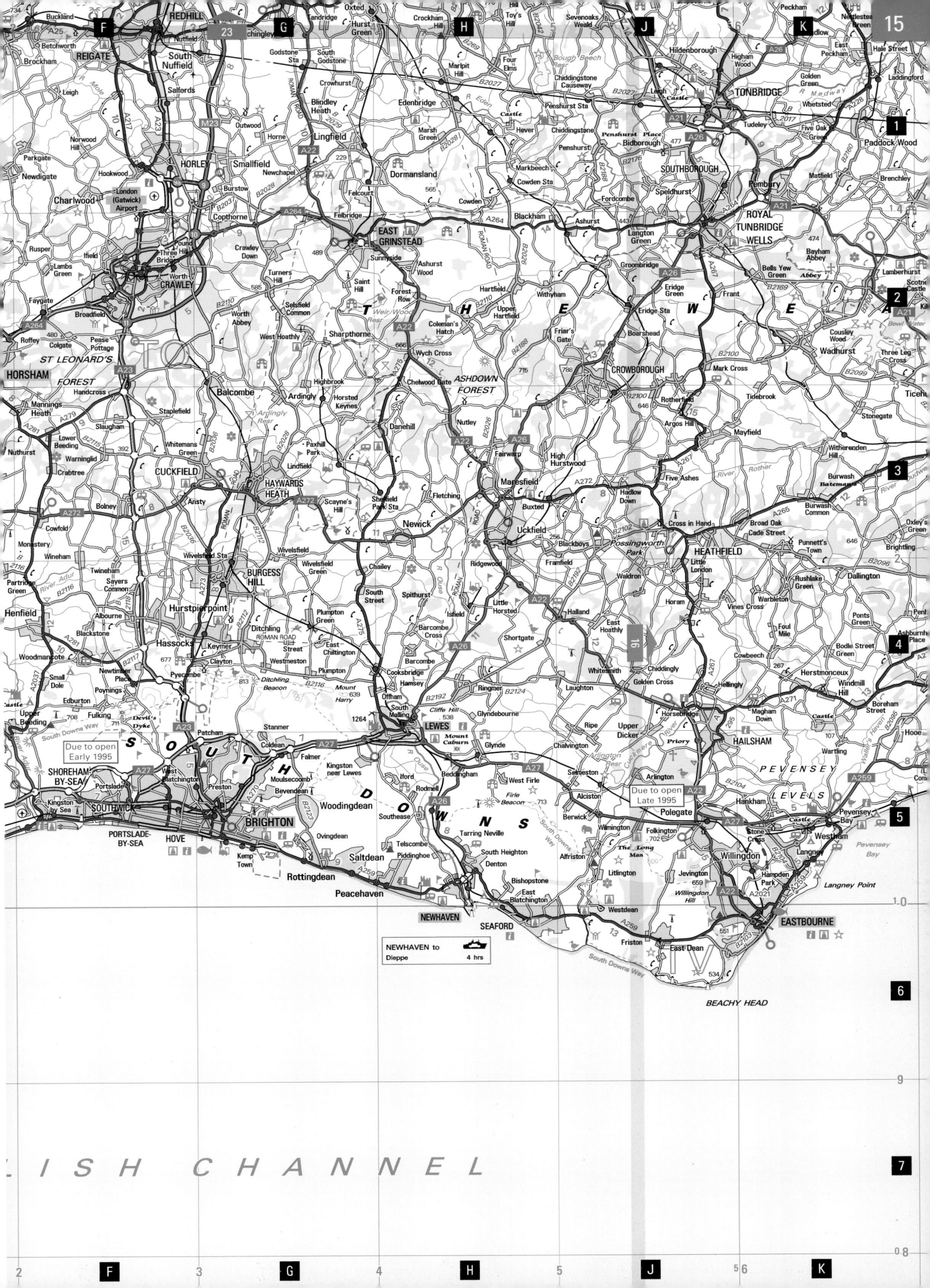

ENGLISH CHANNEL

STRAIT OF DOVER

DOVER to
| Calais | 1 hr |
| Ostend | 4 hrs |

CATAMARAN
| Boulogne-sur-Mer | 40 mins |
| Calais | 40 mins |

| Calais | 30 mins |

(summer only)

FOLKESTONE to
CATAMARAN
Boulogne-sur-Mer   1 hr

Channel Tunnel Terminal

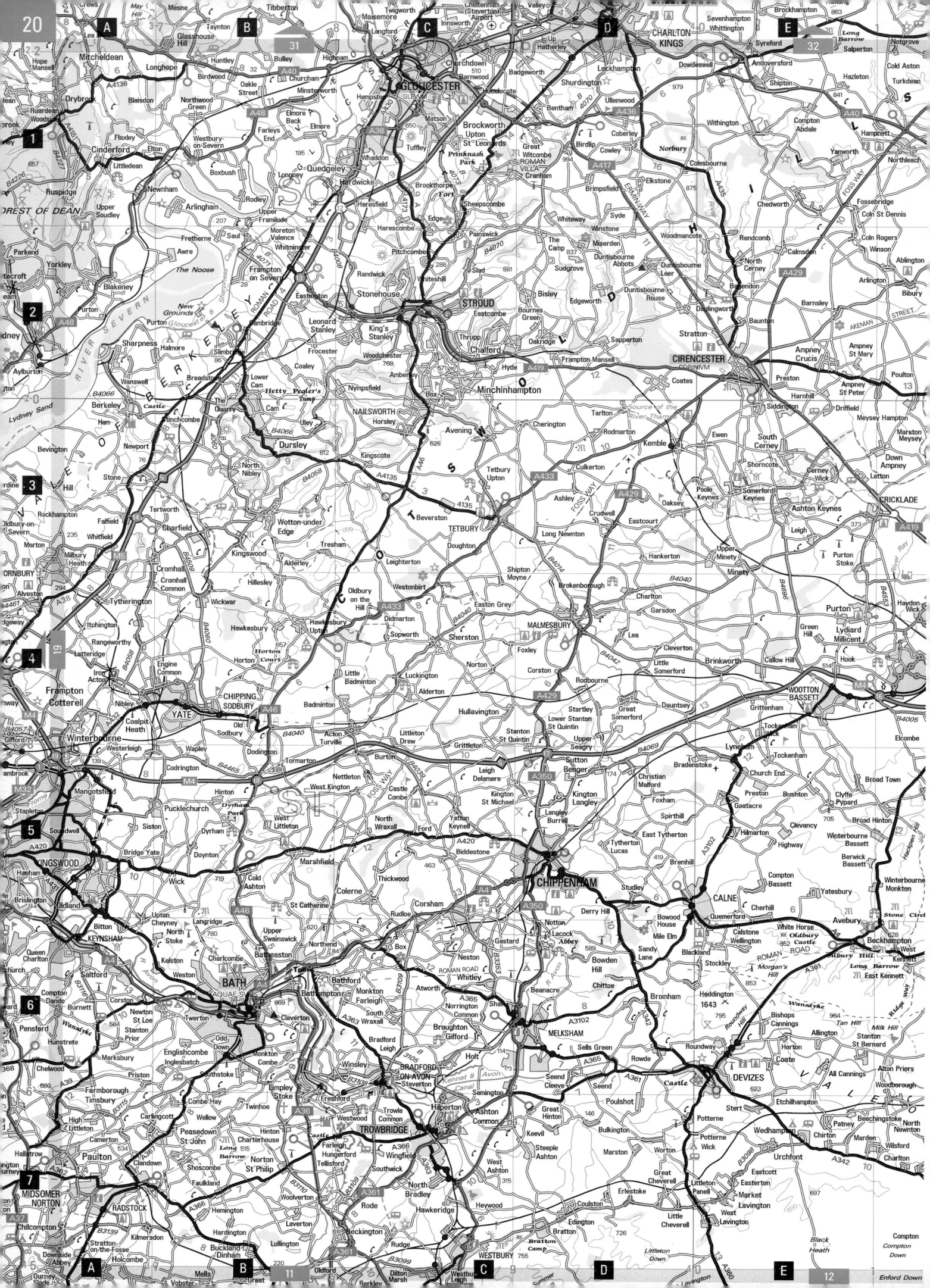

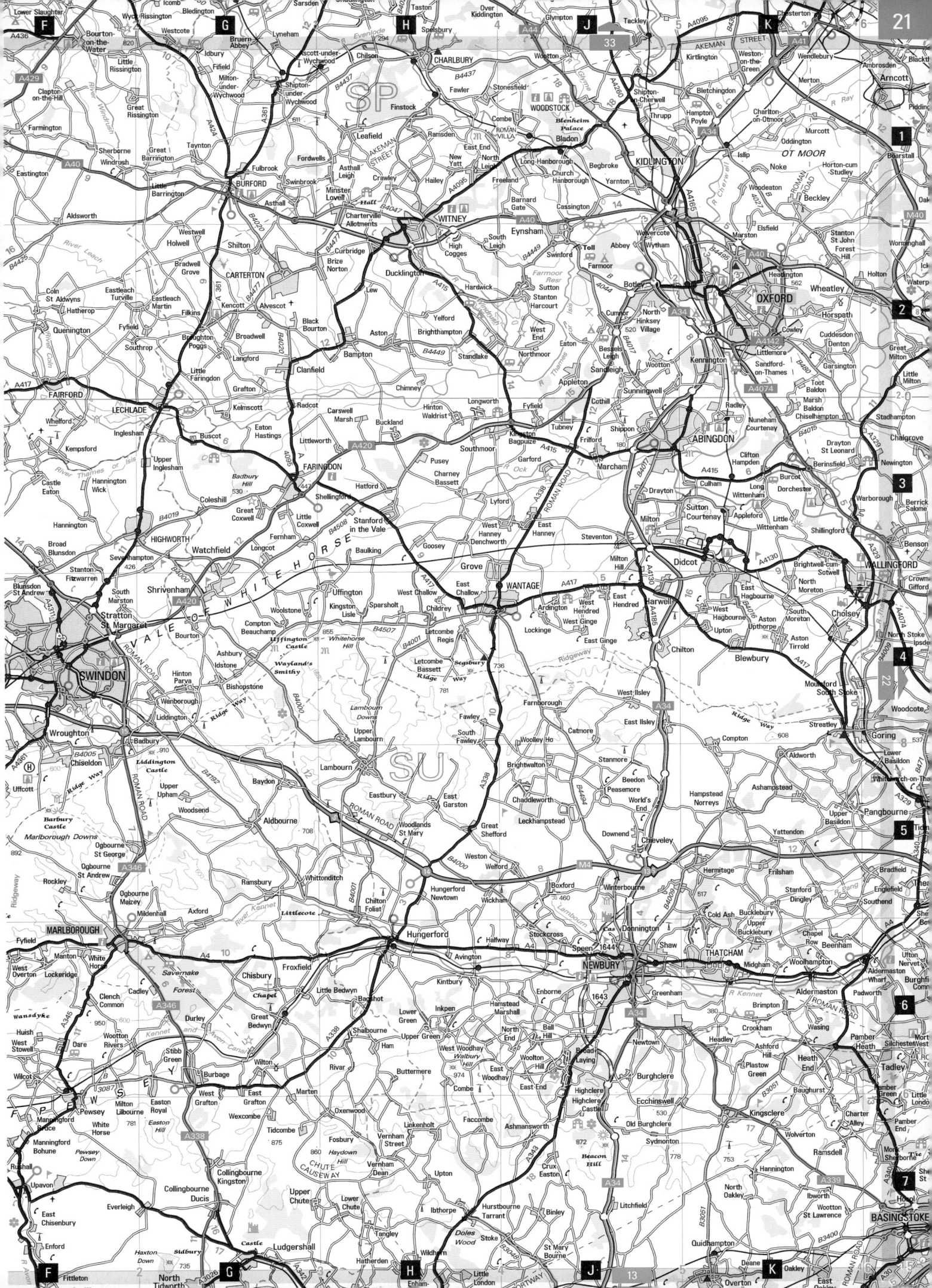

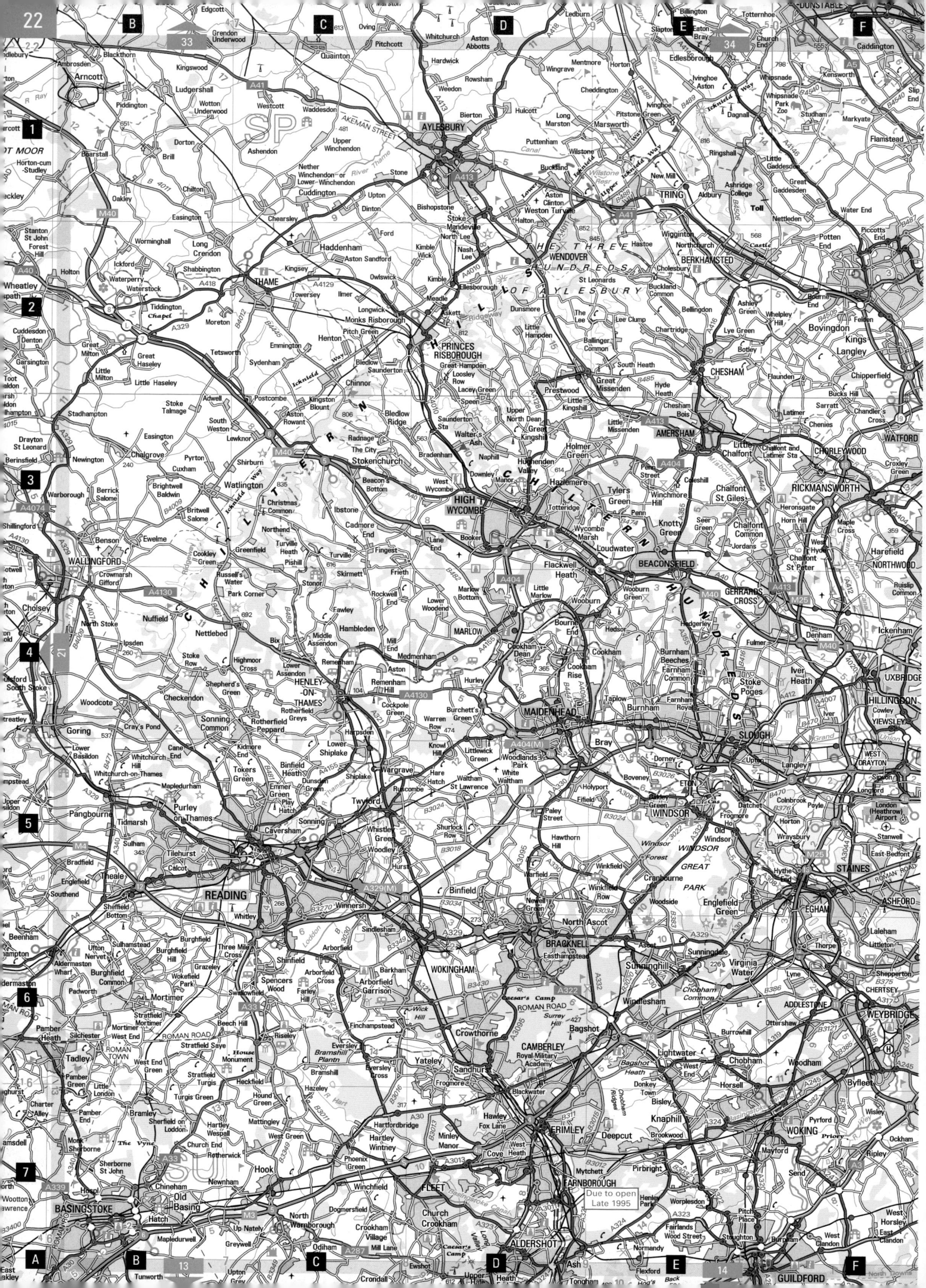

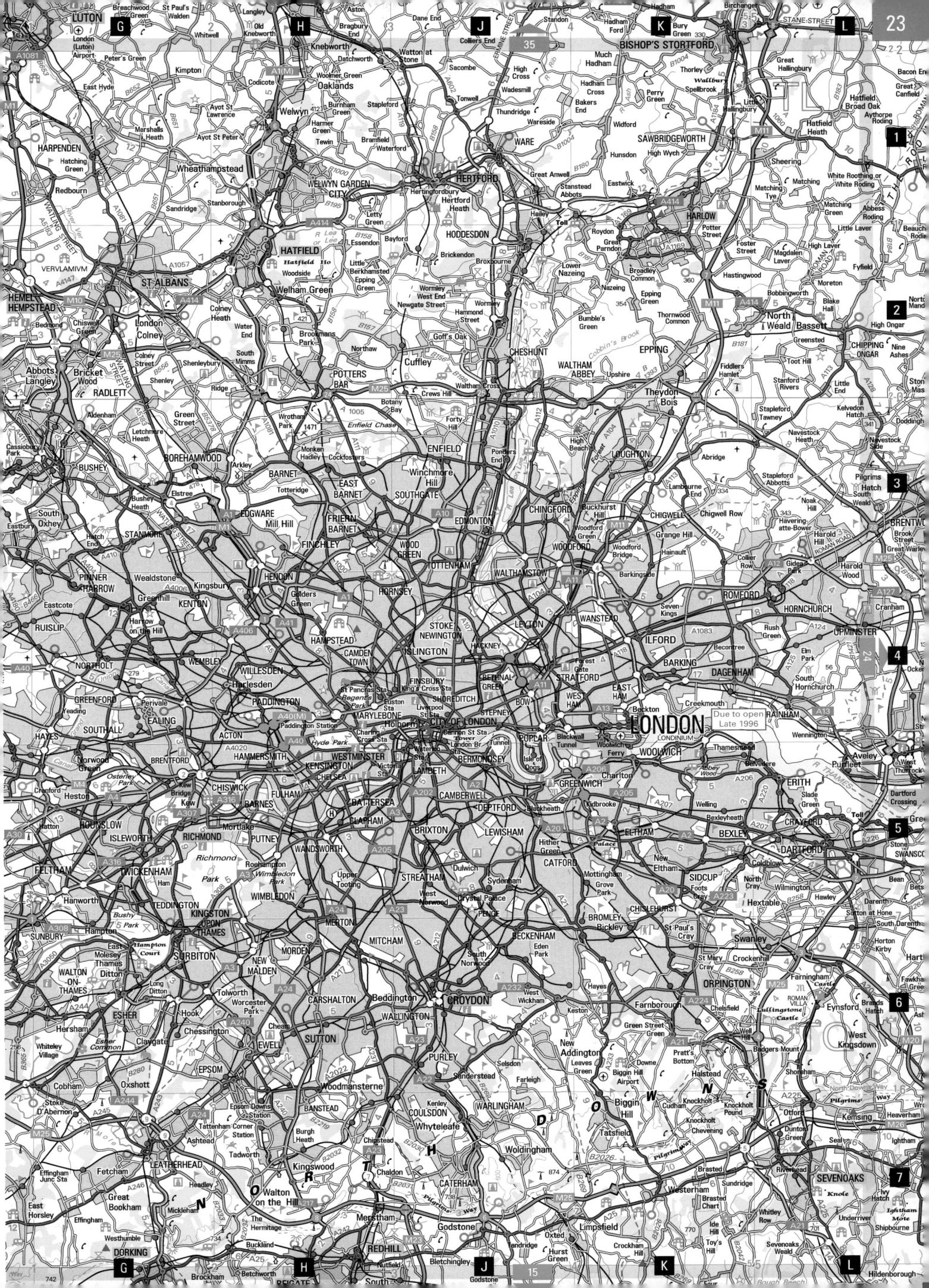

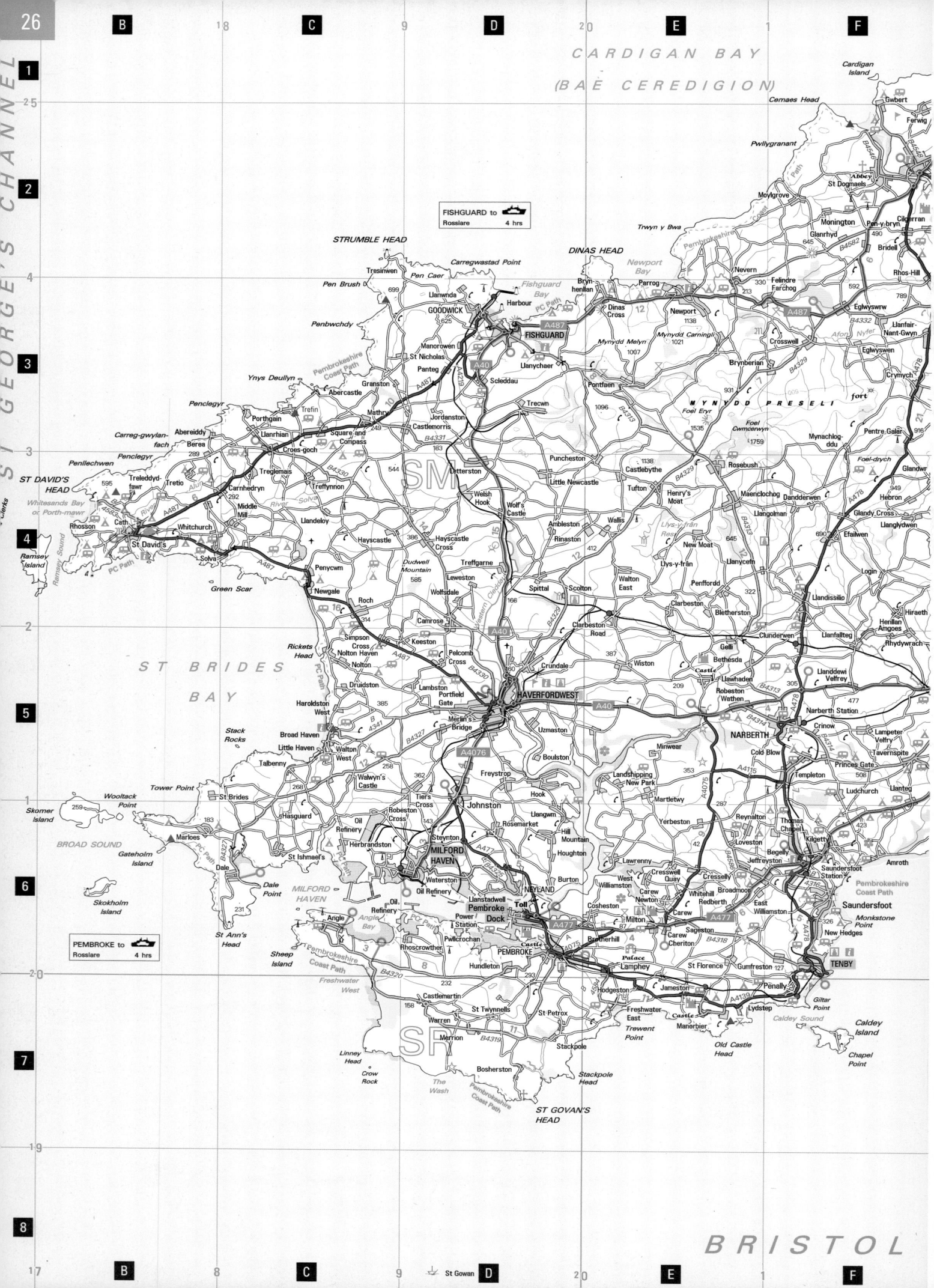

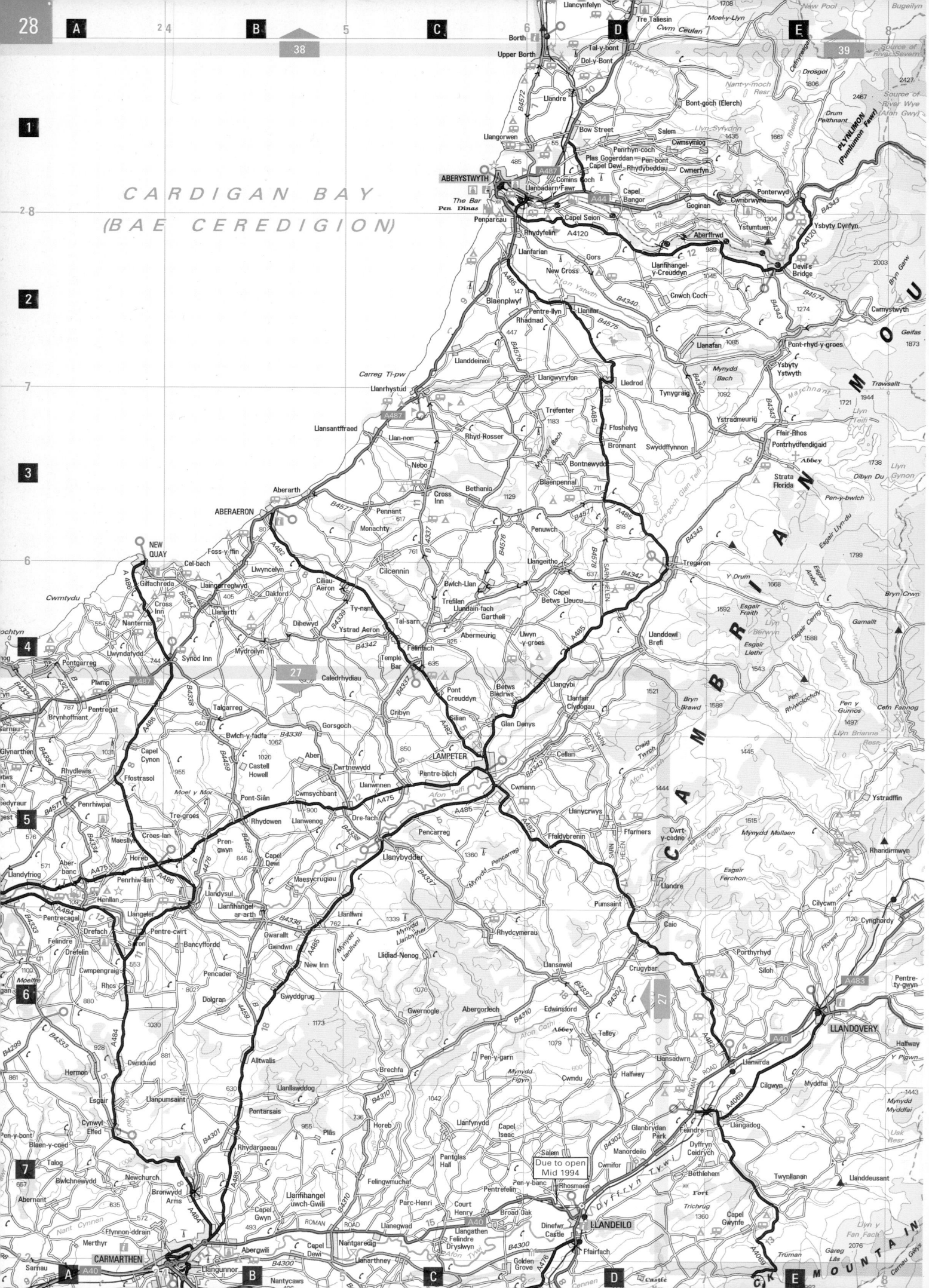

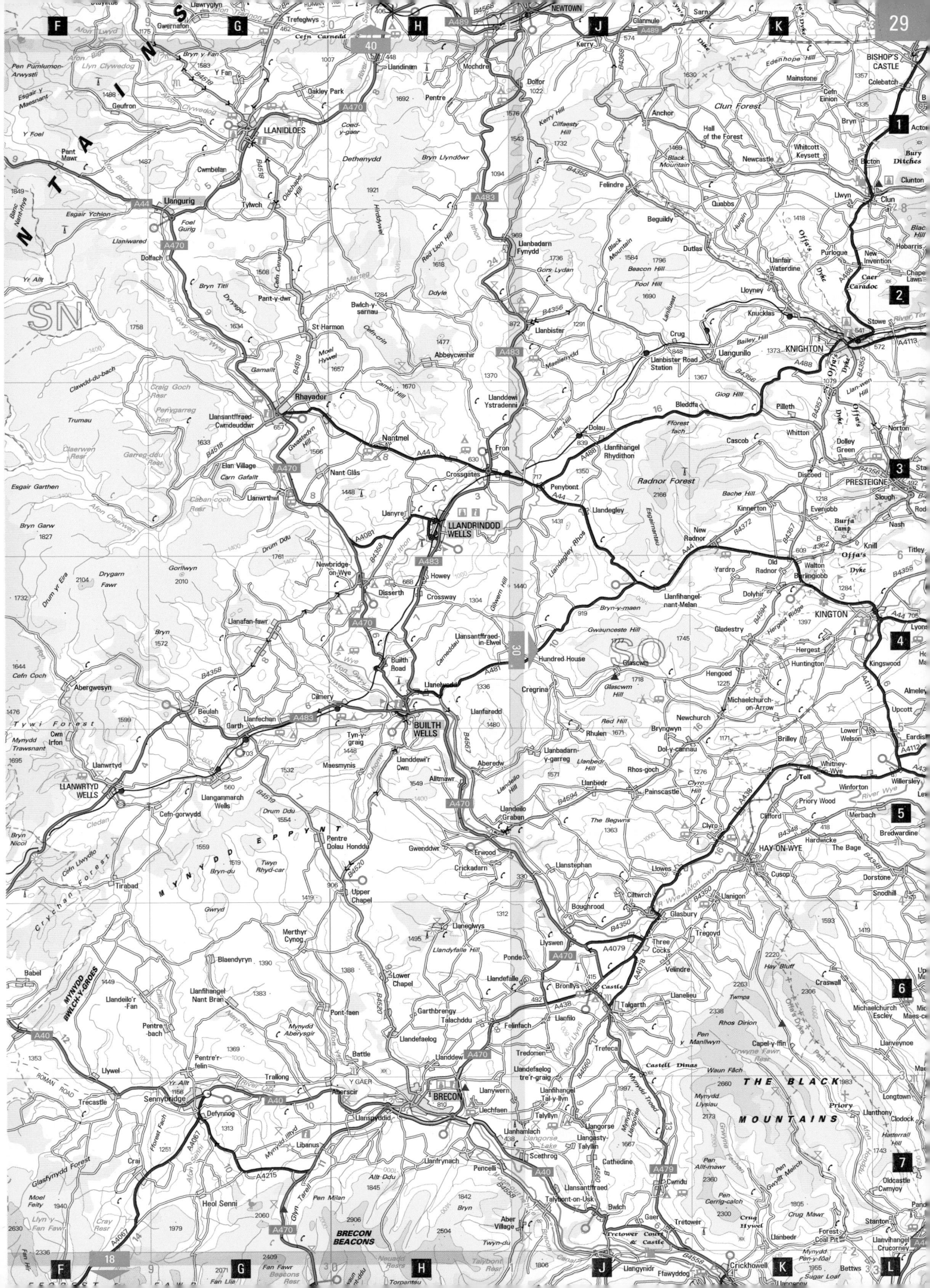

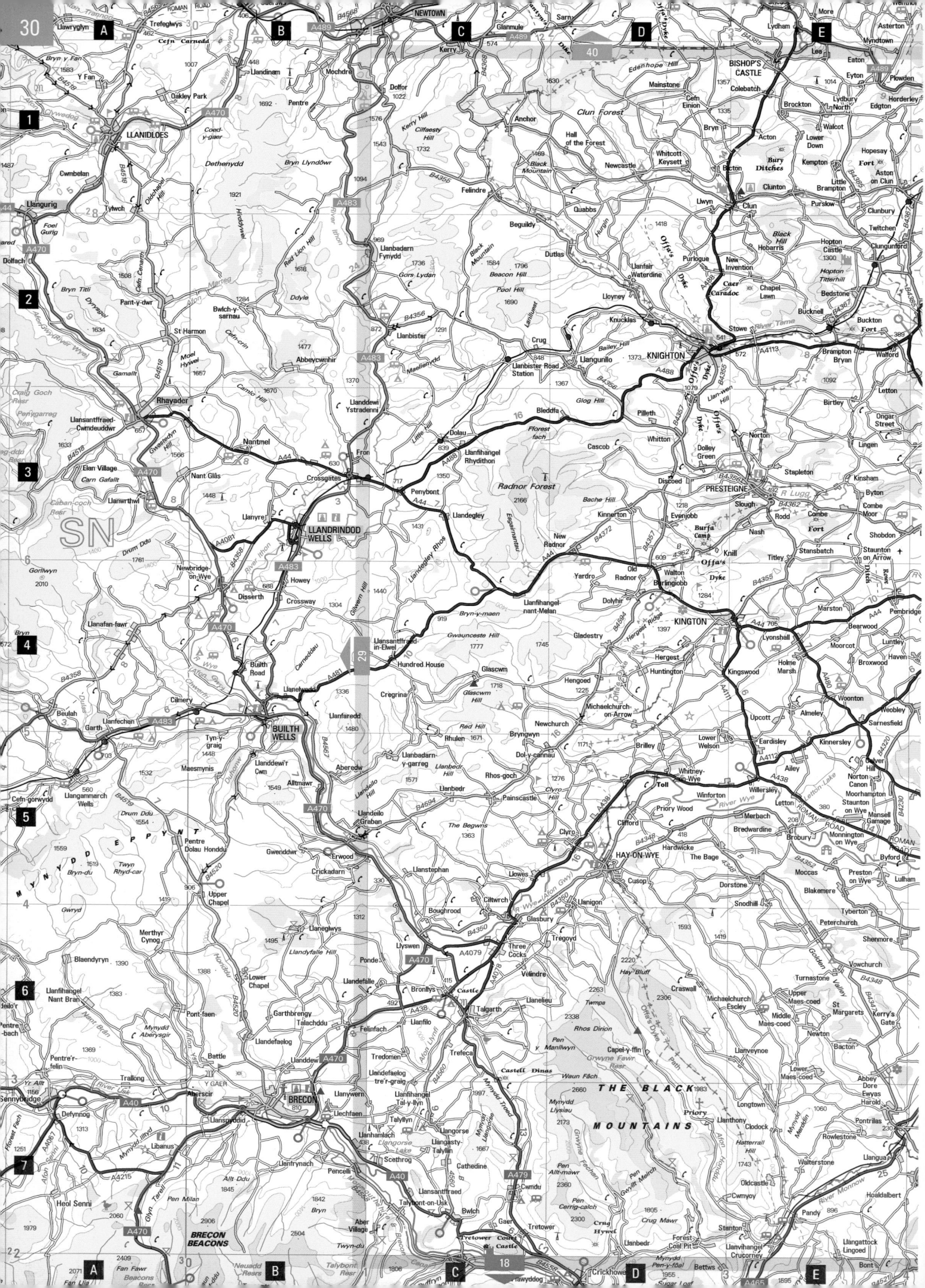

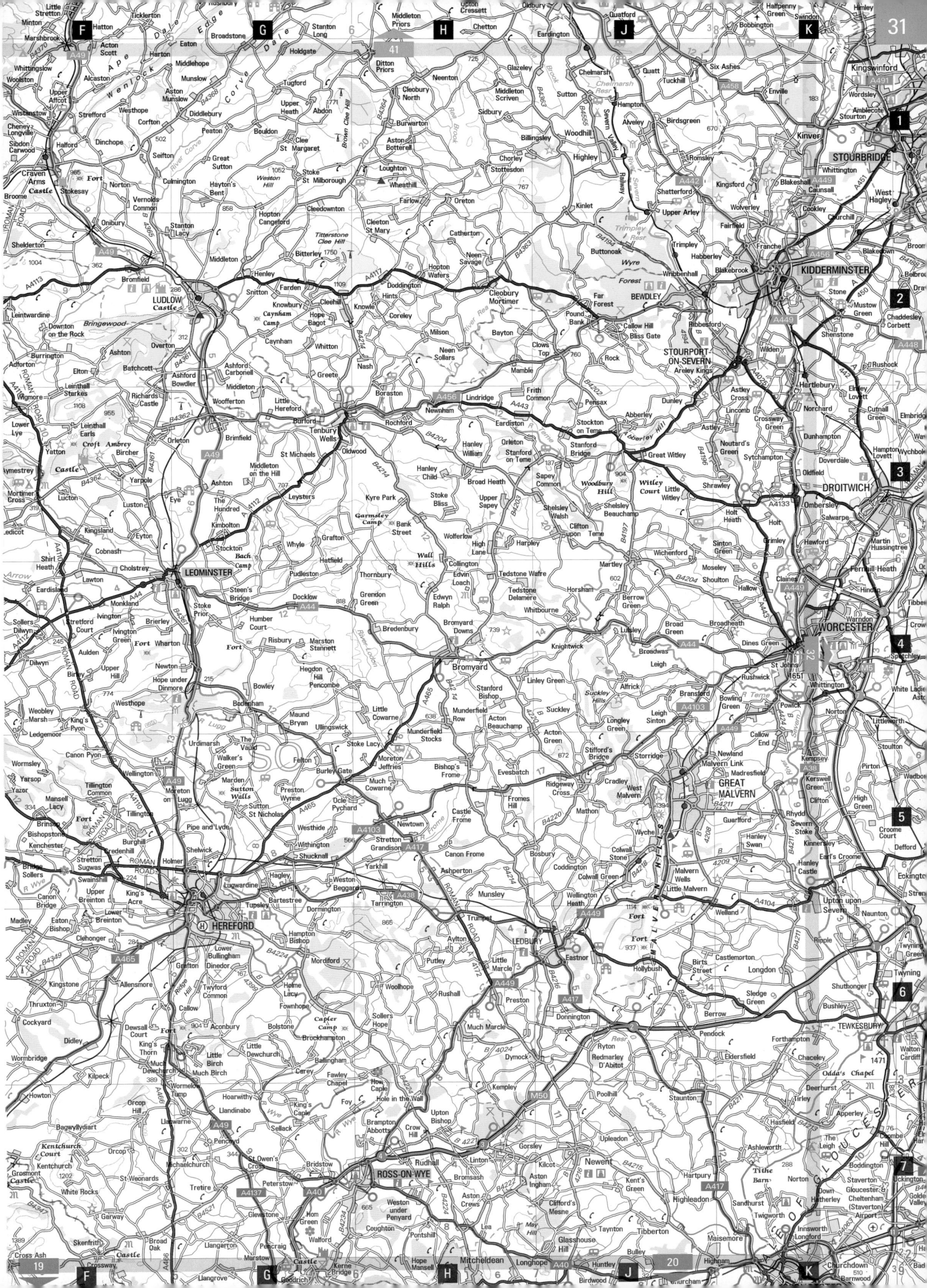

A B C D E

BIRMINGHAM

DUDLEY
WEST BROMWICH
OLDBURY
SMETHWICK
BRIERLEY HILL
Rowley Regis
BLACKHEATH
HALESOWEN
Coleshill

STOURBRIDGE
Kingswinford
Wordsley
Stourton
Amblecote
Lye
Kinver
Wollaston

Harborne
Chad Valley
Edgbaston
Moseley
Acock's Green
Sheldon
Olton
Yardley
Springfield
Hall Green
Bournville
Selly Oak
Woodgate
Northfield
King's Norton
Longbridge
Rubery
Frankley

National Exhibition Centre
Birmingham International Airport
Elmdon
Bickenhill
Marston Green
Hampton in Arden
Four Oaks
Meriden
Eastern Green
Allesley

KIDDERMINSTER
Blakedown
Broome
Belbroughton
Fairfield
Clent
Hagley
West Hagley
Romsley
Holy Cross
Lickey End
Blackwell
Barnt Green
Cofton Hackett
Hopwood
Wythall
Hollywood
Earlswood

SOLIHULL
Whitlock's End
Cheswick Green
Dorridge
Knowle
Bentley Heath
Hockley Heath
Lapworth
Kingswood
Wroxall
Honiley
Beausale

Chaddesley Corbett
Bournheath
Catshill
BROMSGROVE
Stoke Heath
Aston Fields
Tutnall
Alvechurch
Rowney Green
Portway
Wood End
Tanworth-in-Arden
Henley-in-Arden
Preston Bagot
Shrewley
Haseley
Hatton
Old Milverton

DROITWICH
Ombersley
Hadzor
Hanbury
Feckenham
Astwood Bank
Studley
Morton Bagot
Wootton Wawen
Langley
Norton Lindsey
WARWICK
Budbrooke
Longbridge

REDDITCH
Headless Cross
Crabbs Cross
Webheath
Mappleborough Green
Ullenhall
Oldberrow

Hartlebury
Elmley Lovett
Cutnall Green
Upton Warren
Stoke Prior
Wychbold
Upper Bentley
Ham Green
Holberrow Green
Stock Wood
Cookhill
Alcester
King's Coughton
Great Alne
Aston Cantlow
Wilmcote
Snitterfield
Bearley
Edstone
Wolverton
Sherbourne
Barford

WORCESTER
St Johns
Claines
Warndon
Crowle
Himbleton
Huddington
Grafton Flyford
Flyford Flavell
Abberton
Kington
Inkberrow
Abbots Morton
Rous Lench
Church Lench
Iron Cross
Salford Priors
Exhall
Temple Grafton
Ardens Grafton
Billesley
Shottery
Binton
STRATFORD-UPON-AVON
Alveston
Charlecote
Wellesbourne
Loxley
Walton

Powick
Norton
Kempsey
Pirton
Drakes Broughton
Pinvin
Wyre Piddle
Lower Moor
Cropthorne
Charlton
Harvington
Norton
Bishampton
Throckmorton
Peopleton
North Piddle
Naunton Beauchamp
White Ladies Aston
Wadborough
Pershore
Besford
Wick
Fladbury

GREAT MALVERN
Malvern Link
Newland
Madresfield
Kerswell Green
Clifton
High Green
Hanley Swan
Croome Court
Defford
Birlingham
Eckington
Little Comberton
Great Comberton
Bricklehampton
Elmley Castle
Netherton

EVESHAM
Hampton
Wickhamford
Badsey
Bretforton
Aldington
Honeybourne
Mickleton
Pebworth
Broad Marston
Long Marston
Dorsington
Marlcliff
Cleeve Prior
North Littleton
Middle Littleton
South Littleton
Offenham
Bidford-on-Avon
Welford-on-Avon
Barton
Clifford Chambers
Atherstone on Stour
Preston on Stour
Wimpstone
Lower Quinton
Upper Quinton
Meon Hill
Admington
Ilmington
Newbold-on-Stour
Armscote
Tredington
Blackwell
Halford
Idlicote
Pillerton Priors

Upton upon Severn
Welland
Naunton
Ripple
Strensham
Bredon's Norton
Overbury
Kemerton
Conderton
Ashton under Hill
Beckford
Dumbleton
Wormington
Sedgeberrow
Hinton on the Green
Childswickham
Willersey
Saintbury
Weston-sub-Edge
Broadway
Buckland
Laverton
Stanton
Snowshill
Broadway Hill
Chipping Campden
Broad Campden
Paxford
Draycott
Blockley
Batsford
Aston Magna
Lower Lemington
Moreton-in-Marsh
Todenham
Stretton-on-Fosse
Barton-on-the-Heath
Long Compton
Rollright Stones
Little Compton

Longdon
Twyning
Bushley
Tewkesbury
Northway
Great Washbourne
Alderton
Alstone
Teddington
Toddington
Stanway
Didbrook
Hailes Abbey
Wood Stanway
Cutsdean
Condicote
Longborough
Donnington
Evenlode
Broadwell
STOW-ON-THE-WOLD
Upper Swell
Lower Swell
Maugersbury
Icomb
Bledington
Churchill
Kingham
Sarsden

Forthampton
Deerhurst
Apperley
Chaceley
Tirley
Hasfield
Ashleworth
Sandhurst
Norton
Staverton
Gloucester & Cheltenham (Staverton) Airport
Boddington
Uckington
Swindon
Elmstone Hardwicke
Woodmancote
Bishop's Cleeve
Southam
Cleeve Hill
Prestbury
CHELTENHAM
CHARLTON KINGS
Leckhampton
Badgeworth
Shurdington
Dowdeswell
Whittington
Andoversford
Sevenhampton
Brockhampton
Syreford
Hawling
Guiting Power
Temple Guiting
Kineton
Barton
Naunton
Upper Slaughter
Lower Slaughter
Bourton-on-the-Water
Notgrove
Cold Aston
Turkdean
Hazleton
Northleach

Winchcombe
Sudeley Castle
Long Barrow
Charlton Abbots
Didbrook

GLOUCESTER

Due to open Early 1995

1 2 3 4 5 6 7

Motorways/roads shown: M5, M6, M42, M40, M50, A38, A44, A46, A435, A422, A449, A451, A456, A448, A491, A441, A456, A4104, B4211

A B C D E

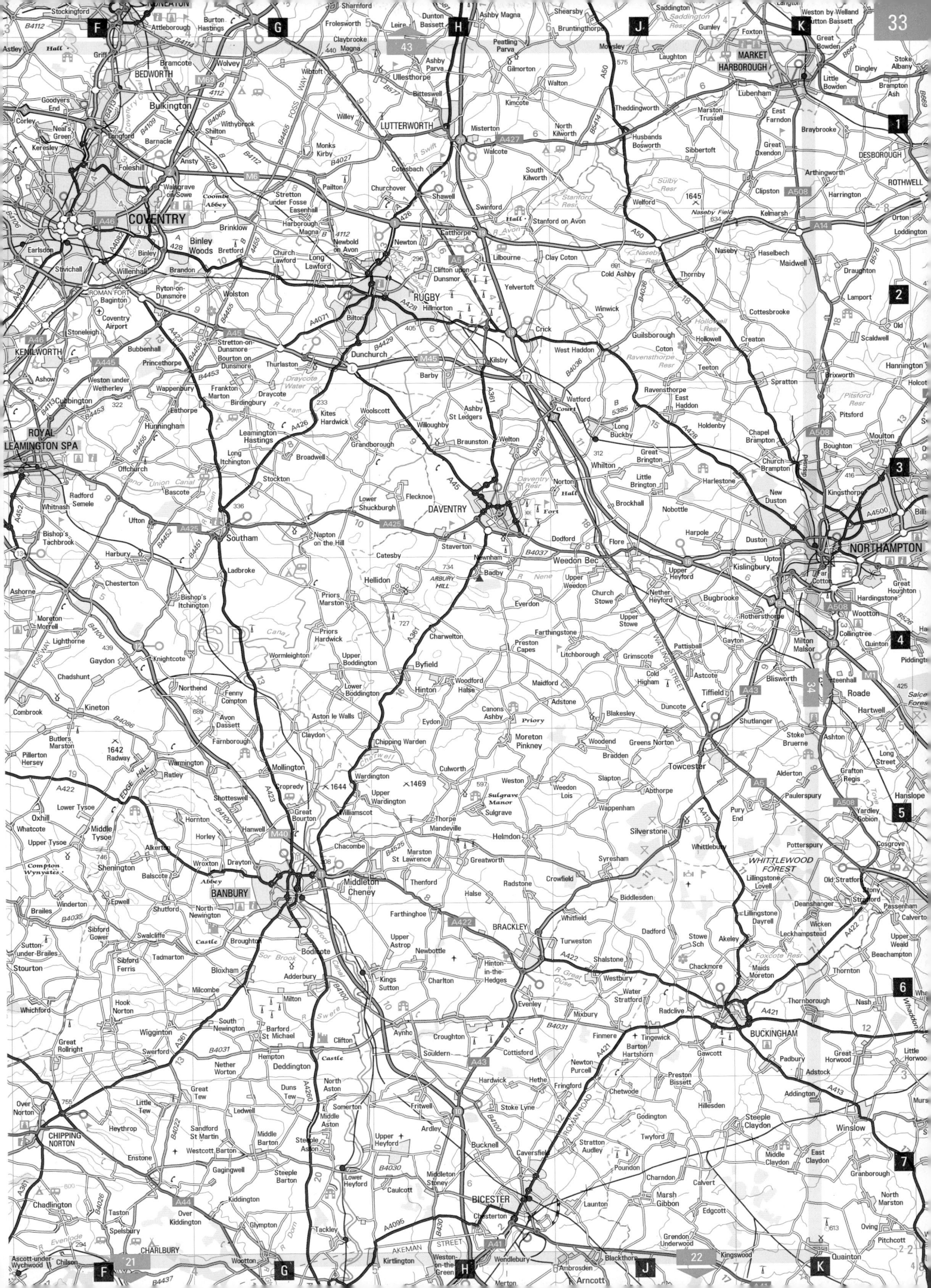

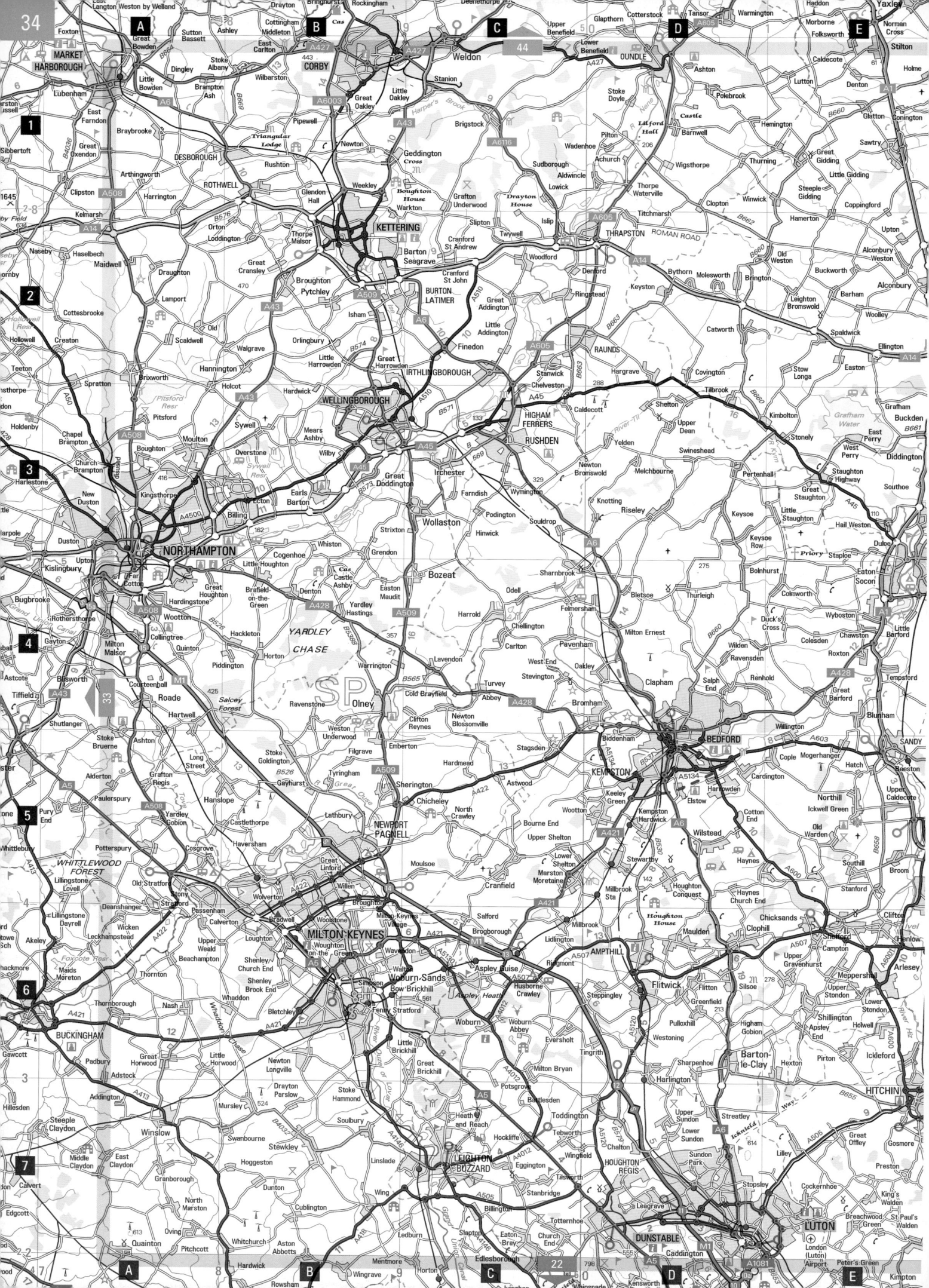

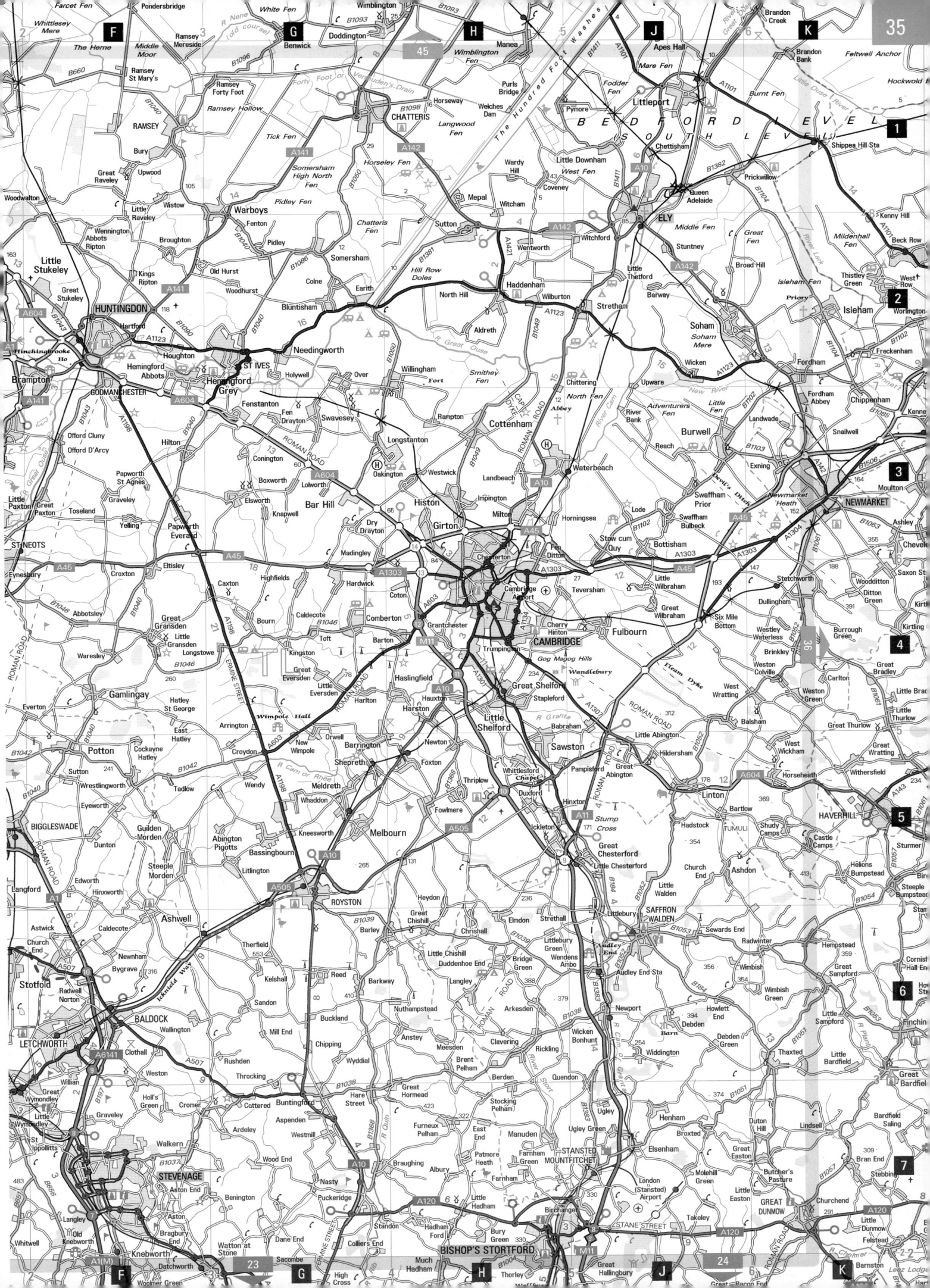

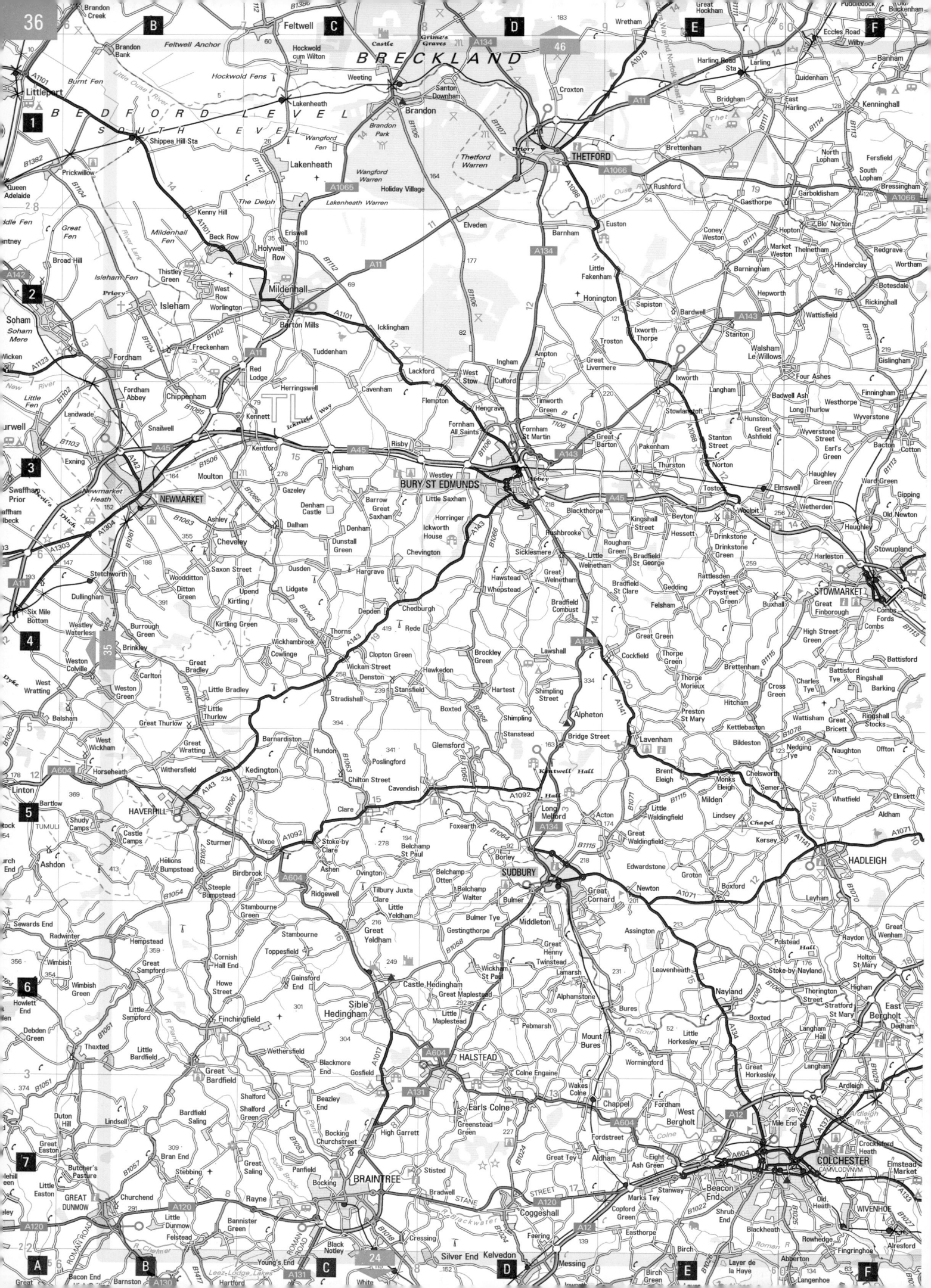

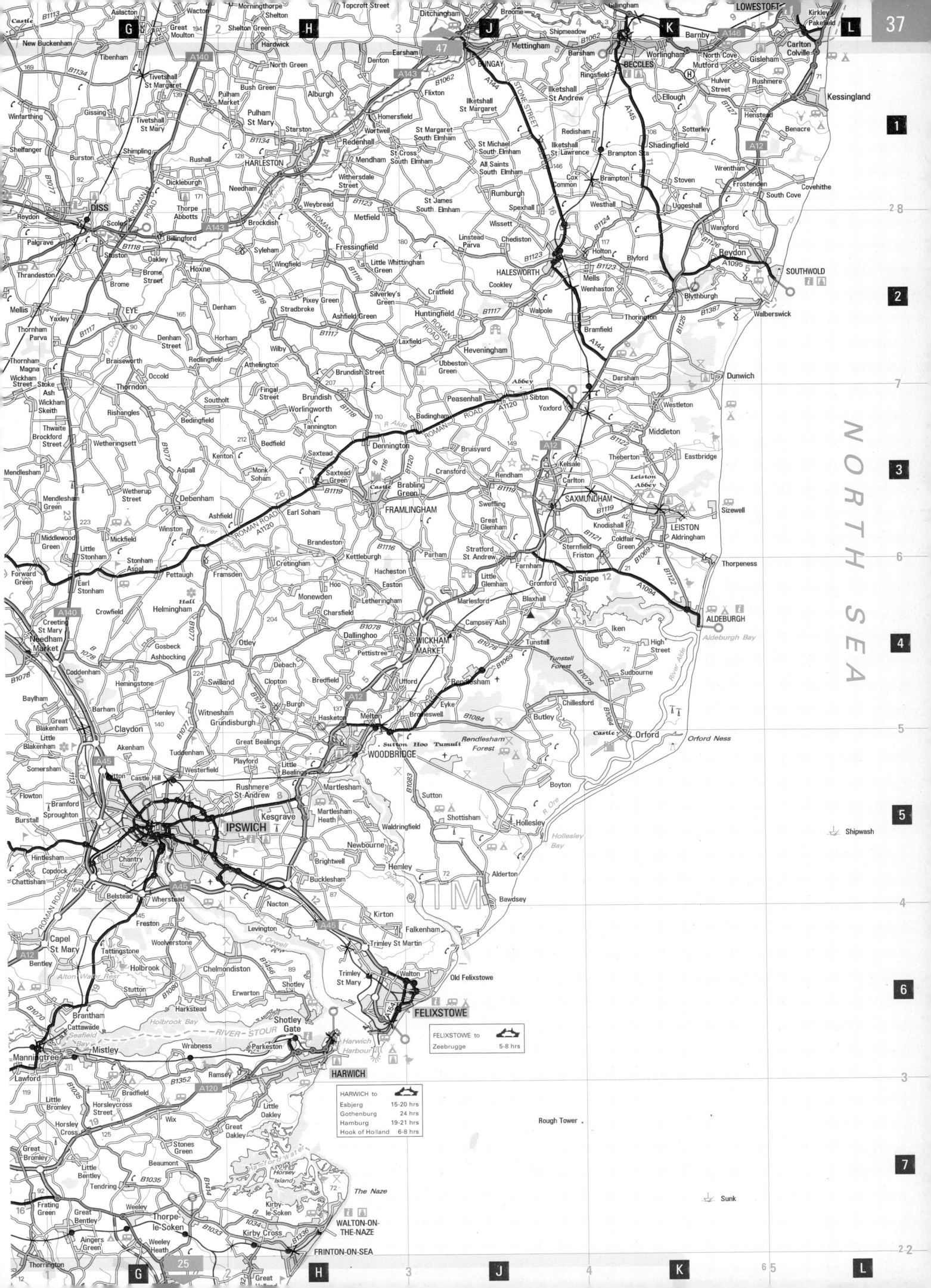

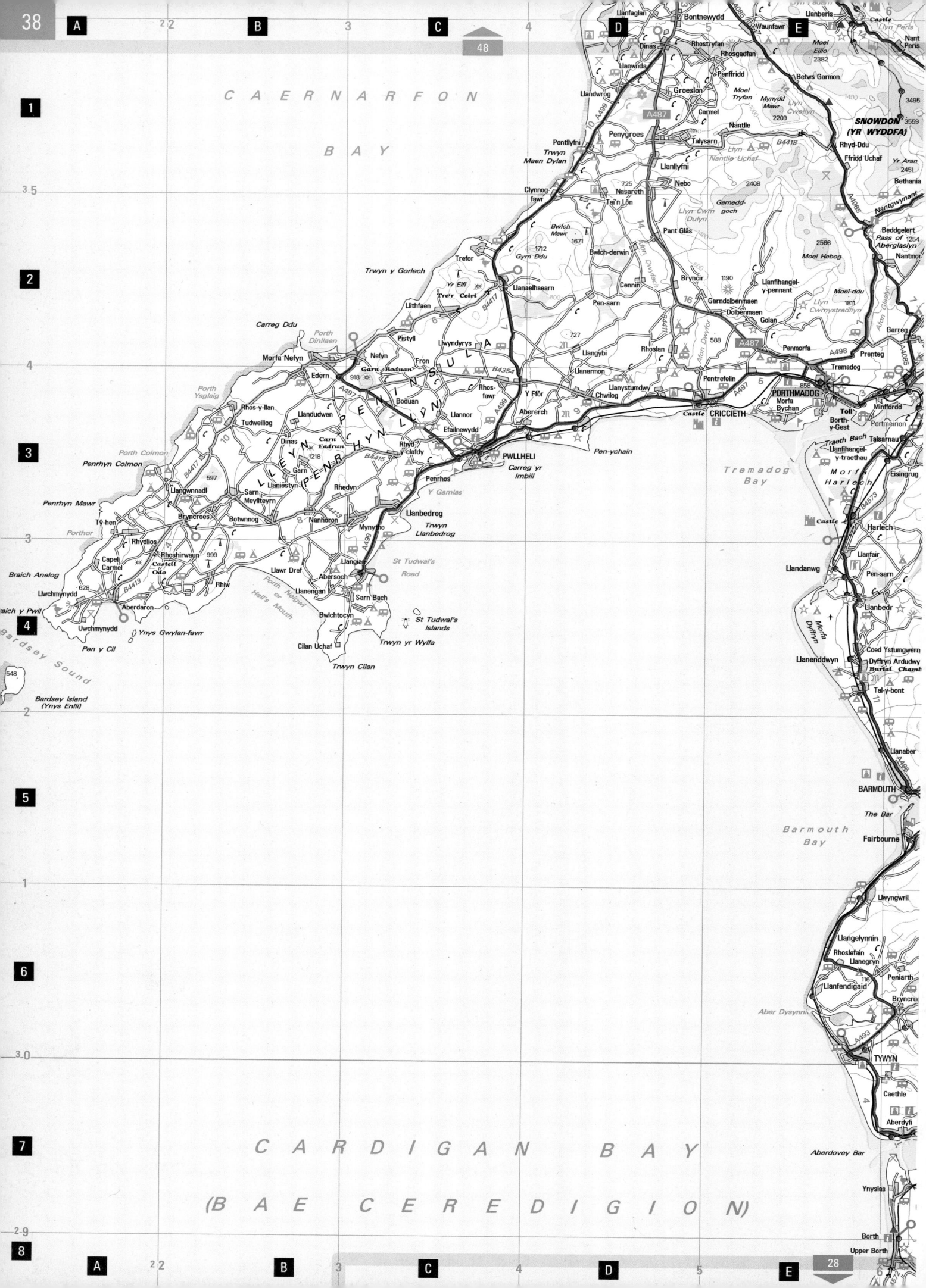

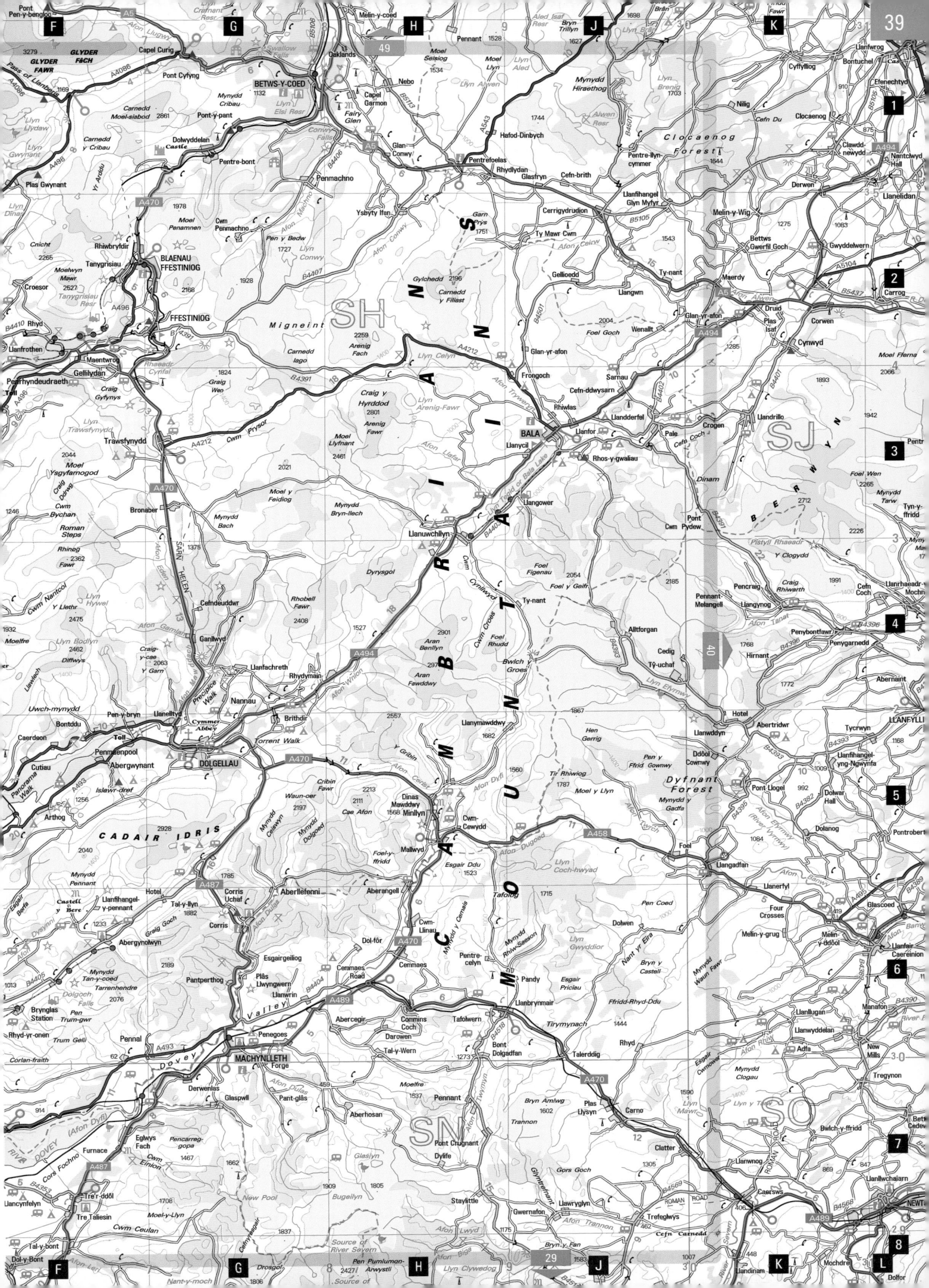

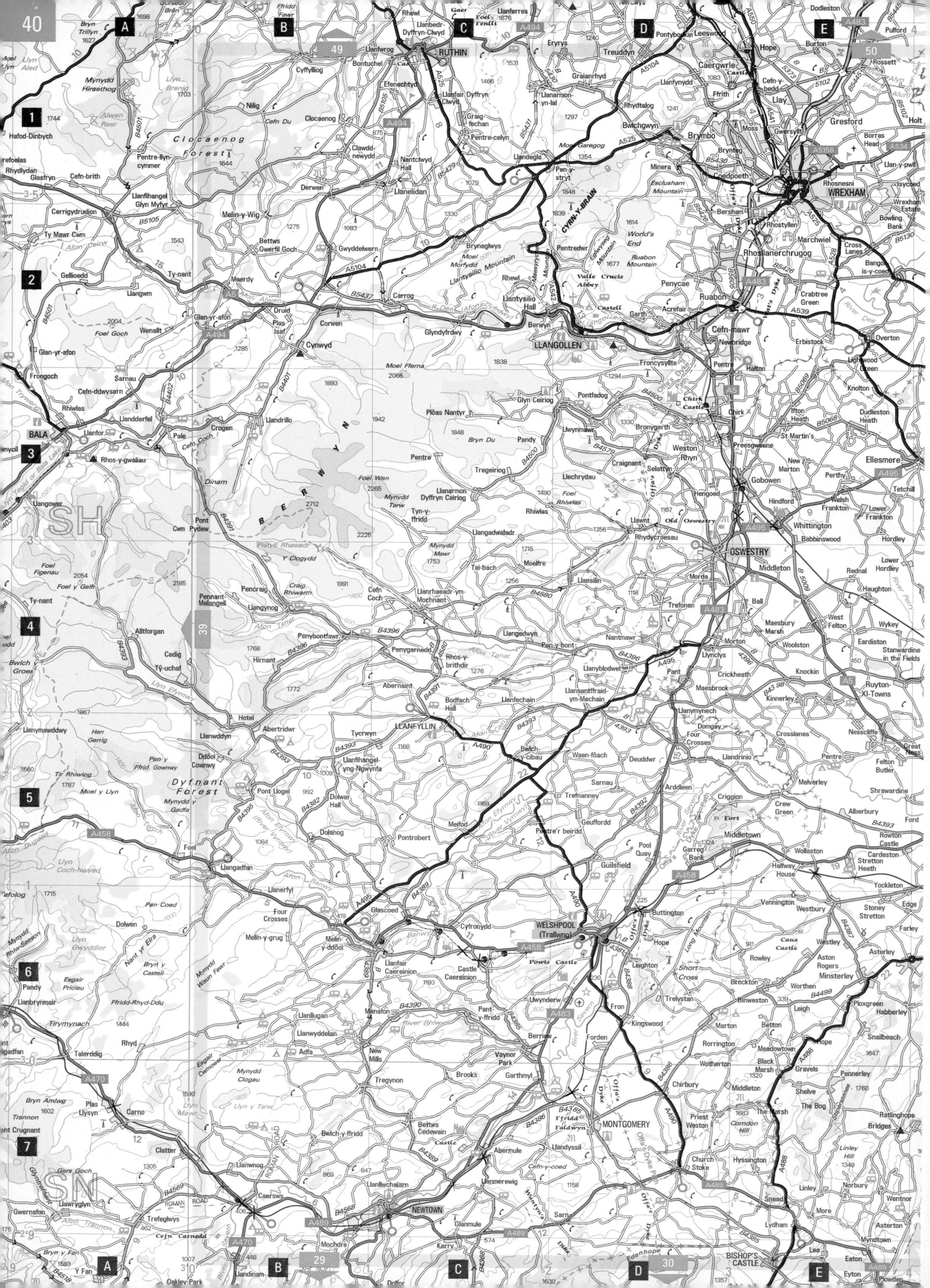

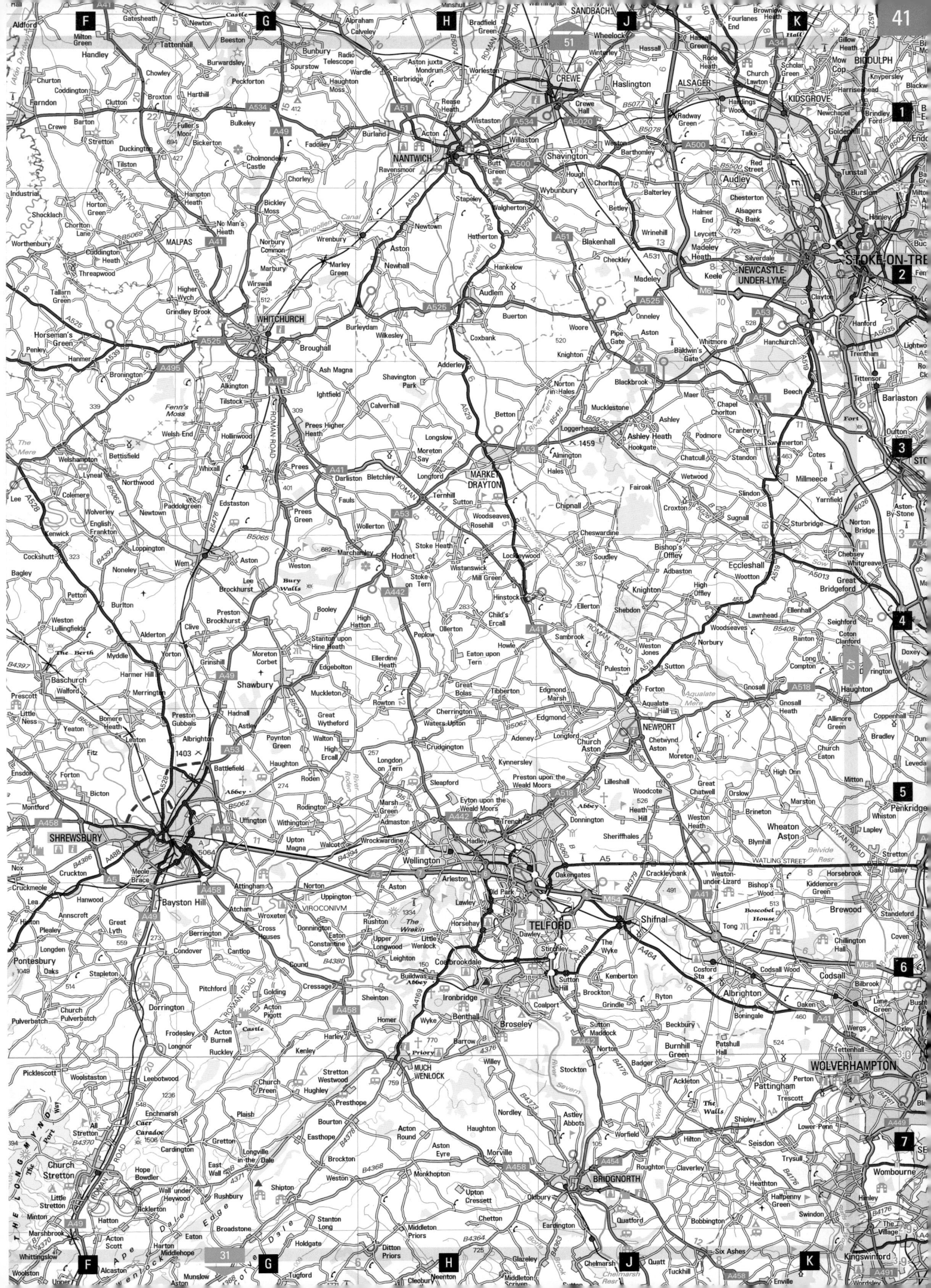

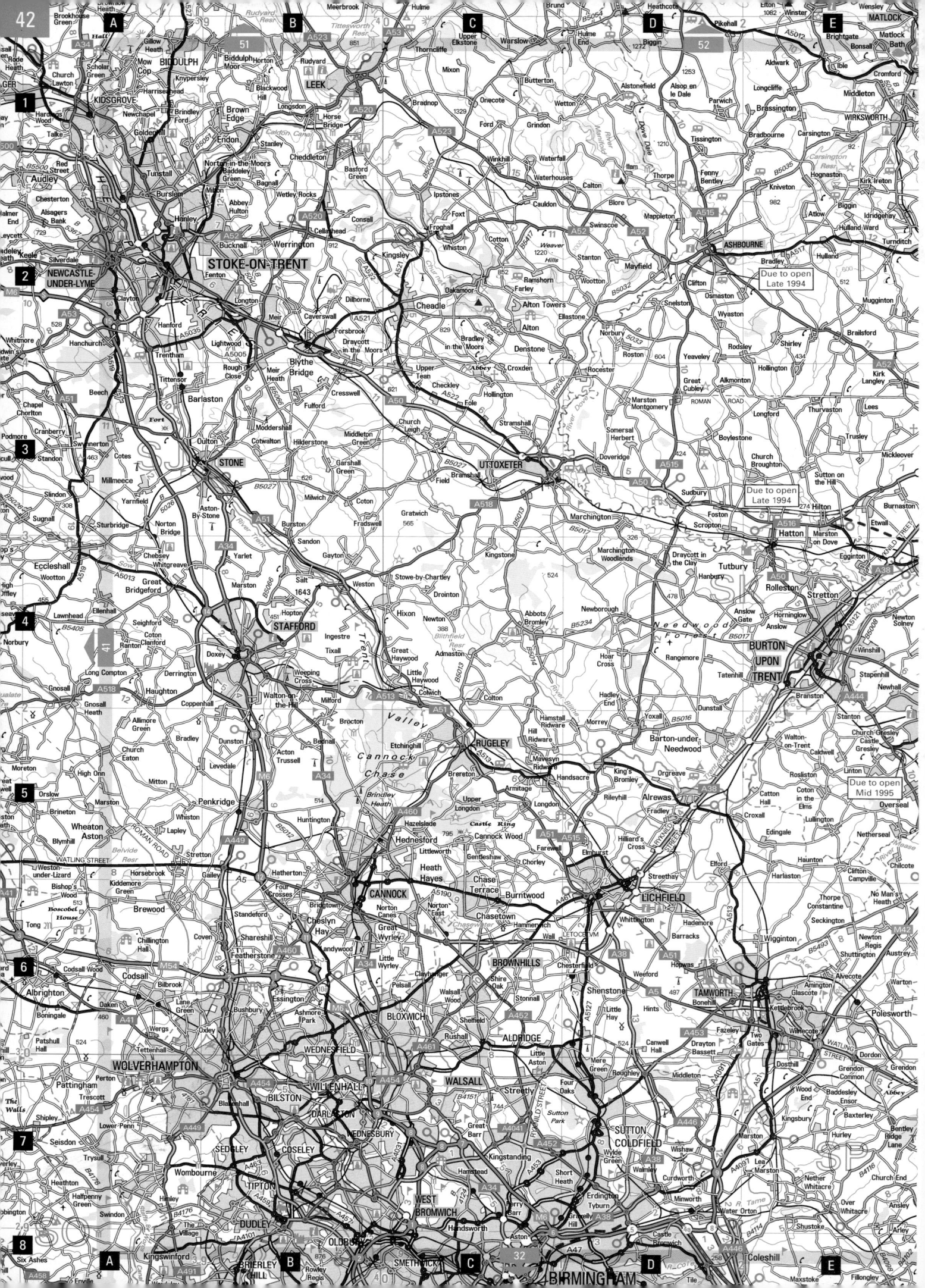

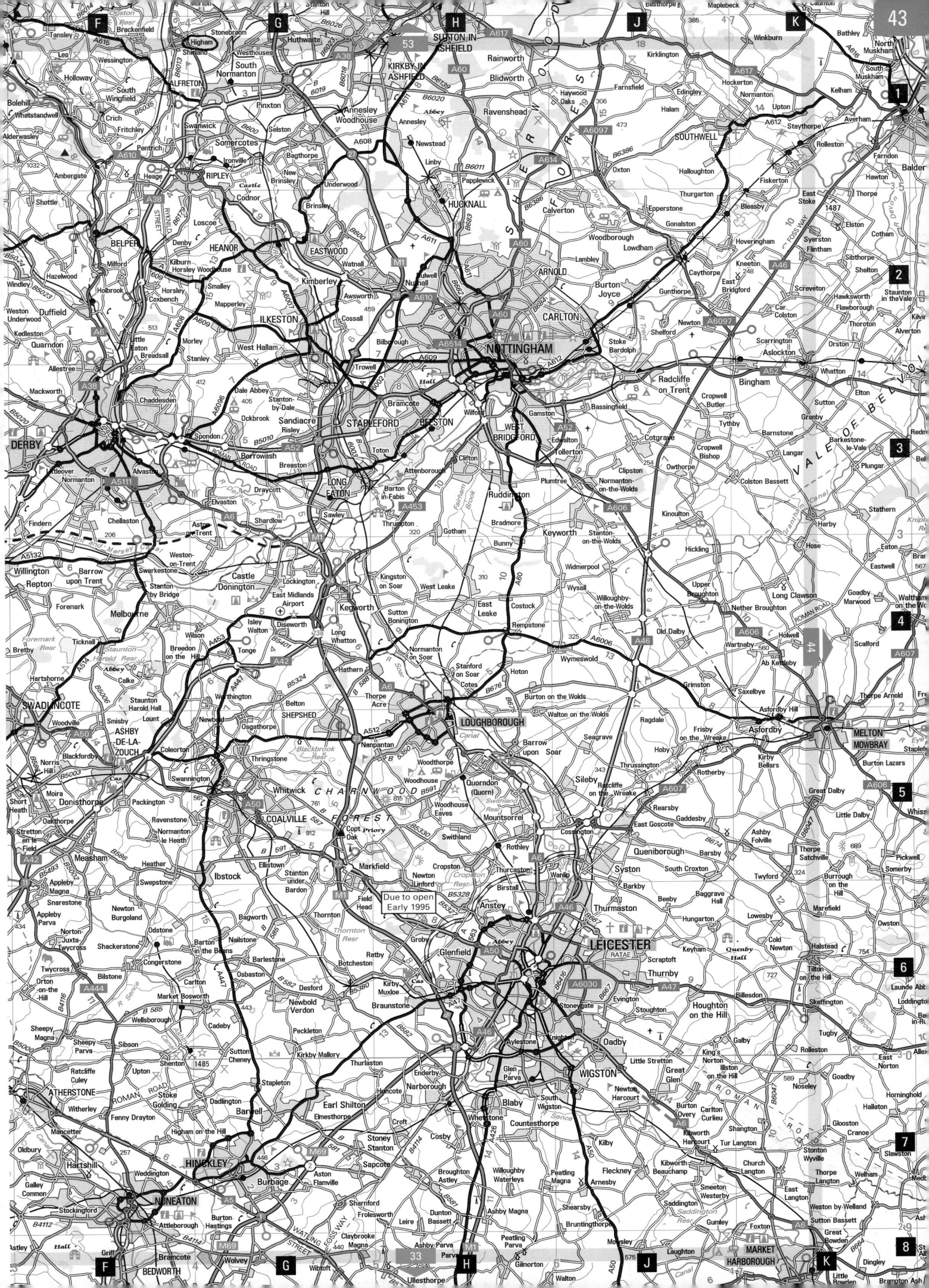

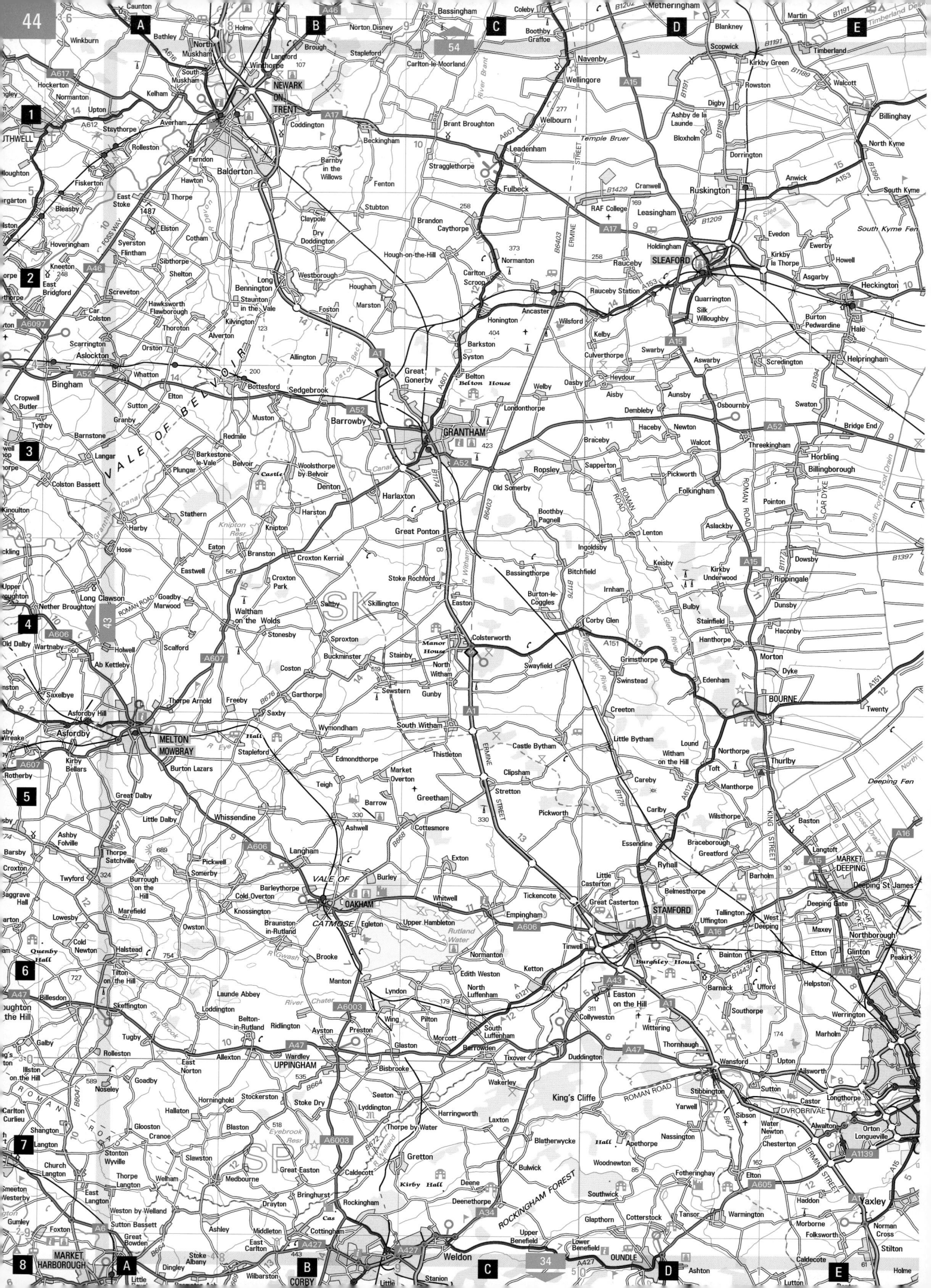

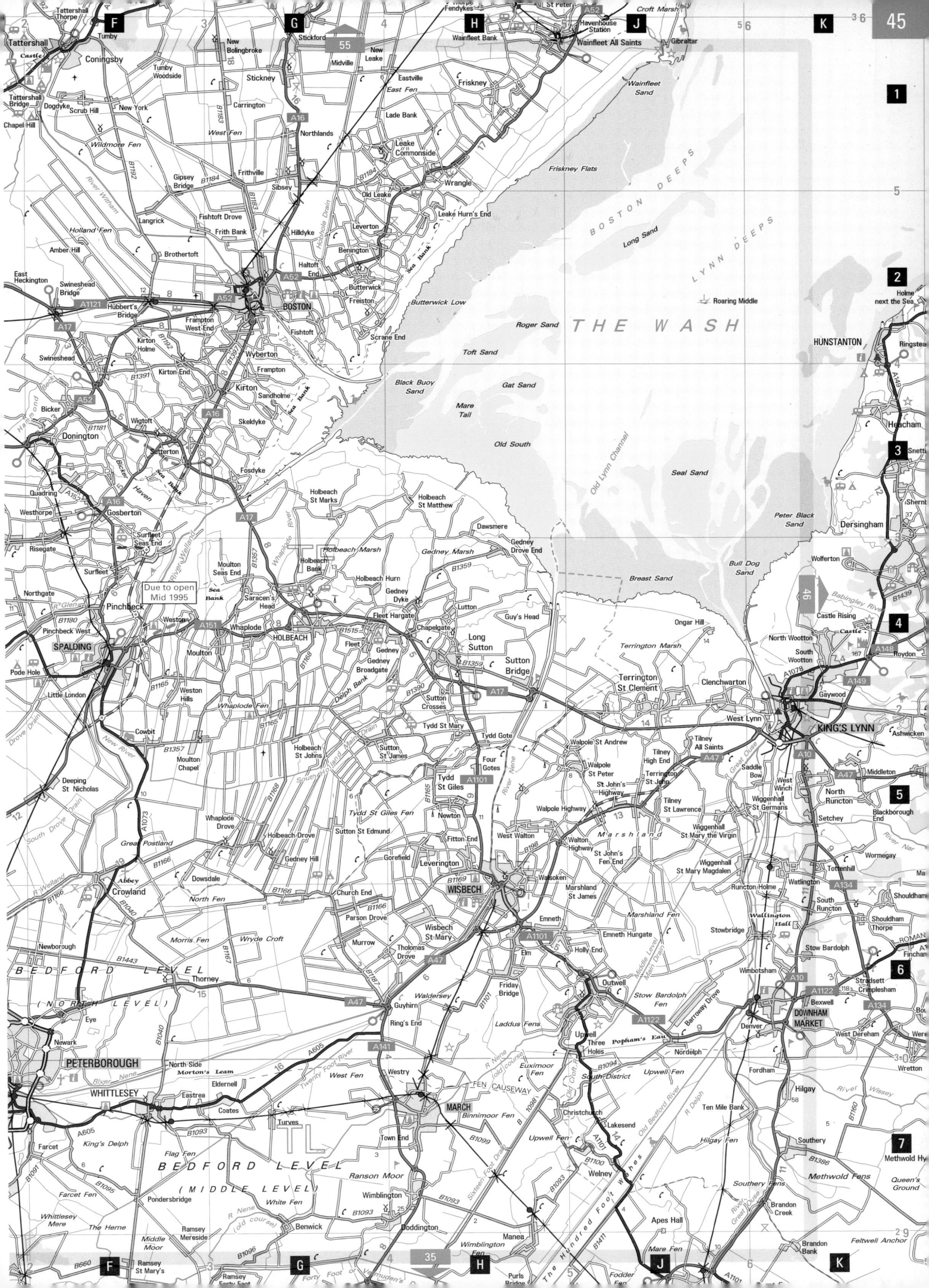

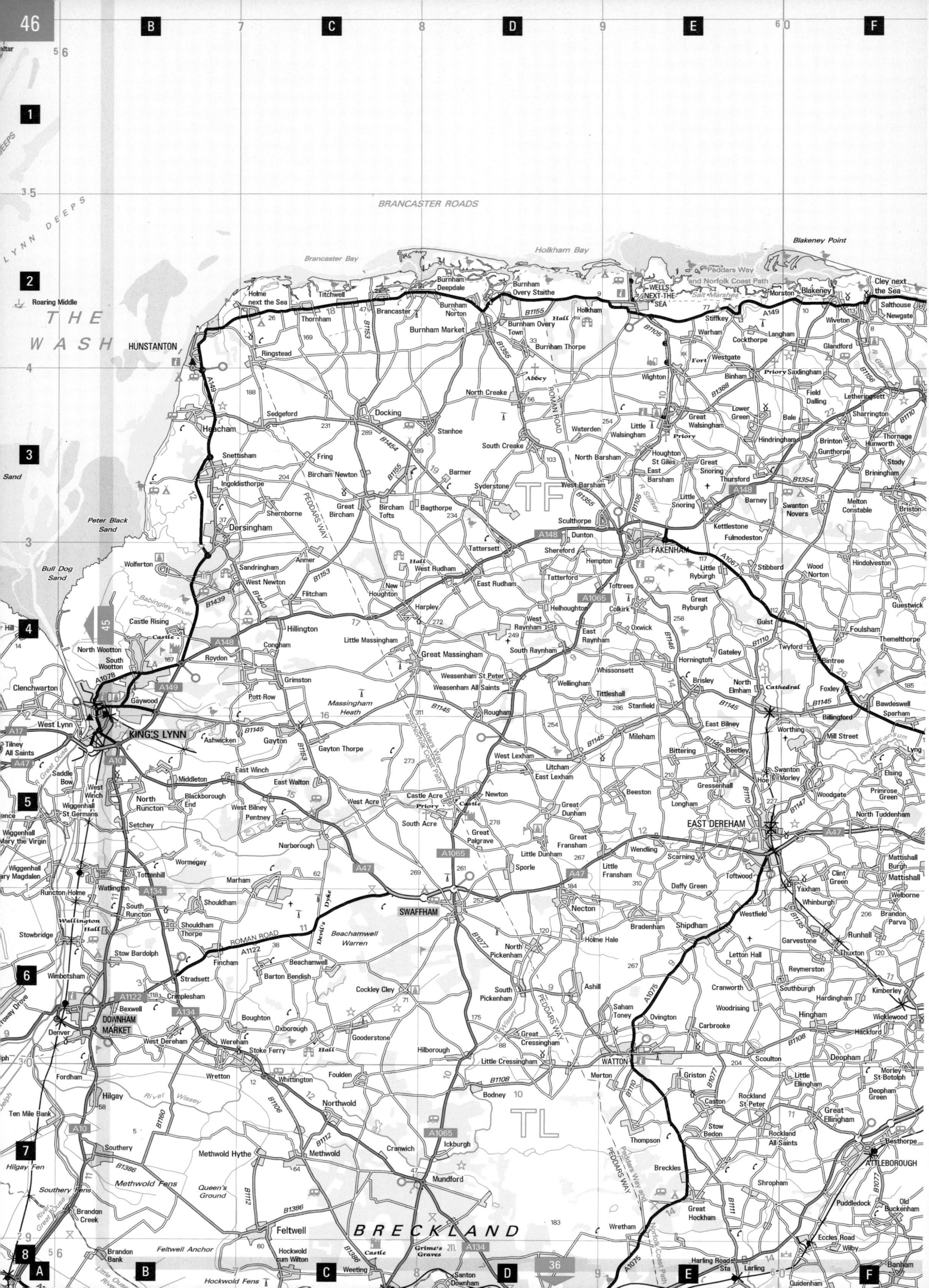

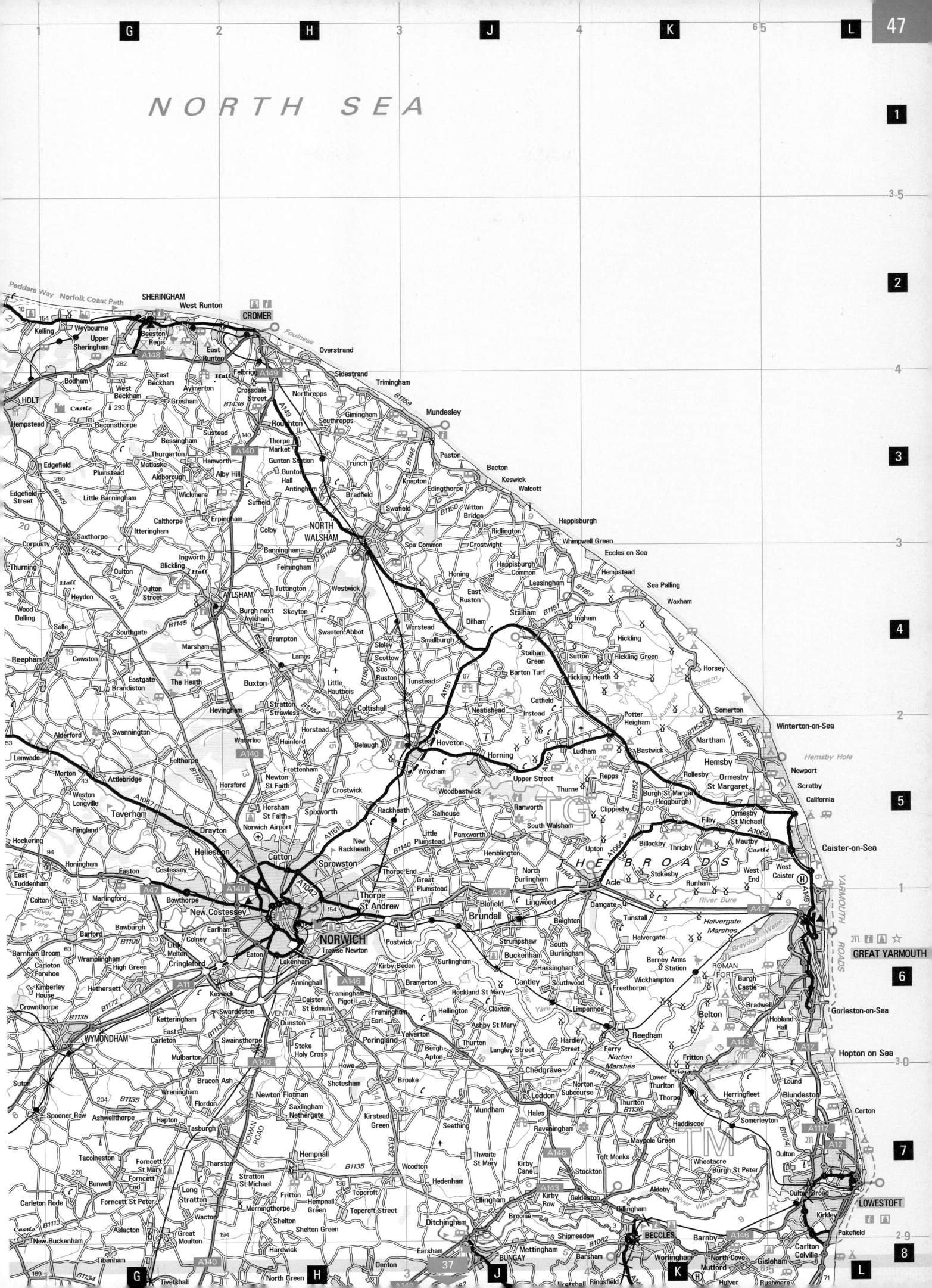

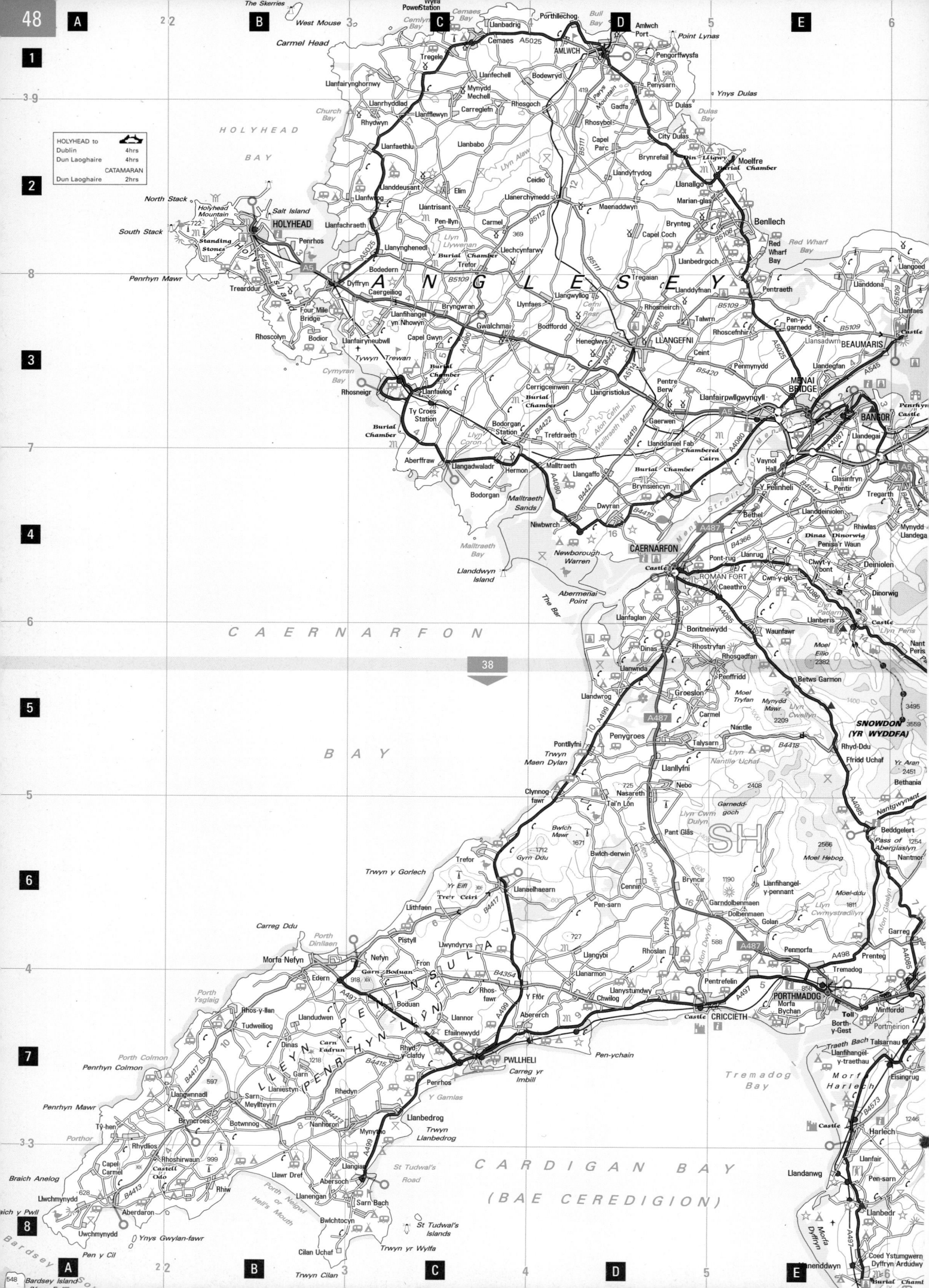

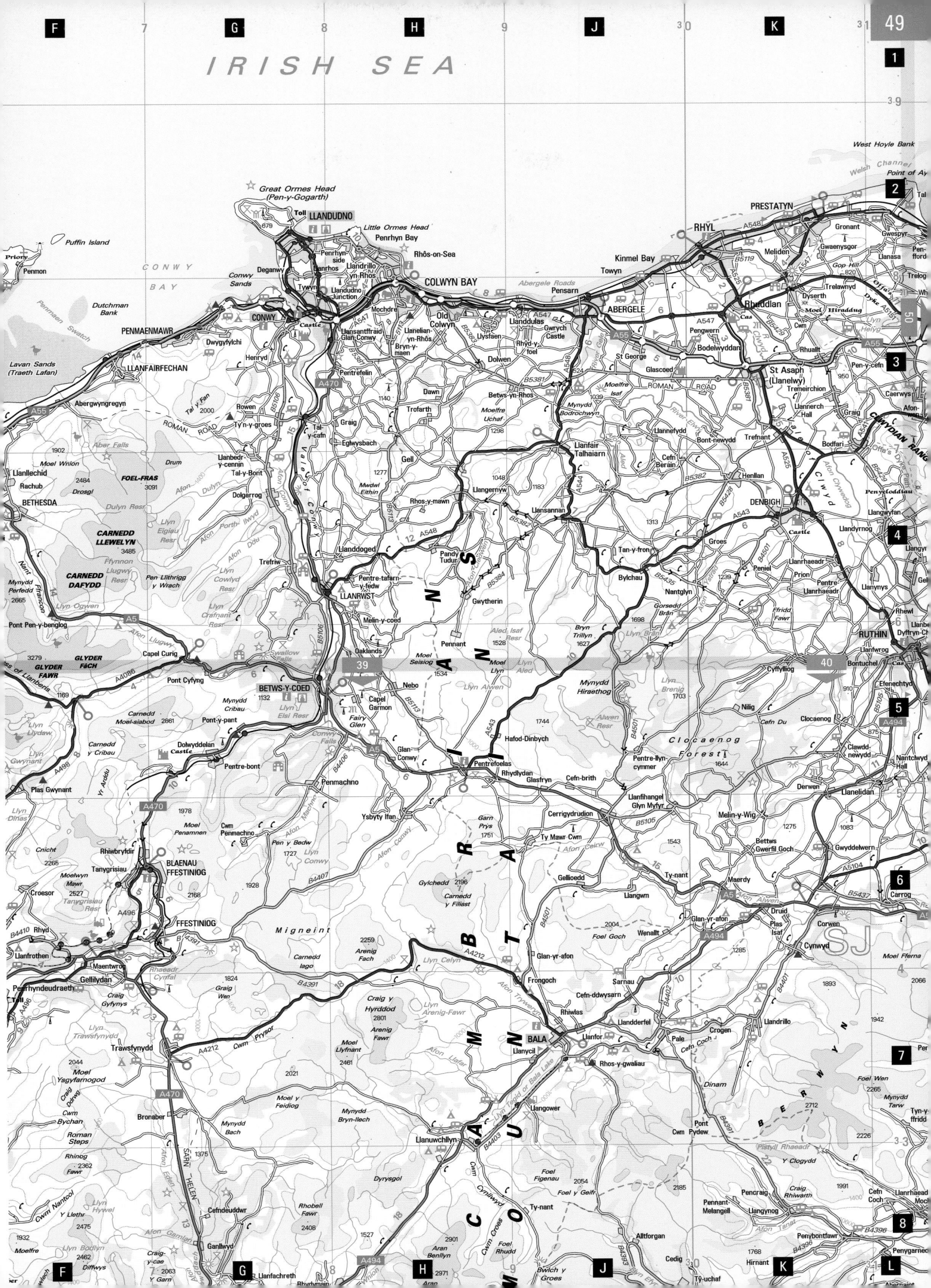

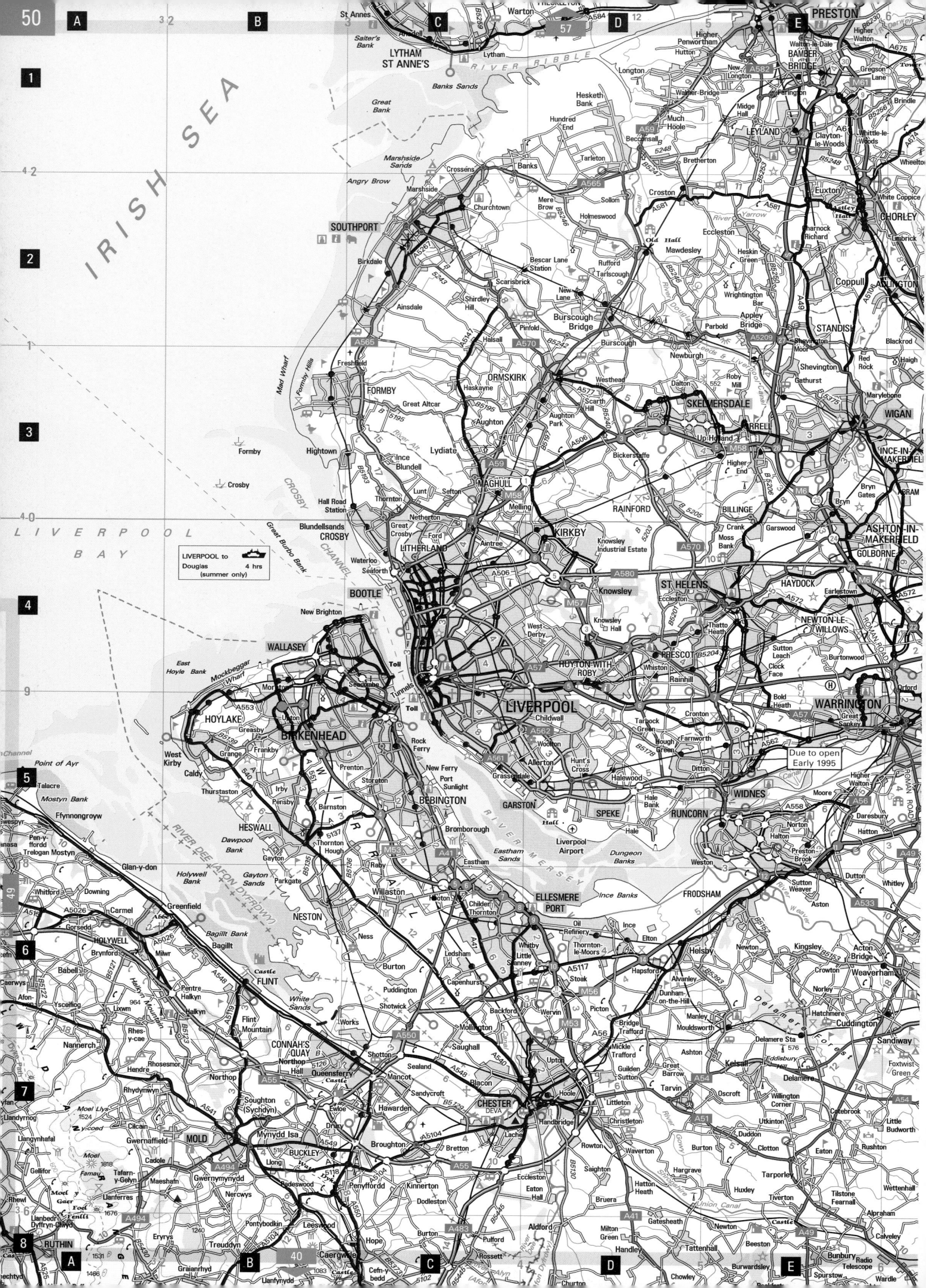

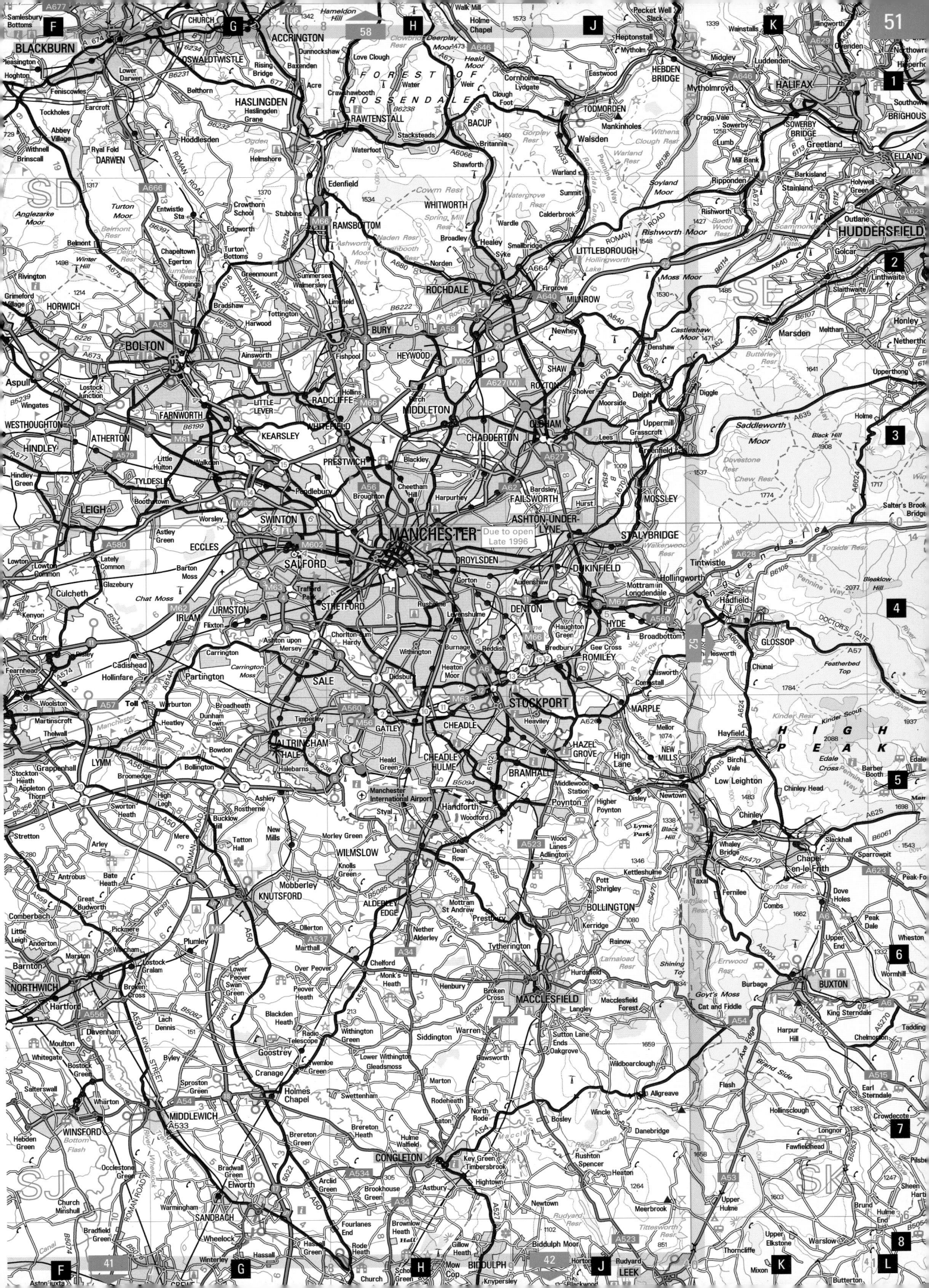

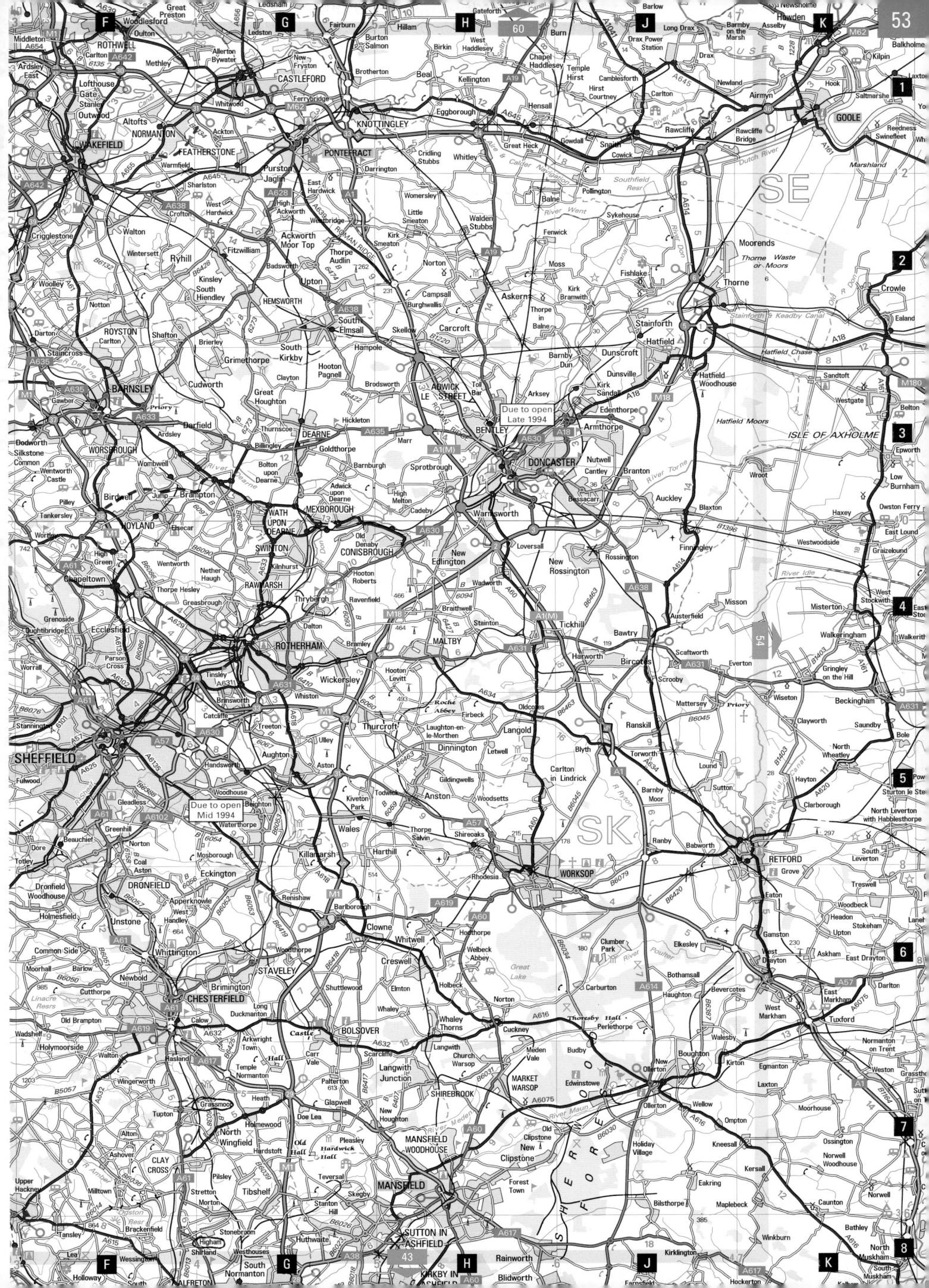

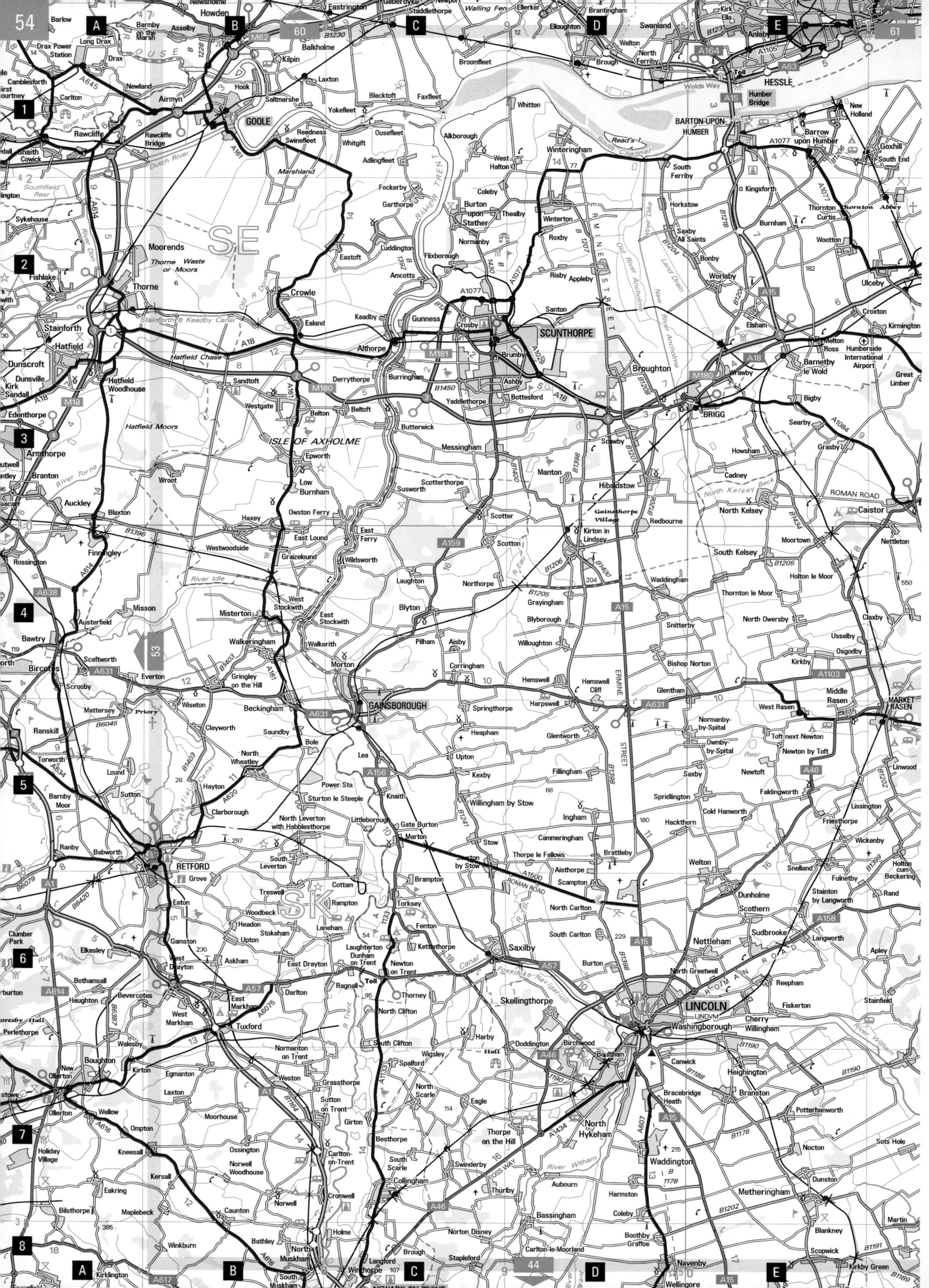

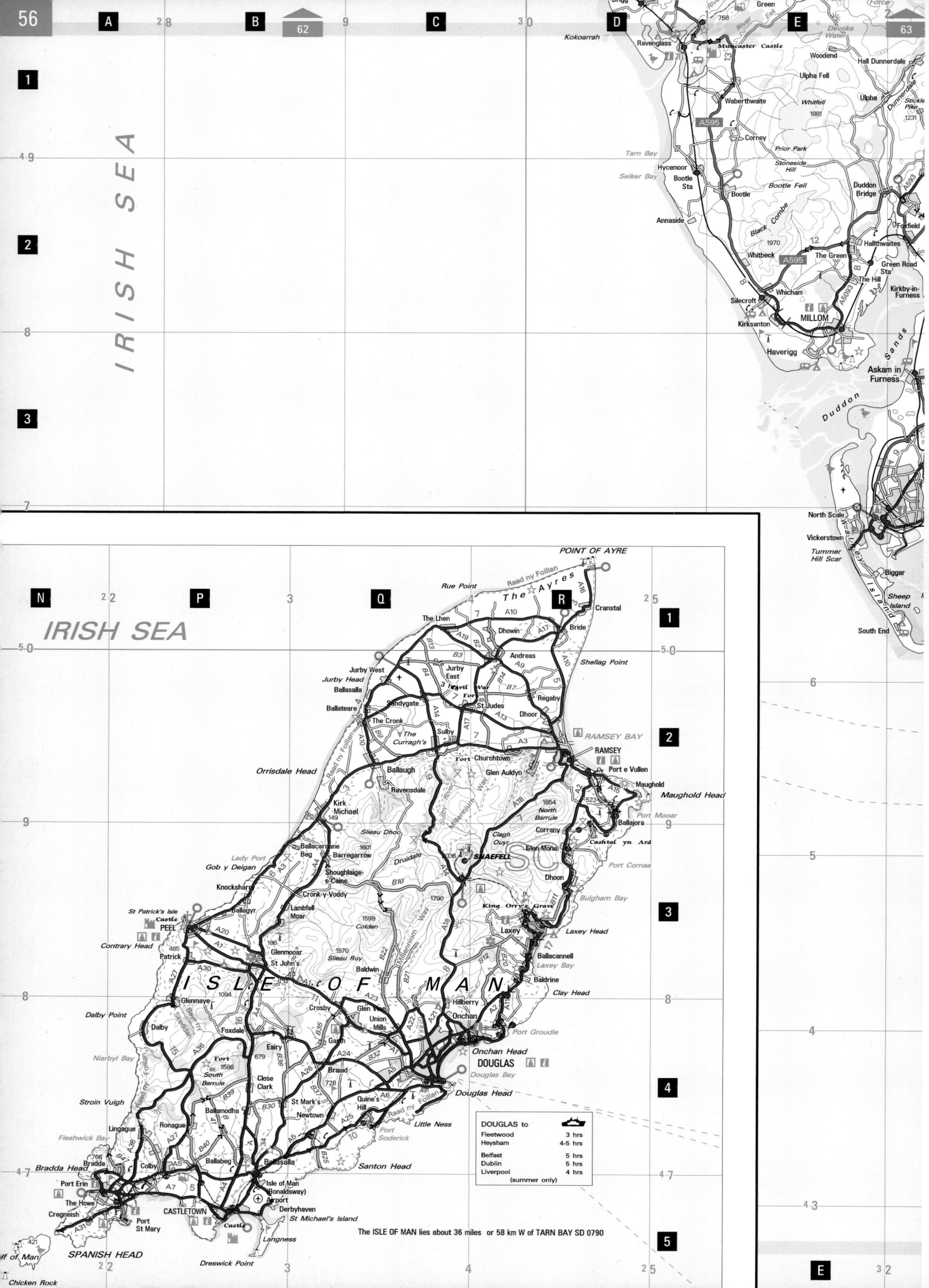

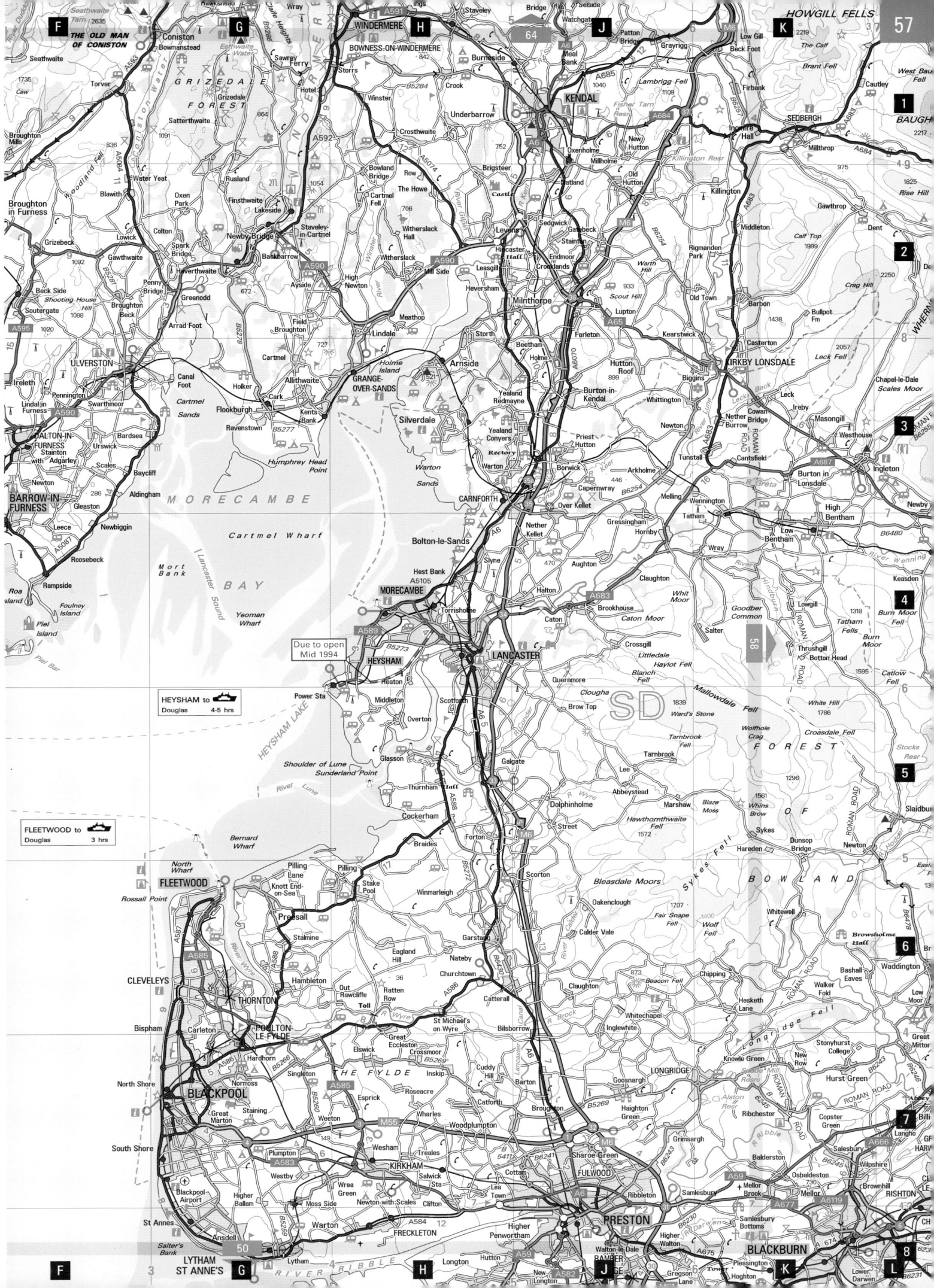

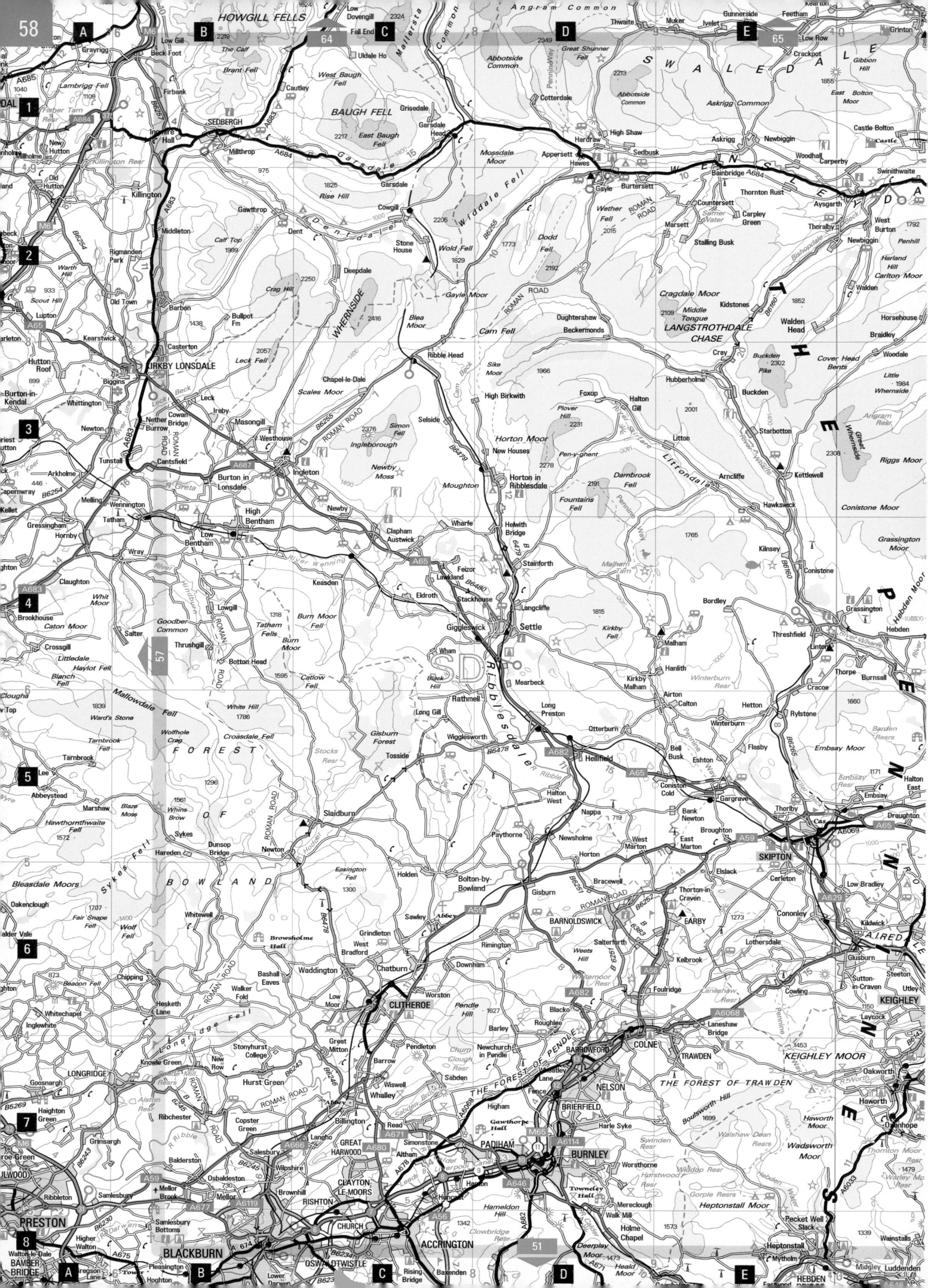

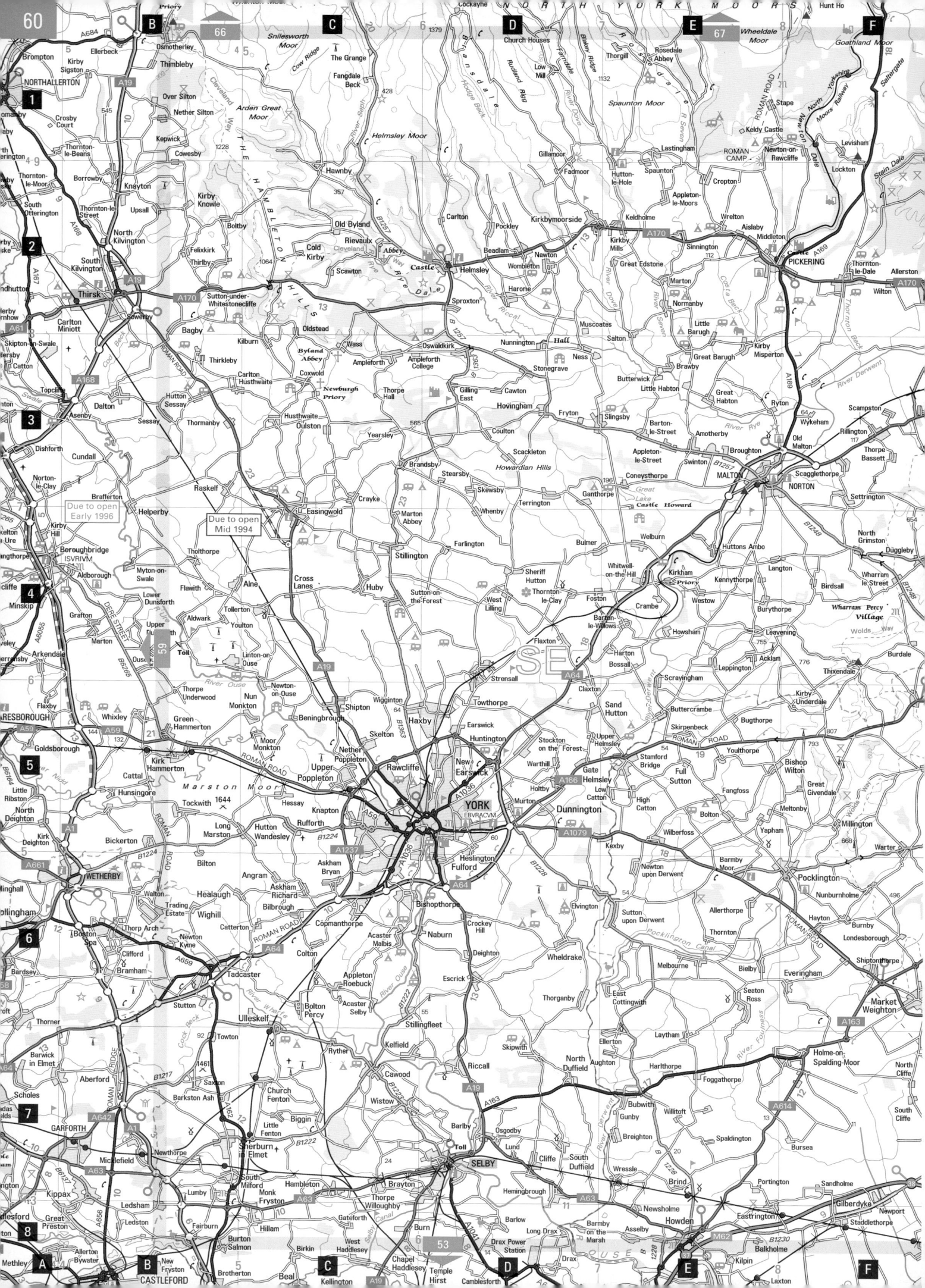

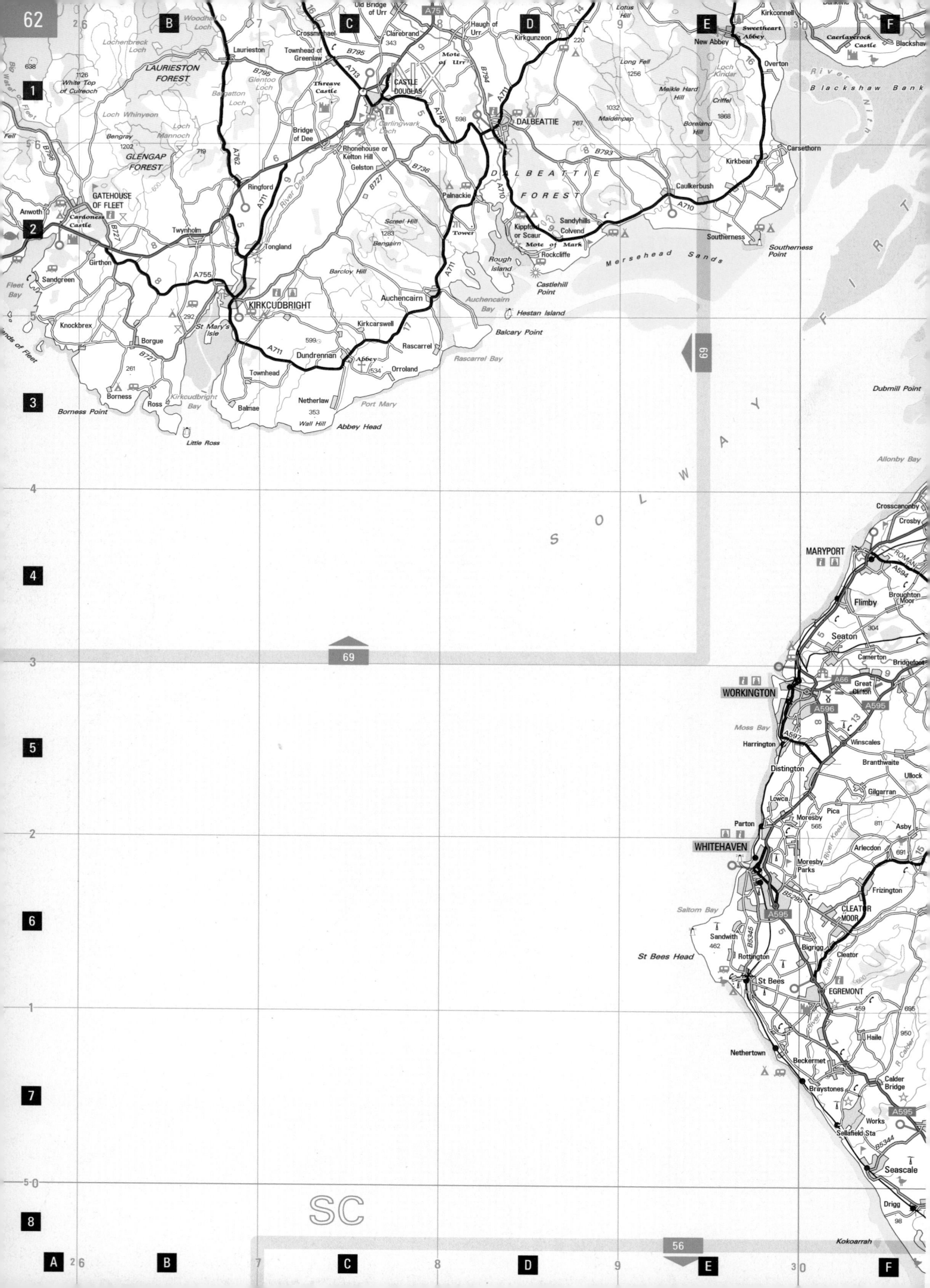

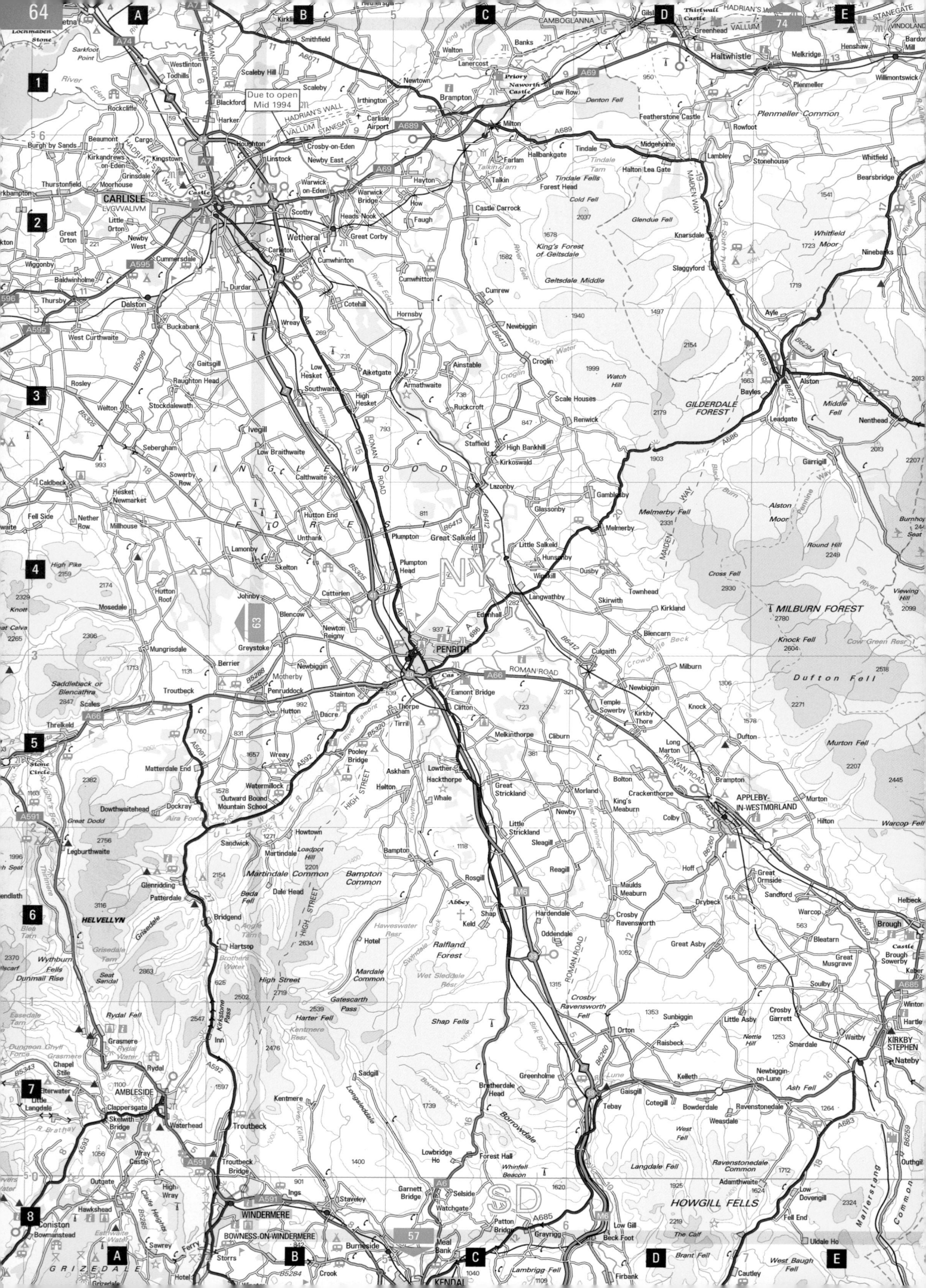

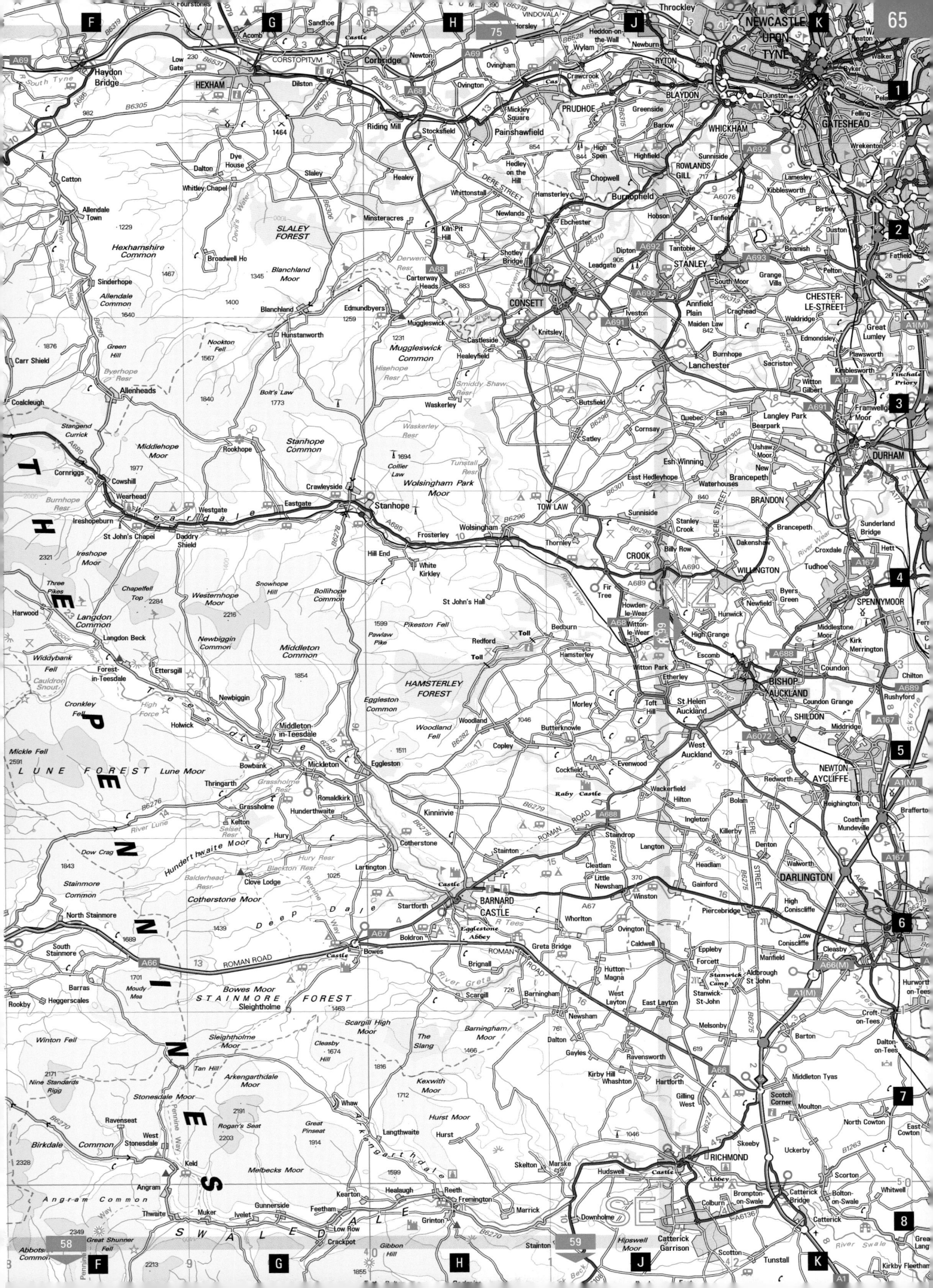

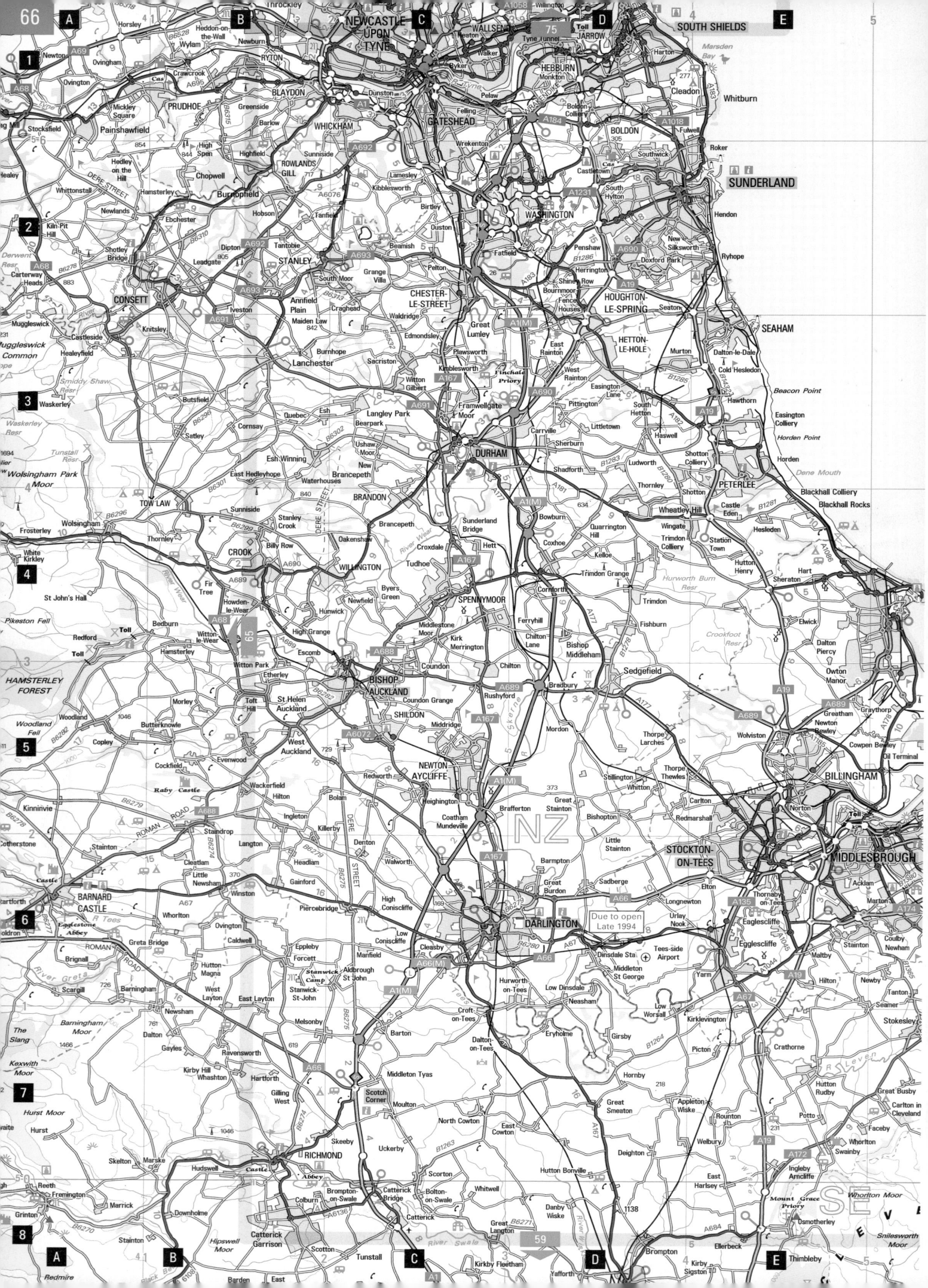

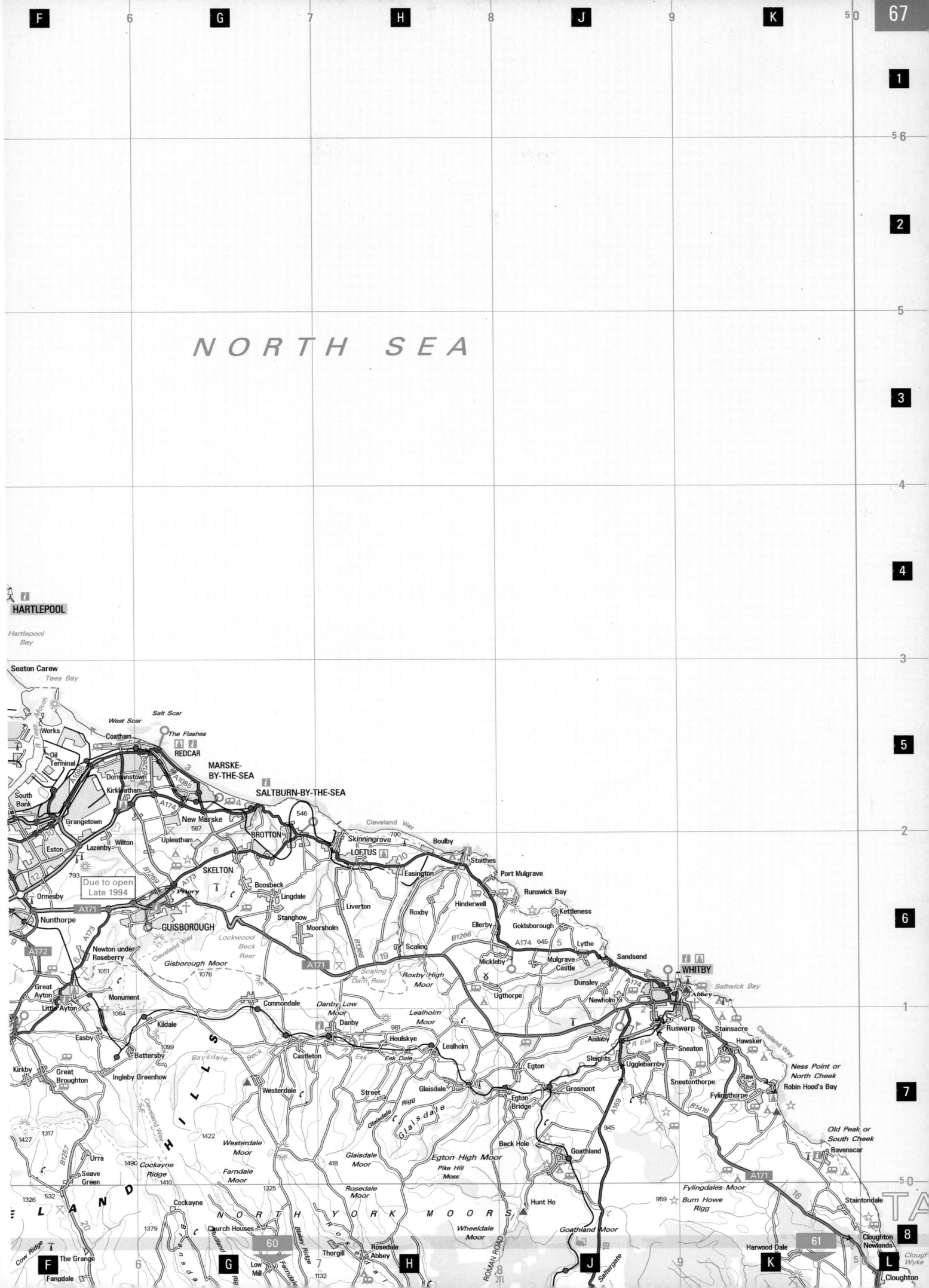

NORTH SEA

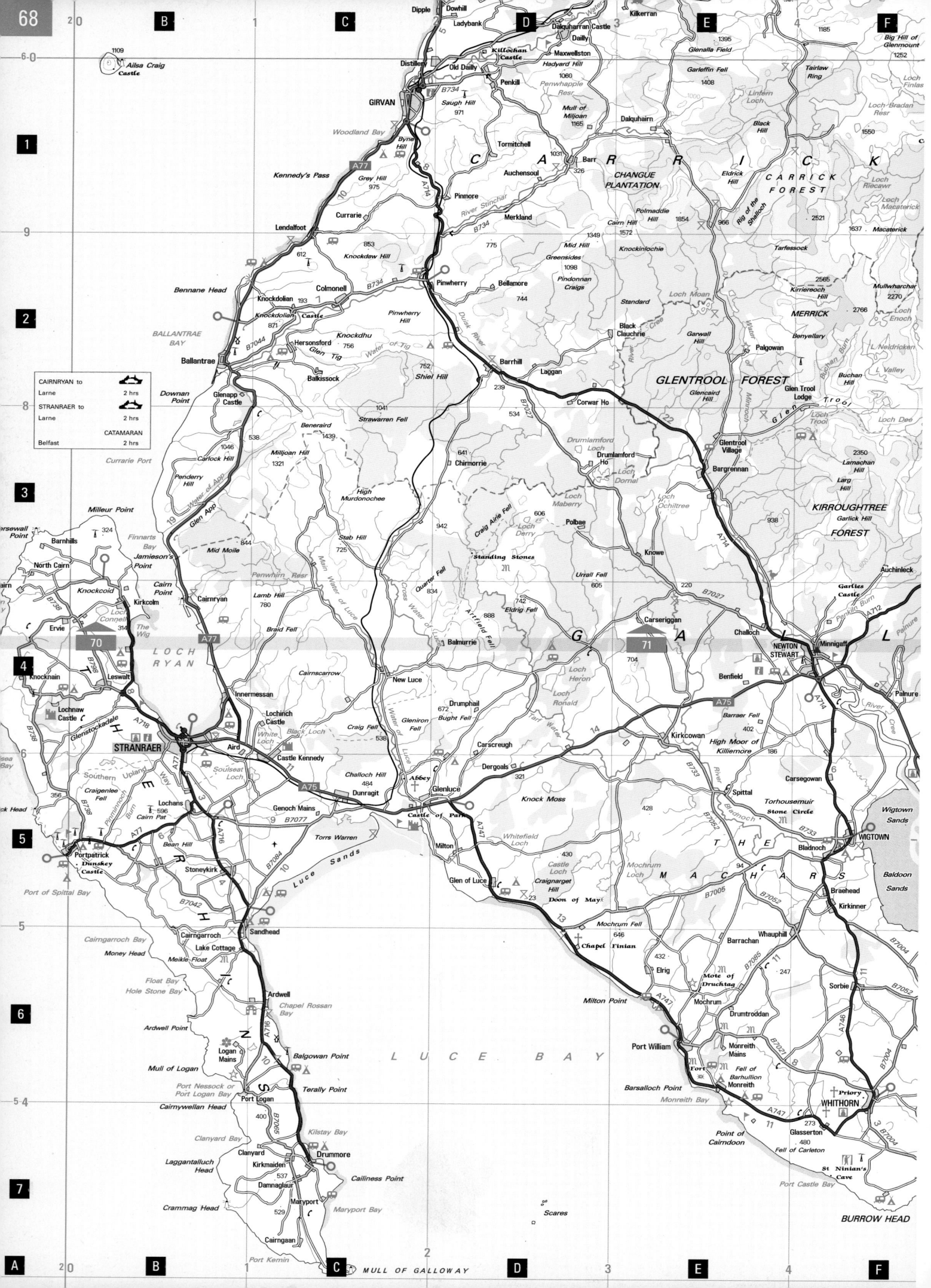

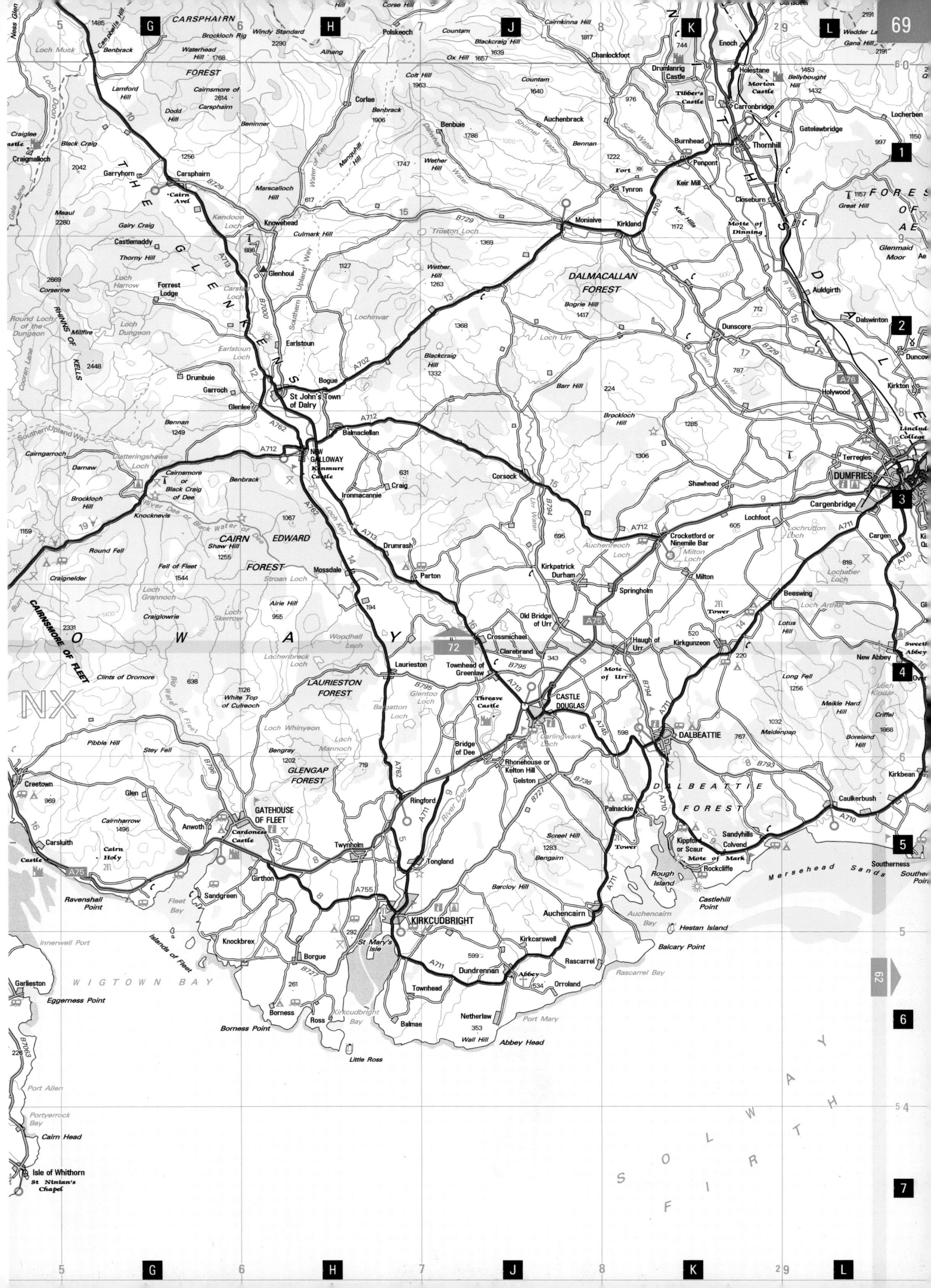

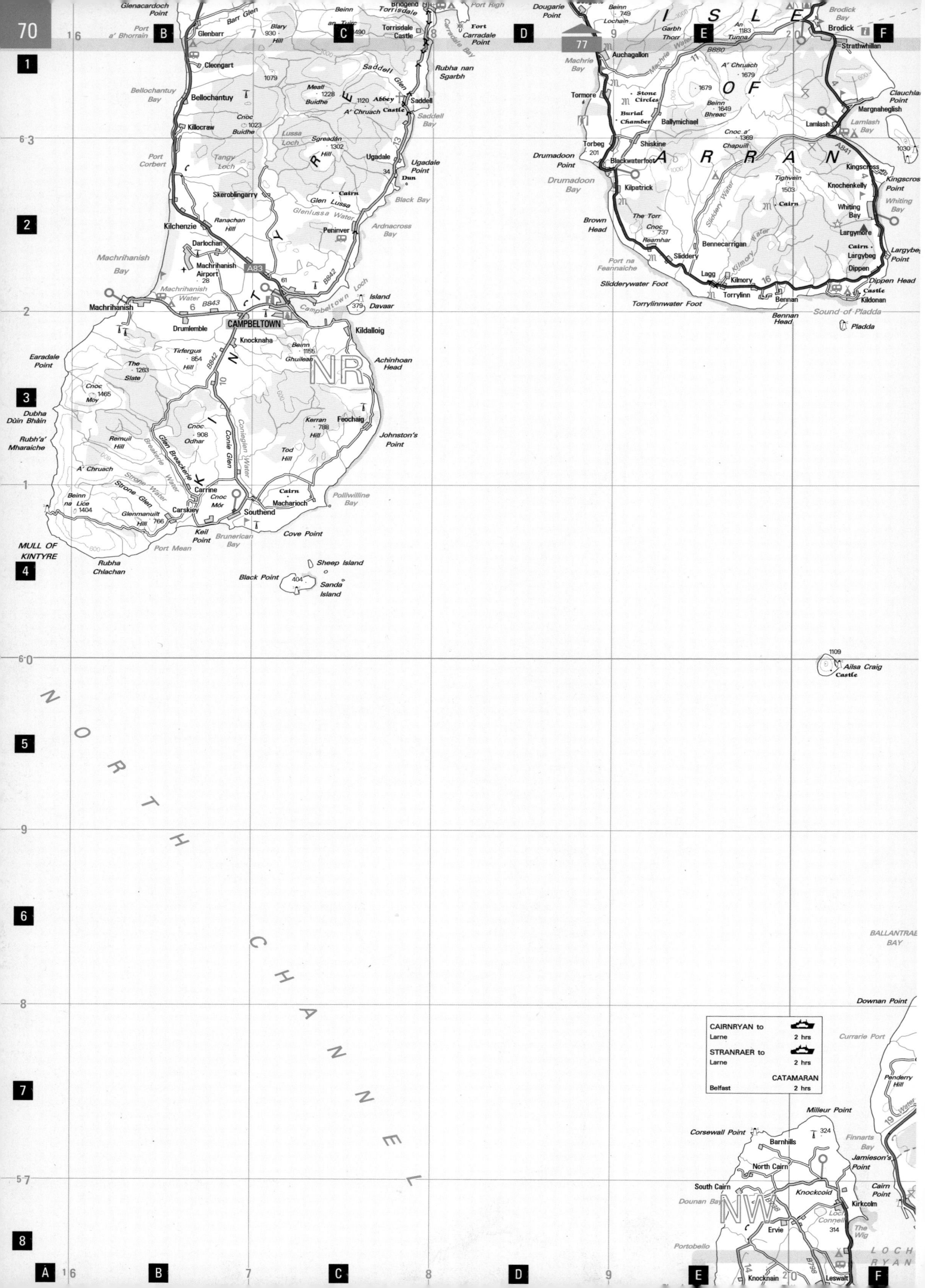

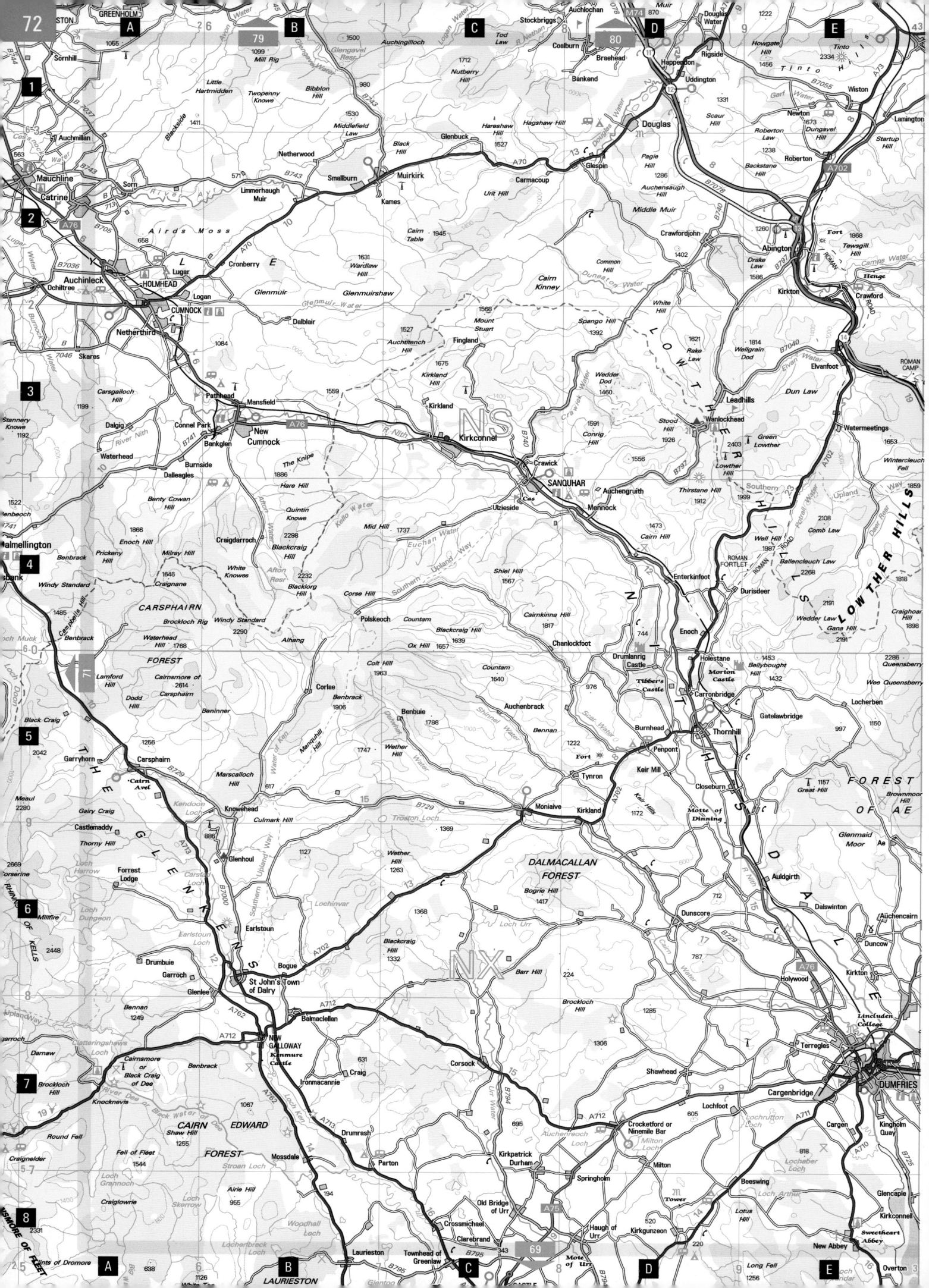

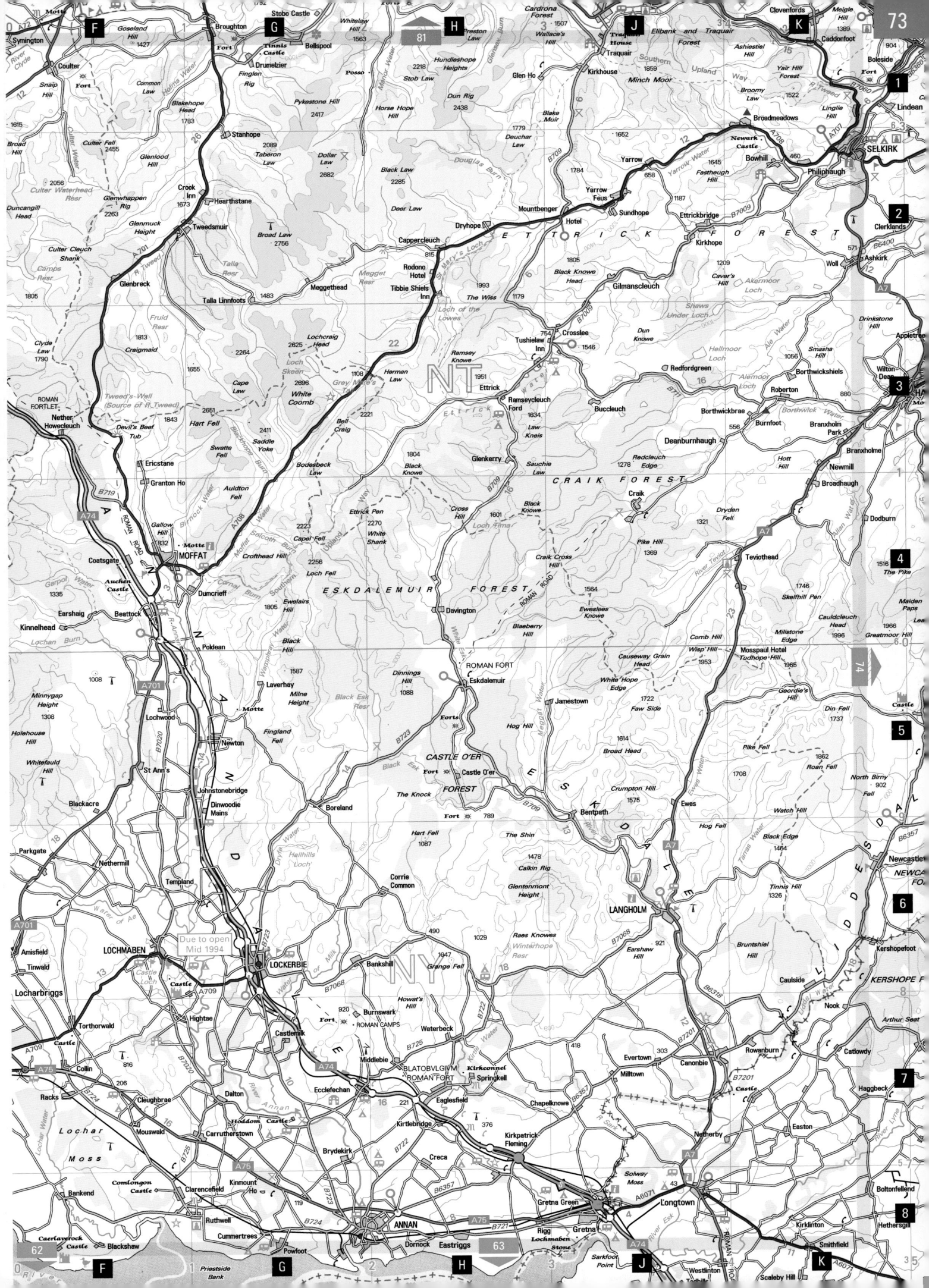

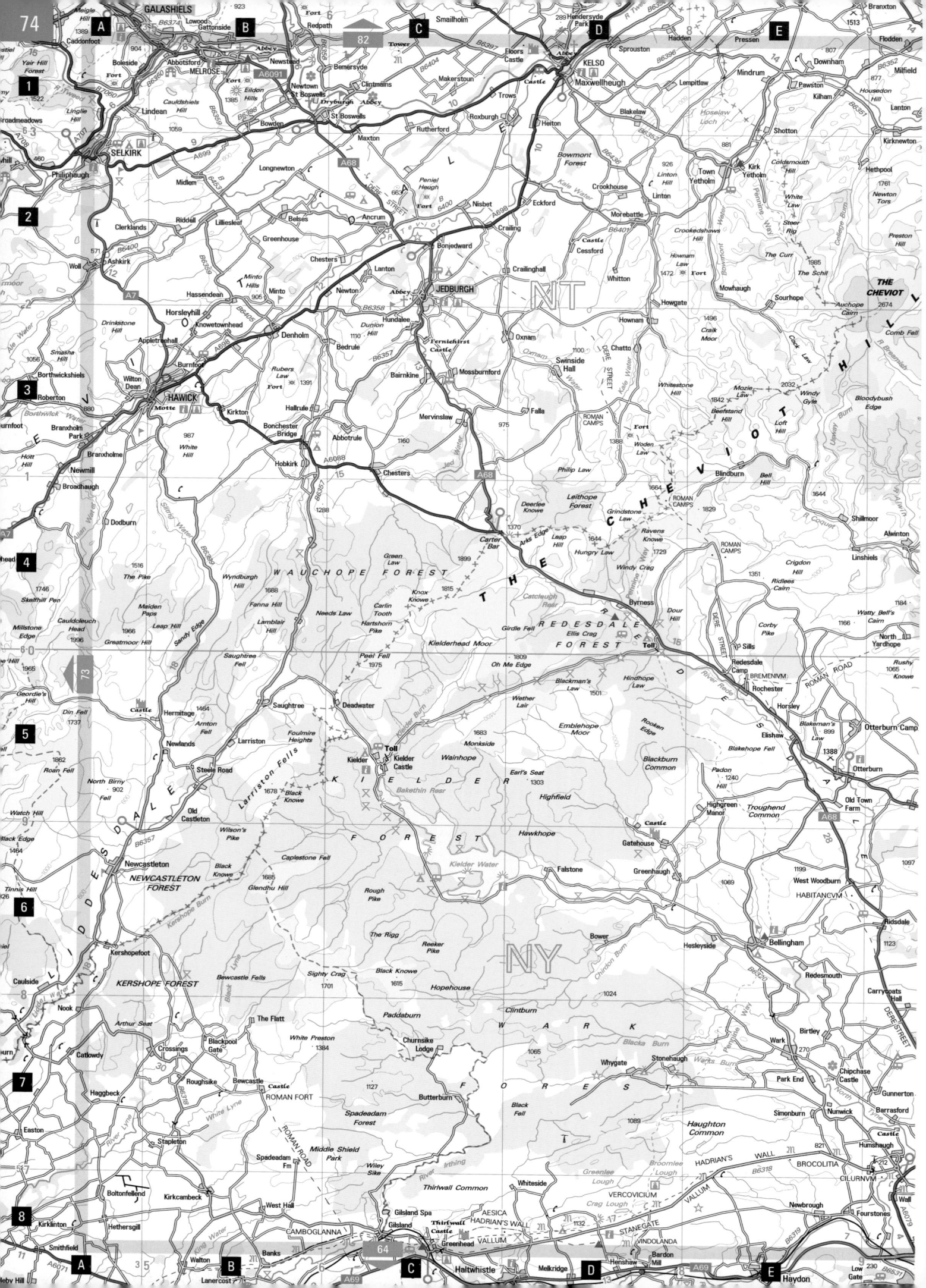

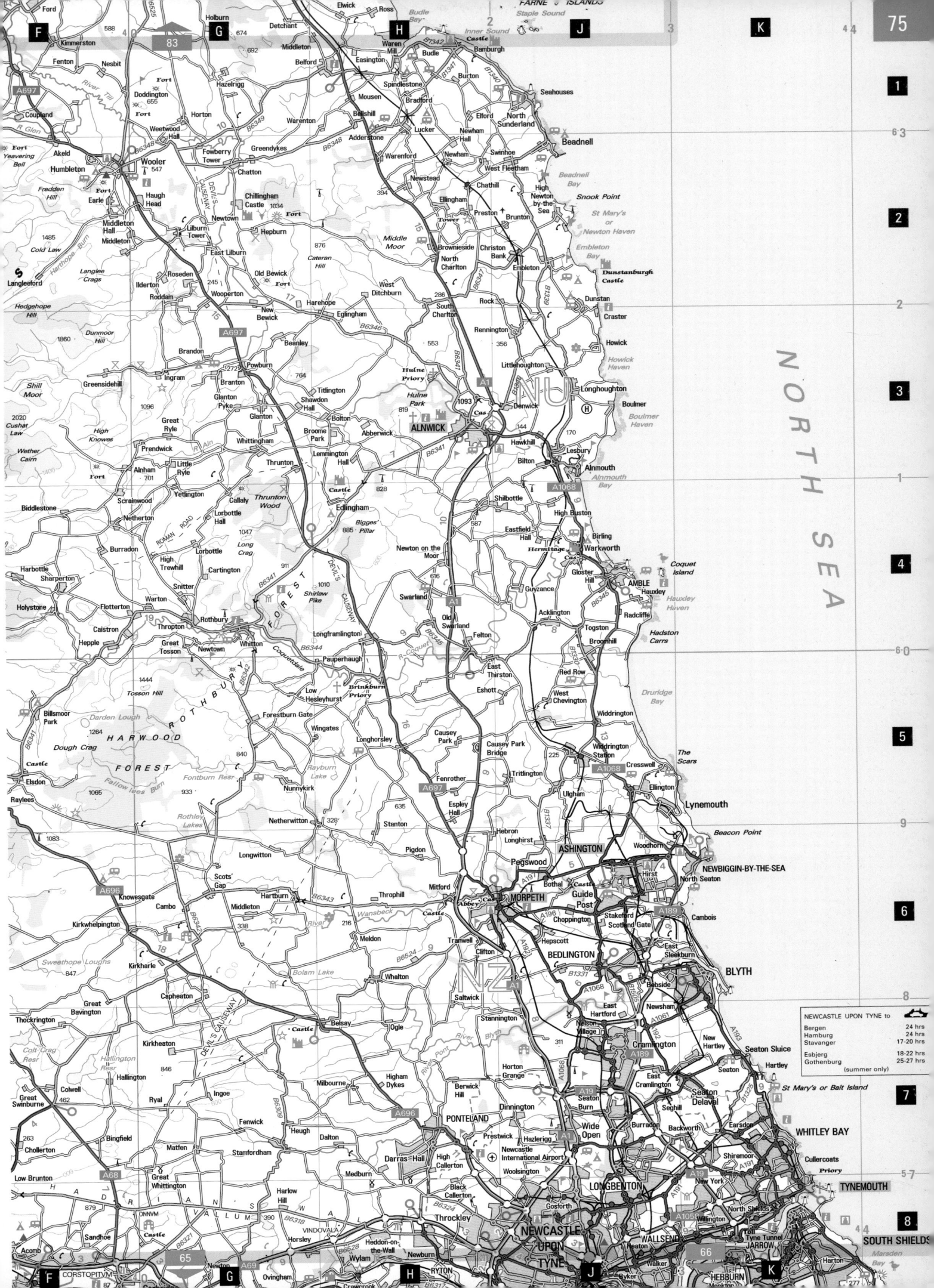

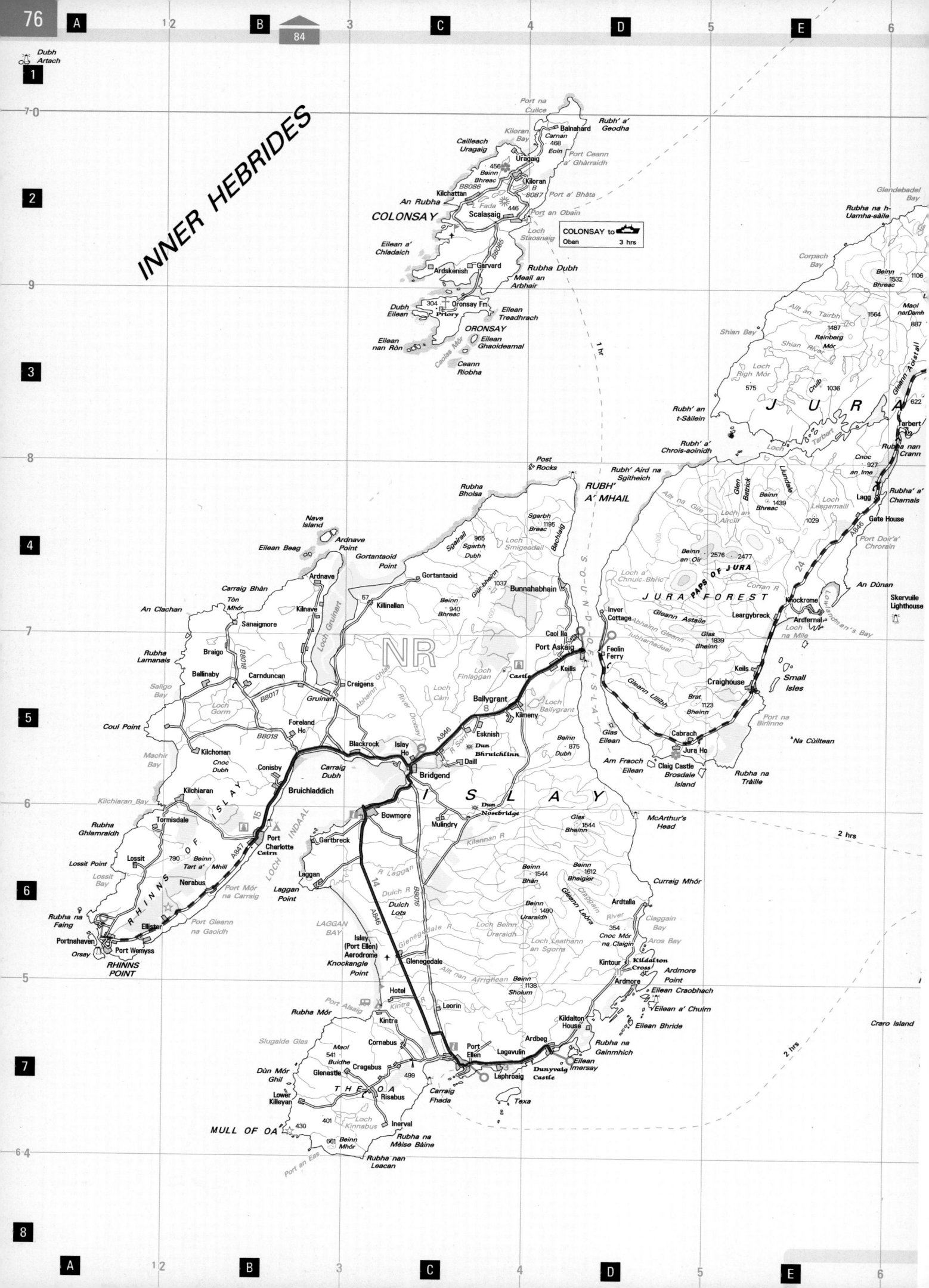

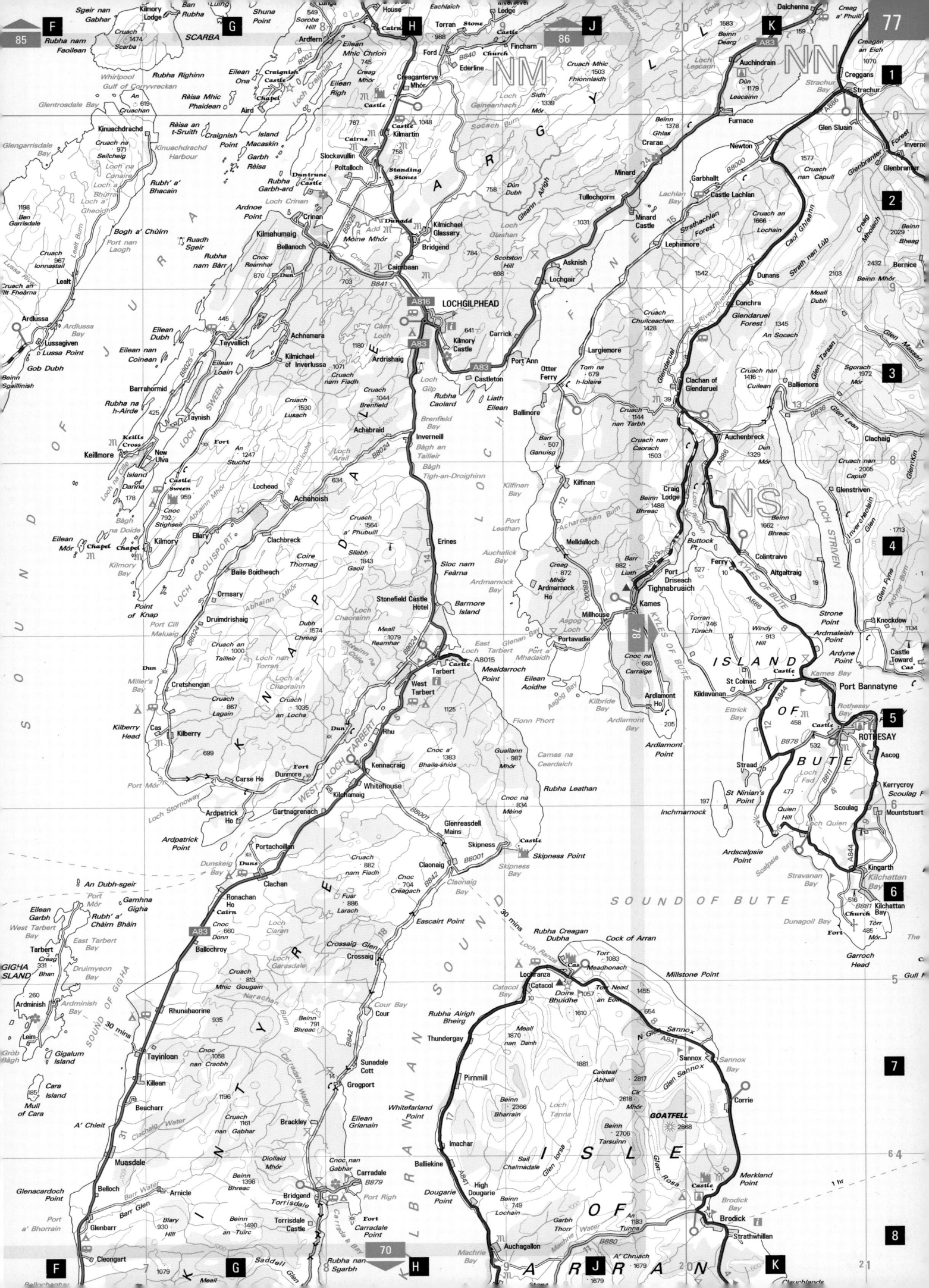

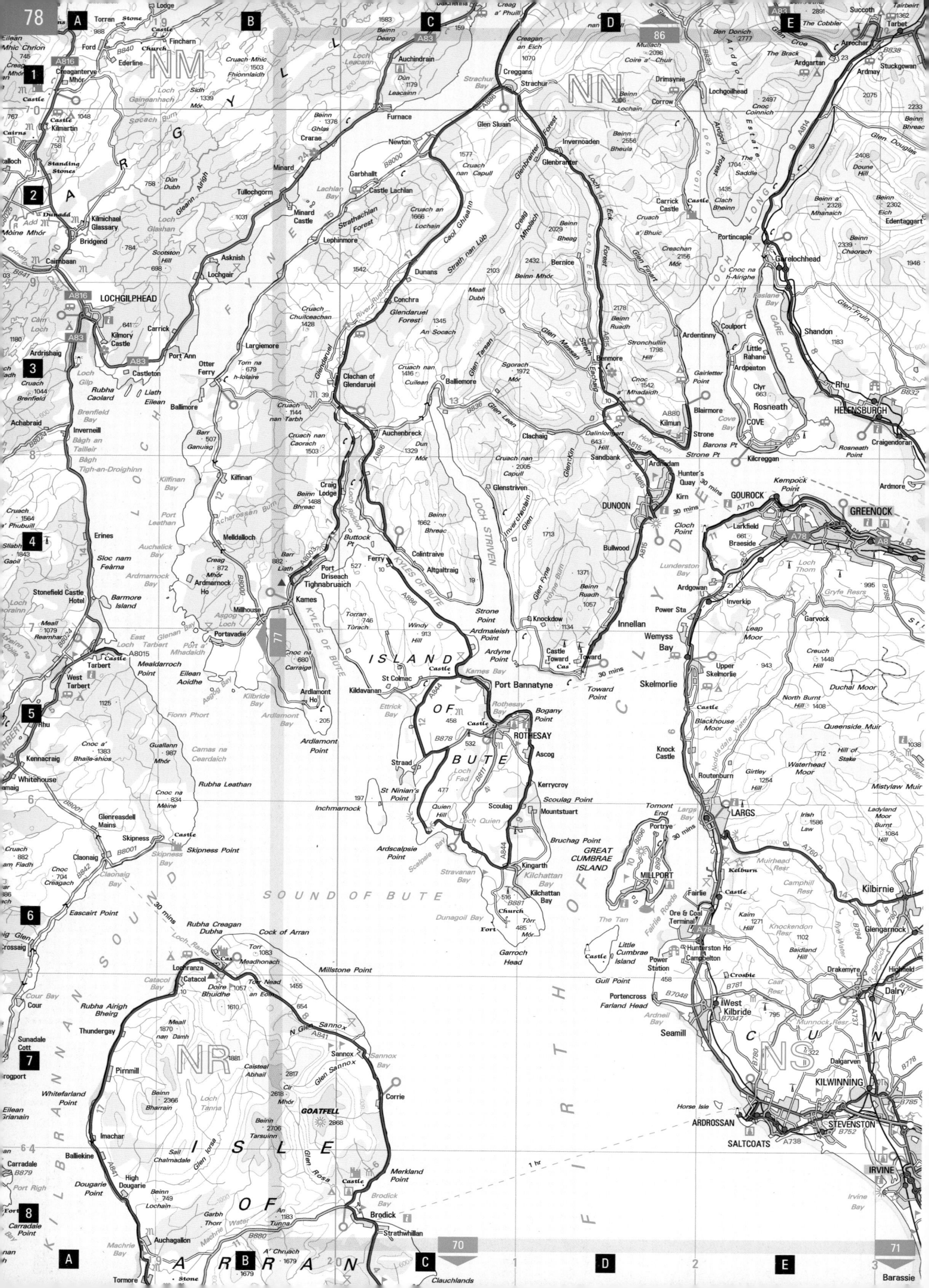

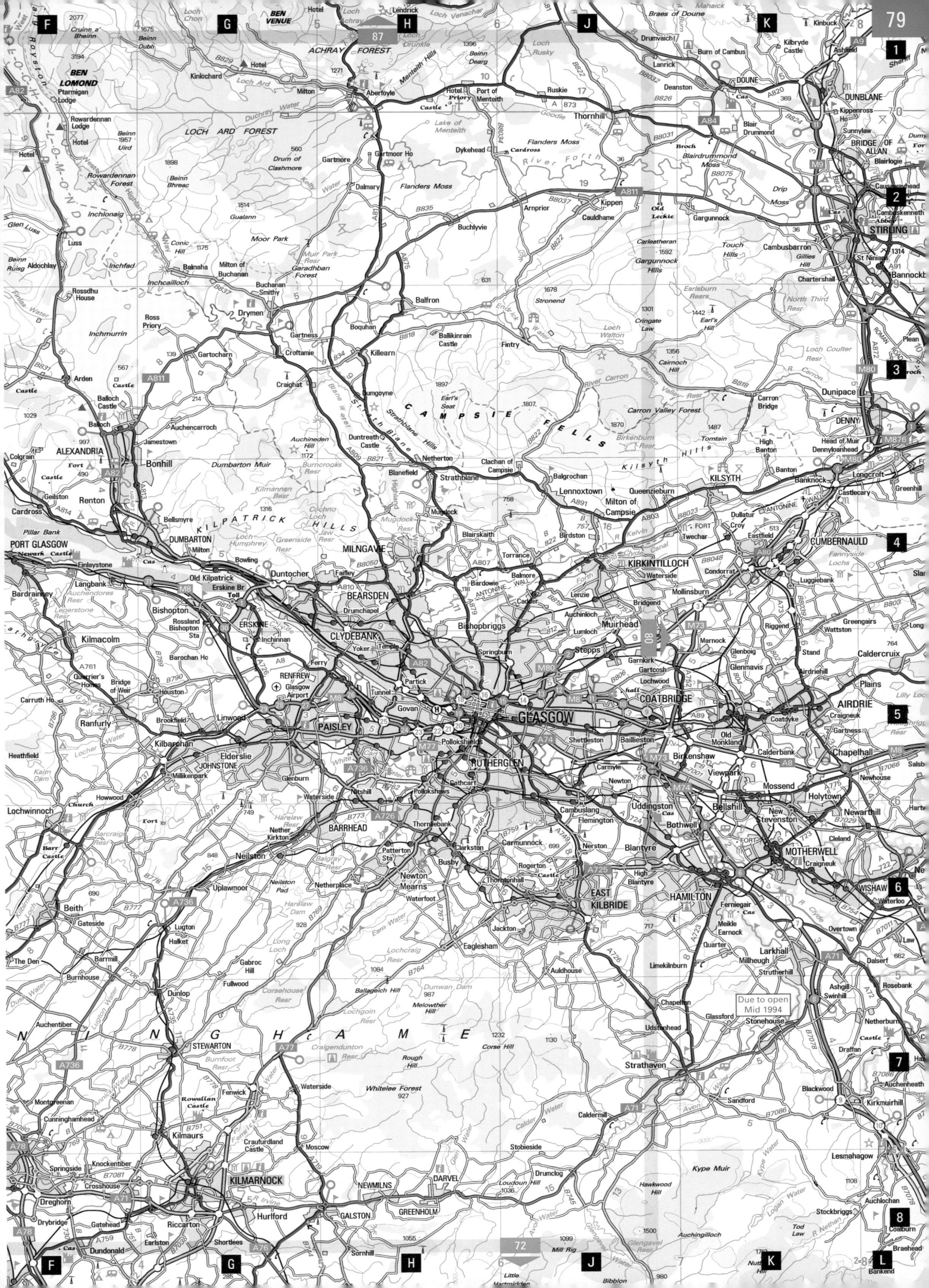

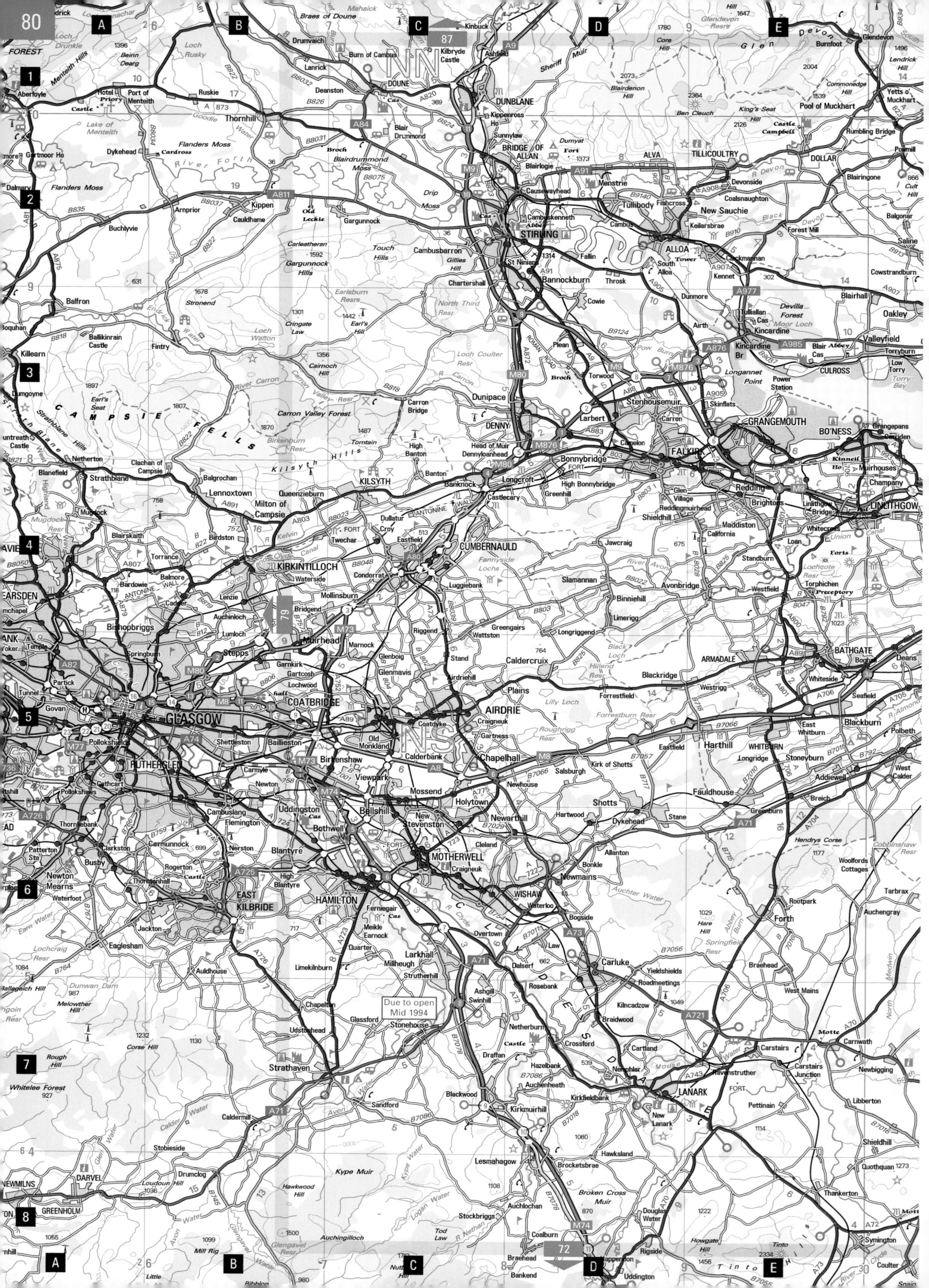

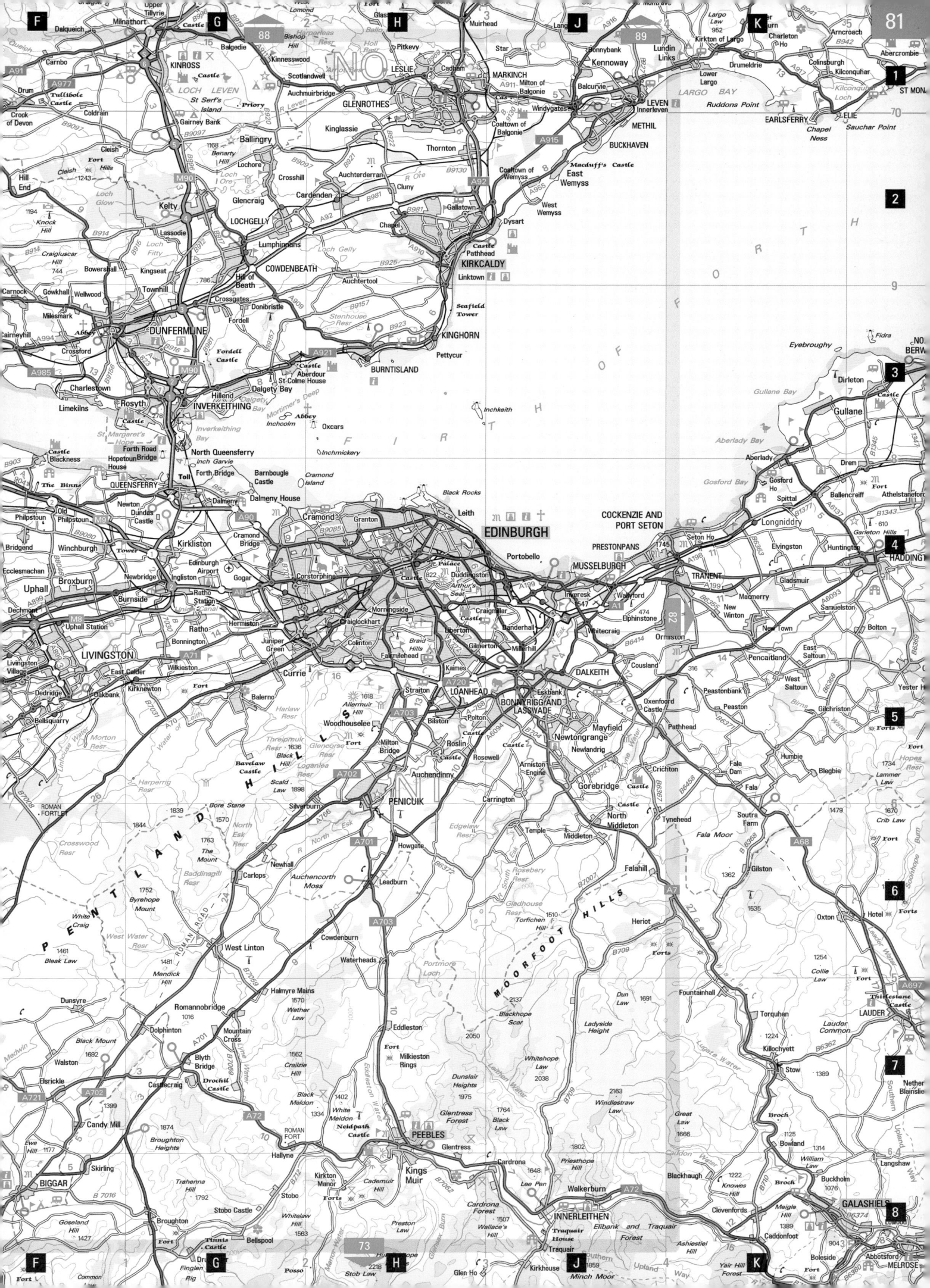

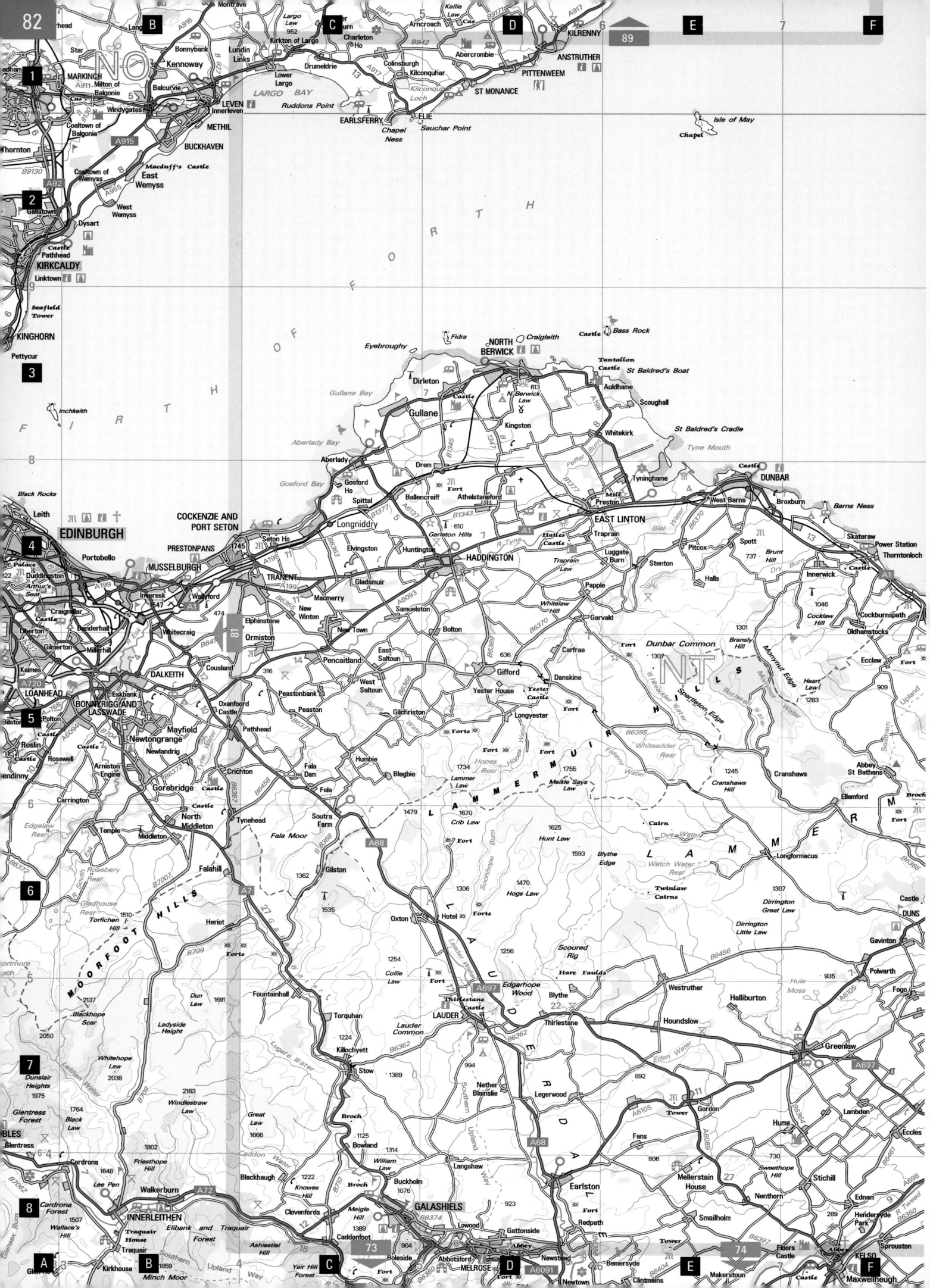

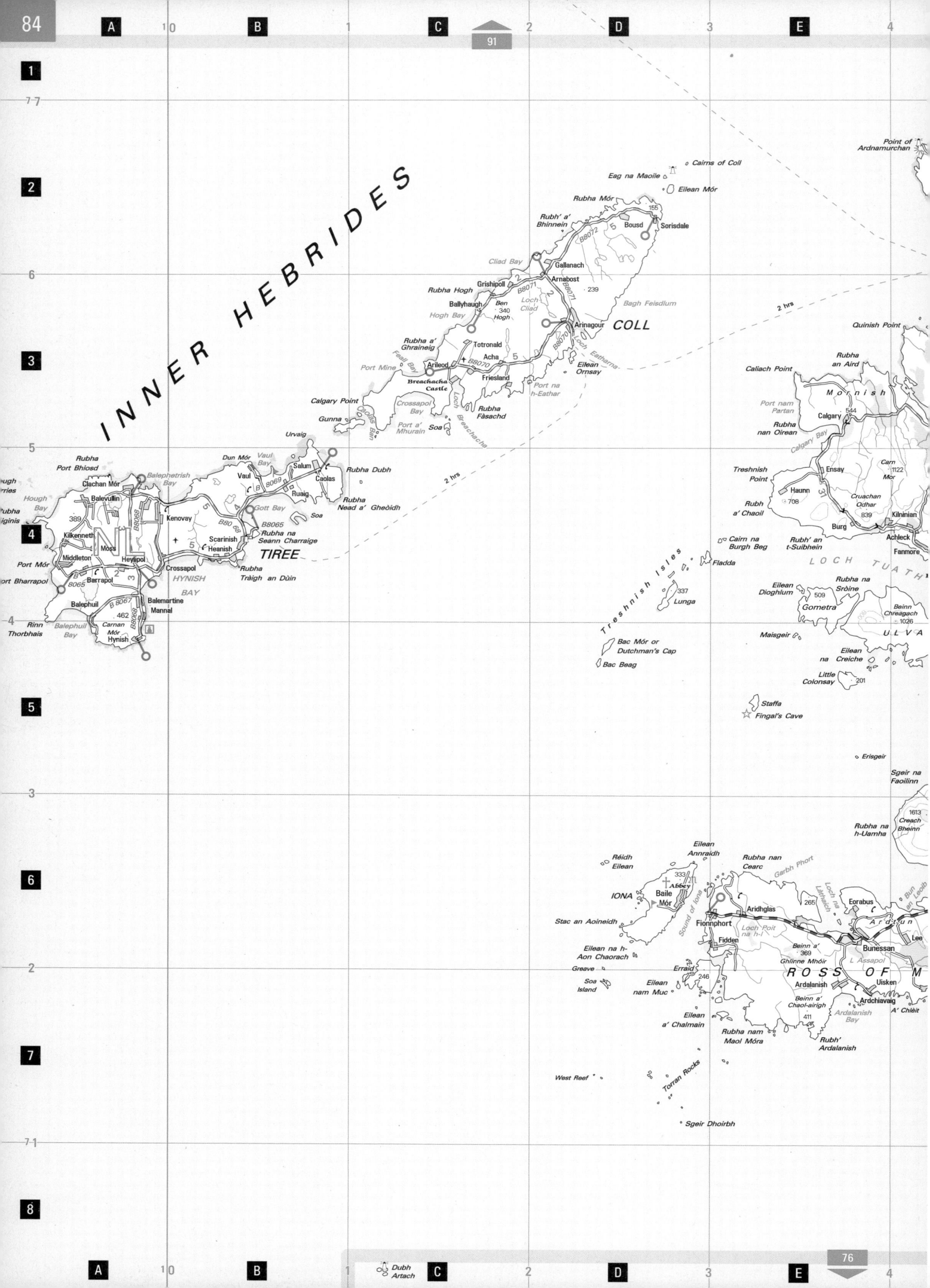

91

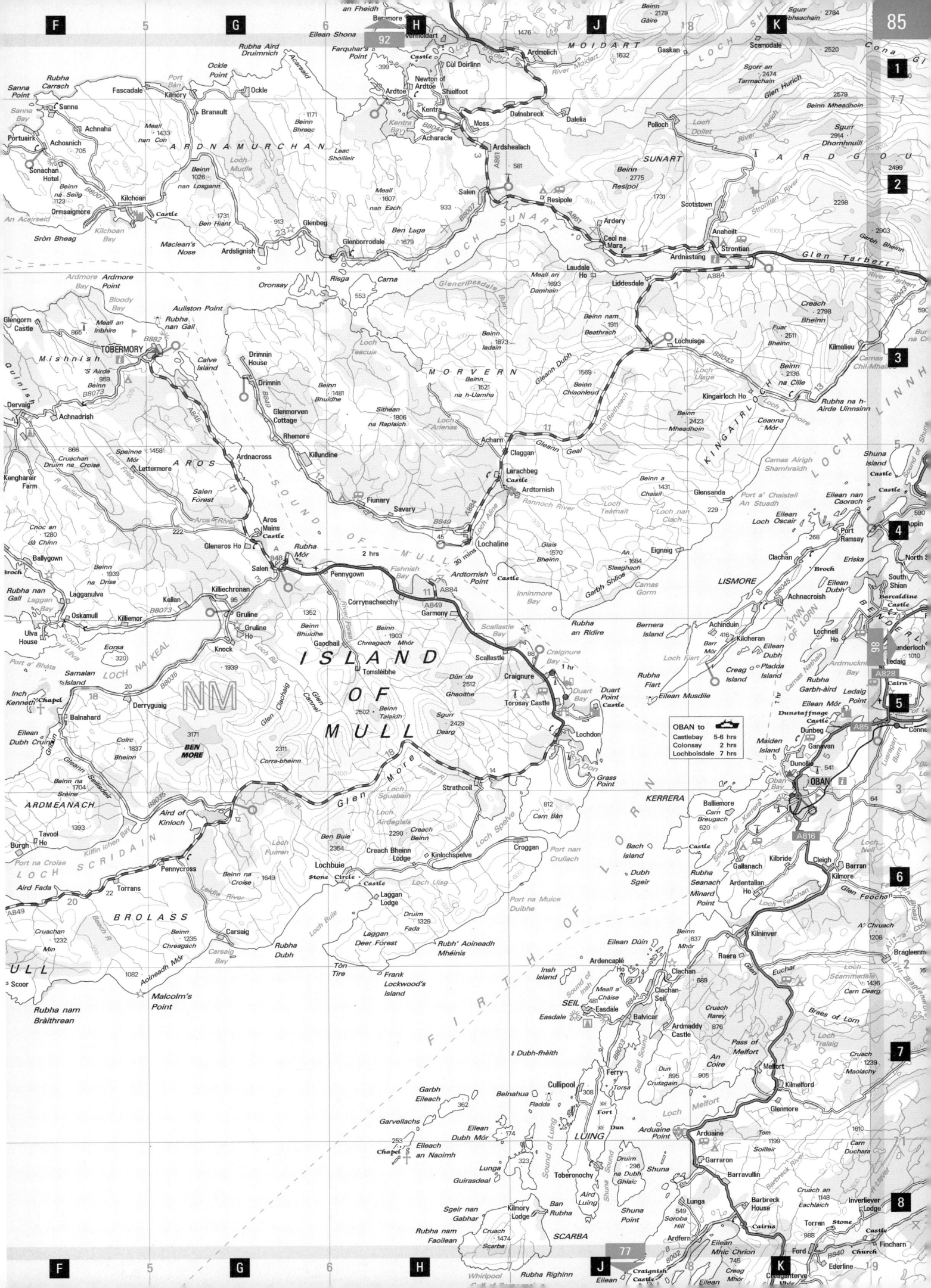

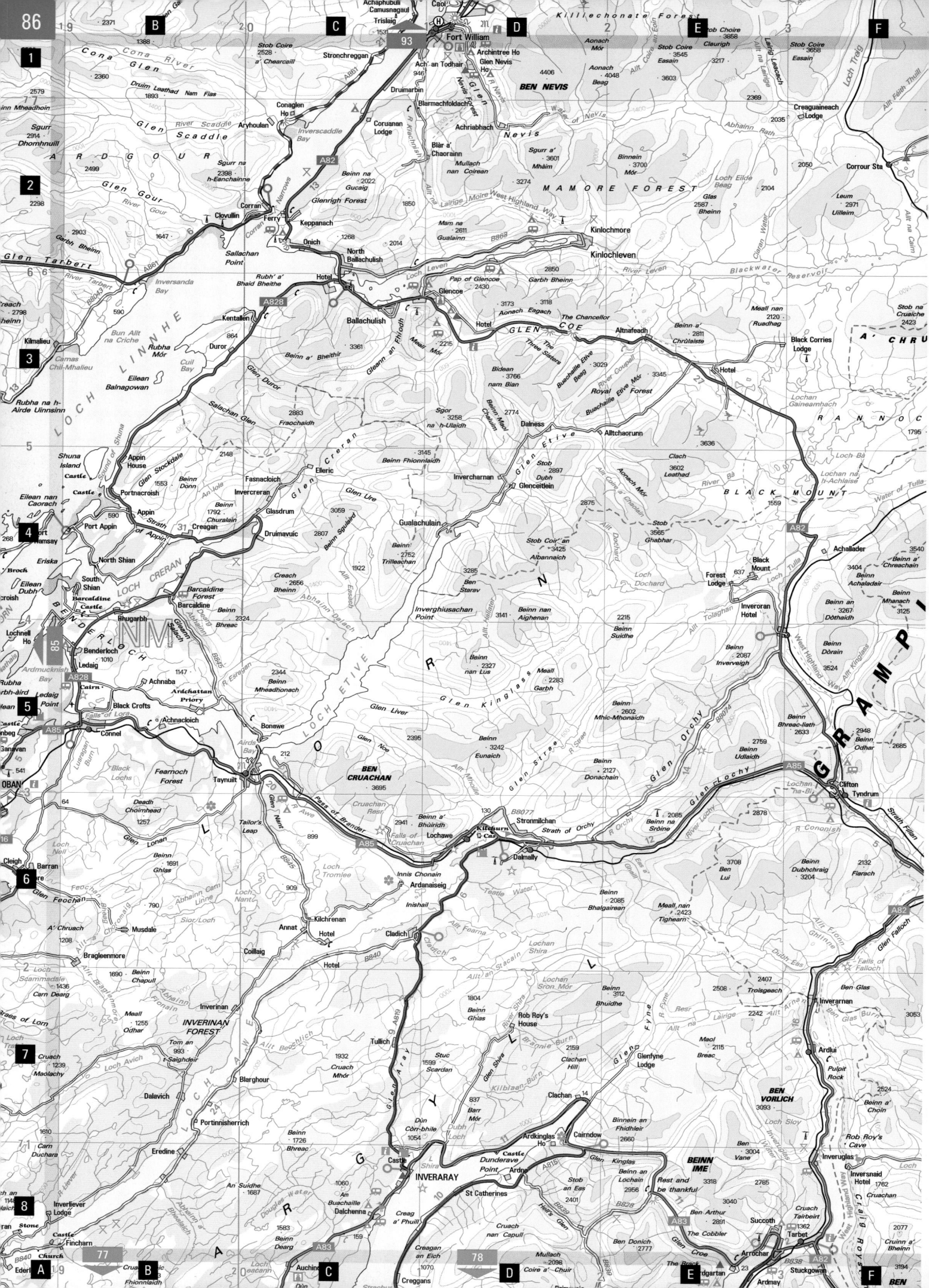

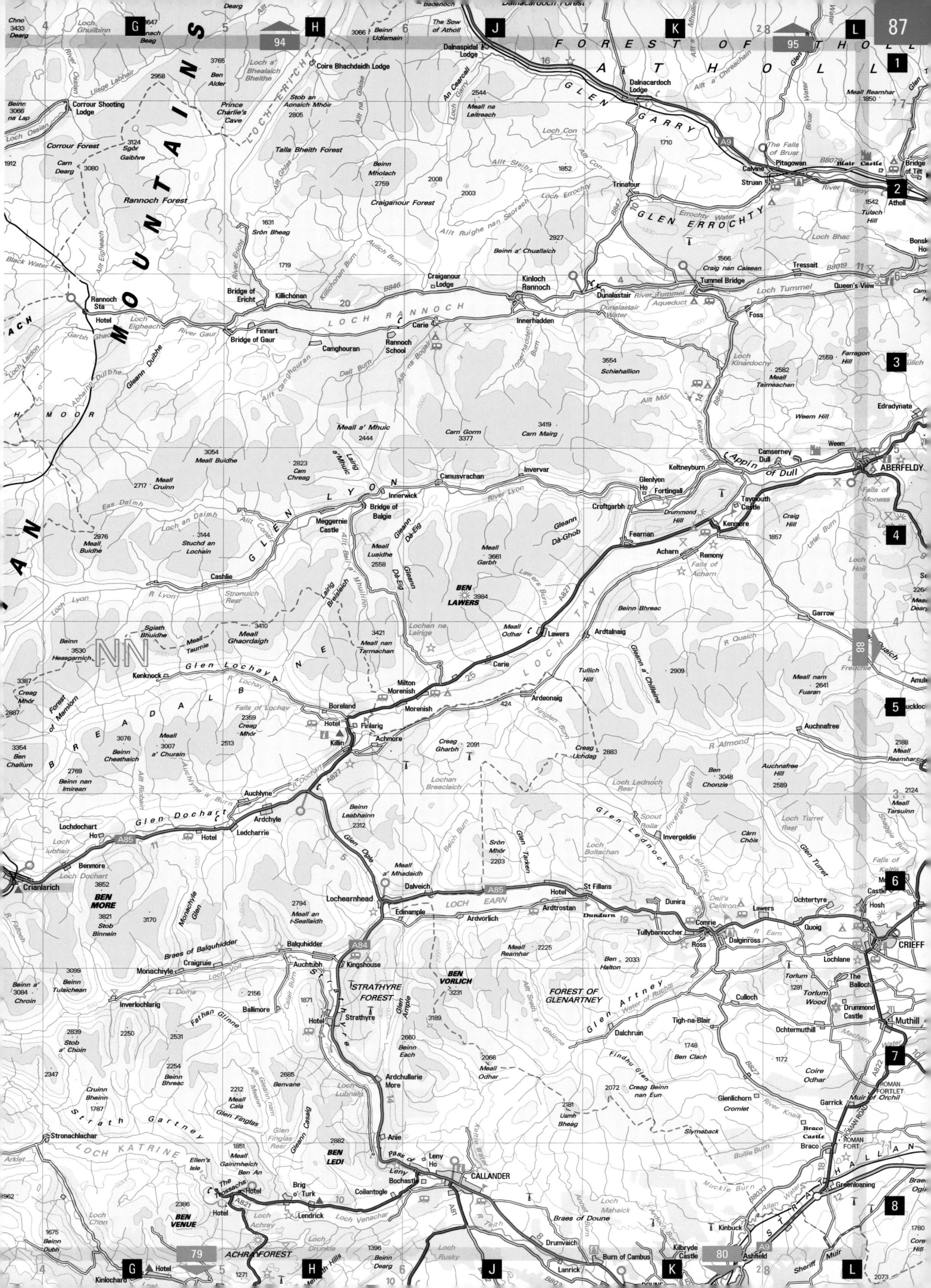

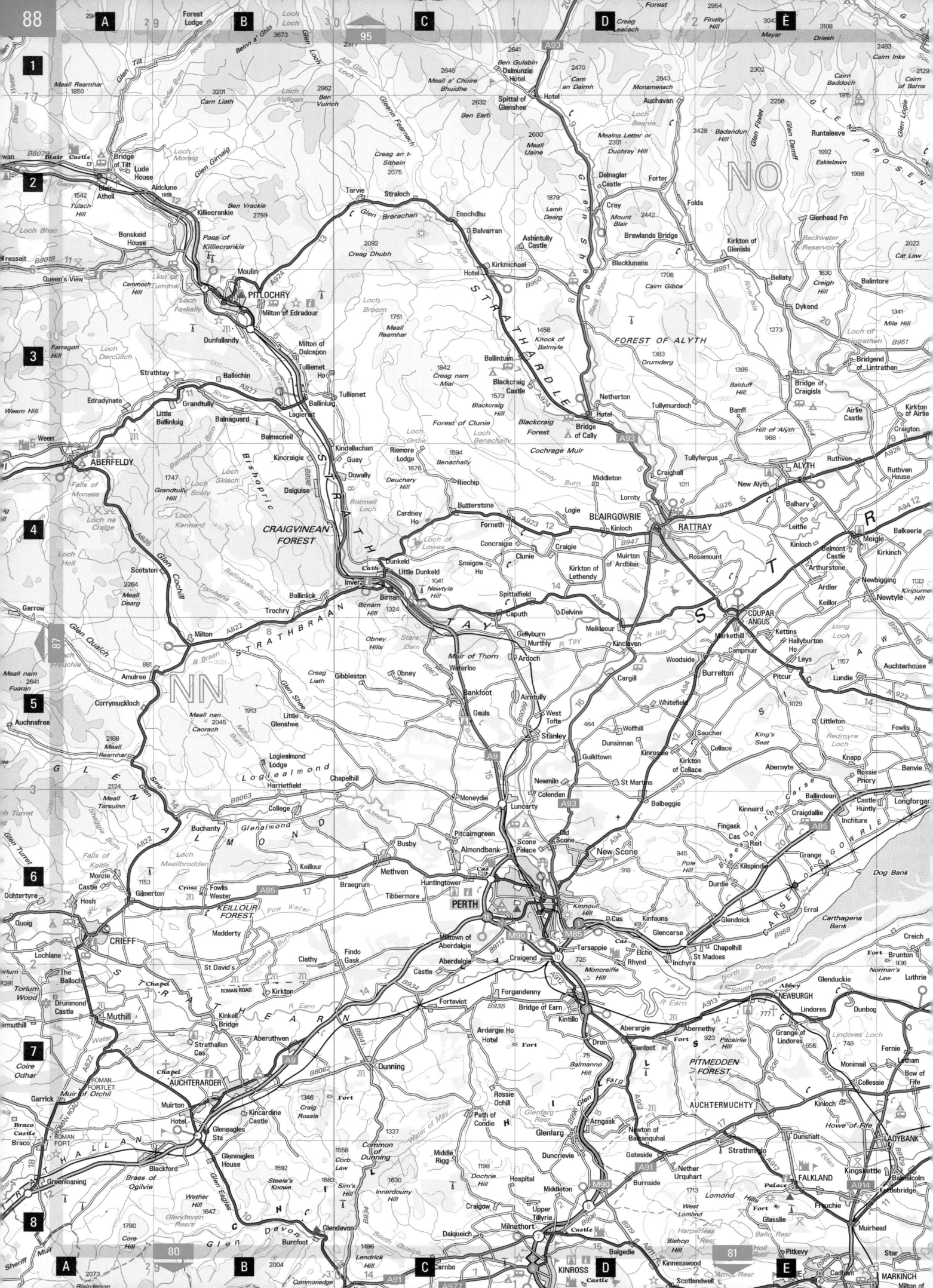

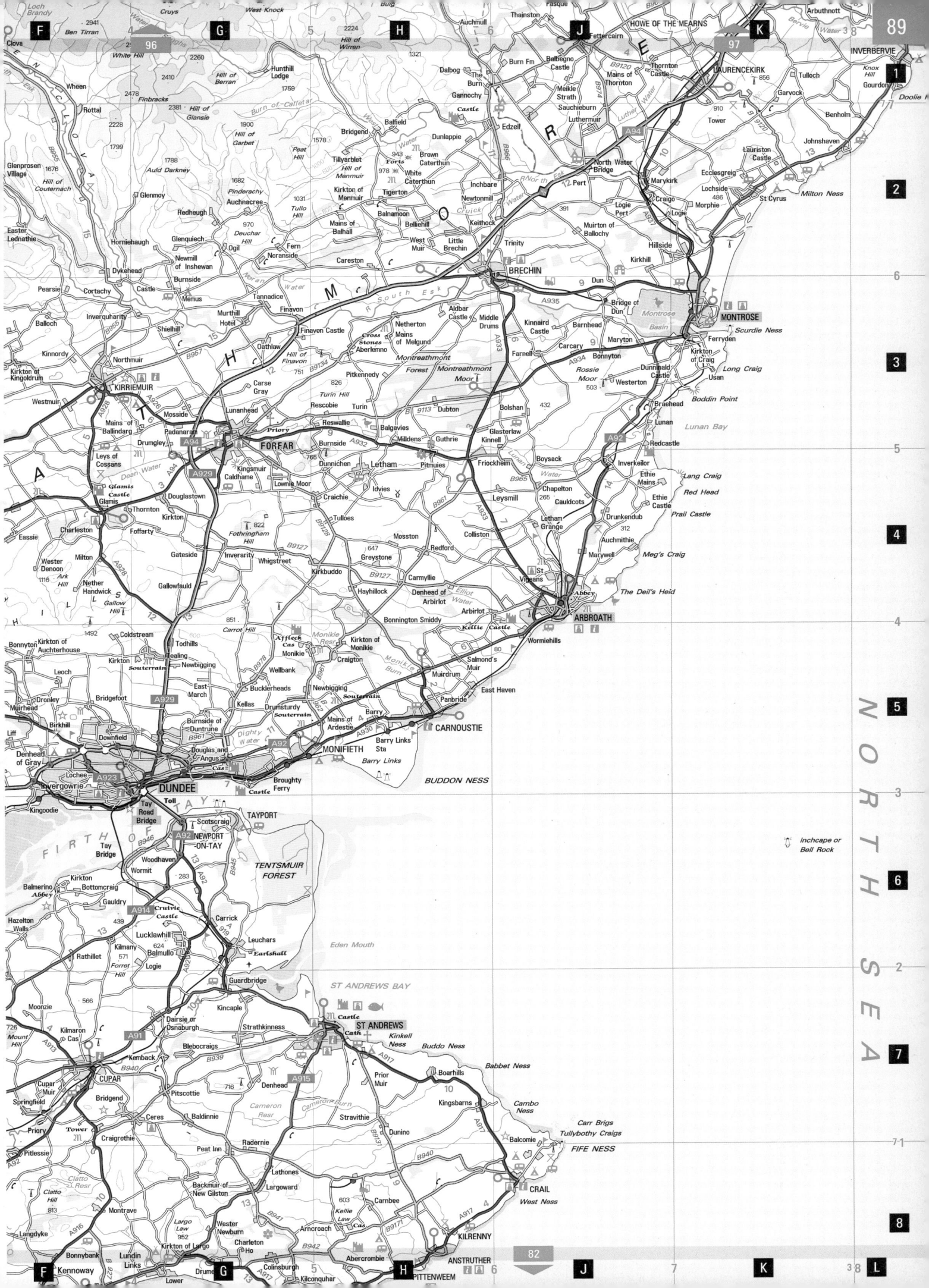

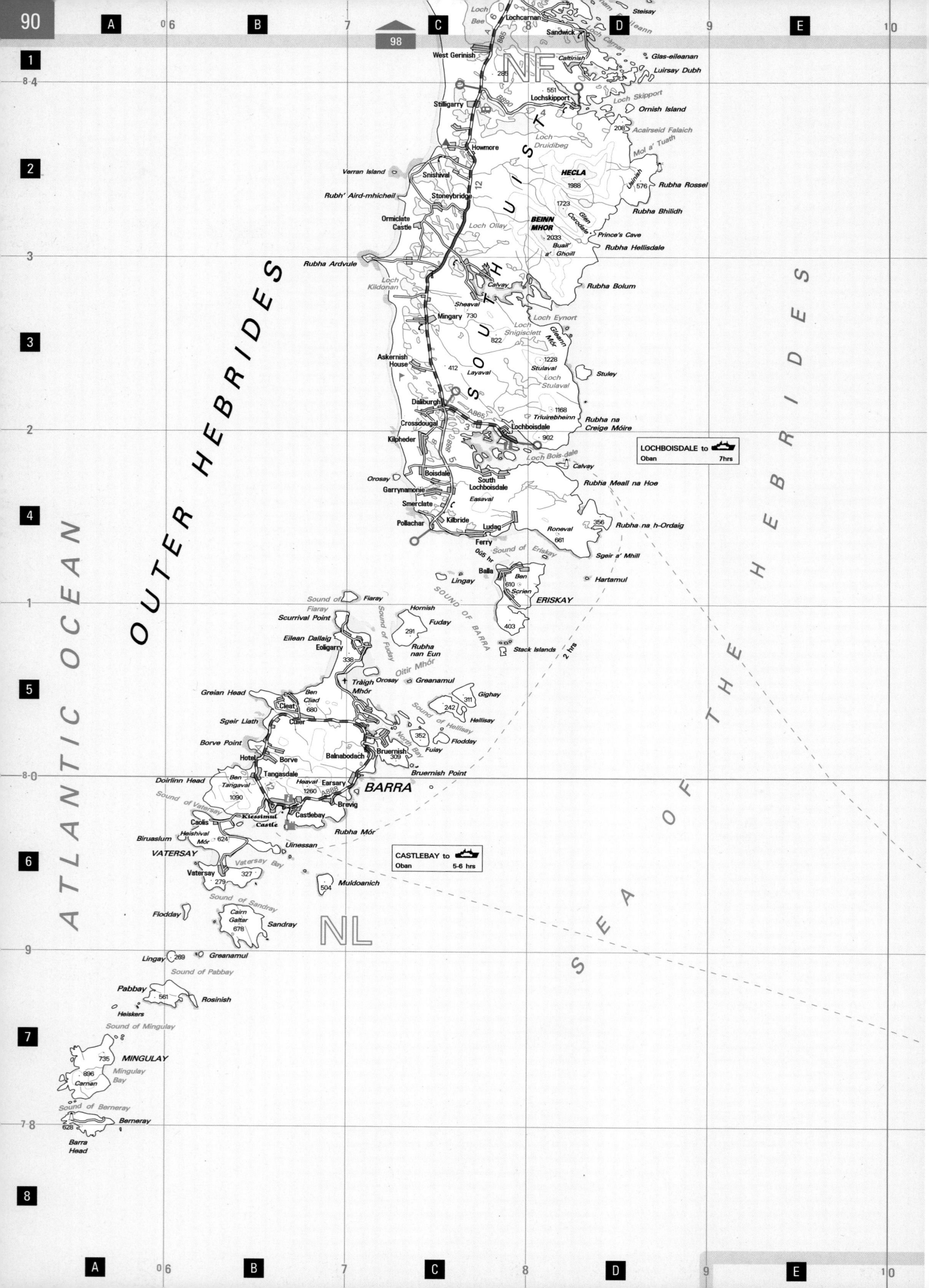

OUTER HEBRIDES

ATLANTIC OCEAN

OUTER HEBRIDES

OF THE HEBRIDES

SEA OF THE HEBRIDES

SOUTH UIST

NF

Loch Bee
Lochcarnan
Sandwick
West Gerinish
Caltinish
Glas-eileanan
Luirsay Dubh
551
Loch Skipport
Lochskipport
Ornish Island
Stilligarry
Loch Druidibeg
208
Acairseid Falaich
Howmore
Mol a' Tuath

HECLA
1988
Usinish
576
Rubha Rossel

Verran Island
Snishival
Stoneybridge
1723
Rubha Bhilidh

Rubh' Aird-mhicheil
Ormiclate Castle
Loch Ollay
BEINN MHOR
2033
Buail a' Ghoill
Prince's Cave
Rubha Hellisdale

Rubha Ardvule
Loch Kildonan
Calvay
Rubha Bolum

Sheaval
Mingary 730

822
Loch Snigisclett
Glearn Mor
Loch Eynort

Askernish House
412
Layaval
1228
Stulaval
Stuley
Loch Stulaval

Daliburgh
Crossdougal
1168
Triuirebheinn
Rubha na Creige Móire

Kilpheder
Lochboisdale
902

Boisdale
South Lochboisdale
Loch Bois-dale
Calvay

Orosay
Garrynamonie
Easaval
Rubha Meall na Hoe

Smerclate
Kilbride
Ludag
Roneval
661
356
Rubha na h-Ordaig

Pollachar
Ferry
Oub hr
Sound of Eriskay
Sgeir a' Mhill

Balla
Ben Scrien 610
Hartamul

Lingay
ERISKAY

Sound of Fiaray
Fiaray
Hornish
Fuday
403

Scurrival Point
291
2 hrs

Eilean Dallaig
Eoligarry
Rubha nan Eun
Stack Islands

338
Oitir Mhór

Greian Head
Tràigh Orosay Mhór
Greanamul

Ben Cliad 680
Gighay
311

Cleat
242
Hallisay

Sgeir Liath
Cuier
352
Floddday
Fuiay

Borve Point
Bruernish
309
North Bay

Hotel
Borve
Balnabodach
Bruernish Point

Tangasdale
Heaval
Earsary
BARRA

Doirlinn Head
Ben Tangaval 1090
1260
Brevig

Caolis
Kiseimul Castle
Castlebay
Rubha Mór

Biruaslum
Heishival Mór 624
Uinessan

VATERSAY
Vatersay Bay
Muldoanich
504

Vatersay 279
327
Sound of Sandray

Flodday
Cairn Galtar 678
Sandray

NL

Lingay 269
Greanamul
Sound of Pabbay

Pabbay
561
Rosinish

Heiskers
Sound of Mingulay

735
MINGULAY
896
Carnan
Mingulay Bay

Sound of Berneray
Berneray
628
Barra Head

LOCHBOISDALE to
Oban   7hrs

CASTLEBAY to
Oban   5-6 hrs

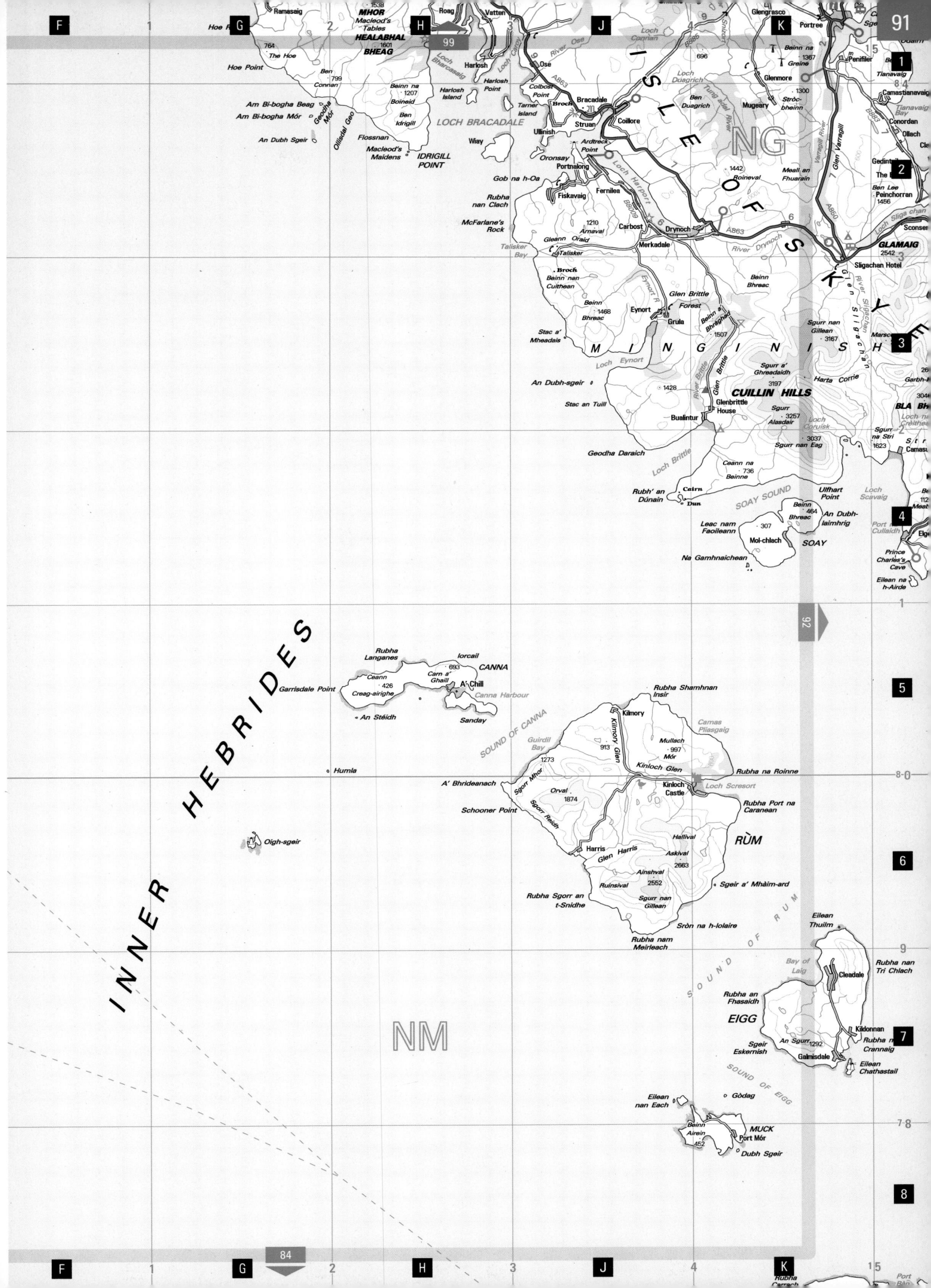

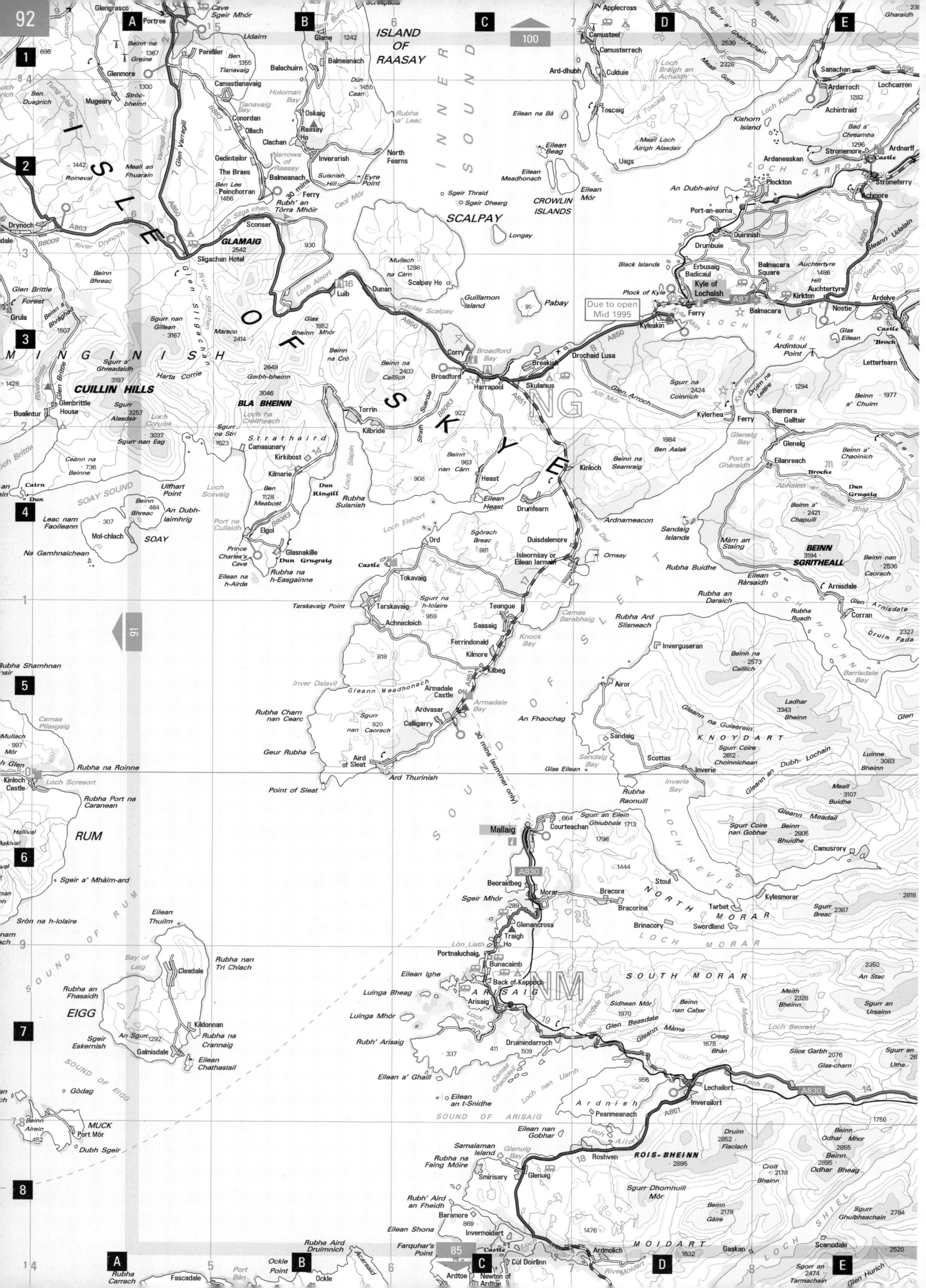

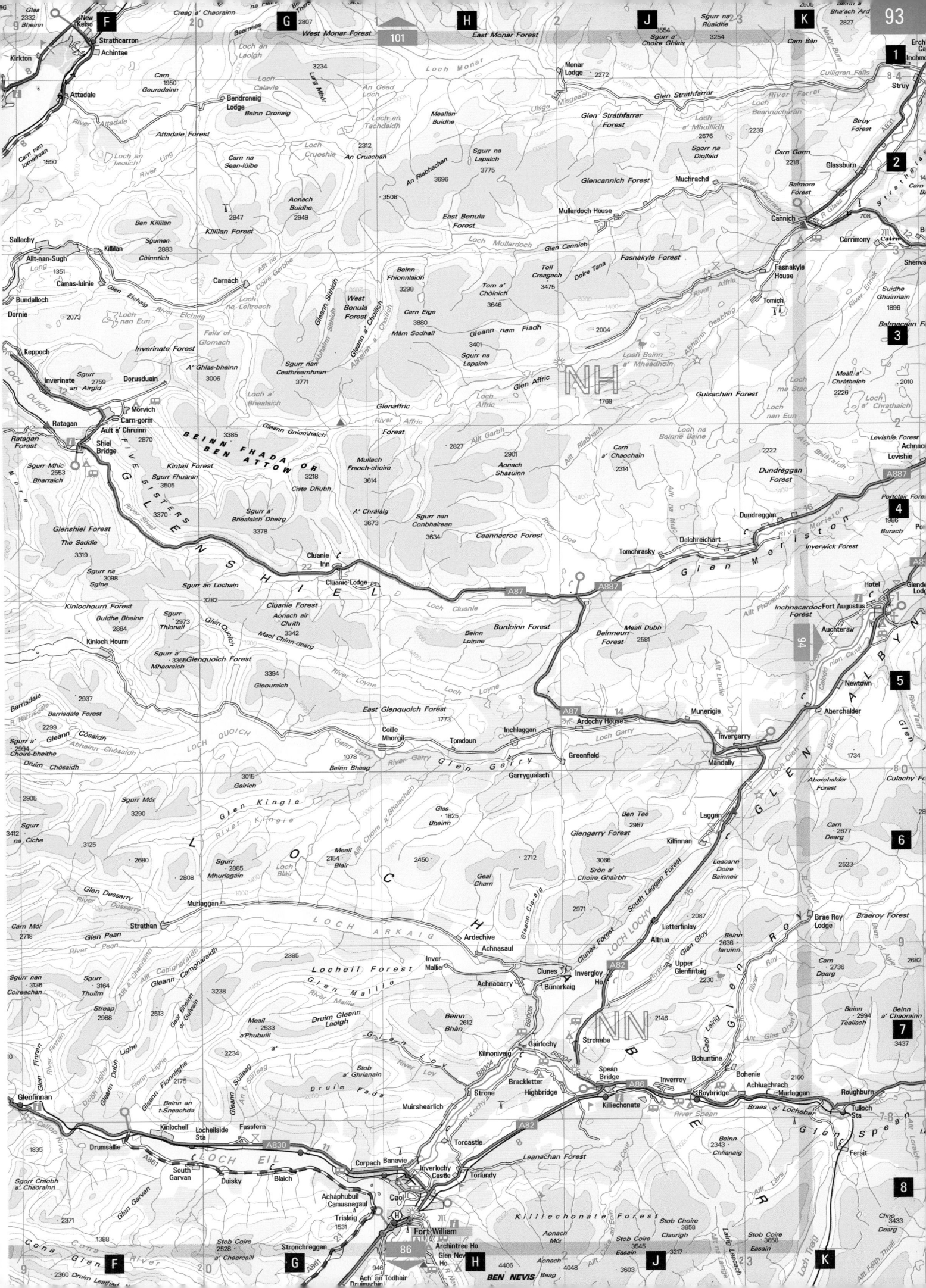

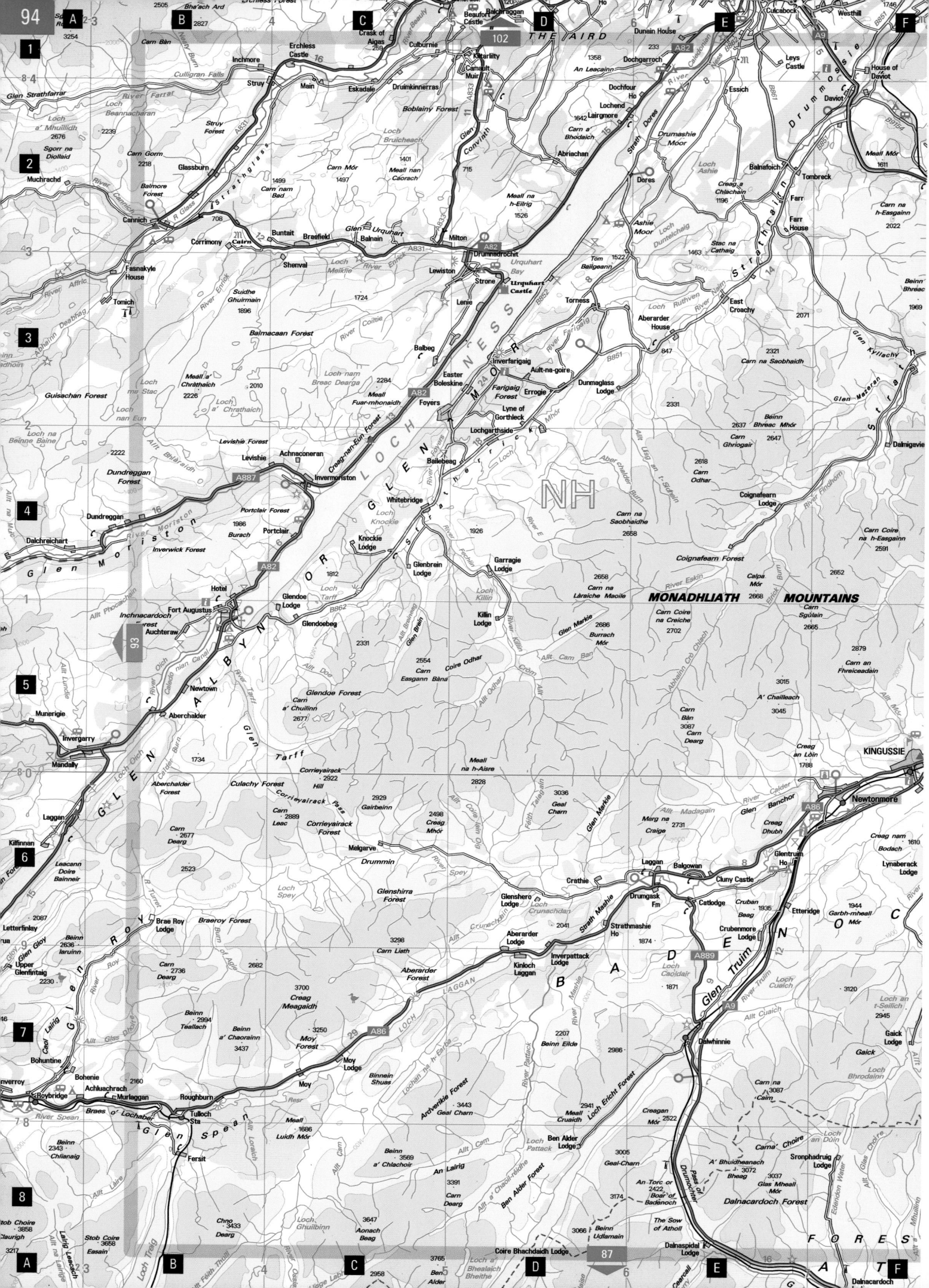

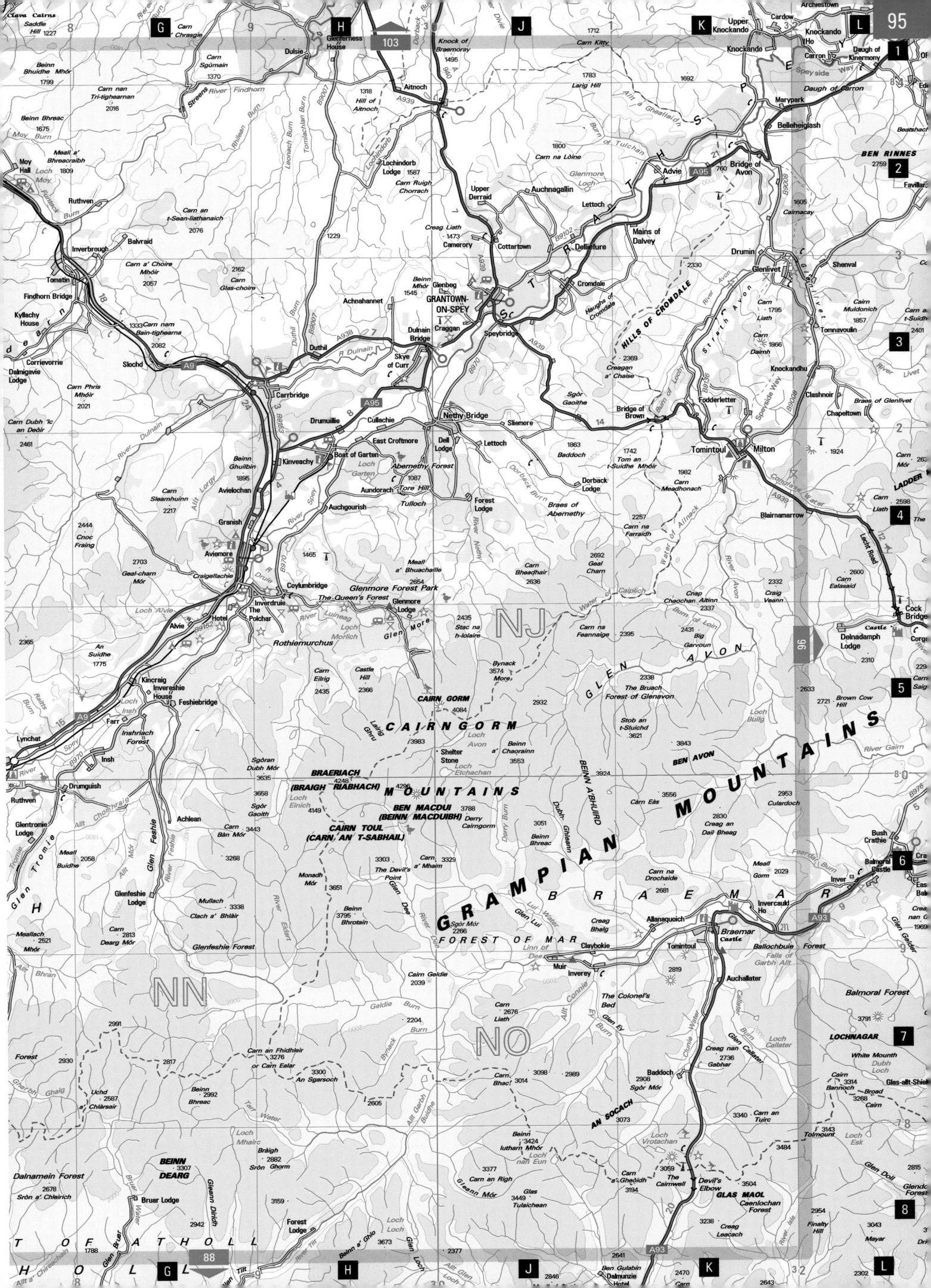

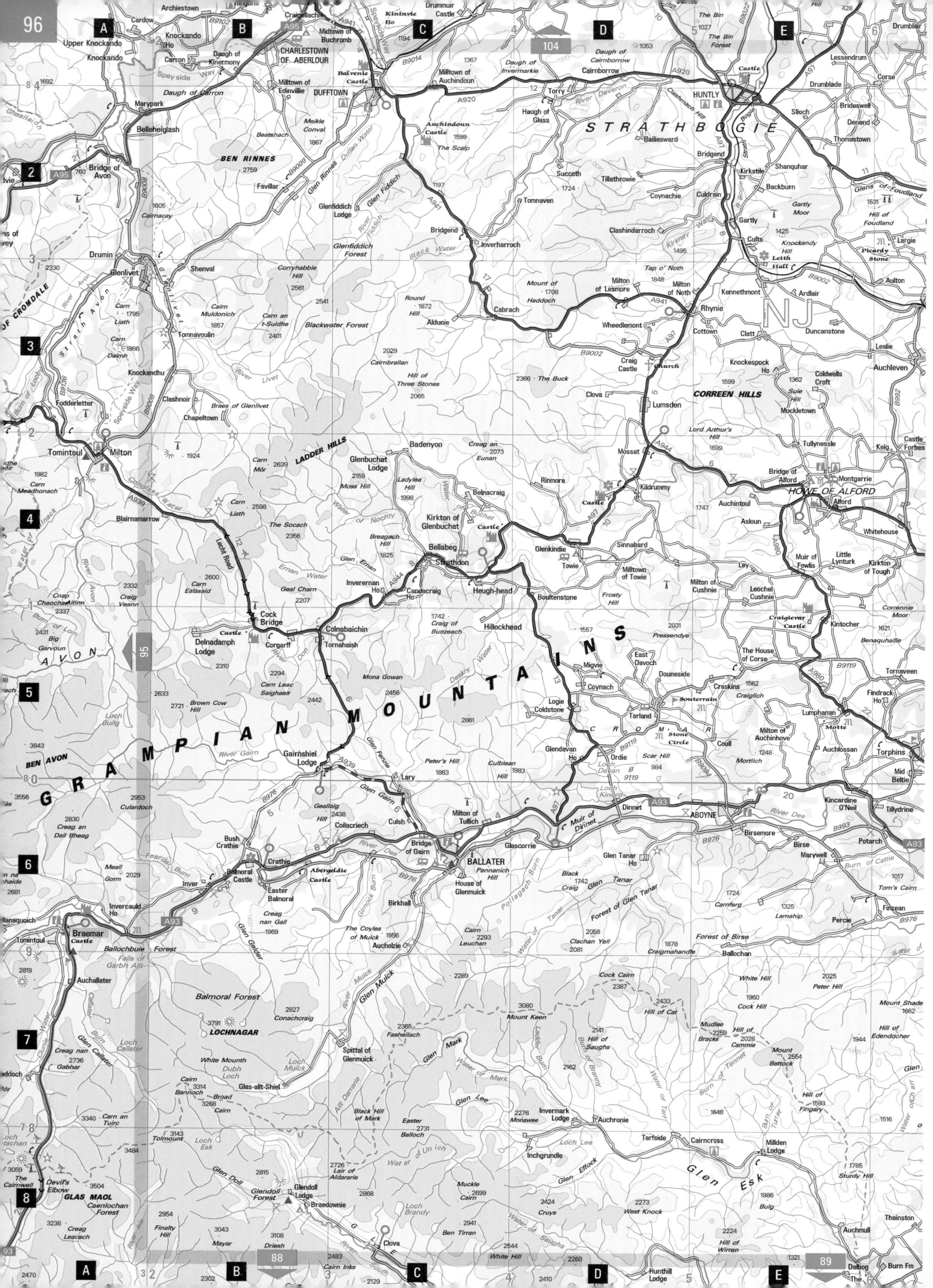

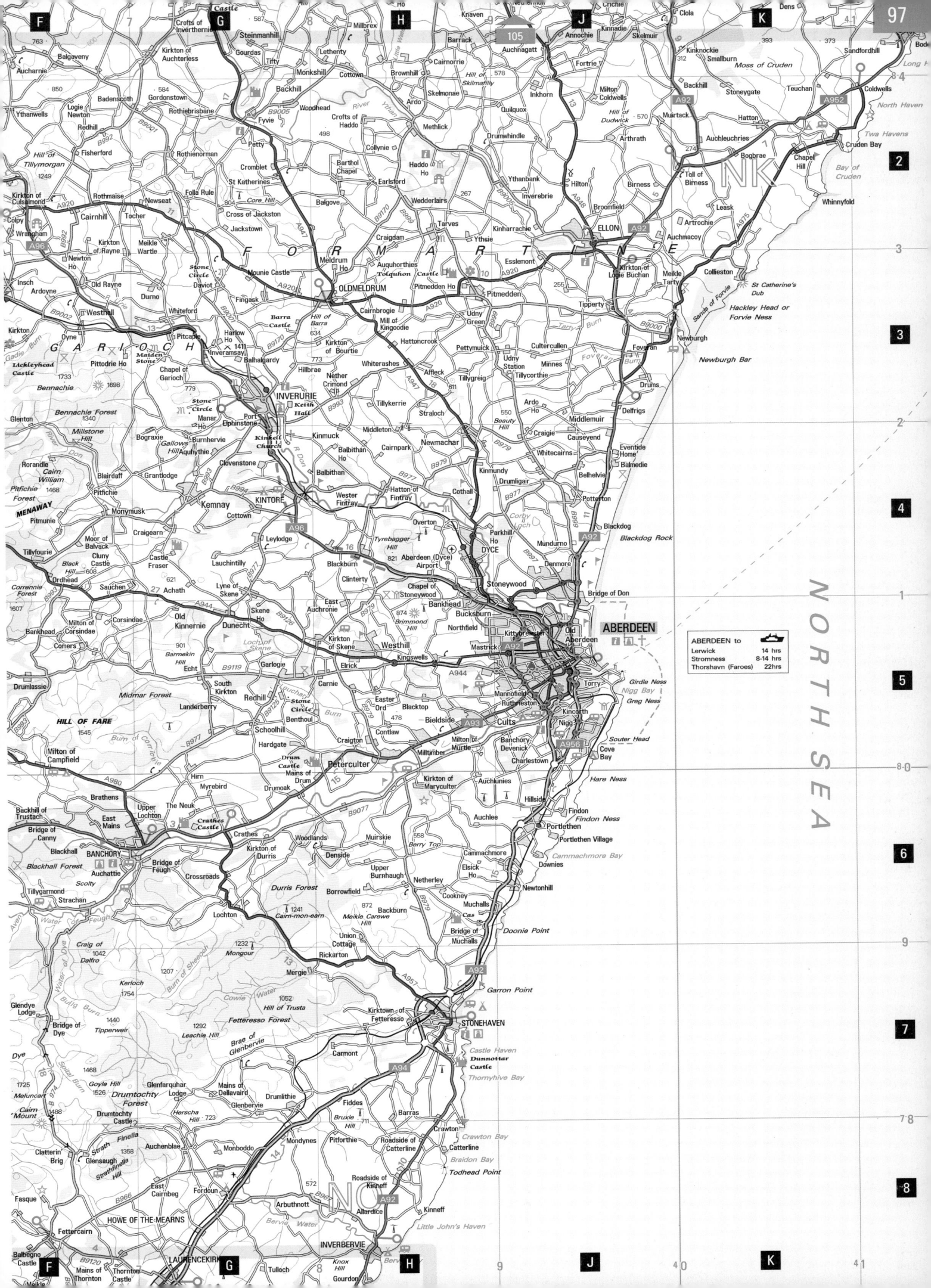

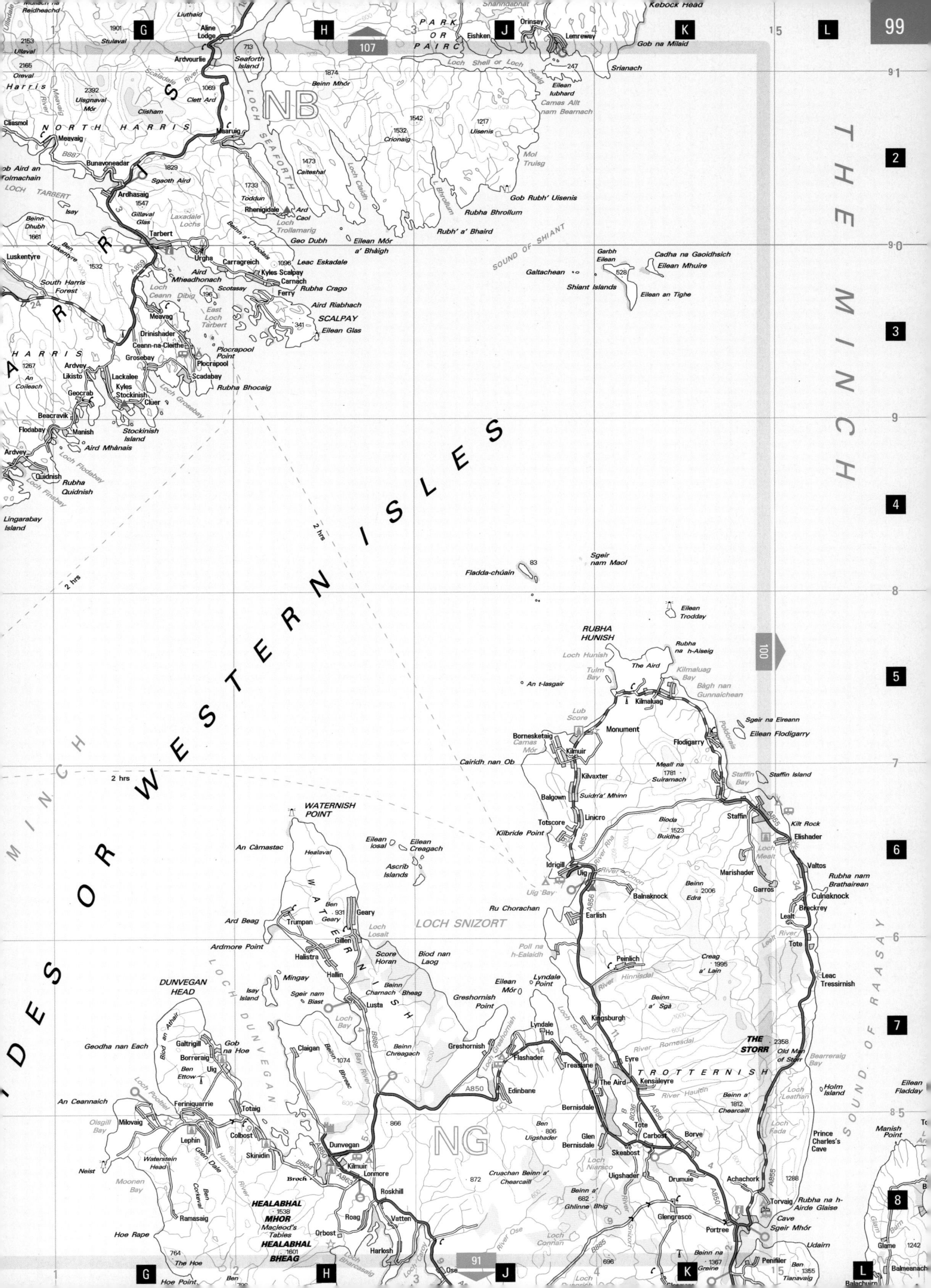

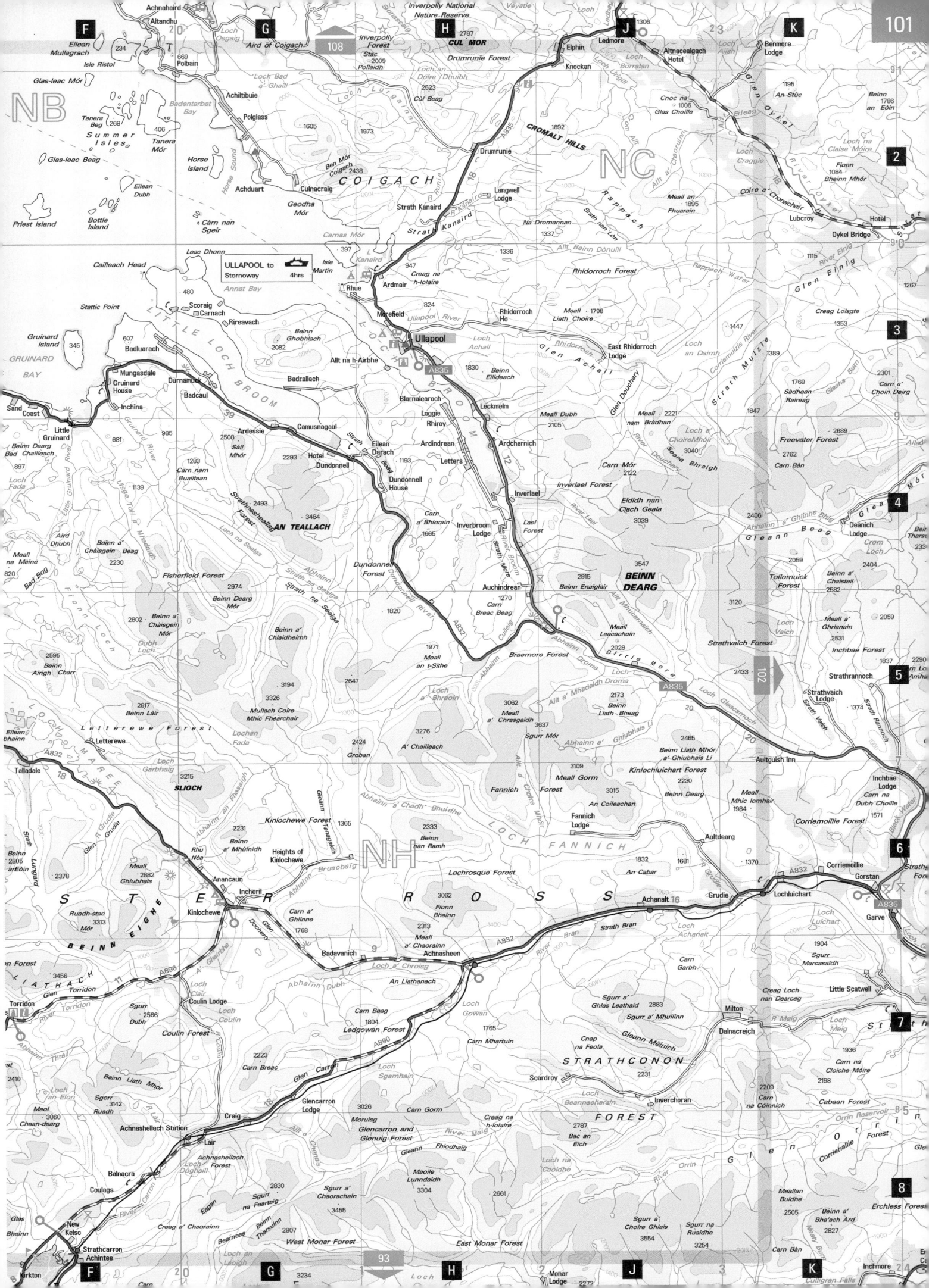

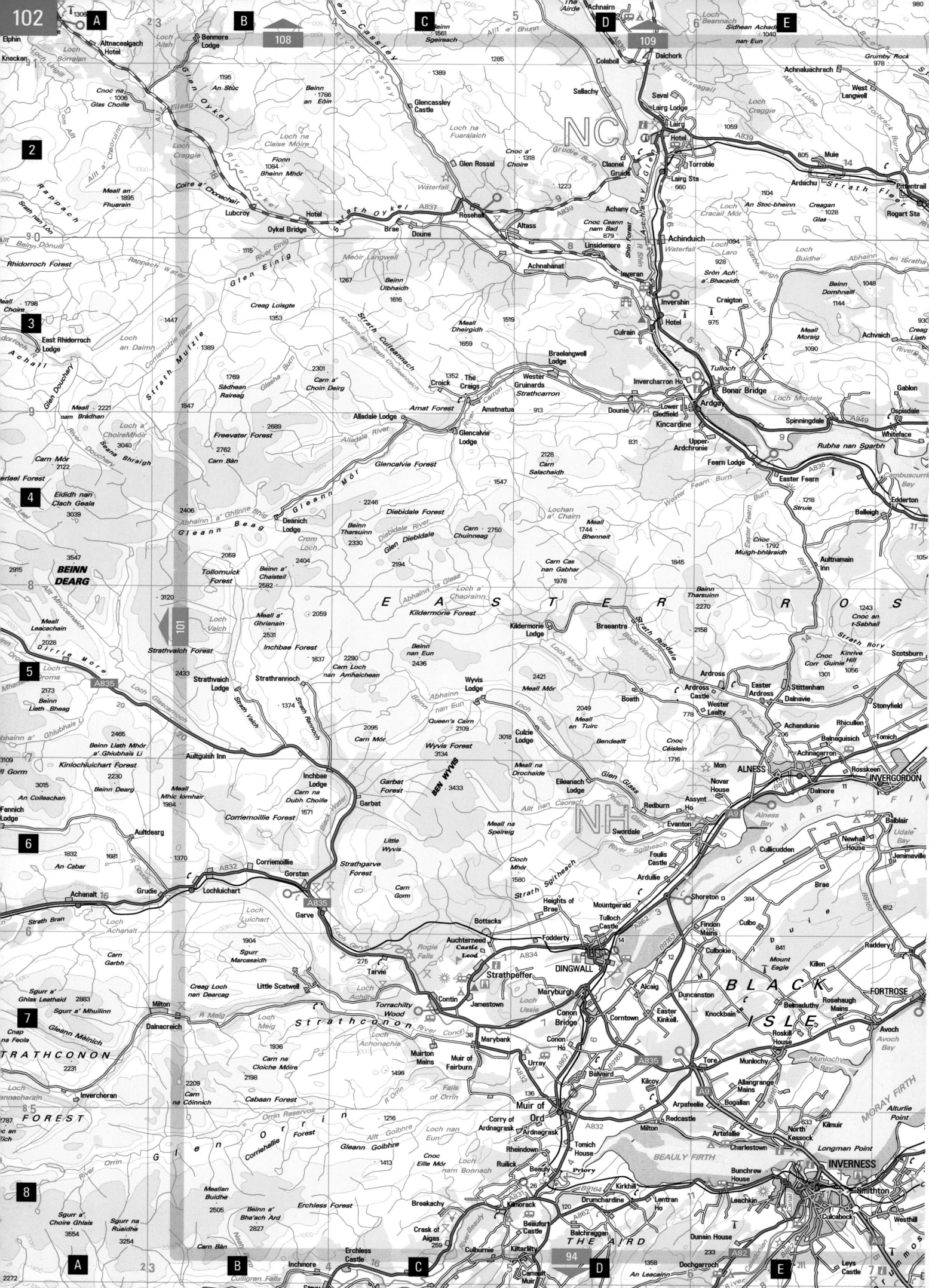

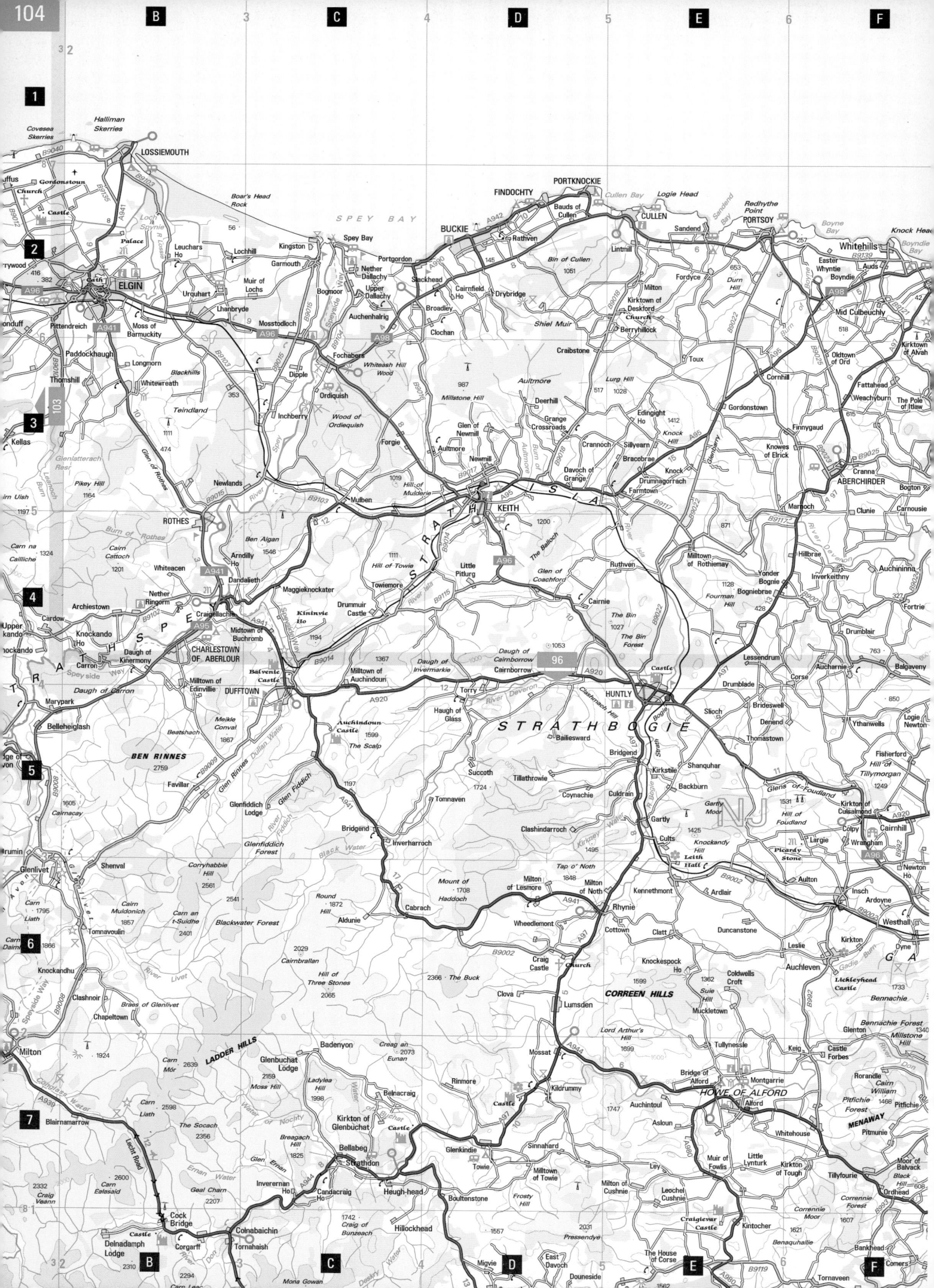

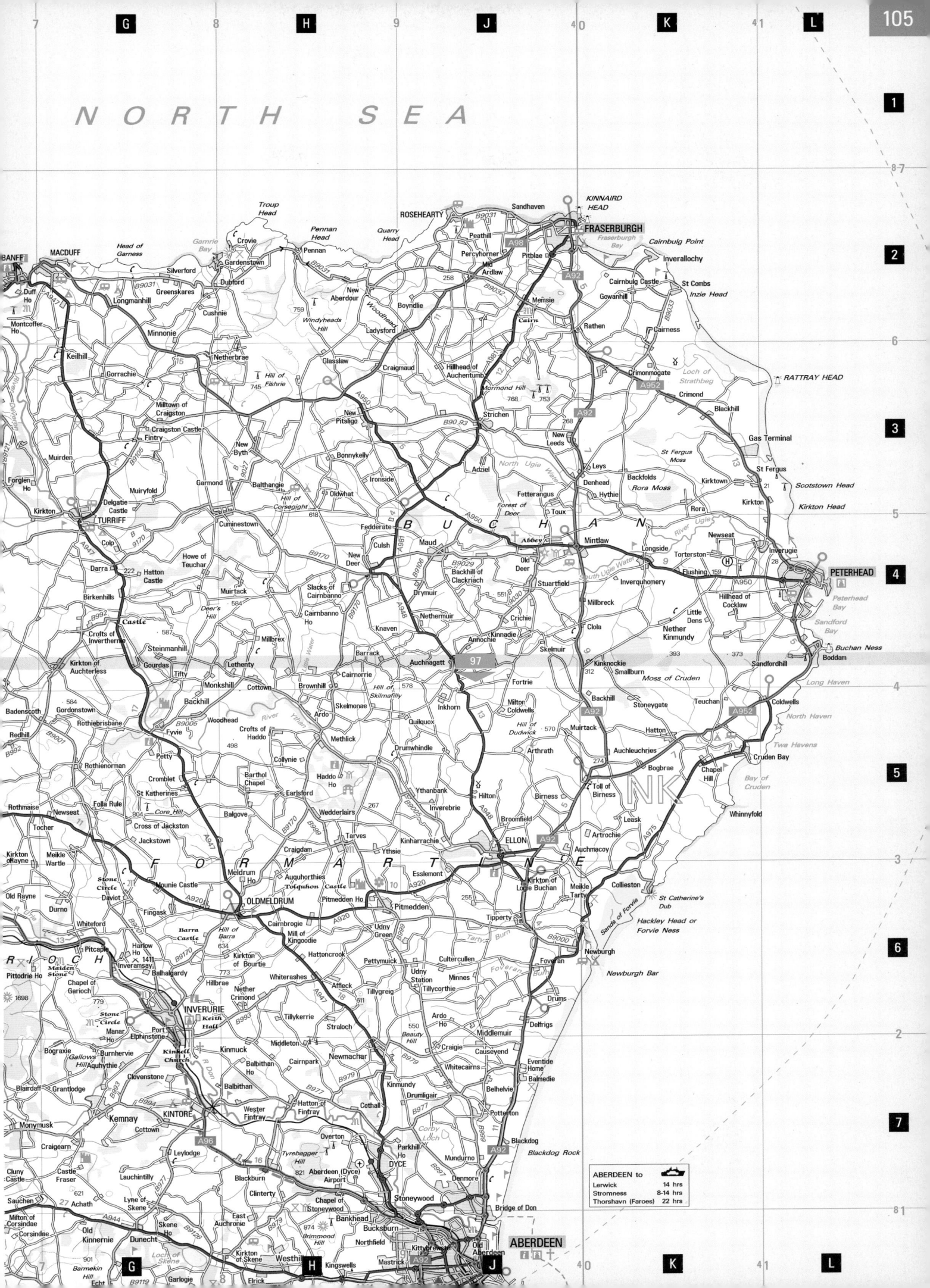

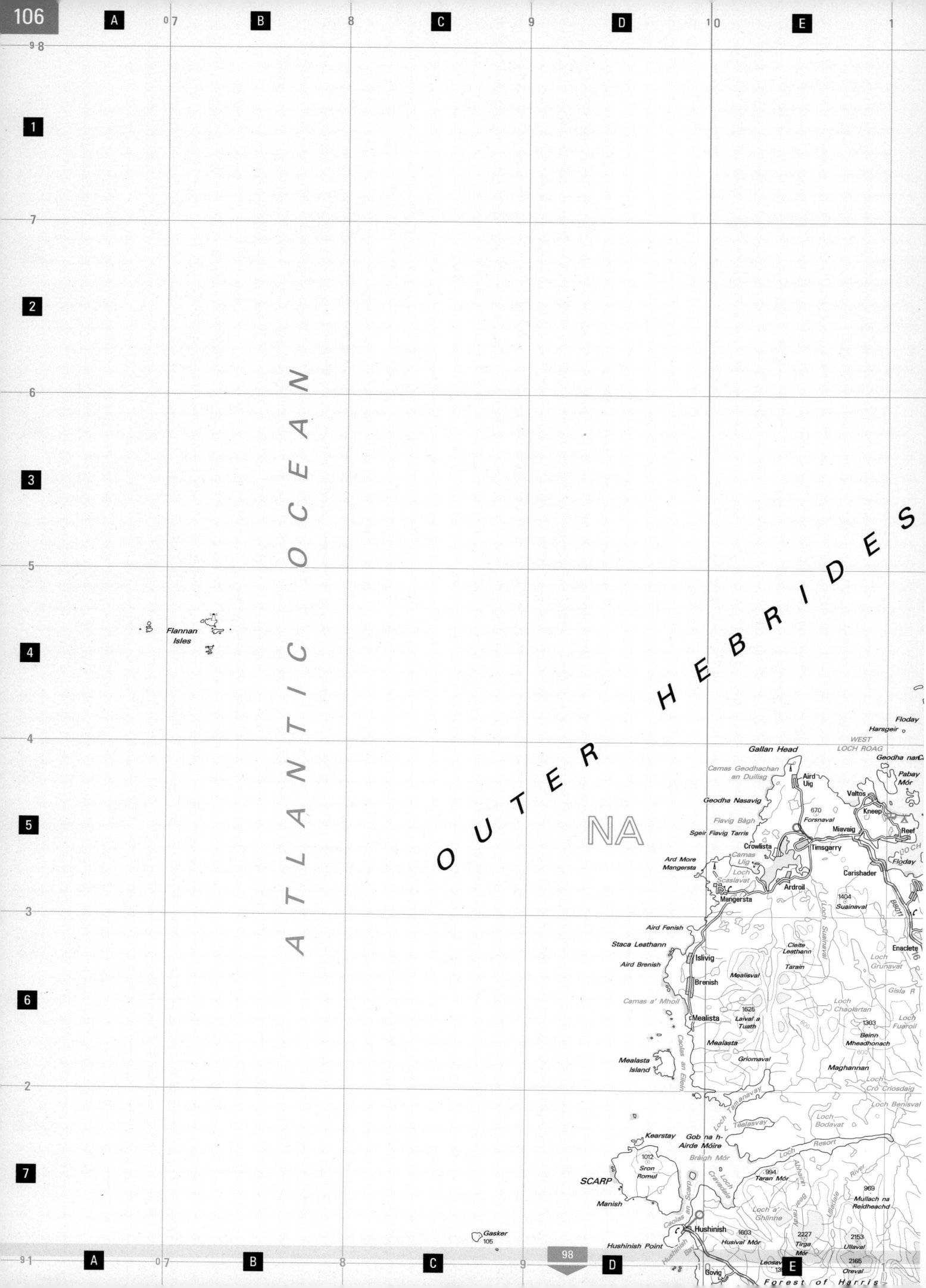

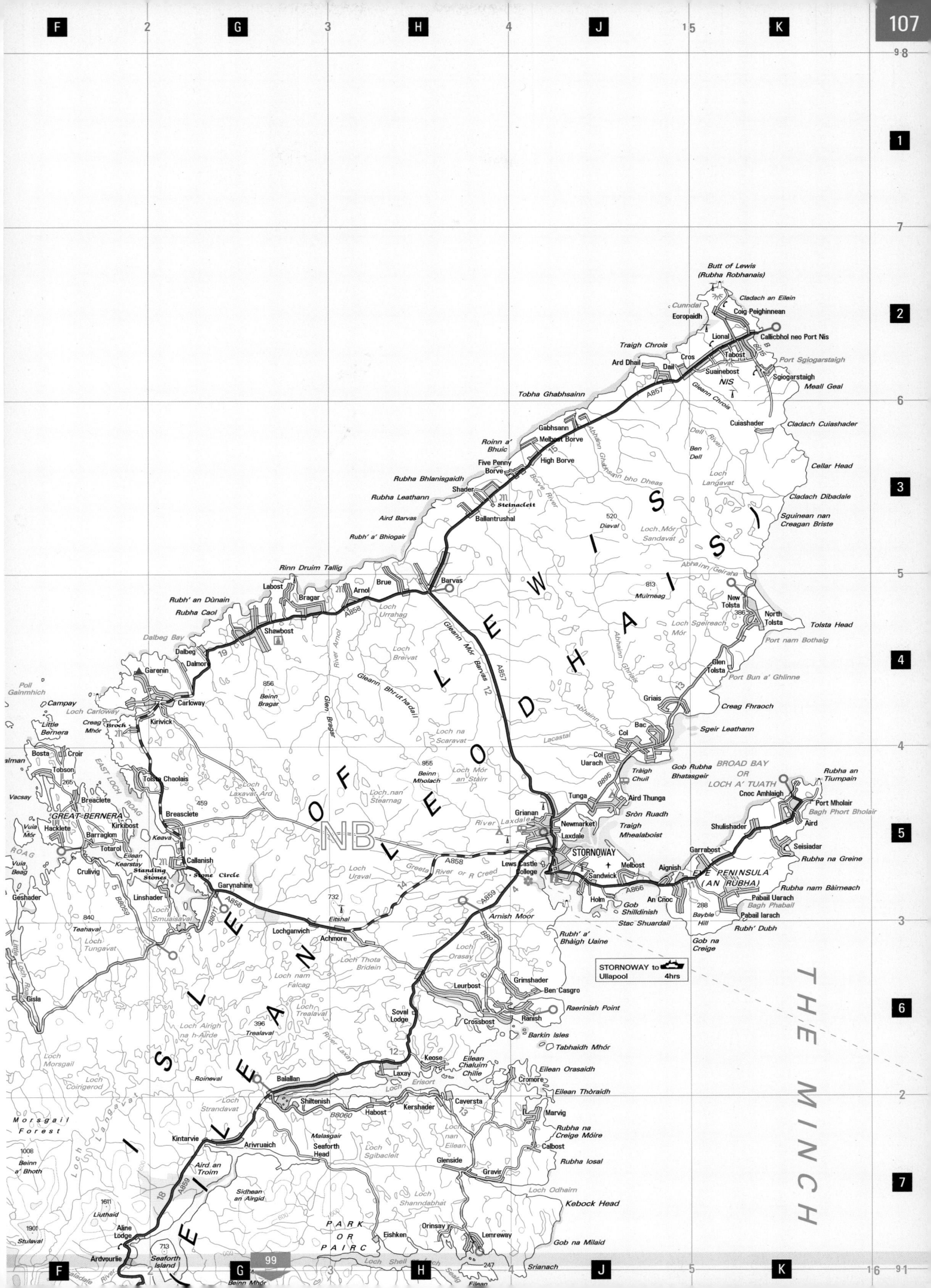

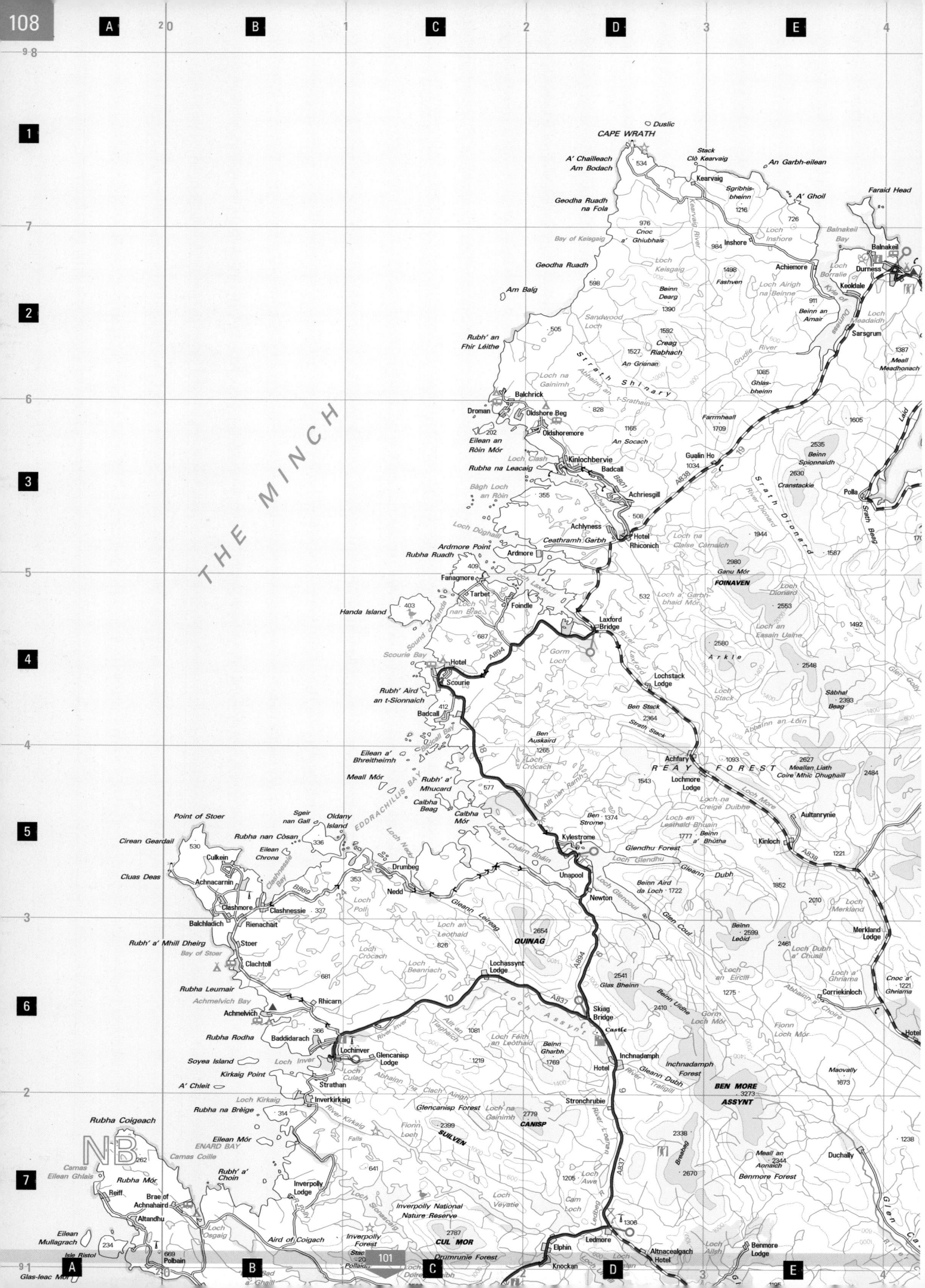

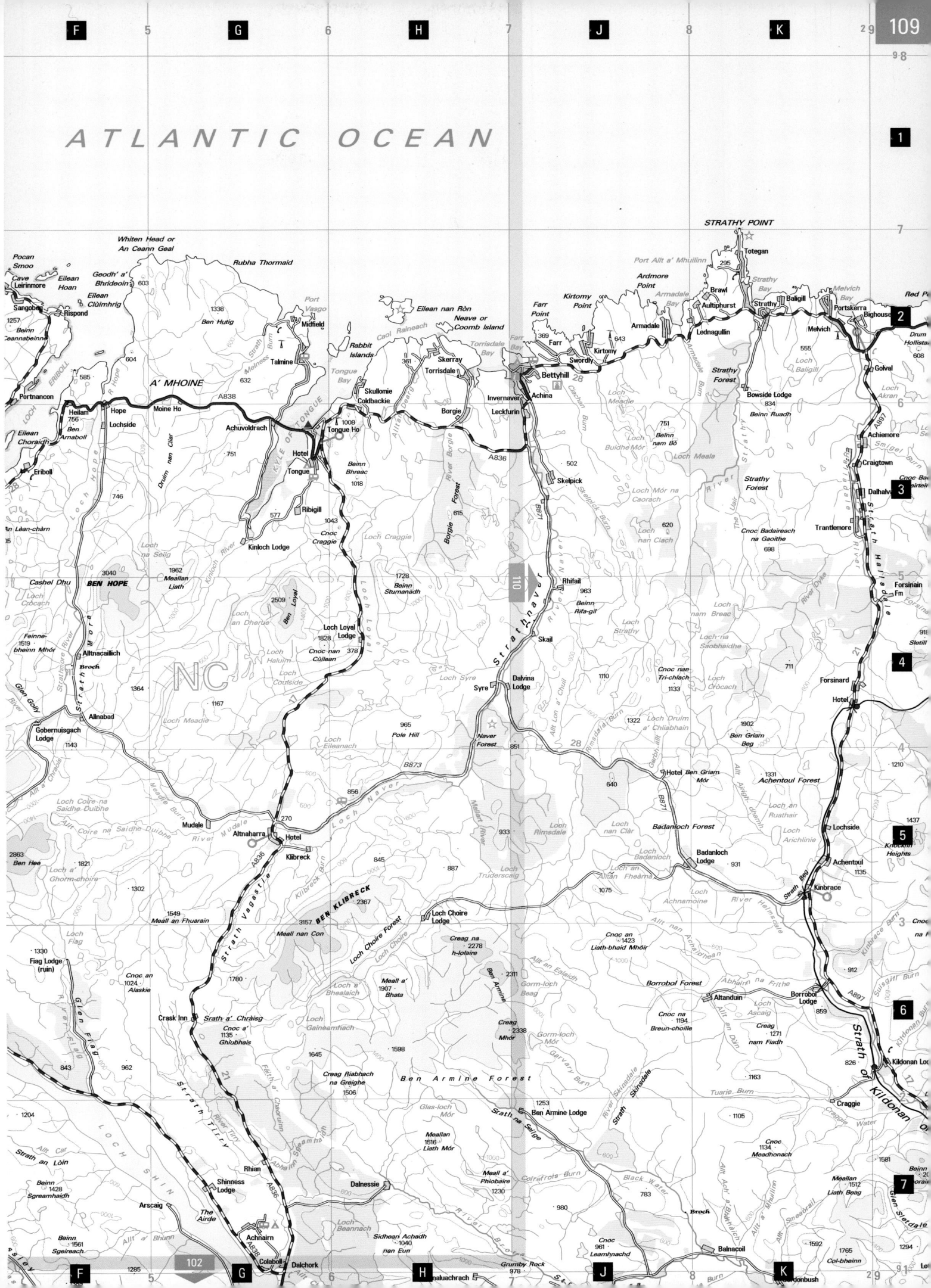

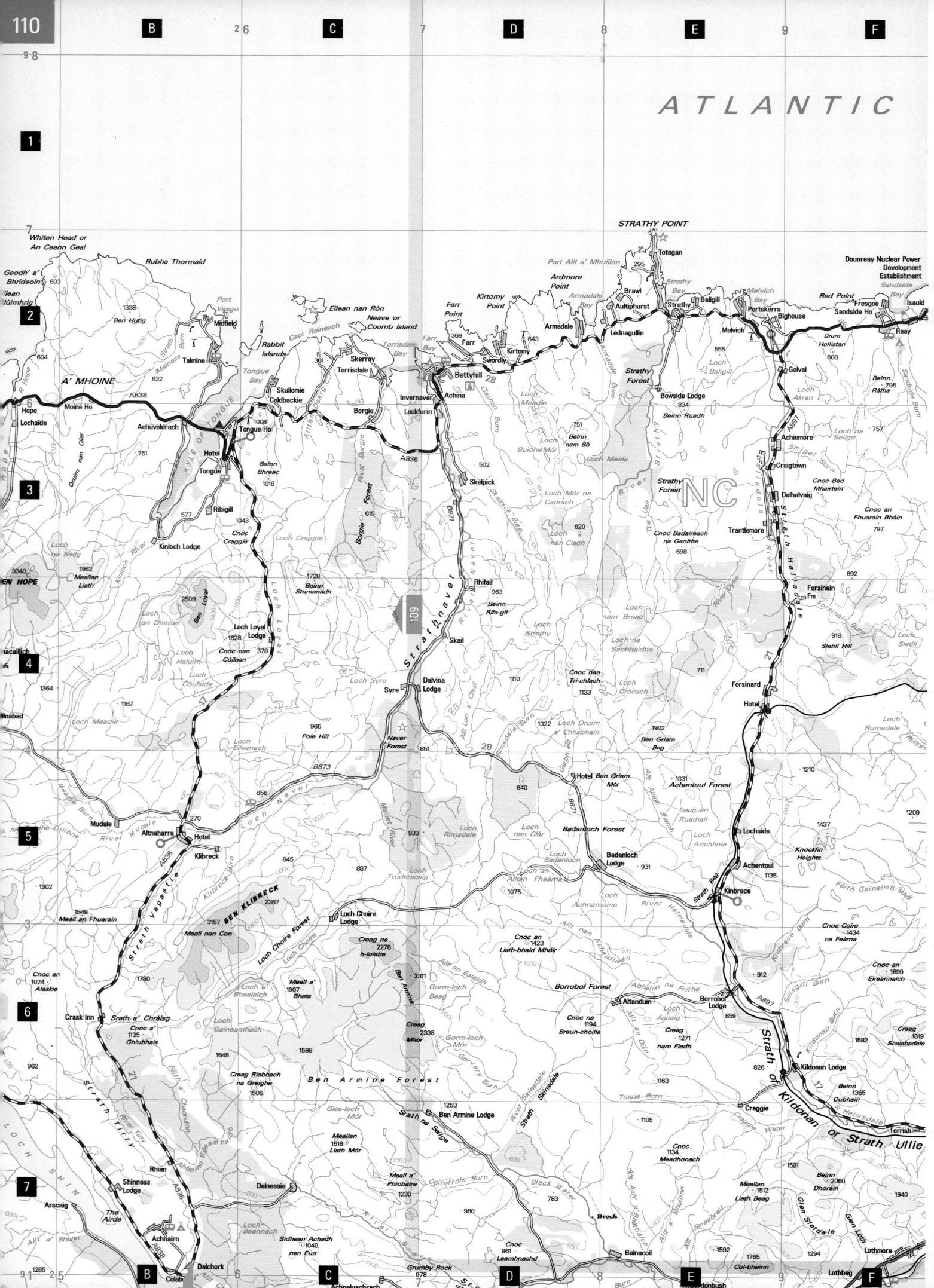

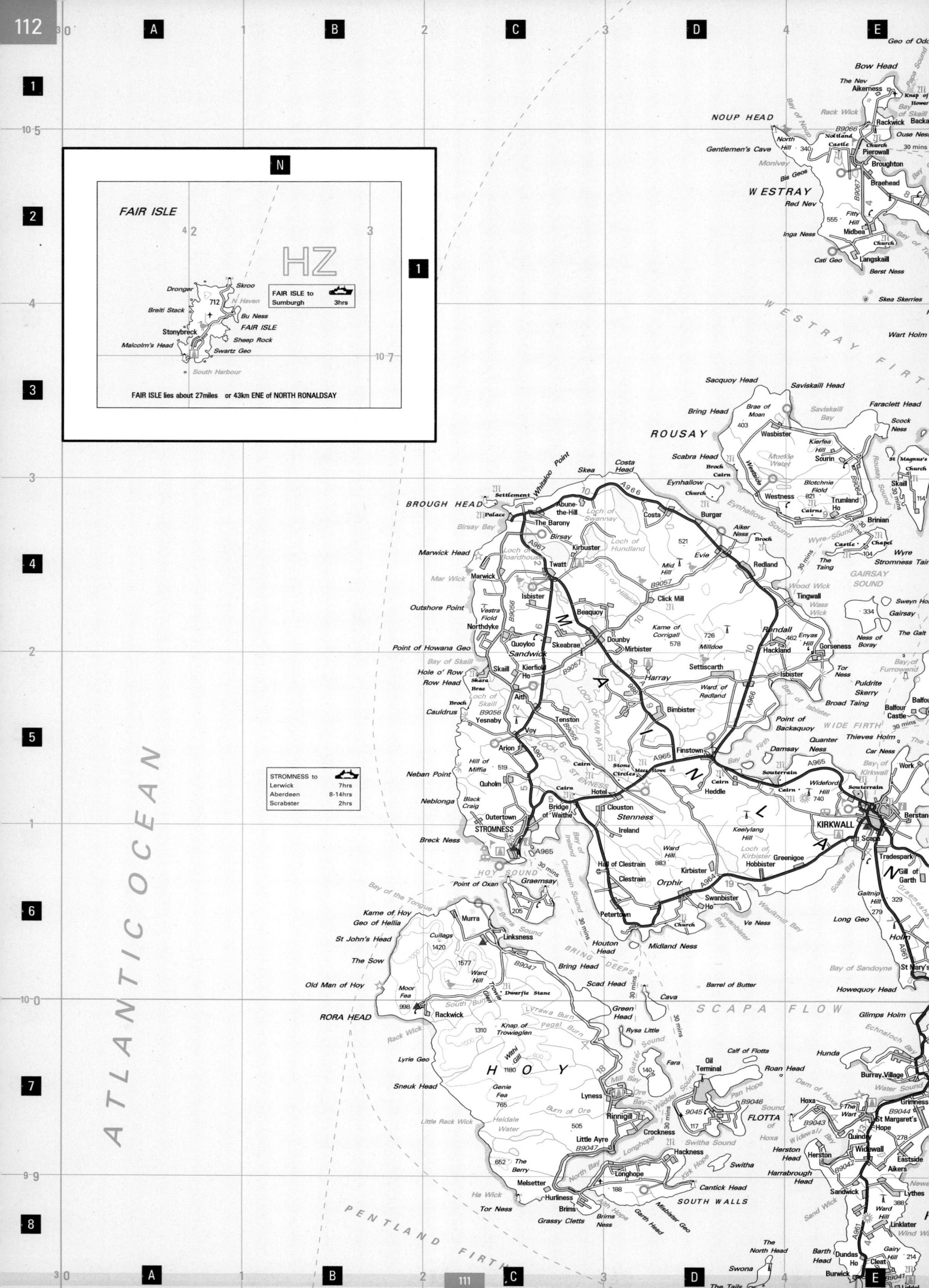

MULL HEAD
The Bore
Veraber
159
North Hill
Neil's Helly
PAPA WESTRAY
Holland
Holm of Papa
Cairn
Chapel
Skaill
Loch of
St Tredwell
Head of Moclett

Garso Wick
Seal Skerry
Point of Sinsoss
NORTH RONALDSAY
Tor Ness
Dennis Head
Hollandstoun
Twinyess
Linklet Bay
Bride's Ness
South Bay
Strom Ness

NORTH RONALDSAY FIRTH

The Riv
Whitemill Bay
Tofts Ness
Holms of Ire
Whitemill Point
Bay of Sandquoy
North Loch
Southvie Bay
THE NORTH SOUND
Scar
Burness
Northwall
START POINT
Roos Wick
North Bay
Otters Wick
Bay of Lopness
Lop Ness
Ness of Brough
Newark
SANDAY
Bay of Brough
Broughtown
Overbister
Cata Sand
163
Bay of Newark
Kettletoft Hotel
Els Ness
Sty Wick
Cairn
Tres Ness
248
Carrick Ho
Cairns
The Wart
216
The Swarf
Calfsound
Braeswick
Quoy Ness
Benstonhall
Stove
Millbounds
Hacks Ness
Stove
SANDAY SOUND
EDAY
291
Fersness Hill
Kirk Taing
Spur Ness
Spurness Sound
30 mins
Holm of Huip
Backaland
Bay of Backaland
Huip Ness
The Ness
335
Ward Hill
Veness
Links Ness
Papa Stronsay
Geo Luon
Odie
Whitehall
Grice Ness
War Ness
Linga Holm
Muckle Green Holm
Mill Bay
Odness
EGILSAY
St Catherine's Bay
Aith
Everbay
STRONSAY
North Taing
Grobister
Kirbuster
Odin Bay
Bay of Bomasty
153
Burgh Head
Rothiesholm
Dishes
Holland
STRONSAY
Bay of Holland
Rothiesholm Head
Greenli Ness
Tor Ness
Lamb Head
Ness of Ork
Bay of Housebay
Edmonstone
Ingale Skerry
Veantrow Bay
Bay of Linton
FIRTH
AUSKERRY SOUND
212
North Taing
SHAPINSAY
The Foot
Auskerry
Helliar Holm
Newlot
South Taing
HY
Haco's Ness
Head of Work
SHAPINSAY SOUND
Bay of Meil
Head of Holland
Rerwick Head
ORKNEY
Linksness
Lea Taing
Hall of Tankerness
The Ness
Den Wick
Mull Head
ISLANDS
Tankerness
Scarva Taing
Brough of Deerness
Deer Sound
285
Marka Ber
Deerness
Skaill
Sandside Bay
Toab
Mirkady Point
Roana Bay
D
Gritley
Point of Ayre
Hamly Hill
Foubister
Newark Bay
240
Upper Sanday
Horse of Copinsay
North Dawn
Braehead
Camy
North Nevi
Corn Holm
Lamb Holm
Cornquoy
South Nevi
Copinsay
Rose Ness
Burray Haas
ND
Northtown
BURRAY
Burray Ness
Southtown
Sea Geo
Rumley Point
Grim Ness
Kirkhouse Point
SOUTH RONALDSAY
Halcro Head

NORTH SEA

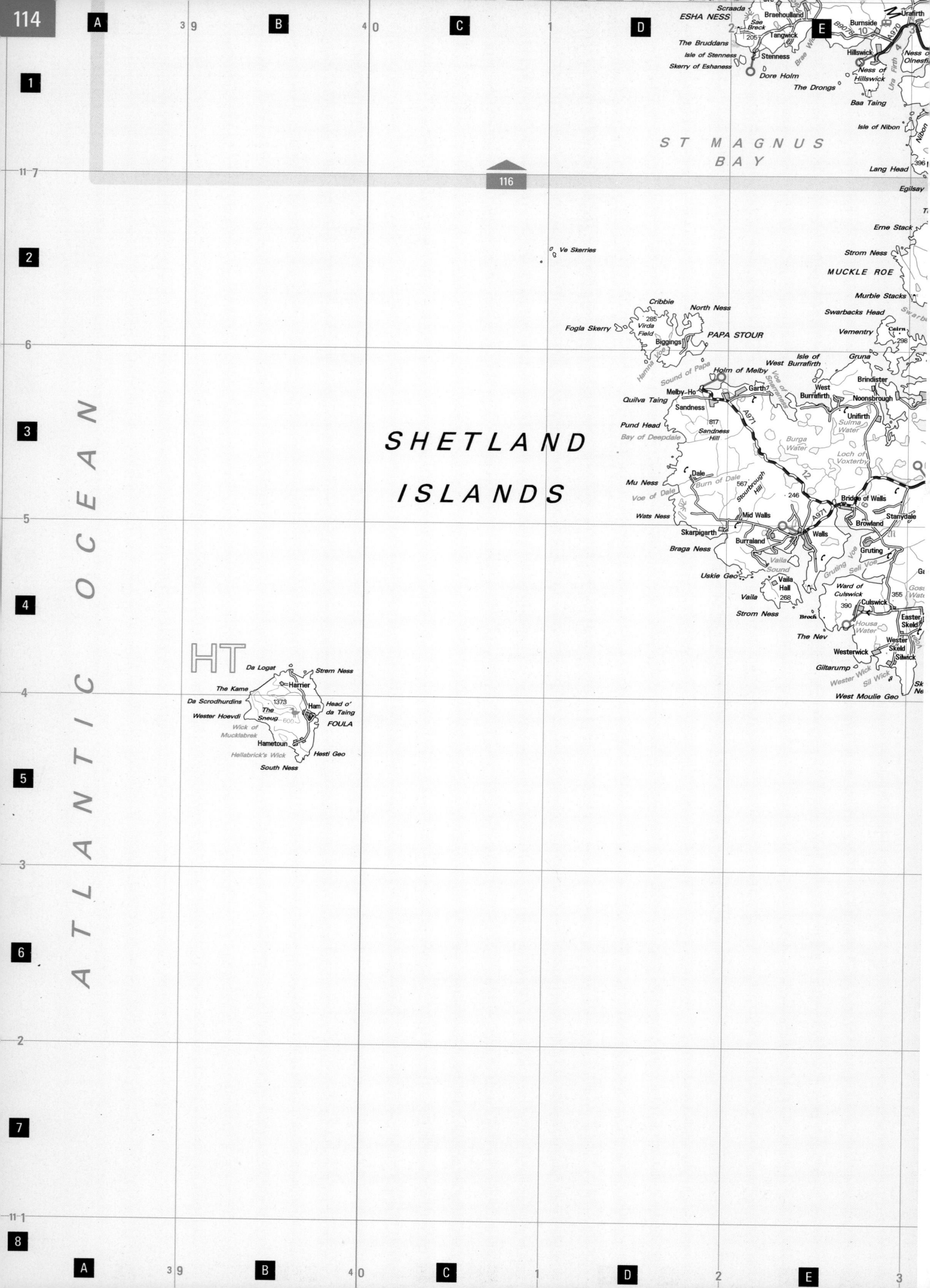

A   39   B   40   C   1   D   E

1

2

3

4

5

6

7

8

ATLANTIC OCEAN

SHETLAND ISLANDS

ST MAGNUS BAY

116

Scraada
ESHA NESS
Sae Breck
205
Tangwick
Braehoulland
Burnside
10
Urafirth

The Bruddans
Isle of Stenness
Skerry of Eshaness
Stenness
Dore Holm
Hillswick
Ness of Hillswick
Ness of Olnesfi

The Drongs

Baa Taing

Isle of Nibon

Nibon

Lang Head
396

Egilsay

Erne Stack

Strom Ness

MUCKLE ROE

Murbie Stacks

Swarbacks Head
Swarb

Vementry
Cairn
298

Ve Skerries

Cribbie
North Ness
285
Virda Field
Biggings
Hamna Voe
Fogla Skerry
PAPA STOUR
Isle of West Burrafirth
Grune

Sound of Papa
Holm of Melby
West Burrafirth
Brindister
Noonsbrough

Melby Ho
Garth
A971
Quilva Taing
Voe of Snarraness
Unifirth
Sulma Water

Sandness
817
Sandness Hill
Burga Water
Loch of Voxterby

Pund Head
Bay of Deepdale

Dale
Burn of Dale
12
Mu Ness
Stourbrough Hill
246
Bridge of Walls
Voe of Dale
567
Stanydale

Wats Ness
Mid Walls
A971
Browland

Skarpigarth
Walls
Gruting

Braga Ness
Burrraland
Gruting Voe
Ga

Uskie Geo
Vaila Sound
Sel Voe

Vaila Hall
Goss Water

Ward of Culswick
355
Vaila
268
Culswick

Strom Ness
Broch
390
Easter Skeld

The Nev
Housa Water
Wester Skeld
Silwick

Giltarump
Westerwick
Sk

Wester Wick
Sil Wick

West Moulie Geo

HT

Da Logat
Strem Ness
The Kame
Harrier
Da Scrodhurdins
1373
Head o' da Taing
Wester Hoevdi
The Sneug
600
Ham
FOULA

Wick of Mucklabrek
Hametoun
Hesti Geo
Hellabrick's Wick
South Ness

11-7
11-1

SHETLAND ISLANDS

ATLANTIC OCEAN

ST MAGNUS BAY

Ramna Stacks

Isle of Fethaland

Garmus Taing

Uyea 231
The Breck Fethaland
Burrier Wick 425 Isbister
Fugla Ness
South Wick North Roe
564

Hevdadale Head Egga Field
Lang Clodie Wick 644 Beorgs of Skelberry Housetter
Gruna Stack Roer Water Collafirth Colla Firth
The Faither Turls Head 740 Quey Firth
Muckle Ossa 351 Ketligill Man o' Scord The Clifts Voe Ollaberry
Heillia Head 1475 Ronas Hill B9079
Ockran Head Stonga Banks Faan Hill
Burries Ness The Brough
South Head RONAS VOE Gluss
Whalwick Taing Gluss Water Heylor Urafirth Gluss Isle
Head of Stanshi Hamna Hamnavoe 567 M Eela Water Bardister
Grind of the Navir Scarff Ura B9078 Burnside Gluss
Scraada Braehoulland
ESHA NESS Sae Breck Burraland
The Bruddans 2057 Tangwick Bree Wick Hillswick Ness of Olnesfirth
Isle of Stenness Stenness Ness of 389 Fugla Ness
Skerry of Eshaness Dore Holm Hillswick Sullom
The Drongs Baa Taing
Isle of Nibon Cairn 270
396 Mangaster
Ve Skerries Lang Head Voxter
Egilsay Mavis Grind
Islesburgh Brae
Turvalds Head 315 Busta Burravoe
Erne Stack Wethersta
Cribbie North Ness Strom Ness Roesound
Fogla Skerry 285 Virda 555 Linga
Field South 229
Biggings Ward Gonfirt
MUCKLE ROE Murbie Stacks Little-ayre
PAPA STOUR Swarbacks Head Swarbacks Minn 272
Vementry Papa East
Isle of Gruna 298 Cairn Little Burrafir
West Burrafirth The Rona B9071
Holm of Melby West Brindister Loch of Vaara
Melby-Ho Garth Burrafirth Noonsbrough Clousta Lamba Water
Quilva Taing Unifirth Sulma Aith Maa Water
Sandness Water 313 Wei
Pund Head 817 Burga Loch of Aithsting
Bay of Deepdale Sandness Water Voxterby Twatt
Hill Westerfield
Dale 567 Bixter Tresta
Mu Ness Burn of Dale Stourbrough Sound
Voe of Dale Hill Bridge of Walls Effirth Russaness
Wats Ness 246 Stanydale Semblister 650 Hill Sandsound
Mid Walls Browland The Firth
Skarpigarth Walls Gruting 437 Garderhouse
Burraland Gruting Voe
Braga Ness Vaila Seli Voe
Uskie Geo Sound

1

2

3

4

5

6

A

B

C

D

Maida Vale

LAUDERDALE ROAD

Maida Vale Hospital for Nervous Diseases

Lord's Cricket Ground

Cricket Museum

London Mosque

(Regent's Canal)

Lisson Green

Lisson Grove

Marylebone Station

Florence Nightingale Hospital

Western Ophthalmic Hospl

Samaritan Hospl for Women

Warwick Avenue

CLIFTON GARDENS

Paddington Green Children's Hospl

Little Venice

HARROW ROAD

Edgware Road (Bakerloo)

Edgware Road (Met., Circle & District Line)

Edgware Road FLYOVER

HARROW ROAD (UNDER)

HARROW ROAD

CHAPEL ST

Paddington

WESTWAY (ELEVATED ROAD)

Bishop's Road Bridge

Paddington Basin

St Mary's Hospital

OLD MARYLEBONE ROAD

Royal Oak

Paddington Station

Paddington

SOUTH WHARF ROAD

NORTH WHARF ROAD

PRAED STREET

The Water Gardens

Synagogue

HALLFIELD

Synagogue

HYDE PARK SQUARE

CONNAUGHT STREET

CONNAUGHT SQUARE

Bayswater

CRAVEN HILL

Bayswater

HYDE PARK GARDENS

St Georges Field

Tyburn Tree (site of)

BAYSWATER ROAD

Lancaster Gate

Westbourne Gate

Victoria Gate

NORTH CARRIAGE DRIVE

North Ride

Black Lion Gate

North Walk

Bayard's Watering Place (site of)

Speke's Monument

Peter Pan Statue

Clock Tower

Kensington Palace

Round Pond

Kensington Gardens

Statue

Temple Lodge

CENTRAL LONDON

Scale 1:10 000, 10 centimetres to 1 kilometre or about 6 inches to 1 mile
For complete street index see pages 125 to 129
Restrictions may not apply at all times and to all vehicles
Les restrictions ne s'appliqueront pas tout le temps et à tous les véhicules

	Main roads / Routes principales
	One way traffic route / Voie de circulation en sens unique
	No access in direction shown / Pas d'accès dans le sens indiquée
	Oxford Street : open to buses and taxis only between 7am and 7pm, Monday to Saturday / *Oxford Street* : interdit à la circulation du lundi au samedi, de 7 heures à 19 heures (sauf autobus et taxis)
	River Bus route / Itinéraire de bus fluvial

Royal Academy of Arts

Horse Guards

	Selected buildings and places of interest / Lieux d'intérêt choisies
i	Information centre / Office de tourisme
	Railway station / Gare
	Underground station / Station de métro
	Bus or coach station / Gare d'autobus ou d'autocar
P	Parking / Parking
+	Hospital with casualty facilities / Hôpital avec équipement pour accidentés

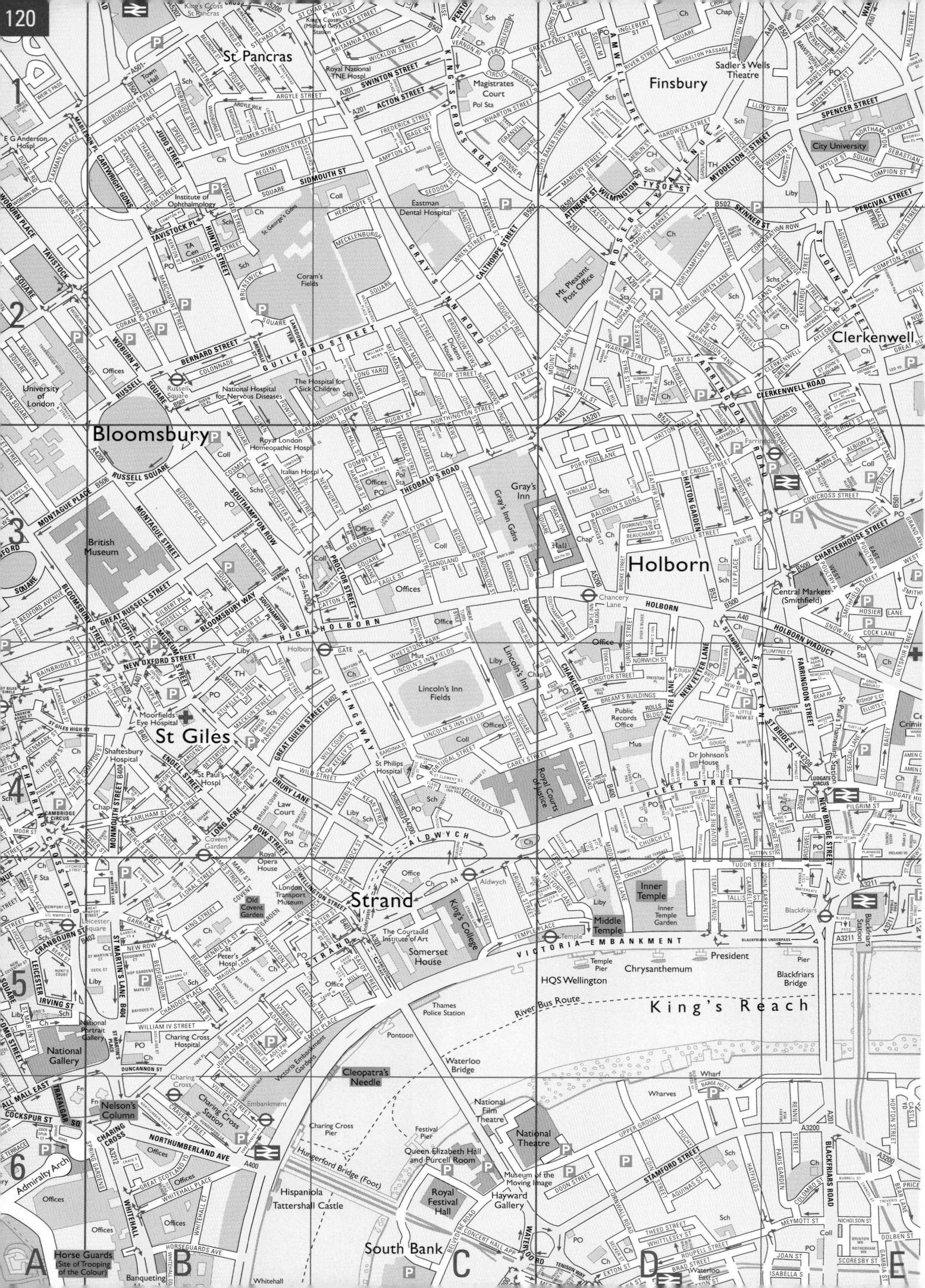

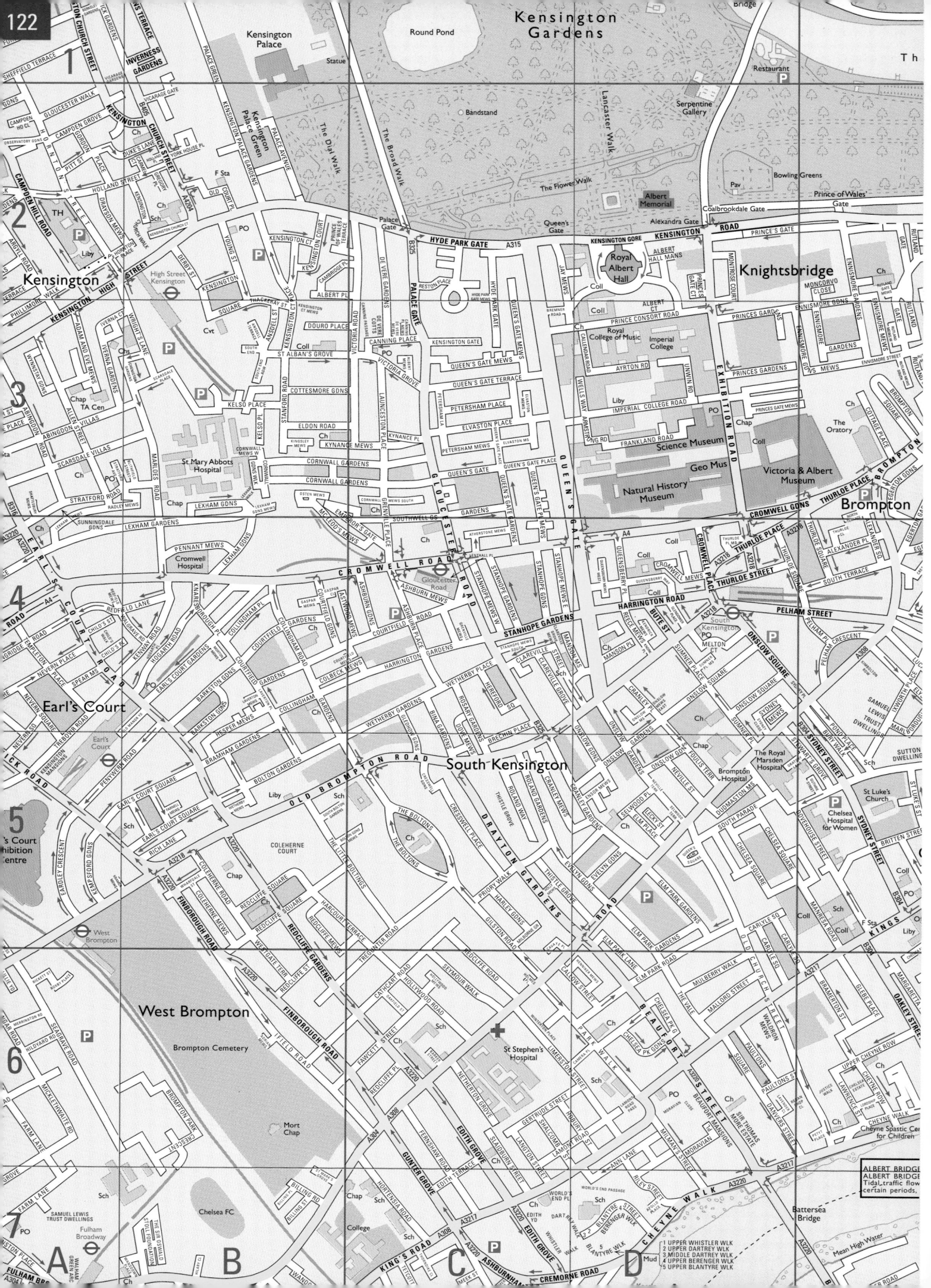

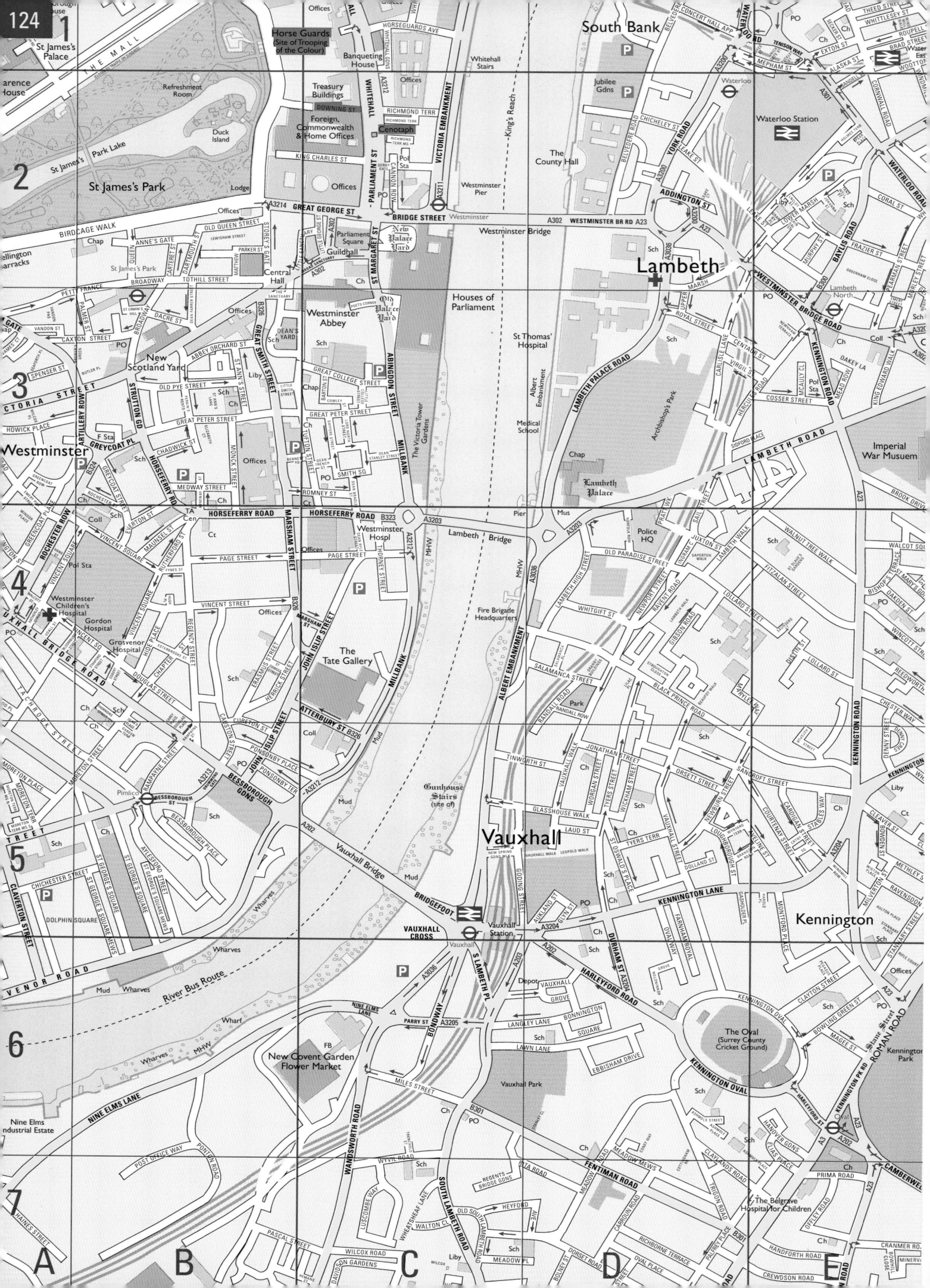

CENTRAL LONDON

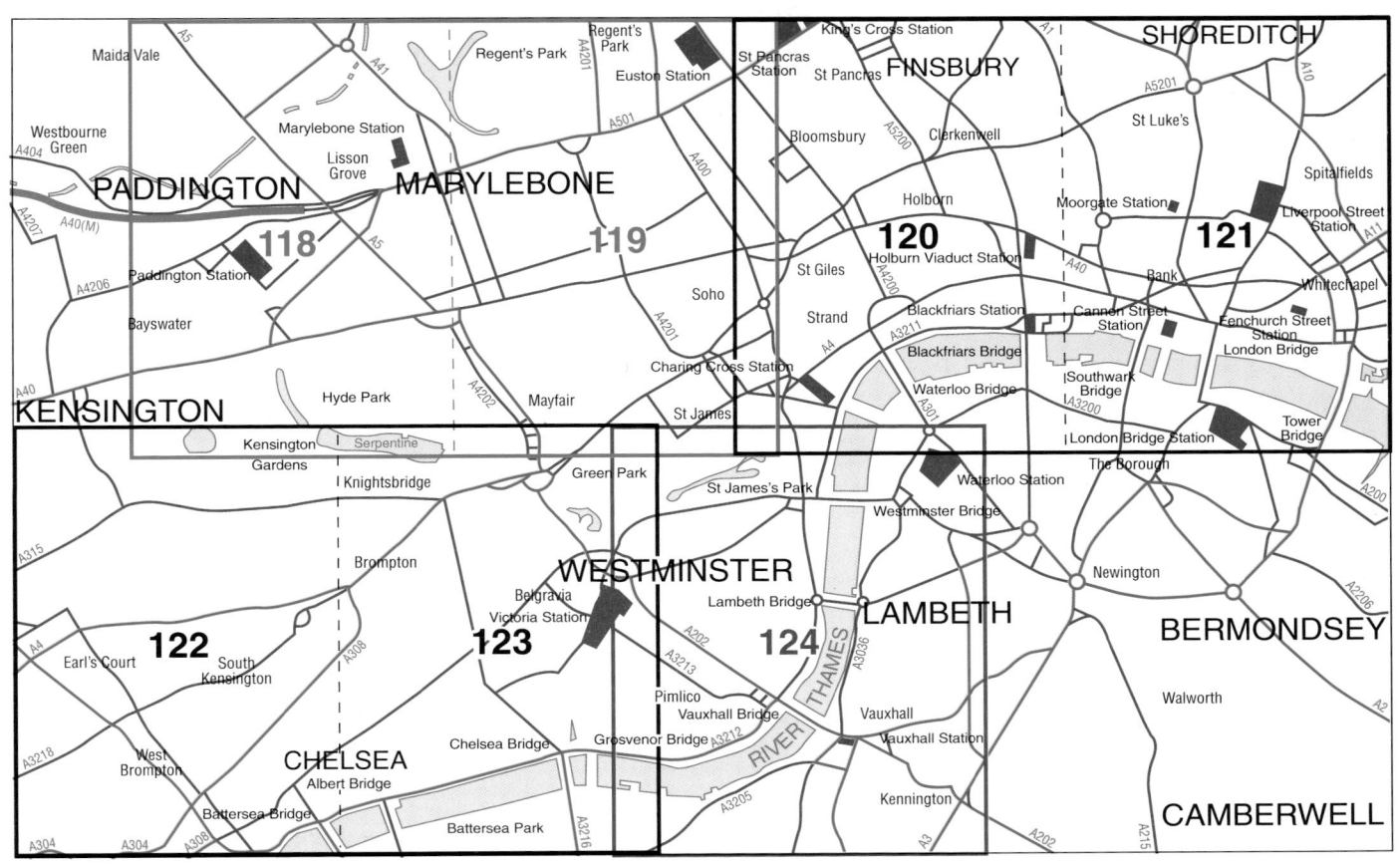

Entries preceded by an asterisk indicate that only the first two letters of the road name have been shown on the map

A

Abbey Orchard St......124 B3
Abchurch La......121 G5
Abchurch Yd......121 G5
Abercorn Pl......118 B1
Aberdeen Pl......118 C2
Abingdon Rd......122 A3
Abingdon St......124 C3
Abingdon Villas......122 A3
Acacia Wlk......122 C7
Achilles Way......119 F6
Acton St......120 C1
Adam and Eve Ct......119 H4
Adam and Eve Mews......122 A3
Adam St......120 B5
Adams Ct......121 G4
Adam's Row......119 F5
Addington St......124 D2
Addle Hill......121 E4
Addle St......121 F3
Adelaide St......120 B5
Adeline Pl......120 A3
Adelphi Terr......120 B5
Adpar St......118 C3
Adrian Mews......122 B6
Agar St......120 B5
Agdon St......120 E2
Air St......119 H5
Airlie Gdns......122 A1
Alaska St......120 D6
Albany Courtyard......119 H5
Albany St......119 G1
Albemarle St......119 H5
Albemarle Way......120 E2
Albert Bridge......123 E6
Albert Bridge Rd......123 F7
Albert Ct......122 D2
Albert Emb......124 C4
Albert Hall Mans......122 D2
Albert Mews......122 C3
Albert Pl......122 B2
Albion Bldgs......121 F3
Albion Cl......118 D5
Albion Mews......118 D5
Albion Pl......121 E3
Albion St......118 D5
Aldermanbury......121 F4
Aldermanbury Sq......121 F3
Alderman's Wlk......121 H3
Alderney St......123 H5
Aldersgate St......121 F3
Aldford St......119 F6
Aldgate......121 J4
Aldgate Ave......121 J4
Aldgate High St......121 J4
Aldwych......120 C4
Alexander Pl......122 C4
Alexander Sq......122 C4
Alfred Mews......119 J3
Alfred Pl......119 J3
Alie St......121 J4
All Souls Pl......119 G3
Allen St......122 A3
Allhallows La......121 G5
Allington St......123 H3
Allsop Pl......119 E2

Alma Sq......118 B1
Alpha Cl......118 D2
Alpha Pl......123 E6
Ambrosden Ave......123 J3
Amen Cnr......120 E4
Amen Ct......120 E4
America Sq......121 J5
America St......121 F6
Ampton Pl......120 C1
Ampton St......120 C1
Amwell St......120 D1
Anchor Yd......121 F2
Anderson St......123 F5
Andrew Borde St......120 A4
Andrews Crosse......120 D4
Angel Ct......121 G4
Angel Ct......119 H6
Angel Ct......124 A1
Angel Pas......121 G5
Angel St......121 F4
Anhalt Rd......123 E7
Anhalt Rd......123 E7
Ann La......122 C6
Anning St......121 H2
Ann's Cl......123 G2
Ansdell St......122 B3
Ansdell Terr......122 B3
Apollo Pl......122 D7
Apothecary St......120 E4
Apple Tree Yd......119 H6
Apple Tree Yd......124 A1
Appold St......121 H3
Apsley Way......123 G2
Aquinas St......120 D6
Arcade The......121 H3
Archer St......119 J5
Archery Cl......118 D4
Arches The......120 B6
Archibald Mews......119 G5
Argon Mews......122 A7
Argyle Sq......120 B1
Argyle St......120 B1
Argyle Wlk......120 B1
Argyll Rd......122 A2
Argyll St......119 H4
Arlington St......119 H6
Arlington St......124 A1
Arlington Way......120 D1
Armstrong Rd......122 D3
Arne St......120 B4
Arneway St......124 B3
Arnold Circ......121 J1
Arthur St......121 G5
Artillery La......121 H3
Artillery Pas......121 J3
Artillery Row......124 B3
Artizan St......121 H4
Arundel St......120 C5
Ascalon St......124 D7
Ashbridge St......118 D2
Ashburn Gdns......122 C4
Ashburn Mews......122 C4
Ashburn Pl......122 C4
Ashburnham Rd......122 C7
Ashby St......120 E1
Ashentree Ct......120 D4
Ashford St......121 H1
Ashland Pl......119 F3
Ashley Pl......123 J3
Ashmill St......118 D3
Ashmole Pl......124 D6

Ashmole St......124 D6
Ashworth Rd......118 A1
Aske St......121 H1
Astell St......123 E5
Astwood Mews......122 C4
Atherstone Mews......122 C4
Atterbury St......124 C4
Attneave St......120 D1
Auckland St......124 D6
Audley Sq......119 F6
Augustus St......119 G1
Austin Friars......121 G4
Austin Friars Sq......121 G4
Austin St......121 J1
Ave Maria La......121 E4
Aveline St......124 E6
Avery Farm Row......123 H4
Avery Row......119 G5
Aybrook St......119 F3
Aylesbury St......120 E2
Aylesford St......124 B5
Ayrton Rd......122 D3

B

Babmaes St......119 J5
Bache's St......121 G1
Back Alley......121 H4
Back Hill......120 D2
Bainbridge St......120 A4
Baird St......121 F2
Baker St......119 E3
Bakers Hall Ct......121 H5
Baker's Mews......119 F4
Baker's Row......120 D2
Balcombe St......118 E2
Balderton St......119 F4
Baldwin St......121 G1
Baldwin's Gdns......120 D3
Balfour Mews......119 F6
Balfour Pl......119 F5
Balfour St......121 G4
Baltic St......121 F2
Banbury Ct......120 B4
Bank End......121 F6
Bankside......121 F5
Banner St......121 F2
Barge House St......120 D6
Barge House St......124 E1
Bark Pl......118 A5
Barkston Gdns......122 B4
Barley Mow Pas......121 E3
Barlow Pl......119 G5
Barnard's Inn......120 D3
Barnby St......119 H1
Barnwood Cl......118 A2
Baroness Rd......121 J1
Barrett St......119 F4
Barter St......120 B3
Bartholomew Cl......121 F3
Bartholomew La......121 G4
Bartholomew Pl......121 F3
Bartlett Ct......120 D4
Bartolomew Sq......121 F2
Barton St......124 C3
Basil St......123 F2
Basil St......123 F2
Basing House Yd......121 H1

Basing Pl......121 H1
Basinghall Ave......121 G4
Basinghall St......121 G4
Bassishaw Highwalk......121 G3
Bastwick St......121 F2
Bateman St......119 J4
Bateman's Bldgs......119 J4
Bateman's Row......121 H2
Bath Ct......120 D2
Bath Pl......121 H1
Bath St......121 G1
Bathurst Mews......118 C5
Bathurst St......118 C5
Battersea Bridge......122 E7
Battersea Bridge Rd......123 E7
Battersea Park Rd......123 J7
Battersea Park Rd......124 A7
Battle Bridge La......121 H6
Bayley St......119 J3
Baylis Rd......124 E2
Bayswater Rd......118 C5
Beak St......119 H5
Bear Alley......120 E4
Bear Gdns......121 F6
Bear La......120 E6
Bear St......120 A5
Beauchamp Pl......123 E3
Beauchamp St......120 D3
Beaufort Gdns......123 F3
Beaufort St......122 D6
Beaufoy Wlk......124 D4
Beaumont Mews......119 F3
Beaumont Pl......119 J2
Beaumont St......119 F3
Bedale St......121 G6
Bedford Ave......120 A3
Bedford Ct......120 B5
Bedford Gdns......122 A1
Bedford Pl......120 B3
Bedford Row......120 C3
Bedford Sq......120 A3
Bedford St......120 B5
Bedford Way......120 A2
Bedfordbury......120 B5
Beech St......121 F3
Beeston Pl......123 H3
Belgrave Mews N......123 G2
Belgrave Mews S......123 G3
Belgrave Mews W......123 G3
Belgrave Pl......123 G3
Belgrave Rd......123 J4
Belgrave Sq......123 G3
Belgrave Yd......123 H3
Bell Inn Yd......121 G4
Bell La......121 J3
Bell St......118 D3
Bell Wharf La......121 F5
Bell Yd......120 D4
Belvedere Rd......124 D2
Bendall Mews......118 D3
Benjamin St......120 E3
Bennett St......119 H6
Bennett St......124 A1
Bennett's Hill......121 F5
Bennett's Yd......124 B3
Bentinck Mews......119 F4
Bentinck St......119 F4
Berenger Wlk......122 D7

Berkeley Gdns......122 A1
Berkeley Mews......119 E4
Berkeley Sq......119 G5
Berkeley St......119 G6
Berners Mews......119 H3
Berners Pl......119 H4
Berners St......119 H4
Berry Pl......120 E1
Berry St......121 E2
Berwick St......119 H4
Bessborough Gdns......124 B5
Bessborough Pl......124 B5
Bessborough St......124 B5
Bethnal Green Rd......121 J2
Betterton St......120 B4
Bevenden St......121 G1
Bevin Way......120 D1
Bevis Marks......121 H4
Bickenhall St......119 E3
Bidborough St......120 B1
Biddulph Rd......118 A1
Billing Pl......122 B7
Billing Rd......122 B7
Billing St......122 B7
Billiter Sq......121 H4
Billiter St......121 H4
Bina Gdns......122 C4
Bingham Pl......119 F3
Binney St......119 F4
Birchin La......121 G4
Bird St......119 F4
Birdcage Wlk......124 B2
Birkenhead St......120 B1
Bishop's Bridge Rd......118 B4
Bishop's Ct......120 E4
Bishop's Ct......120 D4
Bishop's Terr......124 E4
Bishopsgate......121 H3
Bishopsgate Church Yd......121 H4
Black Friars La......121 E4
Black Prince Rd......124 D4
Black Prince Rd......124 D4
Blackall St......121 H2
Blackfriars Bridge......120 E5
Blackfriars Ct......120 E5
Blackfriars Pas......120 E5
Blackfriars Rd......120 E6
Blackfriars Underpass......120 E5
Blacklands Terr......123 F4
Blandford Sq......118 D2
Blandford St......119 F3
Blantyre St......122 D7
Blantyre Wlk......122 D7
Bleeding Heart Yd......120 D3
Blenheim St......119 G4
Blithfield St......122 B3
Bloomfield Pl......118 B3
Bloomfield Pl......119 G5
Bloomfield Terr......123 G5
Bloomfield Villas......118 B3
Bloomburg St......124 A4
Bloomsbury Ct......120 B3
Bloomsbury Pl......120 B3
Bloomsbury Sq......120 B3
Bloomsbury St......120 A3
Bloomsbury Way......120 B3
Blore Ct......119 J5
Blossom St......121 H2
Blue Ball Yd......119 H6

Blue Ball Yd......124 A1
Bolney St......124 D7
Bolsover St......119 G2
Bolt Ct......120 D4
Bolton Gdns......122 B5
Bolton Gdns......122 C5
Bolton Gdns Mews......122 C5
Bolton St......119 G6
Bolton The......122 C5
Bond Ct......121 G4
Bondway......124 C6
Bonhill St......121 G2
Bonnington Sq......124 D6
Boot St......121 H1
Booth's Pl......119 H3
Borer's Pas......121 H4
Boscobel Pl......123 G4
Boscobel St......118 C2
Boston Pl......118 E2
Boswell Ct......120 B3
Boswell St......120 B3
Botolph Alley......121 H5
Botolph La......121 H5
Boundary Pas......121 J2
Boundary St......121 J2
Bourchier St......119 J5
Bourdon Pl......119 G5
Bourdon St......119 G5
Bourlet Cl......119 H3
Bourne St......123 G4
Bourne Terr......118 A3
Bouverie Pl......118 C4
Bouverie St......120 D4
Bow Churchyard......121 F4
Bow La......121 F4
Bow St......120 B4
Bowden St......124 E5
Bowl Ct......121 H2
Bowland Yd......123 F2
Bowling Green La......120 D2
Bowling Green St......124 E6
Bowling Green Wlk......121 H1
Boyce St......120 C6
Boyle St......119 H5
Brackley St......121 F3
Brad St......120 D6
Braden St......118 A2
Bradmead......124 A7
Braham St......121 J4
Braidwood St......121 H6
Bramerton St......122 E6
Bramham Gdns......122 B5
Brandon Mews......121 G3
Brangton Rd......124 D5
Bray Pl......123 F4
Bread St......121 F4
Bream's Bldgs......120 D4
Brechin Pl......122 C4
Bremner Rd......122 C3
Brendon St......118 D4
Bressenden Pl......123 J3
Brewer St......119 H5
Brewer's Green......124 A3
Brewhouse Yd......120 E2
Brick Ct......120 D4
Brick La......121 J2
Brick St......119 G6
Bride Ct......120 E4
Bride La......120 E4
Bridewell Pl......120 E4
Bridford Mews......119 G3

Bridge Pl..............123 H4
Bridge St..............124 C2
Bridgefoot.............124 C6
Bridgewater Sq.........121 F3
Bridgewater St.........121 F3
Bridle Wlk.............119 H5
Brinton Wlk............120 E6
Briset St..............120 E2
Bristol Gdns...........118 A2
Bristol Mews...........118 A2
Britannia St...........120 C1
Britannia Wlk..........121 G1
Britannia Wlk..........121 G1
Britten St.............122 E5
Britton St.............120 E2
Britton's Ct...........120 D4
Broad Ct...............120 B4
Broad Sanctuary........124 C2
Broad St...............121 H3
Broad St Bldgs.........121 H3
Broad Walk The.........118 A6
Broad Walk The.........122 B1
Broad Yd...............120 E2
Broadbent St...........119 G5
Broadley St............118 D3
Broadley Terr..........118 D2
Broadstone Pl..........119 F3
Broadway...............124 B2
Broadwick St...........119 H4
Broken Wharf...........121 F5
Brompton Arcade........123 F2
*Brompton Park Cres....122 B6
Brompton Pl............123 E3
Brompton Rd............122 E3
Brompton Sq............122 E3
Brook Dri..............124 E3
Brook Gate.............119 E5
Brook Mews N...........118 C5
Brook St...............118 C5
Brooke St..............120 D3
Brookes Ct.............120 D3
*Brooke's Market.......120 D3
Brown Hart Gdns........119 F5
Brown St...............118 E4
Browning Cl............118 B2
Browning Mews..........119 F3
Brownlow Mews..........120 C2
Brownlow St............120 C3
Brown's Bldgs..........121 H4
Brune St...............121 J3
Brunswick Gdns.........122 A1
Brunswick Mews.........119 E4
Brunswick Pl...........121 G1
Brunswick Sq...........120 B2
Brushfield St..........121 J3
Bruton La..............119 G5
Bruton Pl..............119 G5
Bruton St..............119 G5
Bryanston Mews E.......118 E3
Bryanston Mews W.......118 E4
Bryanston Pl...........118 E3
Bryanston Sq...........118 E3
Bryanston St...........119 E4
Brydges Pl.............120 B5
Buckingham Arc.........120 B5
Buckingham Gate........123 J3
Buckingham Mews........123 J3
Buckingham Palace Rd...123 H4
Buckingham Pl..........123 J3
Buckingham St..........120 B6
Bucklersbury...........121 G4
Buckley St.............120 D6
Bucknall St............120 B4
Budge Row..............121 G4
Bull Inn Ct............120 B5
Bull Wharf La..........121 F5
Bull's Gdn.............123 E4
Bulls Head Pas.........121 H4
Bulmer Mews............122 A1
Bulstrode Pl...........119 F3
Bulstrode St...........119 F4
Bunhill Row............121 G2
Bunhouse Pl............123 G5
Burdett Mews...........118 A4
Burgon St..............120 E4
Burleigh St............120 C5
Burlington Arc.........119 H5
Burlington Gdns........119 H5
Burne St...............118 D3
Burnsall St............123 E5
Burrell St.............120 E6
Bursar St..............121 H6
Burton Mews............123 G4
Burton Pl..............120 A1
Burton St..............120 A1
Burton St..............119 J2
Burwood Pl.............118 D4
Bury Ct................121 H4
Bury Pl................120 B3
Bury St................121 H4
Bury St................119 J5
Bury St................124 A1
Bury Wlk...............122 E5
Bush La................121 G5
Bute St................122 D4
Butler Pl..............124 B3
Buttesland St..........121 G1
Buxton Ct..............121 F1
Byng Pl...............119 J2
Byward St..............121 H5
Bywater St.............123 F5
Bywell Pl.............119 H3

C

Cabbell St.............118 D3
Cadogan Gate...........123 F4
Cadogan Gdns...........123 F4
Cadogan La.............123 G3
Cadogan Pl.............123 F3
Cadogan Sq.............123 F4
Cadogan St.............123 F4
Caesar St..............121 J1
Cahill St..............121 F2
Cale St................122 E5
Callcott St............122 A1
Callendar Rd...........122 D3
Callow St..............122 D6
Calthorpe St...........120 C2
Calvert Ave............121 J1
Calvert's Bldgs........121 G6
Calvin St..............121 J2
Cambridge Circ.........120 A4
Cambridge Gate.........119 G2
Cambridge Gate Mews....119 G2
Cambridge Pl...........122 C3
Cambridge Sq...........118 D4
Cambridge St...........123 J5
Cambridge Terr.........119 G1
Cambridge Terr Mews....119 G1
Camera St..............122 D6
Camlet St..............121 J2
Camomile St............121 H4
Campden Gr.............122 A2
Campden Hill Gdns......122 A1
Campden Hill Rd........122 A2
Campden House Cl.......122 A2
Campden St.............122 A1
Camperdown St..........121 J4

Candover St............119 H3
Canning Pas............122 C3
Canning Pl.............122 C3
Canning Pl Mews........122 C3
Cannon Row.............124 C2
Cannon St..............121 F5
Canvey St..............121 F6
Capener's Cl...........123 G2
Capland St.............118 C2
Capper St..............119 H2
Carburton St...........119 G2
Cardigan St............124 D5
Cardinal Cap Alley.....121 F6
Cardington St..........119 H1
Carey La...............121 F4
Carey Pl...............124 B4
Carey St...............120 C4
Carlisle Ave...........121 J4
Carlisle La............124 D3
Carlisle Pl............123 J3
Carlos Pl..............119 G5
Carlton Gdns...........119 J6
Carlton Gdns...........124 B1
Carlton House Terr.....119 J6
Carlton House Terr.....124 B1
Carlton St.............119 J5
Carlyle Sq.............122 D6
Carmel Ct..............122 B2
Carmelite St...........120 D5
*Carnaby Ct............119 H4
Carnaby St.............119 H5
Caroline Cl............118 A5
Caroline Gdns..........121 H1
Caroline Pl............118 A5
Caroline Pl Mews.......118 A5
Caroline Terr..........123 G4
Carpenter St...........119 G5
Carriage Dri E.........123 G7
Carriage Dri N.........123 F7
Carrington St..........119 G6
Carroun Rd.............124 D7
Carter La..............121 E4
Carteret St............124 B2
Carthusian St..........121 F3
Carting La.............120 B5
Cartwright Gdns........120 B1
Castellain Rd..........118 A2
Castle Baynard St......121 E5
Castle Baynard St......121 F5
Castle Ct..............121 G4
Castle La..............123 J3
Castle Yd..............121 E6
Castlereagh St.........118 E4
Catton St..............120 C3
Cathcart Rd............122 C6
Cathedral Pl...........121 F4
Cathedral St...........121 G6
Catherine Pl...........123 J3
Catherine St...........120 C5
Catherine Wheel Alley..121 H3
Catherine Wheel Yd.....119 H6
Catherine Wheel Yd.....124 A1
Cato St................118 D4
Catton St..............120 C3
Causton St.............124 B5
Cavaye Pl..............122 C5
Cavendish Ave..........118 C1
Cavendish Cl...........118 C1
Cavendish Ct...........121 H4
Cavendish Mews N.......119 G3
Cavendish Mews S.......119 G3
Cavendish Pl...........119 G4
Cavendish Sq...........119 G4
Caversham St...........123 F6
Caxton St..............124 B3
Cayton Pl..............121 G1
Cayton St..............121 G1
Cecil Ct...............120 B5
Celbridge Mews.........118 A4
Centaur St.............124 D3
Central St.............121 F1
Cerney Mew.............118 C5
Chadwell St............120 D1
Chadwick St............124 B3
Chagford St............118 E2
Chamber St.............121 J5
Chambord St............121 J1
Chance St..............121 J2
Chancel St.............120 E6
Chandos Pl.............120 B5
Chandos St.............119 G3
Change Alley...........121 G4
Chapel Pl..............119 G4
Chapel St..............118 D3
Chapel St..............123 G2
Chapone Pl.............119 J4
Chapter House Ct.......121 F4
Chapter St.............124 B4
Charing Cross..........120 B6
Charing Cross Rd.......120 A5
Charles II St..........119 J6
Charles II St..........124 B1
Charles St.............119 H1
Charles Sq.............121 G1
Charles St.............119 G6
Charlotte Mews.........119 H3
Charlotte Pl...........119 H3
Charlotte Rd...........121 H1
Charlotte St...........119 H3
Charlwood Pl...........124 A4
Charlwood St...........123 J5
Chart St...............121 G1
Charterhouse Bldgs.....121 F2
Charterhouse Mews......121 E3
Charterhouse Sq........121 E3
Charterhouse St........120 E3
Charterhouse St........121 E3
Chatham Ave............121 G1
Cheapside..............121 F4
Chelsea Bridge.........123 H6
Chelsea Bridge Rd......123 G5
Chelsea Emb............123 F6
Chelsea Estate.........122 E6
Chelsea Manor Gdns.....123 E5
Chelsea Manor St.......123 E5
Chelsea Park Gdns......122 D6
Cheltenham Terr........123 F5
Chenies Mews...........119 J2
Chenies St.............119 J3
Cheniston Gdns.........122 B3
Chequer St.............121 F2
Cherry Tree Wlk........121 F2
Chesham Cl.............123 G3
Chesham Mews...........123 G3
Chesham Pl.............123 G3
Chesham St.............123 G3
Chester Cl.............123 H3
Chester Cl N...........119 G1
Chester Cl S...........119 G1
Chester Gate...........119 G1
Chester Mews...........123 H3
Chester Pl.............119 G1
Chester Rd.............119 G1
Chester Row............123 G4
Chester Sq.............123 H4
Chester Sq Mews........123 H3
Chester Terr...........119 G1
Chester Way............124 E4
Chesterfield Gdns......119 G6
Chesterfield Hill......119 G6

Chesterfield St........119 G6
Cheval Pl..............123 E3
Cheyne Gdns............123 E6
Cheyne Mews............123 E6
Cheyne Row.............122 E6
Cheyne Wlk.............122 D7
Cheyne Wlk.............122 E6
Chicheley St...........124 D2
Chichester Rd..........118 A3
Chichester Rents.......120 D4
Chichester St..........124 A5
Child's Pl.............122 A4
Child's St.............122 A4
Child's Wlk............122 A4
Chiltern St............119 F3
Chilworth Mews.........118 C4
Chilworth St...........118 C4
China St...............124 D7
Chiswell St............121 G3
Chitty St..............119 H3
Christchurch St........123 F6
Christchurch Terr......123 F6
Christina St...........121 H2
Christopher Pl.........120 A1
Christopher St.........121 G2
Church Ct..............120 D4
Church Entry...........120 E4
Church Pl..............119 H5
Church St..............118 D2
Churchill Gdns.........123 J5
Churchill Gdns Rd......123 J6
Churchway.............119 J1
Churton Pl.............123 J4
Churton St.............123 J4
Circus Mews............118 E3
Circus Pl..............121 G3
Circus Rd..............118 C1
City Rd................121 E1
City Rd................121 G2
Clabon Mews............123 F4
Clapham Rd.............124 D7
Clare Market...........120 C4
Clarence Gdns..........119 G1
Clarendon Cl...........118 D5
Clarendon Gdns.........118 B2
Clarendon Gr...........119 J1
Clarendon Mews.........118 D5
Clarendon Pl...........118 D5
Clarendon St...........123 H5
Clarendon Terr.........118 B2
Clareville Gr..........122 C4
Clareville Grove Mews..122 C4
Clareville St..........122 C4
Clarges Mews...........119 G6
Clarges St.............119 G6
Clarkes Mews...........119 F3
Clark's Pl.............121 H4
Claverton St...........124 A5
Clay St................119 E3
Claylands Pl...........124 D6
Claylands Rd...........124 D6
Clayton St.............124 E6
Clearwell Dri..........118 A2
Cleaver St.............124 E5
Clements Inn...........120 C4
Clements Inn Pas.......120 C4
Clement's La...........121 G5
Clenston Mews..........118 E4
Clere Pl...............121 G2
Clere St...............121 G2
Clerkenwell Cl.........120 D2
Clerkenwell Green......120 E2
Clerkenwell Rd.........120 E2
Cleveland Gdns.........118 B4
Cleveland Mews.........119 H3
Cleveland Pl...........119 H6
Cleveland Row..........119 H6
Cleveland Sq...........118 B4
Cleveland St...........119 H3
Cleveland Terr.........118 B4
Clifford St............119 H5
Clifford's Inn Pas.....120 D4
Clifton Gdns...........118 B2
Clifton Pl.............118 D4
Clifton St.............121 H2
Clifton Villas.........118 B3
Clink St...............121 G6
Clipstone Mews.........119 H3
Clipstone St...........119 H3
Cliveden Pl............123 G4
Cloak La...............121 G5
Cloth Ct...............121 E3
Cloth Fair.............121 E3
Cloth St...............121 F3
Clothier St............121 H4
Clover Mews............123 F6
Club Row...............121 J2
Coach and Horses Yd....119 H5
Cobb St................121 J3
Cobb's Ct..............120 E4
Cobourg St.............119 H1
Cock Hill..............121 H3
Cock La................120 E3
Cockpit Yd.............120 C3
Cockspur Ct............120 A6
Cockspur St............124 B1
Coin St................120 D6
Colbeck Mews...........122 C4
Colchester St..........121 J4
Coldbath Sq............120 D2
Coleherne Ct...........122 B5
Coleherne Mews.........122 B5
Coleherne Rd...........122 B5
Coleman St.............121 G4
Coleman St Bldgs.......121 G4
Coley St...............120 C2
College Hill...........121 F5
College Hill...........121 F5
College St.............121 F5
Collingham Gdns........122 B4
Collingham Pl..........122 B4
Collingham Rd..........122 B4
Colombo St.............120 E6
Colonnade..............120 B2
Colonnades The.........118 A4
Columbia Rd............121 J1
Colville Pl............119 J3
Commercial St..........121 J3
Compton Cl.............119 G1
Compton Pas............120 E2
Compton Pl.............120 B2
Compton St.............120 E2
Concert Hall App.......120 C6
Conduit Ct.............120 B5
Conduit Mews...........118 C4
Conduit Pas............118 C4
Conduit Pl.............118 C4
Conduit St.............119 G5
Coney Way..............124 D6
Connaught Cl...........118 D4
Connaught Cl...........118 D4
Connaught Mews.........118 E4
Connaught Pl...........118 E4
Connaught Sq...........118 D4
Connaught St...........118 D4
Constitution Hill......123 H2
Conway St..............119 H2

Cooper's Row...........121 J5
Cope Pl................122 A3
Copthall Ave...........121 G4
Copthall Bldgs.........121 G4
Copthall Cl............121 G4
Coptic St..............120 B3
Coral St...............124 E2
Coram St...............120 B2
Corbet Ct..............121 G4
Corbet Pl.............121 J3
Cork St................119 H5
Cork St Mews...........119 H5
Corlett St.............118 D3
Cornhill...............121 G4
Cornwall Gdns..........122 B3
Cornwall Gdns Wlk......122 B3
Cornwall Mews S........122 C3
Cornwall Mews W........122 B3
Cornwall Rd............120 D6
Cornwall Terr Mews.....119 E2
Coronet St.............121 H1
Corporation Row........120 E2
Corsham St.............121 G1
Cosmo Pl..............120 B2
Cosser St..............124 D3
Cosway St..............118 D3
Cottage Pl.............122 E3
Cottesmore Gdns........122 B3
Cottingham Rd..........124 D7
Cotton's La............121 H1
Coulson St.............123 F4
Counter Ct.............121 G6
Counter St.............121 H6
Courtenay Sq...........124 E5
Courtenay St...........124 E5
Courtfield Gdns........122 B4
Courtfield Mews........122 C4
Courtfield Rd..........122 C4
Cousin La..............121 G5
Covent Gdn.............120 B5
Coventry St............119 J5
Cowcross St............120 E3
Cowley St..............124 C3
Cowper St..............121 G2
Cowper's Ct...........121 G4
Craig's Ct.............120 B6
Cramer St..............119 F3
Cranbourn Alley........120 A5
Cranbourn St...........120 A5
Cranley Gdns...........122 D5
Cranley Mews...........122 C5
Cranley Pl.............122 D4
Cranmer Ct.............123 E4
Cranmer Rd.............124 E7
Cranwood St............121 G1
Craven Hill............118 B5
Craven Hill Gdns.......118 B5
Craven Hill Mews.......118 B5
Craven Pas.............120 B6
Craven Rd..............118 C4
Craven St..............120 B6
Craven Terr............118 B5
Crawford Mews..........118 E3
Crawford Pas..........120 D2
Crawford Pl...........118 D3
Crawford St............118 E3
Creechurch La..........121 H4
Creechurch Pl..........121 H4
Creed La...............121 E4
Cremorne Rd............122 D7
Crescent...............121 J5
Crescent Pl............122 E4
Crescent Row...........121 F2
Cresswell Gdns.........122 C5
Cresswell Pl...........122 C5
Crestfield St..........120 B1
Crewdson Rd............124 E7
Cripplegate St.........121 F3
Crispin St.............121 J3
Cromer St..............120 B1
Crompton St............118 C2
Cromwell Gdns..........122 D3
Cromwell Mews..........122 D4
Cromwell Pl...........122 D4
Cromwell Rd............122 B4
Cromwell Rd............122 D4
*Crooked Billet Yd.....121 H1
Crosby Sq..............121 H4
Cross Key Ct...........121 G4
Cross Keys Cl..........119 F3
Cross La...............121 H5
Crosswall..............121 J5
Crown Ct..............121 F4
Crown Ct..............120 B4
Crown Office Row.......120 D5
Crown Pas.............119 H6
Crown Pas.............124 A1
Cruickshank St.........120 D1
Crutched Friars........121 H5
Cubitt St..............120 C1
Culford Gdns...........123 F4
Cullum St..............121 H5
Culross St.............119 F5
Cumberland Gate.......118 E5
Cumberland Gdns.......120 D1
Cumberland Market.....119 G1
Cumberland Pl.........119 G1
Cumberland St.........123 H5
Cundy St...............123 G4
Cunningham Pl.........118 C2
Cureton St.............124 B4
Cursitor St............120 D4
Curtain Pl............121 H2
Curtain Rd............121 H2
Curzon Gate...........119 F6
Curzon Pl............119 F6
Curzon St.............119 G6
Cuthbert St...........118 C2
Cutler St.............121 H4
Cutlers Gdns..........121 H4
Cygnet St.............121 J2
Cypress Pl............119 H2
Cyrus St..............120 E2

D

Dacre St...............124 B3
Dallington St..........121 E2
Damer Terr............122 C7
Dane St...............120 C3
Dansey Pl.............119 J5
Danube St.............123 E5
Danvers St............122 D6
D'arblay St...........119 H4
Dartmouth St..........124 B2
Dartrey Wlk..........122 C7
Daventry St...........118 D3
David Mews............119 F3
Davidson Gdns.........124 C7
Davies Mews...........119 G5
Davies St.............119 G5
De Vere Cotts.........122 C3
De Vere Gdns..........122 C2
De Vere Mews..........122 C3
De Walden St..........119 F3
Dean Bradley St.......124 C3
Dean Farrar St........124 B3
Dean Ryle St..........124 C4

Dean St................119 J4
Dean Stanley St........124 C3
Dean Trench St.........124 C3
Deanery Mews...........119 F6
Deanery St.............119 F6
Dean's Ct.............121 E4
Dean's Mews...........119 G4
Dean's Pl............124 B4
Dean's Yd.............124 B3
Delamere St...........118 A3
Delamere Terr.........118 A3
Delaware Rd...........118 A2
Dell's Mews...........123 J4
Denbigh Mews..........123 J4
Denbigh Pl............123 J5
Denbigh St............123 J5
Denman Pl.............119 J5
Denman St.............119 J5
Denmark Pl............120 A4
Denmark St............120 A4
Denning Cl............118 B1
Denny Cres............124 E5
Denny St..............124 E5
Denyer St.............123 E4
Derby Gate............124 C2
Derby St..............119 F6
Dereham Pl............121 H1
Dering St.............119 G4
Derry St..............122 B2
Desborough Cl.........118 A3
Devereux Ct...........120 D4
Devonport St..........118 D4
Devonshire Cl.........119 G3
Devonshire Mews N.....119 G3
Devonshire Mews S.....119 G3
Devonshire Mews W.....119 G3
Devonshire Pl.........119 F2
Devonshire Pl Mews....119 F3
Devonshire Row........121 H3
Devonshire Row Mews...119 G2
Devonshire Sq.........121 H4
Devonshire St.........119 G3
Devonshire Terr.......118 B4
Diadem Ct.............119 J4
Dial Walk The.........122 B2
Diana Pl..............119 G2
Dilke St..............123 F6
Dingley Pl............121 F1
Dingley Rd............121 F1
Diss St...............121 J1
Distaff La............121 F5
Distin St.............124 E4
Doby Ct...............121 F5
Dolben St.............120 E6
Dolland St............124 D5
Dombey St.............120 C2
Domingo St............121 F2
Dominion St...........121 G3
Donne Pl..............123 E4
Doon St...............120 D6
Doric Way.............119 J1
Dorrington St.........120 D3
Dorset Bldgs..........120 E4
Dorset Cl............118 E3
Dorset Mews...........123 H3
Dorset Pl............124 B5
Dorset Rise...........120 D4
Dorset Sq.............118 E3
Dorset St.............119 F3
Doughty Mews..........120 C2
Doughty St............120 C2
Douglas Pl............124 B4
Douglas St............124 B4
Douro Pl..............122 B3
Dove Mews.............122 C5
Dove Wlk..............123 G5
Dovehouse St..........122 D5
Dover St..............119 H6
Dover St..............119 H5
Dover Yd..............119 H6
Dowgate Hill..........121 G5
Down St...............119 G6
Down St Mews..........119 G6
Downing St............124 C2
D'Oyley St............123 G4
Dragon Yd............120 B4
Drake St..............120 C3
Drapers Gdns..........121 G4
Draycott Ave.........123 E4
Draycott Pl...........123 F4
Draycott Terr.........123 F4
Drayson Mews..........122 A2
Drayton Gdns..........122 C5
Drummond Cres.........119 J1
Drummond Gate.........124 B5
Drummond St...........119 H2
Drury La..............120 B4
Dryden St.............120 B4
Drysdale Pl...........121 H1
Drysdale St...........121 H1
Ducal St..............121 J1
Duchess Mews..........119 G3
Duchess St............119 G3
Duchy St..............120 D6
Duck La...............119 J4
Dudley St.............118 C3
Dudmaston Mews........122 D5
Dufferin Ct...........121 G2
Dufferin St...........121 G2
Dufour's Pl...........119 H4
Duke of Wellington Pl.123 G2
Duke of York St.......119 H6
Duke of York St.......124 A1
Duke St...............119 F4
Duke St...............119 H6
Duke St St James's....119 H6
Duke St St James's....124 A1
Dukes La..............122 B2
Duke's Mews...........119 F4
Duke's Rd.............120 A1
Duke's Yd.............119 F4
Duncannon St..........120 B5
Dunn's Pas............120 B4
Dunraven St...........119 E5
Dunstable Mews........119 F3
Dunster Ct............121 H5
Duplex Ride...........123 F2
Durham House St.......120 B5
Durham Pl.............123 F5
Durham St.............124 D6
Durweston Mews........119 E3
Durweston St..........119 E3
Dyott St..............120 A4
Dyott St..............120 B4
Dysart St.............121 H2

E

Eagle Ct..............120 E3
Eagle Pl..............119 H5
Eagle St..............120 C3
Eardley Cres..........122 A5
Earl St...............121 H3
Earlham St............120 B4
Earl's Court Gdns.....122 B4
Earl's Court Rd.......122 A3
Earl's Court Sq.......122 B5

Earlstoke St..........120 E1
Earnshaw St...........120 A4
Easleys Mews..........119 F4
East Harding St.......120 D4
East Pas..............121 F3
East Poultry Ave......120 E3
East Rd...............121 G1
East Smithfield.......121 J5
Eastbourne Mews.......118 B4
Eastbourne Terr.......118 B4
Eastcastle St.........119 H4
Eastcheap.............121 H5
Eaton Cl..............123 G4
Eaton Gate............123 G4
Eaton La..............123 H4
Eaton Mews N..........123 G3
Eaton Mews S..........123 H3
Eaton Mews W..........123 H3
Eaton Pl..............123 G4
Eaton Row.............123 H3
Eaton Sq.............123 G3
Eaton Terr............123 G4
Eaton Terr Mews.......123 G4
Ebbisham Dr...........124 D6
Ebenezer St...........121 G1
Ebor St...............121 J2
Ebury Bridge..........123 H5
Ebury Bridge Rd.......123 G5
Ebury Mews............123 H4
Ebury Mews E..........123 H4
Ebury Sq.............123 H4
Ebury St..............123 H4
Eccleston Bridge......123 H4
Eccleston Mews........123 G3
Eccleston Pl..........123 H4
Eccleston Sq..........123 H4
Eccleston Sq Mews.....123 H4
Eccleston St..........123 H4
Edge St...............122 A1
Edgware Rd............118 D3
Edith Gr..............122 C7
Edith Terr............122 C7
Edith Yd..............122 C7
Edwards Mews..........119 F4
Effie Pl..............122 A7
Egerton Cres..........123 E4
Egerton Gdns..........122 E3
Egerton Gdns Mews.....123 E3
Egerton Pl............123 E3
Egerton Terr..........123 E3
Elcho St..............123 E7
Elder St..............121 J2
Eldon Rd..............122 B3
Eldon St..............121 G3
Elgin Ave.............118 A1
Elgin Mews N..........118 A1
Elgin Mews S..........118 A1
Elias Pl..............124 E6
Elizabeth Bridge......123 H4
Elizabeth Cl.........118 B2
Elizabeth St..........123 G4
Elliotts Ct...........120 E4
Ellis St..............123 G4
Elm Ct...............120 D5
Elm Park Gdns.........122 D5
Elm Park La...........122 D5
Elm Park Rd...........122 D6
Elm Pl...............122 D5
Elm St...............120 C2
Elm Tree Cl...........118 C1
Elm Tree Rd...........118 C1
Elms Mews.............118 C5
Elnathan Mews.........118 A2
Elvaston Mews.........122 C3
Elvaston Pl...........122 C3
Elverton St...........124 B4
Ely Cottages..........124 D7
Ely Pl...............120 D3
Elystan Pl............123 F5
Elystan St............123 E4
Embankment Gdns.......123 F6
Embankment Pl.........120 B6
Emerald St............120 C3
Emerson St............121 F6
Emery Hill St.........124 A3
Emery St..............124 E3
Empress Pl............122 A5
Endell St.............120 B4
Endsleigh Gdns........119 J2
Endsleigh Pl..........119 J2
Endsleigh St..........119 J2
Enford St.............118 E3
English Grounds.......121 H6
Ennismore Gdns........122 E3
Ennismore Gdns Mews...122 E3
Ennismore Mews........122 E3
Ennismore St.........122 E3
Ensor Mews............122 D5
Epworth St............121 G2
Erasmus St............124 B4
Errol St..............121 G2
Essex Ct.............120 D4
Essex St..............120 D5
Essex Villas..........122 A2
Esterbrooke St........124 B4
Europa Pl............121 F1
Euston Gr.............119 J2
Euston Rd.............119 H2
Euston Sq.............119 J1
Euston St.............119 H1
Evelyn Gdns...........122 D5
Evelyn Yd............119 J4
Ewer St...............121 F6
Excel Ct.............120 A5
Exchange Bldgs........121 H4
Exchange Ct...........120 B5
Exeter St.............120 C5
Exhibition Rd.........122 D3
Exmouth Market........120 D2
Exmouth Mews..........119 H1
Exton St..............120 D6
Eyre St Hill..........120 D2

F

Fairchild Pl..........121 H2
Fairchild St..........121 H2
Fairholt St...........123 E3
Fairlop Pl............118 D1
Falcon Cl............121 E6
Falcon Ct............120 D4
Falconberg Ct.........119 J4
Falconberg Mews.......119 J4
Fann St...............121 F2
Fanshaw St............121 H1
Fareham St............119 J4
Farm La...............122 A7
Farm Pl...............122 A1
Farm St...............119 G5
Farmer St.............122 A1
Farnell Mews..........122 B5
Farnham Pl............121 F6
Farnham Royal.........124 D5
Farringdon La.........120 D2
Farringdon Rd.........120 D2
Farringdon St.........120 E4
Fashion St............121 J3
Faulkner's Alley......120 E3

Fawcett St 122 C6
Featherstone St 121 G2
Fen Ct 121 H4
Fenchurch Ave 121 H4
Fenchurch Bldgs 121 H4
Fenchurch St 121 H5
Fentiman Rd 124 D7
Fernsbury St 120 D1
Fernshaw Rd 122 C6
Fetter La 120 D4
Field Ct 120 C3
Field St 120 C1
Finborough Rd 122 B6
Finch La 121 G4
* Finck St 124 D2
Finsbury Ave 121 G3
Finsbury Circ 121 G3
Finsbury Ct 121 G3
Finsbury Market 121 H3
Finsbury Market 121 H2
Finsbury Pavement 121 G3
Finsbury Sq 121 G3
Finsbury St 121 G3
First St 123 E4
Fish St Hill 121 G5
Fisher St 120 C3
Fisherton St 118 C2
Fitzalan St 124 E4
Fitzhardinge St 119 F4
Fitzmaurice Pl 119 G6
Fitzroy Ct 119 H2
Fitzroy Mews 119 H2
Fitzroy Sq 119 H2
Fitzroy St 119 H2
Flaxman Ct 119 J4
Flaxman Terr 120 A1
Fleet La 120 E4
Fleet Sq 120 C1
Fleet St 120 D4
Flitcroft St 120 A4
Flood St 123 E6
Flood Wlk 123 E6
Floral St 120 B5
Flower and Dean St 121 J3
Fluer De Lis St 121 J2
Foley St 119 H3
Folgate St 121 J3
Fore St 121 G3
Fore St Ave 121 G3
Formosa St 118 A2
Forset St 118 D4
Fort St 121 H3
Fortune St 121 F2
Fosbury Mews 118 A5
Foster La 121 F4
Foubert's Pl 119 H4
Foulis Terr 122 D5
Founders Ct 121 G4
Foundry Mews 119 H2
Fountain Ct 120 D5
Fournier St 121 J3
Fox & Knot St 121 E3
Fox's Yd 121 J2
Frampton St 118 C2
Francis St 123 J3
Frankland Rd 122 D3
Franklin's Row 123 F5
Frazier St 124 E2
Frederic Mews 123 G2
Frederick Cl 118 E5
Frederick Row 120 E1
Frederick St 120 C1
Frederick's Pl 121 G4
French Ordinary Ct 121 H5
French Pl 121 H1
Friar St 120 E4
Friday St 121 F5
Friend St 120 E1
Frith St 119 J4
Frying Pan Alley 121 J3
Fulham Bwy 122 A7
Fulham Rd 122 C6
Fullwood's Mews 121 G1
Fulton Mews 118 B5
Fulwood Pl 120 C3
Furnival St 120 D3
Fynes St 124 B4

G

Gage St 120 B3
Galen Pl 120 B3
Galway St 121 F1
Gambia St 120 E6
Ganton St 119 H4
Garbutt Pl 119 F3
Gard St 121 E1
Garden Ct 120 D5
Garden Rd 118 B1
Garden Terr 124 B5
Garden Wlk 121 H2
Gardeners La 121 F5
Garlick Hill 121 F5
Garnault Mews 120 D1
Garnault Pl 120 D1
Garrett St 121 F2
Garrick St 120 B5
Garrick Yd 120 B5
Gascoigne Pl 121 J1
Gasholder Pl 124 D5
Gaspar Cl 122 B4
Gaspar Mews 122 B4
Gate Mews 123 E2
Gate St 120 C4
Gateforth St 118 D2
Gatesborough St 121 H2
Gateways The 123 E4
Gatliff Rd 123 H5
Gayfere St 124 C3
Gee St 121 F2
Gees Ct 119 F4
George Ct 120 B5
George Inn Yd 121 G6
George Mews 119 H1
George St 119 E4
George Yd 121 G4
George Yd 119 F5
Georgina Gdns 121 J1
Gerald Mews 123 G4
Gerald Rd 123 G4
Gerrard Pl 120 A5
Gerrard St 119 J5
Gertrude St 122 C6
Gibbon's Rents 121 H6
Gilbert Pl 120 B3
Gilbert St 119 F4
Gildea St 119 G3
Gillingham Mews 123 J4
Gillingham Row 123 J4
Gillingham St 123 J4
Gilston Rd 122 C5
Giltspur St 120 E3
Glasgow Terr 123 J5
Glasshouse St 119 H5
Glasshouse Wlk 124 D5
Glasshouse Yd 121 F2
Glebe Pl 122 E6
Gledhow Gdns 122 C4
Glendower Pl 122 D4
Glentworth St 119 E2
Globe Yd 119 G4
Gloucester Ct 121 H5
Gloucester Gdns 118 B4
Gloucester Mews 118 B4
Gloucester Mews W 118 B4
Gloucester Pl 119 E3
Gloucester Pl Mews 119 E3
Gloucester Rd 122 C4
Gloucester Sq 118 D4
Gloucester St 123 J5
Gloucester Terr 118 B4
Gloucester Way 120 D1
Gloucester Wlk 122 A2
Glyde Mews 123 E3
Glyn St 124 D5
Godfrey St 123 E5
Goding St 124 C5
Godliman St 121 F4
Golden La 121 F2
Golden Sq 119 H5
Goldsmith St 121 F4
Goodge Pl 119 H3
Goodge St 119 J3
Goodman's Yd 121 J5
Goodwins Ct 120 B5
Gophir La 121 G5
Gordon Pl 122 A2
Gordon Sq 119 J2
Gordon St 119 J2
Gore St 122 C3
Goring St 121 H4
Gorsuch Pl 121 J1
Gosfield St 119 H3
Goslett Yd 119 J4
Gosset St 121 J1
Goswell Pl 120 E1
Goswell Rd 121 E1
Gough Sq 120 D4
Gough St 120 C2
Goulston St 121 J4
Gower Mews 119 J3
Gower Pl 119 J2
Gower St 119 J2
Gracechurch St 121 G5
Grafton Mews 119 H2
Grafton Pl 119 J1
Grafton St 119 G5
Grafton Way 119 H2
Grafton Way 119 H2
Graham Terr 123 G4
Granby Bldgs 124 D4
Granby Pl 124 E2
Grand Ave 120 E3
Grange Ct 120 C4
Grantham Pl 119 G6
Grantully Rd 118 A1
Granville Pl 119 F4
Granville Sq 120 C1
Granville St 120 C1
Grape St 120 B4
Gravel La 121 J4
Grayfriars Pas 121 E4
Gray's Inn Pl 120 C3
Gray's Inn Rd 120 C2
Gray's Inn Sq 120 D3
Gray's Yd 119 F4
Great Bell Alley 121 G4
Great Castle St 119 G4
Great Castle St 119 H4
Great Central St 118 E3
Great Chapel St 119 J4
Great College St 124 C3
Great Cumberland Mews 118 E4
Great Cumberland Pl 119 E4
Great Eastern St 121 H2
Great George St 124 C2
Great Guildford St 121 F6
Great James St 120 C3
Great Marlborough St 119 H4
Great Maze Pond 121 G6
Great New St 120 D4
Great Newport St 120 B5
Great Ormond St 120 C2
Great Percy St 120 D1
Great Peter St 124 B3
Great Portland St 119 G3
Great Pulteney St 119 H5
Great Queen St 120 B4
Great Russell St 120 A4
Great Russell St 120 B3
Great Scotland Yd 120 B6
Great Smith St 124 B3
Great St Helen's 121 H4
Great St Thomas Apostle 121 F5
Great Suffolk St 121 E6
Great Sutton St 121 E2
Great Swan Alley 121 G4
Great Titchfield St 119 H3
Great Tower St 121 H5
Great Trinity La 121 F5
Great Turnstile 120 C3
Great Winchester St 121 G4
Great Windmill St 119 J5
Greek St 119 J4
Green Arbour Ct 120 E4
Green Dragon Ct 121 G6
Green St 119 F5
Green Terr 120 D1
Greencoat Pl 124 A4
Greencoat Row 124 A3
Greenhill's Rents 120 E3
Greens Ct 119 J5
Greenwell St 119 G2
Gregory Pl 122 B2
Grendon St 118 D2
Grenville Mews 122 C4
Grenville Pl 122 C4
Grenville St 120 B2
Gresham St 121 F4
Gresse St 119 J4
Greville St 120 D3
Grey Eagle St 121 J2
Greycoat Pl 124 B3
Greycoat St 124 B3
Greyhound Ct 120 D5
Greystoke Pl 120 D4
Grindal St 124 E2
Grocers' Hall Ct 121 G4
Groom Pl 123 G3
Grosvenor Bridge 123 H6
Grosvenor Cottages 123 G4
Grosvenor Cres 123 G2
Grosvenor Cres Mews 123 G2
Grosvenor Gdns 123 H3
Grosvenor Gdns Mews E 123 H3
Grosvenor Gdns Mews N 123 H3
Grosvenor Gdns Mews S 123 H3
Grosvenor Hill 119 G5
Grosvenor Pl 123 H2
Grosvenor Rd 123 J6
Grosvenor Sq 119 F5
Grosvenor St 119 G5
Grotto Pas 119 F3
Grove End Rd 118 C1
Grove Gdns 118 D1
Groveland Ct 121 F4
Guildhall Bldgs 121 G4
Guildhall Yd 121 F4
Guildhouse St 123 J4
Guilford Pl 120 C2
Guilford St 120 C2
Guinness Ct 121 F1
Guinness Trust Bldgs 123 F4
Gun St 121 J3
Gunter Gr 122 C7
Gunthorpe St 121 J4
Guthrie St 122 E5
Gutter La 121 F4
Gwynne Pl 120 C1

H

Haberdasher Pl 121 H1
Haberdasher St 121 G1
Haines St 124 A7
Half Moon Ct 121 F3
Half Moon St 119 G6
Halfmoon Pas 121 J4
Halford Rd 122 A6
Halkin Arc 123 G3
Halkin Mews 123 G3
Halkin Pl 123 G3
Halkin St 123 G2
Hall Gate 118 C1
Hall Pl 118 C3
Hall Rd 118 B1
Hall St 120 E1
Hallam Mews 119 G3
Hallam St 119 G3
Hallam St 119 G2
Hallon Gdns 121 J3
Halsey St 123 F4
Ham Yd 119 J5
Hamilton Cl 118 C1
Hamilton Gdns 118 B1
Hamilton Mews 123 H2
Hamilton Pl 123 G1
Hamilton Terr 118 B1
Hammett St 121 J5
Hampden Gurney St 118 E4
Hampstead Rd 119 H1
Hanbury St 121 J3
Hand Ct 120 C3
Handel St 120 B2
Handforth Rd 124 E7
Hanover Gdns 124 E6
Hanover Pl 120 B4
Hanover Sq 119 G4
Hanover St 119 G4
Hanover Terr 118 E1
Hanover Terr Mews 118 E1
Hans Cres 123 F3
Hans Pl 123 F3
Hans Rd 123 F3
Hans St 123 F3
Hanson St 119 H3
Hanway Pl 119 J4
Hanway St 119 J4
Harbet Rd 118 D3
Harcourt St 118 D3
Harcourt Terr 122 C5
Hardwick St 120 D1
Hare Ct 120 D4
Harewood Ave 118 D2
Harewood Pl 119 G4
Harewood Row 118 D3
Harley Gdns 122 C5
Harley Pl 119 G3
Harley St 119 G3
Harleyford Rd 124 D6
Harleyford St 124 E6
Harold Pl 124 E5
Harp Alley 120 E4
Harp La 121 H5
Harp La 121 H5
Harpur St 120 C3
Harriet St 123 F2
Harriet Wlk 123 F2
Harrington Gdns 122 C4
Harrington Rd 122 D4
Harrington St 119 H1
Harrison St 120 B1
Harrow Pl 121 J4
Harrow Rd 118 B3
Harrow Rd Fly 118 D3
Harrowby St 118 D4
Hart St 121 H5
Hartington Rd 124 C7
Hartshorn Alley 121 H4
Harvey's Bldgs 120 B5
Hasker St 123 E4
Hastings St 120 B1
Hatfields 120 D6
Hatherley Gr 118 A4
Hatherley St 124 A4
Hatton Gdn 120 D3
Hatton Pl 120 D3
Hatton Row 118 C2
Hatton St 118 C2
Hatton Wall 120 D3
Haunch of Venison Yd 119 G4
Hay Hill 119 G5
Haydon St 121 J5
Haydon Wlk 121 J4
Hayes Pl 118 D2
Haymarket 119 J5
Haymarket Arc 119 J5
Hayne St 121 E3
Hay's La 121 H6
Hay's Mews 119 G6
Hayward's Pl 120 E2
Headfort Pl 123 G2
Hearn St 121 H2
Heathcote St 120 C1
Heddon St 119 H5
Helmet Row 121 F2
Hemans St 124 C7
Hemans St Estate 124 B7
Hemus Pl 123 E5
Henderson Dri 118 C2
Heneage La 121 H4
Heneage Pl 121 H4
Henniker Mews 122 D6
Henrietta Mews 120 B2
Henrietta Pl 119 G4
Henrietta St 120 B5
Herbal Hill 120 D2
Herbert Cres 123 F3
Herbrand St 120 B2
Hercules Rd 124 E3
Hereford Sq 122 C4
Hermit St 120 E1
Hermitage St 118 C3
Herrick St 124 B4
Hertford Pl 119 H2
Hertford St 119 G6
Hesper Mews 122 B4
Hester Rd 122 E7
Hester Rd 123 E7
Hewett St 121 H2
Heyford Ave 124 D7
Hide Pl 124 B4
High Holborn 120 C3
High Timber St 121 F5
Hilary Cl 122 B7
Hildyard Rd 122 A6
Hill St 119 G6
Hillgate Pl 122 A1
Hillgate St 122 A1
Hills Pl 119 H4
Hind Ct 120 D4
Hinde Mews 119 F4
Hinde St 119 F4
Hobart Pl 123 H3
Hobury St 122 D6
Hocker St 121 J1
Hogarth Ct 121 H5
Hogarth Pl 122 B4
Hogarth Rd 122 B4
Holbein Mews 123 G5
Holbein Pl 123 G4
Holborn 120 D3
Holborn Pl 120 C3
Holburn Viaduct 120 E3
Holford Pl 120 C1
Holford St 120 D1
Holland Pl 122 B2
Holland St 121 E6
Holland St 122 A2
Hollen St 119 J4
Holles St 119 G4
Holly Mews 122 C5
Hollywell Row 121 H2
Hollywood Mews 122 C6
Hollywood Rd 122 C6
Holmead Rd 122 B7
Holmes Pl 122 C6
Holmes Terr 124 E2
Holsworthy Sq 120 C2
Holyrood St 121 H6
Holywell La 121 H2
Homer Row 118 D3
Homer St 118 D3
Honduras St 121 F2
Honey La 121 F4
Hooper's Ct 123 F2
Hop Gdns 120 B5
Hopkins St 119 J4
Hopton St 120 E6
Hornton Pl 122 A2
Hornton St 122 A2
Horse and Dolphin Yd 119 J5
Horse Guards Rd 124 B2
Horse Shoe Alley 121 F6
Horse Shoe Yd 119 G5
Horseferry Rd 124 B4
Horseguards Ave 120 B6
Horselydown La 121 J6
Hortensia Rd 122 C7
Hosier La 120 E3
Hotspur St 124 E5
Houghton St 120 C4
Houndsditch 121 H4
Howard Pl 123 J3
Howick Pl 124 A3
Howie St 123 E7
Howland Mews E 119 H3
Howland St 119 H3
Howley Pl 118 B3
Hoxton Market 121 H1
Hoxton Sq 121 H1
Hudson's Pl 123 J4
Huggin Ct 121 F5
Huggin Hill 121 F5
Hugh Mews 123 H4
Hugh Pl 124 B4
Hugh St 123 H4
Hull st 121 F1
Hungerford Bridge (foot) 120 C6
Hungerford La 120 B6
Hunter St 120 B2
Huntley St 119 J2
Hunt's Ct 120 A5
Huntsworth Mews 118 E2
Hutton St 120 D4
Hyde Park Cnr 123 G2
Hyde Park Cres 118 D4
Hyde Park Gate 122 C2
Hyde Park Gate 122 C2
Hyde Park Gate Mews 122 C2
Hyde Park Gdns 118 D5
Hyde Park Gdns Mews 118 D5
Hyde Park Sq 118 D4
Hyde Park Sq Mews 118 D4
Hyde Park St 118 D4

I

Idol La 121 H5
Ifield Rd 122 B6
Imperial College Rd 122 D3
India St 121 J4
Ingestre Pl 119 H5
Inglebert St 120 D1
Ingram Cl 124 D4
Inigo Pl 120 B5
Inner Circ 119 F1
Inner Temple La 120 D4
Insurance St 120 D1
Inverness Gdns 122 B1
Inverness Mews 118 A5
Inverness Pl 118 A5
Inverness Terr 118 A5
Ireland Yd 120 E4
Irongate Wharf Rd 118 C3
Ironmonger La 121 G4
Ironmonger Pas 121 F1
Ironmonger Row 121 F1
Irving St 120 A5
Isabella St 120 E6
Iverna Ct 122 A3
Iverna Gdns 122 A3
Ives St 123 E4
Ivor Pl 118 E2
Ivybridge La 120 B5
Ixworth Pl 122 E4

J

Jacob's Well Mews 119 F4
James St 119 F4
James St 120 B5
Jameson St 122 A1
Jason Ct 119 F4
Jay Mews 122 C2
Jerdan Pl 122 A7
Jermyn St 119 H6
Jermyn St 124 A1
Jerome Cres 118 D2
Jerome St 121 J2
Jerusalem Pas 120 E2
Jervis Ct 119 G4
Jewry St 121 J4
Joan St 120 E6
Jockey's Fields 120 C3
Johanna St 124 E2
John Adam St 120 B5
John Aird Ct 118 B3
John Carpenter St 120 E5
John Islip St 124 B4
John Prince's St 119 G4
John St 120 C2
John's Mews 120 C2
Johnsons Ct 120 D4
Johnson's Pl 123 J5
Joiner St 121 G6
Jonathan St 124 D5
Jones St 119 G5
Jubilee Pl 123 E5
Judd St 120 B1
Juer St 127 E7
Junction Mews 122 D4
Junction Pl 122 C4
Justice Wlk 126 E6
Juxon St 128 D4

K

Kean St 124 C4
Keats Pl 125 G3
Keeley St 124 C4
Kelso Pl 126 B3
Kemble St 124 C4
Kemp's Ct 123 J4
Kempsford Gdns 126 A5
Kenchester Cl 128 C7
Kendal St 122 D4
Kendall Pl 123 F3
Kendrick Mews 126 D4
Kendrick Pl 126 D4
Kennington Gr 128 D6
Kennington La 128 D5
Kennington La 128 E5
Kennington Oval 128 D6
Kennington Park Rd 128 E6
Kennington Rd 128 E4
Kennington Rd 128 E3
Kenrick Pl 123 F3
Kensington Church Ct 126 B2
Kensington Church St 126 B2
Kensington Church Wlk 126 B2
Kensington Court Mews 126 B3
Kensington Court Pl 126 B3
Kensington Ct 126 B2
Kensington Gate 126 C3
Kensington Gdns Sq 122 A4
Kensington Gore 126 D2
Kensington High St 126 A3
Kensington Mall 126 A1
Kensington Mansions 126 A5
Kensington Palace Gdns 126 B2
Kensington Palace Gdns 126 B1
Kensington Pl 126 A1
Kensington Rd 126 D2
Kensington Sq 126 B3
Kent Pas 122 E1
Kent Terr 122 D1
Kent Yd 127 E2
Kentish Bldgs 125 G6
Kenton St 124 B2
Kenway Rd 126 B4
Keppel Row 125 F6
Keppel St 124 A3
Kibworth St 128 D7
Kiffen St 125 G2
Kimbolton Row 126 E4
King Charles St 128 C2
King Edward St 125 F4
King Edward Wlk 128 E3
King John Ct 125 H2
King Sq 125 F1
King St 125 F4
King St 123 H6
King St 128 A1
King St 124 B5
King William St 125 G5
Kinghorn St 125 F3
Kingly Ct 123 H5
Kingly St 123 H5
King's Arms Yd 125 G4
King's Bench Wlk 124 D4
King's Cross 124 B1
King's Cross Bridge 124 B1
King's Cross Rd 124 C1
King's Head Yd 125 G6
King's Mews 124 C2
King's Rd 126 C7
King's Rd 127 G3
Kings Rd 126 E5
King's Scholars' Pas 127 J4
Kingscote St 124 E5
Kingsley Mews 126 B3
Kingsway 124 C4
Kinnerton Pl N 127 F2
Kinnerton Pl S 127 F2
Kinnerton St 127 G2
Kinnerton Yd 127 G2
Kirby St 124 D3
Kirkman Pl 123 J3
Kirtling St 127 J7
Kirtling St 128 A7
Kirton Gdns 125 J1
Knaresborough Pl 126 B4
Knightrider St 125 E5
Knightsbridge 127 F2
Knightsbridge 127 E2
Knightsbridge Green 127 F2
Knox St 122 E3
Kramer Mews 126 B5
Kynance Mews 126 C3
Kynance Pl 126 C3

L

Lackington St 125 G3
Lamb St 125 J3
Lambeth Bridge 128 C4
Lambeth High St 128 D4
Lambeth Hill 125 F5
Lambeth Mews 128 D4
Lambeth Palace Rd 128 D3
Lambeth Rd 128 E3
Lambeth Wlk 128 D4
Lamb's Bldgs 125 G2
Lamb's Conduit Pas 124 C3
Lamb's Conduit St 124 C2
Lamb's Pas 125 G2
Lamont Rd 126 D6
Lamont Rd Pas 126 D6
Lanark Pl 122 B2
Lanark Rd 122 B1
Lancashire Ct 123 G5
Lancaster Gate 122 B5
Lancaster Mews 122 B5
Lancaster Pl 124 C5
Lancaster Terr 122 C5
Lancelot Pl 127 F2
Lancing St 123 J1
Landon Pl 127 F3
Lanfranc St 128 E3
Langham Pl 123 G3
Langham St 123 G3
Langley Ct 124 B5
Langley La 128 D6
Langley St 124 B4
Langthorn Ct 125 G4
Langton Cl 124 C2
Langton St 126 C6
Lansdowne Rd 123 G6
Lansdowne Terr 124 B2
Laud St 128 D5
Lauderdale Rd 122 A1
Launcelot St 128 E2
Launceston Pl 126 C3
Laurence Pountney Hill 125 G5
Laurence Pountney La 125 G5
Lavender Cl 126 D6
Laverton Mews 126 B4
Laverton Pl 126 B4
Lavington St 125 E6
Lawn La 128 D6
Lawrence La 125 F4
Lawrence St 126 E6
Laxton Pl 123 G2
Laystall St 124 D2
Lazenby Ct 124 B5
Leadenhall Ave 125 H4
Leadenhall Market 125 H4
Leadenhall Pl 125 H4
Leadenhall St 125 H4
Leake Ct 128 D2
Leake St 128 D2
Leather La 124 D3
Lecky St 126 D5
Leeke St 124 C1
Lees Pl 123 F5
Leicester Ct 124 A5
Leicester Pl 124 A5
Leicester Sq 124 A5
Leicester St 123 J5
Leigh Pl 124 D3
Leigh St 124 B1
Leinster Gdns 122 B4
Leinster Mews 122 B5
Leinster Pl 122 B4
Leinster Terr 122 B5
Lennox Gdns 127 F3
Lennox Gdns Mews 127 F4
Lenthal Pl 126 C4
Leo Yd 124 E2
Leonard St 125 H2
Leopards Ct 124 D3
Leopold Wlk 128 D5
Lever St 125 F1
Leverett St 127 E4
Leverington Pl 125 G1
Lewisham St 128 B2
Lexham Gardens Mews 126 B3
Lexham Gdns 126 B5
Lexham Mews 126 A3
Lexham Wlk 126 B3
Lexington St 123 H5
Leyden St 125 J3
Ligonier St 125 J2
Lilac Pl 128 D4
Lilestone St 122 D2
Lillie Rd 126 A6
Lillie Yd 126 A6
Lily Pl 124 D3
Lime St 125 H4
Lime St Pas 125 H4
Limerston St 126 D6
Lincoln St 127 F4
Lincoln's Inn Fields 124 C4
Lindsey St 125 E3
Linhope St 122 E2
Lisle St 124 A5
Lisson Gr 122 D2
Lisson St 122 D3
Litchfield St 124 A5
Little Albany St 123 G2
Little Argyll St 123 H4
Little Boltons The 126 C5
Little Britain 125 F3
Little Chester St 127 H3
Little College La 125 G5
Little College St 128 C3
Little Essex St 124 D5
Little George St 128 C2
Little Marlborough St 123 H4
Little New St 124 D4
Little Newport St 124 A5
Little Portland St 123 H4
Little Russell St 124 B3
Little Sanctuary 128 C2
Little Smith St 128 B3
Little Somerset St 125 J4
Little St James's St 123 H6
Little St James's St 128 A1
Little Titchfield St 123 H3
Little Trinity La 125 F5
Liverpool St 125 H3
Livonia St 123 H4
Lizard St 125 F1
Lloyd Baker St 124 D1
Lloyd Sq 124 D1
Lloyd St 124 D1
Lloyd's Ave 125 H5
Lloyd's Row 124 E1
Lodge Rd 122 D1
Logan Mew 126 A4
Logan Pl 126 A4
Lollard St 128 D4
Lollard St 128 E4
Lombard Ct 125 G5
Lombard La 124 D4
Lombard St 125 G4
Lombardy Pl 122 A5
London Bridge 125 G5
London Bridge St 125 G6
London Mews 122 C4
London St 125 H5
London St 122 C4
London Wall 125 F3
Long Acre 124 B4
Long La 125 E3
Long St 125 J1
Long Yd 124 C2
Longford St 123 G2
Longmore St 127 J4
Longridge Rd 126 A4
Long's Ct 124 A5
Lord Hills Rd 122 A3
Lord North St 128 C3
Lordship Pl 126 E6
Lorenzo St 124 C1
Lorne Cl 122 D1
Lothbury 125 G4
Lots Rd 126 C7
Loughborough St 128 D5
Lovat La 125 H5
Love La 125 F4
Lowdes Ct 123 H4
Lower Belgrave St 127 H3
Lower Grosvenor Pl 127 H3
Lower James St 123 H5
Lower John St 123 H5
Lower Marsh 128 E2
Lower Sloane St 127 G5
Lower Thames St 125 H5
Lowndes Cl 127 G3
Lowndes Pl 127 G3
Lowndes Sq 127 F2
Lowndes St 127 G3
Loxham St 124 B1
Lucan Pl 127 E4
Lucerne Mews 126 A1
Ludgate Bwy 124 E4
Ludgate Circ 124 E4
Ludgate Ct 124 E4
Ludgate Hill 124 E4
Ludgate Sq 124 E4
Ludlow St 125 F2
Luke St 125 H2
Lumley Ct 124 B5
Lumley St 123 F4
Lupus St 127 J5
Luscombe Way 128 C7
Luton St 122 C2
Luxborough St 123 F3

Lyall Mews................123 G3
Lyall Mews W............123 G3
Lyall St.....................123 G3
Lygon Pl....................123 H3
Lyons Pl....................118 C2

M

Mabledon Pl...............120 A1
Mac Farren Pl............119 F2
Macclesfield Rd..........121 F1
Macclesfield St..........119 J5
Macklin St..................120 B4
Mackworth St.............119 H1
Maddox St..................119 H5
Magdalen St...............121 H6
Magee St....................124 E6
Maggie Alley...............120 D4
Maida Ave..................118 B2
Maida Vale.................118 B1
Maiden La...................120 B5
Maidstone Bldgs.........121 G6
Mail Coach Yd............121 H1
Makins St...................123 E4
Malet Pl.....................119 J2
Malet St.....................120 A3
Mall The....................119 J6
Mallord St..................122 D6
Mallory St...................118 D2
Mallow St...................121 G1
Malta St.....................120 E2
Maltravers St..............120 D5
Manchester Sq...........119 F4
Manchester St............119 F3
Mandeville Pl.............119 F4
Manette St.................119 J4
Manningford Cl...........120 E1
Manor St Estate.........123 E6
Manresa Rd................122 E5
Mansell St..................121 J4
Mansfield Mews..........119 G3
Mansfield St...............119 G3
Mansion House Pl.......121 G4
Mansion House St.......121 G4
Manson Mews............122 D4
Manson Pl..................122 D4
Maple Pl....................119 H3
Maple St....................119 H2
Marble Arch...............119 E5
Marchmont St............120 B2
Margaret Ct...............119 H4
Margaret St................119 H4
Margaretta Terr..........120 E6
Margery St..................120 D1
Mark La......................121 H5
Mark St......................121 H2
Mark St......................121 H2
Market Ct...................119 H4
Market Mews..............119 G6
Market Pl...................119 H4
Markham Pl................123 F5
Markham Sq...............123 F5
Markham St................123 E5
*Marlborough Ct.........119 H4
Marlborough Flats.......123 F4
Marlborough Rd..........119 H6
Marlborough St...........122 E4
Marloes Rd.................122 B3
Marshall St.................119 H4
Marsham St.................124 B4
Martin La....................121 G5
Martlett Ct..................120 B4
Marylebone High St.....119 F3
Marylebone La............119 F4
Marylebone Mews.......119 G3
Marylebone Pas..........119 H4
Marylebone Rd...........119 E3
Marylebone St............119 F3
Marylee Way...............124 D4
Mason's Arms Mews....119 G5
Mason's Ave...............121 G4
Mason's St..................121 F1
Mason's Yd.................119 H6
Mason's Yd.................124 A1
Matthew Parker St.......124 B2
Maunsel St..................124 B4
Mayfair Pl...................119 G6
Mays Ct......................120 B5
McAuley Ct.................124 E3
McLeod's Mews...........122 B4
Mead Row...................124 E3
Meadow Mews.............124 D6
Meadow Pl..................124 C7
Meadow Rd.................124 D7
Meard St.....................119 J4
Mecklenburgh Pl.........120 C2
Mecklenburgh Sq........120 C2
Medway St..................124 B3
Meek St......................122 C7
Melbourne Pl..............120 C4
Melbury Rd.................122 A6
Melbury Terr...............118 D2
Melcombe Pl...............118 E3
Melcombe St..............119 E2
Melina Pl....................118 C1
Melon Pl.....................122 A2
Melton Ct...................122 D4
Melton St...................119 J1
Memel Ct....................121 F2
Memel St....................121 F2
Mepham St.................120 D6
Mercer St...................120 C4
Meredith St.................120 E1
Merlin St.....................120 D1
Merrington Rd.............122 A6
Meymott St.................120 E6
Micawber St...............121 F1
Micklethwaite Rd........122 A6
Middle Dartrey Wlk......122 D7
Middle St....................121 F3
Middle Temple La........120 D5
Middle Yd...................121 H6
Middlesex Pas............121 F4
Middlesex St...............121 J4
Middleton Bldgs..........119 H3
Midford Pl..................119 H2
Midhope St.................120 B1
Midland Rd.................120 B1
Milborne Gr................122 C5
Miles Pl.....................118 C3
Miles St.....................124 C6
Milford La...................120 D5
Milford St...................120 D5
Milk St......................121 F4
Mill St......................119 H5
Millbank....................124 C4
Millman Mews.............120 C2
Millman St..................120 C2
Mills Ct.....................121 H1
Milman's St................122 D6
Milner St...................123 F4
Milroy Wlk..................120 E6
Milton Ct....................121 G3
Milton St....................121 G3
Milverton St...............124 E5
Mincing La.................121 H5
Minera Mews..............123 G4
Minories....................121 J5
Mitchell St..................121 F2
Mitre Ct......................120 D4

Mitre Sq.....................121 H4
Mitre St......................121 H4
Modern St...................120 E4
Molyneux St...............118 D3
Monck St....................124 B3
Moncorvo Cl...............122 E2
Monkwell Sq...............121 F3
Monmouth St.............120 B4
Montagu Mansions......119 E3
Montagu Mews N........119 E3
Montagu Mews S........119 E4
Montagu Mews W.......119 E4
Montagu Pl.................119 E3
Montagu Row..............119 E3
Montagu Sq................119 E4
Montagu St.................120 B3
Montclare St...............121 J2
Montford Pl................124 E6
Montpelier Mew...........123 E3
Montpelier Pl..............123 E3
Montpelier Sq.............123 E2
Montpelier St..............123 E2
Montpelier Terr...........123 E3
Montpelier Wlk............123 E3
Montreal Pl.................120 C5
Montrose Ct...............122 D2
Montrose Pl................123 G2
Monument St..............121 G5
Moor La......................121 G3
Moor Pl......................121 G3
Moor St......................120 A4
Moore St....................123 F4
Moorfields..................121 G3
Moorfields Highwalk....121 G3
Moorgate....................121 G3
Moorgate Pl................121 G4
Mora St......................121 F1
Moravian Ct...............122 D6
Moravian Pl................122 D6
Moreland St...............121 E1
Moreton Pl.................124 A5
Moreton St.................124 A5
Moreton Terr...............124 A5
Moreton Terr Mews N...124 A5
Moreton Terr Mews S...124 A5
Morgans La.................121 H6
Morpeth Terr...............123 J4
Mortimer Market.........119 H2
Mortimer St................119 H3
Morton Mews..............122 B4
Morwell St..................119 J3
Moscow Pl..................118 A5
Moscow Rd.................118 A5
Mossop St..................123 E4
Motcomb St................123 G3
Mount Mills................121 E1
Mount Pleasant..........120 D2
Mount Row.................119 G5
Mount St....................119 F5
Moxon St....................119 F3
Mulberry Wlk..............122 D6
Mulready St................118 D2
Mumford Ct................121 F4
Mundy St....................121 H1
Munster Sq.................119 G2
Murphy St...................124 E2
Muscovy St.................121 H5
Museum St.................120 B4
Myddelton Pas............120 D1
Myddelton Sq.............120 D1
Myddelton St..............120 D1
Mylne St.....................120 D1

N

Nantes Pas.................121 J3
Nassau St...................119 H3
Navarre St..................121 J2
Neal St.......................120 B4
Neal's Yd...................120 B4
Neathouse Pl..............123 J4
Nelson Pas.................121 F1
Netherton St...............122 C6
Netley St....................119 H1
Nevern Pl...................122 A4
Nevern Rd..................122 A4
Nevern Sq...................122 A4
Neville St...................122 D5
Neville Terr.................122 D5
New Bond St...............119 G5
New Bridge St.............120 E4
New Broad St..............121 H3
New Burlington Mews...119 H5
New Burlington Pl........119 H5
New Burlington St........119 H5
New Cavendish St........119 G3
New Change.................121 F4
New Charles St...........121 E3
New Compton St.........120 B4
New Coventry St.........120 A5
New Ct......................120 D4
New Fetter La.............120 D4
New Goulston St.........121 J4
New Inn Bwy...............121 H2
New Inn Pas...............120 C4
New Inn Sq.................121 H2
New Inn Yd.................121 H2
New London St............121 H5
New North Pl..............121 H2
New North St..............120 C3
New Oxford St.............120 B4
New Quebec St...........119 E4
New Row....................120 B5
New Spring Gdns Wlk...124 C5
New Sq......................120 C4
New St......................121 H3
New St Sq..................120 D4
New Turnstile..............120 C3
New Union St..............121 G3
Newburgh St...............119 H4
Newburn St.................124 D5
Newbury St.................121 F3
Newcastle Cl..............120 E4
Newcastle Pl..............118 C3
Newcastle Row...........120 D2
Newcombe St.............122 A1
Newgate St.................121 E4
Newman Pas..............119 H3
Newman St.................119 H3
Newman's Ct..............121 G4
Newman's Row............120 C3
Newnham Terr............124 E3
Newport Ct.................120 B4
Newport Pl.................120 A5
Newton St..................120 C3
Nicholas La................121 G5
Nicholson St...............120 E6
Nile St......................121 G1
Nine Elm Ind Estate....123 J6
Noble St.....................121 F4
Noel St......................119 H4
Norfolk Cres...............118 D4
Norfolk Pl...................118 C4
Norfolk Row................124 D4

Norfolk Sq...................118 C4
Norfolk Sq Mews.........118 C4
Norman St...................121 F1
North Audley St...........119 F5
North Bank.................118 D1
North Carriage Dri.......118 D5
North Cres..................119 J3
North Folgate..............121 H3
North Gower St...........119 H1
North Mews.................120 C2
North Row...................119 F5
North Tenter St...........121 J4
North Terr...................122 E3
North Wharf Rd...........118 C3
Northampton Bldgs......120 D2
Northampton Rd..........120 D2
Northampton Sq.........120 E1
Northburgh St.............121 E2
Northcourt..................119 H3
Northington St............120 C2
Northumberland Alley...121 H4
Northumberland Ave....120 B6
Northumberland St......120 B6
Northwick Cl...............118 C2
Northwick Terr............118 C2
Norwich St..................120 D4
Notting Hill Gate.........122 A1
Nottingham Ct............120 B4
Nottingham Pl............119 F3
Nottingham St.............119 F3
Nun Ct......................121 G4
Nutford Pl..................118 E4

O

Oak Tree Rd...............118 D1
Oakden St..................124 E4
Oakey La....................124 E3
Oakfield St.................122 C6
Oakley Gdns...............123 E6
Oakley St...................122 E6
Oat La......................121 F4
Observatory Gdns........122 A2
Odhams Wlk...............120 B4
Offley Rd...................124 E7
Ogle St......................119 H3
Old Bailey..................120 E4
Old Barge House Alley..120 D6
Old Barrack Yd...........123 G2
Old Bldgs....................120 D4
Old Bond St................119 H5
Old Brompton Rd.........122 A5
Old Brompton Rd.........122 D4
Old Burlington St.........119 H5
Old Castle St..............121 J4
Old Cavendish St........119 G4
Old Change Ct............121 F4
Old Church St.............122 D5
Old Compton St..........119 J4
Old Court Pl...............122 B2
Old Fish St Hill...........121 F5
Old Gloucester St........120 C3
Old Jewry...................121 G4
Old Manor Yd.............122 B4
Old Market Sq............121 J1
Old Marylebone Rd......118 D3
Old Nichol St..............121 J2
Old North St...............120 C3
Old Paradise St...........124 D4
Old Park La................123 H1
Old Pye St..................124 B3
Old Quebec St............119 E4
Old Queen St..............124 B2
Old Seacoal La...........120 E4
Old South Lambeth Rd...124 C7
Old St......................120 D4
Old St......................121 G2
Oldbury Pl..................119 F3
Oliver's Yd..................121 G2
Olympia Yd.................118 A5
Omeara St..................121 F6
Ongar Rd....................122 A6
Onslow Mews..............122 D4
Onslow Mews E...........122 D4
Onslow Sq...................122 D4
Onslow St...................120 D2
Onslow Gdns...............122 C5
Orange St...................119 J5
Orange Yd..................119 J4
Oratory La..................122 E5
Orchard St..................119 F4
Orchardson St.............118 C2
Orde Hall St................120 C3
Orme Ct.....................118 A5
Orme Ct Mews............118 A5
Orme La.....................118 A5
Orme Sq.....................118 A5
Ormond Cl..................120 B3
Ormond Mews.............120 B2
Ormond Yd.................119 H6
Ormond Yd.................124 A1
Ormonde Gate............123 F6
Ormonde Pl................123 G4
Orsett St....................124 D5
Orsett Terr.................118 B4
Osbert St....................124 B4
Osnaburgh St..............119 G2
Osnaburgh Terr............119 G2
Ossington Bldgs..........119 F3
Ossulston St...............120 A1
Osten Mews................122 B3
Outer Circ..................119 E2
Outwich St..................121 H4
Oval Pl......................124 D7
Oval Way...................124 D6
Ovington Gdns............123 E3
Ovington Mews............123 E3
Ovington Sq...............123 E3
Ovington St................123 F4
Owen's Ct...................120 E1
Owen's Row................120 E1
Oxendon St................119 J5
Oxford Circ.................119 H4
Oxford Circus Ave.......119 H4
Oxford Ct...................121 G5
Oxford Sq...................118 D4
Oxford St...................119 G4

P

Padbury Ct..................121 J1
Paddington Green........118 C3
Paddington St.............119 F3
Paget St.....................120 E1
Pakenham St..............120 C2
Palace Ave..................122 B2
Palace Ct...................122 C2
Palace Gate................122 C2
Palace Gdns Mews.......122 A1
Palace Gdns Terr.........122 B1
Palace Green...............118 A6
Palace Green...............122 B1
Palace Mews...............123 G4
Palace Pl...................123 J3
Palace St....................123 J3
Palfrey Pl...................124 D7

Palissy St...................121 J1
Pall Mall....................119 J6
Pall Mall....................124 A1
Pall Mall E..................120 A6
Pall Mall E..................124 A1
Pall Mall Pl................119 H6
Pall Mall Pl................124 A1
Palmer St...................124 A3
Pancras La.................121 G4
Panton St...................119 J5
Panyer Alley...............121 F4
Parade The.................123 F7
Paradise Wlk..............123 F6
Pardon St...................120 E2
Paris Gdn...................120 E6
Park Cl......................123 F2
Park Cres...................119 G2
Park Cres Mews E.......119 G2
Park Cres Mews W......119 G2
Park La......................119 F5
Park Mansions Arc......119 H6
Park Pl......................119 H6
Park Pl......................124 C4
Park Pl Villas..............118 B3
Park Rd......................118 E2
Park Rd......................118 D1
Park Road...................118 D2
Park Sq E....................119 G2
Park Sq Mews.............119 G2
Park Sq W...................119 G2
Park St......................121 F6
Park St......................119 F5
Park West Pl...............118 D4
Park Wlk....................122 D6
Parker Mews...............120 B4
Parker St....................120 B4
Parkgate Rd................123 E7
Parliament Sq.............124 C2
Parry St.....................124 C6
Pascal St....................124 B7
Passing Alley..............120 E2
Passmore St...............123 G5
Pater St.....................122 A3
Paternoster Row..........121 F4
Paternoster Sq...........121 F4
Paton St.....................121 F1
Paul St.......................121 H2
Paultons Sq................122 D6
Paultons St................122 D6
Paveley St..................118 D2
Paveley St..................118 D1
Paveley Way...............123 E7
Pavilion Rd.................123 F3
Pavilion St..................123 F3
Pear Pl......................124 E2
Pear Tree Ct...............120 D2
Pear Tree St...............121 F2
Pearman St.................124 E2
Peartree St.................121 F2
Peel Pass....................122 A1
Peel St......................122 A1
Peerless St..................121 G1
Pegasus Pl.................124 E6
Pelham Cres...............122 E4
Pelham Pl...................122 E4
Pelham St...................122 E4
Pemberton Row..........120 D4
Pembroke Cl...............123 G2
Pembroke Rd..............122 A4
Penfold Pl..................118 D3
Penfold St..................118 D3
Penfold St..................118 C2
Pennant Mews............122 B4
Penton Rise................120 C1
Penton St...................120 C1
Penywern Rd..............122 A5
Pepys St.....................121 H5
Percival St..................120 E1
Percy Circ...................120 C1
Percy Mews................119 J3
Percy Pass..................119 J3
Percy St.....................119 J3
Perkins Rents..............124 B3
Perry's Pl...................119 J4
Peter St......................121 J1
Peter St......................119 J5
Peter's Hill.................121 F5
Peter's La...................121 E3
Petersham La..............122 C3
Petersham Mews.........122 C3
Petersham Pl..............122 C3
Peto Pl......................119 G2
Petty France...............124 A3
Petyt Pl......................122 E6
Petyward...................123 E4
Phene St....................123 E6
Philbeach Gdns..........122 A5
Phillimore Wlk............122 A3
Philpot La..................121 H5
Philpot St..................121 H2
Phipp St.....................121 H2
Phoenix Pl..................120 C2
Phoenix St..................120 A4
Piccadilly...................119 H6
Piccadilly...................124 A1
Piccadilly Arc..............119 H6
Piccadilly Arc..............124 A1
Piccadilly Circ............119 J5
Piccadilly Circ............119 H5
Pickard St...................121 E1
Pickering Mews...........118 A4
Pickering Pl...............119 H6
Pickering Pl...............118 C4
Picton Pl....................119 F4
Pilgrim St...................120 E4
Pimlico Rd..................123 G5
Pimlico Wlk.................121 H1
Pindar St....................121 H3
Pindock Mews............118 A2
Pine Apple Ct.............123 J3
Pine St.......................120 D2
Pitfield St...................121 H1
Pitt St......................122 A2
Pitt's Head Mews........119 F6
Platina St....................121 H2
Playhouse Yd..............120 E4
Pleydell St..................120 E4
Plough Ct...................121 G5
Plough St....................121 J4
Plough Yd...................121 H2
Plumber's Pl...............120 D2
Plumptree Ct..............120 E4
Plympton Pl...............118 D2
Plympton St...............118 D2
Poets Corner..............124 C3
Poland St...................119 H4
Pollen St....................119 H4
Pollitt Dri...................124 E7
Pomell Way................121 J4
Pond Pl......................122 E5
Ponsonby Pl...............124 B5
Ponsonby Terr...........124 B5
Pont St......................123 F3
Pont St Mews.............123 F3
Ponton Rd..................124 B7
Pooles Bldgs..............120 D2
*Pope's Head Alley......121 G4
Poplar Pl...................118 A5

Poppins Ct.................120 E4
Porchester Gdn Mews...118 A4
Porchester Gdns.........118 A5
Porchester Mews.........118 A4
Porchester Pl..............118 D4
Porchester Rd.............118 A4
Porchester Sq.............118 A4
Porchester Terr...........118 B5
Porchester Terr N........118 A4
Porchester Wlk............118 A4
Porter St....................119 E3
Porteus Rd.................118 B3
Portland Mews............119 H4
Portland Pl................119 G3
Portman Cl.................119 F4
Portman Mews S.........119 F4
Portman Sq................119 F4
Portman Towers..........119 E4
Portpool La................120 D3
Portsea Mews.............118 D4
Portsea Pl..................118 D4
Portsmouth St............120 C4
Portsoken St...............121 J5
Portugal St.................120 C4
Post Office Ct.............121 G4
Post Office Way..........124 B6
Potters Fields.............121 H6
Poultry......................121 G4
Powis Pl....................120 B2
Praed Mews................118 C4
Praed St....................118 C4
Pratt Wlk...................124 D4
Prescot St..................121 J5
President...................121 F1
Price's St...................121 E6
Prideaux Pl................120 C1
*Priest's Ct................121 F4
Prima Rd....................124 E7
Primrose Hill..............120 D4
Primrose St.................121 H3
Prince Consort Rd.......122 D3
Prince of Wales Pas.....119 H1
Prince of Wales Terr....122 B2
Princelet St................121 J3
Princes Arc.................119 H6
Princes Arc.................124 A1
Princes Gate Ct..........122 D2
Princes Gate Mews......122 D3
Princes Gdns..............122 D3
Prince's St..................121 G4
Princes St...................119 G4
Princeton St...............120 C3
Printer St....................120 D4
Printing House Yd.......121 H1
Priory Wlk...................122 C5
Procter St..................120 C3
Providence Ct.............119 F5
Provost St...................121 G1
Prudent Pas...............121 F4
Pudding La.................121 G5
Puddle Dock................120 E5
Pugh's Pl...................121 H4
Puma Ct....................122 A1
Pump Ct...................120 D4

Q

Quadrangle The..........118 D4
Quadrant Arc..............119 H5
Quaker St..................121 J2
Quality Ct..................120 D4
Quebec Mews.............119 E4
Queen Anne Mews.......119 G3
Queen Anne's Gate.....124 B2
Queen Sq...................120 B3
Queen Sq Pl..............120 B2
Queen St...................119 F5
Queen St...................119 G6
Queen St Pl...............121 F5
Queen Victoria St........121 F5
Queenhithe.................121 F5
Queen's Elm Sq..........122 D5
Queen's Gate..............122 C3
Queen's Gate..............122 C3
Queen's Gate Gdns.....122 C3
Queen's Gate Mews.....122 C3
Queen's Gate Pl..........122 C3
Queen's Gate Pl Mews..122 C3
Queen's Gate Terr.......122 C3
Queen's Gdns.............118 B5
Queen's Head Yd........121 G6
Queen's Mews............118 A5
Queen's Wlk...............119 H6
Queen's Wlk...............124 A1
Queen's Wlk...............119 H2
Queensberry Mews W...122 D4
Queensberry Pl...........122 D4
Queensberry Way........122 D4
Queensborough Mews...118 B5
Queensborough Pas.....118 B5
Queensborough Terr....118 B5
Queenstown Rd...........123 H7
Queensway.................118 A5

R

Rabbit Row.................122 A1
Radley Mews..............122 B3
Radnor Mews..............118 C4
Radnor Pl...................118 D4
Radnor St...................121 F1
Radnor Wlk................123 F5
Radstock St................123 E7
Railway App................121 G6
Railway Pl..................121 H5
Rainsford St...............118 D4
Ralston St..................123 F5
Ramillies Pl...............119 H4
Ramillies St...............119 H4
Rampayne St..............124 B5
Randall Rd..................124 C5
Randall Row...............124 C5
Randolph Ave.............118 B1
Randolph Cres............118 B2
Randolph Mews..........118 B2
Randolph Rd...............118 B2
Ranelagh Br...............118 A3
Ranelagh Gr...............123 G5
Ranston St..................118 D3
Raphael St.................123 F2
Rathbone Pl...............119 J4
Rathbone St...............119 H3
Raven Rd...................124 E1
Ravenscroft St............121 J1
Ravent Rd..................124 D4
Ravey St....................121 H2
Rawlings St................123 F4
Rawstone Pl...............120 E1
Rawstorne St.............120 E1
Ray St......................120 D2
Raynham St................118 D4
Red Lion Pl................124 D5
Red Lion Sq...............120 C3
Red Lion St................120 C3
Red Lion Yd...............119 F6
Red Pl......................119 F5

Redan Pl....................118 A4
Redanchop Cl.............122 E6
Redburn St.................123 F6
Redchurch St.............121 J2
Redcliffe Gdns...........122 B6
Redcliffe Mews...........122 B5
Redcliffe Pl................122 C6
Redcliffe Rd...............122 C5
Redcliffe Sq...............122 B5
Redcliffe St................122 B6
Redcross Way............121 F6
Redesdale St.............123 F6
Redfield La.................122 B4
Redfield Mews............122 A4
Redhill St...................119 G1
Redvers St..................121 H1
Reece Mews...............122 D4
Reeves Mews.............119 F5
Regency St.................124 B4
Regent Pl...................119 H5
Regent Sq..................120 B2
Regent St...................119 J5
Regent St...................119 H5
Regnart Bldgs............119 H2
Relton Mews..............123 E3
Rembrandt Cl............123 G5
Remnant St................120 C4
Rennie St...................120 E6
Reston Pl...................122 C2
Rex Pl......................119 F6
Rhoda St....................121 J2
Rich La.....................122 B5
Richard's Pl...............123 E4
Richardson's Mews.....119 H2
Richbell Pl.................120 C3
Richborne Terr...........124 D7
Richmond Bldgs.........119 J4
Richmond Mews.........119 J4
Richmond Terr............124 C2
Richmond Terr Mews...122 A6
Rickett St...................122 A6
Ridgmount Gdns.........119 J3
Ridgmount Pl.............119 J3
Ridgmount St.............119 J3
Riding House St..........119 H3
Rifle Ct.....................124 E6
Riley St......................122 D7
Rising Sun Ct.............121 E3
Rita Rd......................124 D7
River St......................120 D1
Rivington Pl...............121 H1
Rivington St................121 H1
Robert Adam St..........119 F4
Robert Cl...................118 B2
Robert St...................119 H1
Robert St...................120 B5
Roberts Mews............123 G3
Robinson St...............123 F6
Rochelle St................121 J1
Rochester Row...........124 A4
Rochester St..............124 B3
Rochester Wlk............121 G6
Rodmarton St............119 E3
Roger St....................120 C2
Roland Gdns..............122 C5
Roland Gdns..............122 C5
Roland Way................122 C5
Rolls Bldgs.................120 D4
Rolls Pas....................120 D4
Romilly St..................120 A4
Romney St..................124 C3
Rood La.....................121 H5
Ropemaker St............121 G3
Rosary Gdns..............122 C4
Roscoe St...................121 F2
Rose Alley..................121 F6
Rose and Crown Ct.....121 F4
Rose and Crown Yd.....119 H6
Rose and Crown Yd.....124 A1
Rose St......................120 B5
Rosebery Sq...............120 D3
Rosebery Ave.............120 C2
Rosemoor St..............123 F4
Rosetta Cl..................124 C7
Rosman Pl.................120 D2
Rosman St.................120 D2
Rossmore Rd.............118 D2
Rotherham Wlk...........120 D6
Roupell St..................120 D6
Rowington Cl.............118 A3
Roxby Pl....................122 A6
Royal Arc...................119 H6
Royal Ave..................123 F5
Royal Exchange Ave....121 G4
Royal Exchange Bldgs...121 G4
Royal Hospital Rd.......123 F5
Royal Mint St..............121 J5
Royal Opera Arc.........119 J6
Royal Opera Arc.........124 A1
Royal St....................124 D3
Rufus St....................121 H1
Rugby St....................120 C2
Rupert Ct..................119 J5
Rupert St..................119 J5
Russell Ct..................119 H6
Russell Pl..................124 B5
Russell Sq.................120 B3
Russell St...................120 B5
Russia Ct...................121 F4
Russia Row................121 F4
Rutherford St.............124 B4
Rutland Gate.............122 E2
Rutland Gate Mews.....122 E2
Rutland Gdns.............123 E2
Rutland Gdns Mews....123 E2
Rutland Mews E.........122 E3
Rutland Mews S.........122 E3
Rutland Mews W........122 E3
Rutland St.................123 E3
Ryder Ct....................119 H6
Ryder Ct....................124 A1
Ryder St....................119 H6
Ryder St....................124 A1
Ryder Yd....................119 H6
Ryder Yd....................124 A1
Rysbrack St................123 F3

S

Sackville St................119 H5
Saffron Hill................120 D3
Sage Way...................120 C1
Sail St......................124 D3
St Alban's Gr..............122 B3
St Alban's St..............118 C3
St Alban's St..............119 J5
St Alphage Gdn..........121 F3
St Alphage Highwalk...121 F3
St Andrew St..............120 D3
St Andrew's Hill..........120 E4
St Andrew's Pl...........119 G2
St Andrew's St...........119 J4
St Ann's La................124 B3
St Ann's St................124 B3
St Anselm's Pl...........119 G5
St Barnabas St...........123 G5
St Benet's Pl.............121 G5

St Botolph St.............121 J4
St Bride St...............120 E4
St Bride's Ave............120 E4
St Bride's Pas............120 E4
St Chad's Pl..............120 C1
St Chad's St..............120 B1
St Christopher's Pl.......119 F4
St Clare St...............121 J4
St Clement's Ct...........121 G5
St Clement's La...........120 C4
St Cross St...............120 D3
St Dunstan's Alley........121 H5
St Dunstan's Ct...........120 B4
St Dunstan's Hill.........121 H5
St Dunstan's La...........121 H5
St Ermin's Hill...........124 B3
St George St..............119 G5
St George's Dri...........123 J5
St Georges Field..........118 D4
St George's La............121 G5
St George's Sq............124 B5
St Giles Circ.............119 J4
St Giles High St..........120 A4
St Giles Pl...............120 A4
St Helena St..............120 D1
St Helen's Pl.............121 H4
St James' Ct..............124 A3
St James's App............121 H2
St James's Market.........119 J5
St James's Pas............121 H4
St James's Pl.............119 H6
St James's Pl.............124 A1
St James's Row............120 E2
St James's Sq.............119 J6
St James's St.............124 B1
St James's St.............119 H6
St James's Wlk............120 E2
St John St................120 E2
St John's La..............120 E3
St John's Path............120 E2
St John's Pl..............120 E2
St John's Sq..............120 E2
St John's Wood Rd.........118 C1
St Katharine's Way........121 J5
St Katherine's Row........121 H5
St Leonard's Terr.........123 F5
St Loo Ave................123 E6
St Luke's St..............122 E5
St Margaret St............124 C2
St Margaret's Ct..........121 G6
St Mark's Gr..............122 B7
St Martin's St............120 B5
St Martin's La............120 B5
St Martin's Le Grand......121 F4
St Martin's Pl............120 B5
St Martin's St............120 A5
St Mary at Hill...........121 H5
St Mary Axe...............121 H4
St Mary's Mansions........118 C3
St Mary's Sq..............118 C3
St Mary's Terr............118 C3
St Matthew St.............124 B3
St Michael's Alley........121 G4
St Michael's St...........118 D4
St Mildred's Ct...........121 G4
St Olave's Ct.............121 G4
St Olave's Gdns...........124 E4
St Oswald's Pl............124 D5
St Oswulf St..............124 B4
St Paul's Church Yd.......121 F4
St Paul's Church Yd.......121 F4
St Peter's Alley..........121 G4
St Petersburgh Mews.......118 A5
St Stephen's Row..........121 G4
St Swithin's La...........121 G5
St Thomas St..............121 G6
St Vincent St.............119 F3
Salamanca Pl..............124 D4
Salamanca St..............124 D4
Salamanca St..............124 D4
Sale Pl...................118 A5
Salem Rd..................118 A5
Salisbury Ct..............121 F4
Salisbury Pl..............118 E3
Salisbury Sq..............120 D4
Salisbury St..............118 D2
Salters Hall Ct...........121 G5
Samford St................118 D2
Samuel Lewis Trust
   Dwellings..............122 E4
Samuel Lewis Trust
   Dwellings..............122 A7
Sancroft St...............124 E5
Sanctuary.................124 B3
Sandell St................124 E2
Sandland St...............120 C3
Sandwich St...............120 B1
Sandy's Row...............121 H3
Sans Wlk..................120 E2
Saperton Wlk..............124 D4
Saracen's Head Yd.........121 J4
Sarah St..................121 H1
Sardinia St...............120 C4
Saunders St...............124 E4
Savage Gdns...............121 H5
Saville Row...............119 H5
Savona St.................124 A7
Savoy Bldgs...............120 C5
Savoy Ct..................120 B5
Savoy Hill................120 C5
Savoy Pl..................120 C5
Savoy Row.................120 C5
Savoy St..................120 C5
Savoy Steps...............120 C5
Savoy Way.................120 C5
Scala St..................119 H3
Scarborough St............121 J4
Scarsdale Pl..............122 B3
Scarsdale Villas..........122 A3
School App................121 H1
Sclater St................121 J2
Scoresby St...............120 E6
Scotland Pl...............120 B6
Scotswood St..............120 D2
Scott Ellis Gdns..........118 C1
Scott's Yd................121 G5
Scrutton St...............121 H2
Seacoal La................120 E4
Seaford St................120 B1
Seaforth Pl...............124 A3
Seagrave Rd...............122 A6
Searles Cl................123 E7
Sebastion St..............120 E1
Secker St.................120 D6
Sedding St................123 G4
Seddon St.................120 C1
Sedley Pl.................119 G4
Seething La...............121 H5
Sekforde St...............120 E2
Selwood Pl................122 D5
Selwood Terr..............122 D5
Semley Pl.................123 H4
Senior St.................118 A3
Serjeants' Inn............120 D4
Serle St..................120 C4
Sermon La.................121 F4
Serpentine Rd.............118 F6
Serpentine Rd.............123 F1
Seven Dials...............122 B4

Seville St................123 F2
Seward St.................121 F1
Seymour Mews..............119 F4
Seymour Pl................118 E4
Seymour St................119 E4
Seymour Wlk...............122 C6
Shacklewell St............121 J1
Shad Thames...............121 J6
Shaftesbury Ave...........119 J5
Shaftesbury Mews..........122 A3
Shafto Mews...............123 F3
Shafts Ct.................121 H4
Shalcomb St...............122 C6
Shand St..................121 H6
Shaver's Pl...............119 J5
Shawfield St..............123 E5
Sheba Pl..................121 J2
Sheffield St..............120 C4
Sheffield Terr...........122 A1
Shelton St................120 B4
Shepherd Cl...............119 F5
Shepherd Market...........119 G6
Shepherd St...............119 G6
Shepherdess Pl............121 G1
Shepherds Pl..............119 F5
Sheraton St...............119 J4
Sherborne La..............121 G5
Sherlock Mews.............119 F3
Sherwood St...............119 H5
Shillibeer Pl.............118 D3
Ship Tavern Pas...........121 H5
Shipwright Yd.............121 H6
Shoe La...................120 D4
Shoreditch High St........121 H2
Shorter St................121 J5
Shorts Gdns...............120 B4
Shouldham St..............118 D3
Shroudham Pl..............118 D3
Shroton St................118 D3
Sicilian Ave..............120 B3
Siddon La.................119 E2
Sidford Pl................124 D3
Sidmouth St...............120 C1
Sidney Gr.................120 E1
Silbury St................121 G1
Silk St...................121 F3
Silver Pl.................119 H5
Singer St.................121 G1
Sir Thomas More Estate....122 D6
Sise La...................121 G4
Skin Market Pl............121 F6
Skinner Pl................123 G4
Skinner St................120 D2
Skinners La...............121 F5
Slaidburn St..............122 C6
Sleaford St...............123 J7
Sleaford St...............124 A7
Slingsby Pl...............120 B5
Sloane Ave................123 E4
Sloane Ct E...............123 G5
Sloane Ct W...............123 G5
Sloane Gdns...............123 G4
Sloane Sq.................123 G4
Sloane St.................123 F3
Sloane Terr...............123 G4
Smallbrook Mews...........118 C4
Smart's Pl................120 B4
Smith Sq..................124 C3
Smith St..................123 F5
Smith Terr................123 F5
Smithfield St.............120 E3
Smith's Ct................119 H5
Smith's Ct................119 J5
Snow Hill.................120 E3
Snowden St................121 H2
Soho Sq...................119 J4
Soho St...................119 J4
Soley Mews................120 D1
Somers Cres...............118 D4
South Audley St...........119 F6
South Bolton Gdns.........122 B5
South Carriage Dri........123 F2
South Carriage Dri........123 E2
South Cres................119 J3
South Eaton Pl............123 G4
South End.................122 B3
South End Row.............122 B3
South Lambeth Pl..........124 C6
South Lambeth Rd..........124 C7
South Molton La...........119 G4
South Molton St...........119 G4
South Parade..............122 D5
South Pl..................121 G3
South Pl Mews.............121 G3
South Sq..................120 D3
South St..................119 F6
South Tenter St...........121 J5
South Terr................122 E4
South Wharf Rd............118 C4
South Wlk.................121 G3
Southampton Bldgs.........120 D3
Southampton Pl............120 B3
Southampton Row...........120 B3
Southampton St............120 B5
Southwark Bridge..........121 F5
Southwark St..............121 F6
Southwell Gdns...........122 C4
Southwick Mews............118 D4
Southwick Pl..............118 D4
Southwick St..............118 D4
Southwick Yd..............118 D4
Spafield St...............120 D2
Spanish Pl................119 F4
Spear Mews................122 A4
Speedy Pl.................120 B1
Spencer Pl................120 E1
Spenser St................124 A3
Spital Sq.................121 H3
Spital Yd.................121 H3
Spirimont Pl..............123 F5
Spring Gdns...............120 A6
Spring Gdns...............124 B1
Spring Mews...............119 E3
Spring St.................118 C4
Stable Yd Rd..............123 J2
Stables Way...............124 E5
Stacey St.................120 A4
Stackhouse St.............123 F3
Stadium St................122 C7
Staff St..................121 G1
Stafford Pl...............123 J3
Stafford St...............119 H6
Stafford St...............124 A1
Stafford Terr............122 A2
Stag Pl...................123 J3
Stainer St................121 G6
Staining La...............121 F4
Stalbridge St.............118 D3
Stamford St...............120 D6
Stanbrook Ct..............119 H6
Standard Pl...............121 H1
Stanford Rd...............122 B3
Stanford St...............124 B4
Stanhope Gate.............119 F6
Stanhope Gdns............122 C4
Stanhope Mews E...........122 C4
Stanhope Mews S...........122 C4
Stanhope Mews W...........122 C4
Stanhope Pl...............118 E5

Stanhope Row..............119 G6
Stanhope St...............119 H1
Stanhope Terr.............118 C5
Stanley Cl................124 D6
Stannary Pl...............124 E5
Stannary St...............124 E5
Staple Inn Bldgs..........120 D3
Star Alley................121 H5
Star St...................118 D4
Star Yd...................120 D4
Starcross St..............119 H1
Stationers Hall Ct........120 E4
Stedham Pl................120 B4
Stephen Mews..............119 J3
Stephen St................119 J3
Stephenson Way............119 H2
Sterling St...............123 E3
Stew La...................121 F5
Steward St................121 H3
Stewart's Gr..............122 E5
Stillington St...........124 A4
Stone Bldgs...............120 C3
Stonecutter St............120 E4
Stonehouse Ct............121 H4
Stoney La.................121 J4
Stoney St.................121 G6
Store St..................119 J3
Storey's Gate.............124 B2
Stothard Pl...............121 H3
Stourcliffe St............118 E4
Strand....................120 C5
Strand La.................120 C5
Stratford Pl.............122 B3
Stratford Pl..............119 G4
Stratford Rd..............122 A3
Strathearn Pl.............118 C5
Strathmore Gdns...........122 A1
Stratton St...............119 G6
Streatham St..............120 B4
Stroughton Cl............124 D4
Strout's Pl...............121 J1
Strutton Ground...........124 B3
Strype St.................121 J3
Studio Pl.................123 G3
Stukeley St...............120 B4
Suffolk La................121 G5
Suffolk Pl................119 J5
Suffolk St................119 J6
Suffolk St................124 B1
Sugar Bakers Ct...........121 H4
Sugar Loaf Ct.............121 F5
Summers St................120 D2
Sumner Bldgs..............121 F6
Sumner Pl.................122 D4
Sumner Place Mews.........122 D4
Sumner St.................121 F6
Sun Ct....................121 G4
Sun St....................121 H3
Sun St Pas................121 H3
Sunningdale Gdns..........122 A3
Surrey St.................120 C5
Sussex Gdns...............118 C4
Sussex Mews E.............118 C4
Sussex Mews W.............118 C4
Sussex Pl.................118 H4
Sussex Pl.................122 D4
Sussex Sq.................118 C5
Sussex St.................123 H5
Sutherland Ave............118 A2
Sutherland Ave............118 B1
Sutherland Row............123 H5
Sutherland St.............123 H5
Sutton Dwellings..........122 E5
Sutton Row................119 J4
Suttons Way...............121 G2
Swallow Pas Pl............119 G4
Swallow St................119 H5
Swan Ct...................123 E5
Swan La...................121 G5
Swan Wlk..................123 F6
Swanfield St..............121 J1
Swinton Pl................120 C1
Swinton St................120 C1
Sycamore St...............121 F2
Sydney Cl.................122 D4
Sydney Mews...............122 D4
Sydney Pl.................122 D4
Sydney St.................122 E5
Symons St.................123 F4

T

Tabernacle St.............121 G2
Tachbrook Mews............123 J4
Tachbrook St..............124 A4
Tadema Rd.................122 C7
Talbot Ct.................121 G5
Talbot Sq.................118 C4
Talbot Yd.................121 G6
Tallis St.................120 D5
Tamworth St...............122 A6
Tankerton St..............120 B1
Tanswell St...............124 E2
Taunton Mews..............118 E2
Taunton Pl................118 E2
Tavistock Pl..............120 B2
Tavistock Pl..............120 B2
Tavistock Sq..............120 B5
Tavistock St..............120 C4
Taviton St................120 A2
Tedworth Gdns.............123 F5
Tedworth Sq...............123 F5
Telegraph St..............121 G4
Temple Ave................120 D5
Temple La.................120 D5
Temple Pl.................120 C5
Templeton Pl..............122 A4
Tenison Ct................119 H5
Tenison Way...............120 D6
Tenniel Cl................118 A5
Tenter Ground.............121 J3
Tenterden St..............119 G4
Terminus Pl...............123 H3
Terrace The...............124 D4
Tetcott Rd................122 C7
Thackeray St..............122 B3
Thanet St.................120 B1
Thavie's Inn..............120 D4
Thayer St.................119 F4
The Sir Oswald Stoll
   Foundation.............122 B7
Theed St..................120 D6
Theobald's Rd.............120 C3
Thirleby Rd...............123 J3
Thistle Gr................122 C5
Thistle Gr................122 C5
Thoresby St...............121 F1
Thorndike Cl..............122 C7
Thorndike St..............124 B4
Thorney St................124 C4
Thornhaugh Mews...........120 A2
Thornhaugh St.............120 A2
Thornton Pl...............118 E3
Thrale St.................121 F6
Thrawl St.................121 J3
Threadneedle St...........121 G4

Three Kings Yd............119 G5
Three Nun Ct..............121 F4
Throgmorton Ave...........121 G4
Throgmorton St............121 G4
Thurloe Cl................122 E4
Thurloe Pl................122 D4
Thurloe Place Mews........122 D4
Thurloe Sq................122 D4
Thurloe St................122 D4
Tilney Ct.................121 F2
Tilney St.................119 F6
Timber St.................121 F2
Tinworth St...............124 D5
Tisbury Ct................119 J5
Titchborne Row...........118 D4
Tite St...................123 F6
Tokenhouse Yd.............121 G4
Tolmers Sq................119 H2
Tomlinson Cl..............121 J1
Tompion St................120 E1
Tonbridge St..............120 B1
Tooley St.................121 H6
Tor Gdns..................122 A2
Torrington Pl.............119 J2
Torrington Sq.............120 A2
Tothill St................124 B2
Tottenham Ct Rd...........119 J3
Tottenham Mews............119 H3
Tottenham St..............119 H3
Tower Bridge..............121 J6
Tower Bridge App..........121 J5
Tower Bridge Rd...........121 J6
Tower Hill................121 H5
Tower Royal...............121 F5
Tower St..................120 B4
Toynbee St................121 J3
Trafalgar Rd..............124 C7
Trafalgar Sq..............124 B1
Trafalgar St..............120 B6
Transept St...............118 D3
Trebeck St................119 G6
Trebovir Rd...............122 A4
Tregunter Rd..............122 C5
Trenchold St..............124 C6
Tresham Cres..............118 E2
Treveris St...............120 E6
Trevor Pl.................123 E2
Trevor Sq.................123 E2
Trevor St.................123 E2
Trigon Rd.................124 D7
Trinity Pl................121 J5
Trinity Sq................121 J5
Triton Sq.................119 H2
Trump St..................121 F4
Tryon St..................123 F5
Tuck's Ct.................121 F4
Tudor St..................120 D5
Tufton St.................124 C3
Turks Row.................123 F5
Turnagain La..............120 E3
Turnmill St...............120 E3
Turpentine La............123 H5
Turville St...............121 J2
Tweezer's Alley...........120 D5
Twyford Pl................120 C4
Tyburn Way................119 E5
Tyers Gate................121 H6
Tyers St..................124 D5
Tyne St...................121 J4
Tysoe St..................120 D1

U

Udall St..................124 A4
Ulster Pl.................119 G2
Undershaft................121 H4
Underwood Row.............121 F1
Underwood St..............121 F1
Unicorn Pas...............121 H6
Union Ct..................121 H4
Union St..................121 F6
Union Wlk.................121 J1
University St.............119 H2
Unwin Rd..................122 D3
Upbrook Mews..............118 B4
Upper Belgrave St.........123 G3
Upper Berkeley St.........119 E4
Upper Blantyre Wlk........122 C7
Upper Brook St............119 F5
Upper Cheyne Row..........122 D6
Upper Dartrey Wlk.........122 C7
Upper Grosvenor St........119 F5
Upper Ground..............120 D6
Upper Harley St...........119 F2
Upper James St............119 H5
Upper John St.............119 H5
Upper Marsh...............124 D2
Upper Montague St.........118 E3
Upper St Martin's La......120 B5
Upper Tachbrook St........123 J4
Upper Thames St...........121 F5
Upper Whistler Wlk........122 C7
Upper Wimpole St..........119 F3
Upper Woburn Pl...........120 A1
Uverdale Rd...............122 C7
Uxbridge St...............122 A1

V

Vale Cl...................118 B1
Vale The..................122 D6
Vandon Pas................124 A3
Vandon St.................124 A3
Vandy St..................121 H2
Vane St...................124 A4
Vanston Pl................122 A7
Varndell St...............119 H1
Vauxhall Bridge..........124 C5
Vauxhall Bridge Rd........124 A4
Vauxhall Cross...........124 C5
Vauxhall Gr...............124 D6
Vauxhall St...............124 D5
Vauxhall Wlk..............124 D5
Venables St...............118 C3
Vere St...................119 G4
Vernon Pl.................120 B3
Vernon Rise...............120 C1
Vernon St.................120 C1
Verulam St................120 D3
Vestry St.................121 G1
Viaduct Bldgs.............120 D3
Vicarage Gate............122 B2
Vicarage Gdns............122 A2
Victoria Ave.............121 H3
Victoria Emb..............120 D5
Victoria Emb..............120 C5
Victoria Gdns.............122 A1
Victoria Gr...............122 C3

Victoria Pas..............118 C2
Victoria Rd...............122 C3
Victoria Sq...............123 H3
Victoria Sq...............124 A3
Vigo St...................119 H5
Villiers St...............120 B6
Vince St..................121 G1
Vincent Sq................124 B4
Vincent St................124 B4
Vine Hill.................120 D2
Vine St...................121 J5
Vine St...................119 H5
Vinery Villas.............118 D1
Vineyard Wlk..............120 D2
Virgil Pl.................118 E3
Virgil St.................124 D3
Virginia Rd...............121 J1
Viscount St...............121 F3

W

Waithman St...............120 E4
Wakefield St..............120 B1
Wakley St.................120 E1
Walbrook..................121 G4
Walcot Sq.................124 E4
Walcott St................124 A4
Walden St.................118 H5
Waldron Mews..............122 D6
Walham Gr.................122 A7
Walham Green Arc..........122 A7
Walker's Ct...............119 J5
Wallgrave Rd..............122 B4
Walmer Pl.................118 E3
Walmer St.................118 E3
Walnut Tree Wlk...........124 E4
Walpole St................123 F5
Walton Cl.................124 C7
Walton Pl.................123 E3
Walton St.................123 E3
Wandon Rd.................122 B7
Wandsworth Rd.............124 C7
Wansdown Pl...............122 B7
Wardens Gr................121 F6
Wardour Mews..............119 H4
Wardour St................119 J4
Wardrobe Pl...............121 F4
Wardrobe Terr.............121 E5
Warner Pl.................121 D2
Warner St.................120 D2
Warren Mews...............119 H2
Warren St.................119 H1
Warrington Cres..........118 B2
Warrington Gdns..........118 B2
Warwick Ave...............118 A2
Warwick Ave...............118 B2
Warwick Cres..............118 B3
Warwick House St..........120 A6
Warwick House St..........124 B1
Warwick Pl...............118 B3
Warwick Pl N.............123 J4
Warwick Row...............123 J3
Warwick Sq................120 E4
Warwick Sq Mews..........123 J4
Warwick St................119 H5
Warwick Way...............123 J4
Warwick Yd................121 F2
Water Gdns The............118 D4
Water St..................120 D5
Watergate.................120 E5
Watergate Wlk.............120 B6
Waterloo Bridge..........120 C5
Waterloo Pl...............119 J6
Waterloo Rd...............124 E2
Waterloo Rd...............124 E2
Waterson St...............121 J1
Watling Ct................121 F4
Watling St................121 F4
Watson's Mews.............118 D3
Waverton St...............119 G6
Weaver's La...............121 H6
Weighhouse St.............119 F4
Weir's Pas................120 A1
Welbeck St................119 G4
Welbeck Way...............119 G4
Well Ct...................121 F4
Well Ct...................121 F4
Wellesley Pl..............120 A1
Wellesley Terr...........121 F1
Wellington Bldgs.........123 G5
Wellington Pl...........118 C1
Wellington Rd............118 D1
Wellington Sq............123 F5
Wellington St............120 C5
Wells Mews................119 H4
Wells Sq..................120 C1
Wells St..................119 H4
Wentworth Dwellings.......121 J4
Wentworth St..............121 J3
Wesley St.................119 F3
West Carriage Dri.........118 D6
West Carriage Dri.........123 E1
West Central St...........120 B4
West Cromwell Rd..........122 A4
West Eaton Pl.............123 G4
West Eaton Pl Mews........123 G3
West Halkin St............123 G3
West Harding St...........120 D4
West Mall.................122 A1
West Mews.................123 J4
West Poultry Ave..........120 E3
West Rd...................123 F6
West Smithfield...........120 E3
West St...................120 A4
West Tenter St............121 J4
West Warwick Pl..........123 J4
Westbourne Cres..........118 C5
Westbourne Gdns..........118 A4
Westbourne Gr Terr........118 C5
Westbourne St.............118 C5
Westbourne Terr..........118 B4
Westbourne Terr Mews......118 B3
Westgate Terr............122 B6
Westland Pl...............121 G1
Westminster Bridge........124 C2
Westminster Bridge Rd.....124 E3
Westminster Bldgs.........121 G4
Westmoreland Pl...........123 H5
Westmoreland St...........119 F3
Weston Rise...............120 C1
Weston St.................121 H6
Westway...................118 B3
Wetherby Gdns............122 C4
Wetherby Mews............122 B5
Wetherby Pl..............122 C4
Weymouth Mews.............119 G3
Weymouth St...............119 G3
Wharfedale St.............122 B5
Wharton St................120 C1
Wheatley St...............119 F3
Wheatsheaf La.............124 C7

Wheler St.................121 J2
Whetstone Park...........120 C4
Whichcote St..............120 D6
Whidborne St..............120 B1
Whiskin St................120 E1
Whistler Wlk..............122 C7
Whistlers Ave.............123 E7
Whitby St.................121 J2
Whitcomb Ct...............119 J5
Whitcomb St...............120 A5
White Bear Yd.............120 D2
White Hart St.............121 H3
White Hart St.............124 E4
White Hart Yd.............121 G6
White Horse Alley.........120 E3
White Horse St............119 G6
White Kennett St..........121 H4
White Lion Hill..........121 E5
White Lion St.............119 G5
Whitechapel High St.......121 J4
Whitecross St.............121 G3
Whitecross St.............121 F2
Whitecross St.............121 F3
Whitefriars St............120 D4
Whitehall.................120 B6
Whitehall Ct..............120 B6
Whitehall Gdns...........120 B6
Whitehall Pl..............120 B6
Whitehaven St.............118 D2
Whitehead's Gr...........123 E4
White's Row...............121 J3
Whitfield Pl..............119 H2
Whitfield St..............119 H3
Whitgift St...............124 D4
Whittington Ave..........121 H4
Whittaker St.............123 G4
Whittlesey St.............120 D6
Wickham St................124 D5
Wicklow St................120 C1
Widegate St...............121 H3
Wigmore Pl................119 G4
Wigmore St................119 F4
Wilbraham Pl.............123 G4
Wilcox Cl.................124 C7
Wilcox Rd.................124 C7
Wilcox Rd.................124 C7
Wild Ct...................120 C4
Wild St...................120 C4
Wilfred St................123 J3
Wilkes St.................121 J3
Wilkes St.................121 J3
William IV St.............120 B5
William Mews..............123 F2
William Rd................119 H1
William St................123 F2
Willoughby St............120 B3
Willow Pl................123 J4
Willow St.................121 H2
Wilmington Sq............120 D1
Wilmington St............120 D1
Wilson St.................121 G3
Wilton Cres...............123 G2
Wilton Mews..............123 H3
Wilton Pl................123 G2
Wilton Rd.................123 J4
Wilton Row...............123 G2
Wilton Sq.................123 H3
Wilton St.................123 H3
Wiltshire Cl.............123 F4
Wimpole Mews.............119 G3
Wimpole St...............119 G3
Winchester Mews..........119 F3
Winchester Sq............121 G6
Winchester St............123 H5
Winchester Wlk...........121 G6
Wincott St................124 E4
Windmill St...............119 H5
Windmill St...............119 J3
Windmill Wlk.............120 D6
Windsor Pl...............124 A4
Windsor Terr.............121 F1
Wine Office Ct...........120 D4
Winnett St................119 J5
Winsland Mews............118 C4
Winsland St...............118 C4
Winsley St...............119 H4
Winterton Pl.............122 C6
Withers Pl...............121 F2
Woburn Mews..............120 A2
Woburn Pl................120 B2
Woburn Sq................120 A2
Woburn Wlk...............120 A1
Wood St...................121 F4
Woodbridge St............120 E2
Woodfall St..............123 F5
Woods Mews...............119 F5
Woodstock Mews...........119 F3
Woodstock St.............119 G4
Wootton St................120 D6
Worfield St...............123 E7
Worgan St.................124 D5
World's End Pas..........122 C7
Wormwood St..............121 H4
Worship St................121 H2
Wren St...................120 C2
Wright's La..............122 B3
Wybert St.................119 H2
Wyclif St.................120 E1
Wynard Terr..............124 D6
Wyndham Mews.............118 E3
Wyndham Pl...............118 E3
Wyndham St...............118 E3
Wyndham Yd...............118 E3
Wynnstay Gdns............122 A3
Wynyard Terr.............124 D5
Wyatt St..................120 E1
Wythburn Pl..............118 E4
Wyvil Rd..................124 D6

Y

Yardley St................120 D1
Yarmouth Pl...............119 G6
Yeoman's Row.............123 E3
Yeoman's Row.............123 E3
Yeoman's Yd...............121 J5
York Bldgs...............120 B5
York Bridge..............119 F2
York Gate................119 F2
York House Pl............122 B2
York Pl..................120 B5
York Rd..................124 D2
York St...................118 E3
York Terr E..............119 F2
York Terr W..............119 F2
Yorkshire Grey Yd........120 C3
Young St..................122 B2
Young's Bldgs............121 F2

Z

Zoar St...................121 F6

Aberdeen

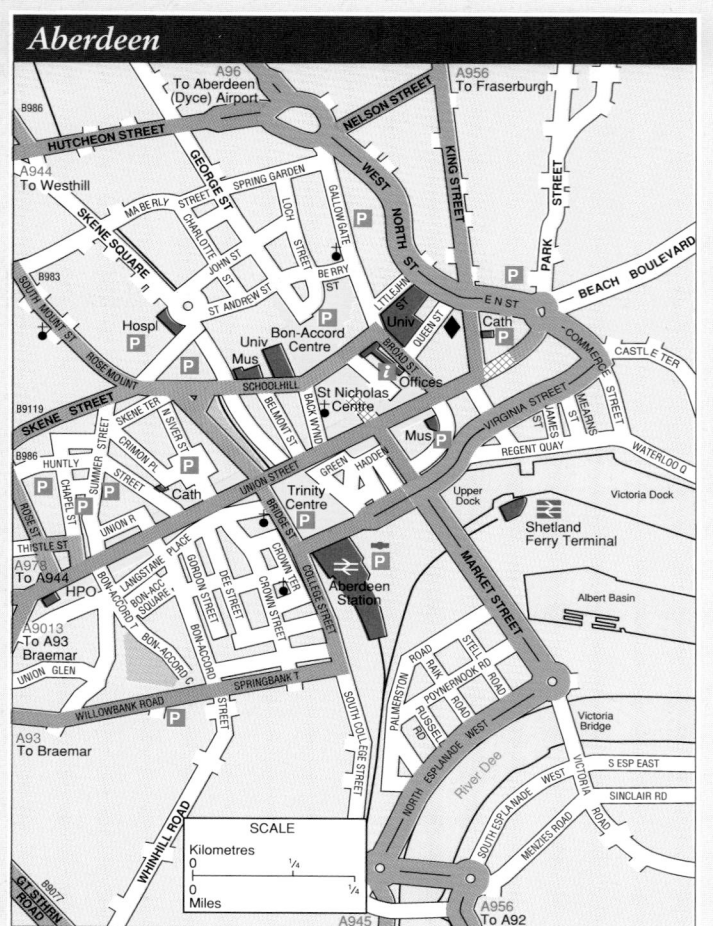

Bath

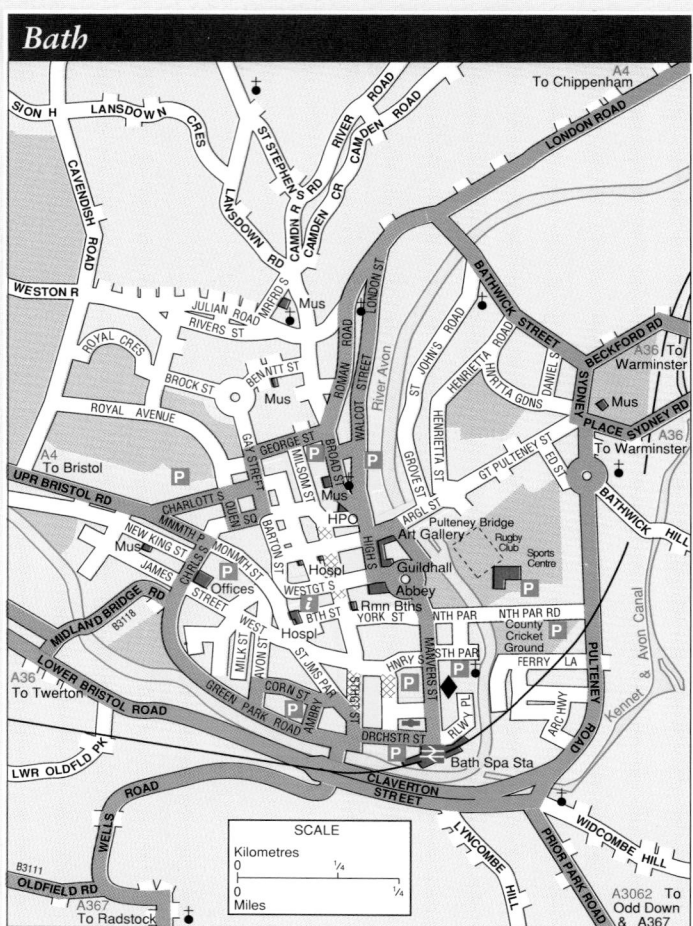

Birmingham

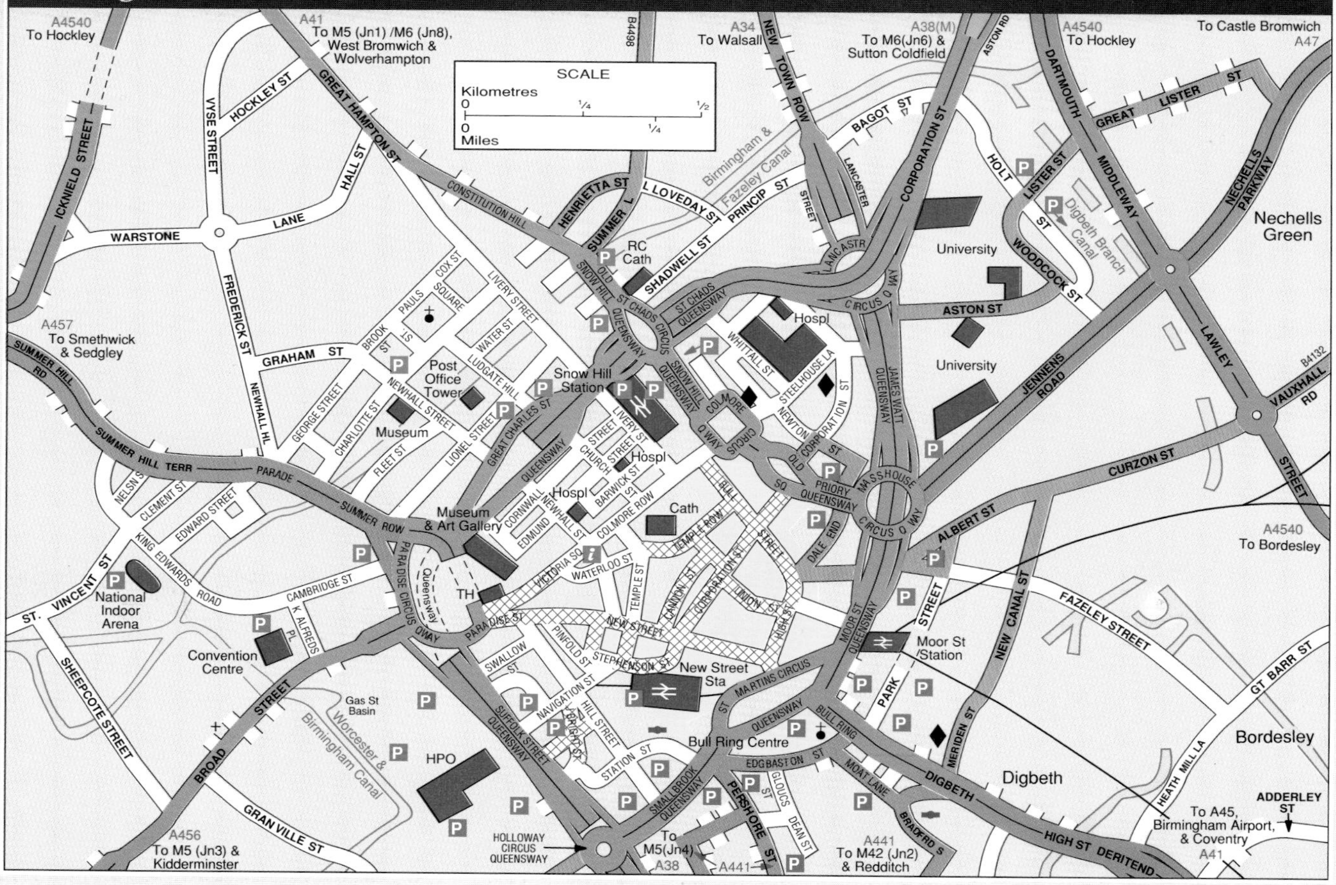

Blackpool

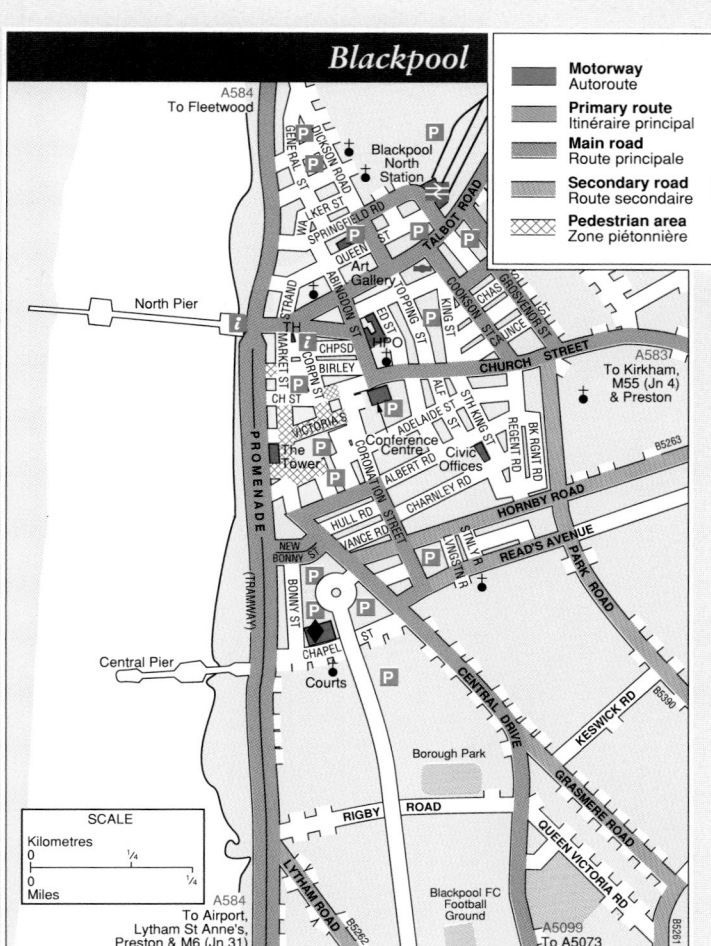

Motorway Autoroute	**Principal shopping centre** Centre commercial
Primary route Itinéraire principal	◆ **Main police station** Commissariat de police
Main road Route principale	⑥ **Motorway junction** Echangeur d'autoroute
Secondary road Route secondaire	**Important building** Edifice important
Pedestrian area Zone piétonnière	HPO **Head Post Office** Bureau de poste principal

TH **Town Hall** Hôtel de ville	**Parking** Parking
Railway station Gare	⊖ **Underground/metro station** Station de métro
Church Eglise	**Bus/coach station** Gare routière
i **Information Centre** Bureau de renseignements	

TOWN PLANS

Bournemouth

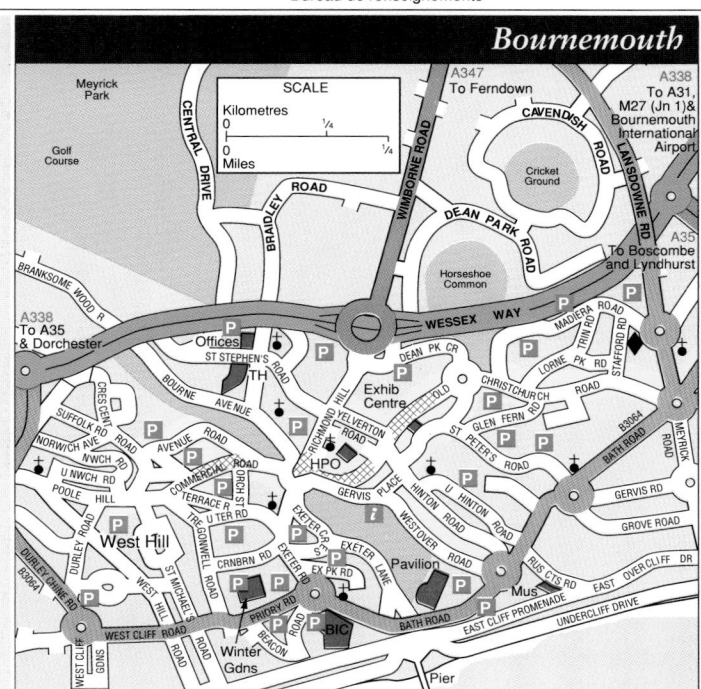

Bradford

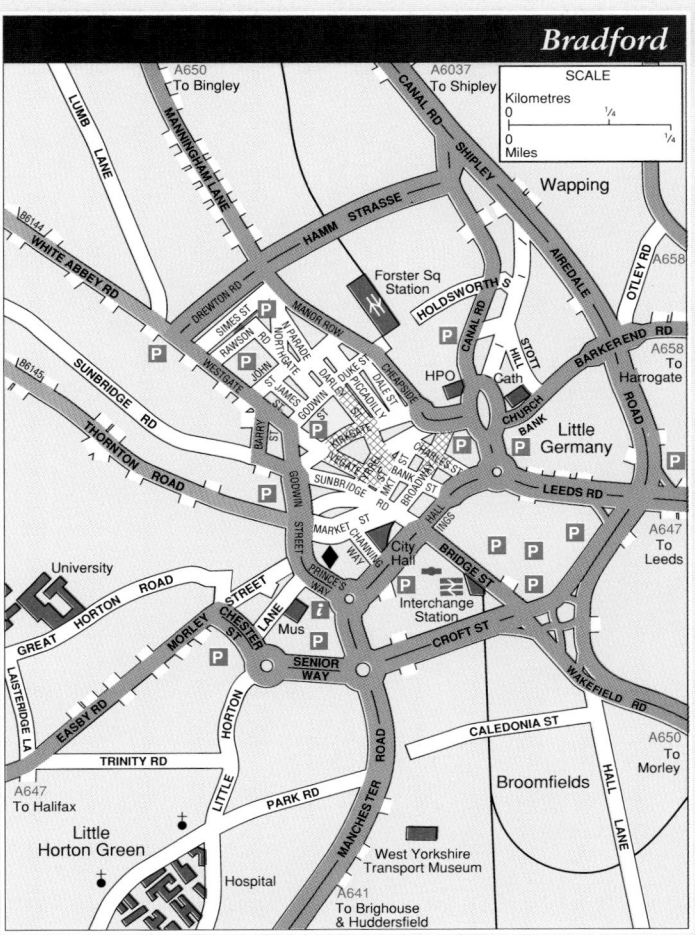

Brighton

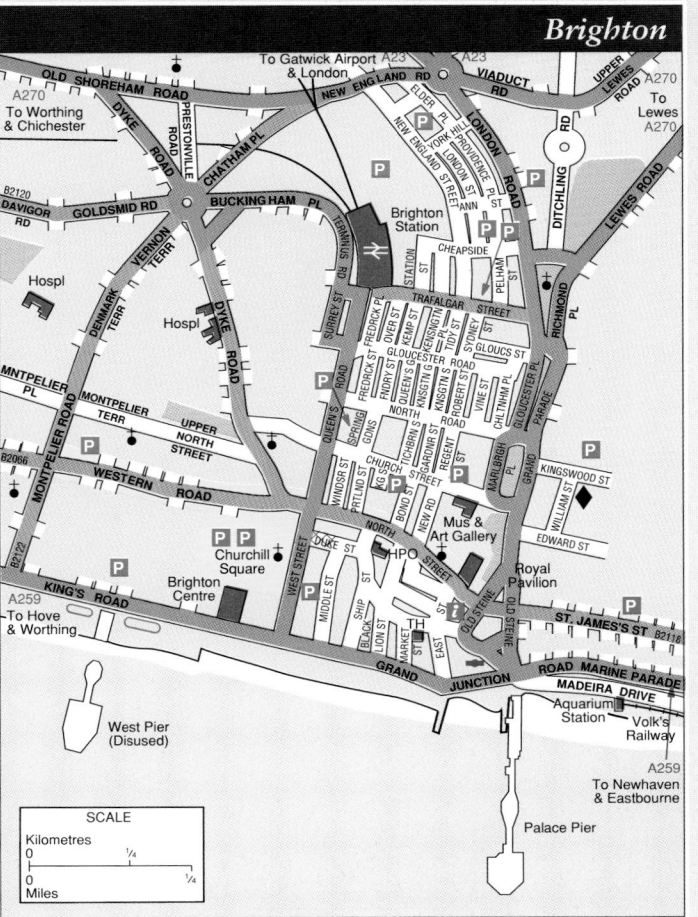

Cambridge

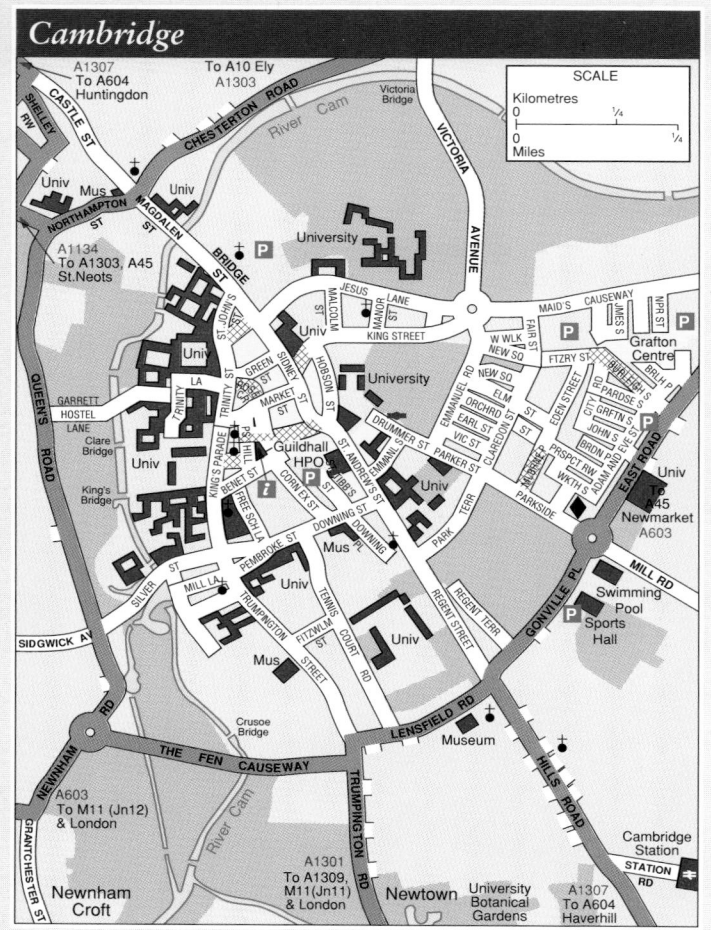

Canterbury

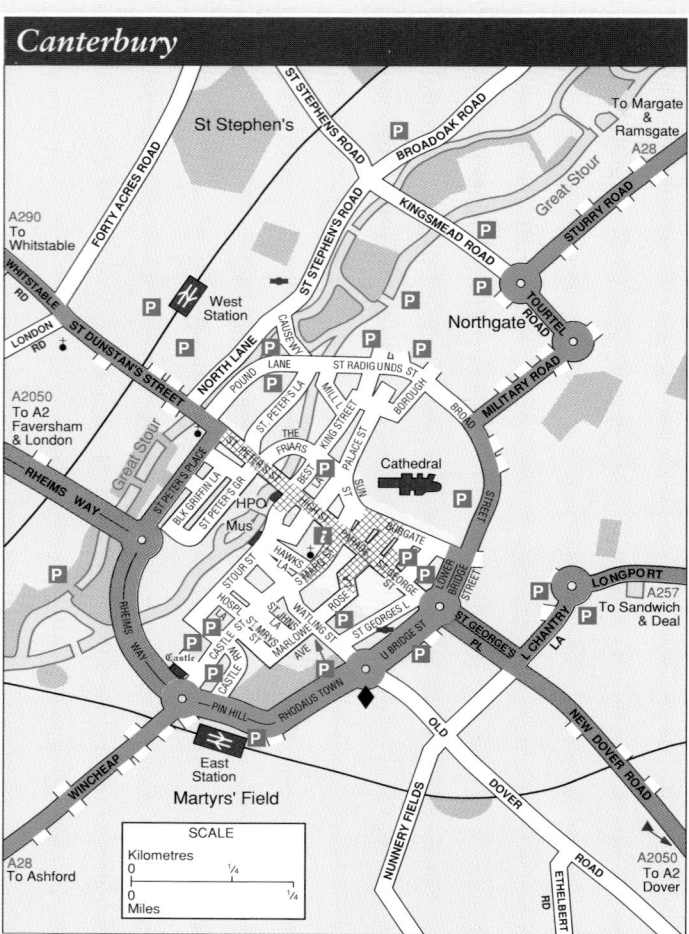

Bristol

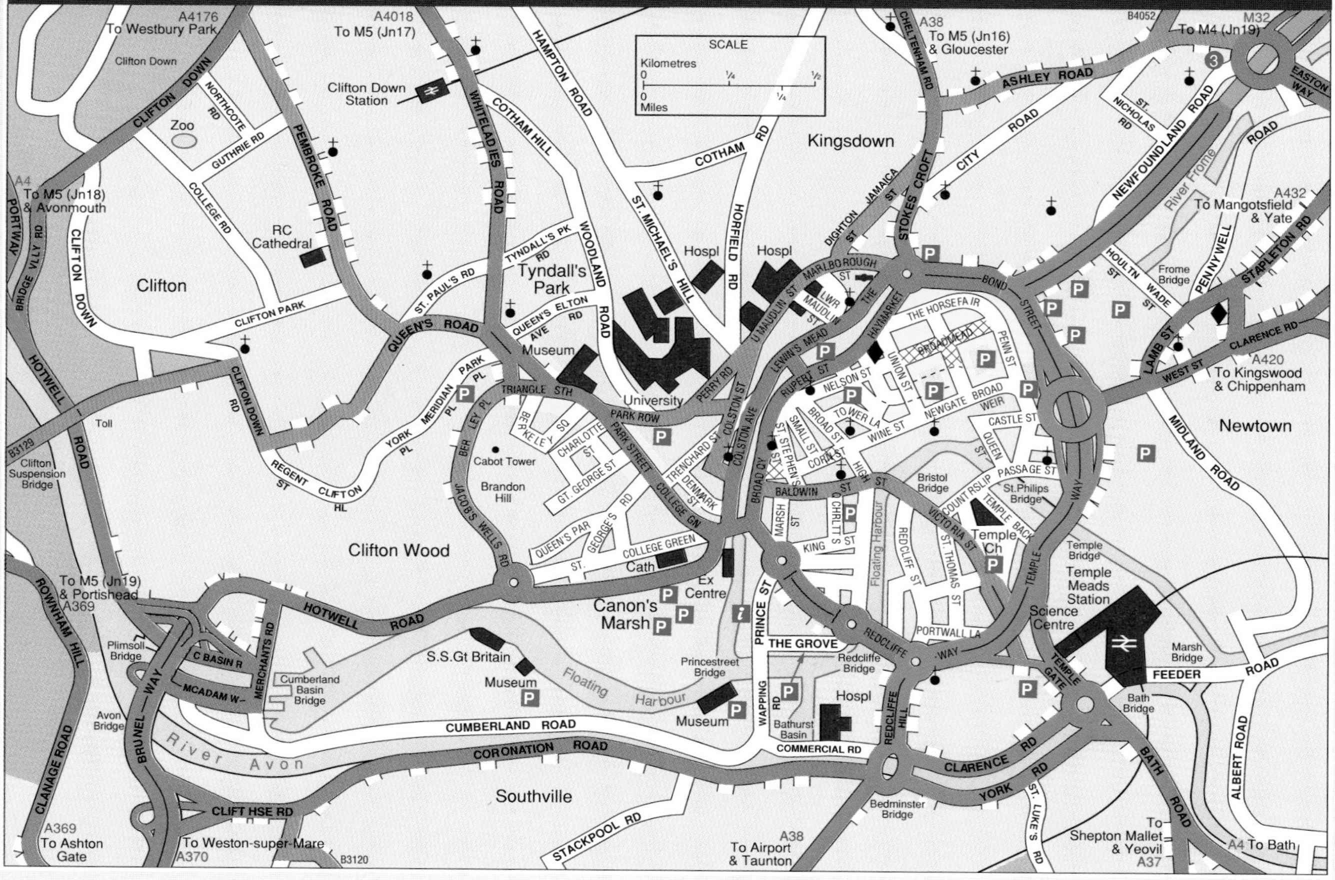

Cheltenham

Chester

Cardiff

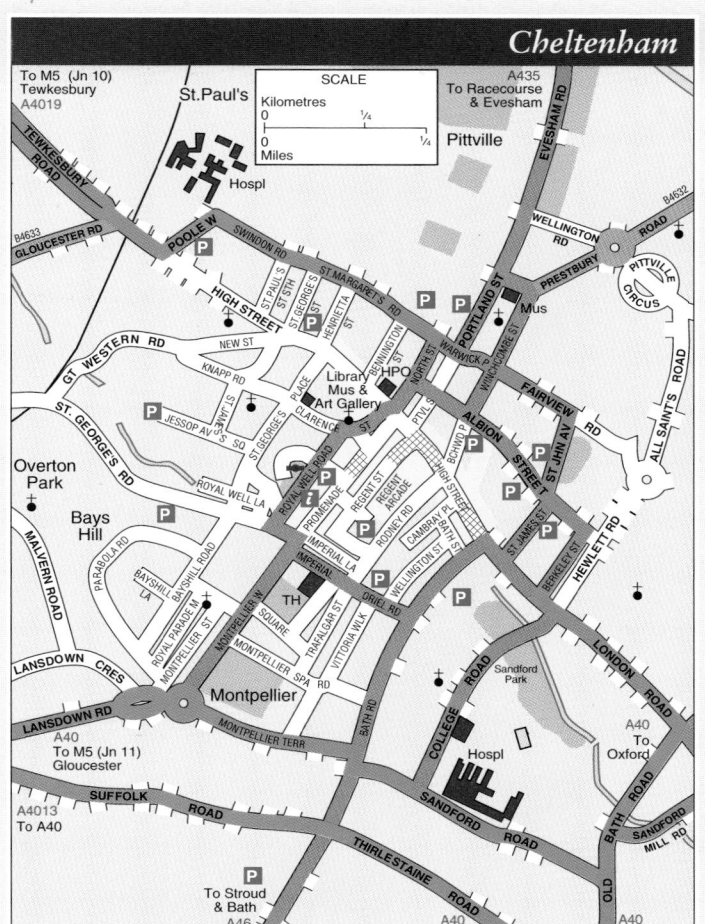

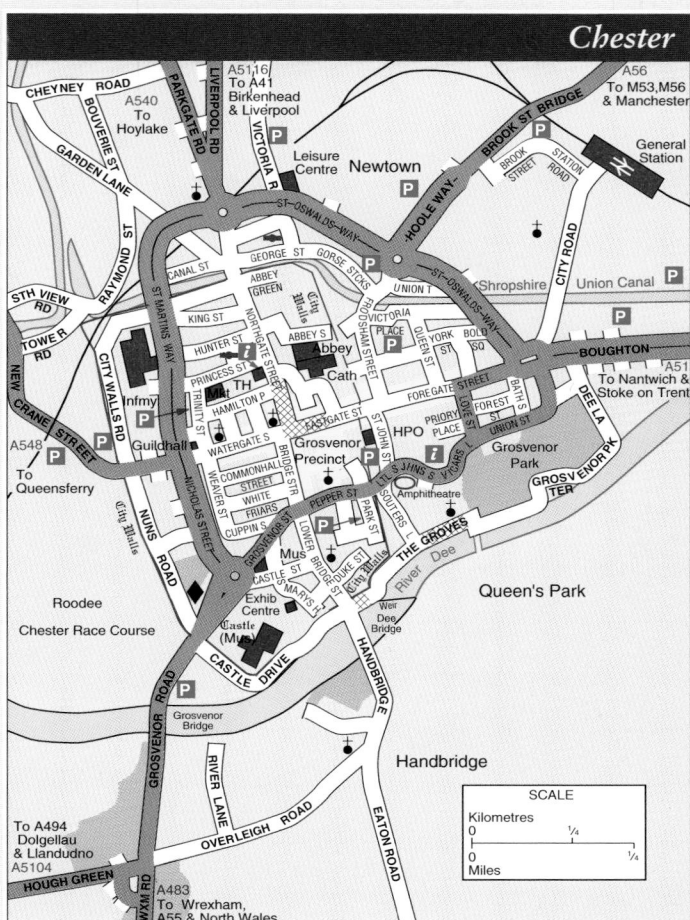

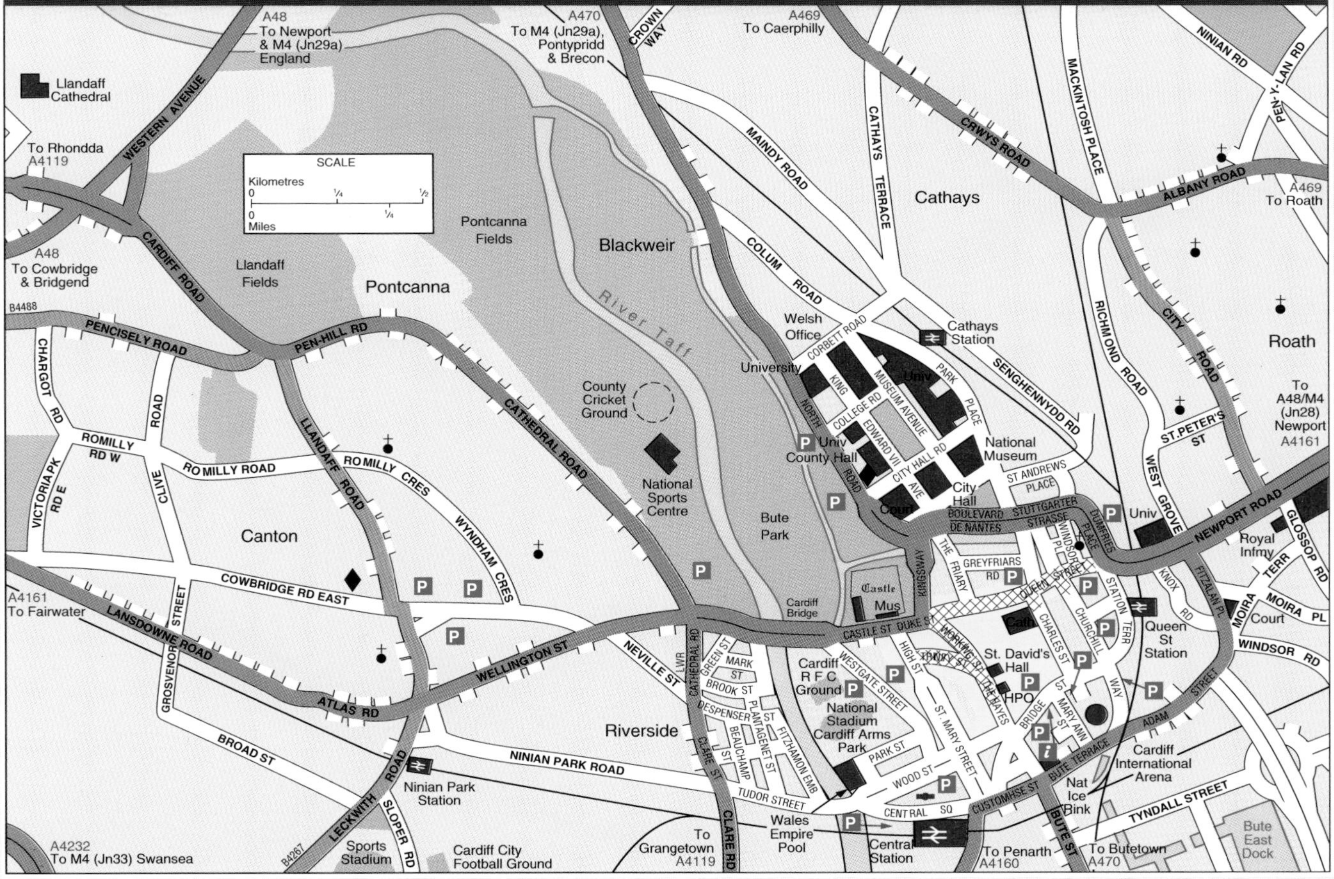

Coventry

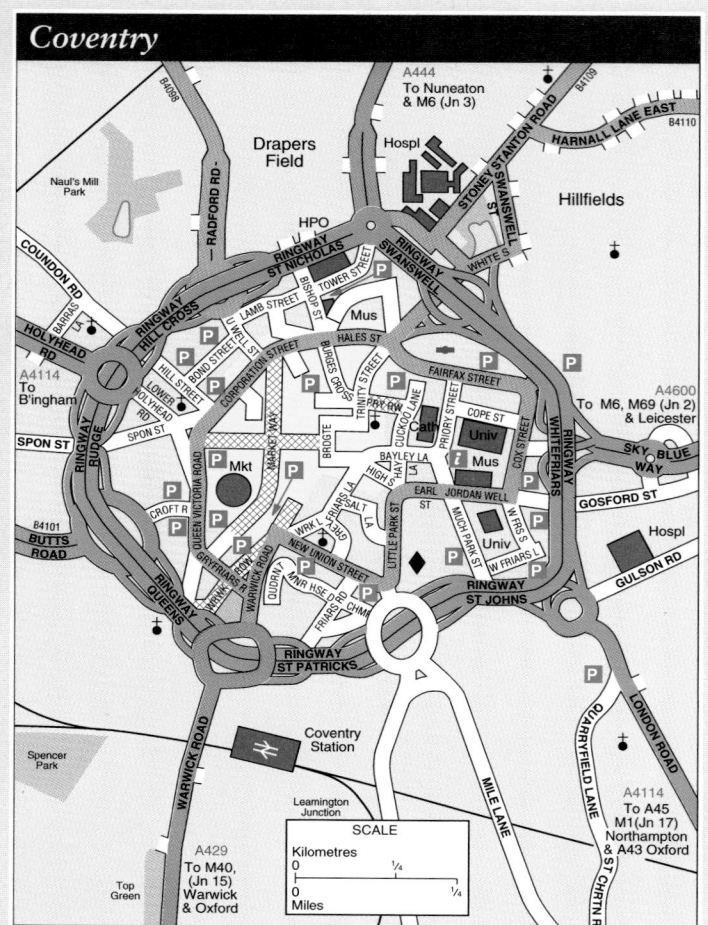

Croydon

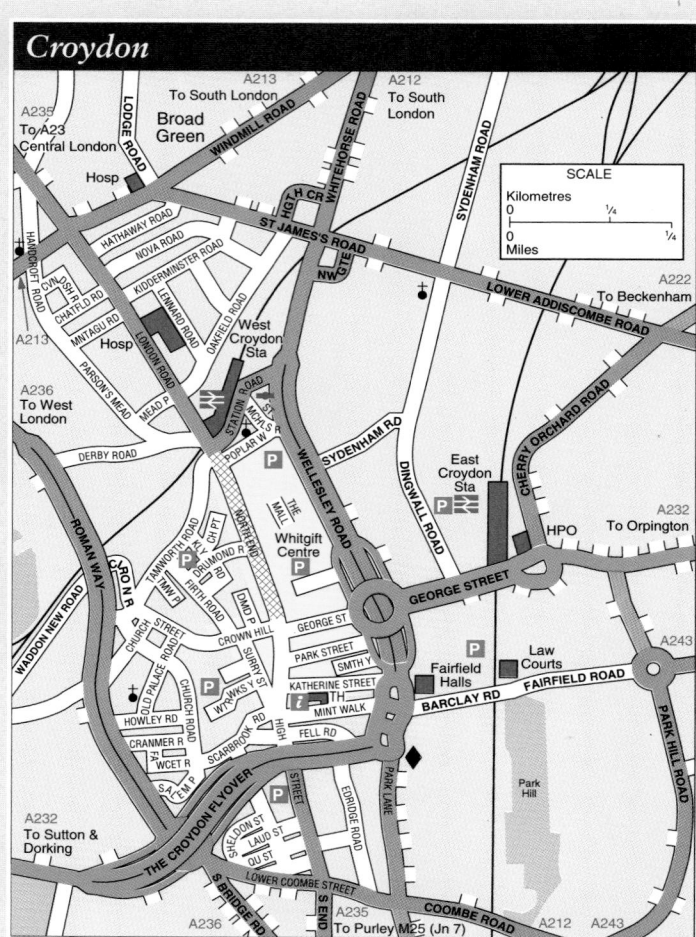

Derby

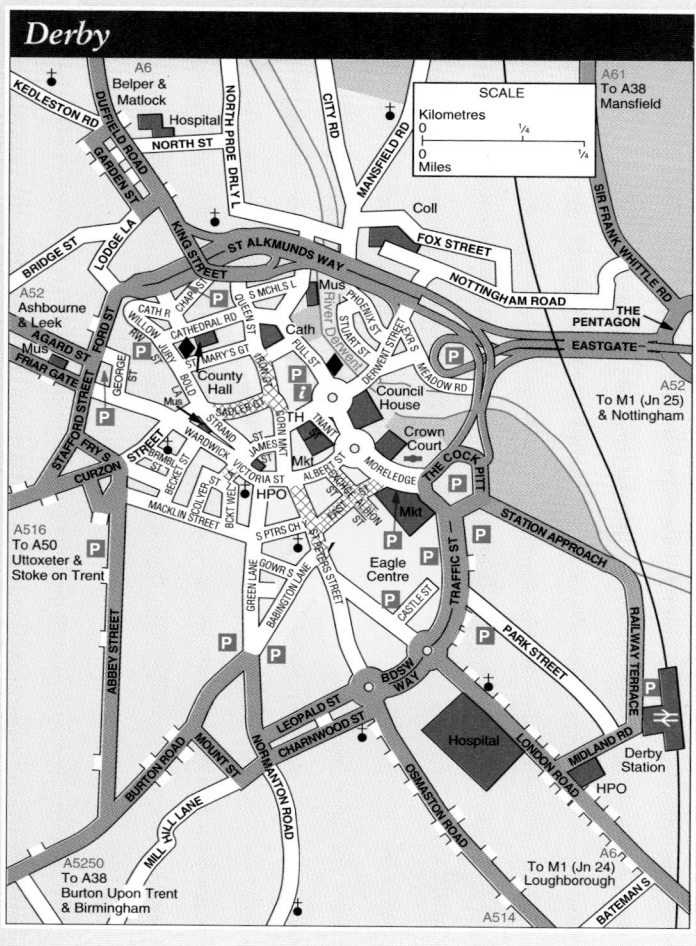

Dundee

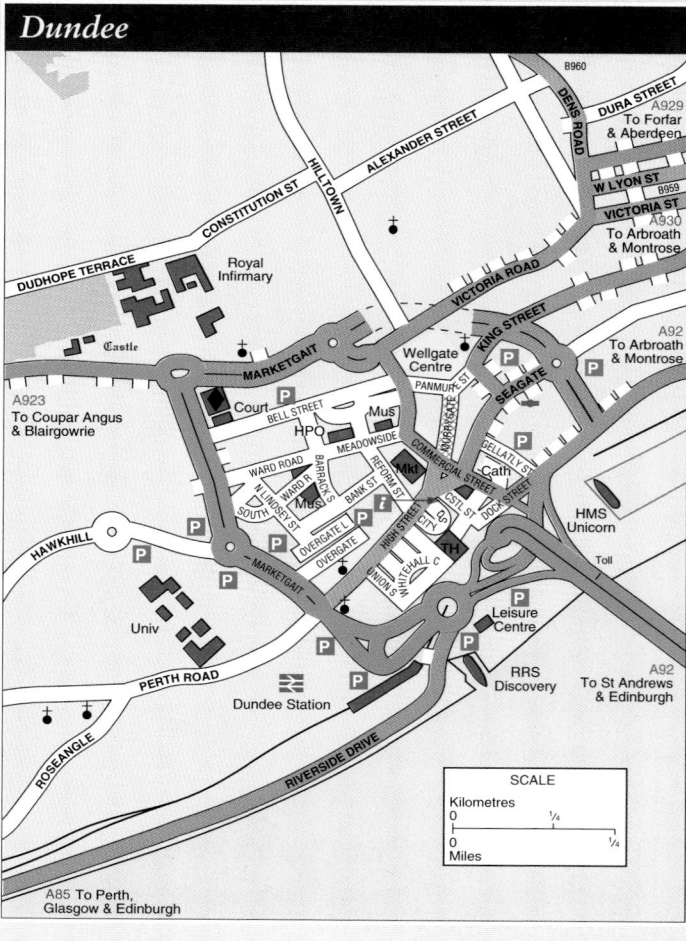

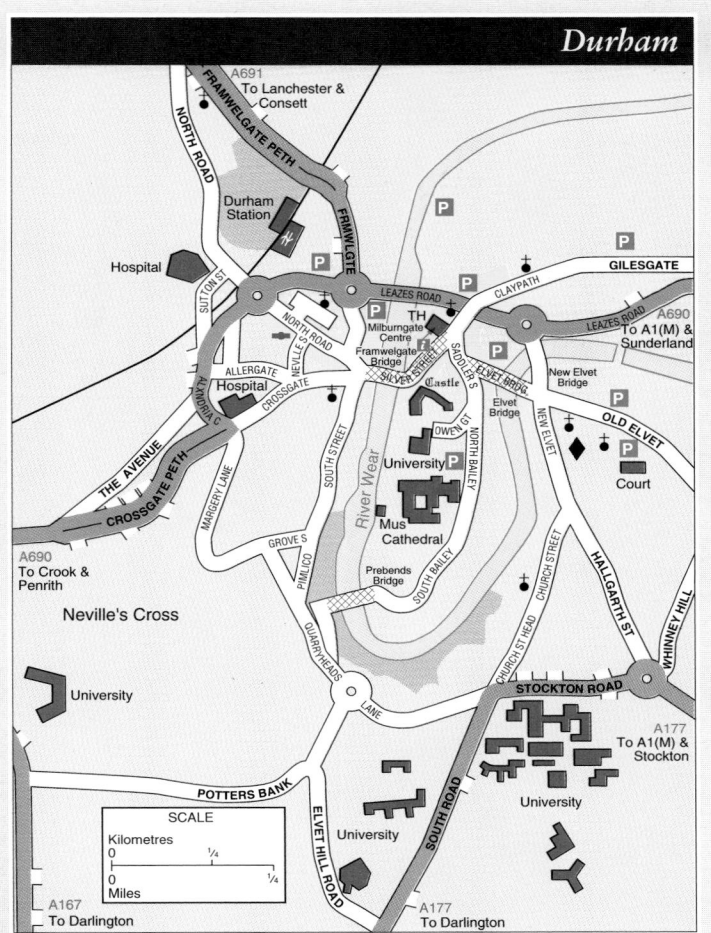

Durham

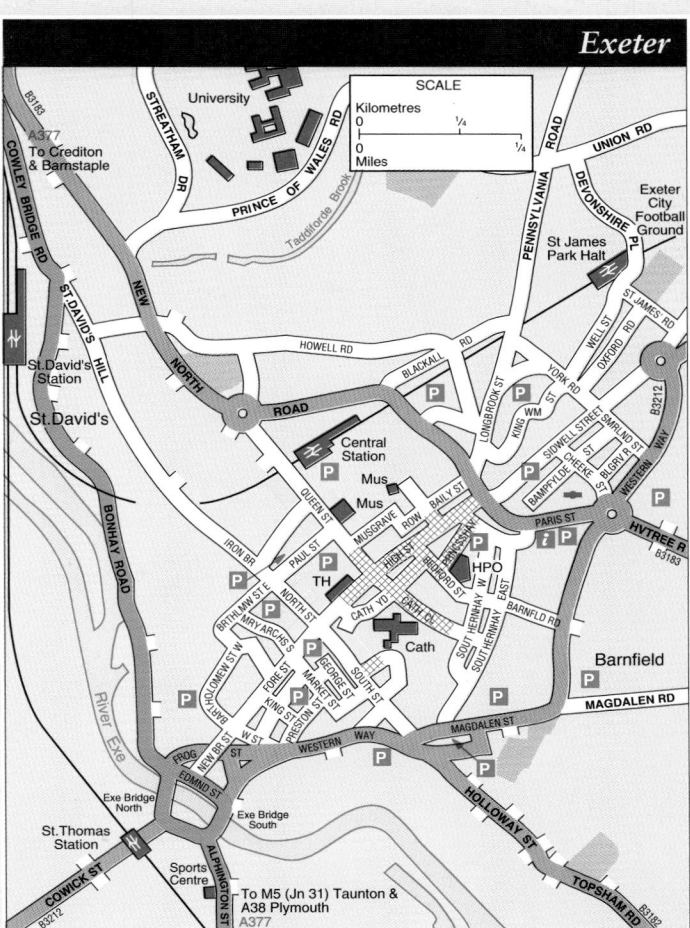

Exeter

Edinburgh

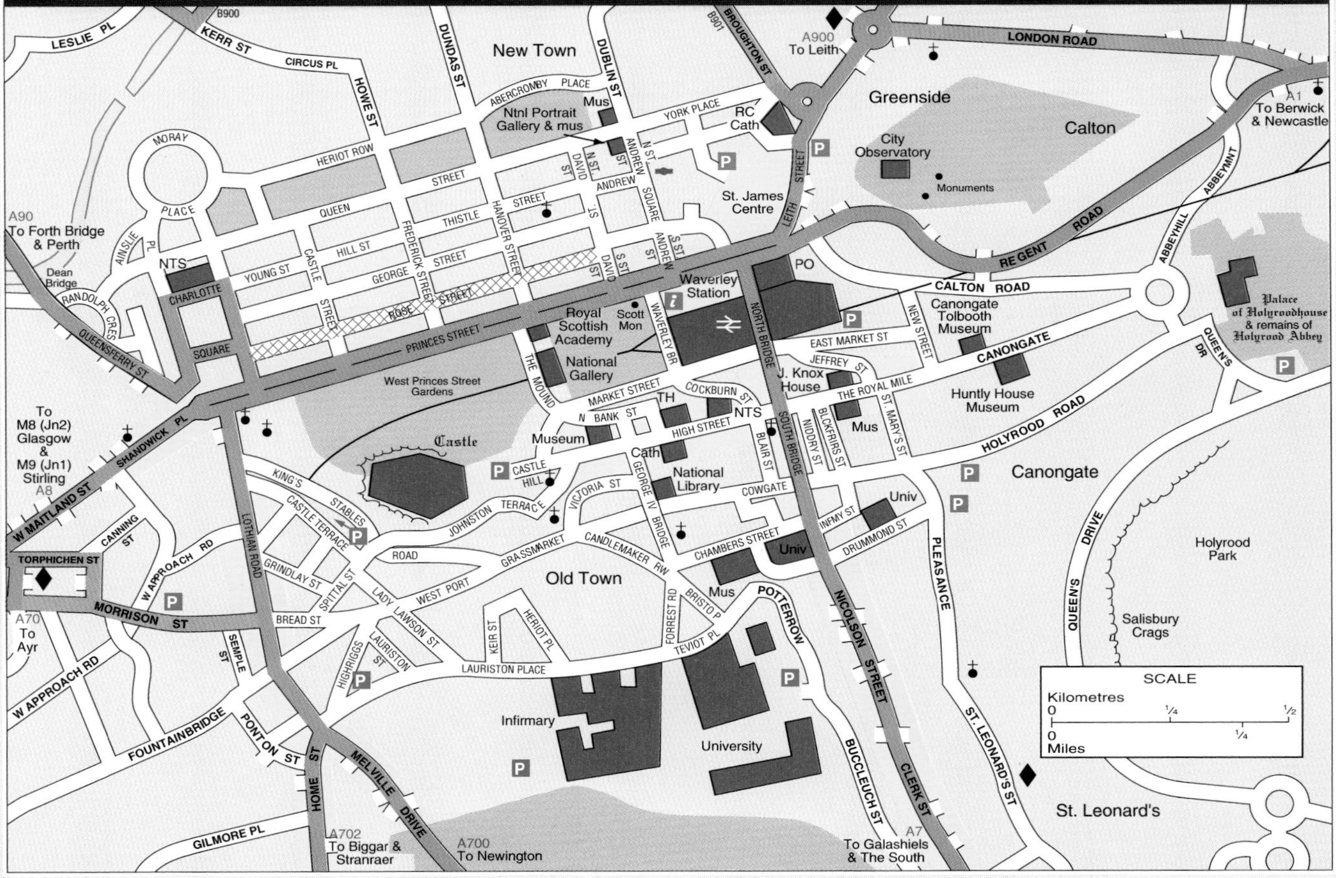

Gloucester

Hull

Glasgow

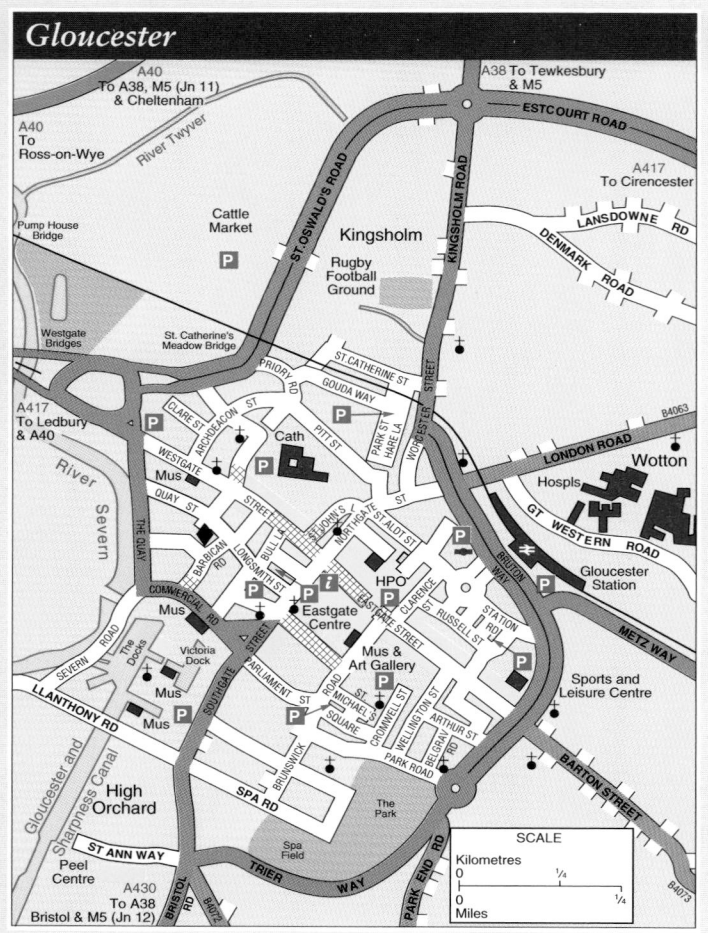

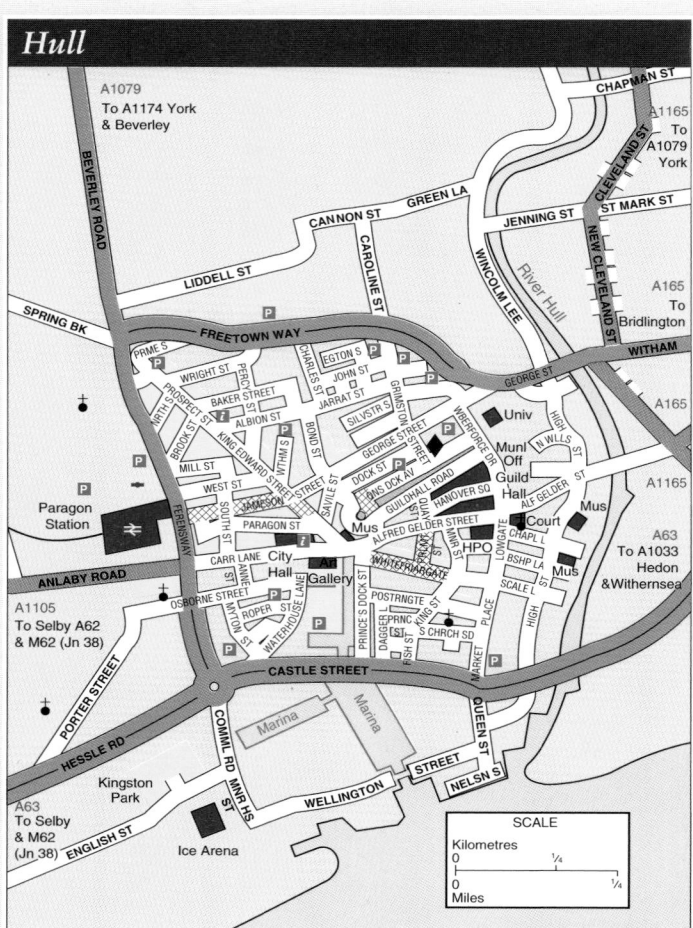

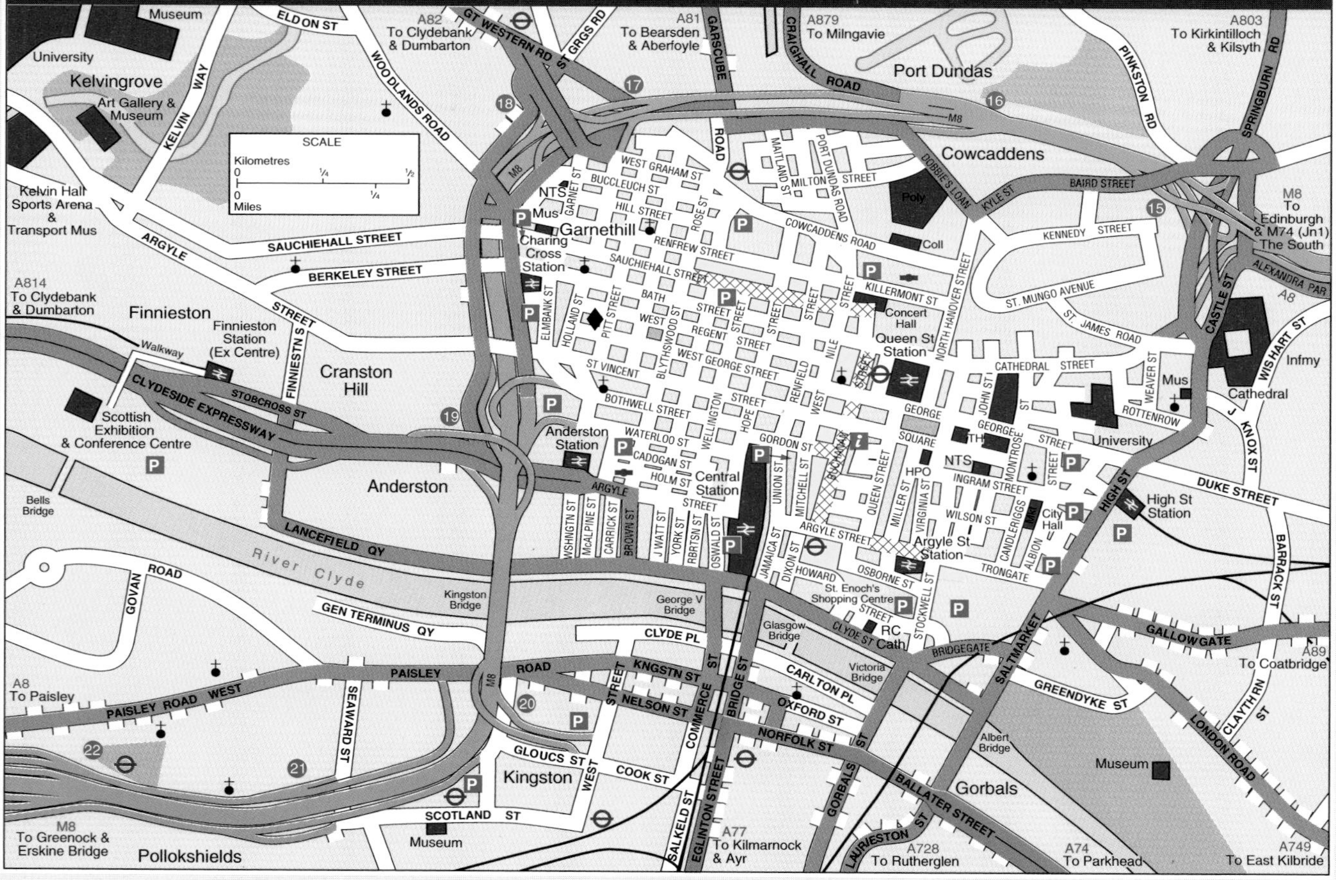

Leeds

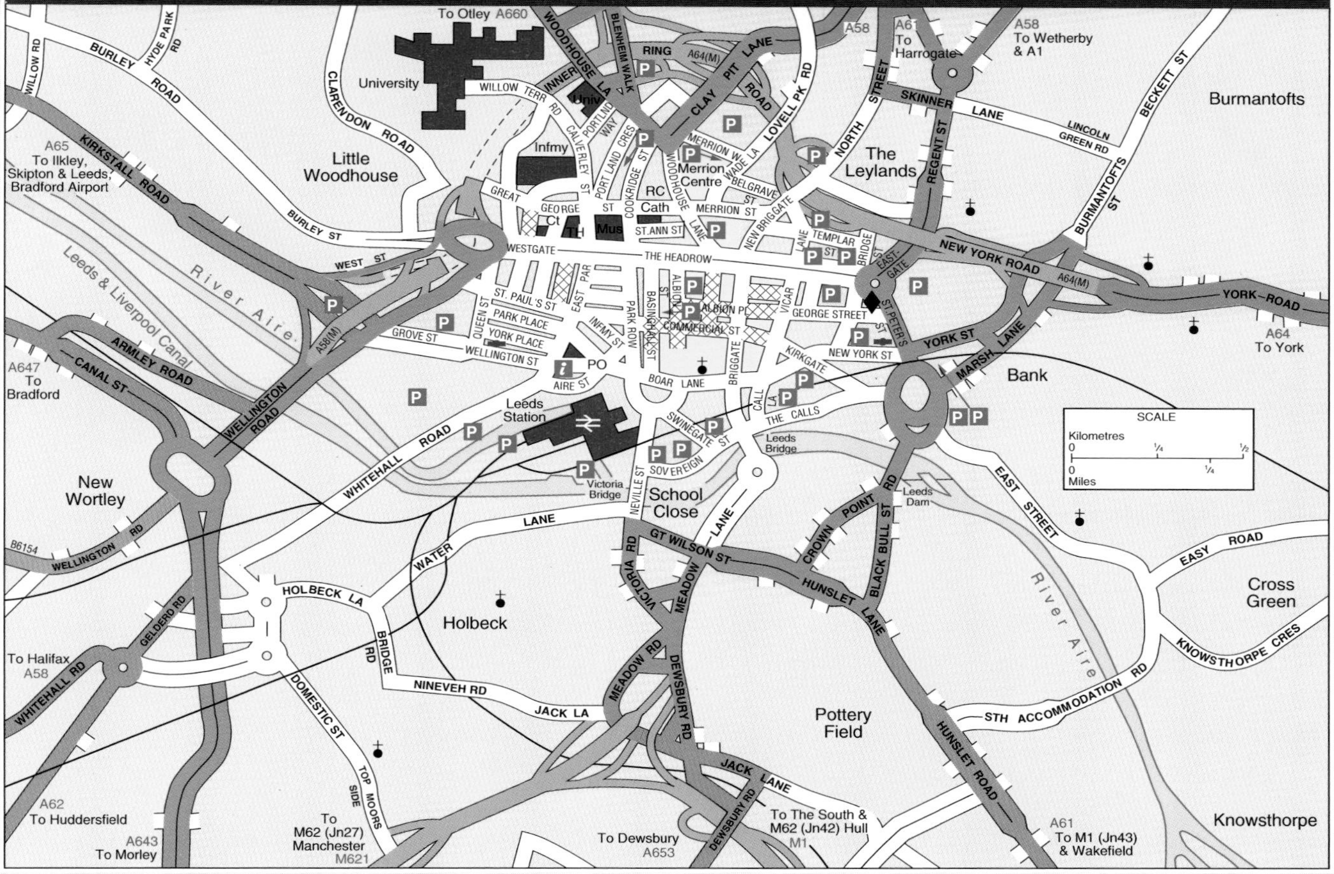

To Otley A660 · Woodhouse La · Ring · A64(M) · A58 · A61 To Harrogate · A58 To Wetherby & A1

University · Little Woodhouse · Burmantofts · Inner La · Blenheim Walk · Clay Pit Lane · Lovell Pk Rd · North St · Skinner Lane · Regent St · Beckett St · Lincoln Green Rd · Burmantofts St

Infmy · RC Cath · Merrion Centre · The Leylands · Willow Terr Rd · Clarendon Road · Portland · Port Land Cres · Cookridge St · Belgrave · Merrion St · New Briggate · Lane · Templar · Gate

A65 To Ilkley, Skipton & Leeds; Bradford Airport · Kirkstall Road · Burley Road · Burley St · West St · George Ct · Geo Mus · St Ann St · Westgate · The Headrow · Albion Pl · Vicar · George Street · East St · New York Road · A64(M) · York Road · A64 To York

Leeds & Liverpool Canal · River Aire · St Paul's · East Par · Park Place · Infmy St · Park Row · Albion · Commercial · Briggate · Call · Kirkgate · New York St · York St · Marsh Lane · Bank

A647 To Bradford · Armley Road · Canal St · Whitehall Road · Wellington Road · Grove St · Queen St · York Place · Wellington St · Aire St · PO · Boar Lane · The Calls · Sovereign · Leeds Bridge · East Street · Easy Road · Cross Green

New Wortley · Wellington Rd · Geldard Rd · Leeds Station · Victoria Bridge · School Close · Crown Point · Black Bull Rd · Leeds Dam · River Aire

B6154 · Water Lane · Holbeck La · Bridge Rd · Gt Wilson St · Victoria Rd · Meadow Rd · Hunslet Lane · Knowsthorpe Cres

To Halifax A58 · Whitehall Rd · Domestic St · Nineveh Rd · Jack La · Dewsbury Rd · Pottery Field · Sth Accommodation Rd · Hunslet Road

Holbeck · Top Moors Side · Jack Lane · Dewsbury Rd

A62 To Huddersfield · A643 To Morley · To M62 (Jn27) Manchester · M621 · To Dewsbury A653 · To The South & M62 (Jn42) Hull · M1 · A61 To M1 (Jn43) & Wakefield · Knowsthorpe

SCALE · Kilometres 0 ¼ ½ · Miles 0 ¼

Liverpool

A5036 To Crosby · A565 To Southport · B5182 · A5038 To Litherland · A59 To Ormskirk & Preston · Scotland Road · Village St · A580 To Manchester · Hospital · A5049 To West Derby · B5188 · Shiel Road

Kingsway (Road Tunnel) · Waterloo Road · Great Howard St · Pall Mall · Vauxhall Road · Fox St · St Anne Street · Everton Brow · Everton Road · West Derby Road · Elm Park · Holt Rd

Leeds Street · Smithfield St · Addison St · Byrom St · Byrom Row · Poly · Hunter St · New Islington · Brunswick Rd · Low Hill · Kensington · A57 To Prescot & St Helens

Bath Street · King Edward St · East St · Pall Mall · Hatton G · Gt Crosshall St · Churchill Way · Art Gallery · London Road · Prescot St · Hall Lane · Durning Rd · A57 · A5047 To M62 (Jn 5) Manchester & St Helens

Moorfields Station · Old Hall St · Cheapside · Vernon St · Dale St · W Brown St · Hall · Lime St Station · Univ · West Derby St · Irvine St · Edge Lane · Overbury St

New Quay · Chapel St · Tithebarn St · Victoria St · St John's La · Lime St · Russell St · Crown St · B5178

Royal Liver Building · Mus · The Strand · Water St · James St · St John's Centre · Copperas Hill · Brownlow Hill · Univ · Grinfield St · Edge Hill · Wavertree Road

Ferry (Foot) · St Nicholas Pl · TH · Brunswick St · Lord St · Church St · Clayton Square · RC Cathedral · Mount Pleasant · Edge Hill Station

James St Station · Paradise · School La · Central Station · Ranelagh St · Renshaw St · Oxford St · Univ · Tunnel Road

Queensway (Mersey Tunnel) · Museum · South John Street · Hanover Street · Bold St · Berry St · Rodney St · Hospl · Grove St · B5178

Tate Gallery · Museum · Albert Dock · Wapping · Duke St · Upper Duke St · Mount St · Catharine St · Hospl · Lodge Lane · B5174

River Mersey · Park La · St James Street · Jamaica Street · Chaloner St · Gt George St · Upper Parliament Street · Mulgrave St · Princes Park · Kingsley Rd · B5173 · A562 To Widnes & Runcorn

A5036 · Parliament St · Cath · Hope St · Upper Princes Rd · B5175 · A561 To Widnes

SCALE · Kilometres 0 ¼ ½ · Miles 0 ¼

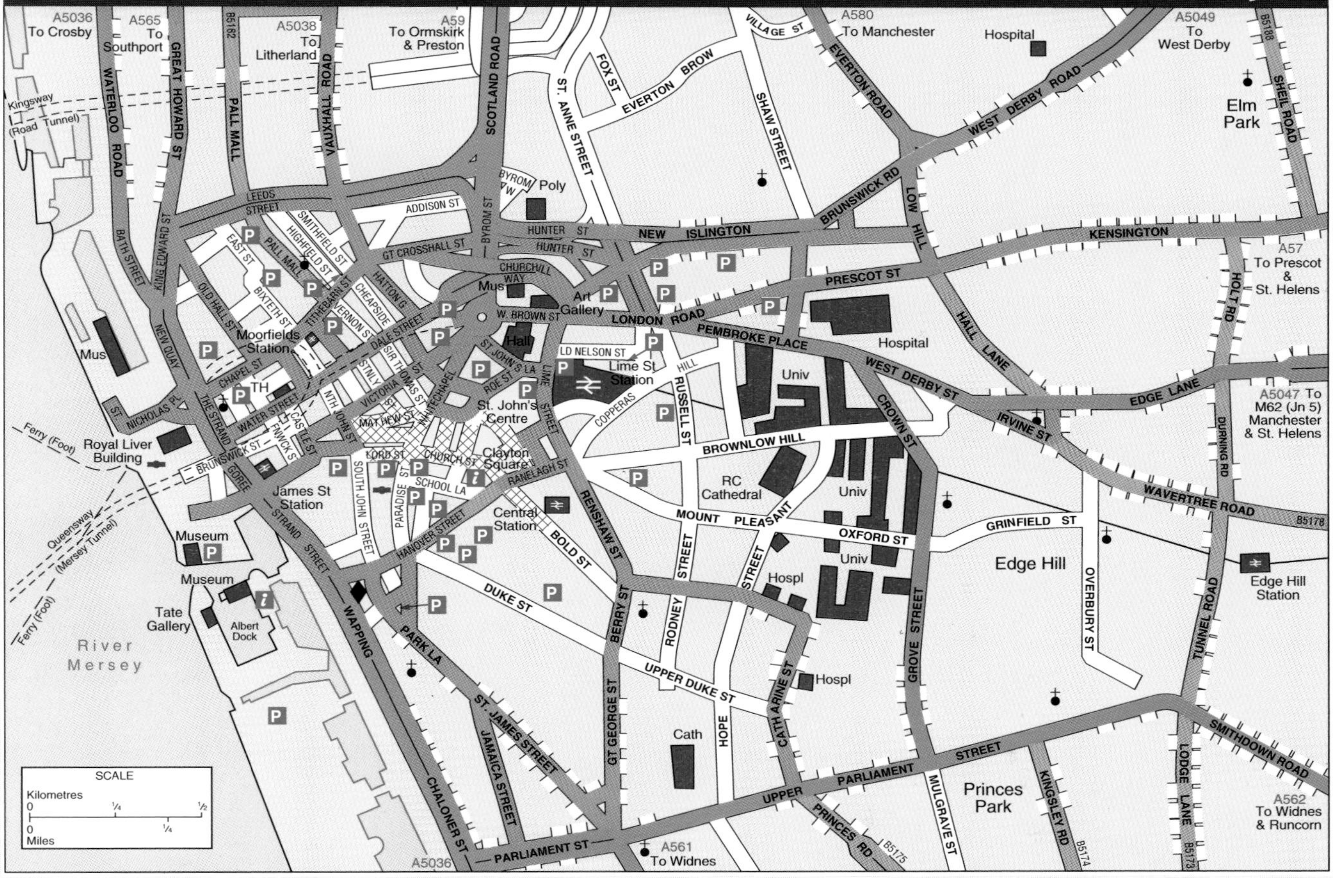

Leicester

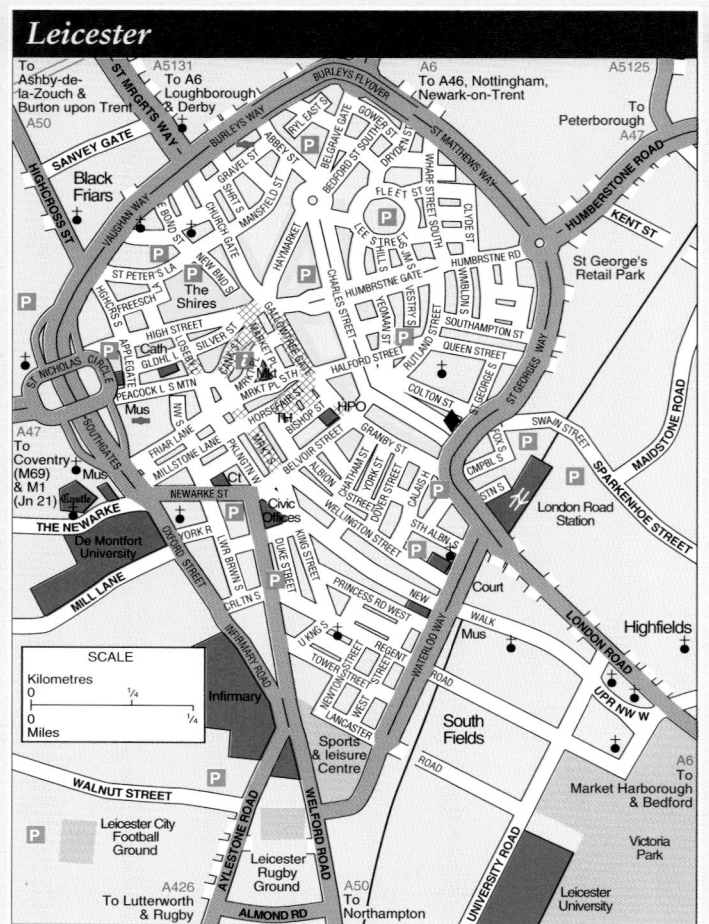

Middlesbrough

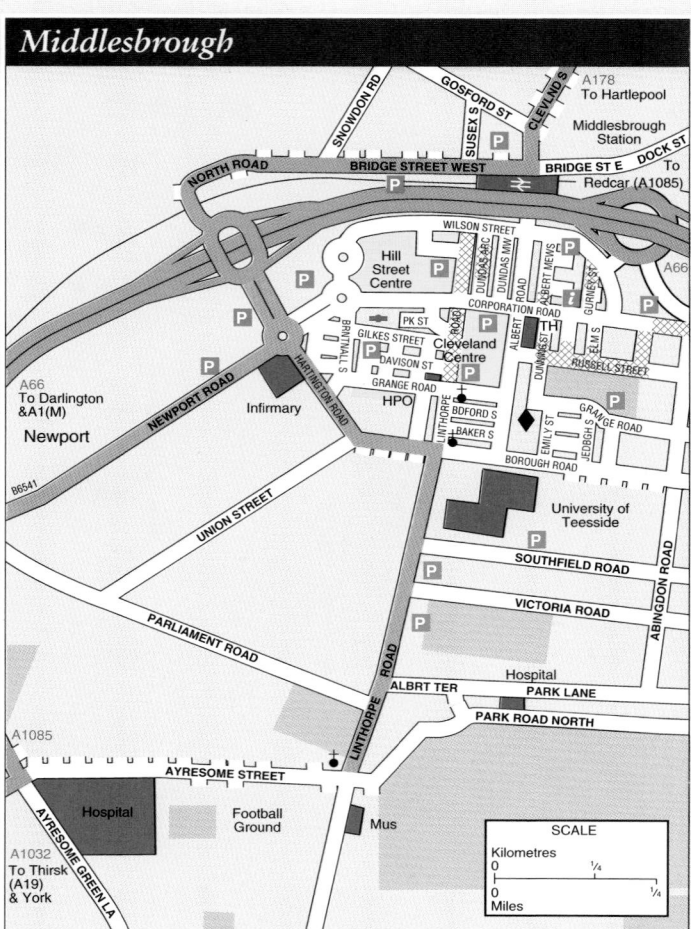

Manchester

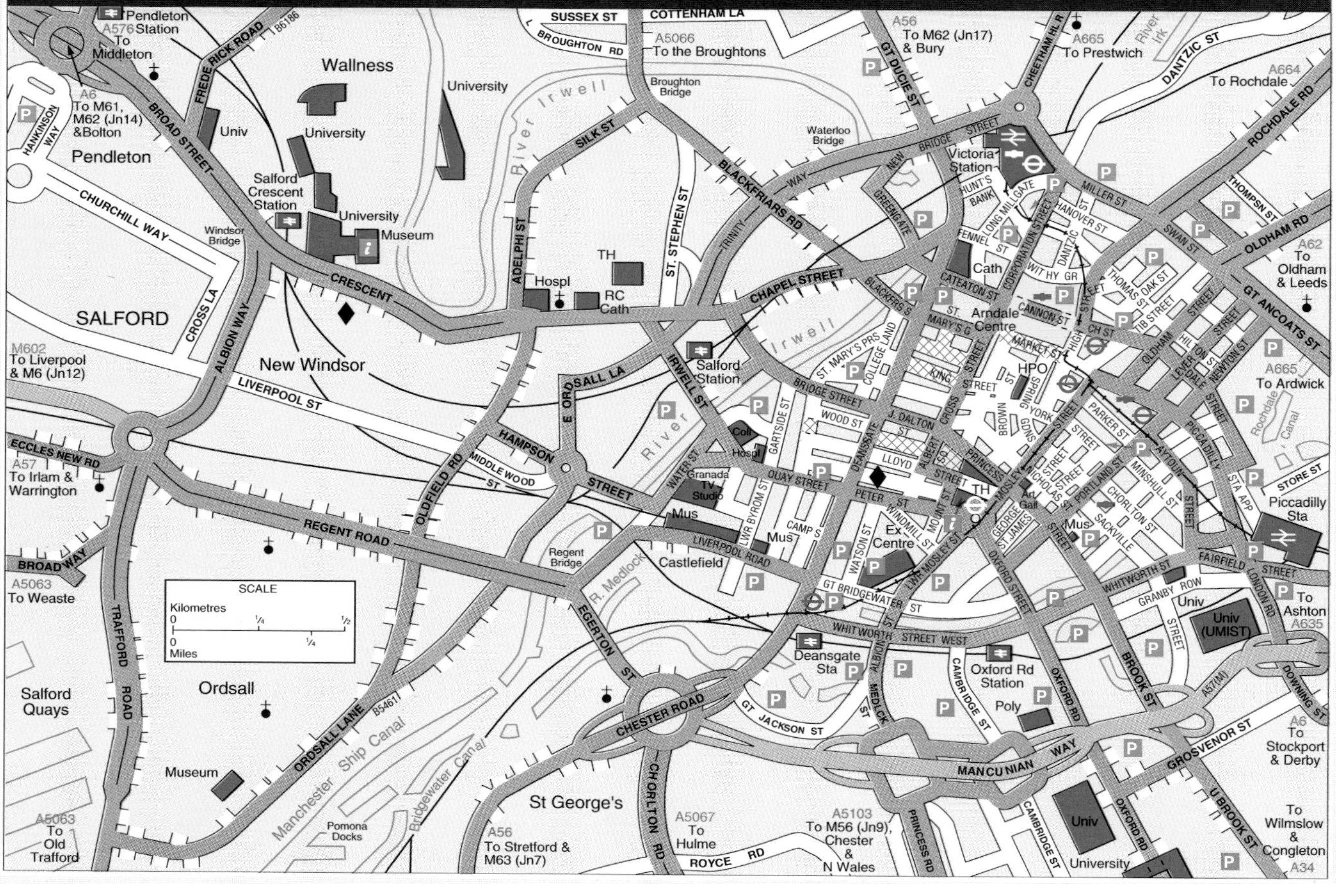

Milton Keynes

Oxford

Newcastle

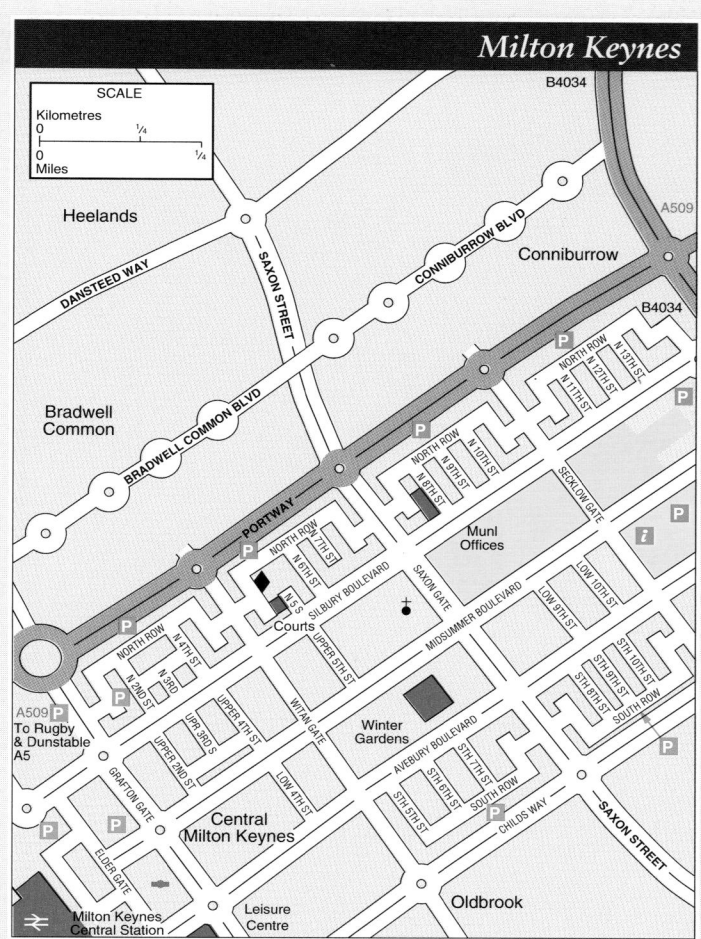

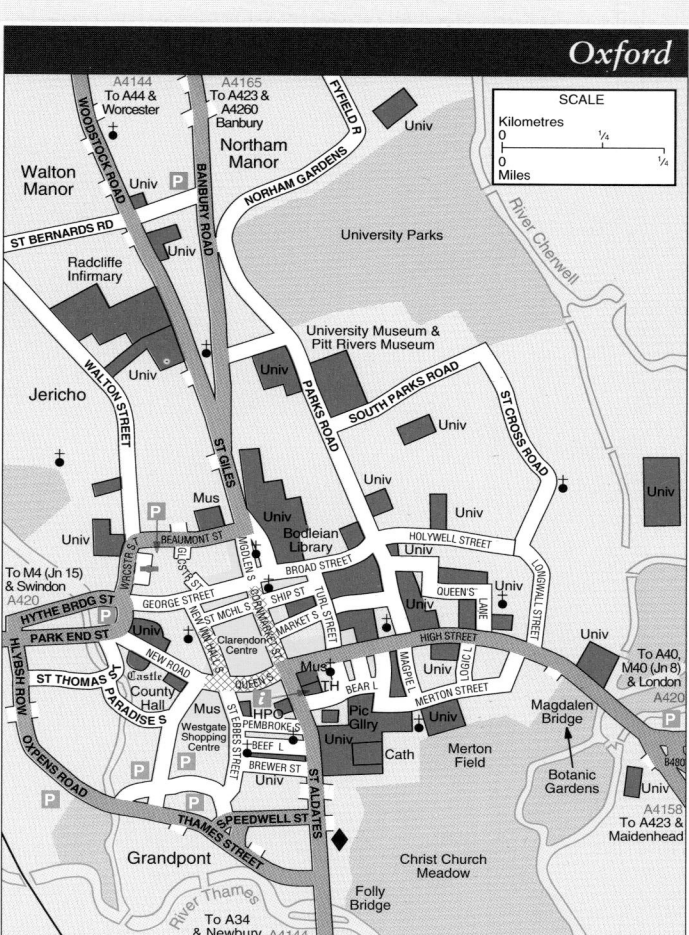

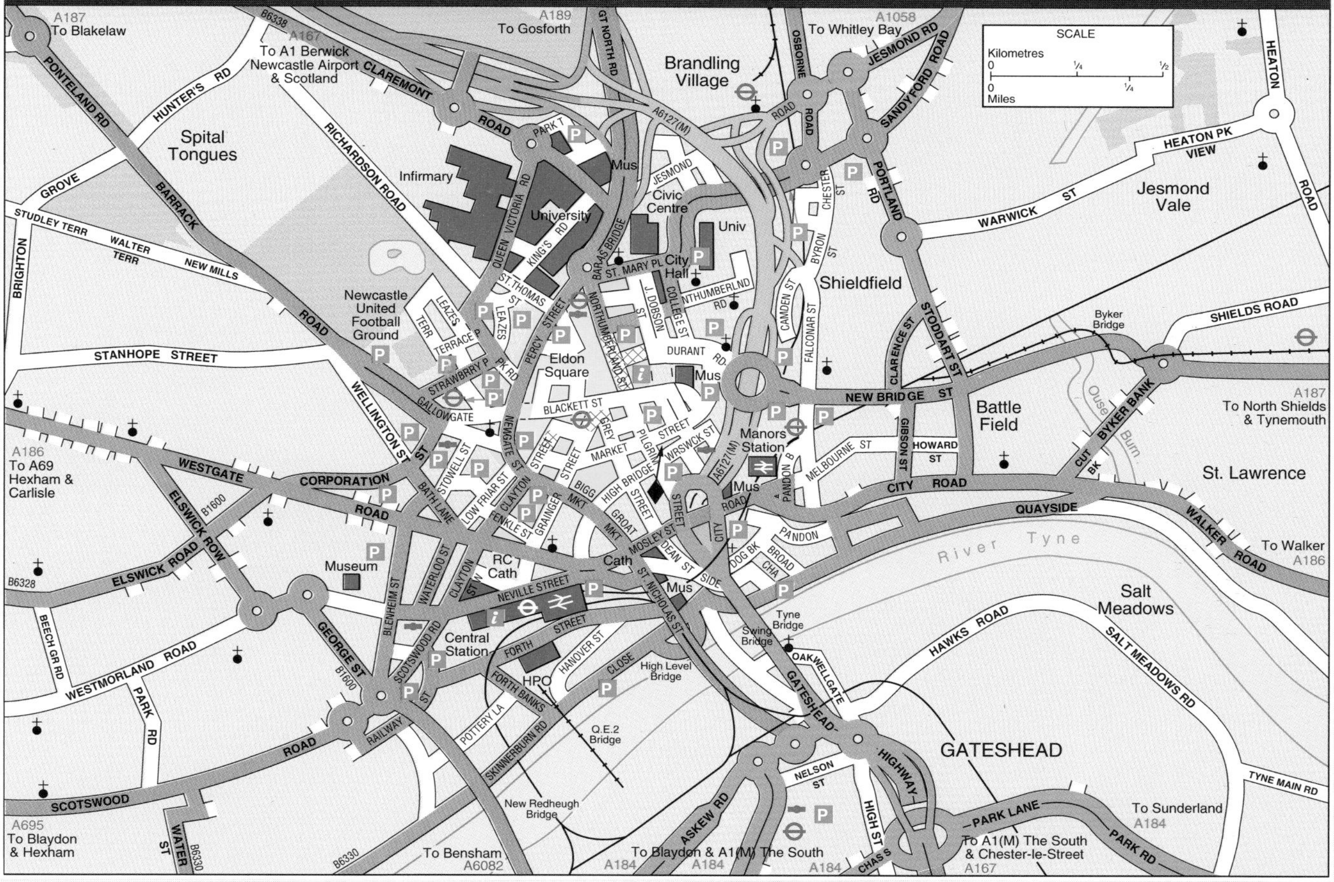

Norwich

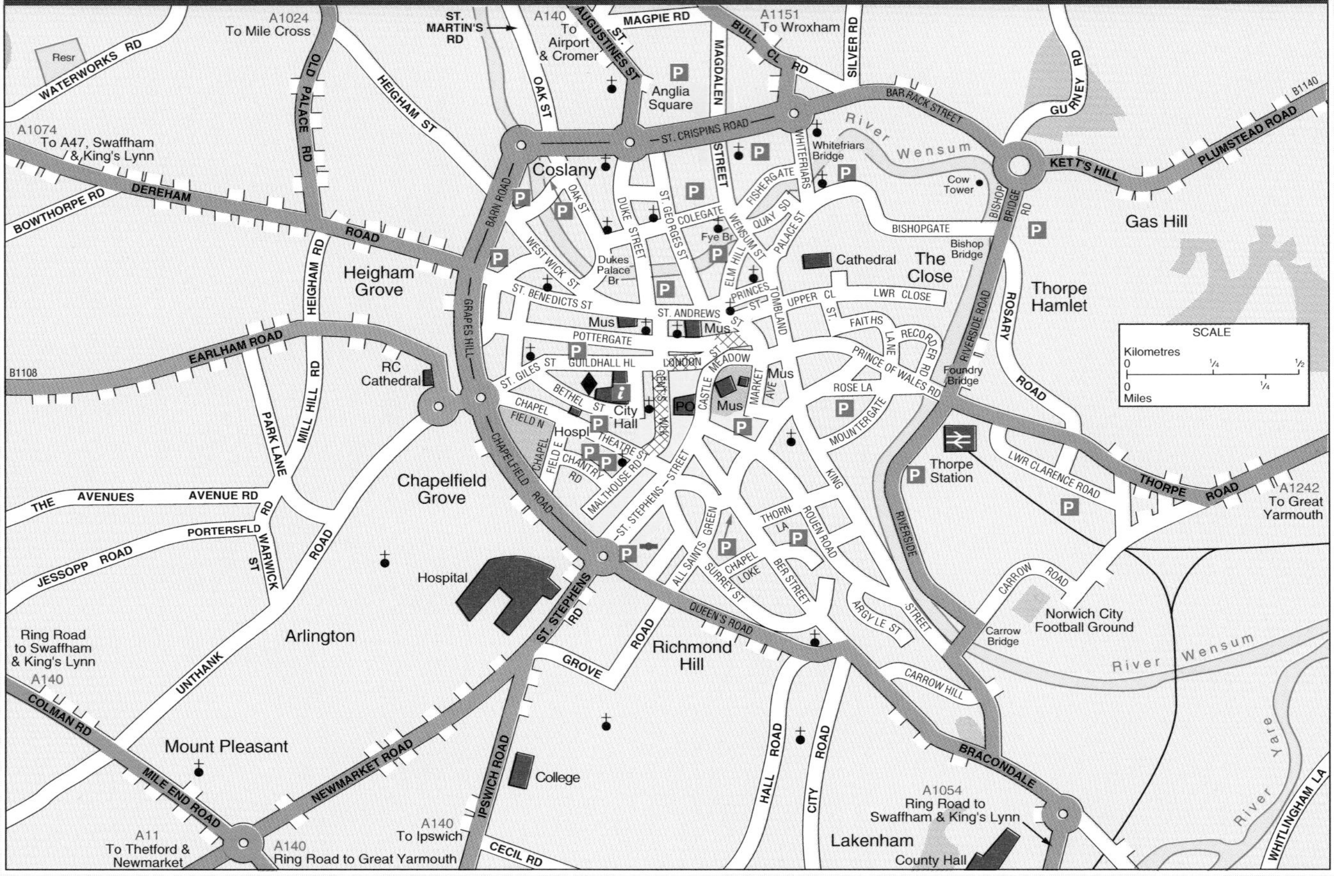

WATERWORKS RD   Resr   A1024 To Mile Cross   ST. MARTIN'S RD   A140 To Airport & Cromer   MAGPIE RD   BULL CL RD   SILVER RD   A1151 To Wroxham

A1074 To A47, Swaffham & King's Lynn   OLD PALACE RD   HEIGHAM ST   ST. AUGUSTINE'S ST   OAK ST   MAGDALEN ST   BARRACK STREET   GURNEY RD   B1140   PLUMSTEAD ROAD

Anglia Square   River Wensum   KETT'S HILL

BOWTHORPE RD   DEREHAM ROAD   HEIGHAM RD   BARN ROAD   ST. CRISPINS ROAD   Coslany   Whitefriars Bridge   Cow Tower   Gas Hill

Heigham Grove   GRAPES HILL   WESTWICK ST   OAK ST   DUKE STREET   ST GEORGES ST   COLEGATE   WENSUM ST   FISHERGATE   QUAY ST   PALACE ST   BISHOPGATE   Bishop Bridge   Thorpe Hamlet

Dukes Palace Br   Fye Br   ELM HILL   Cathedral   The Close   LWR CLOSE   ROSARY ROAD

EARLHAM ROAD   B1108   MILL HILL RD   HEIGHAM RD   RC Cathedral   ST BENEDICTS ST   Mus   POTTERGATE   ST. ANDREWS   PRINCES   TOMBLAND   UPPER CL   FAITHS LANE   RECORDER

CHAPEL FIELD   ST GILES ST   BETHEL ST   GUILDHALL HL   LONDON ST   Mus   City Hall   PO   Mus   RISERSIDE   PRINCE OF WALES RD   Foundry Bridge

PARK LANE   PORTERSFLD RD   WARWICK ST   Hospl   CHANTRY RD   THEATRE   ROSE LA   Mus   MOUNTERGATE   LWR CLARENCE ROAD   THORPE ROAD

THE AVENUES   AVENUE RD   Chapelfield Grove   CHAPELFIELD RD   MALTHOUSE RD   ST STEPHENS ST   Thorpe Station   A1242 To Great Yarmouth

JESSOPP ROAD   Hospital   THORN LA   ROUEN ROAD   KING STREET   CARROW ROAD

Ring Road to Swaffham & King's Lynn   A140   Arlington   ST STEPHENS RD   GROVE ROAD   Richmond Hill   QUEEN'S ROAD   ALL SAINTS GREEN   SURREY ST   BER STREET   ARGYLE ST   RIVERSIDE   Norwich City Football Ground   Carrow Bridge   River Wensum

COLMAN RD   Mount Pleasant   HALL ROAD   CITY ROAD   CARROW HILL   BRACONDALE   River Yare

A11 To Thetford & Newmarket   MILE END ROAD   NEWMARKET ROAD   College   IPSWICH ROAD   A140 To Ipswich   CECIL RD   A140 Ring Road to Great Yarmouth   A1054 Ring Road to Swaffham & King's Lynn   Lakenham   County Hall   WHITLINGHAM LA

SCALE   Kilometres 0 ¼ ½   Miles 0 ¼

Nottingham

A6130   To Eastwood   A610   FOREST ROAD W   WAVERLEY ST   A60 To Mansfield & Worksop   B684   WOODBORO RD   St. Ann's

HARTLEY RD   RADFORD BOULEVARD   ST. PETERS ST   ALFRETON ROAD   FOREST ROAD   Radford   PEEL ST   GILL ST   DRYDEN ST   N SHERWOOD RD   MANSFIELD RD   WOODBORO RD   ST. ANN'S WELL ROAD

CROMWELL STREET   HAMPDEN ST   GOLDSMITH ST   SHAKESPEARE STREET   Trent Univ   Victoria Centre   CARLTON ROAD

WOLLATON ROAD   ILKESTON ROAD   CLARENDON STREET   CHAUCER ST   TALBOT ST   WOLLATON STREET   TH   BURTON ST   S SHERWOOD   BATH ST   HPO

A609 To Ilkeston & Belper   CANNING CIR   DERBY ROAD   U PARLIAMENT ST   LOWER PARLIAMENT ST   MANNERS STREET

RC Cath   REGENT   OXFORD   MAID MARIAN WAY   PARK ROW   ROPEWALK   LONG ROW   PELHM S   CARLTN   GOOSE G   WOOLPCK LA   BARKER GT

The Park   Hospl   R. Hood Centre   S PARADE   WARSER G   FRIAR   FLETCHER GT   PETER G   BRIDLESMITH GT   BELWR   Ice Stad   FISHR

New Lenton   LENTON BOULEVARD   Standard Hill   Hospital   LENTON RD   Mus   HOUNDS G   CASTLE GT   ST MARYS GT   HIGH PAVEMENT   PENNYFOOT ST

Castle   Mus   PEVERIL D   CASTLE RD   Museum   Mus   CLIFF RD   Lace Market   MIDDLE HILL   Broad Marsh Centre   COLLIN ST

DERBY ROAD   Old Lenton   CASTLE BOULEVARD   CANAL STREET   Canal Museum   STATION ST   Nottingham Station   A612 To Grantham

Nottingham Canal   CASTLE BRIDGE   CASTLE ROAD   WILFORD ROAD   QUEEN'S BRIDGE   QUEEN'S ROAD   LONDON ROAD

ABBEY BRIDGE   Castle Marina   LENTON LANE   WATERWAY ST W   CATTLE MKT RD   COUNTY ROAD   Notts County Football Ground   A6011 To A52 Nottingham Airport & Grantham

CLIFTON BOULEVARD   Hospital   ABBEY ST   Meadows   BAY BRIDGE   River Trent   Nottm Forest Football Ground   Trent Bridge   County Cricket Gd

A52 To Stapleford & Derby   Dunkirk   Nottingham University   A6005 To Beeston   BEESTON R   A52 To Grantham & A606 Melton Mowbray   A453 To East Midlands Airport & M1 (Jn24) The South   A60 To West Bridgford & Loughborough

SCALE   Kilometres 0 ¼ ½   Miles 0 ¼

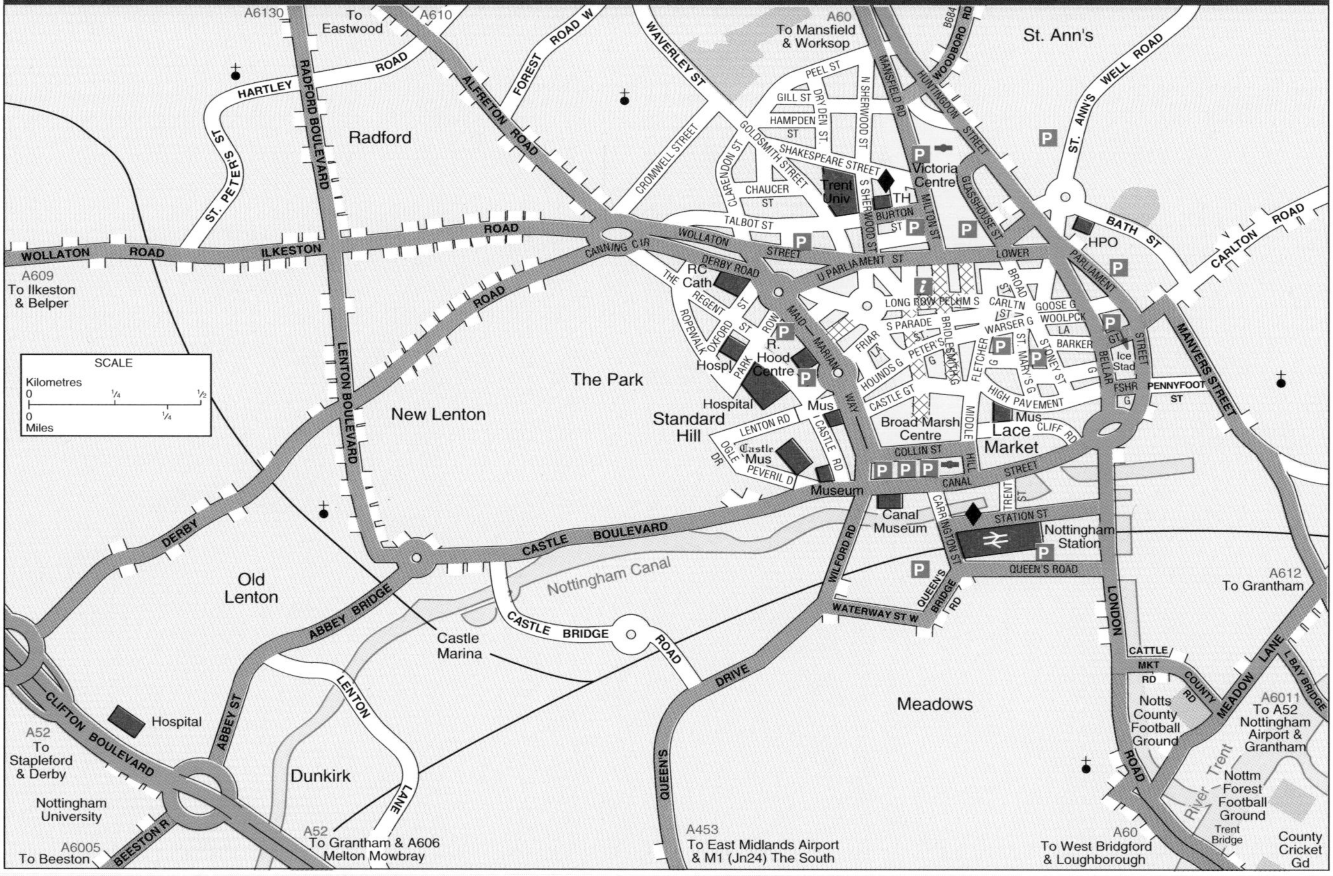

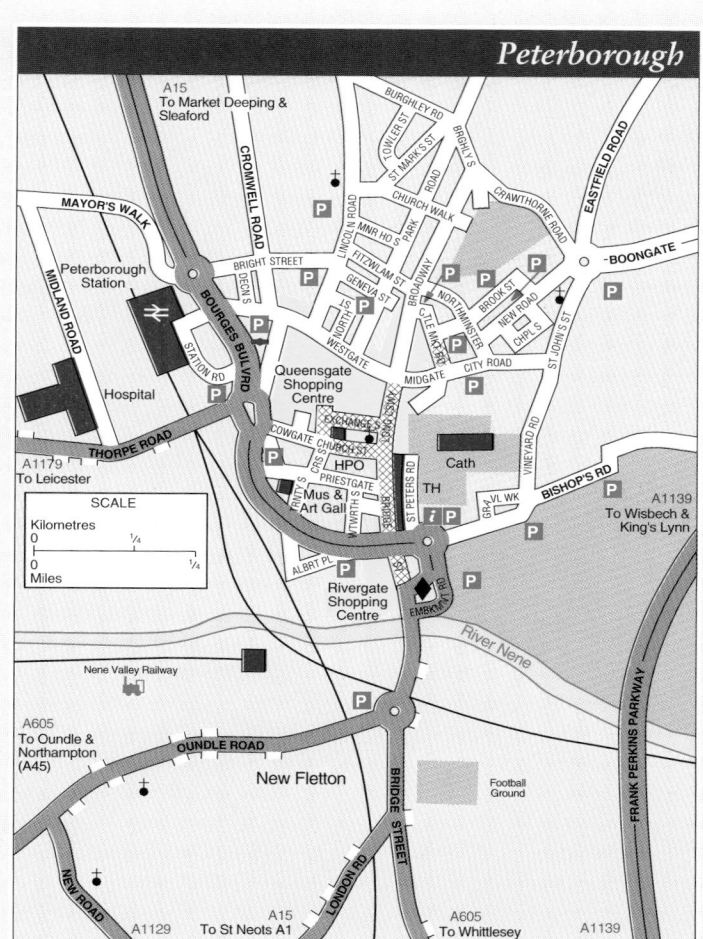

Peterborough

A15 To Market Deeping & Sleaford

MAYOR'S WALK

CROMWELL ROAD

BURGHLEY RD

TOWLER ST

ST MARK'S ST

BRIGHT'S RD

CHURCH WALK

CRAWTHORNE ROAD

EASTFIELD ROAD

BOONGATE

Peterborough Station

MIDLAND ROAD

BOURGES BULVRD

STATION RD

BRIGHT STREET

LINCOLN ROAD

MNR HO S

FITZWLM ST

GENEVA ST

PARK ROAD

NORTHMINSTER

BROADWAY

NEW ROAD

BROOK ST

ST JOHN'S ST

CITY ROAD

BISHOP'S RD

Hospital

Queensgate Shopping Centre

WESTGATE

COWGATE

CHURCH ST

EXCHANGE ST

MIDGATE

CHAPEL ST

Cath

HPO

TH

A1179 To Leicester

THORPE ROAD

SCALE
Kilometres
0   ¼
0   ¼
Miles

PRIESTGATE

ST PETERS RD

Mus & Art Gall

ALBRT PL

Rivergate Shopping Centre

EMBKMNT RD

A1139 To Wisbech & King's Lynn

River Nene

Nene Valley Railway

A605 To Oundle & Northampton (A45)

OUNDLE ROAD

New Fletton

BRIDGE STREET

LONDON ROAD

Football Ground

FRANK PERKINS PARKWAY

NEW ROAD

A1129

A15 To St Neots A1

A605 To Whittlesey

A1139

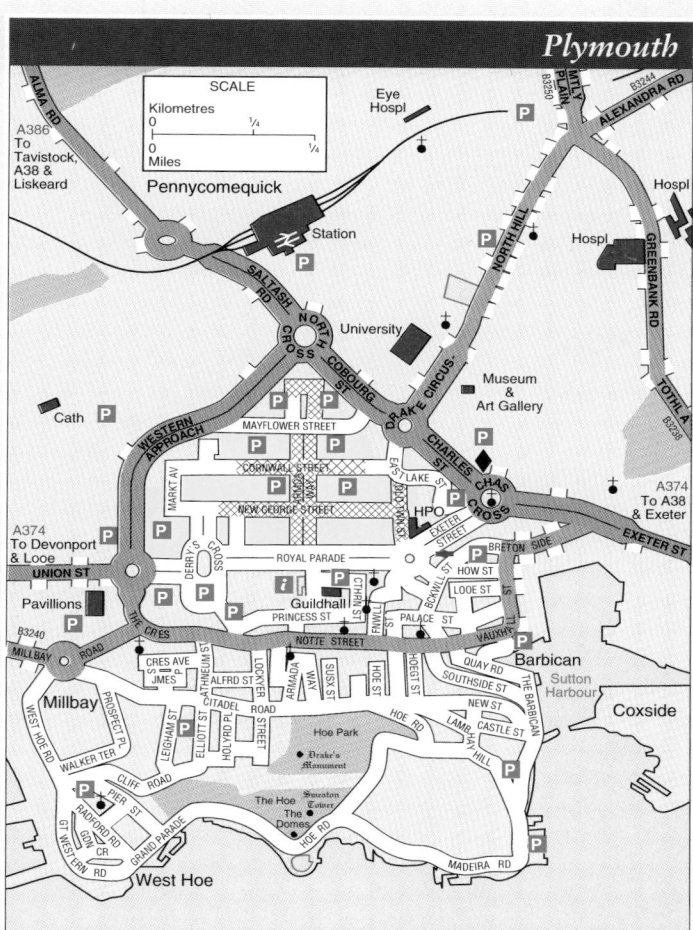

Plymouth

SCALE
Kilometres
0   ¼
0   ¼
Miles

ALMA RD

MTH PLAIN

B3250

ALEXANDRA RD

B3244

A386 To Tavistock, A38 & Liskeard

Eye Hospl

Pennycomequick

Station

SALTASH RD

NORTH CROSS

NORTH HILL

GREENBANK RD

Hospl

Hospl

University

COBURG ST

DRAKE CIRCUS

CHARLES ST

Museum & Art Gallery

TOTHL A

Cath

WESTERN APPROACH

Mayflower Street

Cornwall Street

EAST
LAKE ST

CHAS CROSS

A374 To A38 & Exeter

MARKET AV

New George Street

HPO

EXETER ST

A374 To Devonport & Looe

UNION ST

DERRY'S CROSS

Royal Parade

EXETER STREET

Guildhall

HOW ST

LOOE ST

BRETON SIDE

Pavilions

THE CRES

Princess St

NOTTE STREET

PALACE ST

VAUXHALL ST

QUAY RD

Barbican

B3240

MILLBAY ROAD

CRES AVE

JAMES

ALFRD ST

ARMADA WAY

LOCKER ST

SUSX ST

HOE ST

SOUTHSIDE ST

THE BARBICAN

NEW ST

CASTLE ST

Sutton Harbour

Coxside

Millbay

WEST HOE RD

PROSPECT PL

LEIGHAM ST

CITADEL ROAD

ELLIOTT ST

HOLYRD PL

Hoe Park

Drake's Monument

LAMBHAY HILL

HOE RD

WALKER TER

CLIFF ROAD

PIER ST

GRAND PARADE

The Hoe The Domes

Smeaton Tower

RADFORD RD

GT WESTERN RD

MADEIRA RD

West Hoe

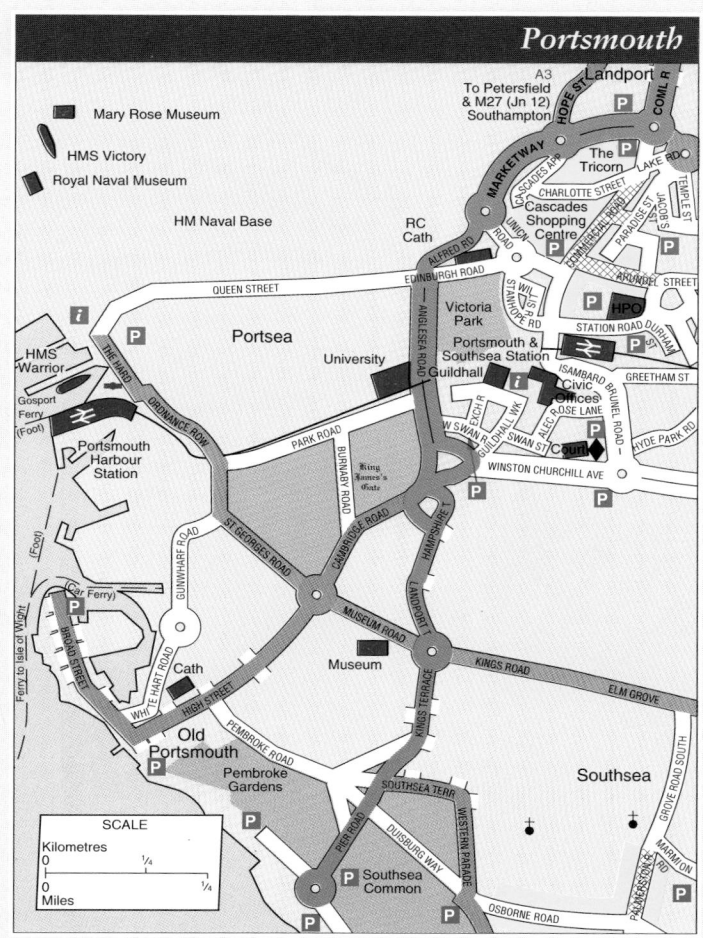

Portsmouth

Mary Rose Museum

HMS Victory

Royal Naval Museum

HM Naval Base

A3 To Petersfield & M27 (Jn 12) Southampton

Landport

HOPE ST

COML R

MARKETWAY

The Tricorn

CASCADES APP

LAKE RD

CHARLOTTE STREET

Cascades Shopping Centre

TEMPLE ST

RC Cath

ALFRED RD

UNION RD

COMMERCIAL RD

PARADISE ST

QUEEN STREET

EDINBURGH ROAD

ARUNDEL STREET

HMS Warrior

Gosport Ferry (Foot)

THE HARD

ANGLESEA ROAD

Victoria Park

Portsea

University

STANHOPE RD

WILTS RD

STATION ROAD

DURHAM

HPO

GREETHAM ST

ORDNANCE ROW

Guildhall

GUILDHALL WK

Portsmouth & Southsea Station

Isambard Brunel ROSE LANE

Civic Offices

Portsmouth Harbour Station

PARK ROAD

BURNABY ROAD

NEW SWAN RD

SWAN ST

Court

HYDE PARK RD

King James's Gate

WINSTON CHURCHILL AVE

GUNWHARF ROAD

ST GEORGES ROAD

CAMBRIDGE ROAD

HAMPSHIRE TCE

LANDPORT

MUSEUM ROAD

KINGS ROAD

ELM GROVE

Ferry to Isle of Wight (Foot)

(Car Ferry)

BROAD STREET

WHTE HART ROAD

HIGH STREET

Cath

Museum

Old Portsmouth

Pembroke Gardens

KINGS TERRACE

PEMBROKE ROAD

SOUTHSEA TERR

Southsea

SCALE
Kilometres
0   ¼
0   ¼
Miles

PIER ROAD

DUISBURG WAY

WESTERN PARADE

Southsea Common

OSBORNE ROAD

GROVE ROAD SOUTH

MARMON

PADDINGTON S

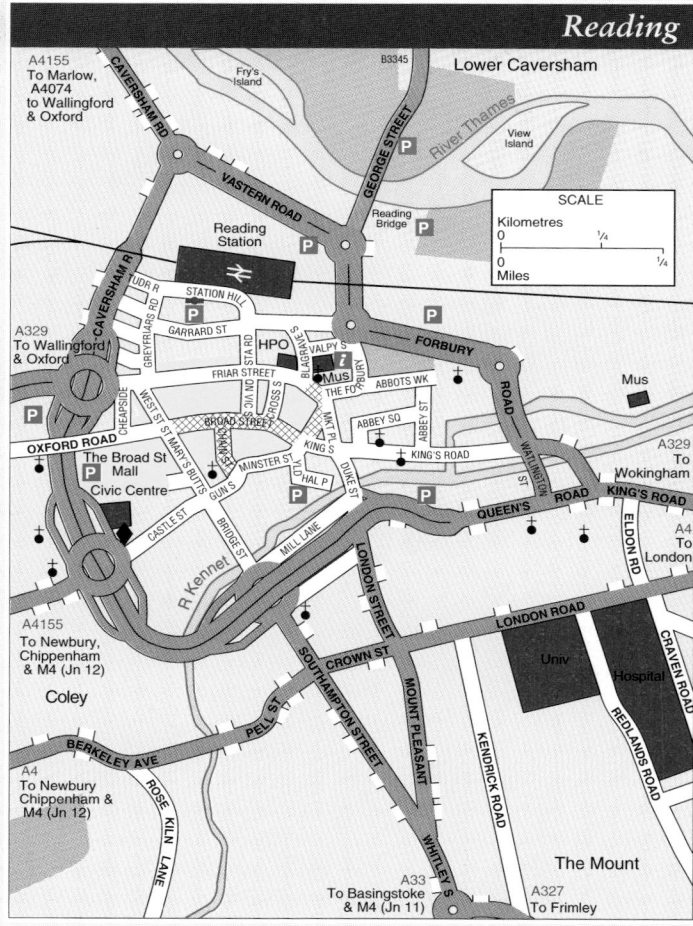

Reading

A4155 To Marlow, A4074 to Wallingford & Oxford

CAVERSHAM RD

Fry's Island

B3345

Lower Caversham

River Thames

GEORGE STREET

View Island

VASTERN ROAD

Reading Station

Reading Bridge

SCALE
Kilometres
0   ¼
0   ¼
Miles

CAVERSHAM R

TUDR R

STATION HILL

STATION RD

GARRARD ST

HPO

VALPY S

FORBURY

A329 To Wallingford & Oxford

GREYFRIARS RD

BLAGRAVE ST

WEST ST

CROSS ST

FRIAR STREET

Mus

ABBOTS WK

Mus

THE FORBURY

OXFORD ROAD

CHEAPSIDE

WEST ST

ST MARY'S BUTTS

MINSTER ST

Broad Street

GUN ST

ABBEY SQ

ABBEY ST

King's Road

A329 To Wokingham

The Broad St Mall

Civic Centre

CASTLE ST

BRIDGE ST

YLD HALL PL

DUKE ST

MKT PL

QUEEN'S ROAD

WATLINGTON ROAD

KING'S ROAD

A4 To London

ELDON RD

R Kennet

A4155 To Newbury, Chippenham & M4 (Jn 12)

Coley

MILL LANE

LONDON STREET

SOUTHAMPTON ST

CROWN ST

LONDON ROAD

MOUNT PLEASANT

Univ

Hospital

CRAVEN ROAD

PELL ST

BERKELEY AVE

A4 To Newbury Chippenham & M4 (Jn 12)

ROSE KILN LANE

WHITLEY ST

KENDRICK RD

REDLANDS ROAD

The Mount

A33 To Basingstoke & M4 (Jn 11)

A327 To Frimley

Salisbury

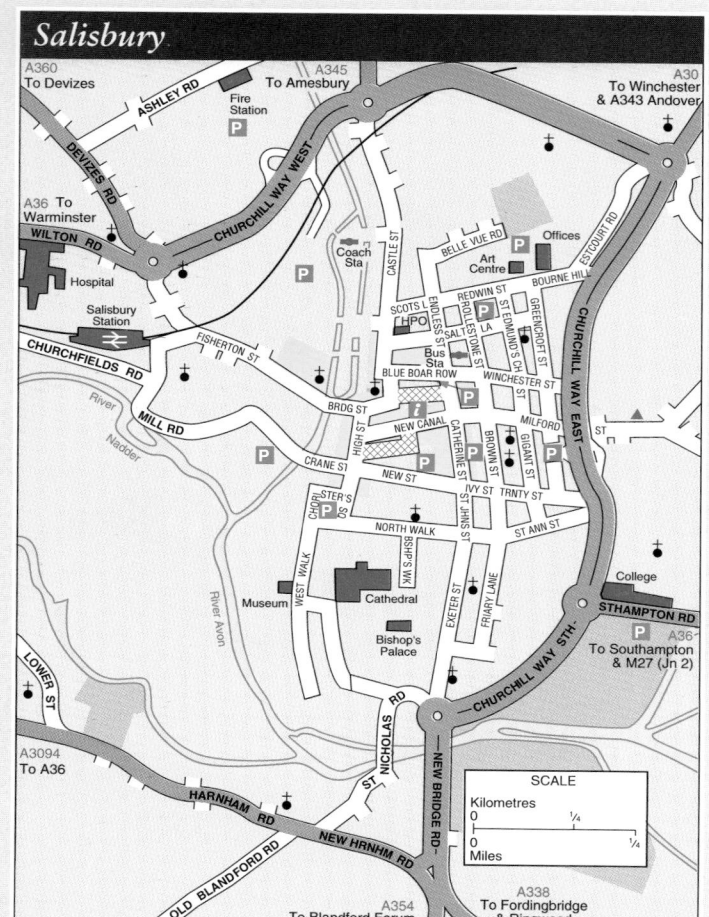

Shrewsbury

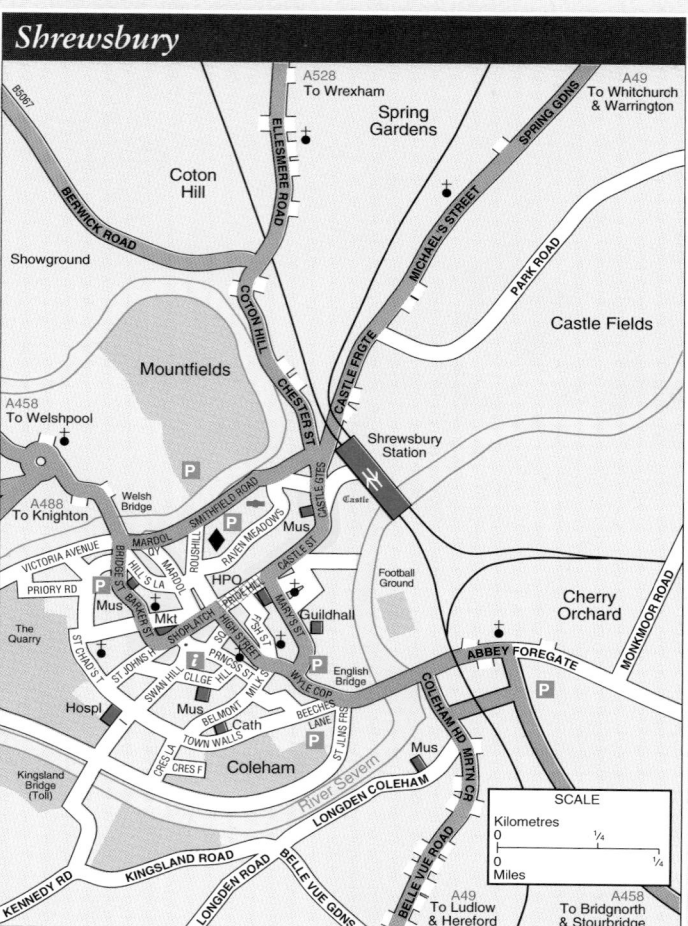

Sheffield

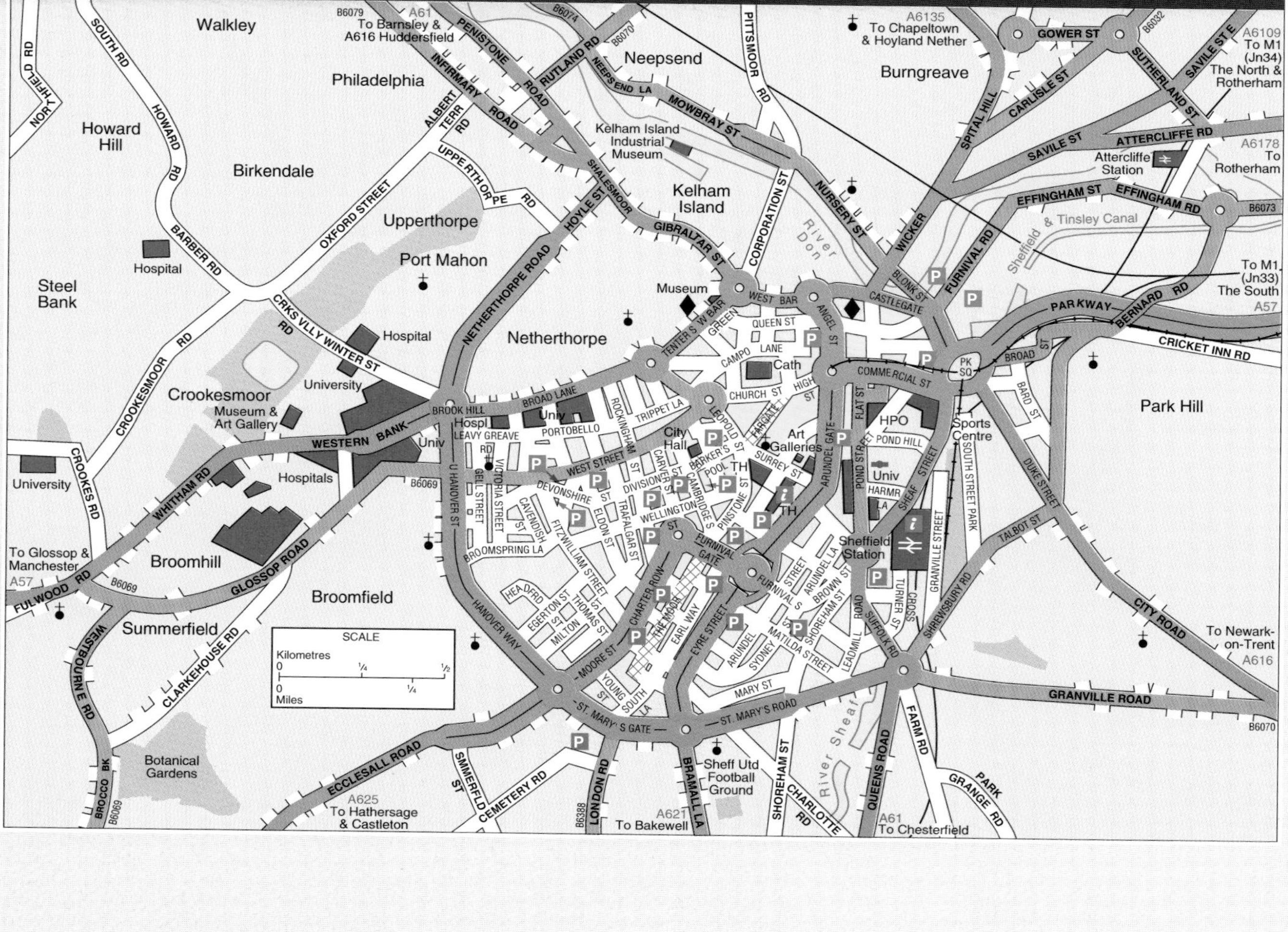

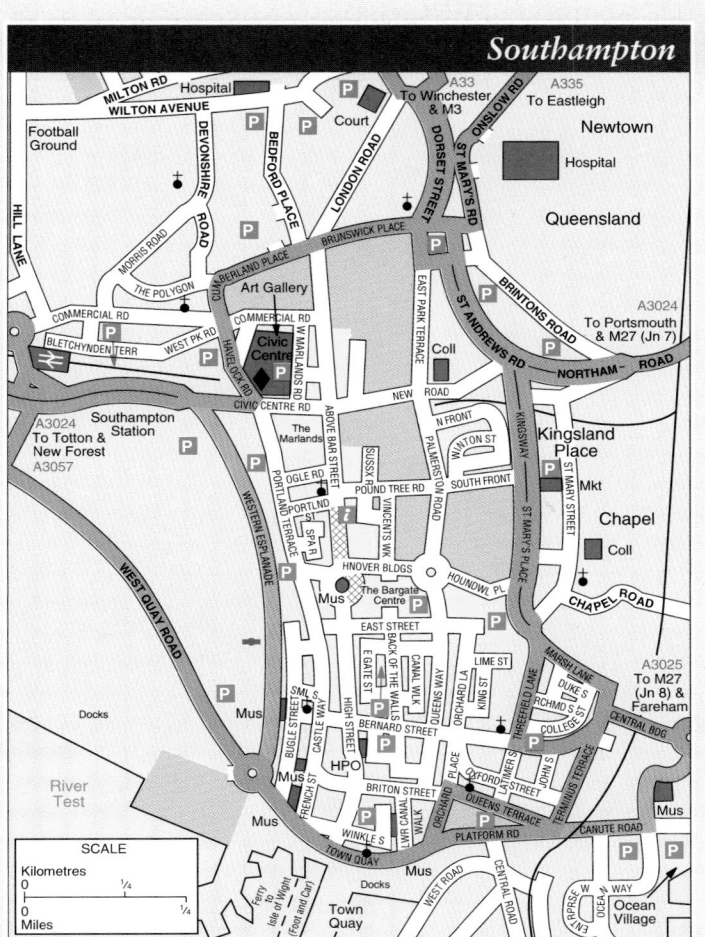

Southampton

Milton Rd · Wilton Avenue · Hospital · Court · Onslow Rd · A33 To Winchester & M3 · A335 To Eastleigh · Newtown · Hospital · Queensland · Morris Road · Devonshire Road · Bedford Place · London Road · Dorset Street · St Mary's Rd · Brunswick Place · Football Ground · Hill Lane · The Polygon · Cumberland Place · Art Gallery · Commercial Rd · St Andrews Rd · Brintons Road · Northam Road · A3024 To Portsmouth & M27 (Jn 7) · East Park Terrace · Coll · Commercial Rd · West Pk Rd · Bletchynden Terr · Civic Centre · Civic Centre Rd · Southampton Station · A3024 To Totton & New Forest · A3057 · The Marlands · Sussex · Ogle Rd · Portland Terrace · Portland Rd · Spar · Pound Tree Rd · Vincents Walk · New Road · N Front · Winton St · Kingsway · St Mary Street · Kingsland Place · Mkt · Chapel · Coll · West Quay Road · Western Esplanade · Above Bar Street · Hnover Bldgs · The Bargate Centre · Mus · East Street · Back of the Walls · Canal Walk · Lime St · Marsh Lane · Chapel Road · A3025 (Jn 8) & Fareham · Queens Way · Orchard La · Duke S · Richmd S St · College St · Central Bog · Docks · Sml S · Bugle Street · Castle Way · High Street · Bernard Street · King Street · Threefield Lane · HPO · Mus · River Test · French St · Orchard Place · Latimer St · John S · Oxford St · Terminus Terrace · Mus · Briton Street · Wr Canal Walk · Queens Terrace · Platform Rd · Winkle S · Town Quay · Mus · Docks · West Road · Central Road · Ferry to Isle of Wight (Foot and Car) · Enterprise W · Ocean Way · Ocean Village · Town Quay · Express W

SCALE
Kilometres 0 — ¼
Miles 0 — ¼

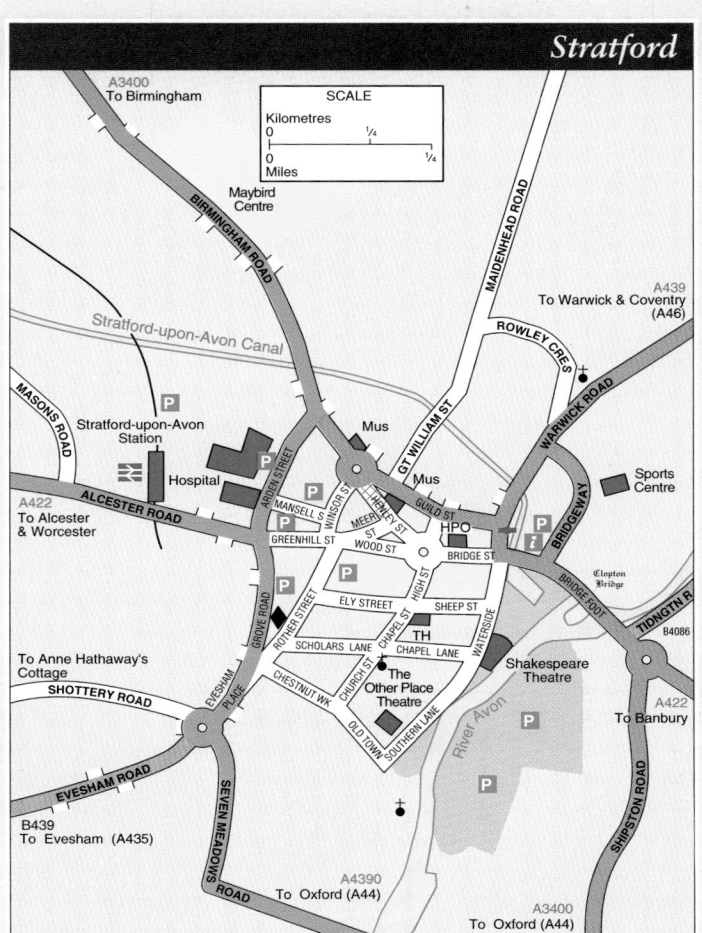

Stratford

A3400 To Birmingham · Birmingham Road · Maybird Centre · Maidenhead Road · Stratford-upon-Avon Canal · Masons Road · Rowley Cres · Warwick Road · A439 To Warwick & Coventry (A46) · Stratford-upon-Avon Station · Hospital · Mus · Mus · Gt William St · Build St · Henley St · Sports Centre · Bridgeway · Clopton Bridge · A422 To Alcester & Worcester · Alcester Road · Mansell St · Windsor St · Meer St · Wood St · Greenhill St · High St · HPO · Bridge St · Tidngtn R · B4086 · Arden Street · Rother Street · Ely Street · Chapel St · Sheep St · Bridge Foot · To Anne Hathaway's Cottage · Scholars Lane · Church St · Chapel Lane · Waterside · Shakespeare Theatre · Shottery Road · Evesham Place · Chestnut Wk · Grove Road · TH · The Other Place Theatre · Old Town · Southern Lane · River Avon · A422 To Banbury · Evesham Road · Seven Meadows Road · B439 To Evesham (A435) · A4390 To Oxford (A44) · A3400 To Oxford (A44)

SCALE
Kilometres 0 — ¼
Miles 0 — ¼

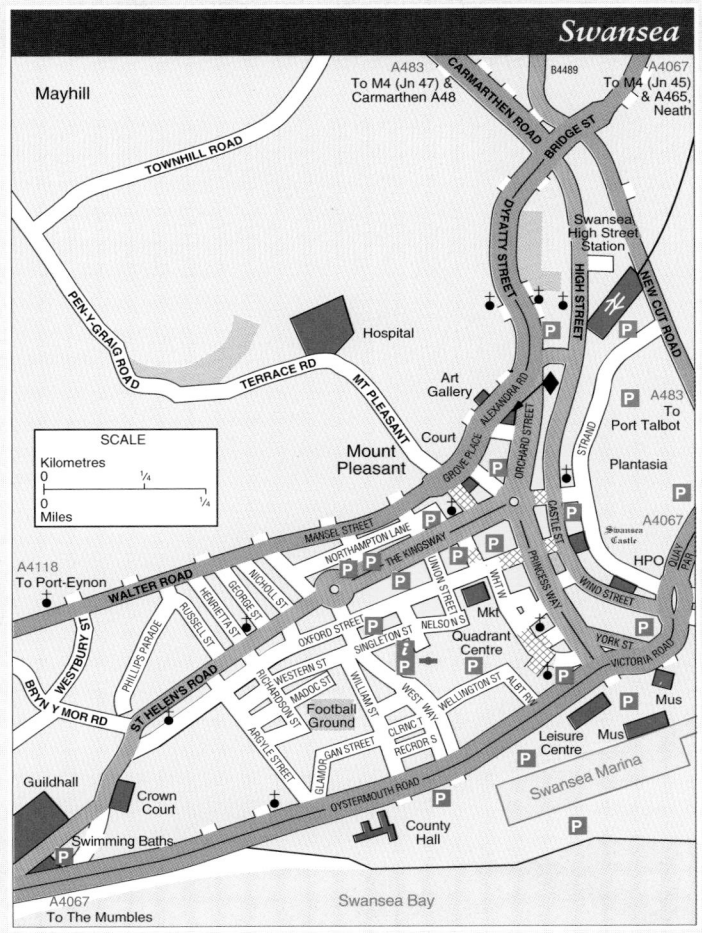

Swansea

Mayhill · A483 To M4 (Jn 47) & Carmarthen A48 · Carmarthen Road · B4489 · Bridge St · A4067 To M4 (Jn 45) & A465, Neath · Townhill Road · D'Fatty Street · High Street · Swansea High Street Station · New Cut Road · Pen-y-Graig Road · Terrace Rd · Hospital · Mt Pleasant · Art Gallery · Court · Strand · A483 To Port Talbot · Mount Pleasant · Plantasia · Mansel Street · Northampton Lane · The Kingsway · Grove Place · Alexandra Rd · Orchard Street · Castle St · Swansea Castle · A4067 · HPO · Quay Park · A4118 To Port-Eynon · Walter Road · Nicholl St · George St · London Road · Whit W · Princess Way · Wind Street · Westbury St · Phillips Parade · Russell St · Henrietta St · Oxford Street · Nelson S · Singleton St · York St · Victoria Road · Bryn y Mor Rd · St Helen's Road · Western St · Madoc S · William St · West Way · Wellington St · Albt St · Quadrant Centre · Mus · Richardson S · Football Ground · Clrnc S · Recrda S · Leisure Centre · Mus · Glamor Street · Gunter Street · Oystermouth Road · Argyle Street · Guildhall · Crown Court · Swimming Baths · County Hall · Swansea Marina · A4067 To The Mumbles · Swansea Bay

SCALE
Kilometres 0 — ¼
Miles 0 — ¼

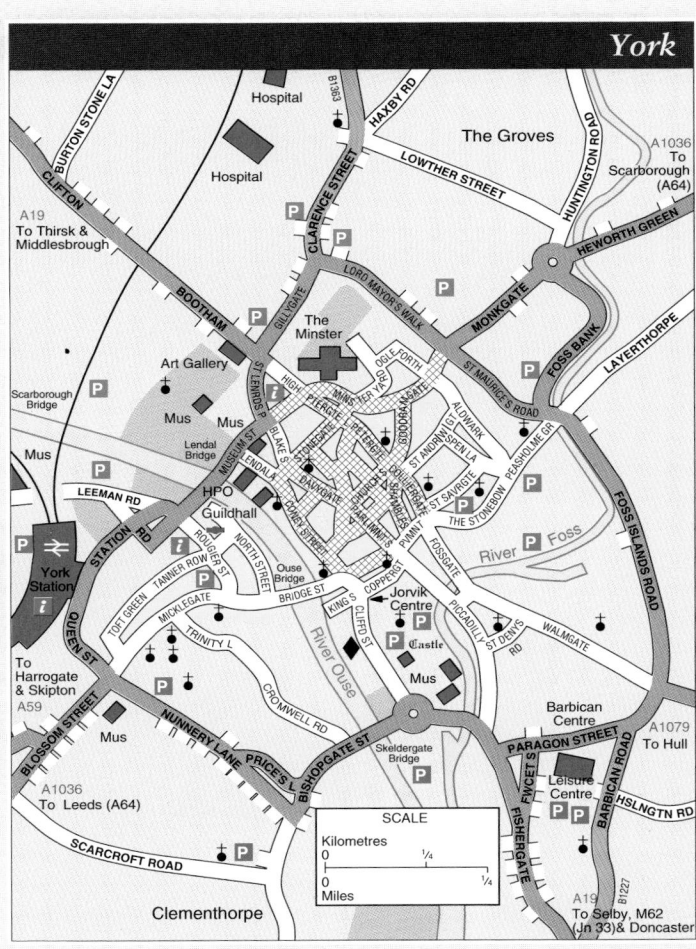

York

Burton Stone La · B1363 · Haxby Rd · Hospital · The Groves · Huntington Road · A1036 To Scarborough (A64) · Hospital · Clifton · Lowther Street · Clarence Street · Heworth Green · A19 To Thirsk & Middlesbrough · Bootham · Lord Mayor's Walk · Monkgate · Foss Bank · Layerthorpe · Gillygate · The Minster · Ogleforth · St Maurice's Rd · Art Gallery · St Leonards · Mus · Mus · Scarborough Bridge · Lendal Bridge · Museum St · Aldwark · Peasholme Gr · Mus · HPO · Guildhall · Davygate · St Andrewsgate · St Saviourgate · Leeman Rd · The Stonebow · Fossgate · River Foss · York Station · Station Rd · Ouse Bridge · Bridge St · King's Copmanthorpe · Jorvik Centre · Piccadilly · Foss Islands Road · To Harrogate & Skipton · Micklegate · Trinity L · Castle · Walmgate · Queen St · River Ouse · Clifford St · Mus · A59 · Cromwell Rd · Barbican Centre · A1079 To Hull · Blossom Street · Nunnery Lane · Price's L · Bishopgate St · Skeldergate Bridge · Paragon Street · Leisure Centre · Fawcet S · Hslngtn Rd · Barbican Rd · A1036 To Leeds (A64) · Fishergate · Scarcroft Road · Clementhorpe · A19 To Selby, M62 (Jn 33) & Doncaster · B1227

SCALE
Kilometres 0 — ¼
Miles 0 — ¼

AIRPORTS

Aberdeen

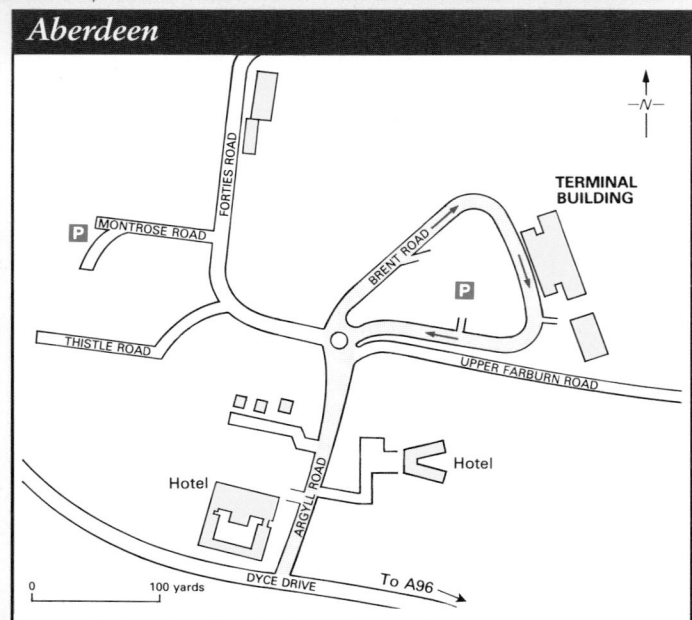

FORTIES ROAD
MONTROSE ROAD
BRENT ROAD
TERMINAL BUILDING
THISTLE ROAD
UPPER FARBURN ROAD
ARGYLL ROAD
Hotel
Hotel
DYCE DRIVE
To A96
0   100 yards

Birmingham International

0   500   1000 ft
(Multistorey)
(Multistorey)
Terminal Building
Hotel
National Exhibition Centre
Eurohub
Rail Link (Elevated)
Bickenhill Lane
Birmingham International Airport
Birmingham International Station
(Long Stay)
(Long Stay)
Fuel Store
Airport Way
To A45
To A45

Stansted

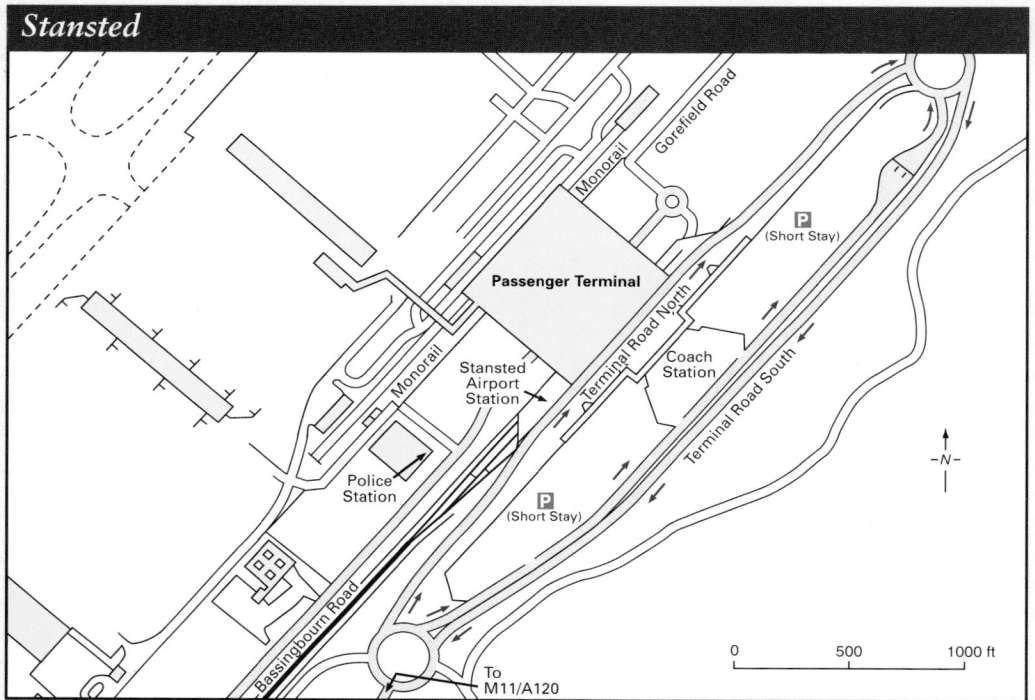

Gorefield Road
Monorail
P (Short Stay)
Passenger Terminal
Terminal Road North
Monorail
Stansted Airport Station
Coach Station
Terminal Road South
Police Station
P (Short Stay)
Bassingbourn Road
To M11/A120
0   500   1000 ft

Edinburgh

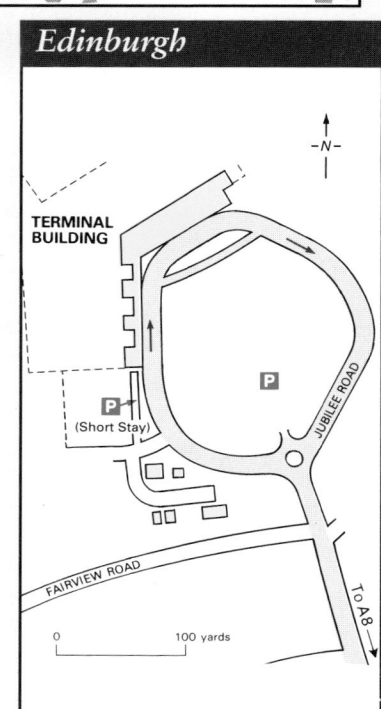

TERMINAL BUILDING
P
P (Short Stay)
JUBILEE ROAD
FAIRVIEW ROAD
To A8
0   100 yards

East Midlands

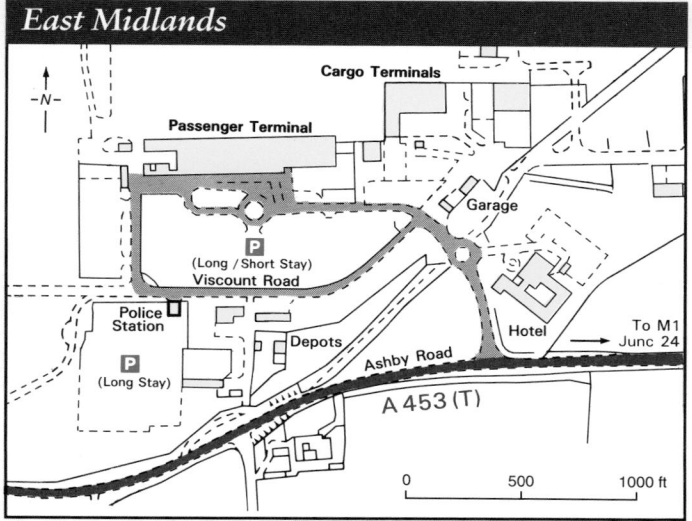

Cargo Terminals
Passenger Terminal
Garage
(Long / Short Stay)
Viscount Road
Police Station
Depots
Hotel
To M1 Junc 24
P (Long Stay)
Ashby Road
A 453 (T)
0   500   1000 ft

Glasgow

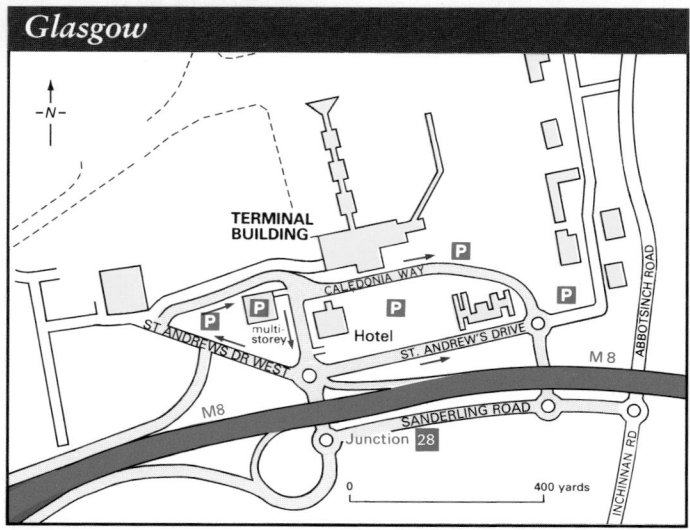

TERMINAL BUILDING
P
CALEDONIA WAY
P
P
multi-storey
Hotel
ST. ANDREWS DR WEST
ST. ANDREW'S DRIVE
M 8
ABBOTSINCH ROAD
M8
SANDERLING ROAD
INCHINNAN RD.
Junction 28
0   400 yards

Gatwick

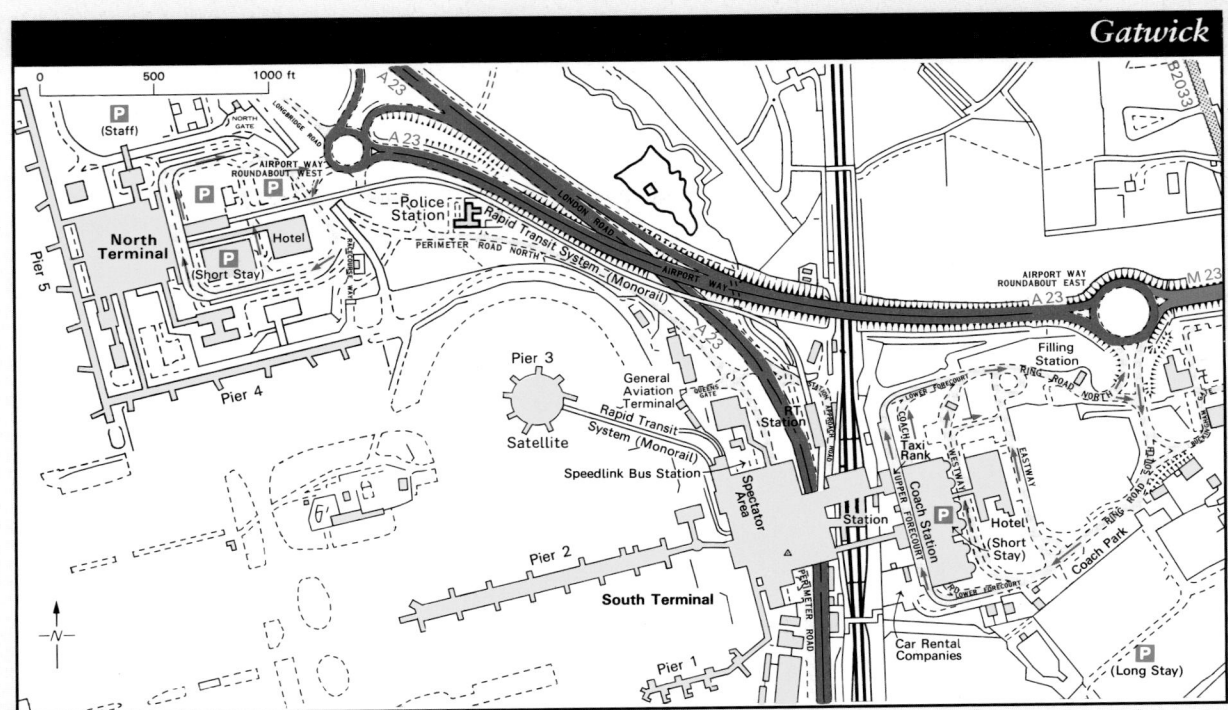

0   500   1000 ft

P (Staff)

NORTH GATE

LONGMORE ROAD

A 23

A 23

AIRPORT WAY ROUNDABOUT WEST

P

LONDON ROAD

RAPID TRANSIT SYSTEM (MONORAIL)

AIRPORT WAY

AIRPORT WAY ROUNDABOUT EAST

M 23

A 23

Police Station

Hotel

P (Short Stay)

North Terminal

Pier 5

PERIMETER ROAD NORTH

Pier 4

Pier 3 Satellite

General Aviation Terminal

WEST GATE

Rapid Transit System (Monorail)

Speedlink Bus Station

RT Station

Spectator Area

Station

Filling Station

Taxi Rank

LOWER FORECOURT

Coach Station

UPPER FORECOURT

Hotel (Short Stay)

RING ROAD NORTH

EASTWAY

WESTWAY

Coach Park

Pier 2

South Terminal

PERIMETER ROAD

Pier 1

Car Rental Companies

P

P (Long Stay)

N

Prestwick

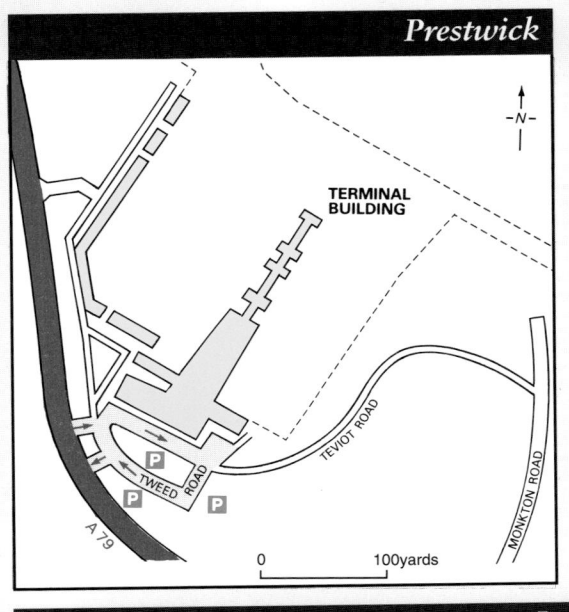

N

TERMINAL BUILDING

TEVIOT ROAD

MONKTON ROAD

TWEED ROAD

P

P

P

A 79

0   100 yards

Manchester

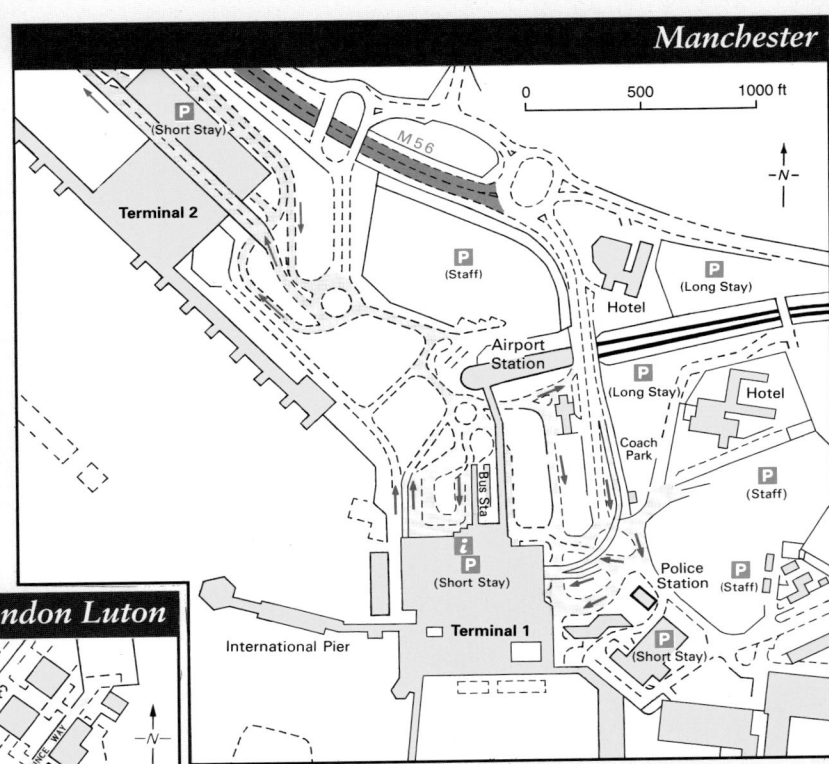

0   500   1000 ft

N

P (Short Stay)

M 56

Terminal 2

P (Staff)

P (Long Stay)

Hotel

Airport Station

P (Long Stay)

Hotel

Coach Park

P (Staff)

Bus Sta

i P (Short Stay)

International Pier

Terminal 1

Police Station

P (Staff)

P (Short Stay)

London Luton

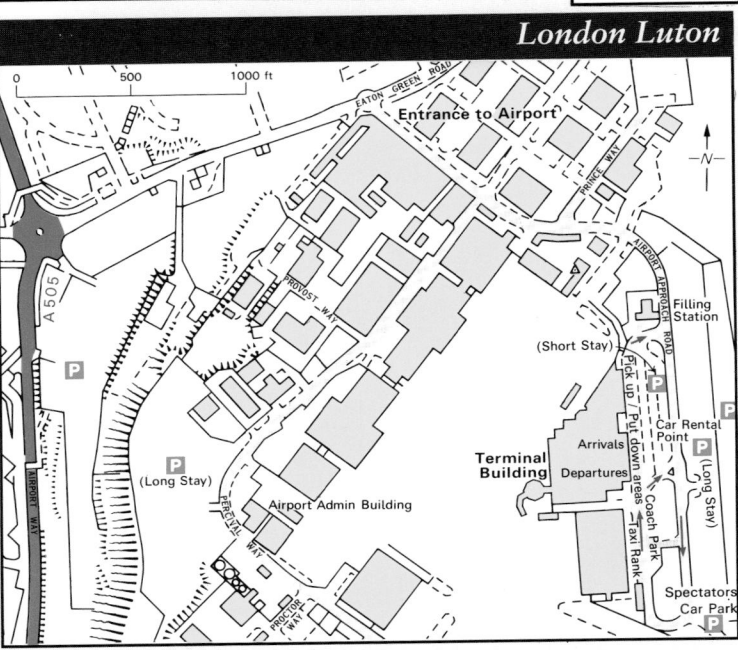

0   500   1000 ft

EATON GREEN ROAD

Entrance to Airport

PRINCE WAY

PROVOST WAY

AIRPORT APPROACH ROAD

Filling Station

(Short Stay)

Pick up

Put down areas

P

Car Rental Point

A 505

P (Long Stay)

Airport Admin Building

PERCIVAL WAY

PROCTOR WAY

AIRPORT WAY

Terminal Building

Arrivals

Departures

Coach Park

Taxi Rank

P (Long Stay)

P

Spectators Car Park

Leeds and Bradford

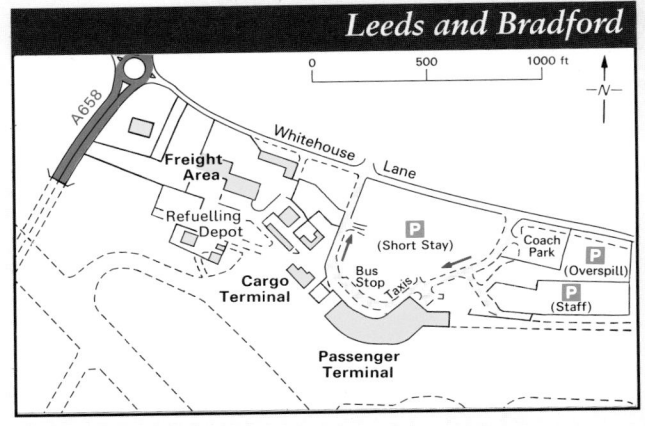

0   500   1000 ft

N

A 658

Freight Area

Whitehouse Lane

Refuelling Depot

(Short Stay)

Coach Park

P (Overspill)

Cargo Terminal

Bus Stop

Taxis

P (Staff)

Passenger Terminal

Heathrow

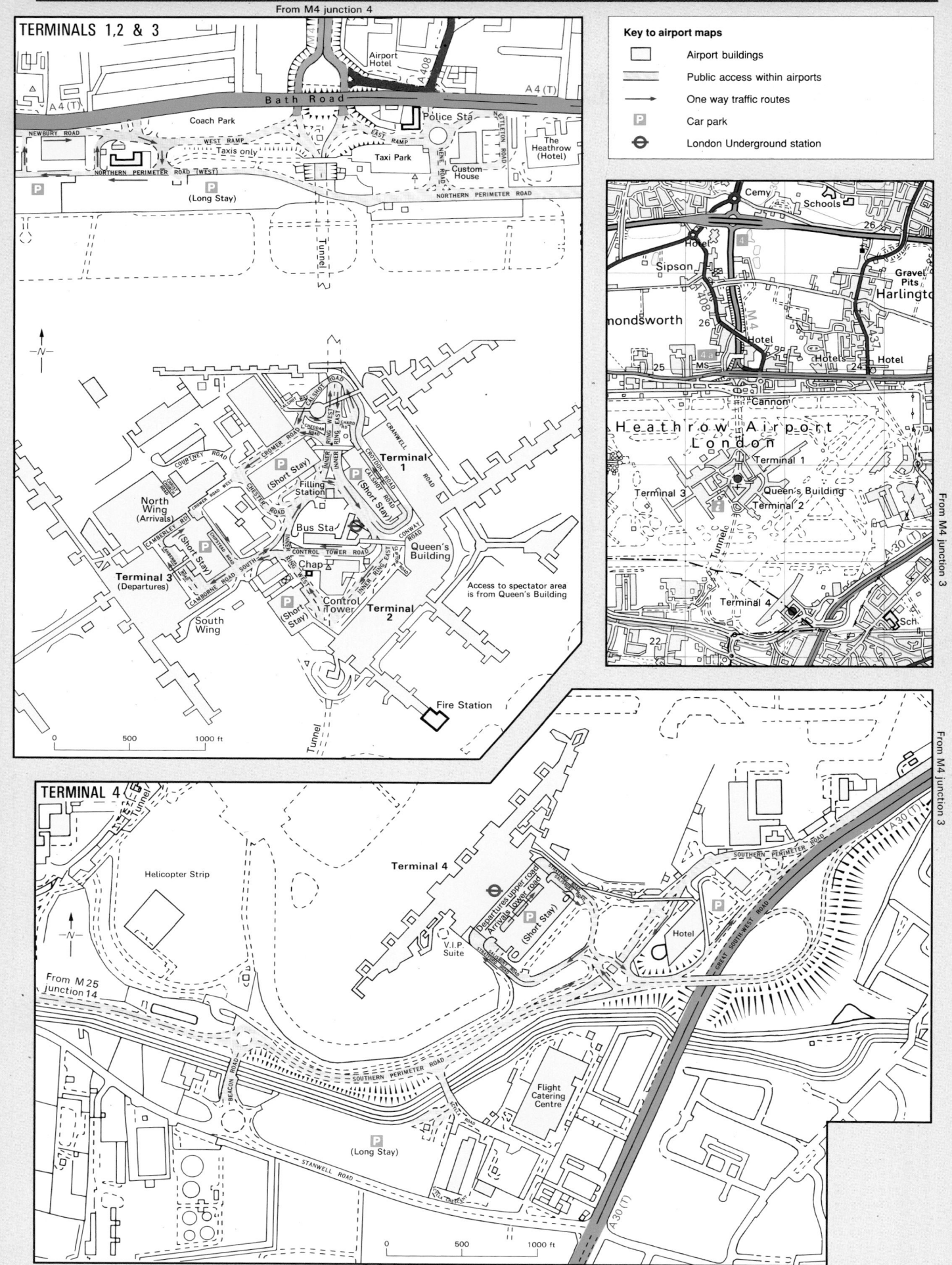

TERMINALS 1,2 & 3

From M4 junction 4

Airport Hotel

Police Sta

The Heathrow (Hotel)

A 4 (T)

A 408

Key to airport maps

Airport buildings

Public access within airports

One way traffic routes

P Car park

London Underground station

Bath Road

Coach Park

NEWBURY ROAD

WEST RAMP

Taxis only

EAST RAMP

Taxi Park

Custom House

NORTHERN PERIMETER ROAD (WEST)

NORTHERN PERIMETER ROAD

P (Long Stay)

Tunnel

N

CRANWELL ROAD

Terminal 1

(Short Stay) P

Filling Station

P (Short Stay)

CROMER ROAD

COURTNEY ROAD

CROYDON ROAD WEST

CHISTLE ROAD

INNER RING WEST

INNER RING EAST

ORCHARD ROAD

CROYDON ROAD

North Wing (Arrivals)

(Short Stay)

CAMBERLEY RD

CROYDON RD

INNER RING SOUTH

Bus Sta

CONTROL TOWER ROAD

Chap

CONWAY ROAD

Queen's Building

Terminal 3 (Departures)

CAMBORNE ROAD

(Short Stay) P

Control Tower

Terminal 2

Access to spectator area is from Queen's Building

South Wing

Fire Station

Tunnel

0   500   1000 ft

Cemy

Schools

26

Sipson

Hotel

4

Gravel Pits

Harlington

A 431

ondsworth

26

25

Hotel

4 a

MS

24

Hotels

Hotel

Cannon

Heathrow Airport London

Terminal 1

Terminal 3

i

Queen's Building

Terminal 2

Tunnel

A 30 (T)

Terminal 4

Sch

22

From M4 junction 3

TERMINAL 4

Tunnel

Helicopter Strip

Terminal 4

SOUTHERN PERIMETER ROAD

A 30 (T)

N

From M25 junction 14

Departures upper road

Arrivals lower road

(Short Stay)

V.I.P. Suite

BEACON ROAD

SOUTHERN PERIMETER ROAD

STANWELL ROAD

P

P (Long Stay)

Flight Catering Centre

Hotel

GREAT SOUTH-WEST ROAD

0   500   1000 ft

From M4 junction 3

CHANNEL TUNNEL TERMINALS

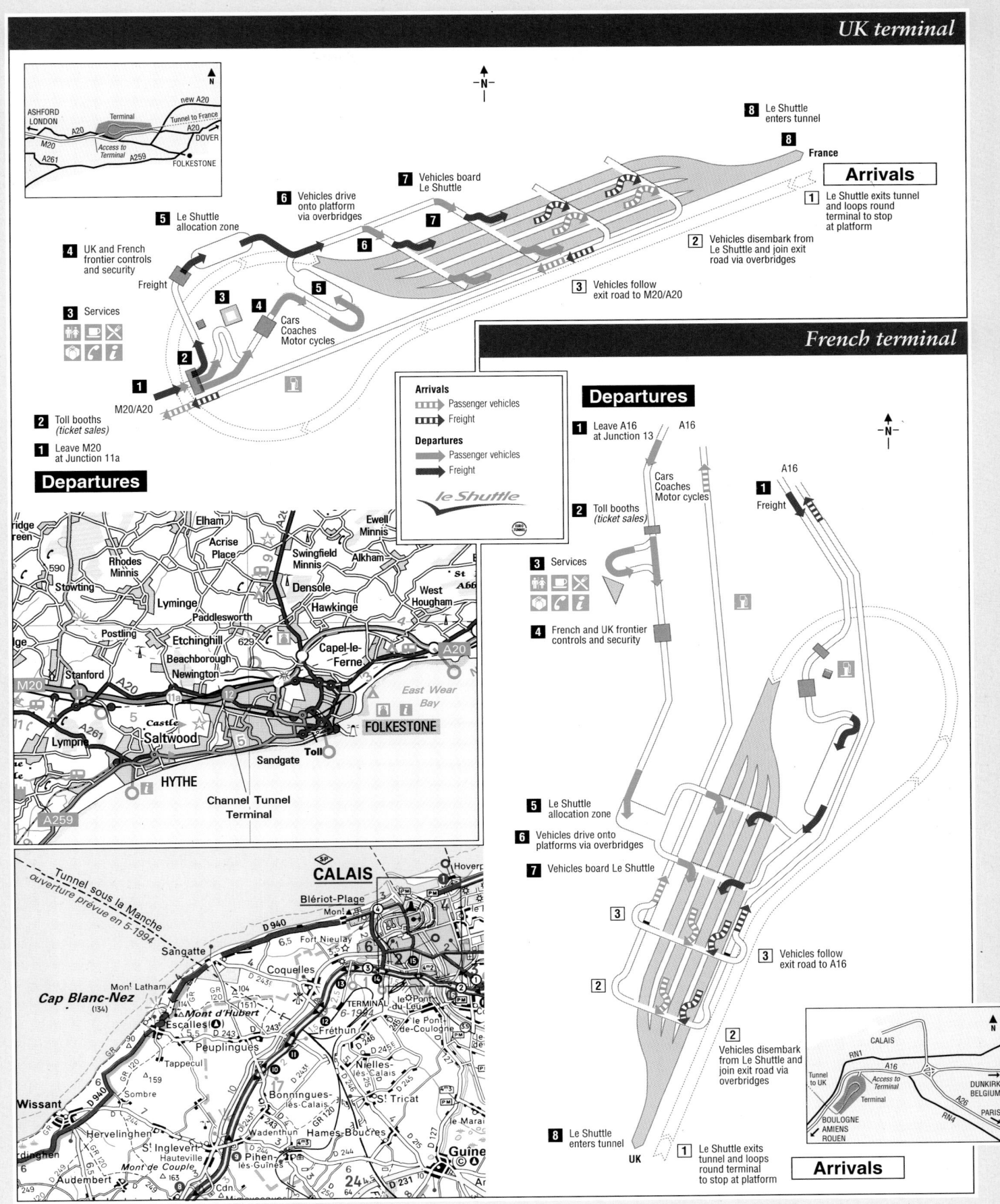

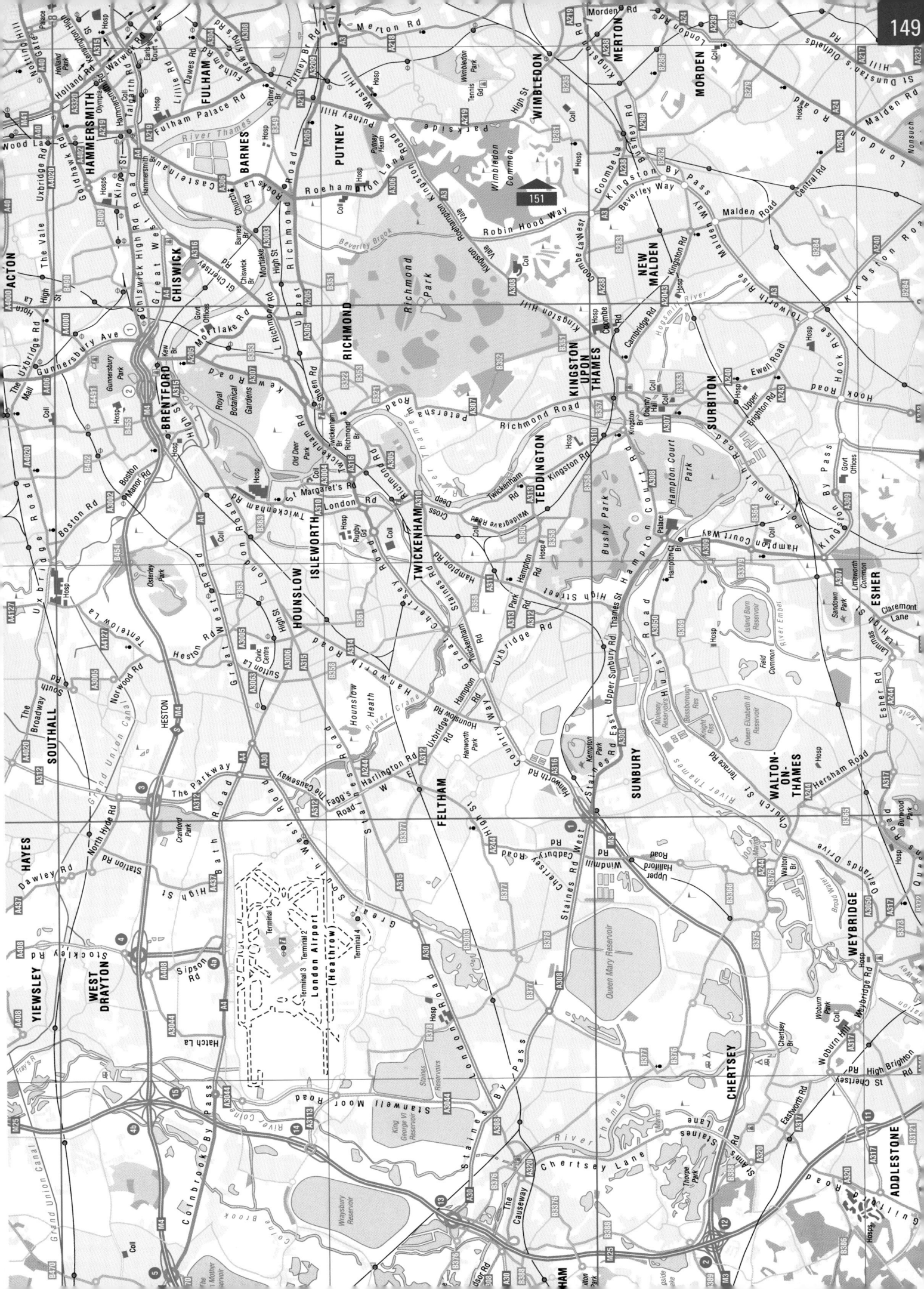

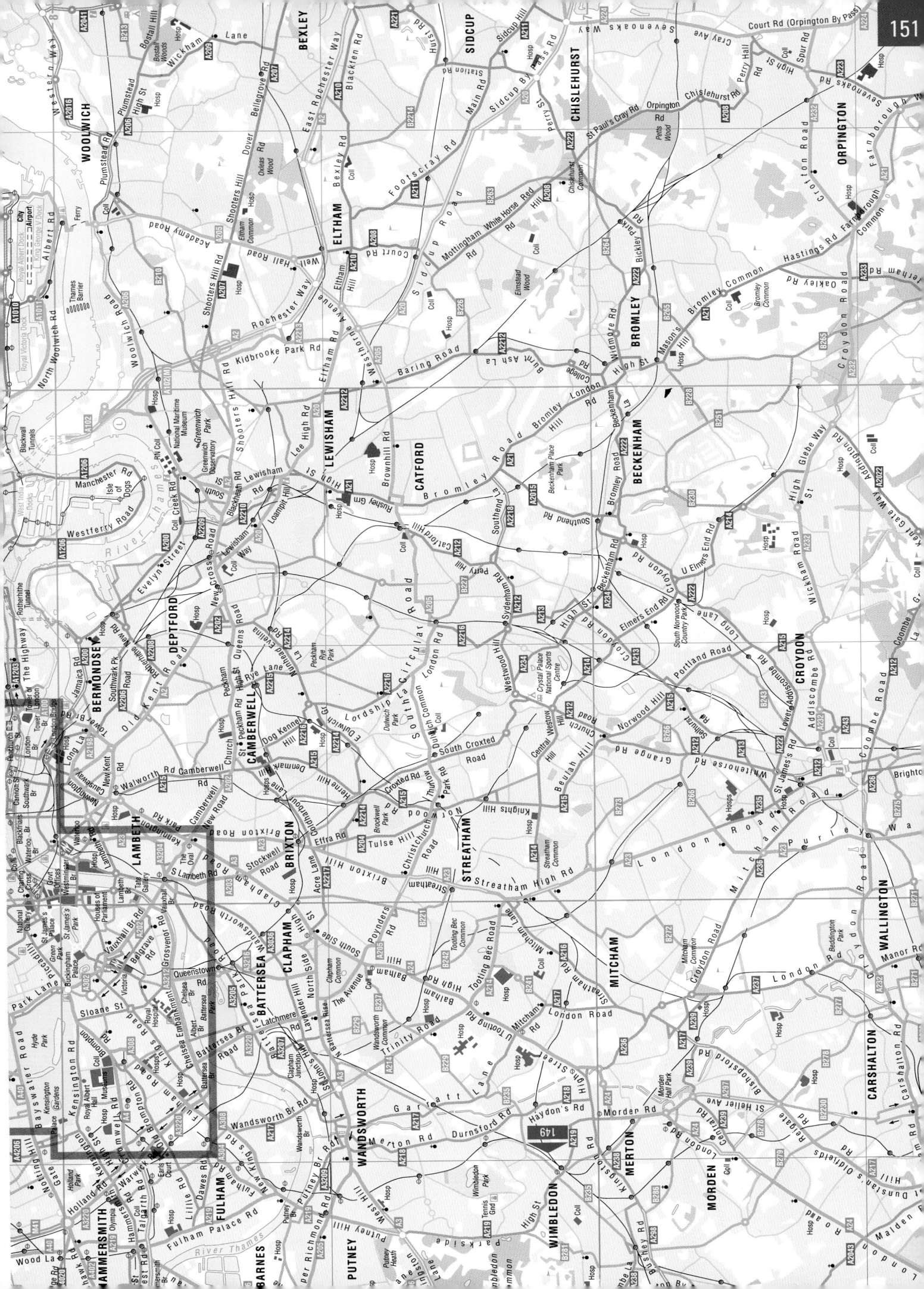

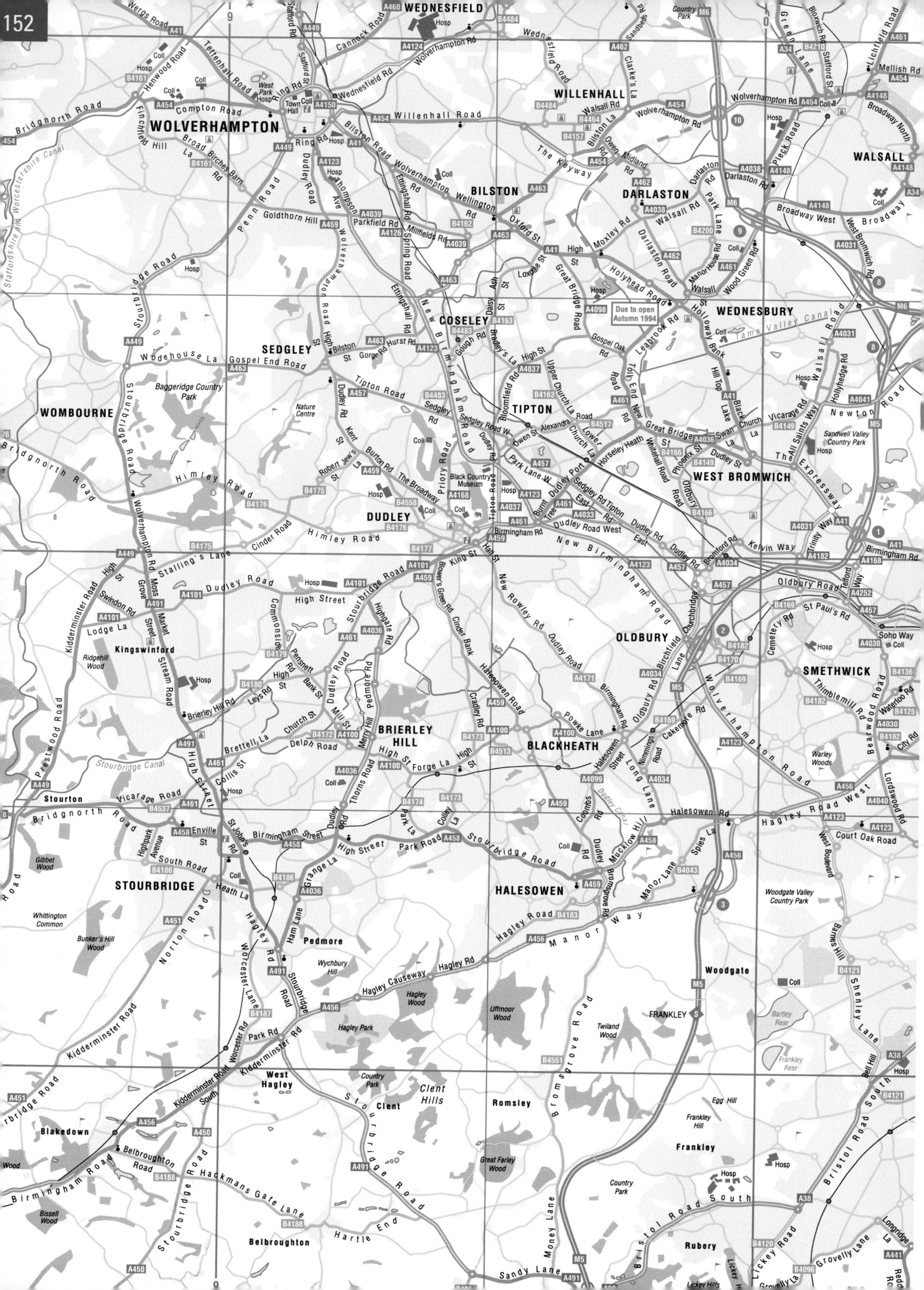

BIRMINGHAM AREA

INCHKEITH

Long Craig

FIRTH OF FORTH

Middle Craigs

Eastern Craigs

PRESTONPANS

Granton Harbour
Leith Docks
Lindsay Rd Commercial
Street Salamander
Street
Hosp
A901
Granton
Road
Ferry
Road
Coll
Coll
Hosp
Inverleith Row
Bonnington
Road
Broughton Rd
Leith Walk
Leith Links
Seafield Road
A199
Hosp
A902 Coll
Coll
Royal Botanic Garden
B900
A900
Portobello Road
B901
Bellvue
A90
Hosp
Queensferry Road
B900
London Rd London Road
A1140
Portobello High St
A6106
B6415
Fisherrow Sands
Ash Lagoons
B1361
MUSSELBURGH
Haddington Road
Wallyford
Mus
Cath
A1 Hosp
Regent
Willowbrae Rd
A199
A6106
Edinburgh Road
N Town Hall
High St
Linkfield Rd
A199
Corstorphine Road
Art Gallery
Coll
Cath
Sandwick
Princes St
Art Galleries
Liby
Castle Univ
Cath Mus
Abbey and Palace of Holyroodhouse
Holyrood Park
Dunsapie Loch
Milton Rd
Milton Rd East
A199
Whitehill
A6905
Newhailes
Road
High St
Hosp
A6094
A1
Rugby Ground
Football Ground
Dalry Road
Lothian
Hosp
A68
Melville Dr
Meadow Park
A7
Commonwealth Pool
Duddingstone Loch
Duddingston Pk
Coll
Newcraighall Rd Street
A1
River Esk
Catherin Rd
A6124
Gorgie Rd
A70
Bruntsfield Place
Morningside Rd
Coll
Hosp
Coll
Hosp
Peffermill Rd
Niddrie Mains Rd
A6905
A6106 South
Duddingston
A1
S
B6415
Whitecraig Road
B6414
Slateford Road
A702
Hosp
Coll
Hosp
Craigmillar Park
Royal Observatory
Univ
Old Dalkeith Rd
A68
Gilmerton Road
A6106
Old Craighall Rd
A720
Salter's Road
A6094
Whitecraig
B6414
Redford Road
Comiston Road
Braid Hills
Liberton Brae
A701
A772
Gilmerton Road
Fernielhill Dr
Drum St
A6094
A6124
Oxgangs Rd
Hosp
Frogston Road West
Frogston Road East
Captain's Road
Burdiehouse Road
Hosps
Gilmerton Road
A772
A7
Gilmerton Rd
Eskbank
Newmills Rd
Lauder Rd
Nature Trail
DALKEITH
A68
Country Park
Leadburn Stratton Rd
B702
LOANHEAD
Melville Dykes Road
Lasswade Road
Eskbank Road
A720
Coll
Easthouses Road
B6482
Glencorse Resr
A702
A703
A701
The Loan
High St
Hosp
A768
High St
Bonnyrigg Road
Newbattle Road
B703
Bryans Road
Suttieslea Road
Mayfield
Pathe
B7006
River North Esk
A6094
BONNYRIGG AND LASSWADE
Cockpen Rd
Murderdean Road
Main St
Newtongrange
Mus
Country Park
River South Esk
B704
A7
Hunterfield Road
B6372
B6367
PENICUIK
B7026
Hosp
B7003
Hosp
Gorebridge
B6372

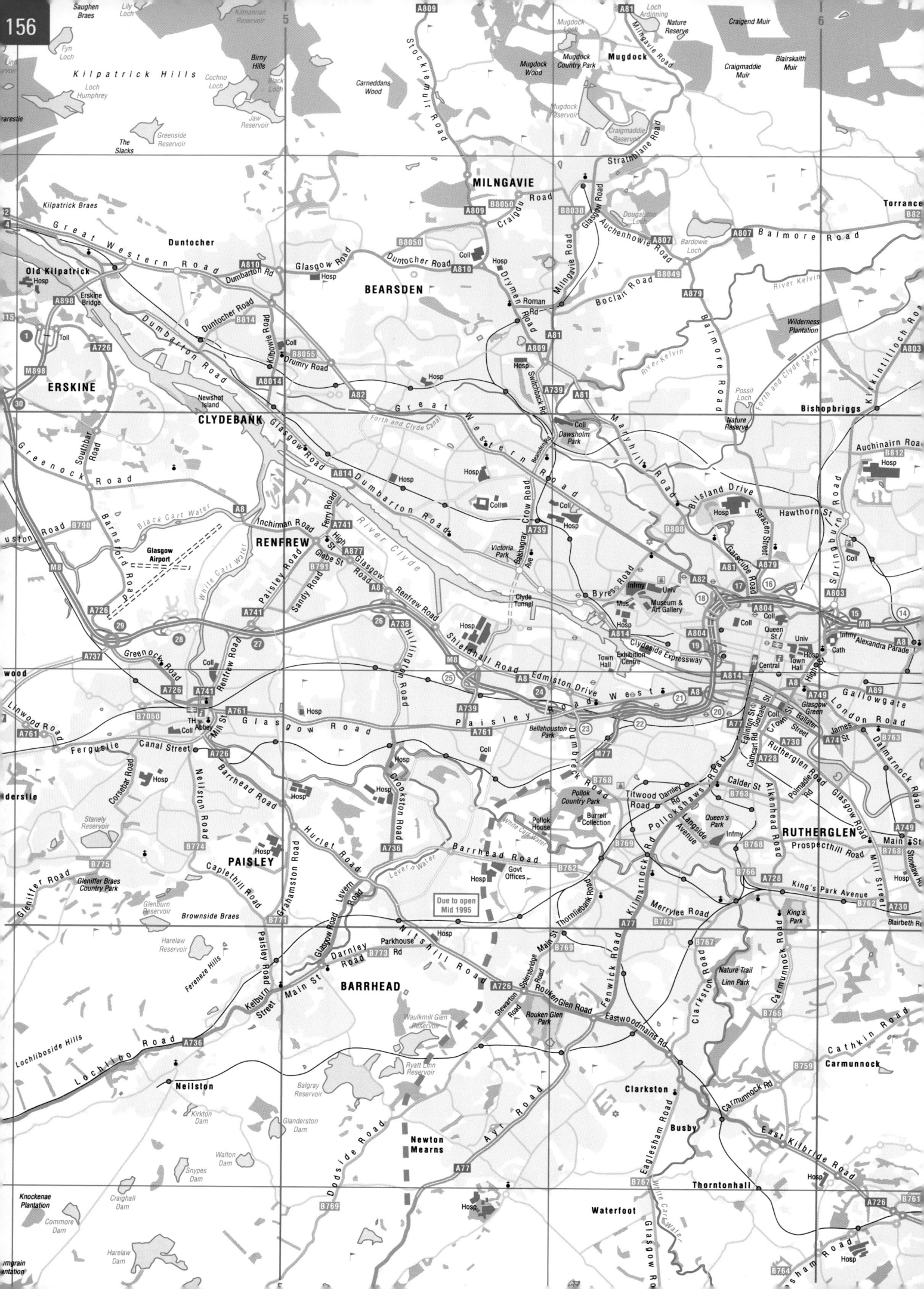

GLASGOW
AREA

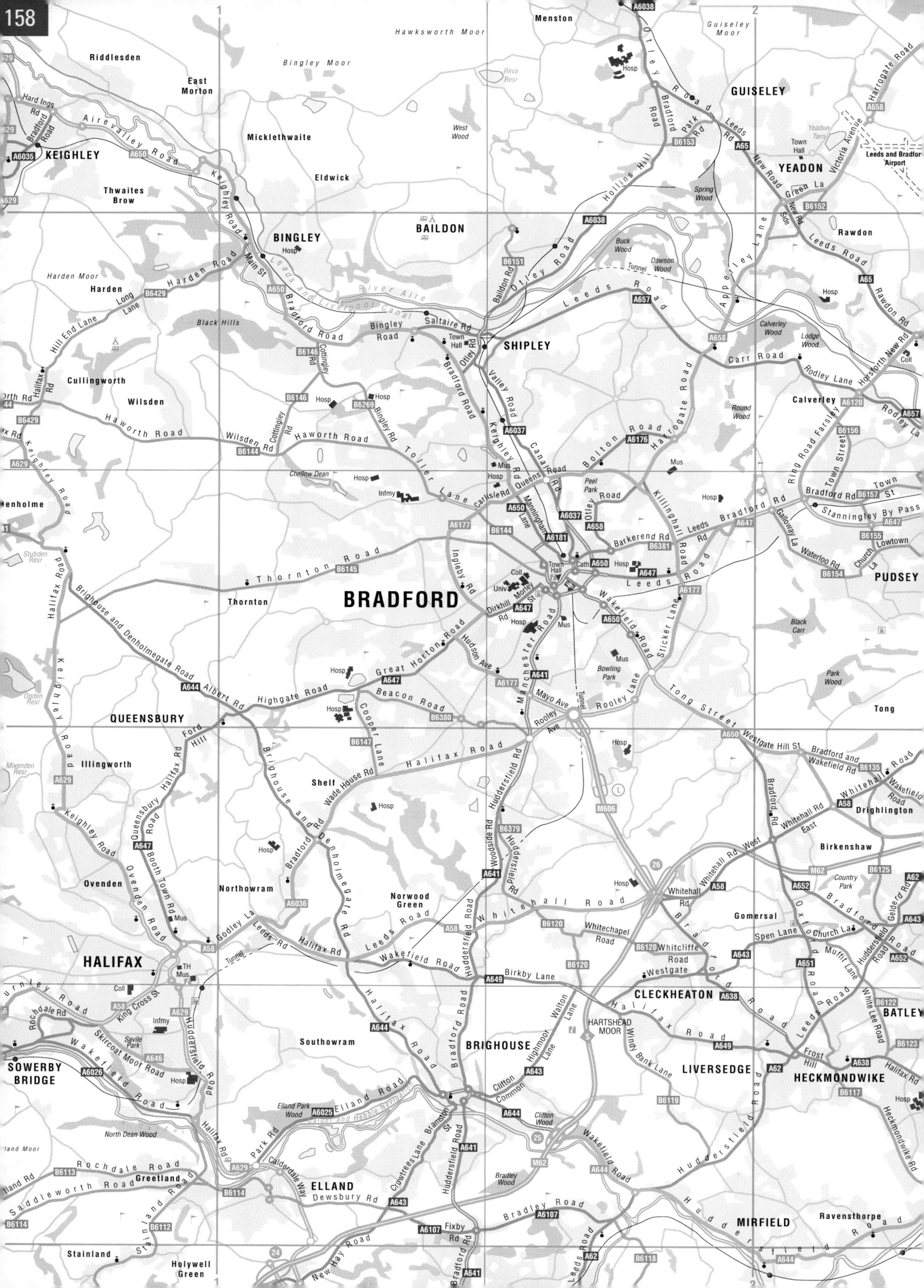

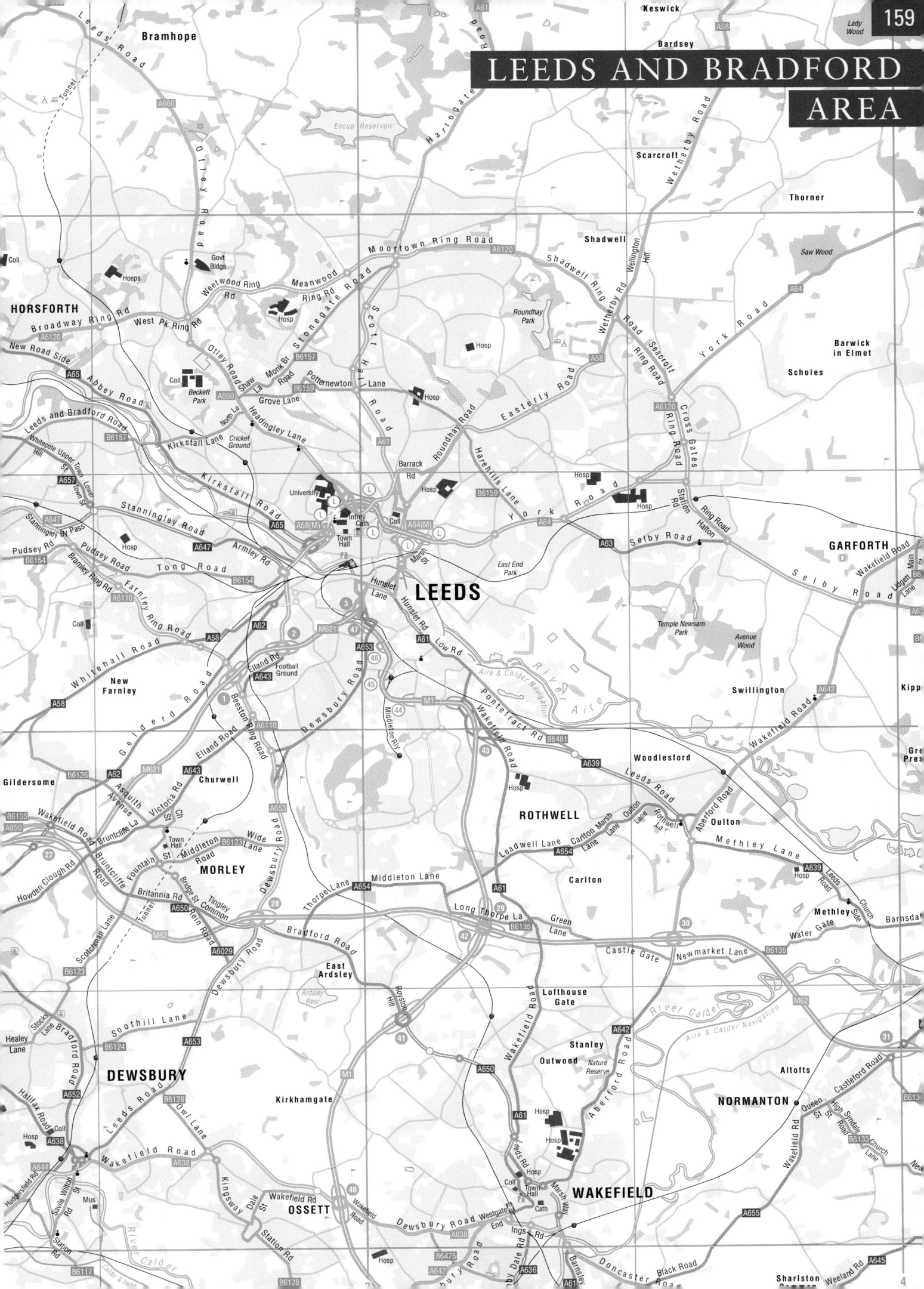

LEEDS AND BRADFORD AREA

LIVERPOOL AREA

MAGHULL

CROSBY

LITHERLAND

KIRKBY

BOOTLE

LLASEY

BIRKENHEAD

HUYTON-WITH-ROBY

PRESCOT

Knowsley Park

White Man's Dam

Reservoir

Croxteth Country Park

Aintree Race Course

Sefton Park

Festival Gardens

River Mersey

Liverpool Airport

Terminal Building

BEBINGTON

Eastham Woods Country Park

Wirral Country Park

Rivacre Valley Country Park

ELLESMERE PORT

Manchester Ship Canal

MANCHESTER AREA

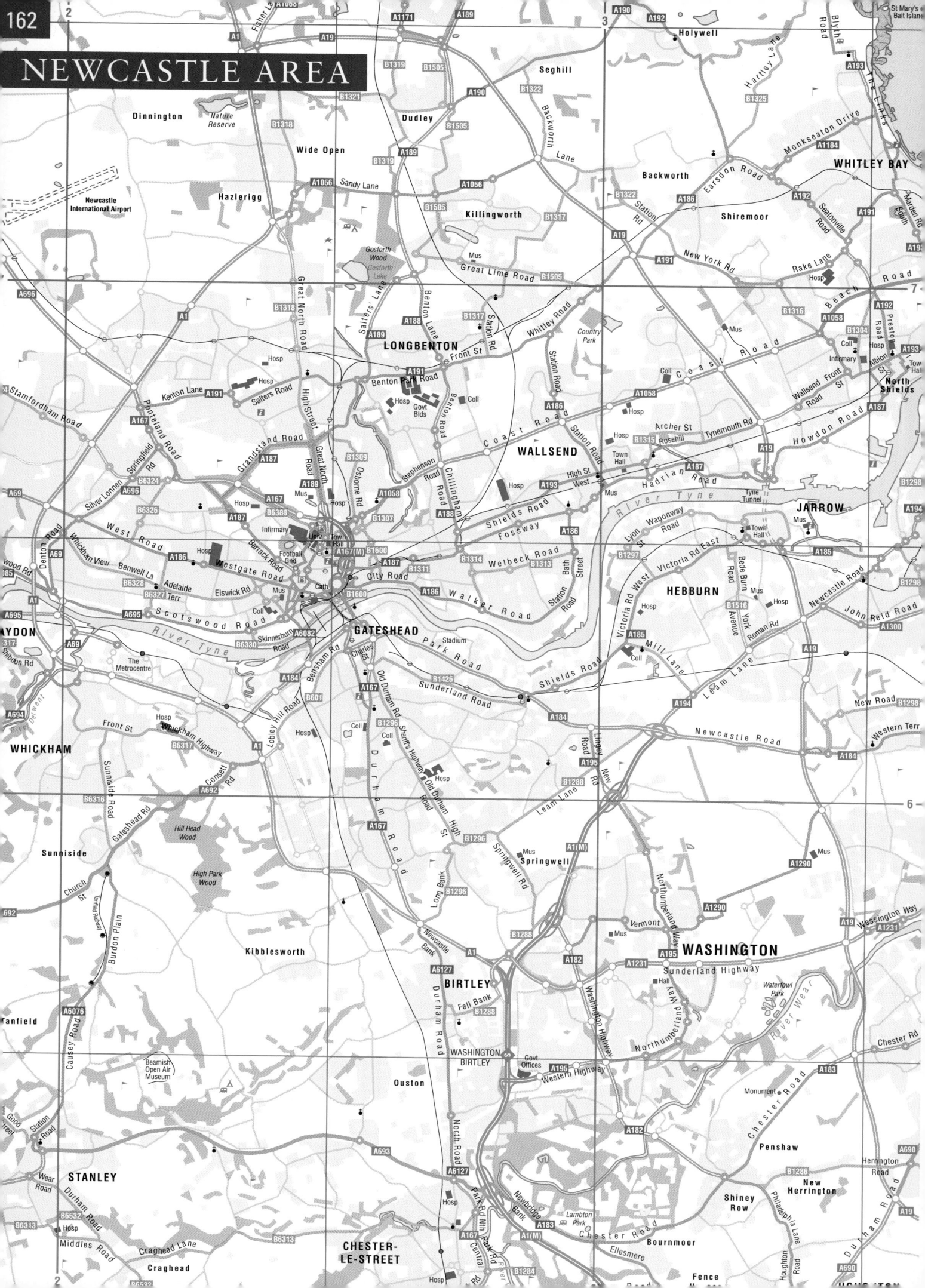

INDEX

How to use this index

For each entry the Atlas page number is listed and an alpha-numeric map reference is given for the grid square in which the name appears.
For example:

Barnstaple......... 9 F2

Barnstaple will be found on page 9, square F2

If you want to give a National Grid Reference to a place or feature, all the information you need is contained on the Atlas map pages. Grid lines appear at 10 kilometre (km) intervals and each carries a reference number (eg 9) in blue. Those 10 km grid lines which fall at the top and bottom and outside edges of each Atlas map page carry an additional smaller reference number (eg 29). This smaller number is the reference of the preceding 100 km grid line.

All 100 km grid lines appear in dark blue and carry a two-figure reference number (eg 20) in blue. The reference letters of the relevant 100 km grid square (eg SS, ST etc) are also printed in blue on every Atlas map page spread.

Thus Barnstaple on page 9 of this Atlas has a National Grid Reference accurate to the nearest 10 km of SS53 where:

SS are the reference letters of the 100 km grid in which Barnstaple lies

5 and **3** are the references for the grid lines running north/south and east/west respectively and which intersect to form the south west corner of the 10 km grid square in which Barnstaple falls.

Barnstaple can be pinpointed more precisely by breaking the 10 km grid square into 10 sub squares of 1 km x 1 km and constructing a four-figure reference SS 5533. The second and fourth figures in the number identify within the 10 km grid square SS53 the imaginary 1 km grid line intervals running north/south and east/west respectively and which intersect to form the south west corner of the 1 km grid square in which the centre of Barnstaple lies. The numbering sequence runs east and north from the south west corner of the country.

A leaflet on the National Grid references system is available from the Information Section, Ordnance Survey, Romsey Road, Maybush, Southampton SO9 4DH.

County names showing abbreviations used in this index

England

Avon	Avon
Bedfordshire	Beds
Berkshire	Berks
Buckinghamshire	Bucks
Cambridgeshire	Cambs
Cheshire	Ches
Cleveland	Cleve
Cornwall	Corn
Cumbria	Cumbr
Derbyshire	Derby
Devon	Devon
Dorset	Dorset
Durham	Durham
East Sussex	E. Susx
Essex	Essex
Gloucestershire	Glos
Greater London	G. Lon
Greater Manchester	G. Man
Hampshire	Hants
Hereford & Worcester	H.& W
Hertfordshire	Herts
Humberside	Humbs
Isle of Wight	I. of W
Kent	Kent
Lancashire	Lancs

Leicester	Leic
Lincolnshire	Lincs
Merseyside	Mers
Norfolk	Norf
North Yorkshire	N. Yks
Northamptonshire	Northnts
Northumberland	Northum
Nottinghamshire	Notts
Oxfordshire	Oxon
Shropshire	Shrops
Somerset	Somer
South Yorkshire	S. Yks
Staffordshire	Staffs
Suffolk	Suff
Surrey	Surrey
Tyne and Wear	T. & W
Warwickshire	Warw
West Midlands	W. Mids
West Sussex	W. Susx
West Yorkshire	W. Yks
Wiltshire	Wilts

Wales

Clwyd	Clwyd
Dyfed	Dyfed
Gwent	Gwent

Gwynedd	Gwyn
Mid Glamorgan	M. Glam
Powys	Powys
South Glamorgan	S. Glam
West Glamorgan	W. Glam

Other Areas

Isle of Man	I. of M
Isles of Scilly	I. Scilly

Scotland *Regions*

Borders	Border
Central	Central
Dumfries & Galloway	D. & G.
Fife	Fife
Grampian	Grampn
Highland	Highl
Lothian	Lothn
Strathclyde	Strath
Tayside	Tays

Scotland *Island Areas*

Orkney	Orkney
Shetland	Shetld
Western Isles	W. Isles

Abbas Combe

Aird Uig

A

Abbas Combe.....11 J3
Abberton, H. & W.....32 B4
Abberton, Essex.....25 G1
Abberwick.....75 H3
Abbess Roding.....24 B1
Abbey.....10 C4
Abbeycwmhir.....29 H2
Abbey Dore.....30 E6
Abbey Hulton.....42 B2
Abbey St Bathans.....82 F5
Abbeystead.....57 J5
Abbeytown.....63 G2
Abbey Village.....51 F1
Abbots Bickington.....8 D4
Abbots Bromley.....42 C4
Abbotsbury.....11 G7
Abbotsham.....8 E3
Abbotskerswell.....5 J3
Abbots Langley.....23 F2
Abbots Leigh.....19 K5
Abbotsley.....35 F4
Abbots Morton.....32 C4
Abbots Ripton.....35 F2
Abbot's Salford.....32 C4
Abbotswood.....13 F3
Abbotts Ann.....13 F1
Abdon.....31 G1
Aber.....27 J2
Aberaeron.....28 B3
Aberaman.....18 E2
Aberangell.....39 H5
Aberargie.....88 D7
Aberarth.....28 B3
Aber-banc.....27 H2
Aberbargoed.....18 F2
Aberbeeg.....19 G2
Abercanaid.....18 E2

Abercarn.....19 G3
Abercastle.....26 C3
Abercegir.....39 H6
Aberchalder.....94 B5
Aberchirder.....104 F3
Abercraf.....18 C1
Abercych.....27 G2
Abercynon.....18 E3
Aberdalgie.....88 C6
Aberdare.....18 E2
Aberdaron.....38 A4
Aberdeen.....97 J5
Aberdour.....81 G3
Aberdulais.....18 B3
Aberdyfi.....38 F7
Aberedw.....29 H5
Abereiddy.....26 B3
Abererch.....38 C3
Aberfan.....18 E2
Aberfeldy.....88 A4
Aberffraw.....48 C4
Aberffrwd.....28 D2
Aberford.....59 K7
Aberfoyle.....79 H1
Abergavenny.....19 H1
Abergele.....49 J3
Abergorlech.....27 K3
Abergwesyn.....29 F4
Abergwili.....27 J4
Abergwynant.....39 F5
Abergwynfi.....18 C3
Abergwyngregyn.....49 F3
Abergynolwyn.....39 F6
Aberhosan.....39 H7
Aberkenfig.....18 C4
Aberlady.....82 C4
Aberlemno.....89 H3
Aberllefenni.....39 G6
Abermeurig.....28 C4
Abermule.....40 C7

Aber-nant, M. Glam.....18 E2
Abernant, Dyfed.....27 H4
Abernethy.....88 D7
Abernyte.....88 E5
Aberporth.....27 G1
Abersoch.....38 C4
Abersychan.....19 G2
Abertillery.....19 G2
Abertridwr, Powys.....40 B5
Abertridwr, M. Glam.....18 F4
Abertysswg.....18 F2
Aberuthven.....88 B7
Aber Village.....30 C7
Aberyscir.....29 H7
Aberystwyth.....28 C1
Abingdon.....21 J3
Abinger Common.....14 E1
Abington.....72 E2
Abington Pigotts.....35 G5
Ab Kettleby.....43 K4
Ablington.....20 F2
Abney.....52 D6
Aboyne.....96 E6
Abram.....50 F3
Abriachan.....94 D2
Abridge.....23 K3
Abthorpe.....33 J5
Abune-the-Hill.....112 C4
Aby.....53 J6
Acaster Malbis.....60 C6
Acaster Selby.....60 C6
Accrington.....58 C8
Achachork.....99 K6
Achahoish.....77 G4
Achanalt.....101 J6
Achandunie.....102 E5
Ach' an Todhair.....86 C1
Achaphubuil.....93 G8
Acharacle.....85 H2
Acharn.....87 K4

Achath.....97 G4
Achfary.....108 D5
Achgarve.....100 E3
Achiemore.....110 E3
Achiltibuie.....101 G2
Achina.....110 D2
Achinduich.....102 D3
Achingills.....111 H2
Achintee.....93 F1
Achintraid.....92 E2
Achleck.....84 F4
Achluachrach.....93 K7
Achlyness.....108 D3
Achmelvich.....108 B6
Achmore, Highld.....92 E2
Achmore, W. Isles.....107 H6
Achnacarnin.....111 G5
Achnacarry.....93 H7
Achnacloich.....92 B5
Achnaconeran.....94 C4
Achnacroish.....85 K4
Achnagarron.....102 E5
Achnahanat.....102 D3
Achnahannet.....95 H3
Achnairn.....109 G7
Achnamara.....77 G3
Achnasaul.....93 H7
Achnasheen.....101 H7
Achreamie.....111 G2
Achriesgill.....108 D3
Achurch.....34 D1
Ackergill.....111 K3
Acklam, N. Yks.....60 E4
Acklam, Cleve.....66 E6
Ackleton.....41 J7
Acklington.....75 J4
Ackton.....53 G1
Ackworth Moor Top.....53 G2
Acle.....47 K5
Acock's Green.....32 D1

Acol.....25 K6
Acomb.....75 F8
Aconbury.....31 G6
Acre.....51 G1
Acrefair.....40 D2
Acton, Suff.....36 D5
Acton, Shrops.....30 E1
Acton, Ches.....41 H1
Acton, G. Lon.....23 H4
Acton Beauchamp.....31 H4
Acton Bridge.....50 E6
Acton Burnell.....41 G6
Acton Green.....31 H4
Acton Pigott.....41 G6
Acton Round.....41 H7
Acton Scott.....41 F8
Acton Trussell.....42 B5
Acton Turville.....20 C4
Adamthwaite.....64 E8
Adbaston.....41 J4
Adber.....11 G3
Adderbury.....33 G6
Adderley.....41 H3
Adderstone.....75 H1
Addiewell.....80 E5
Addingham.....59 F6
Addington, Bucks.....34 A7
Addington, Kent.....24 C7
Addlestone.....22 F6
Addlethorpe.....55 K7
Adeney.....41 J5
Adforton.....30 F2
Adisham.....25 J7
Adlestrop.....32 E7
Adlingfleet.....54 C1
Adlington, Lancs.....50 F2
Adlington, Ches.....51 J5
Admaston, Staffs.....42 C4
Admaston, Shrops.....41 H5

Admington.....32 E5
Adstock.....33 K6
Adstone.....33 H4
Advie.....95 K2
Adwell.....22 B3
Adwick le Street.....53 H3
Adwick upon Dearne.....53 G3
Adziel.....105 J3
Ae.....72 E6
Affleck.....97 H3
Affpuddle.....11 K6
Afon-wen.....50 A4
Agglethorpe.....59 F2
Aignish.....107 J5
Aike.....61 H6
Aikerness.....112 E1
Aikers.....112 E1
Aiketgate.....64 B3
Aikton.....63 H2
Ailey.....30 E5
Ailsworth.....44 F7
Ainderby Quernhow.....59 J2
Ainderby Steeple.....59 J1
Aingers Green.....37 G7
Ainsdale.....50 C2
Ainstable.....64 C3
Ainsworth.....51 G2
Aintree.....50 C4
Aird, D. & G.....68 B4
Aird, Strath.....77 G1
Aird, W. Isles.....107 K5
Aird Mhanais.....99 G4
Aird Mheadhonach.....99 G3
Aird of Sleat.....92 B5
Aird Riabhach.....99 H3
Airdrie.....80 C5
Airdriehill.....80 C5
Aird, The.....99 H4
Aird Thunga.....107 J5
Aird Uig.....106 E5

Airmyn	54	B1
Airntully	88	C5
Airor	92	D5
Airth	80	D3
Airton	58	E5
Aisby, Lincs	54	C4
Aisby, Lincs	44	D3
Aiskew	59	H2
Aislaby, N. Yks	60	E2
Aislaby, N. Yks	67	J7
Aisthorpe	54	D5
Aith, Shetld	115	F3
Aith, Orkney	113	G4
Aithsetter	115	G5
Akeld	75	F2
Akeley	33	K6
Akenham	37	G5
Albaston	4	E2
Alberbury	40	E5
Albourne	15	F4
Albrighton, Shrops	41	F5
Albrighton, Shrops	41	K6
Alburgh	37	H1
Albury, Surrey	14	D1
Albury, Herts	35	H7
Alby Hill	47	G3
Alcaig	102	D7
Alcaston	31	F1
Alcester	32	C4
Alciston	15	J5
Alcombe	10	A1
Alconbury	34	E2
Alconbury Weston	34	E2
Aldborough, Norf	47	G3
Aldborough, N. Yks	59	K4
Aldbourne	21	G5
Aldbrough	61	K7
Aldbrough St John	66	C6
Aldbury	22	E1
Aldclune	88	A2
Aldeburgh	37	K4
Aldeby	47	K7
Aldenham	23	G3
Alderbury	12	D3
Alderford	47	G5
Alderholt	12	D4
Alderley	20	B3
Alderley Edge	51	H6
Aldermaston	21	K6
Alderminster	32	E5
Aldershot	22	D7
Alderton, Northnts	34	A5
Alderton, Wilts	20	C4
Alderton, Glos	32	C6
Alderton, Shrops	41	F4
Alderton, Suff	37	J5
Alderwasley	43	F1
Aldfield	59	H4
Aldford	50	D8
Aldham, Essex	36	E7
Aldham, Suff	36	F5
Aldingbourne	14	C5
Aldingham	57	F3
Aldington, H. & W	32	C5
Aldington, Kent	17	H2
Aldington Frith	17	H2
Aldochlay	79	F2
Aldreth	35	H2
Aldridge	42	C6
Aldringham	37	K3
Aldsworth	21	F1
Aldunie	96	C3
Aldwark, N. Yks	60	B4
Aldwark, Derby	42	E1
Aldwick	14	C6
Aldwincle	34	D1
Aldworth	21	K5
Alexandria	79	F3
Alfardisworthy	8	C4
Alfington	10	C6
Alfold	14	D2
Alford, Grampn	96	E4
Alford, Somer	11	H2
Alford, Lincs	55	J6
Alfreton	43	G1
Alfrick	31	J4
Alfriston	15	J5
Alhampton	11	H2
Alkborough	54	C1
Alkerton	33	F5
Alkham	17	K1
Alkington	41	G3
Alkmonton	42	D3
Allaleigh	5	J4
Allanaquoich	95	K6
Allanton, Strath	80	D6
Allanton, Border	83	G6
Allardice	97	H8
All Cannings	21	F6
Allendale Town	65	F2
Allenheads	65	F3
Allensmore	31	F6
Aller	10	F3
Allerby	63	F4
Allerford	9	K1
Allerston	61	F2
Allerthorpe	60	D6
Allerton	50	D5
Allerton Bywater	53	G1
Allesley	32	E1
Allestree	43	F3
Allexton	44	B6
Allgreave	51	J7
Allhallow-on-Sea	24	E5
Allhallows	24	E5
Alligin Shuas	100	E7
Allimore Green	42	A5
Allington, Lincs	44	B2
Allington, Wilts	21	E2
Allington, Wilts	12	E2
Allington, Wilts	20	E6
Allithwaite	57	G3
Alloa	80	D2
Allonby	63	F3
Alloway	71	J3
All Saints South Elmham	37	J1
All Stretton	41	F7
Alltforgan	39	J4
Alltmawr	29	H5
Allt na h-Airbhe	101	H3
Allt-nan-Sugh	93	F3
Alltwalis	27	J3
Alltwen	18	B2
Almeley	30	E4
Almer	12	B6
Almington	41	J3
Almondbank	88	C6
Almondbury	52	D2
Almondsbury	19	L4
Alne	60	B4
Alness	102	E6
Alnham	75	F3
Alnmouth	75	J3
Alnwick	75	H3
Alphamstone	36	D6
Alpheton	36	D4
Alphington	9	K7
Alport	52	E7
Alpraham	50	E8
Alresford	36	F7
Alrewas	42	D5
Alsager	41	J1
Alsagers Bank	41	K2
Alsop en le Dale	42	D1
Alston	64	E3
Alstone	32	B6
Alstonefield	42	D1
Alswear	9	H3
Altandhu	108	A7
Altarnun	4	C1
Altass	102	D2
Alterwall	111	J2
Altham	58	C7
Althorne	24	F3
Althorpe	54	C3
Altnaharra	109	G5
Altofts	53	F1
Alton, Staffs	42	C2
Alton, Derby	53	F7
Alton, Hants	13	K2
Alton Pancras	11	H5
Alton Priors	20	F6
Altrincham	51	G5
Altrua	93	J6
Alva	80	D2
Alvanley	50	D6
Alvaston	43	F3
Alvechurch	32	C2
Alvecote	42	E6
Alvediston	12	B3
Alveley	31	J1
Alverdiscott	8	F3
Alverstoke	13	J6
Alverstone	13	H7
Alverton	44	A2
Alves	103	K6
Alvescot	21	G2
Alveston, Warw	32	E4
Alveston, Avon	19	L4
Alvie	95	G5
Alvingham	55	H4
Alvington	19	L2
Alwalton	44	E7
Alweston	11	H4
Alwinton	74	F4
Alyth	88	E4
Amatnatua	102	C3
Ambergate	43	F1
Amber Hill	45	F2
Amberley, Glos	20	C2
Amberley, W. Susx	14	D4
Amble	75	J4
Amblecote	32	A1
Ambleside	63	J7
Ambleston	26	E4
Ambrosden	21	L1
Amcotts	54	C2
Amersham	22	E3
Amesbury	12	D1
Amhuinnsuidhe	98	F2
Amington	42	E6
Amisfield	73	F6
Amlwch	48	D1
Amlwch Port	48	D1
Ammanford	27	L5
Amotherby	60	E3
Ampfield	13	G3
Ampleforth	60	C3
Ampney Crucis	20	E2
Ampney St Mary	20	E2
Ampney St Peter	20	E2
Amport	13	F1
Ampthill	34	D6
Ampton	36	C2
Amroth	26	F6
Amulree	88	B5
Anaheilt	85	K2
Anancaun	101	G6
An Ard	100	E5
An Caol	100	C7
Ancaster	44	C2
Anchachork	99	K8
Anchor	30	C1
An Cnoc	107	J5
Ancroft	83	J7
Ancrum	74	C2
Ancton	14	C5
Anderby	55	K6
Anderby Creek	55	K6
Anderson	12	A6
Anderton	51	F6
Andover	13	F1
Andover Down	13	F1
Andoversford	20	E1
Andreas	56	R2
Angersleigh	10	C4
Angle	26	C6
Angmering	14	D5
Angram, N. Yks	60	C6
Angram, N. Yks	65	F8
Ankerville	103	G5
Anlaby	61	H8
Anmer	46	C4
Annan	73	G8
Annaside	56	D2
Annat, Strath	86	C6
Annat, Highld	100	E7
Anna Valley	13	F1
Annbank	71	K2
Annesley	43	H1
Annesley Woodhouse	43	G1
Annfield Plain	66	B2
Annochie	105	J4
Annscroft	41	F6
Ansdell	57	G8
Ansford	11	H2
Ansley	43	F7
Anslow	42	E4
Anslow Gate	42	D4
Anstey, Herts	35	H6
Anstey, Leic	43	H6
Anston	53	H5
Anstruther	82	D1
Ansty, Wilts	12	B3
Ansty, Warw	33	F1
Ansty, W. Susx	15	F3
Ansty, Dorset	11	J5
Anthill Common	13	J4
Anthorn	63	G2
Antingham	47	H3
Antony	4	D4
Antrobus	51	F6
Anwick	44	E1
Anwoth	69	G5
Apes Hall	45	J7
Apethorpe	44	D7
Apley	54	F6
Apperknowle	53	F6
Apperley	32	A7
Appersett	58	D1
Appin	86	B4
Appleby	54	D2
Appleby-in-Westmorland	64	D5
Appleby Magna	43	F5
Appleby Parva	43	F6
Applecross	100	D8
Appledore, Devon	10	B4
Appledore, Devon	8	E2
Appledore, Kent	17	G3
Appleford	21	K3
Appleshaw	13	F1
Applethwaite	63	H5
Appleton-le-Moors	60	E2
Appleton-le-Street	60	E3
Appleton Roebuck	60	C6
Appleton Thorn	51	F5
Appleton Wiske	66	D7
Appletreehall	74	B3
Appletreewick	59	F4
Appley	10	B3
Appley Bridge	50	E3
Apse Heath	13	H7
Apsley End	34	E6
Apuldram	14	B5
Aquhorthies	97	H3
Aquhythie	97	G4
Arabella	103	G5
Arbirlot	89	J4
Arboll	103	G4
Arborfield	22	C6
Arborfield Cross	22	C6
Arborfield Garrison	22	C6
Arbroath	89	J4
Arbuthnott	97	H8
Archiestown	104	B4
Arclid Green	51	G7
Ardachu	102	E2
Ardalanish	84	E7
Ardanaiseig	86	C6
Ardaneaskan	92	E2
Ardarroch	92	E2
Ardbeg	76	D7
Ardcharnich	101	H4
Ardchiavaig	84	E7
Ardchyle	87	H6
Ard Dhail	107	J2
Ard-dhubh	92	D1
Arddleen	40	D5
Ardechive	93	H6
Ardeley	35	G7
Ardelve	92	E3
Arden	79	F3
Ardens Grafton	32	D4
Ardentinny	78	D3
Ardeonaig	87	J5
Ardersier	103	F7
Ardessie	101	G4
Ardfern	85	K8
Ardgay	102	D3
Ardgowan	78	E4
Ardhasaig	99	G2
Ardheslaig	100	D7
Ardindrean	101	H4
Ardingly	15	G3
Ardington	21	J4
Ardivachar	98	C6
Ardivachar Point	98	C8
Ardlair	96	E3
Ardleigh	36	F7
Ardler	88	E4
Ardley	33	H7
Ardlui	86	F7
Ardlussa	77	H1
Ardmair	101	H3
Ardminish	77	F7
Ardmolich	85	J1
Ardnacroish	85	K4
Ardnadam	78	D3
Ardnagrask	102	D8
Ardnarff	92	E2
Ardnastang	85	K2
Ardo	97	H2
Ardoyne	97	F3
Ardrishaig	77	H3
Ardroil	106	E5
Ardross	102	E5
Ardrossan	78	E7
Ardshealach	85	H2
Ardsley	53	F1
Ardsley East	53	F1
Ardtalnaig	87	K5
Ardtoe	85	H1
Ardtornish	85	J4
Ardullie	102	D6
Ardvasar	92	C5
Ardvey, W. Isles	99	F4
Ardvey, W. Isles	99	G3
Ardvourlie	99	G1
Ardwell	68	C6
Areley Kings	31	K2
Argos Hill	16	C3
Aridhglas	84	E6
Arinacrinachd	100	D7
Arinagour	84	D3
Arisaig	92	C7
Arivruaich	107	G7
Arkendale	59	J4
Arkesden	35	H6
Arkholme	57	J3
Arkley	23	H3
Arksey	53	H3
Arkwright Town	53	G6
Arlecdon	62	F6
Arlesey	35	E6
Arleston	41	H5
Arley, Warw	42	F7
Arley, Ches	51	F5
Arlingham	20	B1
Arlington, E. Susx	16	C5
Arlington, Glos	20	F2
Arlington, Devon	9	G1
Armadale, Highld	110	D2
Armadale, Lothn	80	E5
Armathwaite	64	C3
Arminghall	47	H6
Armitage	42	C5
Armscote	32	E5
Armthorpe	53	J3
Arncliffe	58	E3
Arncott	22	B1
Arncroach	89	H8
Arne	12	B7
Arnesby	43	J7
Arnisdale	92	E4
Arnish	100	B8
Arniston Engine	81	J5
Arnol	107	H4
Arnold	43	H2
Arnprior	79	J2
Arnside	57	H3
Arpafeelie	102	E7
Arrad Foot	57	G2
Arram	61	H6
Arrathorne	59	H1
Arreton	13	H7
Arrington	35	G4
Arrochar	78	E1
Arrow	32	C4
Artafallie	102	E8
Aspenden	35	G7
Arthington	59	H6
Arthingworth	34	A1
Arthog	37	F5
Arthrath	97	J2
Arundel	14	D5
Asby	62	F5
Ascog	78	D5
Ascot	22	E6
Ascott-under-Wychwood	21	H1
Asenby	59	J3
Asfordby	43	K5
Asfordby Hill	43	K5
Asgarby, Lincs	44	E2
Asgarby, Lincs	55	H7
Ash, Kent	24	B6
Ash, Surrey	22	D7
Ash, Somer	11	F3
Ash, Kent	25	J7
Ashampstead	21	K5
Ashbocking	37	G4
Ashbourne	42	D2
Ashbrittle	10	B3
Ashburton	5	H3
Ashbury, Devon	8	F6
Ashbury, Oxon	21	G4
Ashby	54	D3
Ashby by Partney	55	J7
Ashby cum Fenby	55	G3
Ashby de la Launde	44	D1
Ashby Folville	43	K5
Ashby-de-la-Zouch	43	F5
Ashby-by-Stone	42	B3
Ashby Magna	43	H7
Ashby Parva	33	H1
Ashby St Ledgers	33	H3
Ashby St Mary	47	J6
Ashchurch	32	B6
Ashcombe	5	K2
Ashcott	11	F2
Ashdon	35	J5
Asheldham	25	F2
Ashen	36	C5
Ashendon	22	B1
Ashfield, Central	80	C1
Ashfield, Suff	37	H3
Ashfield Green	37	H2
Ashford, Devon	9	F2
Ashford, Surrey	22	F5
Ashford, Kent	17	H1
Ashford Bowdler	31	G2
Ashford Carbonell	31	G2
Ashford Hill	21	K6
Ashford in the Water	52	D7
Ashgill	80	C7
Ashill, Devon	10	B4
Ashill, Norf	46	D6
Ashill, Somer	10	E4
Ashingdon	24	E3
Ashington, W. Susx	14	E4
Ashington, Northum	75	J6
Ashkirk	74	A2
Ashleworth	31	K7
Ashley, Northnts	34	A2
Ashley, Cambs	36	B3
Ashley, Glos	20	D3
Ashley, Hants	13	F2
Ashley, Devon	9	G4
Ashley, Ches	51	G5
Ashley, Staffs	41	J3
Ashley Green	22	E2
Ashley Heath, Dorset	12	D5
Ashley Heath, Staffs	41	J3
Ash Magna	41	G3
Ashmansworth	21	J7
Ashmansworthy	8	D4
Ashmore	12	B4
Ashmore Park	42	B6
Ashorne	33	F4
Ashover	53	F7
Ashow	33	F2
Ashperton	31	H5
Ashprington	5	J4
Ash Priors	10	C3
Ashreigney	9	G4
Ashtead	23	G7
Ash Thomas	10	B4
Ashton, Northnts	34	A4
Ashton, Northnts	34	D1
Ashton, Ches	50	E7
Ashton, Corn	2	E7
Ashton, H. & W	31	G3
Ashton Common	20	C7
Ashton in Makerfield	50	E4
Ashton Keynes	20	E3
Ashton under Hill	32	B6
Ashton-under-Lyne	51	J4
Ashton upon Mersey	51	G4
Ashurst, W. Susx	14	E4
Ashurst, Hants	13	F4
Ashurst, Kent	15	J2
Ashurst Wood	15	H2
Ashwater	8	D6
Ashwell, Leic	44	B5
Ashwell, Herts	35	F6
Ashwellthorpe	47	G7
Ashwick	11	H1
Ashwicken	46	C5
Askam in Furness	56	F3
Askern	53	H2
Askerswell	11	G6
Askett	22	D2
Askham, Notts	54	B6
Askham, Cumbr	64	C5
Askham Bryan	60	C6
Askham Richard	60	C6
Asknish	77	J2
Askrigg	58	E1
Askwith	59	G6
Aslackby	44	D3
Aslacton	47	G7
Aslockton	44	A2
Asloun	96	E4
Aspall	37	G3
Aspatria	63	G3
Aspenden	35	G7
Aspley Guise	34	C6
Aspull	50	F3
Asselby	60	E8
Assington	36	E6
Astbury	51	H7
Astcote	33	J4
Asterley	40	E6
Asterton	40	E7
Asthall	21	G1
Asthall Leigh	21	H1
Astley, Warw	43	F8
Astley, Shrops	41	G5
Astley, H. & W	31	J3
Astley Abbots	41	J7
Astley Cross	31	K3
Astley Green	51	G4
Aston, Berks	22	C4
Aston, W. Mids	42	C8
Aston, Derby	52	D5
Aston, Ches	50	E6
Aston, Herts	35	F7
Aston, H. & W	31	F2
Aston, Shrops	41	G4
Aston, S. Yks	53	G5
Aston, Ches	41	H2
Aston, Oxon	21	H2
Aston, Shrops	41	H6
Aston, Staffs	41	J2
Aston Abbotts	34	B7
Aston Botterell	31	H1
Aston-by-Stone	42	B3
Aston Cantlow	32	D3
Aston Clinton	22	D1
Aston Crews	31	H7
Aston End	35	F7
Aston Eyre	41	H7
Aston Fields	32	B3
Aston Flamville	43	G7
Aston Ingham	31	H7
Aston juxta Mondrum	41	H1
Aston le Walls	33	G4
Aston Magna	32	D6
Aston Munslow	31	G1
Aston on Clun	30	E1
Aston-on-Trent	43	G4
Aston Rogers	40	E6
Aston Rowant	22	C3
Aston Sandford	22	C2
Aston Somerville	32	C6
Aston Subedge	32	D5
Aston Tirrold	21	K4
Aston Upthorpe	21	K4
Astwick	35	F6
Astwood	34	C5
Astwood Bank	32	C3
Aswarby	44	D3
Aswardby	55	H6
Atcham	41	G6
Atch Lench	32	C4
Athelhampton	11	J6
Athelington	37	H2
Athelney	10	E3
Athelstaneford	82	D4
Atherington	9	F3
Atherstone	43	F7
Atherstone on Stour	32	E4
Atherton	51	F3
Atlow	42	E2
Attadale	93	F2
Attadale	93	F2
Attenborough	43	H3
Attleborough, Norf	46	F7
Attleborough, Warw	43	F7
Attlebridge	47	G5
Atwick	61	J5
Atworth	20	C6
Auchagallon	70	D1
Aucharnie	97	F1
Auchattie	97	F6
Auchenblae	97	G8
Auchenbrack	72	C5
Auchencairn	70	D1
Auchencarroch	79	G3
Auchencrow	83	G5
Auchengray	80	E6
Auchenhalrig	104	C2
Auchenheath	80	D7
Auchentiber	79	F7
Auchgourish	95	H4
Auchindrain	78	C1
Auchindrean	101	H4
Auchininna	104	F4
Auchinleck	72	A2
Auchinloch	79	J4
Auchleuchries	97	K2
Auchlochan	96	F3
Auchlossan	96	E5
Auchlyne	87	H6
Auchmillan	71	L2
Auchmithie	89	J4
Auchnacree	89	G2
Auchnagallin	95	J2
Auchnagatt	97	J1
Auchterarder	88	B7
Auchteraw	94	B5
Auchterderran	81	H2
Auchterhouse	89	G4
Auchtermuchty	88	E7
Auchterneed	102	C7
Auchtertool	81	H2
Auchtertyre	92	E3
Auchtubh	87	H6
Auckengill	111	K2
Auckley	53	J3
Audenshaw	51	J4
Audlem	41	H2
Audley	41	J1
Auds	104	F2
Aughton, Lancs	50	C3
Aughton, Humbs	60	E7
Aughton, S. Yks	53	G5
Aughton, Lancs	57	J4
Aughton Park	50	D3
Auldearn	103	H7
Aulden	31	F4
Auldhame	82	D3
Auldhouse	79	J6
Ault a' Chruinn	93	F3
Aultbea	100	E4
Aultdearg	101	J6
Aultgrishan	100	D4
Aultiphurst	110	E2
Aultmore	104	D3
Ault-na-goire	94	D3
Aulton	96	F3
Aundorach	95	H4
Aunsby	44	D3
Auquhorthies	97	H3
Aust	19	K4
Austerfield	53	J4
Austrey	42	E6
Austwick	58	C4
Authorpe	55	J5
Authorpe Row	55	K6
Avebury	20	E6
Aveley	24	B4
Avening	20	C3
Averdaron	38	A4
Averffraw	48	C4
Averham	44	A1
Aveton Gifford	5	G5
Avielochan	95	H4
Aviemore	95	G4
Avington	21	H6
Avoch	102	F7
Avon	12	D6
Avonbridge	80	E4
Avon Dassett	33	G4
Avonmouth	19	K5
Avon Wick	5	H4
Awbridge	13	F3
Awkley	19	K4
Awliscombe	10	C5
Awre	20	B2
Awsworth	43	G2
Axbridge	19	J7
Axford, Wilts	21	G5
Axford, Hants	13	J1
Axminster	10	D6
Axmouth	10	D6
Aylburton	19	L2
Ayle	64	D3
Aylesbeare	10	B6
Aylesbury	22	D1
Aylesby	55	G3
Aylesford	24	D7
Aylesham	25	J7
Aylestone	43	H6
Aylmerton	47	G3
Aylsham	47	G4
Aylton	31	H6
Aymestrey	31	F3
Aynho	33	H6
Ayot St Lawrence	23	G1
Ayot St Peter	23	H1
Ayr	71	J2
Aysgarth	58	F2

Ayside....57 G2
Ayston....44 B6
Aythorpe Roding....24 B1
Ayton, N. Yks.....61 G2
Ayton, Border....83 H5
Aywick....117 G4
Azerley....59 H3

B

Babbacombe....5 K3
Babbinswood....40 E3
Babcary....11 G3
Babel....29 F6
Babell....50 A6
Babraham....35 J4
Babworth....53 J5
Bac....107 J4
Backaland....113 F3
Backbarrow....57 G2
Backburn, Grampn.....96 E2
Backburn, Grampn.....97 H6
Backfolds....105 K3
Backford....50 C6
Backhill, Grampn.....97 G2
Backhill, Grampn.....97 K2
Backhill of Clackriach....105 J4
Backhill of Trustach....97 F6
Backies....103 G2
Backlass....111 J3
Backmuir of New Gilston....89 G8
Back of Keppoch....92 C7
Backwell....19 J6
Backworth....75 K7
Bacon End....24 C1
Baconsthorpe....47 G3
Bacton, H. & W.....30 E6
Bacton, Suff.....36 F3
Bacton, Norf.....47 J3
Bacup....51 H1
Badachro....100 D5
Badbury....21 F4
Badby....33 H4
Badcall, Highld.....108 C4
Badcall, Highld.....108 D3
Badcaul....101 G3
Baddeley Green....42 B1
Baddesley Ensor....42 E7
Baddidarach....108 B6
Badenscoth....97 G2
Badger....41 J7
Badgers Mount....23 K6
Badgeworth....20 D1
Badgworth....19 H7
Badicaul....92 D3
Badingham....37 J3
Badlesmere....25 G7
Badluarach....101 F3
Badminton....20 C4
Badninish....103 F3
Badrallach....101 G3
Badsey....32 C5
Badsworth....53 G2
Badwell Ash....36 E3
Bagby....60 B2
Bagendon....20 E2
Bage, The....30 D5
Bagillt....50 B6
Baginton....33 F2
Baglan....18 B3
Bagley....40 F4
Bagnall....42 B1
Bagshot, Surrey....22 E6
Bagshot, Wilts.....21 H6
Bagthorpe, Norf.....46 C3
Bagthorpe, Notts.....43 G1
Bagworth....43 G6
Bagwyllydiart....31 F7
Baildon....59 G7
Baile....98 E4
Bailebeag....94 D4
Baile Boidheach....77 G4
Baile Mor....84 D6
Baillieston....79 J5
Bail Uachdraich....98 D6
Bainbridge....58 E1
Bainton, Cambs.....44 D6
Bainton, Oxon.....21 H2
Bainton, Humbs.....61 G5
Bairnkine....74 C3
Bakers End....23 J1
Baker Street....24 C4
Bakewell....52 E7
Bala....39 J3
Balachuirn....92 B1
Balaglas....98 D7
Balallan....107 G6
Balbeg....94 C3
Balbeggie....88 D6
Balbithan....97 G4
Balblair....102 F6
Balcherry....103 G4
Balchladich....108 B5
Balchraggan....102 D8
Balchrick....108 C2
Balcombe....15 G2
Balcurvie....81 J1
Baldersby....59 J3
Balderstone....58 B7
Balderton....44 B1
Baldhu....2 F5
Baldinnie....89 G7
Baldock....35 F6
Baldrine....56 R3
Baldwin....56 Q3
Baldwinholme....63 J2
Baldwin's Gate....41 J2
Bale....46 F3
Balemartine....84 A4
Balephuil....84 A4
Balerno....81 G5
Balevullin....84 A4
Balfield....89 H2

Balfour....112 E5
Balfron....79 H3
Balgaveny....97 F1
Balgedie....88 D8
Balgonar....80 F2
Balgove....97 H2
Balgowan....94 E6
Balgown....99 J6
Balgrochan....79 J4
Balgy....100 E7
Balhalgardy....97 G3
Baligill....110 E2
Balintore....103 G5
Balintraid....103 F5
Balivanich....98 C7
Balkholme....60 E8
Balkissock....71 G6
Ball....40 E4
Balla....90 C4
Ballabeg....56 P4
Ballacannell....56 R3
Ballacarnane Beg....56 Q3
Ballachulish....86 C3
Ballagyr....56 P3
Ballajora....56 R2
Ballamodha....56 P4
Ballantrushal....107 H3
Ballantrae....71 F6
Ballasalla, I. of M.....56 P5
Ballasalla, I. of M.....56 Q2
Ballater....96 C6
Ballaugh....56 Q2
Balleigh....102 F4
Ballencrieff....82 C4
Ball Hill....21 J6
Balliasta....117 H2
Balliekine....77 H8
Ballig....56 P3
Ballinaby....76 B3
Ballinger Common....22 E2
Ballingham....31 G6
Ballingry....81 G2
Ballinluig....88 B3
Ballintuim....88 D3
Balloch, Strath.....79 F3
Balloch, Highld.....103 F8
Ballochan....96 E6
Balls Cross....14 C3
Ballygown....85 F4
Ballygrant....76 C5
Ballymichael....70 E1
Balmacara....92 E3
Balmacara Square....92 E3
Balmaclellan....72 B7
Balmae....69 H6
Balmaha....79 G2
Balmartin....98 C5
Balmedie....97 J4
Balmerino....89 F6
Balmer Lawn....13 F5
Balmore....79 J4
Balmullo....89 G6
Balnabodach....90 C5
Balnacoil....110 E7
Balnacra....101 F8
Balnaguard....88 B3
Balnaguisich....102 E5
Balnahard....85 F5
Balnain....94 C2
Balnakeil....108 E2
Balnaknock....99 K6
Balnapaling....103 F6
Balne....53 H2
Balquhidder....87 H6
Balranald....98 C6
Balsall Common....32 E2
Balscote....33 F5
Balsham....35 J4
Baltasound....117 H2
Balterley....41 J1
Balthangie....105 H3
Baltonsborough....11 G2
Balvaird....102 D7
Balvicar....85 J7
Balvraid....95 G2
Bamber Bridge....50 E1
Bamburgh....75 H1
Bamford....52 E5
Bampton, Cumbr.....64 C6
Bampton, Oxon.....21 H2
Bampton, Devon.....9 K3
Banavie....93 H8
Banbury....33 G5
Banchory....97 G6
Banchory-Devenick....97 J5
Bancyfelin....27 H5
Bancyffordd....27 J3
Banff....105 F2
Bangor....48 E3
Bangor-is-y-coed....40 E2
Banham....36 F1
Bank....12 E5
Bankend, Strath.....72 D1
Bankend, D. & G.....73 F8
Bankfoot....88 C5
Bankglen....72 A3
Bankhead, Grampn.....97 F5
Bankhead, Grampn.....97 H4
Bank Newton....58 E5
Banknock....80 C4
Banks, Lancs.....50 C1
Banks, Cumbr.....64 C1
Bankshill....73 G6
Bank Street....31 H3
Banningham....47 H4
Bannister Green....36 B7
Bannockburn....80 D2
Banstead....23 H7
Bantham....5 G5
Banton....80 C4
Banton....19 H7
Bapchild....24 F6
Bapton....12 B2
Baramore....92 C8
Barassie....71 J1

Barbaraville....103 F5
Barber Booth....52 D5
Barbon....57 K2
Barbridge....50 F7
Barbrook....9 H1
Barby....33 H2
Barcaldine....86 B4
Barcheston....32 E6
Barcombe....15 H4
Barcombe Cross....15 H4
Barden....59 G1
Bardfield Saling....36 B7
Bardney....54 F7
Bardowie....79 H4
Bardrainney....79 F4
Bardsea....57 G3
Bardsey....59 J6
Bardsley....51 J3
Bardwell....36 E2
Barford, Warw.....32 E3
Barford, Norf.....47 G6
Barford St Martin....12 C2
Barford St Michael....33 G6
Barfrestone....25 J7
Bargoed....18 F3
Bargrennan....71 J7
Barham, Cambs.....34 E2
Barham, Suff.....37 G4
Barham, Kent....25 J7
Bar Hill....35 G3
Barholm....44 D5
Barkby....43 J6
Barkestone-le-Vale....44 A3
Barkham....22 C6
Barking, Suff.....36 F4
Barking, G. Lon.....23 K4
Barkingside....23 K4
Barkisland....52 C2
Barkston....44 C2
Barkston Ash....60 B7
Barkway....35 G6
Barkwith....55 F5
Barlaston....42 A3
Barlavington....14 C4
Barlborough....53 G6
Barlby....60 D7
Barlestone....43 G6
Barley, Lancs.....58 D6
Barley, Herts.....35 G6
Barleythorpe....44 B6
Barling....24 F4
Barlow, N. Yks.....60 D8
Barlow, Derby.....53 F6
Barlow, T. & W.....65 J1
Barmby Moor....60 E6
Barmby on the Marsh....60 D8
Barmer....46 D3
Barmouth....38 F5
Barmpton....66 D6
Barmston....61 J5
Barnack....44 D6
Barnacle....33 F1
Barnard Castle....65 H6
Barnard Gate....21 J1
Barnardiston....36 C5
Barnburgh....53 G3
Barnby....47 K8
Barnby Dun....53 J3
Barnby in the Willows....44 B1
Barnby Moor....53 J5
Barnes....23 H5
Barnetby le Wold....54 E3
Barney....46 E3
Barnham, W. Susx.....14 C5
Barnham, Suff.....36 D2
Barnham Broom....47 F6
Barnhead....89 J3
Barnhill....103 K7
Barningham, Suff.....36 E2
Barningham, Durham.....65 H6
Barnoldby le Beck....55 G3
Barnoldswick....58 D6
Barns Green....14 E3
Barnsley, Glos.....20 E2
Barnsley, S. Yks.....53 F3
Barnstaple....9 F2
Barnston, Mers.....50 B5
Barnston, Essex.....24 C1
Barnstone....43 K3
Barnt Green....32 C2
Barnton....51 F6
Barnwell....20 D1
Barnwood....20 C1
Barony, The....112 C4
Barr....71 H5
Barrachan....68 E6
Barrack....105 H4
Barraglom....107 F5
Barrahormid....77 G3
Barran....85 K6
Barrapol....84 A4
Barras, Cumbr.....65 F6
Barras, Grampn.....97 H7
Barrasford....74 F7
Barravullin....85 K8
Barregarrow....56 Q3
Barrhead....79 H6
Barrhill....71 H6
Barrington, Somer.....10 E4
Barrington, Cambs.....35 G5
Barripper....2 E6
Barrmill....79 F6
Barrock....111 J1
Barrow, Leic.....44 B5
Barrow, Suff.....36 C3
Barrow, Lancs.....58 C7
Barrow, Shrops.....41 H6
Barroway Drove....45 J6
Barrowby....44 B3
Barrowden....44 C6
Barrowford....58 D7
Barrow Gurney....19 K6
Barrow-in-Furness....56 E4
Barrow Street....11 K2

Barrow upon Humber....54 E1
Barrow upon Soar....43 H5
Barrow upon Trent....43 F4
Barry, S. Glam.....18 F6
Barry, Tays.....89 H5
Barry Island....18 F6
Barsby....43 J5
Barsham....47 J8
Barston....32 E2
Bartestree....31 G5
Bartford St Martin....12 C2
Barthol Chapel....97 H2
Barthomley....41 J1
Bartley....13 F4
Bartlow....35 J5
Barton, N. Yks.....66 C7
Barton, Warw.....32 D4
Barton, Glos.....32 D7
Barton, Ches.....41 F1
Barton, Cambs.....35 H4
Barton, Lancs.....57 J7
Barton, Devon.....5 K3
Barton, Norf.....47 K6
Barton Bendish....46 C6
Barton in Fabis....43 H3
Barton Hartshorn....33 J6
Barton in the Beans....43 F6
Barton-le-Clay....34 D6
Barton-le-Street....60 E3
Barton-le-Willows....60 E4
Barton Mills....36 C2
Barton Moss....51 G4
Barton on Sea....12 E6
Barton-on-the-Heath....32 E6
Barton Seagrave....34 B2
Barton Stacey....13 G1
Barton St David....11 G2
Barton Turf....47 J4
Barton-under-Needwood....42 D5
Barton-upon-Humber....54 E1
Barvas....107 H4
Barway....35 J2
Barwell....43 G7
Barwick....11 G4
Barwick in Elmet....59 K7
Baschurch....41 F4
Bascote....33 G3
Basford Green....42 B1
Bashall Eaves....58 C6
Bashley....12 E6
Basildon....24 D4
Basingstoke....22 B7
Baslow....52 E6
Bason Bridge....10 E1
Bassaleg....19 G4
Bassenthwaite....63 H4
Bassett....13 G4
Bassingbourn....35 G5
Bassingfield....43 J3
Bassingham....54 D8
Bassingthorpe....44 C4
Basta....117 G3
Baston....44 E5
Bastwick....47 K5
Batchcott....31 F2
Batchworth....23 F2
Batcombe, Somer.....11 H2
Batcombe, Dorset.....11 H5
Bate Heath....51 F6
Bath....20 B6
Bathampton....20 B6
Bathealton....10 B3
Batheaston....20 B6
Bathford....20 B6
Bathgate....80 E5
Bathley....54 B8
Bathpool....4 C2
Batley....52 E1
Batsford....32 D6
Battersby....67 F7
Battersea....23 H5
Battisford....36 F4
Battisford Tye....36 F4
Battle, E. Susx.....16 E4
Battle, Powys.....29 H6
Battlefield....41 G5
Battlesbridge....24 D3
Battlesden....34 C7
Battleton....9 K3
Battramsley....13 F6
Bauds of Cullen....104 D2
Baughurst....21 K6
Baulking....21 H3
Baumber....55 G6
Baunton....20 E2
Baverstock....12 C2
Bawburgh....47 G6
Bawdeswell....46 F4
Bawdrip....10 E2
Bawdsey....37 J5
Bawtry....53 J4
Baxenden....51 G1
Baxterley....42 E7
Baycliff....57 F3
Baydon....21 G5
Bayford....23 J2
Bayham Abbey....16 C2
Bayhead....98 C6
Bayles....64 E3
Baylham....37 G4
Bayston Hill....41 F6
Bayton....31 H2
Bayworth....21 H2
Beachampton....34 A6
Beachamwell....46 C6
Beachans....103 J8
Beachborough....17 J2
Beachley....19 K3
Beacon....10 C5
Beacon End....36 E7
Beacon's Bottom....22 C3
Beaconsfield....22 E3
Beacravik....99 G3
Beadlam....60 D2
Beadnell....75 J2
Beaford....9 F4
Beal, N. Yks.....53 H1
Beal, Northum.....83 J7

Beaminster....11 F5
Beamish....66 C2
Beamsley....59 F5
Bean....24 B5
Beanacre....20 D6
Beanley....75 G3
Beaquoy....112 C4
Beare Green....14 E1
Bearley....32 D3
Bearpark....66 C3
Bearsbridge....64 E2
Bearsden....79 H4
Bearsted....24 D7
Bearwood....12 C6
Bearwood, H. & W.....30 E4
Beattock....73 F4
Beauchamp Roding....24 B1
Beauchief....53 F5
Beaufort....18 F1
Beaulieu....13 F5
Beauly....102 D8
Beaumaris....48 F3
Beaumont, Essex.....37 G7
Beaumont, Cumbr.....63 J2
Beausale....32 E2
Beaworthy....8 E6
Beazley End....36 C7
Bebington....50 C5
Bebside....75 J6
Beccles....47 K7
Becconsall....50 D1
Beckbury....41 J6
Beckenham....23 J6
Beckermet....62 F7
Beckermonds....58 D2
Beckfoot, Cumbr.....63 F3
Beckfoot, Cumbr.....63 G7
Beck Foot, Cumbr.....57 K1
Beckford....32 B6
Beckhampton....20 E6
Beck Hole....67 J7
Beckingham, Lincs.....44 B1
Beckingham, Notts.....54 B4
Beckington....20 C7
Beckley, E. Susx.....16 F3
Beckley, Oxon.....21 K1
Beck Row....36 B2
Beck Side....57 F2
Beckton....23 K4
Beckwithshaw....59 H5
Becontree....23 K4
Bedale....59 H2
Bedburn....65 J4
Beddau....18 E4
Beddgelert....38 E2
Beddingham....15 H5
Beddington....23 J6
Bedfield....37 H3
Bedford....34 D5
Bedhampton....13 K5
Bedingfield....37 G3
Bedlington....75 J6
Bedlinog....18 E2
Bedmond....23 F2
Bednall....42 B5
Bedrule....74 C3
Bedstone....30 E2
Bedwas....19 F4
Bedworth....33 F1
Bedworth Heath....33 F1
Beeby....43 J6
Beech, Staffs.....42 A3
Beech, Hants.....13 J2
Beech Hill....22 B6
Beechingstoke....20 E7
Beedon....21 J5
Beeford....61 J5
Beeley....52 E7
Beelsby....55 G3
Beenham....21 K6
Beer....10 D7
Beer Crocombe....10 E3
Beer Hackett....11 G4
Beesands....5 J5
Beesby....55 J5
Beeson....5 J5
Beeston, Beds.....34 E5
Beeston, Norf.....46 E5
Beeston, Ches.....50 E8
Beeston, W. Yks.....59 H7
Beeston Regis....47 G2
Beeswing....72 D8
Beetham....57 H3
Beetley....46 E5
Begbroke....21 J1
Begelly....26 F6
Beguildy....30 C2
Beighton, S. Yks.....53 G5
Beighton, Norf.....47 J6
Beith....79 F6
Bekesbourne....25 J7
Belaugh....47 H5
Belbroughton....32 B2
Belchamp Otten....36 D5
Belchamp St Paul....36 C5
Belchamp Walter....36 D5
Belchford....55 G6
Belford....75 H1
Belhelvie....97 J4
Belhinnie....96 C4
Bellabeg....96 C4
Bellanoch....77 G2
Bellasize....60 E7
Bellaty....88 E3
Belleau....55 J6
Bell Busk....58 E5
Belleheiglash....95 K2
Bellerby....59 G1
Bellever....5 G2
Bellfield....71 F8
Bellingdon....22 E2
Bellingham....74 E6
Belloch....77 F8
Bellochantuy....70 B1
Bellsbank....71 K4
Bellshill, Strath.....80 C6
Bellshill, Northum.....75 H1
Bellsmyre....79 G4

Bellspool....81 G8
Bellsquarry....81 F5
Bells Yew Green....16 D2
Belmesthorpe....44 D5
Belmont....51 F2
Belnacraig....96 C4
Belowda....3 H3
Belper....43 F2
Belsay....75 H7
Belses....74 B2
Belsford....5 H4
Belstead....37 G5
Belston....71 J2
Belstone....9 G6
Belthorn....51 G1
Beltinge....25 J6
Beltoft....54 C3
Belton, Humbs.....54 B3
Belton, Lincs.....44 C3
Belton, Leic.....43 G4
Belton, Norf.....47 K6
Belton-in-Rutland....44 B6
Belvedere....23 K5
Belvoir....44 B3
Bembridge....13 J7
Bemersyde....74 B1
Bempton....61 J3
Benacre....37 L1
Benbuie....72 C5
Ben Casgro....107 J6
Benderloch....86 B5
Benenden....16 F2
Bengate....47 J4
Benholm....89 L2
Beningbrough....60 C5
Benington, Lincs.....45 G2
Benington, Herts.....35 G7
Benllech....48 E2
Benmore, Strath.....78 D3
Benmore, Central.....87 G6
Bennacott....6 C6
Bennan....70 E2
Bennecarrigan....70 E2
Benniworth....55 G5
Benover....16 E1
Benson....22 B3
Benthall....41 H6
Bentham....20 D1
Benthoul....97 H5
Bentley, Hants.....14 A1
Bentley, H. & W.....32 B3
Bentley, Warw.....42 E7
Bentley, Suff.....37 G5
Bentley, S. Yks.....53 H3
Bentley, Humbs.....61 H7
Bentley Heath....32 D2
Bentpath....73 J1
Bentworth....13 J1
Benwick....45 G7
Beoley....32 C3
Beoraidbeg....92 C6
Bepton....14 B4
Berden....35 H7
Berea....26 B4
Bere Alston....4 E3
Bere Ferrers....4 E3
Berepper....2 E7
Bere Regis....11 K6
Bergh Apton....47 K6
Berinsfield....21 K3
Berkeley....20 A3
Berkhamsted....22 E2
Berkley....11 K1
Berkswell....32 E2
Bermondsey....23 J5
Bernera....92 E3
Bernisdale....99 K7
Berrick Salome....22 B3
Berriedale....111 H6
Berrier....63 K5
Berriew....40 C6
Berrington, Shrops.....41 G6
Berrington, Northum.....83 J7
Berrow....19 G7
Berrow, H. & W.....31 J6
Berrow Green....31 J4
Berry Hill....19 K1
Berryhillock....104 E2
Berrynarbor....9 F1
Berry Pomeroy....5 J3
Bersham....40 E2
Bersted....14 C5
Berwick....15 J5
Berwick Bassett....20 F5
Berwick Hill....75 H7
Berwick St James....12 C2
Berwick St John....12 B3
Berwick St Leonard....12 B2
Berwick-upon-Tweed....83 H6
Berwyn....40 C2
Besford....20 B5
Bessacarr....53 J3
Bessels Leigh....21 J2
Bessingham....47 G3
Besthorpe, Notts.....54 C7
Besthorpe, Norf.....46 F7
Beswick....61 H6
Betchworth....23 H7
Bethania, Dyfed.....28 C3
Bethania, Gwyn.....39 F1
Bethel....48 E4
Bethersden....17 G1
Bethesda, Dyfed.....26 E5
Bethesda, Gwyn.....49 F4
Bethlehem....28 D7
Bethnal Green....23 J4
Betley....41 J2
Betsham....24 C5
Betteshanger....25 K7
Bettiscombe....10 E6
Bettisfield....41 F3
Betton, Shrops.....40 E6
Betton, Shrops.....41 H3
Bettws, Gwent....19 G1
Bettws, Gwent....19 G3

Bettws Cedewain...40 C7
Bettws Gwerfil Goch...40 B2
Bettws Newydd...19 H2
Bettyhill...110 D2
Betws, M. Glam...18 D4
Betws, Dyfed...27 L5
Betws Bledrws...27 K1
Betws Garmon...38 E1
Betws Ifan...27 H2
Betws-y-Coed...39 G1
Betws-yn-Rhos...49 J3
Beulah, Dyfed...27 G2
Beulah, Powys...29 G4
Bevendean...15 G5
Bevercotes...53 J6
Beverley...61 H7
Beverston...20 C3
Bevington...20 A3
Bewaldeth...63 H4
Bewcastle...74 B7
Bewdley...31 J2
Bewerley...59 G4
Bewholme...61 J5
Bexhill...16 E5
Bexley...23 K5
Bexleyheath...23 K5
Bexwell...46 B6
Beyton...36 E3
Bibury...20 F2
Bicester...33 H7
Bickenhall...10 D4
Bickenhill...32 D1
Bicker...45 F3
Bickerstaffe...50 D3
Bickerton, Ches...41 G1
Bickerton, N. Yks...59 K5
Bickington, Devon...9 F2
Bickington, Devon...5 H2
Bickleigh, Devon...4 F3
Bickleigh, Devon...9 K5
Bickleton...8 F2
Bickley...23 K6
Bickley Moss...41 G2
Bicknacre...24 D2
Bicknoller...10 C2
Bicknor...24 E7
Bickton...12 D4
Bicton, Shrops...30 D1
Bicton, Shrops...41 F5
Bidborough...16 C1
Biddenden...16 F2
Biddenham...34 D4
Biddestone...20 C5
Biddisham...19 H7
Biddlesden...33 J5
Biddlestone...75 F4
Biddulph...42 A1
Biddulph Moor...51 J8
Bideford...8 E3
Bidford-on-Avon...32 D4
Bielby...60 E6
Bieldside...97 H5
Bierley...7 K7
Bierton...22 D1
Bigbury...5 G5
Bigbury-on-Sea...5 G5
Bigby...54 E3
Biggar, Cumbr...56 E4
Biggar, Strath...81 F8
Biggin, N. Yks...60 C7
Biggin, Derby...52 D8
Biggin, Derby...42 E2
Biggings...114 D2
Biggin Hill...23 K7
Biggins...57 K3
Biggleswade...35 E5
Bighton...13 J2
Bignor...14 C4
Bigrigg...63 F6
Big Sand...100 D5
Bigton...115 F6
Bilberry...3 J3
Bilborough...43 H2
Bilbrook...42 A6
Bilbrough...60 C6
Bilbster...111 J3
Bildeston...36 E5
Billericay...24 C3
Billesdon...43 K6
Billesley...32 D4
Billing...34 B3
Billingborough...44 F1
Billinge...50 E3
Billingford, Norf...46 F4
Billingford, Suff...37 G2
Billingham...66 E5
Billinghay...44 E1
Billingley...53 G3
Billingshurst...14 D3
Billingsley...31 J1
Billington, Lancs...58 C7
Billington, Beds...34 C7
Billockby...47 K5
Billy Row...66 B4
Bilsborrow...57 J6
Bilsby...55 J6
Bilsington...17 H2
Bilsthorpe...53 J7
Bilston, W. Mids...42 B7
Bilston, Loth...81 H5
Bilstone...43 F6
Bilting...17 H1
Bilton, N. Yks...60 B5
Bilton, Warw...33 G2
Bilton, Northum...75 J3
Bilton, Humbs...61 J7
Bimbister...112 D5
Binbrook...55 G4
Bincombe...11 H1
Binegar...11 H1
Binfield...22 D5
Binfield Heath...22 C5
Bingfield...75 F7
Bingham...43 K3
Bingley...59 G7

Binham...46 E3
Binley, W. Mids...33 F2
Binley, Hants...21 J7
Binley Woods...33 F2
Binniehill...80 D4
Binstead...13 H6
Binsted...14 A1
Binton...32 D4
Bintree...46 F4
Binweston...40 E6
Birch, Essex...25 F1
Birch, G. Man...51 H3
Bircham Newton...46 C3
Bircham Tofts...46 C3
Birchanger...35 J7
Bircher...31 F3
Birch Green...25 F1
Birchgrove...18 B3
Birchington...25 J6
Birchover...52 E7
Birch Vale...52 C5
Birchwood...54 D7
Bircotes...53 J4
Birdbrook...36 C5
Birdham...14 B5
Birdingbury...33 G3
Birdlip...20 D1
Birdsall...60 F4
Birdsgreen...31 J1
Birdston...79 J4
Birdwell...53 F3
Birdwood...20 B1
Birgham...83 F8
Birkdale...50 C2
Birkenhead...50 C5
Birkenhills...105 G4
Birkenshaw, Strath...80 B5
Birkenshaw, W. Yks...59 H8
Birkhall...96 C6
Birkhill...89 F5
Birkin...53 H1
Birley...31 F4
Birling, Kent...24 C6
Birling, Northum...75 J4
Birlingham...32 B5
Birmingham...32 C1
Birnam...88 C4
Birness...97 J2
Birse...96 E6
Birsemore...96 E6
Birstall...43 H6
Birstall Smithies...52 E1
Birstwith...59 H5
Birts Street...31 J6
Birtley, T. & W...66 C2
Birtley, H. & W...30 E3
Birtley, Northum...74 E7
Bisbrooke...44 B7
Bisham...22 B4
Bishampton...32 B4
Bishop Auckland...66 C5
Bishopbriggs...79 J4
Bishop Burton...61 G7
Bishop Middleham...66 D4
Bishop Monkton...59 J4
Bishop Norton...54 D4
Bishopsbourne...25 H7
Bishops Cannings...20 E6
Bishop's Castle...30 E1
Bishop's Caundle...11 H4
Bishop's Cleeve...32 B7
Bishop's Frome...31 H5
Bishop's Itchington...33 F4
Bishops Lydeard...10 C3
Bishop's Nympton...9 H3
Bishop's Offley...41 J4
Bishop's Stortford...35 H7
Bishop's Sutton...13 J2
Bishop's Tachbrook...33 F3
Bishop's Tawton...9 F2
Bishopsteignton...5 K2
Bishopstoke...13 G4
Bishopston...27 K8
Bishopstone, Wilts...12 C3
Bishopstone, Bucks...22 D1
Bishopstone, H. & W...31 F5
Bishopstone, Wilts...21 G4
Bishopstone, E. Susx...15 H5
Bishop Sutton...19 K7
Bishop's Waltham...13 H4
Bishopswood, Somer...10 D4
Bishop's Wood, Staffs...41 K6
Bishopsworth...19 K6
Bishop Thornton...59 H4
Bishopthorpe...60 C6
Bishopton, Durham...66 D5
Bishopton, Strath...79 G4
Bishop Wilton...60 E5
Bishton...19 H4
Bisley, Glos...20 D2
Bisley, Surrey...22 E7
Bispham...57 G6
Bissoe...2 F5
Bisterne Close...12 E5
Bitchfield...44 C4
Bittadon...9 F1
Bittaford...5 G4
Bittering...46 E5
Bitterley...31 G2
Bitterne...13 G4
Bitteswell...33 H1
Bitton...20 A6
Bix...22 C4
Bixter...115 F3
Blaby...43 H7
Blackacre...73 F5
Blackawton...5 J4
Blackborough...10 B5
Blackborough End...46 B5
Black Bourton...21 G2
Blackboys...15 J3
Blackbrook...41 J3
Blackburn, Lancs...58 B8
Blackburn, Loth...80 E5
Blackburn, Grampn...97 H4

Black Callerton...75 H8
Black Clauchrie...71 H6
Black Crofts...86 B5
Blackden Heath...51 G6
Black Dog, Devon...9 G3
Blackfield...13 G5
Blackford, Tays...88 A8
Blackford, Somer...11 F1
Blackford, Somer...11 H3
Blackford, Cumbr...63 J1
Blackfordby...43 F5
Blackgang...7 J7
Blackhall...97 F6
Blackhall Rocks...66 E4
Blackham...15 J2
Blackhaugh...82 C8
Blackheath, W. Mids...32 B1
Blackheath, Essex...36 F7
Blackheath, G. Lon...23 J5
Blackhill...105 K3
Blackland...20 E6
Blackley...51 H3
Blacklunans...88 D2
Black Marsh...40 E7
Blackmill...18 D4
Blackmoor...14 A2
Blackmore...24 C2
Blackmore End...36 C6
Black Mount...86 E4
Blackness...81 F4
Blacknest...14 A1
Black Notley...36 C7
Blacko...58 D6
Black Pill...27 L7
Blackpool...57 G7
Blackpool Gate...74 B7
Blackridge...80 D5
Blackrock, Strath...76 C5
Blackrock, Gwent...19 G1
Black Rocks...61 H2
Blackrod...50 F2
Blackshaw...62 F1
Blackstone...15 F4
Blackthorn...22 B1
Blackthorpe...36 E3
Blacktoft...54 C1
Blacktop...97 H5
Black Torrington...8 E5
Blackwall Tunnel...23 J5
Blackwater, Hants...22 D6
Blackwater, Corn...2 F5
Blackwater, I. of W...13 H7
Blackwaterfoot...70 D2
Blackwell, H. & W...32 B2
Blackwell, Derby...52 D6
Blackwood, Strath...80 C7
Blackwood, Gwent...19 F3
Blackwood Hill...42 B1
Blacon...50 C7
Bladerstone...57 K7
Bladnoch...68 F5
Bladon...21 J1
Blaenannerch...27 G2
Blaenau Ffestiniog...39 G2
Blaenavon...19 G2
Blaendyryn...29 G6
Blaenffos...27 F3
Blaengarw...18 D3
Blaengwrach...18 C2
Blaengwynfi...18 C3
Blaenpennal...28 D3
Blaenplwyf...28 C2
Blaenporth...27 G2
Blaenrhondda...18 D3
Blaenwaun...27 G4
Blagdon, Devon...5 J3
Blagdon, Avon...19 K7
Blagdon Hill...10 D4
Blaich...93 G8
Blaina...19 G2
Blair Atholl...88 A2
Blairdaff...97 F4
Blairgowrie...88 D4
Blairhall...80 F3
Blairingone...80 E2
Blairlogie...80 D1
Blairmore...78 D3
Blairskaith...79 H4
Blaisdon...20 B1
Blakebrook...31 K2
Blakedown...32 A2
Blakelaw...74 D1
Blakemere...30 E5
Blakeney, Glos...20 A2
Blakeney, Norf...46 F2
Blakenhall, W. Mids...42 B7
Blakenhall, Ches...41 J2
Blakeshall...31 K1
Blakesley...33 J4
Blanchland...65 G2
Blandford Camp...12 B5
Blandford Forum...12 A5
Blandford St Mary...12 A5
Bland Hill...59 H5
Blanefield...79 H4
Blankney...54 E7
Blantyre...80 B6
Blarmachfoldach...86 C2
Blarnalearoch...101 H3
Blashford...12 D5
Blaston...44 B7
Blatherwycke...44 C7
Blawith...57 F2
Blaxhall...37 J4
Blaxton...53 J3
Blaydon...66 B1
Bleadon...19 H7
Blean...25 H6
Bleasby...43 K2
Bleatarn...64 E6
Blebocraigs...89 G7
Bleddfa...30 D3
Bledington...32 E7
Bledlow...22 C2

Bledlow Ridge...22 C3
Blegbie...82 C5
Blencarn...64 D4
Blencogo...63 G3
Blencow...64 B3
Blendworth...13 K4
Blennerhasset...63 G3
Bletchingdon...21 K1
Bletchingley...23 J7
Bletchley, Bucks...34 B6
Bletchley, Shrops...41 H3
Bletherston...26 E4
Bletsoe...34 D4
Blewbury...21 K4
Blickling...47 G4
Blidworth...43 H1
Blindcrake...63 G4
Blindley Heath...15 G1
Blisland...3 K2
Blissford...12 D4
Bliss Gate...31 J2
Blisworth...33 K4
Blockley...32 D6
Blofield...47 J6
Blo' Norton...36 F2
Blore...42 D2
Bloxham...33 G6
Bloxholm...44 D1
Bloxwich...42 C6
Bloxworth...12 A6
Blubberhouses...59 G5
Blue Anchor...10 B1
Blue Bell Hill...24 D6
Blundellsands...50 C4
Blundeston...47 L7
Blunham...34 E4
Blunsdon St Andrew...21 F4
Bluntisham...35 G2
Blyborough...54 D4
Blyford...37 K2
Blymhill...41 K5
Blyth, Notts...53 J5
Blyth, Northum...75 K6
Blyth Bridge...81 G7
Blythburgh...37 K2
Blythe...82 D7
Blyton...54 C4
Boarhills...89 H7
Boarhunt...13 J5
Boarshead...15 J2
Boarstall...22 B1
Boasley Cross...8 F6
Boath...102 D5
Boat of Garten...95 H4
Bobbing...24 E6
Bobbington...41 K7
Bocaddon...4 B4
Bockhampton...11 J6
Bocking...36 C7
Bocking Churchstreet...36 C7
Boddam, Shetld...115 F7
Boddam, Grampn...105 L4
Boddington...32 A7
Bodedern...48 C2
Bodelwyddan...49 K3
Bodenham, Wilts...12 D3
Bodenham, H. & W...31 G4
Bodewryd...48 D1
Bodfari...49 K3
Bodffordd...48 D3
Bodham...47 G2
Bodiam...16 E3
Bodicote...33 G6
Bodieve...3 H2
Bodle Street Green...16 E4
Bodmin...3 J3
Bodney...46 D7
Boduan...38 C3
Bogallan...102 E7
Bogbrae...97 K2
Bogend...71 J1
Boghall...80 E5
Bogmoor...104 B4
Bogniebrae...104 E4
Bognor Regis...14 C6
Bograxie...97 F4
Bog, The...40 E7
Bogton...104 F3
Bohenie...93 J7
Bohortha...3 G6
Bohuntine...93 J7
Boisdale...90 C4
Bojewyan...2 B6
Bolam...66 B5
Bold Heath...50 E6
Boldon...66 D1
Boldre...13 F6
Boldron...65 H6
Bole...54 C5
Bolehill...42 E1
Boleside...74 A1
Bolham...9 K4
Bolham Water...10 C4
Bolingey...2 F5
Bollington, Ches...51 G5
Bollington, Ches...51 H6
Bolney...15 F3
Bolnhurst...34 D4
Bolsover...53 G6
Bolsterstone...52 E4
Bolstone...20 B2
Boltby...60 B2
Bolton, Loth...82 C4
Bolton, Cumbr...64 D5
Bolton, Humbs...60 E5
Bolton, G. Man...51 G3
Bolton, Northum...75 H3
Bolton Abbey...59 F5
Bolton-by-Bowland...58 C6
Boltonfellend...74 A8
Boltongate...63 H3
Bolton-le-Sands...57 H4
Bolton-on-Swale...66 C6
Bolton Percy...60 C6

Bolton upon Dearne...53 G3
Bolventor...4 B2
Bomere Heath...41 F5
Bonar Bridge...102 E3
Bonawe...86 C5
Bonby...54 E2
Boncath...27 G3
Bonchester Bridge...74 B3
Bondleigh...9 G5
Bonehill...42 D6
Bo'Ness...80 E3
Bonhill...79 F4
Boningale...41 K6
Bonjedward...74 C2
Bonkle...80 D6
Bonnington, Northnts...81 G5
Bonnington, Kent...17 H2
Bonnybridge...80 D3
Bonnykelly...105 H3
Bonnyrigg and Lasswade...81 J5
Bonnyton...89 J3
Bonsall...52 E8
Bont...19 H1
Bontddu...39 F5
Bont-goch or Elerch...28 D3
Bontnewydd, Gwyn...48 D4
Bont-newydd, Clwyd...49 K3
Bontuchel...40 B1
Bonvilston...18 E5
Booker...22 D3
Booley...41 G4
Boosbeck...67 G6
Boot...63 G7
Boothby Graffoe...54 D8
Boothby Pagnell...44 C3
Boothstown...51 G3
Bootle, Mers...50 C4
Bootle, Cumbr...56 E2
Boraston...31 H2
Borden...24 E6
Bordley...58 E4
Bordon Camp...14 A2
Boreham, Wilts...12 A1
Boreham, Essex...24 D2
Boreham Street...16 D4
Borehamwood...23 G3
Boreland...73 G5
Borgie...109 H3
Borgue, D. & G...69 H6
Borgue, Highld...111 H6
Borley...36 D5
Bornesketaig...99 J5
Boroughbridge...59 J4
Borough Green...24 C7
Borras Head...40 E1
Borreraig...99 F7
Borrowash...43 G3
Borrowby...59 K2
Borth...38 F7
Borthwickbrae...73 K3
Borthwickshiels...73 K3
Borth-y-Gest...38 E3
Borve, W. Isles...90 B5
Borve, W. Isles...98 E4
Borve, W. Isles...98 F3
Borve, Highld...99 K8
Borwick...57 J3
Bosavern...2 B6
Bosbury...31 H5
Boscastle...8 A6
Boscombe, Dorset...12 D6
Boscombe, Wilts...12 C2
Bosham...14 B5
Bosherston...26 D7
Boskednan...2 C6
Bosley...51 J7
Bossall...60 E4
Bossiney...8 A7
Bossingham...17 J1
Bossington...17 J1
Bosta...107 F4
Bostock Green...51 F7
Boston...45 G2
Boston Spa...59 K6
Boswinger...3 H5
Botallack...2 B6
Botany Bay...23 H3
Botcheston...43 G6
Botesdale...36 F2
Bothal...75 J6
Bothamsall...53 J6
Bothel...63 G4
Bothenhampton...11 F6
Bothwell...80 C6
Botley, Bucks...22 E2
Botley, Hants...13 H4
Botley, Oxon...21 J2
Botolphs...15 E5
Bottacks...102 C6
Bottesford, Leic...44 B3
Bottesford, Humbs...54 C3
Bottisham...35 J3
Bottomcraig...89 F6
Botusfleming...4 E3
Botwnnog...38 B3
Boughrood...30 C6
Boughspring...19 K3
Boughton, Northnts...34 A3
Boughton, Norf...46 B6
Boughton, Notts...53 J7
Boughton Aluph...17 H1
Boughton Lees...17 H1
Boughton Malherbe...17 F1
Boughton Monchelsea...24 D7
Boughton Street...25 G7
Boulby...67 H6
Bouldon...31 G1
Boulmer...75 J3
Boulston...26 D5
Boultham...54 D7
Bourn...35 G4
Bournbrook...44 D4
Bourne End, Beds...34 C5

Bourne End, Bucks...22 D4
Bourne End, Herts...22 F2
Bournemouth...12 C6
Bournes Green...20 D2
Bourneville...32 C1
Bournheath...32 B2
Bournmoor...66 D2
Bourton, Oxon...21 G4
Bourton, Shrops...41 G7
Bourton, Avon...19 H6
Bourton, Dorset...11 J2
Bourton on Dunsmore...33 G2
Bourton-on-the-Hill...32 D6
Bourton-on-the-Water...32 D7
Boveney...22 E5
Boverton...18 D6
Bovey Tracey...5 J2
Bovingdon...22 F2
Bovington Camp...11 K7
Bow, Devon...9 H5
Bow, G. Lon...23 J4
Bowbank...65 G5
Bow Brickhill...34 C6
Bowburn...66 D4
Bowcombe...13 G7
Bowd...10 C6
Bowden, Border...74 B1
Bowden, Devon...5 J5
Bowden Hill...20 D6
Bowderdale...64 D7
Bowdon...51 G5
Bowerchalke...12 C3
Bowermadden...111 J2
Bowers Gifford...24 D4
Bowershall...81 F2
Bowertower...111 J2
Bowes...65 G6
Bowhill...73 K2
Bowithick...82 C7
Bowland Bridge...57 H2
Bowley...31 G4
Bowlhead Green...14 C2
Bowling...79 G4
Bowling Bank...40 E2
Bowling Green...31 K4
Bowmanstead...57 G1
Bowmore...76 C6
Bowness-on-Solway...63 H1
Bowness-on-Windermere...57 H1
Bowsden...83 H7
Bow Street...28 D1
Bowthorpe...47 G6
Box, Glos...20 C2
Box, Wilts...20 C6
Boxbush...20 B1
Boxford, Suff...36 E5
Boxford, Berks...21 J5
Boxgrove...14 C5
Boxley...24 D7
Boxted, Suff...36 D4
Boxted, Essex...36 E6
Boxworth...35 G3
Boylestone...42 D3
Boyndie...104 F2
Boyndlie...105 J2
Boynton...61 J4
Boyton, Wilts...12 B2
Boyton, Corn...8 D6
Boyton, Suff...37 J5
Bozeat...34 C4
Braaid...56 O4
Brabling Green...37 H3
Brabourne...17 J1
Brabourne Lees...17 H1
Brabster...111 K2
Bracadale...91 J2
Braceborough...44 D5
Bracebridge Heath...54 D7
Braceby...44 D3
Bracewell...58 D6
Brackenfield...53 F8
Brackletter...93 H7
Brackley, Strath...77 G7
Brackley, Northnts...33 H6
Bracknell...22 D6
Braco...87 L8
Bracobrae...104 E3
Bracon Ash...47 G7
Bracora...92 D6
Bracorina...92 D6
Bradbourne...42 E1
Bradbury...66 D5
Bradda...56 N4
Bradden...33 J5
Braddock...3 K3
Bradenham, Bucks...22 D3
Bradenham, Norf...46 E6
Bradenstoke...20 E5
Bradfield, Essex...37 G6
Bradfield, Norf...47 H3
Bradfield, Berks...21 L5
Bradfield Combust...36 D4
Bradfield Green...51 F8
Bradfield St Clare...36 E4
Bradfield St George...36 E3
Bradford, Devon...8 E5
Bradford, W. Yks...59 G7
Bradford, Northum...75 H1
Bradford Abbas...11 G4
Bradford Leigh...20 C6
Bradford-on-Avon...20 C6
Bradford-on-Tone...10 C3
Bradford Peverell...11 H6
Brading...14 B7
Bradley, Staffs...42 A5
Bradley, Derby...42 E2
Bradley, Humbs...55 G3
Bradley, Hants...13 J1
Bradley in the Moors...42 C2
Bradmore...43 H3
Bradninch...10 A5
Bradnop...42 C1
Bradpole...11 F6
Bradshaw...51 G2

Bradstone 4 D1
Bradwall Green 51 G7
Bradwell, Bucks 34 B6
Bradwell, Derby 52 D5
Bradwell, Essex 36 D7
Bradwell, Norf 47 L6
Bradwell Grove 21 G2
Bradwell-on-Sea 25 G2
Bradwell Waterside 25 F2
Bradworthy 8 D4
Brae, Shetld 115 F2
Brae, Highld 100 H4
Brae, Highld 102 E6
Braeantra 102 D5
Braefield 94 C2
Braehead, Orkney 112 E2
Braehead, Strath 72 D1
Braehead, Strath 80 E6
Braehead, D. & G 68 F5
Braehead, Tays 89 J3
Braehoulland 116 D5
Braemar 95 K6
Braemore 111 G5
Brae of Achnahaird 108 B7
Brae Roy Lodge 94 B6
Braeside 78 E4
Braes, The 92 B2
Braeswick 113 G3
Brafferton, Durham 66 C5
Brafferton, N. Yks 59 K3
Brafield-on-the-Green ..34 B4
Bragar 107 G4
Bragbury End 35 F7
Braides 57 H5
Braidley 58 F2
Braidwood 80 D7
Brailes 33 F6
Brailsford 42 E2
Braintree 36 C7
Braiseworth 37 G2
Braishfield 13 F3
Braithwaite, Cumbr 62 F5
Braithwaite, Cumbr 63 H5
Braithwell 53 H4
Bramber 15 E4
Bramcote 43 H3
Bramdean 13 J3
Bramerton 47 H6
Bramfield, Herts 23 H1
Bramfield, Suff 37 K2
Bramford 37 G5
Bramhall 51 H5
Bramham 59 K6
Bramhope 59 H6
Bramley, Hants 22 B7
Bramley, Surrey 14 D1
Bramley, S. Yks 53 G4
Brampford Speke 9 K6
Brampton, Cumbr 64 C1
Brampton, Lincs 54 C6
Brampton, Cumbr 64 D5
Brampton, Cambs 35 F2
Brampton, S. Yks 53 G3
Brampton, Norf 47 H4
Brampton, Suff 37 K1
Brampton Abbotts 31 H7
Brampton Ash 34 A1
Brampton Bryan 30 E2
Bramshall 42 C3
Bramshaw 12 E4
Bramshott 14 B2
Brancaster 46 C2
Brancepeth 66 C4
Branchill 103 J7
Branderburgh 104 B1
Brandesburton 61 J6
Brandeston 37 H3
Brandiston 47 G4
Brandon, Suff 36 C1
Brandon, Lincs 44 C2
Brandon, Durham 66 C4
Brandon, Warw 33 G2
Brandon, Northum 75 G3
Brandon Bank 35 K1
Brandon Creek 45 K7
Brandon Parva 46 F6
Brandsby 60 C3
Brane 2 C7
Bran End 36 B7
Branksome 12 C6
Branksome Park 12 C6
Branscombe 10 C7
Bransford 31 J4
Bransgore 12 D6
Branston, Leic 44 B4
Branston, Staffs 42 E4
Branston, Lincs 54 E7
Branstone 13 J7
Brant Broughton 44 C1
Brantham 34 E6
Branthwaite 62 F5
Branthwaite 63 H4
Brantingham 61 G8
Branton, Northum 75 G3
Branton, S. Yks 53 J3
Branxholme 73 K3
Branxholm Park 73 K3
Branxton 83 G8
Brassington 42 E1
Brasted 23 K7
Brasted Chart 23 K7
Brathens 97 F6
Bratoft 55 J7
Brattleby 54 D5
Bratton 20 D7
Bratton Clovelly 8 E6
Bratton Fleming 9 G2
Bratton Seymour 11 H3
Braughing 35 G7
Braunston 33 H3
Braunstone 43 H6
Braunston-in-Rutland ...44 B6
Braunton 8 E2
Brawby 60 D2
Brawl 110 E2

Brawlbin 111 G3
Bray 22 E5
Braybrooke 34 A1
Brayford 9 G2
Bray Shop 4 D2
Braystones 62 F7
Brayton 60 D7
Brazacott 8 C6
Breachwood Green 34 E7
Breaclete 107 F5
Breadsall 43 F3
Breadstone 20 B2
Breage 2 E7
Breakachy 102 C8
Breakish 92 C3
Bream 19 L2
Breamore 12 D4
Brean 19 G7
Brearton 59 J4
Breasclete 107 G5
Breaston 43 G3
Brechfa 27 K3
Brechin 89 H2
Breckles 46 E7
Breckrey 100 B6
Brecon 29 H7
Bredbury 51 J4
Brede 16 F4
Bredenbury 31 H4
Bredfield 37 H4
Bredgar 24 E6
Bredhurst 24 D6
Bredon 32 B6
Bredon's Norton 32 B6
Bredwardine 30 E5
Breedon on the Hill 43 G4
Breich 80 C5
Breighton 60 E7
Bremhill 20 D5
Brenchley 16 D1
Brendon 9 H1
Brenish 106 D6
Brent Eleigh 36 E5
Brentford 23 G5
Brent Knoll 19 H7
Brent Pelham 35 H6
Brentwood 24 B3
Brenzett 17 H3
Brereton 42 C5
Brereton Green 51 G7
Brereton Heath 51 H7
Bressingham 37 F1
Bretby 42 E4
Bretford 33 G2
Bretforton 32 C5
Bretherdale Head 64 C7
Bretherton 50 D1
Brettabister 115 G3
Brettenham, Norf 36 E1
Brettenham, Suff 36 E4
Bretton 50 C7
Brevig 90 B6
Brewham 11 J2
Brewlands Bridge 88 D2
Brewood 42 A6
Briantspuddle 11 K6
Brickendon 23 J2
Bricket Wood 23 G2
Bricklehampton 32 B5
Bride 56 H1
Bridekirk 63 G4
Bridell 26 F2
Bridestowe 8 F7
Brideswell 96 E2
Bridford 9 J7
Bridge 25 H7
Bridge End 44 E3
Bridgefoot, Tays 89 F5
Bridgefoot, Cumbr 62 F5
Bridge Green 35 H6
Bridgemary 13 H5
Bridgend, Strath 80 B4
Bridgend, Grampn 96 C2
Bridgend, Strath 76 C5
Bridgend, M. Glam 18 D4
Bridgend, Grampn 96 E2
Bridgend, Lothn 81 F4
Bridgend, Fife 89 F7
Bridgend, Strath 77 G8
Bridgend, Strath 77 H2
Bridgend, Tays 89 H2
Bridgend, Cumbr 63 J6
Bridgend of Lintrathen .88 E3
Bridge of Alford 96 E4
Bridge of Allan 80 C2
Bridge of Avon 95 K2
Bridge of Brown 95 K3
Bridge of Cally 88 D3
Bridge of Canny 97 F6
Bridge of Dee 69 J4
Bridge of Don 97 J4
Bridge of Don 89 J3
Bridge of Dye 97 F7
Bridge of Earn 88 D7
Bridge of Feugh 97 G6
Bridge of Forss 111 G2
Bridge of Gairn 96 C6
Bridge of Muchalls 97 H6
Bridge of Orchy 86 E5
Bridge of Walls 114 C3
Bridge of Weir 79 F5
Bridgerule 8 C5
Bridges 40 E7
Bridge Sollers 31 F5
Bridge Street 36 D5
Bridgetown 9 K2
Bridge Trafford 50 D6
Bridge Yate 20 A5
Bridgham 36 E1
Bridgnorth 41 J7
Bridgtown 42 B6
Bridgwater 10 E2
Bridlington 61 J4
Bridport 11 F6
Bridstow 31 G7

Brierfield 58 D7
Brierley, H. & W 31 F4
Brierley, S. Yks 53 G2
Brierley, Glos 19 L1
Brierley Hill 32 B1
Brigg 54 E3
Brigham, Cumbr 63 F4
Brigham, Humbs 61 H5
Brighouse 52 D1
Brighstone 13 G7
Brightgate 52 E8
Brighthampton 21 H2
Brightling 16 D3
Brightlingsea 25 G1
Brighton, E. Susx 15 G5
Brighton, Corn 3 H4
Brightons 80 E4
Brightwalton 21 J5
Brightwell 37 H5
Brightwell Baldwin 22 B3
Brightwell-cum-Sotwell .21 K3
Brignall 65 H6
Brig o' Turk 87 H8
Brigsley 55 G3
Brigsteer 57 H2
Brigstock 34 C1
Brill 22 B1
Brilley 30 D5
Brimfield 31 G3
Brimington 53 G6
Brimpsfield 20 D1
Brimpton 21 K6
Brims 112 C8
Brinacory 92 D6
Brind 60 E7
Brindister, Shetld 114 E3
Brindister, Shetld 115 G5
Brindle 50 E1
Brindley Ford 42 A1
Brineton 41 K5
Bringhurst 44 B7
Brington 34 D2
Brinian 112 E4
Briningham 46 F3
Brinkhill 55 H6
Brinkley 35 K4
Brinklow 33 G2
Brinkworth 20 E4
Brinscall 51 F1
Brinsley 43 G2
Brinsop 31 F5
Brinsworth 53 G4
Brinton 46 F3
Brisley 46 E4
Brislington 19 L5
Briston 46 F3
Britannia 51 H1
Britford 13 G3
Brithdir 39 G5
Briton Ferry 18 B3
Britwell Salome 22 B3
Brixham 5 K4
Brixton, Devon 4 F4
Brixton, G. Lon 23 J5
Brixton Deverill 12 A2
Brixworth 34 A2
Brize Norton 21 H2
Broad Blunsdon 21 F3
Broadbottom 51 J4
Broadbridge 14 B5
Broadbridge Heath 14 E2
Broad Campden 32 D6
Broad Chalke 12 C3
Broadclyst 10 A6
Broadford 92 C3
Broad Green 31 J4
Broad Haven 26 C5
Broadheath, G. Man 51 G5
Broad Heath, H. & W ...31 H3
Broadheath, H. & W 31 K4
Broadhembury 10 C5
Broadhempston 5 J3
Broad Hill 35 J2
Broad Hinton 20 F5
Broad Laying 21 J6
Broadley, Grampn 104 C2
Broadley, Lancs 51 H2
Bradley Common 23 K2
Broad Marston 32 D5
Broadmayne 11 J7
Broadmeadows 73 K1
Broadmere 3 J1
Broad Oak, E. Susx 16 D3
Broad Oak, E. Susx 16 F3
Broadoak, Dorset 11 F6
Broad Oak, H. & W 31 F7
Broad Oak, Kent 25 H6
Broad Oak, Dorset 11 J4
Broadstairs 25 K6
Broadstone, Dorset 12 C6
Broadstone, Shrops 41 G8
Broad Street 24 E7
Broad Town 20 E5
Broadwas 31 J4
Broadwater 14 E5
Broadway, H. & W 32 D6
Broadway, Somer 10 E4
Broadwell, Glos 32 E7
Broadwell, Oxon 21 G2
Broadwell, Warw 33 G3
Broadwell, Glos 19 K1
Broadwey 11 H7
Broadwindsor 11 F5
Broadwoodkelly 9 G5
Broadwoodwidger 8 E7
Brobury 30 E5
Brochel 100 B8
Brockbridge 13 J4
Brockdish 37 H2
Brockenhurst 12 E5
Brocketsbrae 80 D8
Brockford Street 37 G3
Brockhall 33 J3
Brockham 15 E1

Brockhampton, Glos 32 C7
Brockhampton, H. & W ..31 G6
Brockholes 52 D2
Brocklesby 55 F2
Brockley 19 J6
Brockley Green 36 D4
Brockton, Shrops 30 E1
Brockton, Shrops 40 E6
Brockton, Shrops 41 G7
Brockton, Shrops 41 J6
Brockweir 19 K2
Brockwood Park 13 J3
Brockworth 20 C1
Brocton 42 B5
Brodick 78 C8
Brodsworth 53 H3
Brogborough 34 C6
Brokenborough 20 D4
Broken Cross, Ches 51 F6
Broken Cross, Ches 51 H6
Bromborough 50 C5
Bromcote 33 G1
Brome 37 G2
Brome Street 37 G2
Bromeswell 37 J4
Bromfield, Shrops 31 F2
Bromfield, Cumbr 63 G3
Bromham, Beds 34 D4
Bromham, Wilts 20 D6
Bromley 23 K6
Bromley Green 17 H2
Brompton, Kent 24 D6
Brompton, N. Yks 61 G2
Brompton, N. Yks 59 J1
Brompton-on-Swale 66 C8
Brompton Ralph 10 B2
Brompton Regis 9 K2
Bromsash 31 H7
Bromsgrove 32 B2
Bromyard 31 H4
Bromyard Downs 31 H4
Bronaber 39 G3
Bronington 41 F3
Bronllys 30 C6
Bronnant 28 D3
Bronwydd Arms 27 J4
Brongarth 40 D3
Brook, Surrey 14 C2
Brook, Hants 12 E4
Brook, Hants 13 F3
Brook, I. of W 13 F7
Brook, Kent 17 H1
Brooke, Leic 44 B6
Brooke, Norf 47 H7
Brookfield 79 G5
Brookhouse 57 J4
Brookhouse Green 51 H7
Brookland 17 G3
Brookmans Park 23 H2
Brookmans 40 C7
Brook Street 24 B3
Brookthorpe 20 C1
Brookwood 22 E7
Broom, Warw 32 C4
Broom, Beds 34 E5
Broome, H. & W 32 B2
Broome, Shrops 30 F1
Broome, Norf 47 J7
Broomedge 51 G5
Broome Park 75 H3
Broomer's Corner 14 E3
Broomfield, Essex 24 D1
Broomfield, Somer 10 D2
Broomfield, Kent 24 E7
Broomfield, Kent 25 H6
Broomfield, Grampn 97 J2
Broomfleet 54 C1
Broom Hill, Dorset 12 C5
Broom Hill, Northum ...75 J4
Brora 103 H2
Broseley 41 H6
Brotherstoft 45 F2
Brotherton 53 G1
Brotton 67 G6
Broubster 111 G2
Brough, Notts 54 C8
Brough, Humbs 54 D1
Brough, Shetld 117 F5
Brough, Shetld 117 G5
Brough, Shetld 115 H2
Brough, Derby 52 D5
Brough, Cumbr 64 E6
Brough, Highld 111 J1
Broughall 41 G2
Brough Sowerby 64 E6
Broughton, Northnts ...34 B2
Broughton, Bucks 34 B5
Broughton, Orkney 112 E2
Broughton, Clwyd 50 C7
Broughton, Humbs 54 D3
Broughton, M. Glam 18 D5
Broughton, N. Yks 60 E3
Broughton, N. Yks 58 E5
Broughton, Cambs 35 F2
Broughton, Hants 13 F2
Broughton, Cumbr 62 F4
Broughton, Oxon 33 G6
Broughton, Border 81 G8
Broughton, G. Man 51 H3
Broughton, Lancs 57 J7
Broughton Astley 43 H7
Broughton Beck 57 F2
Broughton Gifford 20 C6
Broughton Hackett 32 B4
Broughton in Furness ..56 F2
Broughton Mills 57 F1
Broughton Moor 62 F4
Broughton Poggs 21 G2
Broughty Ferry 89 G5
Brown Candover 13 H2
Brown Edge 42 B3
Brownhill, Lancs 58 B7
Brownhill, Grampn 97 H1

Brownhills 42 C6
Brownieside 75 H2
Brownlow Heath 51 H7
Brownston 5 G4
Brow Top 57 J5
Broxbourne 23 J2
Broxburn, Lothn 82 E4
Broxburn, Lothn 81 F4
Broxted 35 J7
Broxton 41 F1
Broxwood 30 E4
Broxa 111 K5
Brue 107 H4
Bruera 50 D7
Bruern Abbey 32 E7
Bruernish 90 C5
Bruichladdich 76 B5
Bruisyard 37 J3
Brumby 54 C3
Brund 52 D7
Brundall 47 J6
Brundish 37 H3
Brundish Street 37 H2
Bruntingthorpe 43 J7
Brunton, Fife 88 F6
Brunton, Northum 75 J2
Brushford, Devon 9 G5
Brushford, Somer 9 K3
Bruton 11 J2
Bryanston 12 A5
Brydekirk 73 G7
Brymbo 40 D1
Brynaman 18 B1
Brynberian 26 F3
Bryncae 18 D4
Bryncethin 18 D4
Byncir 38 D2
Bryn-coch 18 B3
Bryncroes 38 B3
Bryncrug 38 F6
Bryneglwys 40 C2
Brynford 50 A6
Bryn Gates 50 E3
Bryngwran 48 C3
Bryngwyn, Powys 30 C5
Bryngwyn, Gwent 19 H2
Bryn-henllan 26 E3
Brynhoffnant 27 H1
Brynithel 19 G2
Brynmawr 19 F1
Brynmenyn 18 D4
Brynna 18 D4
Brynrefail 48 D2
Brynsadler 18 E4
Brynsiencyn 48 D4
Brynteg, Gwyn 48 D2
Brynteg, Clwyd 40 E1
Bryn, The 19 H2
Bryn-y-maen 49 H3
Bualintur 91 K3
Bualnaluib 100 E3
Bubbenhall 33 F2
Bubwith 60 E7
Buccleuch 73 J3
Buchlyvie 79 H2
Buckabank 63 J3
Buckden, Cambs 35 E3
Buckden, N. Yks 58 E3
Buckenham 47 J6
Buckerell 10 C5
Buckfast 5 H3
Buckfastleigh 5 H3
Buckhaven 81 J2
Buckholm 82 C8
Buckhorn Weston 11 J3
Buckhurst Hill 23 K3
Buckie 104 D2
Buckies 111 H2
Buckingham 33 J6
Buckland, Glos 32 C6
Buckland, Bucks 22 D1
Buckland, Devon 5 G5
Buckland, Herts 35 G6
Buckland, Oxon 21 H3
Buckland, Surrey 23 H7
Buckland, Kent 17 L1
Buckland Brewer 8 E3
Buckland Common 22 E2
Buckland Dinham 20 B7
Buckland Filleigh 8 E5
Buckland in the Moor ..5 H2
Buckland Monochorum ...4 E3
Buckland Newton 11 H5
Buckland St Mary 10 D4
Bucklebury 21 K5
Bucklers Hard 13 G5
Bucklesham 37 H5
Buckley 50 B7
Bucklow Hill 51 G5
Buckminster 44 B4
Bucknall, Staffs 42 B2
Bucknall, Lincs 55 F7
Bucknell, Shrops 30 E2
Bucknell, Oxon 33 H7
Buckpool 97 H5
Buck's Cross 8 D3
Bucks Green 14 D2
Bucks Hill 22 F2
Bucks Horn Oak 14 B1
Buck's Mills 8 D3
Buckton, H. & W 30 E2
Buckton, Northum 83 J8
Buckworth 34 E2
Budbrooke 32 E3
Budby 53 J6
Bude 8 C5
Budlake 10 A5
Budle 83 K8
Budleigh Salterton ...10 B7
Budock Water 3 F6
Buerton 41 H2
Bugbrooke 33 J4

Bugle 3 J4
Bugthorpe 60 E5
Buildwas 41 H6
Builth Road 29 H4
Builth Wells 29 H4
Bulby 44 D4
Buldoo 111 F2
Bulford 12 D1
Bulford Camp 12 D1
Bulkeley 41 G1
Bulkington, Wilts 20 D7
Bulkington, Warw 33 F1
Bulkworthy 8 D4
Bulley 20 B1
Bullwood 78 D4
Bulmer, N. Yks 60 D4
Bulmer, Essex 36 D5
Bulmer Tye 36 D6
Bulphan 24 C4
Bulverhythe 16 E5
Bulwell 43 H2
Bulwick 44 C7
Bumble's Green 23 K2
Bunacaimb 92 C7
Bunarkaig 93 H7
Bunavoneadar 99 G2
Bunbury 50 E8
Bundalloch 93 E3
Bunessan 84 E6
Bungay 47 J8
Bunnahabhain 76 D4
Bunny 43 H4
Buntait 94 C2
Buntingford 35 G7
Bunwell 47 G7
Burbage, Derby 52 C6
Burbage, Wilts 21 G6
Burbage, Leic 43 G7
Burchett's Green 22 D4
Burcombe 12 C2
Burcot 21 K3
Burdale 60 F4
Bures 36 E6
Burford, Oxon 21 G1
Burford, Shrops 31 G3
Burg 84 E4
Burgess Hill 15 G4
Burgh 37 H4
Burgh by Sands 63 J2
Burgh Castle 47 K6
Burghclere 21 J6
Burghead 103 K6
Burghfield 22 B6
Burghfield Common 22 B6
Burghfield Hill 22 B6
Burgh Heath 23 H7
Burghill 31 F5
Burgh le Marsh 55 K7
Burgh next Aylsham ...47 H4
Burgh on Bain 55 G5
Burgh St Margaret or
  Fleggburgh 47 K5
Burgh St Peter 47 K7
Burghwallis 53 H2
Burham 24 D6
Buriton 13 K3
Burland 41 H1
Burlawn 4 B2
Burlescombe 10 B4
Burleston 11 J6
Burley, Leic 44 B5
Burley, Hants 12 E5
Burleydam 41 H2
Burley Gate 31 G5
Burley in Wharfedale .59 G6
Burley Street 12 E5
Burliingobb 30 D4
Burlton 41 F4
Burmarsh 17 J2
Burmington 32 E6
Burn 60 C8
Burnage 51 H4
Burnaston 42 E3
Burnby 60 F6
Burneside 57 J1
Burness 113 G2
Burneston 59 J2
Burnett 20 A6
Burnfoot, Border 74 A3
Burnfoot, Border 73 K3
Burnham, Humbs 54 E2
Burnham, Berks 22 E4
Burnham Deepdale 46 D2
Burnham Green 23 H1
Burnham Market 46 D2
Burnham Norton 46 D2
Burnham-on-Crouch ...25 F3
Burnham-on-Sea 10 E1
Burnham Overy Staithe 46 D2
Burnham Overy Town ..46 D2
Burnham Thorpe 46 D2
Burnhead 72 E5
Burnhervie 97 G4
Burnhill Green 41 J6
Burnhope 66 B3
Burnhouse 79 F6
Burniston 61 H1
Burnley 58 D7
Burnmouth 83 H5
Burn of Cambus 80 C1
Burnopfield 66 B2
Burnsall 58 F4
Burnside, Strath 72 A3
Burnside, Shetld 116 D5
Burnside, Fife 88 D2
Burnside, Lothn 81 F4
Burnside of Duntrune .89 G5
Burntisland 81 H3
Burntwood 42 C6
Burnt Yates 59 H4
Burpham, W. Susx 14 D5
Burpham, Surrey 22 F7
Burradon 75 J7
Burrafirth 117 H1
Burras 2 E6

Burravoe, Shetld............115 F2
Burravoe, Shetld............117 G5
Burray Village............112 E7
Burrelton............88 E5
Burridge............13 H4
Burrill............59 H2
Burringham............54 C3
Burrington, H. & W.............31 F2
Burrington, Devon............9 G4
Burrington, Avon............19 J7
Burrough Green............36 B4
Burrough on the Hill............44 A5
Burrowbridge............10 E2
Burrowhill............22 E6
Burry Green............27 J7
Burry Port............27 J6
Burscough............50 D2
Burscough Bridge............50 D2
Bursea............60 F7
Burshill............61 H6
Bursledon............13 G5
Burslem............42 A2
Burstall............37 F5
Burstock............11 F5
Burston, Staffs............42 B3
Burston, Norf............37 G1
Burstow............15 G1
Burstwick............55 G1
Burtersett............58 D2
Burtle............10 F1
Burton, Somer............10 C1
Burton, Wilts............20 C5
Burton, Ches............50 C6
Burton, Dyfed............26 D6
Burton, Lincs............54 D6
Burton, Dorset............12 D6
Burton, Ches............50 E7
Burton, Northum............75 H1
Burton Agnes............61 J4
Burton Bradstock............11 F7
Burton Constable............61 J7
Burton Fleming............61 H3
Burton Green, Clwyd............50 C8
Burton Green, Warw............32 E2
Burton Hastings............43 G8
Burton-in-Kendal............57 J3
Burton in Lonsdale............58 B3
Burton Joyce............43 J2
Burton Latimer............34 C2
Burton Lazars............44 A5
Burton-le-Coggles............44 C4
Burton Leonard............59 J4
Burton on the Wolds............43 H4
Burton Overy............43 J7
Burton Pedwardine............44 E2
Burton Pidsea............61 K7
Burton Salmon............53 G1
Burton upon Stather............54 C2
Burton upon Trent............42 E4
Burtonwood............50 E4
Burwardsley............41 G1
Burwarton............31 H1
Burwash............16 D3
Burwash Common............16 D3
Burwell, Lincs............55 H6
Burwell, Cambs............35 J3
Bury, W. Susx............14 D4
Bury, Cambs............35 F1
Bury, G. Man............51 H2
Bury, Somer............9 K3
Bury Green............35 H7
Bury St Edmunds............36 D3
Burythorpe............60 E4
Busbridge............14 C1
Busby............79 H6
Buscot............21 G3
Bushbury............42 B6
Bush Crathie............96 B6
Bushey............23 G3
Bushey Heath............23 G3
Bush Green............37 H1
Bushley............32 A6
Bushton............20 E5
Busta............115 F2
Butcher's Pasture............35 K7
Butcombe............19 K6
Butleigh............11 G2
Butleigh Wootton............11 G2
Butlers Marston............33 F4
Butley............37 J4
Butsfield............65 J3
Buttercrambe............60 E4
Butterknowle............65 J5
Butterleigh............10 A5
Buttermere, Cumbr............63 G6
Buttermere, Wilts............21 H6
Buttershaw............59 G8
Butterstone............88 C4
Butterton............42 C1
Butterwick, Humbs............54 C3
Butterwick, N. Yks............60 E3
Butterwick, Lincs............45 G2
Butterwick, N. Yks............61 G3
Butt Green............41 H1
Buttington............40 D6
Buttonoak............31 J2
Buxhall............36 F4
Buxted............15 H3
Buxton, Derby............52 C6
Buxton, Norf............47 H4
Bwlch............30 C7
Bwlch-derwin............38 D2
Bwlchgwyn............40 D1
Bwlch-Llan............28 C4
Bwlchnewydd............27 H4
Bwlchtocyn............38 C4
Bwlch-y-cibau............40 C5
Bwlch-y-fadfa............27 J2
Bwlch-y-ffridd............40 B7
Bwlchygroes............27 G3
Bwlch-y-sarnau............29 H2
Byers Green............66 C4
Byfield............33 H4
Byfleet............22 F6
Byford............30 E5

Bygrave............35 F6
Byker............66 C1
Bylchau............49 J4
Byley............51 G7
Byrness, Northum............74 D4
Byrness, Northum............64 E7
Bythorn............34 D2
Byton............30 E3
Byworth............14 C3

C

Cabourne............55 F3
Cabrach............96 C3
Cadbury............9 K5
Cadbury Barton............9 G4
Cadder............79 J4
Caddington............22 F1
Caddonfoot............73 K1
Cadeby, Leic............43 G6
Cadeby, S. Yks............53 H4
Cadeleigh............9 K5
Cade Street............16 D3
Cadgwith............2 F8
Cadishead............51 G4
Cadle............27 L7
Cadley............21 G6
Cadmore End............22 C3
Cadnam............12 E4
Cadney............54 E3
Cadole............50 B7
Caeathro............48 E4
Caehopkin............18 C1
Caerau, M. Glam............18 C3
Caerau, S. Glam............18 F5
Caerdeon............39 F5
Caergeiliog............48 C3
Caergwrle............40 E1
Caerleon............19 H3
Caer Llan............19 J2
Caernarfon............48 D4
Caerphilly............18 F4
Caersws............40 B7
Caerwent............19 J3
Caerwys............50 A6
Caethle............38 F7
Caio............27 L3
Cairnbaan............77 H2
Cairnborrow............96 D1
Cairnbrogie............97 H3
Cairncross, Tays............96 D8
Cairncross, Border............83 G5
Cairndow............86 D7
Cairneyhill............81 F3
Cairngaan............68 C7
Cairnhill............97 F2
Cairnie............104 D4
Cairnorrie............97 H1
Cairnryan............70 F8
Caister-on-Sea............47 L5
Caistor............54 F3
Caistor St Edmund............47 H6
Caistron............75 F4
Calbost............107 J7
Calbourne............13 G7
Calcot............22 B5
Caldbeck............63 J4
Caldbergh............59 F2
Caldecote, Cambs............34 E1
Caldecote, Herts............35 F6
Caldecote, Cambs............35 G4
Caldecott, Leic............44 B7
Caldecott, Northnts............34 C3
Calderbank............80 C5
Calder Bridge............62 F7
Calderbrook............51 J2
Caldercruix............80 D5
Calder Mains............111 G3
Caldermill............79 J7
Calder Vale............57 J6
Caldicot............19 J4
Caldwell, N. Yks............66 B6
Caldwell, Derby............42 E5
Caldy............50 B5
Caledrhydiau............27 J1
Calfsound............113 F3
Calgary............84 E3
Califer............103 J7
California, Central............80 E4
California, Norf............47 L5
Calke............43 F4
Callakille............100 D5
Callaly............75 G4
Callander............87 J8
Callanish............107 G5
Callestick............2 E4
Callicbhol neo Port Nis............107 K2
Calligarry............92 C5
Callington............4 D3
Callow............31 F6
Callow End............31 K5
Callow Hill, Wilts............20 E4
Callow Hill, H. & W.............31 G3
Callows Grave............31 G3
Calmore............13 F4
Calmsden............20 E2
Calow............53 G6
Calshot............13 G5
Calstock............5 J4
Calstone Wellington............20 E6
Calthorpe............47 G3
Calthwaite............64 B3
Caltron, Staffs............42 D1
Calton, N. Yks............58 E5
Calveley............50 E8
Calver............52 E6
Calver Hill............30 E5
Calverleigh............9 K4

Calverley............59 H7
Calvert............33 J7
Calverton, Bucks............34 A6
Calverton, Notts............43 J2
Calvine............87 L2
Cam............20 B3
Camas-luinie............93 F3
Camastianavaig............92 B2
Camasunary............92 B4
Camault Muir............94 D1
Camb............117 G3
Camber............17 G4
Camberley............22 D6
Camberwell............23 J5
Camblesforth............53 J1
Cambo............75 G6
Cambois............75 K6
Camborne............2 E5
Cambridge, Glos............20 B2
Cambridge, Cambs............35 H4
Cambus............80 D2
Cambusbarron............80 C2
Cambuskenneth............80 D2
Cambuslang............79 J6
Camden Town............23 H4
Camelford............8 B7
Camelon............80 D3
Camelsdale............14 B2
Camerory............95 J2
Camerton, Avon............20 A7
Camerton, Cumbr............62 F4
Cammachmore............97 J6
Cammeringham............54 D5
Campbeltown............70 C2
Campsall............53 H2
Campsey Ash............37 J4
Camp, The............20 D2
Campton............34 E6
Camptown............26 D4
Camrose............26 C4
Camserney............111 J4
Camster............111 K1
Camus Cross............92 D1
Camusnagaul, Highld............101 G4
Camusnagaul, Highld............93 G8
Camusrory............92 E6
Camusteel............100 D8
Camusterrach............92 D1
Canada............12 E4
Canal Foot............57 G3
Candlesby............55 J7
Candy Mill............81 F7
Cane End............22 B5
Canewdon............24 E3
Canisbay............111 K1
Cann............12 A3
Cann Common............12 A3
Cannich............94 B2
Cannington............10 D2
Cannock............42 B5
Cannock Wood............42 C5
Canonbie............73 J7
Canon Bridge............31 F5
Canon Frome............31 H5
Canon Pyon............31 H1
Canons Ashby............33 H4
Canonstown............2 D6
Canterbury............25 H7
Cantley, S. Yks............53 J3
Cantley, Norf............47 J6
Cantlop............41 G6
Canton............18 F5
Cantraydoune............103 F8
Cantraywood............103 F8
Cantsfield............57 K3
Canvey Island............24 D4
Canwick............54 D7
Canworthy Water............8 C6
Caol............93 H8
Caolas............84 B4
Caol Ila............76 D5
Caolis............90 B6
Capel............14 E1
Capel Bangor............28 D1
Capel Betws Lleucu............28 D4
Capel Carmel............38 A4
Capel Coch............48 D2
Capel Curig............49 G5
Capel Cynon............27 H2
Capel Dewi............27 J2
Capel Garmon............39 H1
Capel Gwyn, Gwyn............48 C3
Capel Gwyn, Dyfed............27 J4
Capel Gwynfe............28 E7
Capel Hendre............27 K5
Capel Isaac............27 K4
Capel-le-Ferne............17 K2
Capel Iwan............27 G3
Capel Llanilterne............18 E4
Capel Parc............48 D2
Capel St Mary............37 F6
Capel-y-ffin............30 D6
Capel-y-graig............57 J3
Capenhurst............50 C6
Capernwray............57 J3
Capheaton............75 G6
Cappercleuch............73 H2
Capstone............24 D6
Capton............5 J4
Caputh............88 C3
Carbis Bay............2 D6
Carbost, Highld............91 J2
Carbost, Highld............99 K8
Carbrooke............46 E6
Carburton............53 J6
Car Colston............43 K2
Carcroft............53 H2
Cardenden............81 H2
Cardeston............40 E5
Cardiff............19 F5
Cardigan............26 F2
Cardington, Beds............34 D5
Cardington, Shrops............41 G7
Cardinham............3 K3
Cardow............103 K8
Cardrona............81 J8
Cardross............79 F4
Cardurnock............63 G2

Careby............44 D5
Carew............26 E6
Carew Cheriton............26 E6
Carew Newton............26 E6
Carey............31 G6
Carfrae............82 D5
Cargen............72 E7
Cargenbridge............72 E7
Cargo............63 J2
Cargreen............4 D3
Carham............83 F8
Carhampton............10 B1
Carharrack............2 F5
Carisbrooke............13 G7
Carishader............106 E5
Cark............57 G3
Carlby............44 D5
Carlecotes............52 D3
Carleton, N. Yks............58 E6
Carleton, Lancs............57 G6
Carleton, Cumbr............63 K2
Carleton Forehoe............47 F6
Carleton Rode............47 G7
Carlingcott............20 A7
Carlisle............63 K2
Carloway............107 G3
Carlops............81 G6
Carlton, Cambs............36 B4
Carlton, Beds............34 C4
Carlton, N. Yks............60 D2
Carlton, N. Yks............59 F2
Carlton, Cleve............66 D5
Carlton, W. Yks............53 F1
Carlton, N. Yks............59 F2
Carlton, S. Yks............53 F3
Carlton, Leic............43 F6
Carlton, N. Yks............53 J1
Carlton, Notts............43 J2
Carlton, Suff............37 J3
Carlton Colville............47 L7
Carlton Curlieu............43 J7
Carlton Husthwaite............60 B3
Carlton in Cleveland............66 F7
Carlton in Lindrick............53 H5
Carlton-le-Moorland............44 C1
Carlton Miniott............59 K2
Carlton-on-Trent............54 B7
Carlton Scroop............44 C2
Carluke............80 D6
Carmacoup............72 C2
Carmarthen............27 J4
Carmel, Clwyd............50 A6
Carmel, Gwyn............48 C2
Carmel, Gwyn............38 D1
Carmel, Dyfed............27 K5
Carminish............98 F4
Carmunnock............79 H6
Carmyle............79 J5
Carmyllie............89 H4
Carnaby............61 J4
Carnach, Highld............101 G3
Carnach, Highld............93 G3
Carnach, W. Isles............99 H3
Carnbee............89 H8
Carnbo............81 F1
Carn Brea Village............2 E5
Carne............3 H6
Carnell............71 K1
Carnforth............57 H3
Carn-gorm............93 F3
Carnhedryn............26 C4
Carnhell Green............2 E6
Carnish............98 D6
Carno............39 J7
Carnock............81 F3
Carnon Downs............3 F5
Carnousie............104 F3
Carnoustie............89 H5
Carn Towan............2 B7
Carnwath............80 E7
Carnyorth............2 B6
Carperby............58 F2
Carpley Green............58 E2
Carradale............77 H8
Carragreich............99 G3
Carrbridge............95 H3
Carreglefn............48 C2
Carrick Castle............78 D2
Carriden............81 G3
Carrington, Lincs............45 G1
Carrington, G. Man............51 G4
Carrington, Loth............81 J5
Carrog............40 C2
Carron, Grampn............96 B1
Carron, Central............80 D3
Carronbridge............72 D5
Carr Shield............65 F3
Carrutherstown............73 G7
Carr Vale............53 G7
Carrville............66 D3
Carsaig............85 G6
Carsegowan............68 F5
Carseriggan............62 E2
Carshalton............23 H6
Carsington............42 E1
Carskiey............70 B4
Carsluith............69 F5
Carsphairn............72 A5
Carstairs............80 E7
Carstairs Junction............80 E7
Carswell Marsh............21 H3
Carter's Clay............13 F3
Carterton............21 G1
Carterway Heads............65 H2
Carthew............3 J4
Carthorpe............59 J2
Cartington............75 G4
Cartland............80 D7
Cartmel............57 H2
Cartmel Fell............57 H2
Carway............27 J6
Cas............77 G5
Cascob............30 D3
Cashmoor............12 B4
Cassington............21 J1

Cassiobury Park............23 F3
Castallack............2 C7
Castellau............18 E4
Castell Howell............27 J2
Castell-y-bwch............19 G3
Casterton............57 K3
Castle Acre............46 D5
Castle Ashby............34 B4
Castlebay............90 B6
Castle Bolton............58 F1
Castle Bromwich............42 D7
Castle Bytham............44 C5
Castlebythe............26 E4
Castle Caereinion............40 C6
Castle Camps............36 B5
Castle Carrock............64 C2
Castlecary, Strath............80 C4
Castle Cary, Somer............11 H2
Castle Combe............20 C5
Castlecraig, Highld............103 G6
Castlecraig, Border............81 G7
Castle Donington............43 G4
Castle Douglas............69 J4
Castle Eaton............21 F3
Castle Eden............66 E4
Castleford............53 G1
Castle Frome............31 H5
Castle Gresley............42 E5
Castle Heaton............83 H7
Castle Hedingham............36 C6
Castle Hill............37 G5
Castle Kennedy............68 C5
Castlemartin............26 D7
Castlemilk............79 H6
Castlemorris............26 D3
Castlemorton............31 J6
Castle O'er............73 H5
Castle Rising............46 B4
Castle Side............65 H3
Castlethorpe............34 A5
Castleton, Derby............52 D5
Castleton, Gwent............19 G4
Castleton, N. Yks............67 G7
Castleton, Strath............77 H3
Castletown, T. & W.............66 D2
Castletown, Highld............111 H2
Castletown, I. of M.............56 P5
Caston............46 E7
Castor............44 E7
Catacol............77 J7
Catbrain............19 K4
Catcliffe............53 G5
Catcott............10 E2
Caterham............23 J7
Catesby............33 H4
Catfield............47 J4
Catfirth............115 G3
Catford............23 J5
Catforth............57 H7
Cath............26 B4
Cathcart............79 H5
Cathedine............30 C7
Catherington............13 K4
Catherston............31 H2
Catlodge............94 E6
Catlowdy............73 K7
Catmore............21 J4
Caton............57 H3
Catrine............71 L2
Cat's Ash............19 H3
Catsfield............16 E4
Catshill............32 B2
Cattal............59 K5
Cattawade............37 G6
Catterall............57 H6
Catterick............66 C8
Catterick Bridge............66 C8
Catterick Garrison............66 B8
Catterlen............64 B4
Catterline............97 H8
Catterton............60 C6
Catthorpe............33 H2
Cattistock............11 G6
Catton, Northum............65 F2
Catton, Norf............47 H5
Catton, N. Yks............59 J3
Catwick............61 J6
Catworth............34 D2
Caulcott............33 H7
Cauldhame............79 J2
Cauldon............42 C2
Caulkerbush............69 L5
Caulside............73 K6
Caunsall............32 A1
Caunton............54 B7
Causewayhead............80 D2
Causeway End............9 H1
Causey Park Bridge............75 H5
Cautley............58 B1
Cavendish............36 D5
Cavenham............36 C3
Caversfield............33 H7
Caversham............22 C5
Caversta............107 H7
Caverswall............42 B2
Cawdor............103 G7
Cawood............60 C7
Cawsand............4 E4
Cawston............47 G4
Cawthorne............52 E2
Cawton............60 D3
Caynham............31 G2
Caythorpe, Lincs............44 C2
Caythorpe, Notts............43 J2
Cayton............61 H2
Ceann-na-Cleithe............99 G3
Cefn Berain............49 J4
Cefn-brith............39 J1
Cefn Coch............40 C4
Cefn-coed-y-cymmer............18 E2
Cefn Cribwr............18 C4
Cefn Cross............18 C4
Cefn Einion............30 D1
Cefneithin............27 K5

Cefn Hengoed............18 F3
Cefn-mawr............40 D2
Cefn-y-bedd............40 E1
Cefn-y-pant............27 F4
Ceint............48 D3
Cellan............27 L2
Cellarhead............42 B2
Cemaes............39 H6
Cemmaes............39 H6
Cemmaes Road............39 H6
Cenarth............27 G2
Cennin............38 D2
Ceres............89 G7
Cerne Abbas............11 H5
Cerney Wick............20 E3
Cerrigceinwen............48 D3
Cerrigydrudion............39 J2
Cessford............74 D2
Chaceley............32 A6
Chackmore............33 J6
Chacombe............33 G5
Chadderton............51 J3
Chaddesden............43 F3
Chaddesley Corbett............32 A2
Chaddleworth............21 J5
Chadlington............33 F7
Chadshunt............33 F4
Chad Valley............32 C1
Chadwell St Mary............24 C5
Chadwick End............32 E2
Chaffcombe............10 E4
Chagford............9 H7
Chailey............15 G4
Chainhurst............16 E1
Chalbury Common............12 C5
Chaldon............23 J7
Chaldon Herring or
  East Chaldon............11 J7
Chale............7 J7
Chale Green............7 J7
Chalfont Common............22 F3
Chalfont St Giles............22 E3
Chalfont St Peter............22 F3
Chalford............20 C2
Chalgrove............22 B3
Chalk............24 C5
Challacombe............9 J1
Challoch............71 J8
Challock............25 G7
Chalton, Beds............34 D7
Chalton, Hants............13 K4
Chalvington............15 J5
Champany............80 F4
Chandler's Cross............22 F3
Chandler's Ford............13 G3
Channerwick............115 G6
Chantry, Suff............37 G5
Chantry, Somer............11 J1
Chapel............81 H2
Chapel Allerton, Somer............19 J7
Chapel Allerton, W. Yks............59 J7
Chapel Amble............3 H1
Chapel Brampton............33 K3
Chapel Chorlton............41 K3
Chapel-en-le-Frith............52 C5
Chapelgate............45 H4
Chapel Haddlesey............53 H1
Chapelhall............80 C5
Chapelhill, Tays............88 C3
Chapel Hill, Lincs............45 F1
Chapel Hill, Grampn............97 K2
Chapel Hill, Gwent............19 K2
Chapelknowe............73 J7
Chapel Lawn............30 E2
Chapel-le-Dale............58 C3
Chapel of Garioch............97 G3
Chapel of Stoneywood............97 H4
Chapel Row............21 K6
Chapel Stile............63 J7
Chapel St Leonards............55 K6
Chapelton, Strath............80 B7
Chapelton, Devon............9 F3
Chapelton, Tays............89 J4
Chapeltown, Grampn............96 B3
Chapeltown, S. Yks............53 F4
Chapeltown, Lancs............51 G2
Chapmanslade............11 K1
Chapmans Well............8 D6
Chappel............36 D7
Chard............10 E5
Chardstock............10 E5
Charfield............20 B3
Charing............17 G1
Charing Heath............17 G1
Charingworth............32 E6
Charlbury............21 H1
Charlcombe............20 B6
Charlecote............32 E4
Charles............9 G2
Charleston............89 F4
Charlestown, Highld............100 E5
Charlestown, Highld............102 E8
Charlestown, Fife............81 F3
Charlestown, Dorset............11 H8
Charlestown, Corn............3 J4
Charlestown, Grampn............97 J5
Charlestown of Aberlour............104 B4
Charles Tye............36 F4
Charlesworth............52 C4
Charlton, Wilts............12 B3
Charlton, W. Susx............14 B4
Charlton, H. & W.............32 C5
Charlton, Wilts............20 D4
Charlton, Wilts............20 E4
Charlton, Northnts............33 H6
Charlton, G. Lon............23 K5
Charlton Abbots............32 C7
Charlton Adam............11 G3
Charlton-All-Saints............12 D3
Charlton Horethorne............11 H3
Charlton Kings............32 B7
Charlton Mackrell............11 G3
Charlton Marshall............12 B5
Charlton Musgrove............11 J2

Charlton-on-Otmoor	21 K1	Chickerell	11 H7
Charlwood	15 F1	Chicklade	12 B2
Charlynch	10 D2	Chicksands	34 E6
Charminster	11 H6	Chicksgrove	12 B3
Charmouth	10 E6	Chidden	13 J4
Chandon	33 J7	Chiddingfold	14 C2
Charney Bassett	21 H3	Chiddingly	16 C4
Charnock Richard	50 E2	Chiddingstone	15 H1
Charsfield	37 H4	Chideock	11 F6
Charter Alley	21 K7	Chidham	14 A5
Charterhouse	19 J7	Chieveley	21 J5
Chartershall	80 D2	Chignall Smealy	24 C1
Charterville Allotments	21 H1	Chignall St James	24 C2
Chartham	25 H7	Chigwell	23 K3
Chartham Hatch	25 H7	Chigwell Row	23 K3
Chartridge	22 E2	Chilbolton	13 F2
Chart Sutton	24 D7	Chilcombe	11 G6
Charwelton	33 H4	Chilcompton	19 L7
Chase Terrace	42 C6	Chilcote	42 E5
Chasetown	42 C6	Childer Thornton	50 C6
Chastleton	32 E7	Child Okeford	11 K4
Chatburn	58 C4	Childrey	21 H4
Chatcull	41 J3	Child's Ercall	41 H4
Chatham	24 D6	Childswickham	32 C6
Chathill	75 H2	Childwall	50 D5
Chattenden	24 D5	Chilfrome	11 G6
Chatteris	35 G1	Chilgrove	14 B4
Chattisham	37 F5	Chilham	25 G7
Chatto	74 D3	Chillaton	4 E1
Chatton	75 G2	Chillenden	25 J7
Chawleigh	9 H4	Chillerton	13 G7
Chawston	34 E4	Chillesford	37 J4
Chawton	13 K2	Chillingham	75 G2
Cheadle, Staffs	42 C2	Chillington, Somer	10 E4
Cheadle, G. Man	51 H5	Chillington, Devon	5 H5
Cheadle Hulme	51 H5	Chilmark	12 B2
Cheam	23 H6	Chilson	21 H1
Chearsley	22 C1	Chilsworthy, Devon	8 D5
Chebsey	42 A4	Chilsworthy, Corn	4 C2
Checkendon	22 B4	Chilthorne Domer	11 G4
Checkley, Staffs	42 C3	Chilton, Bucks	22 B1
Checkley, Ches	41 J2	Chilton, Durham	66 C5
Chedburgh	36 C4	Chilton, Oxon	21 J4
Cheddar	19 J7	Chilton Cantelo	11 G3
Cheddington	22 E1	Chilton Foliat	21 H5
Cheddleton	42 B1	Chilton Lane	66 D4
Cheddon Fitzpaine	10 D3	Chilton Polden	10 E2
Chedgrave	47 J7	Chilton Street	36 C5
Chedington	11 F5	Chilton Trinity	10 D2
Chediston	37 J2	Chilworth, Surrey	14 D1
Chedworth	20 E1	Chilworth, Hants	13 G4
Chedzoy	10 E2	Chimney	21 H2
Cheeseman's Green	17 H2	Chineham	22 B7
Cheetham Hill	51 H3	Chingford	23 J3
Cheldon	9 H4	Chinley	52 C5
Chelford	51 H6	Chinley Head	52 C5
Chellaston	43 F3	Chinnor	22 C2
Chellington	34 C4	Chipnall	41 J3
Chelmarsh	31 J1	Chippenham, Cambs	36 B3
Chelmondiston	37 H6	Chippenham, Wilts	20 D5
Chelmorton	52 D6	Chipperfield	22 F2
Chelmsford	24 D2	Chipping, Herts	35 G6
Chelsea	23 H5	Chipping, Lancs	57 K6
Chelsfield	23 K6	Chipping Campden	32 D6
Chelsworth	36 E5	Chipping Hill	24 E1
Cheltenham	32 B7	Chipping Norton	33 F7
Chelveston	34 C3	Chipping Ongar	23 L2
Chelvey	19 J6	Chipping Sodbury	20 B4
Chelwood	19 L6	Chipping Warden	33 G5
Chelwood Gate	15 H3	Chipstable	10 B3
Cheney Longville	31 F1	Chipstead	23 H7
Chenies	22 F3	Chirbury	40 D7
Chepstow	19 K3	Chirk	40 D3
Cherhill	20 E5	Chirnside	83 G6
Cherington, Glos	20 D3	Chirnsidebridge	83 G6
Cherington, Warw	32 E6	Chirton	20 E7
Cheriton, Devon	10 C5	Chisbury	21 G6
Cheriton, Hants	13 H3	Chiselborough	11 F4
Cheriton, W. Glam	27 J7	Chiseldon	21 F5
Cheriton Bishop	9 H6	Chiselhampton	21 K3
Cheriton Fitzpaine	9 J5	Chislehurst	23 K5
Cherrington	41 H4	Chislet	25 J6
Cherry Burton	61 G6	Chiswell Green	22 G2
Cherry Hinton	35 H4	Chiswick	23 H5
Cherry Willingham	54 E6	Chisworth	51 J4
Chertsey	22 F6	Chitcomb	13 H3
Cheselbourne	11 J6	Chithurst	14 B3
Chesham	22 E2	Chittering	35 H2
Chesham Bois	22 E3	Chitterne	12 B1
Cheshunt	23 J2	Chittlehamholt	9 G3
Cheslyn Hay	42 B6	Chittlehampton	9 G3
Chessington	23 G6	Chittoe	20 D6
Chester	50 D7	Chivenor	8 F2
Chesterblade	11 H1	Chobham	22 E6
Chesterfield, Staffs	42 D6	Cholderton	12 E1
Chesterfield, Derby	53 F6	Cholesbury	22 E2
Chester-le-Street	66 C2	Chollerton	75 F7
Chesters, Border	74 C2	Cholsey	21 K4
Chesters, Border	74 C3	Cholstrey	31 F4
Chesterton, Cambs	44 E7	Choppington	75 J6
Chesterton, Warw	33 F4	Chopwell	65 J2
Chesterton, Cambs	35 H3	Chorley, Staffs	42 C5
Chesterton, Oxon	33 H7	Chorley, Lancs	50 E2
Chesterton, Staffs	41 K2	Chorley, Ches	41 G1
Chestfield	25 H6	Chorley, Shrops	31 H1
Cheswardine	41 J4	Chorleywood, Herts	22 F3
Cheswick	83 J7	Chorleywood, Bucks	22 F3
Cheswick Green	32 D2	Chorlton	41 J1
Chetnole	11 H5	Chorlton-cum-Hardy	51 H4
Chettiscombe	9 K4	Chorlton Lane	41 F2
Chettisham	35 J1	Chowley	41 F1
Chettle	12 B4	Chrishall	35 H6
Chetton	41 H7	Christchurch, Dorset	12 D6
Chetwode	33 J7	Christchurch, Cambs	45 H7
Chetwynd Aston	41 J5	Christchurch, Glos	19 K1
Cheveley	36 B3	Christian Malford	20 D5
Chevening	23 K7	Christleton	50 D7
Chevington	36 C4	Christmas Common	22 C3
Chevington Drift	75 J5	Christon	19 H7
Chevithorne	10 A4	Christon Bank	75 J2
Chew Magna	19 K6	Christow	9 J7
Chew Stoke	19 K6	Chudleigh	5 J2
Chewton Mendip	19 K7	Chudleigh Knighton	5 J2
Chicheley	34 C5	Chulmleigh	9 G4
Chichester	14 B5	Chunal	52 C4

Church	58 C8	Claughton, Lancs	57 J6
Churcham	20 B1	Claverdon	32 D3
Church Aston	41 J5	Claverham	19 J6
Church Brampton	33 K3	Clavering	35 H5
Church Broughton	42 E3	Claverley	41 J7
Church Cove	2 F8	Claverton	20 B6
Church Crookham	22 D7	Clawdd-newydd	40 B1
Churchdown	32 A7	Clawton	8 D6
Church Eaton	41 K5	Claxby, Lincs	54 F4
Church End, Hants	22 B7	Claxby, Lincs	55 J6
Church End, Beds	34 C7	Claxton, N. Yks	60 D4
Churchend, Essex	36 B7	Claxton, Norf	47 J6
Church End, Wilts	20 E5	Claybokie	95 J6
Church End, Beds	35 E6	Claybrooke Magna	33 G1
Church End, Warw	42 E7	Clay Coton	33 H2
Churchend, Essex	25 G3	Clay Cross	53 F7
Church End, Essex	35 J5	Claydon, Suff	37 G4
Church End, Cambs	45 G6	Claydon, Oxon	33 G4
Church Fenton	60 C7	Claygate	23 G6
Church Gresley	42 E5	Claygate Cross	24 C7
Church Hanborough	21 J1	Clayhanger, Devon	10 B3
Church Houses	67 G8	Clayhanger, W. Mids	42 C6
Churchill, H. & W	32 A2	Clayhidon	10 C4
Churchill, Devon	10 D5	Clayock	111 H3
Churchill, Oxon	32 E7	Claypole	44 B2
Churchill, Avon	19 J7	Clayton, Staffs	42 A2
Churchinford	10 D4	Clayton, S. Yks	53 G3
Church Knowle	6 D6	Clayton, W. Susx	15 G4
Church Langton	43 K7	Clayton, W. Yks	59 G7
Church Lawford	33 G2	Clayton-le-Moors	58 C7
Church Lawton	41 K1	Clayton-le-Woods	50 E1
Church Leigh	42 C3	Clayton West	52 E2
Church Lench	32 C4	Clayworth	54 B5
Church Minshull	51 F7	Cleadale	92 A7
Church Norton	14 B6	Cleadon	66 D1
Churchover	33 H1	Clearwell	19 K2
Church Preen	41 G7	Cleasby	66 C6
Church Pulverbatch	41 F6	Cleat, W. Isles	90 B5
Churchstanton	10 C4	Cleat, Orkney	112 E4
Church Stoke	40 D7	Cleatlam	65 J6
Churchstow	5 H5	Cleator	62 F6
Church Stowe	33 J4	Cleator Moor	62 F6
Church Street	24 D5	Cleckheaton	52 D1
Church Stretton	41 F7	Cleedownton	31 G1
Churchtown, Mers	50 C2	Cleehill	31 G2
Churchtown, Lancs	57 H6	Clee St Margaret	31 G1
Churchtown, I. of M	56 R2	Cleethorpes	55 H3
Church Village	18 E4	Cleeton St Mary	31 H2
Church Warsop	53 H7	Cleeve	19 J6
Churt	14 B2	Cleeve Hill	32 B7
Churton	41 F1	Cleeve Prior	32 C5
Churwell	59 H8	Clehonger	31 F6
Chwilog	38 D3	Cleigh	85 K6
Chyandour	2 C6	Cleish	81 F2
Cilan Uchaf	38 B4	Cleland	80 C6
Cilcain	50 A7	Clench Common	21 F6
Cilcennin	28 C3	Clenchwarton	45 J4
Cilfrew	18 B2	Clent	32 B2
Cilfynydd	18 E3	Cleobury Mortimer	31 H2
Cilgerran	27 F2	Cleobury North	31 H1
Cilgwyn	28 E7	Clephanton	103 G2
Ciliau-Aeron	28 C4	Clerklands	74 B2
Cilmaengwyn	18 B2	Clestrain	112 D6
Cilmery	29 H4	Cleughbrae	73 F7
Cilrhedyn	27 G3	Clevancy	20 E5
Ciltwrch	30 C5	Clevedon	19 J5
Cilwendeg	27 G3	Cleveleys	57 G6
Cilybebyll	18 B2	Cleverton	20 D4
Cilycwm	28 E5	Clewer	19 J7
Cinderford	20 A1	Cley next the Sea	46 F2
Cirencester	20 E2	Cliasmol	99 F2
City Dulas	48 D2	Cliburn	64 C5
City of London	23 J4	Cliddesden	13 J1
City, The	22 C3	Cliffe, Kent	24 D5
Clachaig	78 D3	Cliffe, N. Yks	60 D7
Clachan, Highld	92 B2	Cliff End	17 F4
Clachan, Strath	77 H6	Cliffe Woods	24 D5
Clachan, Strath	85 J7	Clifford, H. & W	30 D5
Clachan, Strath	85 K4	Clifford, W. Yks	59 K6
Clachan-a-Luib	98 D6	Clifford Chambers	32 D4
Clachan of Campsie	79 J4	Clifford's Mesne	31 J7
Clachan of Glendaruel	78 B3	Cliffs End	25 K6
Clachan-Seil	85 J7	Clifton, Cumbr	64 C5
Clachbreck	77 G4	Clifton, Derby	42 D2
Clachtoll	108 B6	Clifton, Beds	34 E6
Clackmannan	80 E2	Clifton, Central	86 F5
Clacton-on-Sea	25 H1	Clifton, Oxon	33 G6
Claddach Kirkibost	98 C6	Clifton, Notts	43 H3
Claggan	85 H4	Clifton, Lancs	57 H7
Claigan	90 H7	Clifton, Northum	75 J6
Claines	32 A4	Clifton, Avon	19 K5
Clandown	20 A7	Clifton, H. & W	31 K5
Clanfield, Oxon	21 G2	Clifton Campville	42 E5
Clanfield, Hants	13 J4	Clifton Hampden	21 K3
Clanville	13 F1	Clifton Reynes	34 C4
Clanyard	68 C7	Clifton upon Dunsmore	33 H2
Claonaig	77 H6	Clifton upon Teme	31 J3
Claonel	102 D2	Climping	14 C5
Clapgate	12 C5	Clint	59 H5
Clapham, N. Yks	58 C4	Clint Green	46 F5
Clapham, Beds	34 D4	Clintmains	74 C1
Clapham, W. Susx	14 D5	Clippesby	47 K5
Clapham, G. Lon	23 H5	Clipsham	44 C5
Clappers	83 H6	Clipston, Notts	43 J3
Clappersgate	63 J7	Clipston, Northnts	33 K1
Clapton	11 F5	Clitheroe	58 C6
Clapton-in-Gordano	19 J5	Clive	41 G4
Clapton-on-the-Hill	21 F1	Clivocast	117 H2
Clapworthy	9 G3	Clixby	55 F2
Clarbeston	26 E4	Clocaenog	40 B1
Clarbeston Road	26 E4	Clochan	104 D2
Clarborough	54 B5	Clock Face	50 E4
Clardon	111 H2	Cloddymoss	103 H6
Clare	72 C8	Cloddock	30 E7
Clarebrand	72 C8	Clola	105 K4
Clarencefield	73 F8	Clophill	34 D6
Clarkston	79 H6	Clopton, Northnts	34 D1
Clashmore, Highld	108 B5	Clopton, Suff	37 H4
Clashmore, Highld	103 F4	Clopton Green	36 C4
Clashnessie	108 B5	Close Clark	56 P4
Clashnoir	96 B3	Closeburn	72 D5
Clatt	96 E3	Clothall	35 F6
Clatter	39 J7	Clotton	50 E7
Clatworthy	10 B2	Clough Foot	51 J1
Claughton, Lancs	57 J4	Cloughton	61 H1
		Cloughton Newlands	61 H1

Clousta	115 F3	Colby, I. of M	56 P4
Clouston	112 D5	Colchester	36 F7
Clova	96 C8	Cold Ash	21 K5
Clovelly	8 D3	Cold Ashby	33 J2
Clovenfords	82 C8	Cold Ashton	20 B5
Clovenstone	97 G4	Cold Aston	21 F1
Clovullin	86 C2	Coldbackie	109 H2
Clowne	53 G6	Coldblow	23 L5
Clows Top	31 J2	Cold Brayfield	34 C4
Cluer	99 G3	Coldean	15 G5
Clun	30 E1	Coldeast	5 J2
Clunbury	30 E1	Colden Common	13 G3
Clunderwen	26 F5	Coldfair Green	37 K3
Clunes	93 J1	Cold Hanworth	54 E5
Clungunford	30 E2	Coldharbour	14 E1
Clunie	104 F3	Cold Hesledon	66 E3
Clunton	30 E1	Cold Higham	33 J4
Cluny	81 H2	Coldingham	83 H5
Clutton, Ches	41 F1	Cold Kirby	60 C2
Clutton, Avon	19 L7	Cold Newton	43 K6
Clwyt-y-bont	48 E4	Cold Norton	24 E2
Clydach, W. Glam	18 A2	Cold Overton	44 B5
Clydach, Gwent	19 G1	Coldred	17 K1
Clydach Vale	18 D3	Coldridge	9 G5
Clydebank	79 H5	Coldstream	83 G8
Clydey	27 G3	Coldwaltham	14 D4
Clyffe Pypard	20 E5	Coldwells	97 L2
Clynder	78 E3	Coldwells Croft	96 E3
Clynelish	103 G2	Cole	11 H2
Clynnog-fawr	38 D2	Colebatch	30 E1
Clyro	30 D5	Colebrook	10 B5
Clyst Honiton	10 A6	Colebrooke	9 H5
Clyst Hydon	10 B5	Coleburn	66 C8
Clyst St George	10 A7	Coleby, Humbs	54 C2
Clyst St Lawrence	10 B5	Coleby, Lincs	54 D7
Clyst St Mary	10 A6	Coleford, Somer	11 H1
Clyth	111 J5	Coleford, Devon	9 H5
Cnoc Amhlaigh	107 K5	Coleford, Glos	19 K1
Cnwch Coch	28 D2	Colehill	12 C5
Coad's Green	4 C2	Coleman's Hatch	15 H2
Coal Aston	53 F6	Colemere	41 F3
Coalbrookdale	41 H6	Colemore	88 D6
Coalburn	72 D1	Coleorton	43 G5
Coalcleugh	65 F3	Colerne	20 C5
Coaley	20 B2	Colesbourne	20 D1
Coalpit Heath	20 A4	Colesden	34 E4
Coalport	41 H6	Coleshill, Bucks	22 E3
Coalsnaughton	80 E2	Coleshill, Warw	42 E8
Coaltown of Balgonie	81 J2	Coleshill, Oxon	21 G3
Coaltown of Wemyss	81 J2	Colgate	15 G2
Coalville	43 G5	Colgrain	78 F3
Coast	101 J3	Colinsburgh	82 C1
Coatbridge	80 C5	Colinton	81 H5
Coatdyke	80 C5	Colintraive	78 C4
Coate	20 E6	Colkirk	46 E4
Coates, Glos	20 D2	Collafirth	116 E4
Coates, Cambs	45 G7	Collaton St Mary	5 J4
Coatham	67 F5	Collessie	88 E7
Coatham Mundeville	66 C5	Collier Row	23 K3
Coatsgate	73 F4	Colliers End	35 G7
Cobbaton	9 G3	Collier Street	16 E1
Coberley	20 D1	Collieston	97 K3
Cobham, Kent	24 C5	Collin	73 F7
Cobham, Surrey	23 G6	Collingbourne Ducis	21 G7
Cobnash	31 F3	Collingbourne Kingston	21 G7
Cockayne	67 G8	Collingham, Notts	54 C7
Cockayne Hatley	35 F5	Collingham, W. Yks	59 J6
Cock Bridge	96 B5	Collington	31 H3
Cockburnspath	82 F4	Collingtree	34 A4
Cock Clarks	24 E2	Colliston	89 J4
Cockenzie and Port Seton	82 C4	Collyweston	44 C6
Cockerham	57 H5	Colmonell	71 G6
Cockerington	55 H4	Colmworth	34 E4
Cockermouth	63 G4	Colnabaichin	96 B5
Cockernhoe	34 E7	Colnbrook	22 F5
Cockfield, Suff	36 E4	Colne, Lancs	58 D6
Cockfield, Durham	65 J5	Colne, Cambs	35 G2
Cockfosters	23 H3	Colne Engaine	36 D6
Cocking	14 B4	Colney	47 G6
Cockington	5 J3	Colney Heath	23 H2
Cocklake	11 F1	Colney Street	23 G2
Cockley Beck	63 H7	Coln Rogers	20 E2
Cockley Cley	46 C6	Coln St Aldwyns	21 F2
Cockpole Green	22 C4	Coln St Dennis	20 E1
Cockshutt	41 F4	Colpy	97 F2
Cockthorpe	46 E2	Colsterdale	59 G2
Cockwood	5 K1	Colsterworth	44 C4
Cockyard	31 F6	Colston Bassett	43 J3
Coddenham	37 G4	Coltfield	103 K6
Coddington, Notts	44 B1	Coltishall	47 H4
Coddington, Ches	41 F1	Colton, Staffs	42 C4
Coddington, H. & W	31 J5	Colton, N. Yks	60 C6
Codford St Mary	12 B2	Colton, Cumbr	57 G2
Codford St Peter	12 B1	Colton, Norf	47 G6
Codicote	23 H1	Col Uarach	107 J5
Codnor	43 G2	Colvend	69 K5
Codrington	20 B5	Colvister	117 J2
Codsall	42 A6	Colwall Green	31 J5
Codsall Wood	41 K6	Colwall Stone	31 J5
Coedely	18 E4	Colwell	75 F7
Coedkernew	19 G4	Colwich	42 C4
Coedpoeth	40 D1	Colwinston	18 D5
Coed-y-paen	19 H3	Colworth	14 C5
Coed Ystumgwern	38 D2	Colwyn Bay	49 H3
Coelbren	18 C1	Colyford	10 D6
Coffinswell	5 J3	Colyton	10 D6
Cofton Hackett	32 C2	Combe, H. & W	30 E3
Cogenhoe	34 B3	Combe, Berks	21 H6
Coggeshall	36 D7	Combe, Oxon	21 J1
Coig Peighinnean	107 K2	Combe Florey	10 C2
Coilacriech	96 C6	Combe Hay	20 B7
Coille Mhorgil	93 H5	Combeinteignhead	5 K2
Coillore	91 J2	Combe Martin	8 F1
Coity	18 D4	Combe Moor	30 E3
Col	107 J4	Combe Raleigh	10 C5
Colaboll	102 D1	Comberbach	51 F6
Colan	3 G3	Comberton, H. & W	30 E3
Colaton Raleigh	10 B7	Comberton, Cambs	35 G4
Colbost	99 H8	Combe St Nicholas	10 E4
Colburn	66 B8	Combpyne	10 D6
Colby, Cumbr	64 D5	Combrook	33 G4
Colby, Norf	47 H3	Combs, Derby	52 C6
		Combs, Suff	36 E4
		Combs Ford	36 F4
		Combwich	10 D1
		Comers	97 F5

Commins Coch 39 H6
Commondale 67 G6
Common Moor 4 C3
Common Side 53 F6
Common, The 12 E2
Compstall 51 J4
Compton, W. Susx. 14 A4
Compton, Surrey 14 C1
Compton, Wilts. 21 F7
Compton, Hants. 13 G3
Compton, Devon 5 J3
Compton, Berks. 21 K5
Compton Abbas. 12 A4
Compton Abdale 20 E1
Compton Bassett 20 E5
Compton Beauchamp 21 G4
Compton Bishop 19 H7
Compton Chamberlayne ...12 C3
Compton Dando 19 L6
Compton Dundon 11 F2
Compton Martin 19 K7
Compton Pauncefoot 11 H3
Compton Valence 11 G6
Comrie 87 K6
Conchra 78 C3
Conderton 32 B6
Condicote 32 D7
Condorrat 80 C4
Condover 41 F6
Coneyhurst 14 E3
Coneysthorpe 60 E3
Coney Weston 36 E2
Congerstone 43 F6
Congham 46 C4
Congleton 51 H7
Congresbury 19 J6
Conicavel 103 H7
Coningsby 45 F1
Conington, Cambs. 34 E1
Conington, Cambs. 35 G3
Conisbrough 53 H4
Conisby 76 B5
Conisholme 55 J4
Coniston, Humbs. 61 J7
Coniston, Cumbr. 63 J8
Coniston Cold 58 E5
Conistone 58 E4
Connah's Quay 50 B7
Connel 86 B5
Connel Park 72 B3
Connor Downs 2 D6
Conon Bridge 102 D7
Cononley 58 E6
Conordan 92 B2
Consall 42 B2
Consett 65 J2
Constable Burton 59 G1
Constantine 2 F7
Contin 102 C7
Conwy 49 G3
Conyer 25 F6
Cookbury 8 E5
Cookham 22 D4
Cookham Dean 22 D4
Cookham Rise 22 D4
Cookhill 32 C4
Cookley, Suff. 37 J2
Cookley, H. & W. 31 K1
Cookley Green 22 B3
Cookney 97 H6
Cooksbridge 15 H4
Cooksmill Green 24 C2
Coolham 14 E3
Cooling 24 D5
Coombe, Corn. 8 C4
Coombe, Corn. 3 H4
Coombe Bissett 12 D3
Coombe Hill 32 A7
Coombe Keynes 11 K7
Coombes 15 E5
Copdock 37 G5
Copford Green 36 E7
Copister 117 F5
Cople 34 E5
Copley 65 H5
Coplow Dale 52 D6
Copmanthorpe 60 C6
Coppathorne 8 C5
Coppenhall 42 B5
Copperhouse 2 D6
Coppingford 34 E1
Copplestone 9 H5
Coppull 50 E2
Copsale 14 E3
Copster Green 58 B7
Copt Heath 32 D2
Copt Hewick 59 J3
Copthorne 15 G2
Copt Oak 43 G5
Copythorne 13 F4
Corbridge 65 G1
Corby 34 B1
Corby Glen 44 C4
Coreley 31 H2
Corfe 10 D4
Corfe Castle 11 C6
Corfe Mullen 12 B6
Corfton 31 F1
Corgarff 96 B5
Corhampton 13 J3
Corlae 72 B5
Corley 33 F1
Corley Ash 32 E1
Corley Moor 32 E1
Cornelly 18 C4
Corney 56 E1
Cornforth 21 D4
Cornhill 104 E3
Cornhill-on-Tweed 83 G8
Cornholme 51 J1
Cornriggs 65 F3
Cornsay 65 J3
Corntown 102 D7
Cornwell 32 E7

Cornwood 5 G4
Cornworthy 5 J4
Corpach 93 G8
Corpusty 47 G3
Corran, Highld. 86 C2
Corran, Highld. 92 E5
Corrany 56 R3
Corrie 78 C7
Corrie Common 73 H6
Corriemoillie 102 B6
Corrimony 94 B2
Corringham, Lincs. 54 C4
Corringham, Essex 24 D4
Corris 39 G6
Corris Uchaf 39 G6
Corry 92 C3
Corry of Ardnagrask ...102 D8
Corscombe 11 G5
Corse 96 F1
Corsham 20 C5
Corsindae 97 F5
Corsley 11 K1
Corsley Heath 11 K1
Corsock 72 C7
Corston, Avon. 20 A6
Corston, Wilts. 20 D4
Corstorphine 81 G4
Corton, Wilts. 12 B1
Corton, Suff. 47 L7
Corton Denham 11 H3
Corwen 40 B2
Coryton, Essex 24 D4
Coryton, Devon. 8 E7
Cosby 43 H7
Coseley 42 B7
Cosgrove 34 A5
Cosham 13 J5
Cosheston 26 E6
Cossall 43 G2
Cossington, Somer. 10 E1
Cossington, Leic. 43 J5
Costa 112 D4
Costessey 47 G5
Costock 43 H4
Coston 44 B4
Cotebrook 50 E7
Cotegill 64 D7
Cotehill 64 B2
Cotes, Leic. 43 H4
Cotes, Staffs. 41 K3
Cotesbach 33 H1
Cotgrave 43 J3
Cothall 97 H4
Cotham 44 A2
Cothelstone 10 C2
Cotherstone 65 H6
Cothill 21 J3
Cotleigh 10 D5
Coton, Staffs. 42 B3
Coton, Cambs. 35 H4
Coton, Northnts. 33 J2
Coton Clanford 42 A4
Coton in the Elms 42 E5
Cott 5 H3
Cottam, Notts. 54 C5
Cottam, Lancs. 57 J7
Cottartown 95 J2
Cottenham 35 H3
Cotterdale 58 D1
Cottered 35 G7
Cotterstock 44 D7
Cottesbrooke 33 K2
Cottesmore 44 C5
Cottingham, Northnts. ..44 B7
Cottingham, Humbs. 61 H7
Cottisford 33 H6
Cotton, Staffs. 42 C2
Cotton, Suff. 36 F3
Cotton End 34 D5
Cottown, Grampn. 96 E3
Cottown, Grampn. 97 G4
Cottown, Grampn. 97 H1
Cotwalton 42 B3
Coughton, Warw. 32 C3
Coughton, H. & W. 31 G7
Coulags 101 F8
Coulby Newham 66 F6
Coull 96 E5
Coulport 78 E3
Coulsdon 23 J7
Coulston 20 D7
Coulter 73 F1
Coulton 60 D3
Cound 41 G6
Coundon 66 C5
Coundon Grange 66 C5
Countersett 58 E2
Countess Wear 9 K7
Countesthorpe 43 H7
Countisbury 9 H1
Coupar Angus 88 E4
Coupland 75 F1
Cour 77 H7
Courteachan 92 C6
Courteenhall 34 A4
Court Henry 27 K4
Courtsend 25 G3
Courtway 10 D2
Cousland 81 J5
Cousley Wood 16 D2
Cove, Hants. 22 D7
Cove, Strath. 78 E3
Cove, Highld. 100 V4
Cove, Devon. 9 K4
Cove Bay 97 J5
Covehithe 37 L1
Coven 42 B6
Covenham St Bartholomew .55 H4
Covenham St Mary 55 H4
Coventry 33 F2
Coverack 3 F8
Coverham 59 G2
Covington 34 D2
Cowan Bridge 58 B3

Cowbeech 16 D4
Cowbit 45 F5
Cowbridge 18 D5
Cowden 15 H1
Cowdenbeath 81 G2
Cowes 13 G6
Cowesby 60 B2
Cowfold 15 F3
Cowgill 58 C2
Cowick 53 J1
Cowie 80 D1
Cowley, Glos. 20 D1
Cowley, Oxon. 21 K2
Cowley, G. Lon. 22 F4
Cowley, Devon. 9 K6
Cowling, N. Yks. 58 E6
Cowling, N. Yks. 59 H2
Cowlinge 36 C4
Cowpen Bewley 66 C6
Cowplain 13 J4
Cowshill 65 F3
Cowstrandburn 81 F2
Coxbank 41 H2
Coxbench 43 F2
Cox Common 37 K1
Coxheath 24 D7
Coxhoe 66 D4
Coxley 11 G1
Coxwold 60 C3
Coychurch 18 D5
Coylumbridge 95 H4
Coynach 96 D5
Crabbs Cross 32 C3
Crabtree 15 F3
Crabtree Green 40 E2
Crackenthorpe 64 D5
Crackington 8 B6
Cracklebank 41 J5
Crackpot 58 E1
Cracoe 58 E4
Cradley 31 J5
Crafthole 4 D4
Craggan 95 J3
Cragg Vale 52 C1
Craghead 66 C2
Crai 29 F7
Craichie 89 H4
Craig, D. & G. 72 B7
Craig, Highld. 101 G8
Craig Castle 96 D3
Craigcefnparc 27 L6
Craigdam 97 H2
Craigearn 97 G4
Craigellachie 104 B4
Craigendoran 78 F3
Craighouse 76 E5
Craigie, Grampn. 97 J4
Craigie, Strath. 71 K1
Craiglockhart 81 H4
Craigmaud 105 H3
Craigmillar 81 H4
Craignant 40 D3
Craigneuk, Strath. 80 C5
Craigneuk, Strath. 80 C6
Craignure 85 J5
Craigo 89 J2
Craigrothie 89 F7
Craigton, Tays. 88 F3
Craigton, Grampn. 97 H5
Craigton, Tays. 89 H5
Craigtown 110 E3
Craik 73 J4
Crail 89 J8
Crailing 74 C2
Crailinghall 74 C2
Crakehall 59 H1
Cramalt 73 G2
Crambe 60 E4
Cramlington 75 J7
Cramond 81 G4
Cramond Bridge 81 G4
Cranage 51 G7
Cranberry 41 K3
Cranborne 12 C4
Cranbourne 22 E5
Cranbrook 16 E2
Cranbrook Common 16 E2
Cranfield 34 C5
Cranford St Andrew 34 C2
Cranford St John 34 C2
Cranham, G. Lon. 24 B4
Cranham, Glos. 20 C1
Crank 50 E4
Cranleigh 14 D2
Cranmore, I. of W. 13 F6
Cranmore, Somer. 11 H1
Cranna 104 F3
Crannoch 104 D3
Cranoe 44 A7
Cransford 37 J3
Cranshaws 82 E5
Cranstal 56 R1
Crantock 3 F3
Cranwell 44 D2
Cranwich 46 C7
Cranworth 46 E6
Crapstone 4 F3
Craskins 96 E5
Crask of Aigas 102 C8
Craster 75 J3
Craswall 30 D6
Cratfield 37 J2
Crathes 97 G6
Crathie, Grampn. 96 B6
Crathie, Highld. 94 D6
Crathorne 66 E7
Craven Arms 31 F1
Crawcrook 65 J1
Crawford 72 E2
Crawfordjohn 72 D2
Crawick 72 C3
Crawleside 65 G3
Crawley, W. Susx. 15 F2
Crawley, Hants. 13 G2

Crawley, Oxon. 21 H1
Crawley Down 15 G2
Crawshawbooth 51 H1
Crawton 97 H8
Cray 58 D3
Crayke 60 C3
Cray's Pond 22 B4
Creacombe 9 J4
Creagorry 98 C8
Creagton 33 K2
Creca 73 H7
Credenhill 31 F5
Crediton 9 J5
Creech St Michael 10 D3
Creed 3 H5
Creekmouth 23 K4
Creeting St Mary 36 F4
Creeton 44 D4
Creetown 69 F5
Creggans 78 C1
Cregneish 56 N5
Cregrina 30 C4
Creich 88 F6
Creigiau 18 E4
Cremyll 4 C4
Cressage 41 G6
Cresselly 26 E6
Cressing 36 C7
Cresswell, Staffs. 42 B3
Cresswell, Northum. ...75 J5
Cresswell Quay 26 E6
Creswell 53 H6
Cretingham 37 H3
Cretshengan 77 G5
Crewe, Ches. 41 F1
Crewe, Ches. 41 J1
Crew Green 40 E5
Crewkerne 11 F5
Crews Hill 23 J3
Crianlarich 87 F6
Cribyn 27 K1
Criccieth 38 E3
Crich 43 F1
Crichie 105 J4
Crichton 81 J5
Crick, Northnts. 33 H2
Crick, Gwent 19 J3
Crickadarn 29 H5
Cricket St Thomas 10 E5
Crickheath 40 D4
Crickhowell 19 G1
Cricklade 20 F3
Cridling Stubbs 53 H1
Crieff 88 A6
Criggion 40 D5
Crigglestone 53 F2
Crimond 105 K3
Crimplesham 46 B6
Crinan 77 G2
Cringleford 47 G6
Crinow 26 F5
Cripplesease 2 D6
Cripp's Corner 16 E3
Crockenhill 23 L6
Crockernwell 9 H6
Crockerton 12 A1
Crocketford or Ninemile Bar ..72 D7
Crockey Hill 60 D6
Crockham Hill 23 K7
Crockleford Heath 36 F7
Croeserw 18 C3
Croes-goch 26 C3
Croesor 39 F2
Croesyceiliog 19 H3
Croesyceiliog 27 J5
Croes-y-mwyalch 19 H3
Croft, Ches. 51 F4
Croft, Leic. 43 H7
Croft, Lincs. 55 K7
Croftamie 79 G3
Crofton 53 F2
Croft-on-Tees 66 C7
Crofts of Benachielt .111 H5
Crofts of Haddo 97 H2
Crofts of Inverthernie .105 G4
Crofty 27 K7
Croggan 85 J6
Croglin 64 C3
Croir 107 F5
Cromarty 103 F6
Cromdale 95 J3
Cromer, Herts. 35 F7
Cromer, Norf. 47 H2
Cromford 42 E1
Cromhall 20 A3
Cromhall Common 20 A4
Cromore 107 J6
Cromra 94 D6
Cromwell 54 B7
Cronberry 72 B2
Crondall 22 A1
Cronk, The 56 Q2
Cronk-y-Voddy 56 Q3
Cronton 50 D5
Crook, Durham. 66 B4
Crook, Cumbr. 57 H1
Crookham, Northum. 83 H8
Crookham, Berks. 21 K6
Crookham Village 22 C7
Crookhouse 74 D2
Crooklands 57 J2
Crook of Devon 81 F1
Cropredy 33 G5
Cropston 43 H5
Cropthorne 32 B5
Cropton 60 E2
Cropwell Bishop 43 J3
Cropwell Butler 43 J3
Cros, W. Isles 107 K2
Crosby, Humbs. 54 C2
Crosby, Mers. 50 C4
Crosby, Cumbr. 62 F4
Crosby, I. of M. 56 Q4

Crosby Garrett 64 E7
Crosby-on-Eden 64 B2
Crosby Ravensworth 64 D6
Croscombe 11 G1
Cross, Somer. 19 J7
Crossapol 84 A4
Cross Ash 19 J1
Crossbost 107 H6
Crosscanonby 62 F4
Crossdale Street 47 H3
Crossdougal 90 C3
Crossens 50 C2
Crossford, Strath. 80 D7
Crossford, Fife. 81 F3
Crossgates, Fife. 81 G3
Crossgates, Powys 29 H3
Crossgill 57 J4
Cross Green, Devon. 8 D7
Cross Green, Suff. 36 E4
Crosshands, Dyfed 27 F4
Cross Hands, Dyfed 27 K5
Crosshill, Fife. 81 G2
Crosshill, Strath. 71 J4
Crosshouse 79 F8
Cross Houses 41 G6
Crossings 74 B7
Cross in Hand 16 C3
Cross Inn, Dyfed 28 A4
Cross Inn, Dyfed 28 C3
Cross Inn, M. Glam. ...18 E4
Crosskeys 19 G3
Crosskirk 111 G1
Cross Lanes, N. Yks. ..60 C4
Cross Lanes, Clwyd 40 E2
Crosslanes, Shrops. ...40 E5
Crosslee 73 J3
Crossmichael 72 C8
Crossmoor 57 H7
Cross of Jackston 97 G2
Crossroads 97 G6
Crossway 19 J1
Crossway Green 31 K3
Crossways 11 J7
Crosswell 27 F3
Crosthwaite 57 H1
Croston 50 D2
Crostwick 47 J3
Crostwight 47 J3
Crovie 105 H2
Crowan 2 E6
Crowborough 15 J2
Crowcombe 10 C2
Crowdecote 52 D7
Crowfield, Suff. 37 G4
Crowfield, Northnts. ..33 J5
Crow Hill 31 H7
Crowhurst, E. Susx. ...16 E4
Crowhurst, Surrey 15 G1
Crowland 45 F5
Crowlas 2 D6
Crowle, Humbs. 54 B2
Crowle, H. & W. 32 B4
Crowlista 106 C3
Crowmarsh Gifford 22 B4
Crownhill 4 E4
Crownthorpe 47 F6
Crowthorne 22 D6
Crowton 50 E6
Croxall 42 D5
Croxdale 66 C4
Croxden 42 C3
Croxley Green 22 F3
Croxton, Norf. 36 D1
Croxton, Humbs. 54 E4
Croxton, Cambs. 35 F4
Croxton, Staffs. 41 J3
Croxton Kerrial 44 B4
Croxton Park 44 B4
Croy, Strath. 80 C4
Croy, Highld. 103 F8
Croyde 8 E2
Croydon, Cambs. 35 G5
Croydon, G. Lon. 23 J6
Cruckmeole 41 F6
Cruckton 41 F5
Cruden Bay 97 K2
Crudgington 41 H5
Crudwell 20 D3
Crug 30 C2
Crugmeer 3 H2
Crugybar 27 L3
Cruliyig 107 F5
Crumlin 19 G3
Crundale, Dyfed 26 D5
Crundale, Kent. 17 H1
Cruwys Morchard 9 J4
Crux Easton 21 J7
Crwbin 27 J5
Crychan 26 F3
Cromra 94 D6
Crynant 18 B2
Cuaig 100 D7
Cubbington 33 F3
Cubert 3 F4
Cublington 34 B7
Cuckfield 15 G3
Cucklington 11 J3
Cuckney 53 H6
Cuddesdon 21 K2
Cuddington, Bucks. 22 C1
Cuddington, Ches. 50 E6
Cuddington Heath 41 F2
Cuddy Hill 57 H7
Cudham 23 K7
Cudliptown 4 F7
Cudworth, Somer. 10 E4
Cudworth, S. Yks. 53 F3
Cuffley 23 J2
Culbo 102 E6
Culbokie 102 E7
Culburnie 94 C1
Culcabock 102 E8
Culcharry 103 G7
Culcheth 51 F4
Cul Doirlinn 85 H1

Culdrain 96 E2
Culduie 92 D1
Culford 36 D2
Culgaith 64 D5
Culham 21 K3
Culkein 108 B5
Culkerton 20 D3
Cullachie 95 H3
Cullen 104 E2
Cullercoats 75 K7
Cullicudden 102 E6
Cullingworth 59 F7
Cullipool 85 J7
Cullivoe 117 G2
Cullompton 10 B5
Culmington 31 F1
Culmstock 10 C4
Culnacraig 101 G2
Culnaknock 100 B6
Culrain 102 D3
Culross 80 E3
Culroy 71 J3
Culsh 105 H4
Culswick 114 E4
Cultercullen 97 J3
Cults, Grampn. 96 E2
Cults, Grampn. 97 H5
Culverstone Green 24 C6
Culverthorpe 44 D2
Culworth 33 H5
Culzie 80 C4
Cumberlow Green 35 G7
Cumberworth 55 K6
Cuminestown 105 H3
Cummersdale 63 J2
Cummertrees 73 G8
Cummingstown 103 K6
Cumnock 72 A2
Cumnor 21 J2
Cumrew 64 C2
Cumwhinton 64 B2
Cumwhitton 64 C2
Cundall 59 K3
Cunninghamhead 79 F7
Cunnister 117 G3
Cupar 89 F7
Cupar Muir 89 F7
Curbar 52 E6
Curbridge, Oxon. 21 H2
Curbridge, Hants. 13 H4
Curdridge 13 H4
Curdworth 42 D7
Curland 10 D4
Currie 81 G5
Curry Mallet 10 E3
Curry Rivel 10 E3
Curtisden Green 16 E1
Curtisknowle 5 H4
Cury 2 E7
Cushnie 105 G2
Cushuish 10 C2
Cusop 30 D5
Cutiau 39 F5
Cutnall Green 32 A3
Cutsdean 32 C6
Cutthorpe 53 F6
Cuxham 22 B3
Cuxton 24 D6
Cuxwold 55 F3
Cwm, Gwent 19 F2
Cwm, Clwyd 49 K3
Cwmafan 18 B3
Cwmaman 18 E3
Cwmann 27 K2
Cwmavon 19 G2
Cwmbach, M. Glam. 18 E2
Cwmbach, Dyfed 27 G4
Cwmbelan 29 G1
Cwmbran 19 G3
Cwmcarn 19 G3
Cwmcarvan 19 J2
Cwm-Cewydd 39 H5
Cwm-Cou 27 G2
Cwmdare 18 D2
Cwmdu, Powys 30 C7
Cwmdu, Dyfed 27 L3
Cwmduad 27 H3
Cwmerfyn 28 D1
Cwmfelin Boeth 27 F5
Cwmfelinfach 19 F3
Cwmfelin Mynach 27 G4
Cwmffrwd 27 J5
Cwmgwrach 18 C2
Cwm Irfon 29 F5
Cwmisfael 27 J5
Cwm-Llinau 39 H6
Cwmllynfell 18 B1
Cwmparc 18 D3
Cwmpengraig 27 H3
Cwm Penmachno 39 G2
Cwmsychbant 27 J2
Cwmsymlog 28 D1
Cwmtillery 19 G2
Cwm-twrch Isaf 18 B1
Cwm-twrch Uchaf 18 B1
Cwm-y-glo 48 E4
Cwmyoy 30 E7
Cwmystwyth 28 E2
Cwrt 27 J2
Cwrtnewydd 27 J2
Cwrt-y-cadno 28 D5
Cwrt-y-gollen 19 G1
Cyffylliog 40 B1
Cyfronydd 40 C6
Cymer, W. Glam. 18 C3
Cymmer, M. Glam. 18 E3
Cynghordy 28 F6
Cynwyd 40 B2
Cynwyl Elfed 27 H4

D

Dacre, Cumbr. 64 B5
Dacre, N. Yks. 59 G4

Dacre Banks.....59 G4
Daddry Shield.....65 F4
Dadford.....33 J6
Dadlington.....43 G7
Dafen.....27 K6
Dagenham.....23 L4
Daglingworth.....20 D2
Dagnall.....22 E1
Dail.....107 J2
Daily.....71 H4
Dairsie or Osnaburgh.....89 G7
Dalavich.....86 B7
Dalbeattie.....69 K4
Dalbeg.....107 G4
Dalblair.....72 B3
Dalby.....56 P4
Dalchalloch.....87 K2
Dalchenna.....86 C8
Dalchreichart.....93 J4
Dalderby.....55 G7
Dale, Shetld.....114 D3
Dale, Dyfed.....26 C6
Dale Abbey.....43 G3
Dale Head.....64 B6
Dalgarven.....78 E7
Dalgety Bay.....81 G3
Dalginross.....87 K6
Dalhalvaig.....110 E3
Dalham.....36 C3
Daliburgh.....90 C3
Dalkeith.....81 J5
Dallas.....103 K7
Dalleagles.....71 L3
Dallinghoo.....37 H4
Dallington.....16 D4
Dalmally.....86 D6
Dalmary.....79 H2
Dalmellington.....71 K4
Dalmeny.....81 G4
Dalmore, Highld.....102 E6
Dalmore, W. Isles.....107 G4
Dalnabreck.....85 J2
Dalnacreich.....101 K7
Dalnavie.....102 E5
Dalreavoch.....103 F2
Dalry.....78 E7
Dalrymple.....71 J3
Dalserf.....80 C6
Dalston.....63 J2
Dalswinton.....72 E6
Dalton, Lancs.....50 D3
Dalton, Northum.....65 G2
Dalton, S. Yks.....53 G4
Dalton, D. & G......73 G7
Dalton, Northum.....75 H7
Dalton, N. Yks.....65 J7
Dalton, N. Yks.....59 K3
Dalton-in-Furness.....57 F3
Dalton-le-Dale.....66 E3
Dalton-on-Tees.....66 C7
Dalton Piercy.....66 E4
Dalwhinnie.....87 H2
Dalwood.....10 D5
Damerham.....12 D4
Damgate.....47 K6
Damnaglaur.....68 C7
Danbury.....24 D2
Danby.....67 H7
Danby Wiske.....66 D8
Danderhall.....81 J5
Danebridge, Staffs.....51 J7
Danebridge, Ches.....51 J7
Dane End.....35 G7
Danehill.....15 H3
Darenth.....24 B5
Daresbury.....50 E5
Darfield.....53 G3
Dargate.....25 G6
Darite.....4 C3
Darlaston.....42 B7
Darlingscote.....32 E5
Darlington.....66 C6
Darliston.....41 G3
Darlton.....54 B6
Darowen.....39 H6
Darra.....105 G4
Darras Hall.....75 H7
Darrington.....53 G1
Darsham.....37 K3
Dartford.....23 L5
Dartford Crossing.....24 B5
Dartington.....5 H3
Dartmeet.....5 G2
Dartmouth.....5 J4
Darton.....53 F2
Darvel.....79 H8
Darwen.....51 F1
Datchet.....22 E5
Datchworth.....23 H1
Daugh of Kinermony.....96 B1
Dauntsey.....20 D4
Davenham.....51 F6
Daventry.....33 H3
Davidstow.....8 B7
Davington.....73 H4
Daviot, Highld.....94 F2
Daviot, Grampn.....97 G3
Davoch of Grange.....104 D2
Dawley.....41 H6
Dawlish.....5 K2
Dawlish Warren.....5 K2
Dawn.....49 H3
Daws Heath.....24 E4
Dawsmere.....45 H3
Daylesford.....32 E7
Ddol Cownwy.....40 B5
Deal.....25 K7
Dean, Cumbr.....62 F5
Dean, Somer.....11 H1
Dean, Devon.....5 H3
Dean, Hants.....13 H4
Deanburnhaugh.....73 J3
Deane.....21 K7
Deanland.....12 B4
Dean Prior.....5 H3

Dean Row.....51 H5
Deans.....80 F5
Deanscales.....63 F5
Deanshanger.....34 A6
Deanston.....80 C1
Dearham.....62 F4
Dearne.....53 G3
Debach.....37 H4
Debden.....35 J6
Debden Green.....35 J6
Debenham.....37 G3
Dechmont.....81 F4
Deddington.....33 G6
Dedham.....36 F6
Deene.....44 C7
Deenethorpe.....44 C7
Deepcut.....22 E7
Deepdale.....58 C2
Deeping Gate.....44 E6
Deeping St James.....44 E6
Deeping St Nicholas.....45 F5
Deerhill.....104 D3
Deerhurst.....32 A7
Defford.....32 B5
Defynnog.....29 G7
Deganwy.....49 G3
Deighton, N. Yks.....60 D6
Deighton, N. Yks.....66 D7
Deiniolen.....48 E4
Delabole.....8 A7
Delamere.....50 E7
Delfrigs.....97 J3
Delliefure.....95 J2
Delph.....51 J3
Dembleby.....44 D3
Denbigh.....49 K4
Denbury.....5 J3
Denby.....43 F2
Denby Dale.....52 E3
Denchworth.....21 H3
Denford.....34 C2
Dengie, Essex.....25 F2
Dengie, Essex.....25 F2
Denham, Suff.....36 C3
Denham, Bucks.....22 F4
Denham, Suff.....37 G2
Denham Green.....22 F4
Denham Street.....37 G2
Denhead, Fife.....89 G7
Denhead, Grampn.....105 K3
Denholm.....74 B3
Denholme.....59 F7
Denmead.....13 J4
Denmore.....97 J4
Denne Park.....14 E3
Dennington.....37 H3
Denny.....80 D3
Dennyloanhead.....80 D3
Denshaw.....51 J2
Denside.....97 H6
Densole.....17 K1
Denston.....36 C4
Denstone.....42 C2
Dent.....58 C2
Den, The.....78 F6
Denton, Lincs.....44 B3
Denton, Northnts.....34 B4
Denton, Durham.....66 C6
Denton, Cambs.....34 E1
Denton, N. Yks.....59 G6
Denton, Norf.....37 H1
Denton, E. Susx.....15 H5
Denton, G. Man.....51 J4
Denton, Kent.....17 K1
Denton, Oxon.....21 K2
Denver.....45 K6
Denwick.....75 J3
Deopham.....46 F6
Deopham Green.....46 F7
Depden.....36 C4
Deptford, Wilts.....12 C2
Deptford, G. Lon.....23 J5
Derby.....43 F3
Derbyhaven.....56 P5
Deri.....18 F2
Derrington.....42 A4
Derryguaig.....85 F5
Derry Hill.....20 D5
Derrythorpe.....54 C3
Dersingham.....46 B3
Dervaig.....85 F3
Derwen.....40 B1
Desborough.....34 B1
Desford.....43 G6
Detchant.....83 J8
Detling.....24 D7
Deuddwr.....40 D5
Devauden.....19 J3
Devil's Bridge.....28 E2
Devizes.....20 E6
Devonport.....4 E4
Devonside.....80 E2
Devoran.....3 F6
Dewlish.....11 J6
Dewsbury.....52 E1
Dhoon.....56 R3
Dhoor.....56 R2
Dhowin.....56 R1
Dial Post.....14 E4
Dibden.....13 G5
Dibden Purlieu.....13 G5
Dickleburgh.....37 G1
Didbrook.....32 C6
Didcot.....21 K4
Diddington.....35 E3
Diddlebury.....31 G1
Didley.....31 F6
Didmarton.....20 C4
Didsbury.....51 H4
Didworthy.....5 G3
Digby.....44 D1
Diggle.....52 C3
Dihewyd.....28 A4
Dilham.....47 J4

Dilhorne.....42 B2
Dilston.....65 G1
Dilton Marsh.....11 K1
Dilwyn.....31 F4
Dinas, Gwyn.....38 B3
Dinas, Gwyn.....48 D5
Dinas, Dyfed.....27 G3
Dinas Cross.....26 E3
Dinas Mawddwy.....39 H5
Dinas Powys.....18 F5
Dinchope.....31 F1
Dinder.....11 G1
Dinedor.....31 G6
Dingestow.....19 J1
Dingley.....34 A1
Dingwall.....102 D7
Dinnet.....96 D6
Dinnington, Somer.....10 F4
Dinnington, S. Yks.....53 H5
Dinnington, T. & W......75 J7
Dinorwig.....48 E4
Dinton, Bucks.....22 C1
Dinton, Wilts.....12 C2
Dinworthy.....8 B4
Dippen.....70 F2
Dippenhall.....14 B1
Dipple.....104 C3
Diptford.....5 H4
Dipton.....65 J2
Dirleton.....82 D3
Discoed.....30 D3
Diseworth.....43 G4
Dishes.....113 G4
Dishforth.....59 J3
Disley.....51 J5
Diss.....37 G2
Disserth.....29 H4
Distington.....62 F5
Ditcheat.....11 H2
Ditchingham.....47 J7
Ditchling.....15 G4
Dittisham.....5 J4
Ditton, Ches.....50 D5
Ditton, Kent.....24 D7
Ditton Green.....36 B4
Ditton Priors.....41 H8
Dixton, Glos.....32 B6
Dixton, Gwent.....19 K1
Dlengrasco.....99 K8
Dobwalls.....4 C3
Doccombe.....9 H7
Dochgarroch.....94 E1
Docking.....46 C3
Docklow.....31 G4
Dockray.....63 J5
Doddinghurst.....24 B3
Doddington, Lincs.....54 D6
Doddington, Northum.....75 F1
Doddington, Kent.....25 F7
Doddington, Shrops.....31 H2
Doddington, Cambs.....45 H7
Doddiscombsleigh.....9 J7
Dodford, H. & W......32 B2
Dodford, Northnts.....33 J3
Dodington.....20 B4
Dodleston.....50 C7
Dodworth.....53 F3
Doe Lea.....53 G7
Dogmersfield.....22 C7
Dog Village.....10 A6
Dogyke.....45 F1
Dolanog.....40 B5
Dolau.....30 C3
Dolbenmaen.....38 E2
Dolfach.....29 G2
Dolfor.....30 C1
Dolgarrog.....49 G4
Dolgellau.....39 G5
Dolgran.....27 J3
Doll.....103 G2
Dollar.....80 E2
Dolley Green.....30 D3
Dolphinholme.....57 J5
Dolphinton.....81 G7
Dolton.....9 F4
Dolwen.....49 H3
Dolwyddelan.....39 G1
Dol-y-cannau.....30 D5
Dolyhir.....30 D4
Domgay.....40 D5
Doncaster.....53 H3
Donhead St Andrew.....12 B3
Donhead St Mary.....12 B3
Donibristle.....81 G3
Donington on Bain.....55 G5
Donisthorpe.....43 F5
Donkey Town.....22 E6
Donnington, W. Susx.....14 B5
Donnington, Glos.....32 D7
Donnington, Shrops.....41 G6
Donnington, Shrops.....41 J5
Donnington, Berks.....21 J6
Donnington, H. & W......31 J6
Donyatt.....10 E4
Doonfoot.....71 J3
Doonholm.....71 J3
Dorchester, Dorset.....11 H6
Dorchester, Oxon.....21 K3
Dordon.....42 E6
Dore.....53 F5
Dores.....94 D2
Dorking.....14 E1
Dormansland.....15 H1
Dormanstown.....67 F5
Dormington.....31 G5
Dormston.....32 B4
Dorney.....22 E5
Dornie.....92 E3
Dornoch.....103 F4
Dornock.....73 H8
Dorridge.....32 D2
Dorrington, Lincs.....44 D1
Dorrington, Shrops.....41 F6

Dorsington.....32 D5
Dorstone.....30 E5
Dorton.....22 B1
Dosthill.....42 E6
Doublebois.....4 B3
Doughton.....20 C3
Douglas, Strath.....72 D1
Douglas, I. of M......56 Q4
Douglas and Angus.....89 G5
Douglastown.....89 G4
Douglas Water.....80 D8
Doulting.....11 H1
Dounby.....112 C4
Doune.....80 C1
Douneside.....96 D5
Dounie.....102 D3
Dove Holes.....52 C6
Dovenby.....63 F4
Dover.....17 L1
Doverdale.....32 A3
Doveridge.....42 D3
Dowdeswell.....20 E1
Dowland.....9 F4
Dowlish Wake.....10 E4
Down Ampney.....20 F3
Downderry.....4 D4
Downe.....23 K6
Downend, I. of W......13 H7
Downend, Berks.....21 J5
Downfield.....89 F5
Downgate.....4 D2
Downham, Lancs.....58 C6
Downham, Essex.....24 D3
Downham, Northum.....74 E1
Downham Market.....45 K6
Down Hatherley.....32 A7
Downholme.....65 J8
Downies.....97 J6
Downley.....22 D3
Downs.....18 F5
Downside Abbey.....20 A7
Down St Mary.....9 H5
Downton, Wilts.....12 D3
Downton, Hants.....12 E6
Downton on the Rock.....31 F2
Dowsby.....44 E3
Dowsdale.....45 F5
Dowthwaitehead.....63 J5
Doxey.....42 B4
Doxford Park.....66 D2
Doynton.....20 B5
Draethen.....19 G4
Draffan.....80 C7
Drakeland Corner.....4 F4
Drakemyre.....78 E6
Drakes Broughton.....32 B5
Draughton, Northnts.....34 A2
Draughton, N. Yks.....58 F5
Drax.....53 J1
Draycote.....33 G2
Draycott, Glos.....32 D6
Draycott, Derby.....43 G3
Draycott, Somer.....19 J7
Draycott in the Clay.....42 D4
Draycott in the Moors.....42 B2
Drayton, H. & W......32 B2
Drayton, Leic.....44 B7
Drayton, Somer.....10 F3
Drayton, Norf.....47 G5
Drayton, Oxon.....33 G5
Drayton, Oxon.....21 J3
Drayton, Hants.....13 J5
Drayton Bassett.....42 D6
Drayton Parslow.....34 B7
Drayton St Leonard.....21 K3
Drefach, Dyfed.....27 H3
Dre-fach, Dyfed.....27 K2
Drefach, Dyfed.....27 K5
Drefelin.....27 H3
Dreghorn.....79 F8
Drem.....82 D4
Drewsteignton.....9 H6
Driby.....55 H6
Driffield, Glos.....20 E3
Driffield, Humbs.....61 H5
Drift.....2 C7
Drigg.....62 F8
Drighlington.....59 H8
Drimnin.....85 G3
Drimpton.....11 F5
Drinkstone.....36 E3
Drinkstone Green.....36 E3
Droitwich.....32 A3
Droman.....108 C3
Dron.....88 D7
Dronfield.....53 F6
Dronfield Woodhouse.....53 F6
Drongan.....71 K3
Droxford.....13 J4
Droylsden.....51 J4
Druid.....40 B2
Druidston.....26 C5
Druimarbin.....86 C1
Druimdrishaig.....77 G4
Druimindarroch.....92 C7
Drum.....81 F1
Drumbeg.....108 C5
Drumblade.....96 E1
Drumbuie.....92 D2
Drumchapel.....79 H4
Drumchardine.....102 D8
Drumchork.....100 E4
Drumclog.....79 J8
Drumelzier.....73 G1
Drumfearn.....92 C4
Drumgley.....89 G3
Drumguish.....95 F6
Drumin.....95 K2
Drumlassie.....97 G5
Drumlemble.....70 B3

Drumligair.....97 J4
Drumlithie.....97 G7
Drummore.....68 C7
Drumnadrochit.....94 D3
Drumoak.....97 G6
Drums.....97 J3
Drumsallie.....93 F8
Drumsturdy.....89 G5
Drumuie.....99 K8
Drumuillie.....95 H3
Drumwhindle.....97 J2
Drury.....50 B7
Drybeck.....64 D6
Drybridge, Grampn.....104 D2
Drybridge, Strath.....79 F8
Drybrook.....19 L1
Dryhope.....73 H2
Drymen.....79 G3
Drymuir.....105 J4
Drynoch.....91 K2
Dubford.....105 G2
Dubton.....83 H7
Duchally.....108 F1
Duckington.....41 F1
Ducklington.....21 H2
Duck's Cross.....34 E4
Duddenhoe End.....35 H6
Duddingston.....81 H4
Duddington.....44 C6
Duddleswell.....15 H3
Duddleston Heath.....40 E3
Dudley, W. Mids.....42 B7
Dudley, T. & W......75 J7
Duffield.....43 F2
Duffryn, W. Glam.....18 C3
Duffryn, Gwent.....19 G4
Dufftown.....96 C1
Duffus.....103 K6
Dufton.....64 D5
Duggleby.....60 F4
Duirinish.....92 D2
Duisky.....93 G8
Dukestown.....18 F1
Dukinfield.....51 J4
Dulas.....48 D2
Dulcote.....11 G1
Dulford.....10 B5
Dull.....87 L4
Dullingham.....35 K4
Dulnain Bridge.....95 H3
Duloe, Corn.....4 C4
Duloe, Beds.....34 E3
Dulsie.....95 H1
Dulverton.....9 K3
Dulwich.....23 J5
Dumbarton.....79 F4
Dumbleton.....32 C6
Dumcrieff.....73 G4
Dumfries.....72 E7
Dumgoyne.....79 H3
Dummer.....13 H1
Dunan.....92 B3
Dunball.....10 E1
Dunbar.....82 F3
Dunbeath.....111 H6
Dunblane.....80 C1
Dunbog.....88 E2
Duncanston.....102 D7
Duncanstone.....96 E3
Dunchideock.....9 J7
Dunchurch.....33 G2
Duncote.....33 J4
Duncow.....72 E6
Duncrievie.....88 D8
Duncton.....14 C4
Dundee.....89 G5
Dundon.....11 F2
Dundonald.....71 J1
Dundonnell.....101 G4
Dundraw.....63 H3
Dundreggan.....93 K4
Dundrennan.....69 J6
Dundry.....19 K6
Dunecht.....97 G5
Dunfermline.....81 F3
Dunford Bridge.....52 E3
Dunham-on-the-Hill.....50 D6
Dunham on Trent.....54 C6
Dunhampton.....31 K3
Dunham Town.....51 G5
Dunholme.....54 E6
Dunino.....89 H7
Dunipace.....80 D3
Dunkeld.....88 C4
Dunkeswell.....10 C5
Dunkirk.....25 G7
Dunk's Green.....24 C7
Dunley.....31 J3
Dunlop.....79 G7
Dunmore, Central.....80 D3
Dunmore, Strath.....77 G5
Dunnet.....111 J1
Dunnichen.....89 H4
Dunning.....88 C7
Dunnington, Warw.....32 C4
Dunnington, N. Yks.....60 D5
Dunnington, Humbs.....61 J5
Dunnockshaw.....51 H1
Dunollie.....85 K5
Dunoon.....78 D4
Dunragit.....68 C5
Duns.....83 F6
Dunscore.....72 D6
Dunscroft.....53 J3
Dunsden Green.....22 C5
Dunsfold.....14 D2
Dunsford.....9 J7
Dunshalt.....88 E7
Dunsley.....67 J6

Dunsmore.....22 D2
Dunsop Bridge.....58 B5
Dunstable.....34 D7
Dunstall.....42 D4
Dunstall Green.....36 C3
Dunstan.....75 J3
Dunster.....10 A1
Duns Tew.....33 G7
Dunston, Staffs.....42 B5
Dunston, T. & W......66 C1
Dunston, Lincs.....54 E7
Dunston, Norf.....47 H6
Dunsville.....53 J3
Dunswell.....61 H7
Dunterton.....4 D2
Duntisbourne Abbots.....20 D2
Duntisbourne Leer.....20 D2
Duntisbourne Rouse.....20 D2
Duntish.....11 H5
Duntocher.....79 G4
Dunton, Bucks.....34 B7
Dunton, Norf.....46 D3
Dunton, Beds.....35 F5
Dunton Bassett.....43 H7
Dunton Green.....23 L3
Dunure.....71 H3
Dunvant.....27 K7
Dunvegan.....99 H8
Dunwich.....37 K2
Durdar.....63 K2
Durham.....66 C3
Durisdeer.....72 D4
Durleigh.....10 D2
Durley, Wilts.....21 G6
Durley, Hants.....13 H4
Durnamuck.....101 G3
Durness.....108 F2
Durno.....97 G3
Durran.....111 H2
Durrington, Wilts.....12 D1
Durrington, W. Susx.....14 C5
Dursley.....20 B3
Durston.....10 D3
Durweston.....11 K5
Dury.....115 G2
Duston.....33 K3
Duthil.....95 H3
Dutlas.....30 D2
Duton Hill.....35 K7
Dutton.....50 E6
Duxford.....35 H5
Dwygyfylchi.....49 G3
Dwyran.....48 D4
Dyce.....97 H4
Dye House.....65 G2
Dyffryn, Gwyn.....48 B3
Dyffryn, M. Glam.....18 C3
Dyffryn Ardudwy.....38 E4
Dyffryn Ceidrych.....28 E7
Dyffryn Cellwen.....18 C1
Dyke, Devon.....8 D3
Dyke, Lincs.....44 E4
Dyke, Grampn.....103 H7
Dykehead, Strath.....80 D6
Dykehead, Tays.....89 F2
Dylife.....39 H7
Dymchurch.....17 J3
Dymock.....31 J6
Dyrham.....20 B5
Dysart.....81 J2
Dyserth.....49 K3

E

Eagland Hill.....57 H6
Eagle.....54 C7
Eaglescliffe.....66 E6
Eaglesfield, Cumbr.....63 F5
Eaglesfield, D. & G......73 H7
Eaglesham.....79 H6
Eairy.....56 P4
Eakring.....53 J7
Ealand.....54 B2
Ealing.....23 G4
Eamont Bridge.....64 C5
Earby.....58 E6
Earcroft.....51 F1
Eardington.....41 J7
Eardisland.....31 F4
Eardisley.....30 E5
Eardiston, Shrops.....40 E4
Eardiston, H. & W......31 H3
Earith.....35 G2
Earle.....75 F2
Earlestown.....50 E4
Earlham.....47 G6
Earlish.....99 J6
Earls Barton.....34 B3
Earls Colne.....36 D7
Earl's Croome.....32 A5
Earlsdon.....33 F2
Earlsferry.....82 C2
Earlsfield.....97 H2
Earl's Green.....36 F3
Earl Shilton.....43 G7
Earl Soham.....37 H3
Earl Sterndale.....52 C7
Earlston, Border.....82 D8
Earlston, Strath.....79 G8
Earl Stonham.....37 G4
Earlswood, Warw.....32 D2
Earlswood, Gwent.....19 J3
Earnley.....14 B6
Earsairy.....90 C6
Earsdon.....75 K7
Earsham.....47 J8
Earswick.....60 D5
Eartham.....14 C5
Easby.....67 F7
Easdale.....85 J7
Easebourne.....14 B3
Easenhall.....33 G2

Easington, Bucks.............22 B1
Easington, Northum..........75 H1
Easington, Humbs............55 H2
Easington, Cleve............67 H6
Easington Lane..............66 D3
Easingwold..................60 C4
Easole Street...............25 J7
Eassie......................89 F4
East Aberthaw...............18 E6
East Allington...............5 H5
East Anstey..................9 J3
East Ashling................14 B5
East Auchronie..............97 H5
East Barkwith...............55 F5
East Barming................24 D7
East Barnet.................23 H3
East Barsham................46 E3
East Beckham................47 G3
East Bedfont................23 F5
East Bergholt...............36 F6
East Bilney.................46 E5
East Blatchington...........15 H5
East Boldre.................13 F5
Eastbourne..................16 D6
East Brent..................19 H7
Eastbridge..................37 K3
East Bridgford..............43 J2
East Buckland................9 G2
East Budleigh...............10 B7
East Burrafirth............115 F3
East Burton.................11 K7
Eastbury, Herts.............23 F3
Eastbury, Berks.............21 H5
East Calder.................81 F5
East Carleton...............47 G6
East Carlton................44 B8
East Chaldon or
  Chaldon Herring...........11 J7
East Challow................21 H4
East Chiltington............15 G4
East Chinnock...............11 F4
East Chisenbury.............21 F7
Eastchurch..................25 F5
East Clandon................22 F7
East Claydon................33 K7
East Coker..................11 G4
Eastcombe, Glos.............20 C2
East Combe, Somer...........10 C2
East Compton................11 H1
Eastcote, W. Mids...........32 D2
Eastcote, G. Lon............23 G4
Eastcott, Corn...............8 C4
Eastcott, Wilts.............20 E7
East Cottingwith............60 E6
Eastcourt...................20 D3
East Cowes..................13 H6
East Cowton.................66 D7
East Cramlington............75 J7
East Creech.................12 B7
East Croachy................94 E3
East Davoch.................96 D5
East Dean, W. Susx..........14 C4
East Dean, E. Susx..........16 C6
East Dean, Hants............12 E3
East Dereham................46 E5
East Down....................9 G1
East Drayton................54 B6
East End, Dorset............12 B6
East End, Kent..............16 F2
East End, Hants.............13 F6
East End, Oxon..............21 H1
East End, Herts.............35 H7
East End, Avon..............19 J5
East End, Hants.............21 J6
Easter Ardross.............102 E5
Easter Balmoral.............96 B6
Easter Boleskine............94 D3
Easter Compton..............19 K4
Easter Fearn...............102 E4
Eastergate..................14 C5
Easter Kinkell.............102 D7
Easter Lednathie............89 F2
Eastern Green...............32 E2
Easter Ord..................97 H5
Easter Quarff..............115 G5
Easter Skeld...............114 F4
Easterton...................20 E7
Eastertown..................19 H7
East Farleigh...............24 D7
East Farndon................33 K1
East Ferry..................54 C4
Eastfield, Strath...........80 C4
Eastfield, Strath...........80 D5
Eastfield, N. Yks...........61 H2
East Garston................21 H5
Eastgate, Norf..............47 G4
Eastgate, Durham............65 G4
East Ginge..................21 J4
East Goscote................43 J5
East Grafton................21 G6
East Grimstead..............12 E3
East Grinstead..............15 G2
East Guldeford..............17 G3
East Haddon.................33 J3
East Hagbourne..............21 K4
East Halton.................55 F2
Eastham, Mers...............50 C5
East Ham, G. Lon............23 K4
Easthampstead..............22 D6
East Hanney.................21 J3
East Hanningfield...........24 D2
East Hardwick...............53 G2
East Harling................36 E1
East Harlsey................61 E8
East Harptree...............19 K7
East Hartford...............75 J7
East Harting................14 A4
East Hatley..................35 F4
East Hauxwell...............59 G1
East Haven..................89 H5
East Heckington.............45 E2
East Hedleyhope.............65 J3
East Hendred................21 J4
East Heslerton..............61 G3
East Hoathly................15 J4

Easthope....................41 G7
Easthorpe...................36 E7
East Horrington.............11 G1
East Horsley................23 F7
East Huntspill..............10 E1
East Hyde...................23 G1
East Ilsley.................21 J4
Eastington, Glos............20 B2
Eastington, Glos............21 F1
Eastington, Devon............9 H5
East Kennett................20 F6
East Keswick................59 J6
East Kilbride...............79 J6
East Kirkby.................55 H7
East Knighton...............11 K7
East Knoyle.................12 A2
East Lambrook...............11 F4
East Lamington.............103 F5
East Langdon................17 L1
East Langton................43 K7
East Langwell..............102 F2
East Lavington..............14 C4
East Layton.................66 B7
Eastleach Martin............21 G2
Eastleach Turville..........21 F2
East Leake..................43 H4
Eastleigh, Hants............13 G4
East Leigh, Devon............9 G5
East Lexham.................46 D5
East Lilburn................75 G2
Eastling....................25 F7
East Linton.................82 D4
East Liss...................14 A3
East Lound..................54 B4
East Lulworth...............12 A7
East Mains..................97 F6
East Malling................24 C7
East Marden.................14 B4
East Markham................54 B6
East Marton.................58 E5
East Meon...................13 J3
East Mersea.................25 G1
East Molesey................23 G6
East Morden.................12 B6
East Morton.................59 G6
Eastney.....................13 J6
Eastnor.....................31 J6
East Norton.................44 A6
East Oakley.................21 K7
East Ogwell..................5 J2
Easton, Dorset..............6 A7
Easton, Lincs...............44 C4
Easton, Cambs...............34 E2
Easton, Somer...............11 G1
Easton, Norf................47 G5
Easton, Hants...............13 H2
Easton, Suff................37 H4
Easton, Devon................9 H7
Easton, Cumbr...............73 K7
Easton Grey.................20 C4
Easton-in-Gordano...........19 K5
Easton Maudit...............34 B4
Easton on the Hill..........44 D6
Easton Royal................21 G6
East Ord....................83 H6
East Panson..................8 D6
East Peckham................16 D1
East Pennard................11 G2
East Perry..................34 E3
East Portlemouth............5 H6
East Prawle..................5 H6
East Preston................14 D5
East Putford.................8 D4
East Quantoxhead............10 C1
East Rainton................66 D3
East Ravendale..............55 G4
East Raynham................46 D4
Eastrea.....................45 F7
Eastriggs...................73 H8
Eastrington.................60 E7
East Rudham.................46 D4
East Runton.................47 G2
East Ruston.................47 J4
Eastry......................25 K7
East Saltoun................82 C5
Eastside, Orkney...........112 E7
East Sleekburn..............75 J6
East Stockwith..............54 B4
East Stoke, Notts...........44 A2
East Stoke, Dorset..........12 A7
East Stour..................11 J3
East Stourmouth.............25 J6
East Stratton...............13 H2
East Studdal................17 L1
East Taphouse................4 B3
East-the-Water...............8 E3
East Tilbury................24 C5
East Tisted.................13 K2
East Torrington.............55 F5
East Tuddenham..............46 F5
East Tytherley..............12 E3
East Tytherton..............20 D5
East Village.................9 J5
Eastville...................45 H1
East Wall...................41 G7
East Walton.................46 C5
Eastwell....................44 A4
East Wellow.................13 F3
Eastwell Park...............17 H1
East Wemyss.................81 J2
East Whitburn...............80 E5
Eastwick....................23 K1
East Williamston............26 E6
East Winch..................46 B5
East Wittering..............14 A6
East Witton.................59 G2
Eastwood, Essex.............24 E4
Eastwood, Notts.............43 G2
East Woodhay................21 J6
East Worldham...............13 K2
Eathorpe....................33 F3
Eaton, Leic.................44 A4
Eaton, Notts................54 B6

Eaton, Ches.................50 E7
Eaton, Shrops...............40 E8
Eaton, Shrops...............41 G2
Eaton, Norf.................47 H6
Eaton, Ches.................51 H7
Eaton, Oxon.................21 J2
Eaton Bishop................31 F6
Eaton Bray..................34 C7
Eaton Constantine...........41 G6
Eaton Hastings..............21 G3
Eaton Socon.................34 E4
Eaton upon Tern.............41 H4
Ebberston...................61 F2
Ebbesbourne Wake............12 B3
Ebbw Vale...................19 F2
Ebchester...................65 J2
Ebford......................10 A7
Ebnal.......................40 E1
Ebrington...................32 D5
Ecchinswell................21 J7
Ecclaw......................82 F5
Ecclefechan.................73 G7
Eccles, Kent................24 D6
Eccles, Border..............82 F7
Eccles, G. Man..............51 G4
Ecclesfield.................53 F4
Eccleshall..................41 K4
Ecclesmachan................81 F4
Eccles on Sea...............47 K4
Eccles Road.................46 F7
Eccleston, Mers.............50 D4
Eccleston, Ches.............50 D7
Eccleston, Lancs............50 E2
Eccup.......................59 H6
Echt........................97 G5
Eckford.....................74 D2
Eckington, H. & W...........32 B5
Eckington, Derby............53 G6
Ecton.......................34 B3
Edale.......................52 D5
Edburton....................15 F4
Edderton...................102 F4
Eddistone...................81 H7
Eddlesbridge................15 H1
Edenbridge..................15 H1
Edenfield...................51 H2
Edenhall....................64 C4
Edenham.....................44 D4
Eden Park...................23 J6
Edensor.....................52 E6
Edenthorpe..................53 J3
Edentown....................38 B3
Edgbaston...................32 C1
Edgcott.....................33 J7
Edge........................40 E6
Edge, Glos..................20 C2
Edgebolton..................41 G4
Edge End....................19 K1
Edgefield...................47 F3
Edgefield Street............47 F3
Edgeworth...................20 D2
Edgmond.....................41 J5
Edgmond Marsh...............41 J4
Edgton......................30 E1
Edgware.....................23 H3
Edgworth....................51 G2
Edinbane....................99 J7
Edinburgh...................81 H4
Edingale....................42 E5
Edingley....................43 J1
Edingthorpe.................47 J3
Edington, Wilts.............20 D7
Edington, Somer.............10 E2
Edithmead...................10 E1
Edith Weston................44 C6
Edlesborough................22 E1
Edlingham...................75 H4
Edlington...................55 G6
Edmondsham..................12 C4
Edmondsley..................66 C3
Edmondthorpe................44 B5
Edmonstone.................113 F4
Edmonston...................23 J3
Edmundbyers.................65 H2
Ednam.......................82 F8
Edney Common................24 C2
Edrom.......................83 G6
Edstaston...................41 G3
Edstone.....................32 D3
Edvin Loach.................31 H4
Edwalton....................43 H3
Edwardstone.................36 E5
Edwinsford..................27 L3
Edwinstowe..................53 J7
Edworth.....................35 F5
Edwyn Ralph.................31 H4
Edzell......................89 J2
Efail Isaf..................18 E4
Efailnewydd.................38 C3
Efailwen....................26 F4
Efenechtyd..................40 C1
Effingham...................23 G7
Effirth....................115 F3
Efford.......................9 J5
Egerton, Kent...............17 G1
Egerton, G. Man.............51 G2
Egerton Forstal.............17 F1
Eggborough..................53 H1
Eggesford Station...........9 G4
Eggington...................34 C7
Egginton....................42 E4
Egglescliffe................66 E6
Eggleston...................65 G5
Egham.......................22 F5
Egleton.....................44 B6
Eglingham...................75 H3
Egloshayle...................3 J2
Egloskerry...................8 C7
Eglwysbach..................49 H3
Eglwys-Brewis...............18 E6
Eglwys Fach.................39 F7
Eglwyswrw...................26 F3
Egmanton....................54 B7
Egremont....................62 F6
Egton.......................67 J7
Egton Bridge................67 J7
Eight Ash Green.............36 E7

Eilanreach..................92 E4
Eilean Darach..............101 H4
Eilean Glas.................99 H3
Eilean Iarmain or Isleornsay..92 C4
Eishken....................107 H7
Eisingrug...................38 F3
Elan Village................29 G3
Elberton....................19 L4
Elburton.....................4 F4
Elcombe.....................21 F4
Eldersfield.................31 K6
Elderslie...................79 G5
Eldroth.....................58 C4
Eldwick.....................59 G6
Elerch or Bont-goch.........28 D1
Elford, Staffs..............42 D5
Elford, Northum.............75 H1
Elgin......................104 B2
Elgol.......................92 B4
Elham.......................17 J1
Elie........................82 C1
Elim........................48 C2
Eling.......................13 F4
Elishader..................100 B6
Elishaw.....................74 E5
Elkesley....................53 J6
Elkstone....................20 D1
Elland......................52 D1
Ellary......................77 G4
Ellastone...................42 D2
Ellemford...................82 F5
Ellenhall...................41 K4
Ellen's Green...............14 D2
Ellerbeck...................59 K1
Ellerby.....................67 H6
Ellerdine Heath.............41 H4
Ellerker....................61 G8
Ellerton, Humbs.............60 E7
Ellerton, Shrops............41 J4
Ellesborough................22 D2
Ellesmere...................40 F3
Ellesmere Port..............50 C6
Ellingham, Northum..........75 H2
Ellingham, Norf.............47 J7
Ellingstring................59 G2
Ellington, Cambs............34 E2
Ellington, Northum..........75 J5
Ellisfield..................13 J1
Ellistown...................43 G5
Ellon.......................97 J2
Ellough.....................37 J1
Elloughton..................54 D1
Ellwood.....................19 K2
Elm.........................45 H6
Elmbridge...................32 B3
Elmdon, W. Mids.............32 D1
Elmdon, Essex...............35 H6
Elmdon Heath................32 D1
Elmesthorpe.................43 G7
Elmhurst....................42 D5
Elmley Castle...............32 B5
Elmley Lovett...............32 A3
Elmore......................20 B1
Elmore Back.................20 B1
Elm Park....................23 L4
Elmscott.....................8 C3
Elmsett.....................36 F5
Elmstead Market.............37 F7
Elmsted.....................17 J1
Elmstone....................25 J6
Elmstone Hardwicke..........32 B7
Elmswell....................36 E3
Elmton......................53 H6
Elphin.....................108 D7
Elphinstone.................81 J4
Elrick......................97 H5
Elrig.......................68 E6
Elsdon......................75 F5
Elsecar.....................53 F3
Elsenham....................35 J7
Elsfield....................21 K1
Elsham......................55 E2
Elsing......................46 F5
Elslack.....................58 E6
Elsrickle...................81 F7
Elstead.....................14 C1
Elsted......................14 B4
Elston......................44 A2
Elstone......................9 G4
Elstow......................34 D5
Elstree.....................23 G3
Elstronwick.................61 K7
Elswick.....................57 H7
Elsworth....................35 G3
Elterwater..................63 J7
Eltham......................23 K5
Eltisley....................35 F4
Elton, Notts................44 A3
Elton, Glos.................20 B1
Elton, Ches.................50 D6
Elton, Cambs................44 D7
Elton, Cleve................66 E6
Elton, Derby................52 E7
Elton, H. & W...............31 F2
Elvanfoot...................72 E3
Elvaston....................43 G3
Elveden.....................36 D2
Elvingston..................82 C4
Elvington, N. Yks...........60 F6
Elvington, Kent.............25 J7
Elwick, Cleve...............66 E4
Elwick, Northum.............83 K8
Elworth.....................51 G7
Elworthy....................10 B2
Ely, S. Glam................18 F5
Ely, Cambs..................35 J1
Emberton....................34 B5
Embleton, Cumbr.............63 G4
Embleton, Northum...........75 J2
Embo.......................103 G3
Emborough...................19 L7
Embsay......................58 F5
Emery Down..................12 E5
Emley.......................52 E2
Emmer Green.................22 C5

Emmington...................22 C2
Emneth......................45 H6
Emneth Hungate..............45 J6
Empingham...................44 C6
Empshott....................14 A2
Emsworth....................13 K5
Enaclete...................107 F6
Enborne.....................21 J6
Enchmarsh...................41 G7
Enderby.....................43 H7
Endmoor.....................57 J2
Endon.......................42 B1
Enfield.....................23 J3
Enford......................21 F7
Engine Common...............20 A4
Englefield..................22 B5
Englefield Green............22 E5
English Bicknor.............19 K1
Englishcombe................20 B6
English Frankton............41 F4
Enham-Alamein...............13 F1
Enmore......................10 D2
Ennerdale Bridge............62 F6
Enochdhu....................88 C2
Ensbury.....................12 C6
Ensdon......................41 F5
Ensis........................9 F3
Enstone.....................33 F7
Enterkinfoot................72 D4
Enville.....................31 K1
Eochar......................98 C8
Eoligarry...................90 C5
Eorabus.....................84 E6
Eoropaidh..................107 K2
Epperstone..................43 J2
Epping......................23 K2
Epping Green, Herts.........23 H2
Epping Green, Essex.........23 K2
Eppleby.....................66 B6
Epsom.......................23 H6
Epwell......................33 F5
Epworth.....................54 B8
Erbistock...................40 E2
Erbusaig....................92 D3
Erdington...................42 D7
Eredine.....................86 B3
Ericstane...................73 F3
Eridge Green................16 C2
Eriswell....................36 C2
Erith.......................23 L5
Erlestoke...................20 D7
Ermington....................5 G4
Erpingham...................47 G3
Errogie.....................94 D3
Errol.......................88 E6
Erskine.....................79 G4
Erskine Bridge..............79 G4
Erwarton....................37 H6
Erwood......................29 H5
Eryholme....................66 D7
Eryrys......................50 B8
Escomb......................66 B4
Escrick.....................60 D6
Esgairgeiliog...............39 G6
Esh.........................66 B3
Esher.......................23 G6
Eshott......................75 J5
Eshton......................58 E5
Esh Winning.................66 B3
Eskadale....................94 C2
Eskbank.....................81 J5
Eskdale Green...............63 G7
Eskdalemuir.................73 H5
Esknish.....................76 C5
Esprick.....................57 H7
Essendine...................44 D5
Essendon....................23 H2
Essich......................94 E2
Esslemont...................97 J3
Eston.......................67 F6
Etal........................83 H8
Etchilhampton...............20 E6
Etchingham..................16 E3
Etchinghill, Staffs.........42 C5
Etchinghill, Kent...........17 J2
Etherley....................66 B5
Eton........................22 E5
Etteridge...................94 E6
Ettersgill..................65 F5
Ettington...................32 E5
Etton, Cambs................44 E6
Etton, Humbs................61 G6
Ettrick.....................73 H3
Ettrickbridge...............73 J2
Etwall......................42 E3
Euston......................36 D2
Euxton......................50 E2
Evanton....................102 E6
Evedon......................44 D2
Evelix.....................103 F3
Evenjobb....................30 D3
Evenley.....................33 H6
Evenlode...................32 E7
Evenwood...................65 J5
Everbay....................113 G4
Evercreech..................11 H2
Everdon.....................33 H4
Everingham..................60 F6
Everleigh...................21 G7
Everley.....................67 J8
Eversholt...................34 C6
Evershot....................11 G5
Eversley....................22 C6
Eversley Cross..............22 C6
Everton, Hants..............12 E6
Everton, Beds...............35 F4
Everton, Notts..............53 J4
Evertown....................73 J7
Evesbatch...................31 H5
Evesham.....................32 C5
Evington....................43 J6
Ewden Village...............52 E4
Ewell.......................23 H6
Ewell Minnis................17 K1

Ewelme......................22 B3
Ewen........................20 E3
Ewenny......................18 D5
Ewerby......................44 E2
Ewes........................73 J5
Ewhurst.....................14 D1
Ewhurst Green...............16 E3
Ewloe.......................50 C7
Eworthy......................8 E6
Ewshot......................14 B1
Ewyas Harold................30 E7
Exbourne.....................9 F6
Exbury......................13 G5
Exebridge....................9 K3
Exelby......................59 H2
Exeter.......................9 K6
Exford.......................9 J2
Exhall......................32 D4
Exminster....................9 K7
Exmouth......................5 L1
Exnaboe....................115 F7
Exning......................35 K3
Exton, Devon................10 A7
Exton, Leic.................44 C5
Exton, Hants................13 J3
Exton, Somer.................9 K2
Eyam........................52 E6
Eydon.......................33 H4
Eye, H. & W.................31 F3
Eye, Cambs..................45 F6
Eye, Suff...................37 G2
Eyemouth....................83 H5
Eyeworth....................35 F5
Eyhorne Street..............24 E7
Eyke........................37 J4
Eynesbury...................34 E4
Eynort......................91 J3
Eynsford....................23 L6
Eynsham.....................21 J2
Eype........................11 F6
Eyre........................99 K7
Eythorne....................17 K1
Eyton, Shrops...............30 E1
Eyton, H. & W...............31 F3
Eyton upon the Weald Moors..41 H5

F

Faccombe....................21 H7
Faceby......................66 E7
Faddiley....................41 G1
Fadmoor.....................60 D2
Faerdre.....................18 A2
Faifley.....................79 H4
Failand.....................19 K5
Failford....................71 K2
Failsworth..................51 H3
Fairbourne..................38 F5
Fairburn....................53 G1
Fairfield...................32 B2
Fairford....................21 F2
Fairlands...................22 E7
Fairlie.....................78 E6
Fairlight...................16 F4
Fairmile....................10 B6
Fairmilehead................81 H5
Fair Oak, Hants.............13 G4
Fairoak, Staffs.............41 J3
Fairseat....................24 C6
Fairstead...................24 D1
Fairwarp....................15 H3
Fairy Cross..................8 E3
Fakenham....................46 E3
Fala........................82 C5
Fala Dam....................82 C5
Falahill....................81 J6
Faldingworth................54 E5
Falfield....................20 A3
Falkenham...................37 H6
Falkirk.....................80 D3
Falkland....................88 E8
Fallin......................74 D3
Falmer......................15 G5
Falmouth.....................3 G6
Fanagmore..................108 C4
Fangdale Beck...............60 C1
Fangfoss....................60 E5
Fanmore.....................84 F4
Fans........................82 E7
Far Cotton..................34 A4
Farden......................31 G2
Fareham.....................13 H5
Farewell....................42 C5
Far Forest..................31 J2
Faringdon...................21 G3
Farington...................50 E1
Farleigh, Surrey............23 J6
Farleigh, Avon..............19 J6
Farleigh Hungerford.........20 C7
Farleigh Wallop.............13 J1
Farlesthorpe................55 J6
Farleton....................57 J2
Farley, Staffs..............42 C2
Farley, Wilts...............12 E3
Farley, Shrops..............40 E6
Farley Green................14 D1
Farley Hill.................22 C6
Farleys End.................20 B1
Farlington..................60 D4
Farlow......................31 H1
Farmborough.................20 A6
Farmcote....................32 C7
Farmington..................21 F1
Farmoor.....................21 J2
Farmtown...................104 E3
Farnborough, Hants..........22 D7
Farnborough, Warw...........33 G5
Farnborough, G. Lon.........23 K6
Farncombe...................14 C1
Farndish....................34 C3

Farndon, Notts....................44 A1
Farndon, Ches....................41 F1
Farnell..............................89 J3
Farnell, Surrey...................14 B1
Farnham, Dorset.................12 B4
Farnham, Essex..................35 H7
Farnham, Suff....................37 J3
Farnham, N. Yks.................59 J4
Farnham Common...............22 E4
Farnham Green...................35 H7
Farnham Royal...................22 E4
Farningham........................23 L6
Farnley.............................59 H6
Farnley Tyas......................52 D2
Farnsfield..........................43 J1
Farnworth, Ches.................50 E5
Farnworth, G. Man..............51 G3
Farr, Highld......................110 D2
Farr, Highld........................94 E2
Farringdon.........................10 B6
Farrington Gurney...............19 L7
Farsley..............................59 H7
Farthinghoe.......................33 H6
Farthingstone.....................33 J4
Farway..............................10 C6
Fascadale..........................85 G1
Fasnacloich........................86 C4
Fassfern............................93 G8
Fatfield.............................66 D2
Fattahead.........................104 F3
Faugh..............................64 C2
Fauldhouse........................80 E5
Faulkbourne.......................24 D1
Faulkland...........................20 B7
Fauls.................................41 G3
Faversham.........................25 G6
Favillar.............................96 B2
Fawfieldhead......................52 C7
Fawkham Green...................24 B6
Fawler..............................21 H1
Fawley, Bucks....................22 C4
Fawley, Hants.....................13 G5
Fawley, Berks.....................21 H4
Fawley Chapel....................31 G7
Faxfleet............................54 C1
Faygate.............................15 F2
Fazeley.............................42 E6
Fearby...............................59 G2
Fearnan.............................87 K4
Fearnbeg..........................100 D5
Fearnhead.........................51 F4
Fearnmore........................100 D6
Featherstone, Staffs............42 B6
Featherstone, W. Yks..........53 G1
Feckenham.........................32 C3
Fedderate........................105 H4
Feering..............................36 D7
Feetham.............................65 G8
Feizor...............................58 C4
Felbridge...........................15 G2
Felbrigg.............................47 H3
Felcourt............................15 G1
Felden..............................22 F2
Felindre, Powys..................30 C1
Felindre, Dyfed...................28 C7
Felindre, Dyfed...................27 H3
Felindre, W. Glam...............27 L6
Felindre Farchog.................26 F3
Felinfach...........................29 H6
Felinfoel............................27 K6
Felixkirk............................60 B2
Felixstowe.........................37 H6
Fell End............................64 E8
Felling..............................66 C1
Fell Side............................63 J4
Felmersham......................34 C4
Felmingham........................47 H4
Felpham............................14 C6
Felsham.............................36 E4
Felstead............................36 B7
Feltham.............................23 G5
Felthorpe..........................47 G5
Felton, H. & W....................31 G5
Felton, Northum..................75 H4
Felton, Avon......................19 K6
Felton Butler......................40 E5
Feltwell............................46 C7
Fence................................58 D7
Fence Houses.....................66 D2
Fencote.............................59 H1
Fen Ditton.........................35 H3
Fen Drayton.......................35 G3
Fen End.............................32 E2
Feniscowles.......................51 F1
Feniton..............................10 C6
Fenny Bentley.....................42 D1
Fenny Bridges.....................10 C6
Fenny Compton...................33 G4
Fenny Drayton....................43 F7
Fenny Stratford...................34 B6
Fen Pitton..........................35 H3
Fenrother...........................75 H5
Fenstanton.........................35 G3
Fenton, Staffs.....................42 A2
Fenton, Lincs.....................44 B1
Fenton, Lincs.....................54 C6
Fenton, Northum..................75 H4
Fenton, Cambs....................35 G2
Fenwick, Strath...................79 G6
Fenwick, Northum................75 G7
Fenwick, S. Yks..................53 H4
Fenwick, Northum................83 J7
Feochaig............................70 C3
Feock.................................3 G6
Feolin Ferry.......................76 D5
Feriniquarrie......................99 F2
Fern..................................89 G2
Ferndale.............................18 E3
Ferndown..........................12 C5
Ferness............................103 H4
Fernham.............................21 G3
Fernhill Heath.....................32 A4
Fernhurst...........................14 B3

Ferniegair..........................80 C6
Fernilea.............................91 J2
Fernilee.............................52 C6
Ferrensby..........................59 J4
Ferrindonald.......................92 C5
Ferring...............................14 D5
Ferrybridge........................53 G1
Ferryden............................89 K3
Ferryhill............................66 C4
Ferryside...........................27 H5
Fersfield............................36 F1
Fersit...............................94 B8
Ferwig...............................26 F2
Feshiebridge......................95 G5
Fetcham.............................23 G7
Fetterangus......................105 J3
Fettercairn.........................97 F8
Fewston.............................59 G5
Ffairfach............................27 L4
Ffaldybrenin.......................27 L2
Ffarmers............................27 L2
Ffawyddog..........................19 G1
Ffestiniog...........................39 G2
Fforest...............................27 K6
Fforest-fach........................27 L7
Ffostrasol..........................27 H2
Ffrith...............................40 D1
Ffrynnon-ddrain...................27 J4
Ffynnongroyw......................50 A5
Fidden..............................84 E6
Fiddington, Glos..................32 B6
Fiddington, Somer................10 D1
Fiddleford..........................11 K4
Fiddlers Hamlet...................23 K2
Field..................................42 C3
Field Broughton...................57 G2
Field Dalling.......................46 F3
Field Head.........................43 G6
Fifehead Magdalen...............11 J3
Fifehead Neville...................11 J4
Fifield, Berks.......................22 E5
Fifield, Oxon.......................21 G1
Figheldean..........................12 D1
Filby..................................47 K5
Filey.................................61 J2
Filgrave.............................21 G2
Filkins..............................21 G2
Filleigh, Devon.....................9 G3
Filleigh, Devon.....................9 H4
Fillingham..........................54 D5
Fillongley...........................32 E1
Filton...............................19 L5
Fimber...............................61 F4
Fincham.............................46 B6
Finchdean...........................13 K4
Finchampstead....................22 C6
Finchingfield.......................36 B6
Finchley.............................23 H3
Findern..............................43 F3
Findhorn..........................103 J6
Findochty.........................104 D2
Findon, W. Susx..................14 E5
Findon, Grampn...................97 J6
Finedon..............................34 C2
Fingal Street.......................37 H3
Fingask.............................97 G3
Fingest..............................22 C3
Finghall.............................59 G2
Fingland............................72 C3
Fingringhoe........................36 F7
Finmere..............................33 J6
Finningham.........................36 F3
Finningley..........................53 J4
Finnygaud........................104 F3
Finsbay..............................99 F4
Finsbury............................23 J4
Finsthwaite.........................57 G2
Finstock.............................21 H1
Finstown...........................112 D5
Fintry, Grampn..................105 G3
Fintry, Strath......................79 J3
Finzean..............................96 F6
Fionnphort..........................84 E6
Firbank..............................57 K1
Firbeck.............................53 H5
Firgrove.............................51 J2
Firsby...............................55 J7
Firth................................117 F5
Fir Tree.............................65 J4
Fishbourne, W. Susx............14 B5
Fishbourne, I. of W..............13 H6
Fishburn............................66 D4
Fishcross...........................80 E2
Fisherford..........................97 F2
Fisher's Pond......................13 G3
Fisherstreet........................14 C2
Fisherton, Highld...............103 F7
Fisherton, Strath..................71 H3
Fishguard...........................26 D3
Fishlake.............................53 J2
Fishpool.............................51 H3
Fishtoft..............................45 G2
Fishtoft Drove.....................45 G2
Fishwick............................83 H6
Fiskavaig...........................91 J2
Fiskerton, Lincs...................54 E6
Fiskerton, Notts..................43 K1
Fittleton............................12 D1
Fittleworth.........................14 D4
Fitton End..........................45 H5
Fitz..................................41 F5
Fitzhead............................10 C3
Fitzwilliam.........................53 G2
Fiunary.............................85 H4
Five Ashes.........................16 C3
Fivehead............................10 E3
Five Oak Green....................16 D1
Five Oaks...........................14 D3
Five Penny Borve................107 J3
Five Roads.........................27 J6
Flackwell Heath..................22 D4
Fladbury.............................32 B5
Fladdabister......................115 G3
Flagg................................52 D7
Flamborough......................61 K3

Flamstead..........................22 F1
Flansham............................14 C5
Flasby...............................58 E5
Flash.................................52 C7
Flashader............................99 J7
Flaunden............................22 F2
Flawborough.......................44 A2
Flawith..............................60 B4
Flax Bourton.......................19 K6
Flaxby...............................59 J5
Flaxley..............................20 A1
Flaxpool.............................10 C2
Flaxton..............................60 D4
Fleckney............................43 J7
Flecknoe............................33 H3
Fleet, Hants........................22 D7
Fleet, Lincs........................45 G4
Fleet Hargate......................45 G4
Fleetwood...........................57 G6
Fleggburgh or
  Burgh St Margaret............47 K5
Flemingston........................18 E5
Flemington.........................79 J6
Flempton............................36 D2
Fletching............................15 H3
Flexbury..............................8 C5
Flexford.............................22 E7
Flicham..............................46 C4
Flimby................................62 F4
Flimwell.............................16 E2
Flint..................................50 B6
Flintham.............................44 A2
Flint Mountain.....................50 B6
Flinton...............................61 K7
Flitcham.............................46 C4
Flitton...............................34 D6
Flitwick.............................34 D6
Flixborough........................54 C2
Flixton, G. Man...................51 G4
Flixton, N. Yks....................61 H3
Flixton, Suff.......................37 J1
Flockton.............................52 E2
Flodabay.............................99 F4
Flodden..............................83 H8
Flookburgh.........................57 G3
Flordon..............................46 F4
Flore.................................33 J3
Flotterton...........................75 F4
Flowton..............................37 F5
Flushing, Corn......................3 G6
Flushing, Grampn...............105 K4
Flyford Flavell......................32 B4
Fobbing..............................24 D4
Fochabers.........................104 C3
Fochriw..............................18 F2
Fockerby............................54 C2
Fodderty...........................102 D7
Foel...................................39 J5
Foggathorpe........................60 E7
Fogo..................................82 F7
Foindle.............................108 C4
Folda..................................88 D2
Fole...................................42 C3
Foleshill.............................33 F1
Folke..................................11 H4
Folkestone..........................17 K2
Folkingham..........................44 D3
Folkington...........................16 C5
Folksworth..........................44 E8
Folkton...............................61 H3
Folla Rule...........................97 G2
Follifoot.............................59 J5
Folly Gate............................9 F6
Fonthill Bishop....................12 B2
Fonthill Gifford....................12 B2
Fontmell Magna....................12 A4
Fontwell.............................14 C5
Foolow...............................52 D6
Foots Cray..........................23 K5
Forcett...............................66 B6
Ford, Staffs.........................42 C1
Ford, Bucks.........................22 C2
Ford, Mers..........................50 C4
Ford, Wilts..........................20 C5
Ford, Glos...........................32 C4
Ford, W. Susx......................14 D5
Ford, Shrops.......................41 F5
Ford, Strath.........................77 H1
Ford, Devon..........................5 H5
Ford, Northum......................83 H8
Fordcombe..........................16 C2
Fordell...............................81 G3
Forden...............................40 D6
Ford End............................24 C1
Forder Green........................5 H3
Fordham, Cambs...................35 B2
Fordham, Essex....................36 E7
Fordham, Norf......................45 K7
Fordingbridge.......................12 D4
Fordon...............................61 H3
Fordoun..............................97 G8
Ford Street, Somer................10 C4
Fordstreet, Essex..................36 E7
Fordwells............................21 H1
Fordwich.............................25 H7
Fordyce............................104 E2
Foremark............................43 F4
Forest................................16 C2
Forestburn Gate...................75 G5
Forestfield..........................80 D5
Forest Gate..........................23 K4
Forest Green.......................14 E1
Forest Head........................64 C2
Forest Hill..........................21 K2
Forest-in-Teesdale................65 F5
Forest Mill.........................80 E2
Forest Row..........................15 H2
Forestside...........................14 A4
Forest Town........................53 H7
Forfar................................89 G3
Forgandenny........................88 C7
Forge Side..........................19 G2
Forgie..............................104 C3
Formby...............................50 B3
Forncett End.......................47 G7

Forncett St Mary..................47 G7
Forncett St Peter..................47 G7
Forneth..............................88 C4
Fornham All Saints...............36 D3
Fornham St Martin................36 D3
Forres.............................103 J7
Forsbrook...........................42 B2
Forse...............................111 J5
Forsinard..........................110 E4
Forston..............................11 H6
Fort Augustus.......................94 B5
Forteviot............................88 C7
Fort George.......................103 F7
Forth.................................80 E6
Forthampton........................32 A6
Forth Road Bridge, Fife.........81 G4
Forth Road Bridge, Loth........81 G4
Fortingall...........................87 K4
Forton, Somer......................10 E5
Forton, Shrops.....................41 F5
Forton, Lancs......................57 H5
Forton, Staffs......................41 J4
Fortrie, Grampn..................104 F4
Fortrie, Grampn....................97 J1
Fortrose...........................102 F7
Fortuneswell........................6 A7
Fort William.........................93 H8
Forty Hill...........................23 J3
Forward Green......................37 F4
Fosbury..............................21 H7
Fosdyke.............................45 G3
Foss..................................87 K3
Fossebridge.........................20 E1
Foss-y-ffin..........................28 B3
Foster Street.......................23 K2
Foston, Lincs.......................44 B2
Foston, Derby......................42 D3
Foston, N. Yks......................60 D4
Foston on the Wolds..............61 J5
Fotherby.............................55 H4
Fotheringhay.......................44 D7
Foubister..........................113 F6
Foul Mile...........................16 D4
Foulden, Norf......................46 C7
Foulden, Border....................83 H6
Foul Mile...........................16 D4
Foulridge............................58 D6
Foulsham............................46 F4
Fountainhall........................82 C7
Four Ashes..........................36 F2
Four Crosses, Staffs.............42 B6
Four Crosses, Powys.............40 B6
Four Crosses, Powys.............40 D5
Four Elms............................15 H1
Four Forks...........................10 D2
Four Gotes..........................45 H5
Four Lanes............................2 E6
Fourlanes End......................51 H8
Four Marks..........................13 J2
Four Mile Bridge..................48 B3
Four Oaks, W. Mids..............42 D7
Four Oaks, W. Mids..............32 E1
Four Oaks, E. Susx...............16 F3
Fourpenny.........................103 G3
Four Throws.........................16 E3
Fovant...............................12 C3
Foveran..............................97 J3
Fowey..................................3 K4
Fowlis...............................88 F5
Fowlis Wester......................88 B6
Fowlmere...........................35 H5
Fownhope...........................31 G6
Foxdale..............................56 P4
Foxearth.............................36 D5
Foxfield.............................56 F2
Foxham...............................20 D5
Foxhole...............................3 H4
Foxholes.............................61 H3
Fox Lane.............................22 D7
Foxley, Wilts.......................20 C4
Foxley, Norf.........................46 F4
Foxt...................................42 C2
Foxton, Cambs......................35 H5
Foxton, Leic.........................43 K8
Foxtwist Green......................51 F7
Foxup..................................58 D3
Foyers................................94 C3
Fraddon...............................3 H4
Fradley................................42 D5
Fradswell............................42 B3
Fraisthorpe..........................61 J4
Framfield............................15 H3
Framingham Earl...................47 H6
Framingham Pigot.................47 H6
Framlingham.........................37 H3
Frampton, Lincs....................45 G3
Frampton, Dorset..................11 H6
Frampton Cotterell................20 A4
Frampton Mansell..................20 D2
Frampton on Severn..............20 B2
Frampton West End...............45 G2
Framsden............................37 G4
Framwellgate Moor...............66 C3
Franche..............................31 K2
Frankby...............................50 B5
Frankley.............................32 B1
Frankton.............................33 G2
Frant..................................16 C2
Fraserburgh.......................105 J2
Frating Green.......................37 F7
Fratton...............................13 H5
Freathy................................4 D4
Freckenham..........................36 B2
Freckleton............................57 H4
Freebirch.............................. ...
Freeby................................44 B4
Freefolk..............................21 J1
Freeland..............................21 J1
Freester............................115 G3
Freethorpe..........................47 K6
Freiston..............................45 G2
Fremington, Devon.................8 F7
Fremington, N. Yks...............65 H4
Fremington, Strath................79 J6
Frenchbeer............................9 G7
Frensham............................14 B1

Fresgoe.............................110 F2
Freshfield...........................50 B3
Freshford............................20 B6
Freshwater...........................13 F7
Freshwater East....................26 E7
Fressingfield........................37 H2
Freston...............................37 G6
Freswick...........................111 K2
Fretherne...........................20 B2
Frettenham..........................47 H5
Freuchie..............................88 E8
Friar's Gate.........................15 H2
Friday Bridge.......................45 H6
Fridaythorpe........................60 F5
Friern Barnet.......................23 H3
Friesthorpe..........................54 E5
Frieth.................................22 C3
Frilford...............................21 J3
Frilsham.............................21 K5
Frimley...............................22 D7
Frindsbury...........................24 D6
Fring..................................46 C3
Fringford.............................33 J7
Frinsted..............................24 E7
Frinton-on-Sea.....................37 H7
Friockheim...........................89 H4
Frisby on the Wreake............43 J5
Friskney..............................45 H1
Friston, E. Susx...................16 C6
Friston, Suff.........................37 K3
Fritchley.............................43 F1
Fritham...............................12 E4
Frith Bank...........................45 G2
Frith Common.......................31 H3
Frithelstock...........................8 E4
Frithville.............................45 G1
Frittenden...........................16 F1
Fritton, Norf.........................47 H7
Fritton, Norf.........................47 K6
Fritwell...............................33 H7
Frizington............................62 F6
Frocester............................20 B2
Frodesham............................41 G6
Frodsham............................50 E6
Froggatt..............................52 E6
Froghall..............................42 C2
Frogmore............................22 D6
Frolesworth..........................43 H7
Frome.................................11 J1
Fromes Hill..........................31 H5
Frome St Quintin..................11 G5
Fron, Gwyn..........................38 C3
Fron, Powys.........................40 D6
Fron, Powys.........................29 H3
Fron, Powys.........................40 D2
Froncysyllte.........................40 D2
Frongoch............................39 J3
Frosterley...........................65 H4
Froxfield............................21 G6
Froxfield Green....................13 K3
Fryerning............................24 C2
Fryton................................60 D3
Fulbeck..............................44 C1
Fulbourn.............................35 J4
Fulbrook.............................21 G1
Fulford, Staffs......................42 B3
Fulford, Somer.....................10 D3
Fulford, N. Yks.....................60 D6
Fulham...............................23 H5
Fulking...............................15 F4
Fuller's Moor.......................41 F1
Fuller Street.......................24 D1
Fullerton.............................13 F2
Fulletby..............................55 G6
Full Sutton..........................60 E5
Fulmer................................22 E4
Fulmodeston........................46 E3
Fulnetby.............................54 E6
Fulstow..............................55 H4
Fulwell..............................66 D2
Fulwood, S. Yks...................53 F5
Fulwood, Lancs.....................57 J7
Funtington............................14 B5
Funtley................................13 H5
Funzie..............................117 H3
Furnace..............................78 C1
Furneux Pelham....................35 H7
Furzebrook...........................12 B7
Furzehill.............................10 D4
Fyfett.................................10 D4
Fyfield, Essex......................24 B2
Fyfield, Hants......................12 E1
Fyfield, Wilts.......................21 F6
Fyfield, Glos........................21 G2
Fyfield, Oxon.......................21 J3
Fylingthorpe........................67 K7
Fyvie.................................97 G2

G

Gabhsann..........................107 J3
Gabroc Hill..........................79 G6
Gaddesby............................43 J5
Gadfa.................................48 D2
Gaer..................................30 C7
Gaer-fawr...........................19 J3
Gaerllwyd............................19 J3
Gaerwen..............................48 D3
Gagingwell...........................33 G7
Gailey................................42 B5
Gainford.............................66 B6
Gainsborough.......................54 C5
Gainsford End......................36 C6
Gairloch............................100 E5
Gairlochy.............................93 H7
Gaisgill...............................64 D7
Gaitsgill.............................63 J3
Galashiels...........................82 C8
Galby.................................43 J6
Galgate...............................57 H5
Galhampton..........................11 H3
Gallatown............................81 H2

Galley Common......................43 F7
Galleywood...........................24 D2
Gallowfauld.........................89 G4
Galltair.............................92 E3
Galmisdale..........................92 A7
Galmpton, Devon....................5 G5
Galmpton, Devon....................5 J4
Galphay..............................59 H3
Galston..............................79 H8
Galtrigill............................99 G7
Gamblesby...........................64 D4
Gamlingay...........................35 F4
Gamston, Notts......................54 B6
Gamston, Notts......................43 J3
Ganarew..............................19 K1
Ganllwyd.............................39 G4
Ganstead.............................61 J7
Ganthorpe...........................60 D3
Ganton...............................61 G3
Garbat..............................102 C6
Garbhallt............................78 C2
Garboldisham.......................36 F1
Gardenstown......................105 H2
Garderhouse......................115 F4
Gare Hill.............................11 J7
Garforth..............................59 K7
Gargrave.............................58 E5
Gargunnock..........................80 C2
Garlieston...........................69 F6
Garlogie..............................97 G5
Garmond...........................105 H3
Garmouth...........................104 C2
Garn..................................38 B3
Garnant...............................18 A1
Gardonbenmaen.....................38 D2
Garnett Bridge......................64 C8
Garnkirk.............................79 J5
Garn-yr-erw..........................19 G1
Garrabost...........................107 K5
Garras..................................2 F7
Garreg................................38 F2
Garreg Bank.........................40 D5
Garrigill.............................64 E3
Garros...............................100 A6
Garrygualach.........................93 H5
Garrynamonie.......................90 C4
Garsdale.............................58 C2
Garsdale Head......................58 C1
Garsdon..............................20 D4
Garshall Green......................42 B3
Garsington...........................21 K2
Garstang.............................57 H6
Garswood............................50 E4
Gartcosh.............................80 B5
Garth, M. Glam.....................18 C3
Garth, Clwyd........................40 D2
Garth, Powys........................29 G5
Garth, I. of M.......................56 Q4
Garthbrengy.........................29 H6
Gartheli..............................28 C4
Garthmyl............................40 C7
Garthorpe, Leic......................44 B4
Garthorpe, Humbs.................54 C2
Gartly.................................96 E2
Gartmore............................79 H2
Gartocharn..........................79 G3
Garton...............................61 K7
Garton-on-the-Wolds...............61 G5
Gartymore.........................111 G7
Garvald...............................82 D4
Garvard..............................76 C2
Garve...............................102 B6
Garvestone..........................46 F6
Garvock...............................89 K1
Garway...............................31 F7
Garynahine........................107 G5
Gastard...............................20 C6
Gasthorpe............................36 E1
Gatcombe.............................13 G7
Gatebeck.............................57 J2
Gate Burton..........................54 C5
Gateforth.............................60 C8
Gatehead.............................79 H7
Gate Helmsley.......................60 D5
Gatehouse of Fleet.................69 H5
Gatelawbridge......................72 E5
Gateley...............................46 E4
Gatenby...............................59 J2
Gateshead.............................66 C1
Gatesheath...........................50 D7
Gateside, Fife.......................88 D8
Gateside, Strath....................79 F6
Gateside, Strath....................89 G4
Gateside, Tays......................89 F6
Gathurst.............................50 E3
Gatley................................51 H5
Gattonside...........................82 D8
Gauldry..............................89 F6
Gaunt's Common...................12 C5
Gautby...............................55 F6
Gavinton.............................82 F6
Gawber...............................53 F3
Gawcott.............................33 J6
Gawsworth............................51 H7
Gawthorp............................58 B3
Gawthwaite.........................57 F2
Gaydon...............................33 F4
Gayhurst.............................34 B5
Gayle.................................58 D2
Gayles................................65 J7
Gay Street...........................14 D3
Gayton, Staffs.......................42 B4
Gayton, Mers........................50 B5
Gayton, Norf.........................46 C5
Gayton, Northnts....................33 K4
Gayton le Marsh....................55 J5
Gayton Thorpe.......................46 C5
Gaywood.............................46 B4
Gazeley..............................36 C3
Geary.................................99 H6
Gedding.............................36 E4
Geddington.........................34 B1

Gedintailor ... 92 B2
Gedney ... 45 H4
Gedney Broadgate ... 45 H4
Gedney Drove End ... 45 H4
Gedney Dyke ... 45 H4
Gedney Hill ... 45 G5
Gedney Marsh ... 43 G4
Gee Cross ... 51 J4
Geise ... 111 H2
Geldeston ... 47 J7
Gelli ... 26 E5
Gellifor ... 50 A7
Gelligaer ... 18 F3
Gellilydan ... 39 F3
Gellioedd ... 39 J2
Gellywen ... 27 G4
Gelston ... 69 J5
Gentleshaw ... 42 C5
Geocrab ... 99 G3
Georgeham ... 8 E2
George Nympton ... 9 H3
Georgia ... 2 C6
Germansweek ... 8 E6
Germoe ... 2 D7
Gerrans ... 3 G6
Gerrards Cross ... 22 F4
Geshader ... 106 F5
Gestingthorpe ... 36 D6
Geuffordd ... 40 D5
Geufron ... 29 F1
Gibraltar ... 55 K8
Gidea Park ... 23 L3
Gidleigh ... 9 G7
Gifford ... 82 D5
Giggleswick ... 58 D4
Gilberdyke ... 60 F8
Gilchriston ... 82 C5
Gilcrux ... 63 G4
Gildersome ... 59 H8
Gildingwells ... 53 H5
Gileston ... 18 E6
Gilfach Goch ... 18 D4
Gilfachreda ... 28 B4
Gilgarran ... 62 F5
Gillamoor ... 60 D1
Gilling East ... 60 D3
Gillingham, Kent ... 24 D6
Gillingham, Dorset ... 11 K3
Gillingham, Norf ... 47 K7
Gilling West ... 66 B7
Gillow Heath ... 51 H8
Gills ... 111 K1
Gilmanscleuch ... 73 J2
Gilmerton, Tays ... 88 A6
Gilmerton, Lothn ... 81 H5
Gilmorton ... 33 H1
Gilsland ... 74 C8
Gilsland Spa ... 74 C8
Gilston ... 82 C6
Gilwern ... 19 G1
Gimingham ... 47 H3
Gipping ... 36 F3
Gipsey Bridge ... 45 F1
Girlsta ... 115 G3
Girsby ... 66 D7
Girthon ... 69 H5
Girton, Notts ... 54 C7
Girton, Cambs ... 35 H3
Girvan ... 71 G5
Gisburn ... 58 D6
Gisla ... 107 F6
Gisleham ... 37 L1
Gislingham ... 36 F2
Gissing ... 37 G1
Gittisham ... 10 C6
Gladestry ... 30 D4
Gladsmuir ... 82 C4
Glais ... 18 B2
Glaisdale ... 67 H7
Glame ... 100 B8
Glamis ... 89 F4
Glanaman ... 18 A1
Glandford ... 46 F2
Glandwr, Dyfed ... 27 F4
Glandwr, Gwent ... 19 G2
Glangrwyney ... 19 G1
Glanmule ... 40 C7
Glanrhyd ... 26 F2
Glanton ... 75 G3
Glanton Pyke ... 75 G3
Glanvilles Wootton ... 11 H5
Glan-y-don ... 50 A6
Glan-yr-afon ... 40 B2
Glapthorn ... 44 D7
Glapwell ... 53 G7
Glasbury ... 30 C6
Glascoed, Powys ... 40 C6
Glascoed, Gwent ... 19 H2
Glascoed, Clwyd ... 49 J3
Glascote ... 42 E6
Glascwm ... 30 C4
Glasdrum ... 86 C4
Glasfryn ... 39 J1
Glasgow ... 79 H5
Glasinfryn ... 48 E4
Glasnakille ... 92 B4
Glaspwll ... 39 G7
Glassburn ... 94 B2
Glasserton ... 68 F7
Glassford ... 80 C7
Glasshouse Hill ... 31 J7
Glasshouses ... 59 G4
Glasslaw ... 105 H3
Glasson, Cumbr ... 63 H1
Glasson, Lancs ... 57 H5
Glassonby ... 64 C4
Glaston ... 44 B6
Glastonbury ... 11 F2
Glatton ... 34 E1
Glazebury ... 51 F4
Glazeley ... 31 J1
Gleadless ... 53 F5
Gleadsmoss ... 51 H7
Gleaston ... 57 F3
Glemsford ... 36 D5

Glenancross ... 92 C6
Glenastle ... 76 C7
Glen Auldyn ... 56 R2
Glenbarr ... 77 F8
Glenbeg ... 85 G2
Glen Bernisdale ... 99 K8
Glenbervie ... 97 G7
Glenboig ... 80 C5
Glenborrodale ... 85 H2
Glenbreck ... 73 F2
Glenbuck ... 72 C2
Glenburn ... 79 G5
Glencaple ... 72 E8
Glencarse ... 88 D6
Glencoe ... 86 D3
Glencraig ... 81 G2
Glendevon ... 88 B8
Glendoebeg ... 94 C5
Glenegedale ... 76 C6
Glenelg ... 92 E4
Glenfarg ... 88 D7
Glenfield ... 43 H6
Glenfinnan ... 93 F7
Glenfoot ... 88 D7
Glengarnock ... 78 F6
Glengrasco ... 99 K8
Glenkerry ... 73 H3
Glenkindie ... 96 D4
Glenlee ... 72 B6
Glenlivet ... 95 K3
Glenluce ... 68 C5
Glenmavis ... 80 C5
Glenmaye ... 56 P4
Glenmore ... 91 K1
Glenmoy ... 89 G2
Glen of Newmill ... 104 D3
Glen Parva ... 43 H7
Glenprosen Village ... 88 F2
Glenreasdell Mains ... 77 H6
Glenridding ... 63 J6
Glenrothes ... 81 H1
Glenside ... 107 H7
Glentham ... 54 E4
Glenton ... 97 F3
Glentress ... 81 H8
Glen Trool Lodge ... 71 K6
Glentrool Village ... 71 J7
Glentworth ... 54 C5
Glenuig ... 92 C8
Glen Village ... 80 D4
Glen Vine ... 56 Q4
Glespin ... 72 D2
Gletness ... 115 G3
Glewstone ... 31 G7
Glinton ... 44 E6
Glooston ... 44 A7
Glossop ... 52 C4
Gloster Hill ... 75 J4
Gloucester ... 20 C1
Gloup ... 117 G2
Glusburn ... 58 F6
Gluss ... 116 E5
Glympton ... 33 G7
Glynarthen ... 27 H2
Glyn Ceiriog ... 40 D3
Glyncoch ... 18 E3
Glyncorrwg ... 18 C3
Glynde ... 15 H5
Glyndebourne ... 15 H4
Glyndyfrdwy ... 40 C2
Glyn Neath ... 18 C2
Glynogwr ... 18 D4
Glyntaff ... 18 E4
Gnosall ... 41 K4
Gnosall Heath ... 41 K4
Goadby ... 44 A7
Goadby Marwood ... 44 A4
Goatacre ... 20 E5
Goathill ... 11 H4
Goathland ... 67 J7
Goathurst ... 10 D2
Gobowen ... 40 E3
Godalming ... 14 C1
Godington ... 33 J7
Godmanchester ... 35 F2
Godmanstone ... 11 H6
Godmersham ... 25 G7
Godney ... 11 F1
Godolphin Cross ... 2 E6
Godre'r-graig ... 18 B2
Godshill, Hants ... 12 D4
Godshill, I. of W. ... 7 K6
Godstone ... 23 J7
Goff's Oak ... 23 J2
Gogar ... 81 G4
Goginan ... 28 D1
Golan ... 38 E2
Golant ... 3 K4
Golberdon ... 4 D2
Golborne ... 50 F4
Golcar ... 52 D2
Goldcliff ... 19 H4
Golden Cross ... 15 J4
Golden Green ... 16 D1
Golden Grove ... 27 K5
Goldenhill ... 42 A1
Golden Pot ... 13 K1
Golden Valley ... 32 B7
Golders Green ... 23 H4
Goldhanger ... 24 F2
Golding ... 41 G6
Goldsborough, N. Yks ... 59 J5
Goldsborough, N. Yks ... 67 J6
Goldsithney ... 2 D6
Goldthorpe ... 53 G3
Gollanfield ... 103 G3
Golspie ... 103 G2
Gomeldon ... 12 D2
Gomersal ... 52 E1
Gomshall ... 14 D1
Gonalston ... 43 J2
Gonfirth ... 115 F2
Good Easter ... 24 C1
Gooderstone ... 46 C6

Goodleigh ... 9 F2
Goodmanham ... 61 F6
Goodnestone, Kent ... 25 G6
Goodnestone, Kent ... 25 J7
Goodrich ... 19 K1
Goodrington ... 5 J4
Goodwick ... 26 D3
Goodworth Clatford ... 13 F1
Goole ... 54 B1
Goonbell ... 2 F5
Goonhavern ... 3 F4
Gooseham ... 8 C4
Goosetrey ... 51 G7
Goosey ... 21 H3
Goosnargh ... 57 J7
Goostrey ... 51 G6
Gordon ... 82 E7
Gordonbush ... 103 G2
Gordonstown, Grampn ... 104 E3
Gordonstown, Grampn ... 97 G2
Gorebridge ... 81 J5
Gorefield ... 45 H5
Goring ... 21 L4
Goring-by-Sea ... 14 E5
Gorleston-on-Sea ... 47 L6
Gorran Haven ... 3 J5
Gors ... 28 D2
Gorsedd ... 50 A6
Gorseinon ... 27 K7
Gorseness ... 112 E5
Gorsgoch ... 27 J1
Gorslas ... 27 K5
Gorsley ... 31 H7
Gorstan ... 102 B6
Gorton ... 51 H4
Gosbeck ... 37 G4
Gosberton ... 45 F3
Gosfield ... 36 C7
Gosforth, Cumbr ... 62 F7
Gosforth, T. & W. ... 75 J8
Gosmore ... 34 E7
Gosport ... 13 J6
Gossabrough ... 117 G4
Goswick ... 83 J7
Gotham ... 43 H3
Gotherington ... 32 B7
Goudhurst ... 16 E2
Goulceby ... 55 G6
Gourdas ... 97 G1
Gourdon ... 89 L1
Gourock ... 78 E4
Govan ... 79 H5
Goveton ... 5 H5
Govig ... 98 F2
Govilon ... 19 G1
Gowanhill ... 105 K2
Gowdall ... 53 J1
Gowerton ... 27 K7
Gowkhall ... 81 F3
Goxhill, Humbs ... 54 F1
Goxhill, Humbs ... 61 J6
Graffham ... 14 C4
Grafham ... 34 E3
Grafton, H. & W. ... 31 F6
Grafton, Oxon ... 21 G2
Grafton, H. & W. ... 31 G3
Grafton, N. Yks ... 59 K4
Grafton Flyford ... 32 B4
Grafton Regis ... 34 A5
Grafton Underwood ... 34 C1
Grafty Green ... 16 F1
Graianrhyd ... 40 D1
Graig, Gwyn ... 49 H3
Graig, Clwyd ... 49 K3
Graig-fechan ... 40 C1
Graig Penllyn ... 18 D5
Grain ... 24 E5
Grainsby ... 55 G4
Grainthorpe ... 55 H4
Graizelound ... 54 B4
Grampound ... 3 H5
Grampound Road ... 3 H4
Gramsdale ... 98 D7
Granborough ... 34 A7
Granby ... 44 A3
Grandborough ... 33 G3
Grandtully ... 88 B3
Grange, Mers ... 50 B5
Grange, Cumbr ... 63 H6
Grange Crossroads ... 104 D3
Grange Hall ... 23 K3
Grange Moor ... 52 E2
Grangemouth ... 80 E3
Grange-over-Sands ... 57 H3
Grangepans ... 80 E2
Grange, The ... 60 C1
Grangetown ... 67 F5
Grange Villa ... 66 C2
Granish ... 95 G4
Gransmoor ... 61 J5
Granston ... 26 C3
Grantchester ... 35 H4
Grantham ... 44 C3
Grantley ... 59 H4
Grantlodge ... 97 G4
Granton ... 81 H4
Grantown-on-Spey ... 95 J3
Grantshouse ... 83 G5
Grappenhall ... 51 F5
Grasby ... 54 E3
Grasmere ... 63 J7
Grascroft ... 51 J3
Grasscroft ... 51 J3
Grassendale ... 50 C5
Grassholme ... 65 G5
Grassington ... 58 F4
Grassmoor ... 53 G7
Grassthorpe ... 54 B7
Grateley ... 12 E1
Gratwich ... 42 C3
Graveley, Cambs ... 35 F3
Graveley, Herts ... 35 F7
Gravelly Hill ... 42 D7
Gravels ... 40 E6
Graveney ... 25 G6
Gravesend ... 24 C5

Gravir ... 107 H7
Grayingham ... 54 D4
Grayrigg ... 64 C8
Grays ... 24 C5
Grayshott ... 14 B2
Grayswood ... 14 C2
Graythorp ... 66 F5
Grazeley ... 22 B6
Greasbrough ... 53 G4
Greasby ... 50 B5
Great Abington ... 35 J5
Great Addington ... 34 C2
Great Alne ... 32 D4
Great Altcar ... 50 C3
Great Amwell ... 23 J1
Great Asby ... 64 D6
Great Ashfield ... 36 F3
Great Ayton ... 67 F6
Great Baddow ... 24 D2
Great Bardfield ... 36 B6
Great Barford ... 34 E4
Great Barr ... 42 C7
Great Barrington ... 21 G1
Great Barrow ... 50 D7
Great Barton ... 36 D3
Great Barugh ... 60 E3
Great Bavington ... 75 F6
Great Bealings ... 37 H5
Great Bedwyn ... 21 G6
Great Bentley ... 37 G7
Great Bircham ... 46 C3
Great Blakenham ... 37 G4
Great Bolas ... 41 H4
Great Bookham ... 23 G7
Great Bosullow ... 2 C6
Great Bourton ... 33 G5
Great Bowden ... 34 A1
Great Bradley ... 36 B4
Great Braxted ... 24 E1
Great Bricett ... 36 F4
Great Brickhill ... 34 C6
Great Bridgeford ... 42 A4
Great Brington ... 33 J3
Great Bromley ... 37 F7
Great Broughton ... 67 F7
Great Budworth ... 51 F6
Great Burdon ... 66 D6
Great Burstead ... 24 C3
Great Busby ... 66 F7
Great Canfield ... 24 B1
Great Carlton ... 55 J5
Great Casterton ... 44 D6
Great Chart ... 17 G1
Great Chatwell ... 41 J5
Great Chesterford ... 35 J5
Great Cheverell ... 20 D7
Great Chishill ... 35 H6
Great Clacton ... 25 H1
Great Clifton ... 62 F5
Great Coates ... 55 G2
Great Comberton ... 32 B5
Great Corby ... 64 B2
Great Cornard ... 36 D5
Great Coxwell ... 21 G3
Great Cransley ... 34 B2
Great Cressingham ... 46 D6
Great Crosby ... 50 C4
Great Cubley ... 42 D3
Great Dalby ... 44 A5
Great Doddington ... 34 B3
Great Dunham ... 46 D5
Great Dunmow ... 35 K7
Great Durnford ... 12 D2
Great Easton, Leic ... 44 B7
Great Easton, Essex ... 35 K7
Great Eccleston ... 57 H6
Great Edstone ... 60 E2
Great Ellingham ... 46 F7
Great Elm ... 11 J1
Great Eversden ... 35 G4
Great Finborough ... 36 F4
Greatford ... 44 D5
Great Fransham ... 46 D5
Great Gaddesden ... 22 F1
Great Gidding ... 34 E1
Great Givendale ... 60 F5
Great Glemham ... 37 J3
Great Glen ... 43 J7
Great Gonerby ... 44 B3
Great Gransden ... 35 F4
Great Green ... 36 E4
Great Habton ... 60 E3
Great Hallingbury ... 23 L1
Greatham, Hants ... 14 A2
Greatham, Cleve ... 66 E5
Great Hampden ... 22 D2
Great Harrowden ... 34 B2
Great Harwood ... 58 C7
Great Haseley ... 22 B2
Great Hatfield ... 61 J6
Great Haywood ... 42 C4
Great Heck ... 53 H1
Great Henny ... 36 D6
Great Hinton ... 20 D7
Great Hockham ... 46 E7
Great Holland ... 25 J1
Great Horkesley ... 36 E7
Great Hormead ... 35 H6
Great Horwood ... 34 A6
Great Houghton, Northnts ... 34 A4
Great Houghton, S. Yks ... 53 G3
Great Hucklow ... 52 D6
Great Kelk ... 61 J5
Great Kimble ... 22 D3
Great Langton ... 59 H1
Great Leighs ... 24 D1
Great Limber ... 55 F3
Great Linford ... 34 B5
Great Livermore ... 36 D2
Great Longstone ... 52 E6
Great Lumley ... 66 C3
Great Lyth ... 41 F6
Great Malvern ... 31 J5
Great Maplestead ... 36 D6
Great Marton ... 57 G7

Great Massingham ... 46 C4
Great Milton ... 22 B2
Great Missenden ... 22 D2
Great Mitton ... 58 C7
Great Mongeham ... 25 K7
Great Moulton ... 47 G7
Great Musgrave ... 64 E6
Great Ness ... 40 E5
Great Oakley, Northnts ... 34 B1
Great Oakley, Essex ... 37 G7
Great Offley ... 34 E7
Great Ormside ... 64 E6
Great Orton ... 63 J2
Great Oxendon ... 33 K1
Great Palgrave ... 46 D5
Great Pardon ... 23 K2
Great Paxton ... 35 F3
Great Plumstead ... 47 J5
Great Ponton ... 44 C3
Great Preston ... 59 K8
Great Raveley ... 35 F1
Great Rissington ... 21 F1
Great Rollright ... 33 F6
Great Ryburgh ... 46 E4
Great Ryle ... 75 G3
Great Saling ... 36 C7
Great Salkeld ... 64 C4
Great Sampford ... 36 B6
Great Sankey ... 50 E5
Great Saxham ... 36 C3
Great Shefford ... 21 H5
Great Shelford ... 35 H4
Great Smeaton ... 66 D7
Great Snoring ... 46 E3
Great Somerford ... 20 D4
Great Stainton ... 66 D5
Great Stambridge ... 24 F3
Great Staughton ... 34 E3
Great Steeping ... 55 J7
Great Stonar ... 25 K7
Greatstone-on-Sea ... 17 H3
Great Strickland ... 64 C5
Great Stukeley ... 35 F2
Great Sturton ... 55 G6
Great Swinburne ... 75 F7
Great Tew ... 33 F7
Great Tey ... 36 D7
Great Thurlow ... 36 B4
Great Torrington ... 8 E4
Great Tosson ... 75 G4
Great Totham, Essex ... 24 E1
Great Totham, Essex ... 24 E1
Great Wakering ... 25 F4
Great Waldingfield ... 36 E5
Great Walsingham ... 46 E3
Great Waltham ... 24 C1
Great Warley ... 24 B3
Great Washbourne ... 32 B6
Great Welnetham ... 36 D4
Great Wenham ... 36 F6
Great Whittington ... 75 G7
Great Wigborough ... 25 F1
Great Wilbraham ... 35 J4
Great Wishford ... 12 C2
Great Witcombe ... 20 D1
Great Witley ... 31 J3
Great Wolford ... 32 E6
Greatworth ... 33 H5
Great Wratting ... 36 B5
Great Wymondley ... 35 F7
Great Wyrley ... 42 B6
Great Wytheford ... 41 G5
Great Yarmouth ... 47 L6
Great Yeldham ... 36 C6
Greenburn ... 80 E5
Greendykes ... 75 G2
Greenfield, Clwyd ... 50 A6
Greenfield, Oxon ... 22 C3
Greenfield, Beds ... 34 D6
Greenfield, G. Man ... 51 J3
Greenfield, Highld ... 93 J5
Greenford ... 23 G4
Greengairs ... 80 C4
Greenham ... 21 J6
Green Hammerton ... 60 B5
Greenhaugh ... 74 D6
Greenhead ... 64 D1
Greenhill, Central ... 80 D4
Green Hill, Wilts ... 20 E4
Greenhill, S. Yks ... 53 F5
Greenhill, G. Lon ... 23 G4
Greenhithe ... 24 B5
Greenholm ... 79 H8
Greenholme ... 64 C7
Greenhow Hill ... 59 G4
Greenigoe ... 112 E6
Greenland ... 111 J2
Greenlaw ... 82 F7
Greenloaning ... 87 L8
Greenmount ... 51 G2
Greenmow ... 115 G6
Greenock ... 78 E4
Greenodd ... 57 G2
Green Ore ... 19 K7
Greenside ... 65 J1
Greensidehill ... 75 F3
Greenskares ... 105 G2
Greens Norton ... 33 J5
Greenstead Green ... 36 D7
Greensted ... 23 L2
Green Street Green ... 23 K6
Green, The, Wilts ... 12 A3
Green, The, Cumbr ... 56 E2
Greenwich ... 23 K5
Greet ... 32 C6
Greete ... 31 G2
Greetham, Leic ... 44 C5
Greetham, Lincs ... 55 H6
Greetland ... 52 C1
Gregson Lane ... 50 E1
Greinton ... 11 F2
Grendon, Northnts ... 34 B3
Grendon, Warw ... 42 E7

Grendon Common ... 42 E7
Grendon Green ... 31 G4
Grendon Underwood ... 33 J7
Grenitote ... 98 D5
Grenoside ... 53 F4
Gresford ... 40 E1
Gresham ... 47 G3
Greshornish ... 99 J3
Gressenhall ... 46 E5
Gressingham ... 57 J4
Greta Bridge ... 65 H3
Gretna ... 73 J8
Gretna Green ... 73 J8
Gretton, Northnts ... 44 B7
Gretton, Glos ... 32 C6
Gretton, Shrops ... 41 G7
Grewelthorpe ... 59 H3
Greygarth ... 59 G3
Greysouthen ... 62 F5
Greystoke ... 64 B4
Greystone ... 89 H4
Greywell ... 22 C7
Griais ... 107 J4
Grianan ... 107 J5
Griff ... 33 F1
Griffithstown ... 19 G3
Grike ... 63 F6
Grimeford Village ... 50 F2
Grimethorpe ... 53 G3
Griminish ... 98 C3
Grimister ... 117 F3
Grimley ... 31 K3
Grimness ... 112 E7
Grimoldby ... 55 H5
Grimsargh ... 57 J7
Grimsby ... 55 G3
Grimscote ... 33 J4
Grimscott ... 8 C5
Grimshader ... 107 J6
Grimston, Norf ... 46 C4
Grimston, Leic ... 43 J4
Grimstone ... 11 H6
Grindale ... 61 J3
Grindiscol ... 115 G5
Grindle ... 41 J6
Grindleford ... 52 E6
Grindleton ... 58 C6
Grindley Brook ... 41 G2
Grindlow ... 52 D6
Grindon, Staffs ... 42 C1
Grindon, Northum ... 83 H7
Gringley on the Hill ... 54 B4
Grinsdale ... 63 J2
Grinshill ... 41 G4
Grinton ... 65 H4
Grisedale ... 58 C1
Gristhorpe ... 61 H2
Griston ... 46 E7
Grittenham ... 20 E4
Grittleton ... 20 C4
Grizebeck ... 57 F2
Grizedale ... 57 G1
Grobister ... 113 G4
Groby ... 43 H6
Groes, W. Glam ... 18 A4
Groes, Clwyd ... 49 K4
Groes-faen ... 18 E4
Groeslon ... 38 D1
Grogport ... 77 H7
Gromford ... 37 J4
Gronant ... 49 K2
Groombridge ... 15 J2
Grosebay ... 99 G3
Grosmont, Gwent ... 30 F7
Grosmont, N. Yks ... 67 J7
Groton ... 36 E5
Grove, Dorset ... 6 A7
Grove, Notts ... 54 B6
Grove, Oxon ... 21 J3
Grove, Kent ... 25 J6
Grove Park ... 23 K5
Grovesend ... 27 K6
Grudie ... 101 K6
Gruids ... 102 D2
Gruline ... 85 G4
Grumbla ... 2 C7
Grunasound ... 115 F5
Grundisburgh ... 37 H4
Gruting ... 114 E4
Guardbridge ... 89 G7
Guarlford ... 31 K5
Guestling Green ... 16 F4
Guestwick ... 46 F4
Guide Post ... 75 J6
Guilden Morden ... 35 F5
Guilden Sutton ... 50 D7
Guildford ... 14 C1
Guildtown ... 88 D5
Guilsborough ... 33 J2
Guilsfield ... 40 D5
Guisborough ... 67 G6
Guiseley ... 59 G6
Guist ... 46 E4
Guiting Power ... 32 C7
Gullane ... 82 C3
Gulval ... 2 C6
Gulworthy ... 26 F6
Gumley ... 43 J7
Gunby, Lincs ... 44 C4
Gunby, Humbs ... 60 E7
Gundleton ... 13 J2
Gunn ... 9 G2
Gunnerside ... 65 G8
Gunnerton ... 74 F7
Gunness ... 54 C2
Gunnislake ... 4 E2
Gunnista ... 115 H4
Gunthorpe, Norf ... 46 F3
Gunthorpe, Notts ... 43 J2
Gunwalloe Fishing Cove ... 2 E7
Gurnard ... 13 G6
Gurney Slade ... 11 H1
Gurnos ... 18 B2
Gussage All Saints ... 12 C4

Gussage St Michael.........12 B4
Guston.....................17 L1
Gutcher...................117 G3
Guthrie....................89 H3
Guyhirn....................45 G6
Guy's Head.................45 H4
Guy's Marsh................11 K3
Guyzance...................75 J4
Gwaelod-y-Garth............18 F4
Gwaenysgor.................49 K2
Gwalchmai..................48 C3
Gwaun-Cae-Gurwen...........18 B1
Gwbert.....................26 F1
Gweek......................2 F7
Gwehelog...................19 H2
Gwenddwr...................29 H5
Gwennap....................2 F5
Gwenter....................2 F8
Gwernaffield...............50 B7
Gwernesney.................19 J2
Gwernogle..................27 K3
Gwernymynydd...............50 B7
Gwersyllt..................40 E1
Gwespyr....................49 L2
Gwinear....................2 D6
Gwithian...................2 D5
Gwyddelwern................40 B2
Gwyddgrug..................27 J3
Gwytherin..................49 H4

H

Habberley, Shrops..........40 E6
Habberley, H. & W..........31 K2
Habost, W. Isles..........107 H7
Habrough...................55 F2
Haccombe...................5 J2
Haceby.....................44 D3
Hacheston..................37 J4
Hackford...................46 F6
Hackforth..................59 H1
Hacklete..................107 F5
Hackleton..................34 B4
Hackness, Orkney..........112 D7
Hackness, N. Yks...........61 G1
Hackney....................23 J4
Hackthorn..................54 D5
Hackthorpe.................64 C5
Haconby....................44 E4
Hadden.....................83 F8
Haddenham, Bucks...........22 C2
Haddenham, Cambs...........35 H2
Haddington.................82 D4
Haddiscoe..................47 K7
Haddon.....................44 E7
Hademore...................42 D6
Hadfield...................52 C4
Hadham Cross...............23 K1
Hadham Ford................35 H7
Hadleigh, Essex............24 E4
Hadleigh, Suff.............36 F5
Hadley.....................41 H5
Hadley End.................42 D4
Hadlow.....................24 C7
Hadlow Down................15 J3
Hadnall....................41 G4
Hadstock...................35 J5
Hadzor.....................32 B3
Haffenden Quarter..........17 F1
Hafod-Dinbych..............39 H1
Haggbeck...................74 A7
Haggerston.................83 J7
Hagley, H. & W.............32 B1
Hagley, H. & W.............31 G5
Hagworthingham.............55 H7
Haigh......................50 F3
Haighton Green.............57 J7
Haile......................62 F7
Hailes.....................32 C6
Hailey, Oxon...............21 H1
Hailey, Herts..............23 J1
Hailsham...................16 C5
Hail Weston................34 E3
Hainault...................23 K3
Hainford...................47 H5
Hainton....................55 F5
Haisthorpe.................61 J4
Halam......................43 J1
Halberton..................10 B4
Halcro....................111 J2
Hale, Hants................12 D4
Hale, Ches.................50 D5
Hale, Lincs................44 E2
Hale, G. Man...............51 G5
Hale Bank..................50 D5
Halebarns..................51 G5
Hales, Staffs..............41 J3
Hales, Norf................47 J7
Halesowen..................32 B1
Hales Place................25 H7
Hale Street................16 D1
Halesworth.................37 J2
Halewood...................50 D5
Halford, Warw..............32 E5
Halford, Shrops............31 F1
Halfpenny Green............41 K7
Halfway, Powys.............29 F6
Halfway, Berks.............21 J6
Halfway, Dyfed.............27 L3
Halfway House..............40 E5
Halfway Houses.............25 F5
Halifax....................52 C1
Halistra...................99 H7
Halket.....................79 G6
Halkirk...................111 H3
Halkyn.....................50 B6
Halland....................15 J4
Hallaton...................44 A4
Hallatrow..................19 L7
Hallbankgate...............64 C2
Hallen.....................19 K4

Hall Green.................32 D1
Halliburton................82 E7
Hallin.....................99 H7
Halling....................24 D6
Hallington.................75 F7
Hall of the Forest.........30 D1
Halloughton................43 J1
Hallow.....................31 K4
Hallrule...................74 B3
Halls......................82 E4
Hallthwaites...............56 E2
Hallworthy..................8 B7
Hallyne....................81 G7
Halmer End.................41 K2
Halmore....................20 A2
Halmyre Mains..............81 G7
Halnaker...................14 C5
Halsall....................50 C2
Halse, Somer...............10 C3
Halse, Northnts............33 H5
Halsetown...................2 D6
Halsham....................55 G1
Halsinger...................8 F2
Halstead, Leic.............44 A6
Halstead, Essex............36 D6
Halstead, Kent.............23 K6
Halstock...................11 G5
Haltham....................55 G7
Haltoft End................45 G2
Halton, Bucks..............22 D1
Halton, Clwyd..............40 E3
Halton, Ches...............50 E5
Halton, Lancs..............57 J4
Halton East................58 F5
Halton Gill................58 D3
Halton Holegate............55 J7
Halton Lea Gate............64 D2
Halton West................58 D5
Haltwhistle................64 E1
Halvergate.................47 K6
Halwell.....................5 H4
Halwill.....................8 E6
Halwill Junction...........8 E5
Ham, Glos..................20 A3
Ham, Shetld...............114 B5
Ham, G. Lon................23 G5
Ham, Wilts.................21 H6
Ham, Highld...............111 J1
Hambleden..................22 C4
Hambledon, Surrey..........14 C2
Hambledon, Hants...........13 J4
Hamble-le-Rice.............13 G5
Hambleton, N. Yks..........60 C7
Hambleton, Lancs...........57 G6
Hambridge..................10 E3
Hambrook, W. Susx..........14 A5
Hambrook, Avon.............19 L5
Hameringham................55 H7
Hamerton...................34 E2
Hametoun..................114 B5
Ham Green, H. & W..........32 C3
Ham Green, Avon............19 K5
Hamilton...................80 C6
Hammersmith................23 H5
Hammerwich.................42 C6
Hammond Street.............23 J2
Hammoon...................11 K4
Hamnavoe, Shetld..........115 F5
Hamnavoe, Shetld..........117 G5
Hampden Park...............16 D5
Hampnett...................20 F1
Hampole....................53 H2
Hampreston.................12 C6
Hampstead..................23 H4
Hampstead Norreys..........21 K5
Hampsthwaite...............59 H5
Hampton, H. & W............32 C5
Hampton, G. Lon............23 G6
Hampton, Shrops............31 J1
Hampton Bishop.............31 G6
Hampton Heath..............41 F2
Hampton in Arden...........32 E1
Hampton Lovett.............32 A3
Hampton Lucy...............32 E4
Hampton on the Hill........32 E3
Hampton Poyle..............21 K1
Hamsey.....................15 H4
Hamstall Ridware...........42 D5
Hamstead, W. Mids..........42 C7
Hamstead, I. of W..........13 F6
Hamstead Marshall..........21 J6
Hamsterley, Durham.........65 J2
Hamsterley, Durham.........65 J4
Ham Street, Somer..........11 G2
Hamstreet, Kent............17 H2
Hamworthy..................12 B6
Hanbury, H. & W............32 B3
Hanbury, Staffs............42 D4
Hanchurch..................41 K2
Handbridge.................50 D7
Handcross..................15 F3
Handforth..................51 H5
Handley....................41 F1
Handsacre..................42 C5
Handsworth, W. Mids........42 C7
Handsworth, S. Yks.........53 G5
Hanford....................42 A2
Hanging Langford...........12 C2
Hanham.....................19 L5
Hankelow...................41 H2
Hankerton..................20 D3
Hankham....................16 D5
Hanley.....................42 A2
Hanley Castle..............31 K5
Hanley Child...............31 H3
Hanley Swan................31 K5
Hanley William.............31 H3
Hanlith....................58 E4
Hanmer.....................41 F3
Hannington, Northnts.......34 B2
Hannington, Wilts..........21 F3
Hannington, Hants..........21 K7
Hannington Wick............21 F3
Hanslope...................34 B5

Hanthorpe..................44 D4
Hanwell....................33 G5
Hanwood....................41 F6
Hanworth, Norf.............47 G3
Hanworth, G. Lon...........23 G5
Happendon..................72 D1
Happisburgh................47 J3
Happisburgh Common.........47 J4
Hapsford...................50 D6
Hapton, Lancs..............58 C7
Hapton, Norf...............47 G7
Harberton...................5 H4
Harbertonford...............5 H4
Harbledown.................25 H7
Harborne...................32 C1
Harborough Magna...........33 G2
Harbottle..................75 F4
Harbury....................33 F4
Harby, Leic................44 A3
Harby, Notts...............54 C6
Harcombe...................10 C6
Harden.....................59 F7
Hardendale.................64 C6
Hardgate...................97 G5
Hardham....................14 D4
Hardhorn...................57 G7
Hardingham.................46 F6
Hardingstone...............34 A4
Hardings Wood..............41 K1
Hardington.................20 B7
Hardington Mandeville......11 G4
Hardington Marsh...........11 G5
Hardley....................13 G5
Hardley Street.............47 J6
Hardmead...................34 C5
Hardraw....................58 D1
Hardstoft..................53 G7
Hardway, Somer.............11 J2
Hardway, Hants.............13 J5
Hardwick, Northnts.........34 B3
Hardwick, Bucks............22 D1
Hardwick, Cambs............35 G4
Hardwick, Oxon.............21 H2
Hardwick, Oxon.............33 H7
Hardwick, Norf.............47 H8
Hardwicke, Glos............32 B7
Hardwicke, Glos............20 C1
Hardwicke, H. & W..........30 D5
Hareby.....................55 H7
Harefield..................22 F3
Hare Hatch.................22 D5
Harehope...................75 G2
Harescombe.................20 C1
Haresfield.................20 C1
Hare Street................35 G7
Harewood...................59 J6
Harford.....................5 G4
Hargrave, Suff.............36 C4
Hargrave, Northnts.........34 D2
Hargrave, Ches.............50 D7
Harker.....................63 J1
Harkstead..................37 G6
Harlaston..................42 E5
Harlaxton..................44 B3
Harlech....................38 E3
Harlesden..................23 H4
Harleston, Suff............36 F3
Harleston, Norf............37 H1
Harleston, Devon............5 H5
Harlestone.................33 K3
Harle Syke.................58 D7
Harley.....................41 G6
Harlington.................34 D6
Harlosh....................91 H1
Harlow.....................23 K1
Harlow Hill................75 G8
Harlsey....................66 E8
Harlthorpe.................60 E7
Harlton....................35 G4
Harman's Cross..............6 D6
Harmby.....................59 G2
Harmer Green...............23 H1
Harmer Hill................41 F4
Harmston...................54 D7
Harnham....................12 D3
Harnhill...................20 E2
Harold Hill................23 L3
Haroldston West............26 C5
Haroldswick...............117 H1
Harold Wood................23 L3
Harome.....................60 D2
Harpenden..................23 G1
Harpford...................10 B6
Harpham....................61 H4
Harpley, Norf..............46 C4
Harpley, H. & W............31 H3
Harpole....................33 J3
Harpsdale.................111 H3
Harpsden...................22 C4
Harpswell..................54 D5
Harpurhey..................51 H3
Harpur Hill................52 C6
Harrapool..................92 C3
Harrietfield...............88 B6
Harrietsham................24 E7
Harrington, Northnts.......34 A1
Harrington, Cumbr..........62 E5
Harrington, Lincs..........55 H6
Harringworth...............44 C2
Harriseahead...............42 A1
Harrogate..................59 J5
Harrold....................34 C4
Harrow.....................23 G4
Harrowbarrow................4 E2
Harrowden..................34 D5
Harrow on the Hill.........23 G4
Harston, Leic..............44 B3
Harston, Cambs.............35 H4
Hart.......................66 E4
Hartburn...................75 G6
Hartest....................36 C4
Hartfield..................15 H2
Hartford, Cambs............35 F2
Hartford, Ches.............51 F6

Hartfordbridge.............22 C7
Hartford End...............24 C1
Harthill, Strath...........80 E5
Harthill, Ches.............41 G1
Harthill, S. Yks...........53 G5
Hartington.................52 D7
Hartland....................8 C3
Hartland Quay...............8 C3
Hartlebury.................31 K2
Hartlepool.................66 F4
Hartley, Kent..............24 C6
Hartley, Kent..............16 E2
Hartley, Cumbr.............64 E7
Hartley, Northum...........75 K7
Hartley Wespall............22 B7
Hartley Wintney............22 C7
Hartlip....................24 E6
Harton, T. & W.............66 D1
Harton, N. Yks.............60 E4
Harton, Shrops.............31 F1
Hartpury...................31 K7
Hartshill..................43 F7
Hartshorne.................43 F4
Hartsop....................63 K6
Hartwell...................34 A4
Hartwood...................80 D6
Harvel.....................24 C6
Harvington.................32 C5
Harwell....................21 J4
Harwich....................37 H6
Harwood, Durham............65 F4
Harwood, G. Man............51 G2
Harwood Dale...............61 G1
Harworth...................53 J4
Hascombe...................14 C1
Haselbech..................33 K2
Haselbury Plucknett........11 F4
Haseley....................32 E3
Haselor....................32 D4
Hasfield...................31 K7
Hasguard...................26 C6
Haskayne...................50 C3
Hasketon...................37 H4
Hasland....................53 F7
Haslemere..................14 C2
Haslingden.................51 G1
Haslingden Grane...........51 G1
Haslingfield...............35 H4
Haslington.................41 J1
Hassall....................41 J1
Hassall Green..............51 G8
Hassall Street.............17 H1
Hassendean.................74 B2
Hassingham.................47 J6
Hassocks...................15 G4
Hassop.....................52 E6
Hastigrow.................111 J2
Hastingleigh...............17 H1
Hastings...................16 F5
Hastingwood................23 K2
Hastoe.....................22 E2
Haswell....................66 D3
Hatch, Wilts...............12 B3
Hatch, Hants...............22 B7
Hatch, Beds................34 E5
Hatch Beauchamp............10 E3
Hatch End..................23 G3
Hatching Green.............23 G1
Hatchmere..................50 E6
Hatcliffe..................55 G3
Hatfield, H. & W...........31 G4
Hatfield, Herts............23 H2
Hatfield, S. Yks...........53 J3
Hatfield Broad Oak.........23 L1
Hatfield Heath.............23 L1
Hatfield Peverel...........24 D1
Hatfield Woodhouse.........53 J3
Hatford....................21 H3
Hatherden..................21 H7
Hatherleigh.................9 F5
Hathern....................43 H4
Hatherop...................20 F2
Hathersage.................52 E5
Hatherton, Staffs..........42 B5
Hatherton, Ches............41 H2
Hatley St George...........35 F4
Hatt........................4 D3
Hattingley.................13 J2
Hatton, Warw...............32 E3
Hatton, Derby..............42 E3
Hatton, Ches...............50 E5
Hatton, G. Lon.............23 F5
Hatton, Lincs..............55 F6
Hatton, Shrops.............41 F7
Hatton, Grampn.............97 K2
Hattoncrook................97 H3
Hatton Heath...............50 D7
Hatton of Fintray..........97 H5
Haugham....................55 H5
Haugh Head.................75 G2
Haughley...................36 F3
Haughley Green.............36 F3
Haugh of Glass.............96 D2
Haugh of Urr...............72 D8
Haughton, Staffs...........42 A4
Haughton, Shrops...........40 E4
Haughton, Shrops...........41 G5
Haughton, Shrops...........41 H7
Haughton, Notts............53 J6
Haughton Green.............51 J4
Haughton Moss..............41 G1
Haunton....................42 E5
Hauxley....................75 J4
Hauxton....................35 H4
Havant.....................13 K5
Haven......................30 F4
Havenstreet................13 H6
Haverfordwest..............26 D5
Haverhill..................36 B5
Haverigg...................56 E3
Havering-atte-Bower........23 L3
Haversham..................34 B5
Haverthwaite...............57 G2
Hawarden...................50 C7

Hawes......................58 D2
Hawford....................31 K3
Hawick.....................74 B3
Hawkchurch................10 E5
Hawkedon...................36 C4
Hawkeridge.................20 C7
Hawkerland.................10 B7
Hawkesbury.................20 B4
Hawkesbury Upton...........20 B4
Hawkes End.................32 E1
Hawkhill...................75 J3
Hawkhurst..................16 E2
Hawkinge...................17 K1
Hawkley....................13 K3
Hawkridge...................9 J2
Hawkshead..................63 J8
Hawksland..................80 D8
Hawkswick.................58 E3
Hawksworth, Notts..........44 A2
Hawksworth, W. Yks.........59 G6
Hawkwell...................24 E3
Hawley, Hants..............22 D7
Hawley, Kent...............23 L5
Hawling....................32 C7
Hawnby.....................60 C2
Haworth....................58 F7
Hawsker....................67 K7
Hawstead...................36 D4
Hawthorn...................66 E3
Hawthorn Hill..............22 D5
Hawton.....................44 A1
Haxby......................60 D5
Haxey......................54 B4
Haydock....................50 E4
Haydon.....................11 H4
Haydon Bridge..............65 F1
Haydon Wick................21 F4
Haye........................4 D3
Hayes, G. Lon..............23 F4
Hayes, G. Lon..............23 K6
Hayfield...................52 C5
Hayle.......................2 D6
Haynes.....................34 D5
Haynes Church End..........34 D5
Hay-on-Wye.................30 D5
Hayscastle.................26 C4
Hayscastle Cross...........26 D4
Hayton, Notts..............54 B5
Hayton, Cumbr..............64 C2
Hayton, Humbs..............60 F6
Hayton, Cumbr..............63 G3
Hayton's Bent..............31 G1
Haytor Vale.................5 H2
Haywards Heath.............15 G3
Haywood Oaks...............43 J1
Hazelbank..................80 D7
Hazelbury Bryan............11 J5
Hazeley....................22 C7
Hazel Grove................51 J5
Hazelrigg..................75 G1
Hazelslade.................42 C5
Hazelwood..................43 F2
Hazlemere..................22 D3
Hazlerigg..................75 J7
Hazleton...................20 E1
Heacham....................46 B3
Headbourne Worthy..........13 G2
Headcorn...................16 F1
Headingley.................59 H7
Headington.................21 K2
Headlam....................66 B6
Headless Cross.............32 C3
Headley, Hants.............14 B2
Headley, Surrey............23 H7
Headley, Hants.............21 K6
Head of Muir...............80 D3
Headon.....................54 B6
Heads Nook.................64 B2
Heage......................43 F1
Healaugh, N. Yks...........60 C6
Healaugh, N. Yks...........65 H8
Heald Green................51 H5
Healey, N. Yks.............59 G2
Healey, Lancs..............51 H2
Healey, Northum............65 H2
Healeyfield................65 H3
Healing....................55 G2
Heamoor.....................2 C6
Heanish....................84 B4
Heanor.....................43 G2
Heanton Punchardon..........8 F2
Heapham....................54 C5
Hearthstane................73 G2
Heasley Mill................9 H2
Heast......................92 C4
Heath, S. Glam.............19 F5
Heath, Derby...............53 G7
Heath and Reach............34 C7
Heathcote..................52 D7
Heath End, Hants...........14 B1
Heath End, Hants...........21 K6
Heathfield, E. Susx........16 C3
Heathfield, Somer..........10 C3
Heathfield, Strath.........78 F5
Heathfield, Devon...........5 J2
Heath Hayes................41 J5
Heath Hill.................41 J5
Heath House................11 F1
Heath, The.................47 G4
Heathton...................41 K7
Heatley....................51 G5
Heaton, Lancs..............57 H4
Heaton, Staffs.............51 J7
Heaton, T. & W.............75 J8
Heaton Moor...............51 H4
Heaverham..................24 B7
Heaviley...................51 J5
Hebburn....................66 D1
Hebden.....................58 F4
Hebden Bridge..............51 J1
Hebden Green...............51 F7
Hebron.....................22 C6
Heckfield..................22 C6
Heckington.................44 E2

Heckmondwike...............52 E1
Heddington.................20 D6
Heddle....................112 D5
Heddon-on-the-Wall.........75 H8
Hedenham...................47 J7
Hedge End..................13 G4
Hedgerley..................22 E4
Hedging....................10 E3
Hedley on the Hill.........65 H2
Hednesford................42 C5
Hedon......................61 J8
Hedsor.....................22 E4
Hegdon Hill................31 G4
Heggerscales...............65 F6
Heglibister...............115 F3
Heighington, Durham........66 C5
Heighington, Lincs.........54 E7
Heights of Brae...........102 D6
Heights of Kinlochewe.....101 G6
Heiton.....................74 D1
Helbeck....................64 E6
Hele, Devon................10 A5
Hele, Devon.................9 F1
Helensburgh................78 E3
Helford.....................2 F7
Helhoughton................46 D4
Helions Bumpstead..........36 B5
Helland.....................3 J2
Hellesdon..................47 H5
Hellidon...................33 H4
Hellifield.................58 D5
Hellingly..................16 C4
Hellington.................47 J6
Hellister.................115 F4
Helmdon....................33 H5
Helmingham................37 G4
Helmsdale.................111 G7
Helmshore..................51 G1
Helmsley...................60 D2
Helperby...................59 K4
Helperthorpe...............61 G3
Helpringham................44 E2
Helpston...................44 E6
Helsby.....................50 D6
Helston.....................2 E7
Helstone....................3 J1
Helton.....................64 C5
Helwith Bridge.............58 D4
Hemblington...............47 J5
Hemel Hempstead............22 F2
Hemingbrough...............60 D7
Hemingby...................55 G6
Hemingford Abbots..........35 F2
Hemingford Grey............35 F2
Hemingstone...............37 G4
Hemington, Somer...........20 B7
Hemington, Northnts........34 D1
Hemley.....................37 H5
Hempholme..................61 H6
Hemphall...................47 H7
Hempnall Green.............47 H7
Hemppriggs................103 K5
Hempstead, Essex...........36 B6
Hempstead, Norf............47 G3
Hempstead, Norf............47 K4
Hempsted...................20 C1
Hempton, Norf..............46 E4
Hempton, Oxon..............33 G6
Hemsby.....................47 K5
Hemswell...................54 D4
Hemswell Cliff.............54 D5
Hemsworth..................53 G2
Hemyock....................10 C4
Henbury, Ches..............51 H6
Henbury, Avon..............19 K5
Hendon, T. & W.............66 E2
Hendon, G. Lon.............23 H4
Hendre.....................50 A7
Hendy......................27 K6
Heneglwys..................48 D3
Henfield...................15 F4
Hengoed, Shrops............40 D3
Hengoed, Powys.............30 D4
Hengoed, M. Glam...........18 F3
Hengrave..................36 D3
Henham.....................35 J7
Henley, W. Susx............14 B3
Henley, Somer..............11 F2
Henley, Shrops.............31 G2
Henley, Suff...............37 G4
Henley-in-Arden............32 D3
Henley-on-Thames...........22 C4
Henley Park................22 F7
Henllan, Dyfed.............27 H2
Henllan, Clwyd.............49 K4
Henllan Amgoed.............26 F4
Henllys....................19 G3
Henlow.....................34 E6
Hennock.....................5 J1
Henryd.....................49 G3
Henry's Moat...............26 E4
Hensall....................53 H1
Henshaw....................64 E1
Henstead...................37 K1
Henstridge.................11 J4
Henstridge Marsh...........11 J3
Henton, Oxon...............22 C2
Henton, Somer..............19 J7
Henwood.....................4 C2
Heogan....................115 G4
Heol Senni.................29 G2
Heol-y-Cyw.................18 D4
Hepburn....................75 G2
Hepple.....................75 F4
Hepscott...................75 J5
Heptonstall................58 E8
Hepworth, W. Yks...........52 D3
Hepworth, Suff.............36 E2
Herbrandston...............26 C6
Hereford...................31 G5
Hergest....................30 D4
Heriot.....................81 J6
Hermiston..................81 G4
Hermitage, W. Susx.........14 A5
Hermitage, Border..........74 B5

176 Hermitage, Dorset Huttons Ambo

Hermitage, Dorset 11 H5
Hermitage, Berks 21 K5
Hermitage, The 23 H7
Hermon, Gwyn 48 C4
Hermon, Dyfed 27 G3
Hermon, Dyfed 27 H3
Herne 25 H6
Herne Bay 25 H6
Herner 9 F3
Hernhill 25 G6
Herodsfoot 4 C3
Herongate 24 C3
Heronsgate 22 F3
Herriard 13 J1
Herringfleet 47 K7
Herringswell 36 C3
Herrington 66 D2
Hersden 25 J6
Hersham 23 G6
Herstmonceux 16 D4
Herston 112 E7
Hertford 23 J1
Hertford Heath 23 J1
Hertingfordbury 23 J1
Hesketh Bank 50 D1
Hesketh Lane 57 K6
Hesket Newmarket 63 J4
Heskin Green 50 E2
Hesleden 66 E4
Heslington 60 D5
Hessay 60 C5
Hessenford 4 D4
Hessett 36 E3
Hessle 54 E1
Hest Bank 57 H4
Heston 23 G5
Heswall 50 B5
Hethe 33 H7
Hethersett 47 G6
Hethersgill 74 A8
Hethpool 74 E2
Hett 66 C4
Hetton 58 E5
Hetton-le-Hole 66 D3
Heugh 75 G7
Heugh-head 96 C4
Heveningham 37 J2
Hever 15 H1
Heversham 57 H2
Hevingham 47 G4
Hewelsfield 19 K2
Hewish, Somer 11 F5
Hewish, Avon 19 J6
Hexham 65 G1
Hextable 23 L5
Hexton 34 E6
Hexworthy 5 G2
Heybridge, Essex 24 C3
Heybridge, Essex 24 E2
Heybridge Basin 24 E2
Heybrook Bay 4 E5
Heydon, Norf 47 G4
Heydon, Cambs 35 H5
Heydour 44 D3
Heylipol 84 A4
Heylor 116 D4
Heysham 57 H4
Heyshott 14 B4
Heytesbury 12 B1
Heythrop 33 F7
Heywood, Wilts 20 C7
Heywood, G. Man 51 H2
Hibaldstow 54 D3
Hickleton 53 G3
Hickling, Notts 43 J4
Hickling, Norf 47 K4
Hickling Green 47 K4
Hickling Heath 47 K4
Hidcote Boyce 32 D5
High Ackworth 53 G2
Higham, Suff 36 C3
Higham, Kent 24 D5
Higham, Lancs 58 D7
Higham, Suff 36 F6
Higham, Derby 53 F8
Higham Dykes 75 H7
Higham Ferrers 34 C3
Higham Gobion 34 E6
Higham on the Hill 43 F7
Highampton 8 E5
High Wood 16 D1
High Beach 23 K3
High Bentham 58 B4
High Bickington 9 G3
High Birkwith 58 D3
High Blantyre 80 B6
High Bonnybridge 80 D4
High Borve 107 J3
High Bradfield 52 E4
Highbridge, Somer 10 E1
Highbridge, Highld 93 H7
Highbrook 15 G2
Highburton 52 D2
Highbury 11 H1
High Buston 75 J4
High Callerton 75 H7
High Catton 60 E5
Highclere 21 J6
Highcliffe 12 E6
High Cogges 21 H2
High Coniscliffe 66 C6
High Cross, Herts 23 J1
High Cross, Hants 13 K3
High Dougarie 77 H8
High Easter 24 C1
High Ellington 59 G2
Higher Ashton 9 J7
Higher Ballam 57 G7
Higher Ercall 41 G5
Higher End 50 E3
Higher Penwortham 57 J8
Higher Poynton 51 J5
Higher Tale 10 B5
Higher Town 2 P2
Higher Walreddon 4 E2
Higher Walton, Lancs 50 E1
Higher Walton, Ches 50 E5
Higher Wych 41 F2
Highfield, Strath 78 F6
Highfield, T. & W 65 J2
Highfields 35 G4
High Garrett 36 C7
High Grange 66 B4
High Green, H. & W 32 A5
High Green, S. Yks 53 F4
High Green, Norf 47 G6
High Halden 17 F2
High Halstow 24 D5
High Ham 11 F2
High Hatton 41 H4
High Hesket 64 B3
High Hoyland 52 E2
High Hunsley 61 G7
High Hurstwood 15 H3
High Lane, H. & W 31 H3
High Lane, G. Man 51 J5
High Laver 23 L2
Highleadon 31 J7
High Legh 51 G5
Highleigh 14 B6
Highley 31 J1
High Littleton 19 L7
High Melton 53 H3
Highmoor Cross 22 C4
Highmoor Hill 19 J4
Highnam 20 B1
High Newton 57 H2
High Newton-by-the-Sea 75 J2
High Offley 41 J4
High Ongar 24 B2
High Onn 41 K5
High Roding 24 C1
High Salvington 14 E5
High Shaw 58 D1
High Spen 65 J2
Highsted 24 F6
High Street, Corn 3 H4
High Street, Suff 37 K4
High Street Green 36 F4
Hightae 73 F7
Hightown, Mers 50 C3
Hightown, Ches 51 H7
High Toynton 55 G7
High Trewhill 75 G4
Highway, Wilts 20 E5
Highway, Corn 3 K4
Highworth 21 G3
High Wray 63 J8
High Wych 23 K1
High Wycombe 22 D3
Hilborough 46 D6
Hildenborough 16 C1
Hildersham 35 J5
Hilderstone 42 B3
Hilderthorpe 61 J4
Hilgay 45 K7
Hill 19 L3
Hillam 60 C8
Hillberry 56 Q4
Hillbrae, Grampn 104 F4
Hillbrae, Grampn 97 G3
Hill Brow 14 A3
Hilldyke 45 G2
Hill End, Fife 81 F2
Hillend, Fife 81 G3
Hill End, Durham 65 H4
Hillerton 9 H6
Hillesden 33 J7
Hillesley 20 B4
Hillfarrance 10 C3
Hill Head, Hants 13 H5
Hillhead, Strath 71 K3
Hillhead, Devon 5 K4
Hillhead of Auchentumb 105 J3
Hillhead of Cocklaw 105 K4
Hilliard's Cross 42 D5
Hilliclay 111 H2
Hillingdon 22 F4
Hillington 46 C4
Hillmorton 33 H2
Hill Mountain 26 D6
Hillockhead 96 C5
Hill of Beath 81 G2
Hill of Fearn 103 G5
Hill Ridware 42 C5
Hillside, Shetld 115 G2
Hillside, Grampn 97 J6
Hillside, Tays 89 K2
Hillswick 116 D5
Hill, The 56 E2
Hilmarton 20 E5
Hilperton 20 C7
Hilsea 13 J5
Hilton, Durham 66 B5
Hilton, Derby 42 E3
Hilton, Cumbr 64 E5
Hilton, Cleve 66 E6
Hilton, Cambs 35 F3
Hilton, Grampn 97 J2
Hilton, Dorset 11 J5
Hilton, Shrops 41 J7
Hilton of Cadboll 103 G5
Himbleton 32 B4
Himley 42 A7
Hincaster 57 J2
Hinckley 43 G7
Hinderclay 36 F2
Hinderwell 67 H6
Hindford 40 E3
Hindhead 14 B2
Hindley 51 F3
Hindley Green 51 F3
Hindlip 32 A4
Hindolveston 46 F4
Hindon 12 B2
Hindringham 46 E3
Hingham 46 F6
Hinkley Point Power Station 10 D1
Hinstock 41 H4
Hintlesham 37 F5
Hinton, Avon 20 B5
Hinton, Hants 12 E6
Hinton, Shrops 41 F6
Hinton, Northnts 33 H4
Hinton Ampner 13 H3
Hinton Blewett 19 K7
Hinton Charterhouse 20 B7
Hinton-in-the-Hedges 33 H6
Hinton Martell 12 C5
Hinton on the Green 32 C5
Hinton Parva 21 G4
Hinton St George 11 F4
Hinton St Mary 11 J4
Hinton Waldrist 21 H3
Hints, Staffs 42 D6
Hints, Shrops 31 H2
Hinwick 34 C3
Hinxhill 17 H1
Hinxton 35 H5
Hinxworth 35 F5
Hipperholme 52 D1
Hirn 97 G5
Hirnant 40 B4
Hirst 75 J6
Hirst Courtney 53 J1
Hirwaun 18 D2
Hiscott 9 F3
Histon 35 H3
Hitcham 36 E4
Hitchin 34 E7
Hither Green 23 J5
Hittisleigh 9 H6
Hixon 42 C4
Hoaden 25 J7
Hoaldalbert 30 E7
Hoar Cross 42 D4
Hoarwithy 31 G7
Hoath 25 J6
Hobarris 30 E2
Hobbister 112 D6
Hobkirk 74 B3
Hobson 66 B2
Hoby 43 J5
Hockering 46 F5
Hockerton 43 K1
Hockley 24 E3
Hockley Heath 32 D2
Hockliffe 34 C7
Hockwold cum Wilton 36 C1
Hockworthy 10 B4
Hoddesdon 23 J2
Hoddlesden 51 G1
Hodgeston 26 E7
Hodnet 41 H4
Hodthorpe 53 H6
Hoe 46 E5
Hoe Gate 13 J4
Hoff 64 D6
Hoggeston 34 B7
Hoghton 50 F1
Hognaston 42 E1
Hogsthorpe 55 K6
Holbeach 45 G4
Holbeach Bank 45 G4
Holbeach Drove 45 G5
Holbeach Hurn 45 G4
Holbeach St Johns 45 G5
Holbeach St Marks 45 G3
Holbeach St Matthew 45 H3
Holbeck 53 H6
Holberrow Green 32 C4
Holbeton 5 G4
Holborn 23 J4
Holbrook, Derby 43 F2
Holbrook, Suff 37 G6
Holburn 83 J8
Holbury 13 G5
Holcombe, Somer 11 H1
Holcombe, Devon 5 K2
Holcombe Rogus 10 B4
Holcot 34 A3
Holden 58 C6
Holdenby 33 J3
Holdgate 41 G8
Holdingham 44 D2
Hole in the Wall 31 H7
Holemoor 8 E5
Holford 10 C1
Holker 57 G3
Holkham 46 D2
Hollacombe, Devon 8 D5
Hollacombe, Devon 9 G4
Holland-on-Sea 25 J1
Hollandstoun 113 H1
Hollesley 37 J5
Hollinfare 51 F4
Hollingbourne 24 E7
Hollington, Staffs 42 C3
Hollington, Derby 42 E3
Hollington, E. Susx 16 E4
Hollingworth 52 C4
Hollins 51 H3
Hollinsclough 52 C7
Hollinwood 41 G3
Holloway 43 F1
Hollowell 33 J2
Holl's Green 35 F7
Hollybush, Gwent 18 F2
Hollybush, Strath 71 J3
Hollybush, H. & W 31 J6
Holly End 45 H6
Hollym 55 H1
Hollywood 32 C2
Holm 107 J5
Holmbury St Mary 14 E1
Holme, Notts 54 C8
Holme, W. Yks 52 D3
Holme, Cambs 35 E1
Holme, Cumbr 57 J3
Holme Chapel 58 D8
Holme Hale 46 D6
Holme Lacy 31 G6
Holme Marsh 30 E4
Holme next the Sea 46 C2
Holme-on-Spalding-Moor 60 F7
Holme on the Wolds 61 G6
Holmer 31 G5
Holmer Green 22 E3
Holmes Chapel 51 G7
Holmesfield 53 F6
Holmeswood 50 D2
Holmewood 53 G7
Holmfirth 52 D3
Holmhead 72 A2
Holmpton 55 H1
Holmrook 62 F8
Holmsgarth 115 G4
Holne 5 H3
Holnest 11 H5
Holsworthy 8 D5
Holsworthy Beacon 8 D5
Holt, Dorset 12 C5
Holt, Wilts 20 C6
Holt, Clwyd 41 F1
Holt, Norf 46 F3
Holt, H. & W 31 K3
Holtby 60 D5
Holt End 32 C3
Holt Heath 31 K3
Holton, Somer 11 H3
Holton, Suff 37 K2
Holton, Oxon 21 L2
Holton cum Beckering 54 F5
Holton le Clay 55 G3
Holton le Moor 54 E4
Holton St Mary 36 F6
Holwell, Herts 34 E6
Holwell, Oxon 21 G2
Holwell, Dorset 11 J4
Holwell, Leic 43 K4
Holwick 65 G5
Holworth 11 J7
Holybourne 13 K1
Holy Cross 32 B2
Holyhead 48 B2
Holy Island 83 K7
Holymoorside 53 F7
Holyport 22 D5
Holystone 75 F4
Holytown 80 C5
Holywell, Clwyd 50 A6
Holywell, Corn 2 F4
Holywell, Cambs 35 G2
Holywell, Dorset 11 G5
Holywell Green 52 C2
Holywell Lake 10 C3
Holywell Row 36 C2
Holywood 72 E6
Homer 41 H6
Homersfield 37 H1
Hom Green 31 G7
Homington 12 D3
Honeybourne 32 D5
Honeychurch 9 G5
Honey Hill 25 H6
Honiley 32 E2
Honing 47 J4
Honingham 47 G5
Honington, Lincs 44 C2
Honington, Suff 36 E2
Honington, Warw 32 E5
Honiton 10 C5
Honley 52 D2
Hoo 37 H4
Hooe, E. Susx 16 D5
Hooe, Devon 4 F4
Hook, Humbs 54 B1
Hook, Hants 22 C7
Hook, Dyfed 26 D5
Hook, Wilts 20 E4
Hook, G. Lon 23 G6
Hooke 11 G5
Hookgate 41 J3
Hook Norton 33 F6
Hookway 9 J6
Hookwood 15 F1
Hoole 50 D7
Hoo St Werburgh 24 D5
Hooton Levitt 53 H4
Hooton Pagnell 53 G3
Hooton Roberts 53 G4
Hope, Clwyd 50 C8
Hope, Derby 52 D5
Hope, Powys 40 D6
Hope, Shrops 40 E6
Hope, Devon 5 G5
Hope Bagot 31 G2
Hope Bowdler 41 F7
Hopeman 103 K6
Hope Mansell 19 L1
Hopesay 30 E1
Hope under Dinmore 31 G4
Hopton, Staffs 42 B4
Hopton, Suff 36 E2
Hopton Cangeford 31 G1
Hopton Castle 30 E2
Hopton on Sea 47 L6
Hopton Wafers 31 H2
Hopwas 42 D6
Hopwood 32 C2
Horam 16 C4
Horbling 44 E3
Horbury 52 E2
Horden 66 E3
Horderley 31 F1
Hordle 12 E6
Hordley 40 E3
Horeb, Dyfed 27 H2
Horeb, Dyfed 27 K4
Horham 37 H2
Horkstow 54 D2
Horley, Surrey 15 F1
Horley, Oxon 33 G5
Hornblotton Green 11 G2
Hornby, N. Yks 66 D7
Hornby, Lancs 57 J4
Horncastle 55 G7
Hornchurch 23 L4
Horncliffe 83 H7
Horndean 13 K4
Horndon on the Hill 24 C4
Horne 15 G1
Horn Hill 22 F3
Horning 47 J5
Horninghold 44 B7
Horninglow 42 E4
Horningsea 35 H3
Horningsham 11 K1
Horningtoft 46 E4
Hornish Point 98 C8
Hornsby 64 C2
Hornsea 61 K6
Hornsey 23 J4
Hornton 33 F5
Horrabridge 4 F3
Horringer 36 D3
Horse Bridge, Staffs 42 B1
Horsebridge, E. Susx 16 C4
Horsebridge, Hants 13 F2
Horsebrook 42 A5
Horsehay 41 H6
Horseheath 35 K5
Horsehouse 58 F2
Horsell 22 E7
Horseman's Green 41 F2
Horseway 35 H1
Horsey 47 K4
Horsford 47 G5
Horsforth 59 H7
Horsham, W. Susx 14 E2
Horsham, H. & W 31 J4
Horsham St Faith 47 H5
Horsington, Lincs 55 F7
Horsington, Somer 11 J3
Horsley, Glos 20 C3
Horsley, Northum 74 E5
Horsley, Derby 43 F2
Horsley, Northum 75 G8
Horsley Cross 37 G7
Horsleycross Street 37 G7
Horsleyhill 74 B3
Horsley Woodhouse 43 F2
Horsmonden 16 E1
Horspath 21 K2
Horstead 47 H5
Horsted Keynes 15 G3
Horton, Staffs 42 B1
Horton, Northnts 34 B4
Horton, Avon 20 B4
Horton, Dorset 12 C5
Horton, Lancs 58 D5
Horton, Bucks 22 E1
Horton, Somer 10 E4
Horton, Wilts 20 E6
Horton, Berks 22 F5
Horton, Northum 75 G1
Horton, W. Glam 27 J8
Horton-cum-Studley 21 K1
Horton Green 41 F2
Horton Heath 13 G4
Horton in Ribblesdale 58 D3
Horton Kirby 24 B6
Horwich 51 F2
Horwood 8 F3
Hose 43 K4
Hosh 88 A6
Hostingfield 35 H4
Hoswick 115 G6
Hotham 61 F7
Hothfield 17 G1
Hoton 43 H4
Hough 41 J1
Hougham 44 B2
Hougharry 98 C5
Hough Green 50 D5
Hough-on-the-Hill 44 C2
Houghton, W. Susx 14 D4
Houghton, Dyfed 26 D6
Houghton, Cambs 35 F2
Houghton, Hants 13 F2
Houghton, Cumbr 63 K2
Houghton Conquest 34 D5
Houghton-le-Spring 66 D3
Houghton on the Hill 43 J6
Houghton Regis 34 D7
Houghton St Giles 46 E3
Houlskye 67 H7
Hound Green 22 C7
Houndslow 82 E7
Houndwood 83 G5
Hounslow 23 G5
Housetter 116 E4
Houston 79 G5
Houstry 111 H5
Hove 15 F5
Hoveringham 43 J2
Hoveton 47 J5
Hovingham 60 D3
How 64 C2
How Caple 31 H6
Howden 60 E8
Howden-le-Wear 65 J4
Howe, Norf 47 H7
Howe, Highld 111 K2
Howe Green 24 D2
Howell 44 E2
Howe of Teuchar 105 G4
Howe Street, Essex 36 B6
Howe Street, Essex 24 C1
Howe, The, Cumbr 57 H2
Howe, The, I. of M 56 N5
Howey 29 H4
Howgate, Border 74 D2
Howgate, Lothn 81 H6
Howick 75 J3
Howle 41 H4
Howlett End 35 J6
Howmore 90 C2
Hownam 74 D3
Howsham, Humbs 54 E3
Howsham, N. Yks 60 E4
Howton 31 F7
Howtown 64 B6
Howwood 79 F5
Hoxa 112 E7
Hoxne 37 G2
Hoylake 50 B5
Hoyland 53 F3
Hoyland Swaine 52 E3
Hubberholme 58 E3
Hubbert's Bridge 45 F2
Huby, N. Yks 60 C4
Huby, N. Yks 59 H6
Hucclecote 20 C1
Hucking 24 E7
Hucknall 43 H2
Huddersfield 52 D2
Huddington 32 B4
Hudswell 65 J7
Huggate 61 F5
Hughenden Valley 22 D3
Hughley 41 G7
Hugh Town 2 P2
Huish, Devon 9 F4
Huish, Wilts 21 F6
Huish Champflower 10 B3
Huish Episcopi 11 F3
Hulcott 22 D1
Hulland 42 E2
Hulland Ward 42 E2
Hullavington 20 C4
Hullbridge 24 E3
Hulme End 52 D8
Hulme Walfield 51 H7
Hulver Street 37 K1
Humber Bridge 54 E1
Humber Court 31 G4
Humberston 55 H3
Humbie 82 C5
Humbleton, Northum 75 F2
Humbleton, Humbs 61 K7
Hume 82 F7
Humshaugh 74 F7
Huna 111 K1
Huncoat 58 C7
Huncote 43 H7
Hundalee 74 C3
Hunderthwaite 65 G5
Hundleby 55 H7
Hundleton 26 D6
Hundon 36 C5
Hundred Acres 13 H4
Hundred End 50 D1
Hundred House 30 C4
Hundred, The 31 G3
Hungarton 43 J6
Hungerford 21 H6
Hungerford Newtown 21 H5
Hunmanby 61 H3
Hunningham 33 F3
Hunsdon 23 K1
Hunsingore 59 K5
Hunsonby 64 C4
Hunspow 111 J1
Hunstanton 46 B2
Hunstanworth 65 G3
Hunston, W. Susx 14 B5
Hunston, Suff 36 E3
Hunstrete 19 L6
Hunt End 32 C3
Hunter's Quay 78 D4
Huntingdon 35 F2
Huntingfield 37 J2
Huntington, Staffs 42 B5
Huntington, Lothn 82 C4
Huntington, H. & W 30 D4
Huntington, N. Yks 60 D5
Huntingtower 88 C6
Huntley 20 B1
Huntly 96 E1
Hunton, Kent 16 E1
Hunton, N. Yks 59 G1
Hunt's Cross 50 D5
Huntsham 10 B3
Huntspill 10 E1
Huntworth 10 E2
Hunwick 66 B4
Hunworth 46 F3
Hurdsfield 51 J6
Hurley, Berks 22 D4
Hurley, Warw 42 E7
Hurlford 79 G8
Hurliness 112 C8
Hurn 12 D6
Hursley 13 G3
Hurst, Berks 22 C5
Hurst, N. Yks 65 H7
Hurst, G. Man 51 J3
Hurstbourne Priors 13 G1
Hurstbourne Tarrant 21 H7
Hurst Green, Lancs 58 B7
Hurst Green, E. Susx 16 E3
Hurst Green, Surrey 23 J7
Hurstpierpoint 15 F4
Hurworth-on-Tees 66 D6
Hury 65 G6
Husbands Bosworth 33 J1
Husborne Crawley 34 C6
Hushinish 106 D7
Husthwaite 60 C3
Hutcherleigh 5 H4
Huthwaite 53 G8
Huttoft 55 K6
Hutton, Cumbr 64 B5
Hutton, Essex 24 C3
Hutton, Lancs 50 D1
Hutton, Border 83 H6
Hutton, Avon 19 H7
Hutton Bonville 66 D7
Hutton Buscel 61 G2
Hutton Conyers 59 J3
Hutton Cranswick 61 H5
Hutton End 64 B4
Hutton Henry 66 E4
Hutton-le-Hole 60 E1
Hutton Magna 65 J6
Hutton Roof, Cumbr 57 J3
Hutton Roof, Cumbr 63 J4
Hutton Rudby 66 E7
Huttons Ambo 60 E4

Hutton Sessay
Kinnerton, Powys
177

Hutton Sessay 60 B3
Hutton Wandesley 60 C5
Huxley 50 E7
Huyton-with-Roby 50 D4
Hycemoor 56 D2
Hyde, Glos 20 C2
Hyde, Hants 12 D4
Hyde, G. Man 51 J4
Hyde Heath 22 E2
Hydestile 14 C1
Hynish 84 A5
Hyssington 40 E7
Hythe, Hants 13 G5
Hythe, Kent 17 J2
Hythe End 22 F5
Hythie 105 K3

I

Ibberton 11 J5
Ible 42 E1
Ibsley 12 D5
Ibstock 43 G5
Ibstone 22 C3
Ibthorpe 21 H7
Ibworth 21 K7
Ickburgh 46 D7
Ickenham 22 F4
Ickford 22 B2
Ickham 25 J7
Ickleford 34 E6
Icklesham 16 F4
Ickleton 35 H5
Icklingham 36 C2
Ickwell Green 34 E5
Icomb 32 E7
Idbury 32 E7
Iddesleigh 9 F5
Ide 9 J6
Ideford 5 J2
Ide Hill 23 K7
Iden 17 G3
Iden Green 16 F2
Idlicote 32 E5
Idmiston 12 E2
Idridgehay 42 E2
Idrigill 99 J6
Idstone 21 G4
Ifield 15 F2
Ifold 14 D2
Iford 15 H5
Ifton Heath 40 E3
Ightfield 41 G3
Ightham 24 B7
Iken 37 K4
Ilam 42 D1
Ilchester 11 G3
Ilderton 75 G2
Ilford 23 K4
Ilfracombe 8 F1
Ilkeston 43 G2
Ilketshall St Andrew 37 J1
Ilketshall St Lawrence 37 J1
Ilketshall St Margaret 37 J1
Ilkley 59 G6
Illey 32 B1
Illingworth 59 F8
Illogan 2 E5
Illston on the Hill 43 K7
Ilmer 22 C2
Ilmington 32 E5
Ilminster 10 E4
Ilsington 5 H2
Ilston 27 K7
Ilton, Somer 10 E4
Ilton, N. Yks 59 G3
Immingham 55 F2
Impington 35 H3
Ince 50 D6
Ince Blundell 50 C3
Ince-in-Makerfield 50 E3
Inchbare 89 J2
Inchberry 104 C3
Incheril 101 G6
Inchina 101 F3
Inchinnan 79 G5
Inchlaggan 93 H5
Inchmore 94 B1
Inchnadamph 108 D6
Inchture 88 E6
Indian Queens 3 H4
Ingatestone 24 C3
Ingbirchworth 52 E3
Ingestre 42 B4
Ingham, Suff 36 D2
Ingham, Lincs 54 D5
Ingham, Norf 47 J4
Ingleby Arncliffe 66 E7
Ingleby Greenhow 67 F7
Inglesbatch 20 B6
Inglesham 21 G3
Ingleton, N. Yks 58 B3
Ingleton, Durham 66 B5
Inglewhite 57 J6
Ingliston 81 G4
Ingoe 75 G7
Ingoldisthorpe 46 B3
Ingoldmells 55 K7
Ingoldsby 44 D3
Ingram 75 G3
Ingrave 24 C3
Ings 64 B8
Ingst 19 K4
Ingworth 47 G4
Inkberrow 32 C4
Inkhorn 97 J2
Inkpen 21 H6
Inkstack 111 J1
Innellan 78 D4
Innerleithen 81 J8
Innerleven 81 J1
Innermessan 68 B4
Innerwick, Lothn 82 F4
Innerwick, Tays 87 H4
Innsworth 32 A7
Insch 97 F3
Insh 95 G5
Inskip 57 H7
Instow 8 E2
Inver, Grampn 96 B6
Inver, Highld 103 G4
Inverailort 92 D7
Inveralligin 100 E7
Inverallochy 105 K2
Inveramsay 97 G3
Inveran 102 D3
Inveraray 86 C8
Inverarish 92 B2
Inverarity 89 G4
Inverarnan 86 F7
Inverasdale 100 E4
Inverbervie 89 L1
Inverbrough 95 G2
Inverchoran 101 J7
Invercreran 86 C4
Inverdruie 95 H4
Inverebrie 97 J2
Inveresk 81 J4
Inverey 95 J7
Inverfarigaig 94 D3
Invergarry 93 K5
Invergordon 102 F6
Invergowrie 89 F5
Inverguseran 92 D5
Inverharroch 96 C2
Inverie 92 D6
Inverinate 93 F3
Inverkeilor 89 J4
Inverkeithing 81 G3
Inverkeithny 104 F4
Inverkip 78 E4
Inverkirkaig 108 B7
Invermoidart 92 C8
Invermoriston 94 C4
Invernaver 110 D2
Inverness 102 E8
Inverquhomery 105 K4
Inverroy 93 J7
Invershin 102 D3
Inverugie 105 L4
Inveruglas 86 F8
Inverurie 97 G3
Invervar 87 J4
Inwardleigh 9 F6
Inworth 24 E1
Iping 14 B3
Ipplepen 5 J3
Ipsden 22 B4
Ipstones 42 C1
Ipswich 37 G5
Irby 50 B5
Irby in the Marsh 55 J7
Irby upon Humber 55 F3
Irchester 34 C3
Ireby, Lancs 58 B3
Ireby, Cumbr 63 H4
Ireland, Orkney 112 D6
Ireland, Shetld 115 F6
Ireleth 57 F3
Ireshopeburn 65 F4
Irlam 51 G4
Irnham 44 D4
Iron Acton 20 A4
Ironbridge 41 H6
Iron Cross 32 C4
Ironmacannie 72 B7
Ironside 105 H3
Ironville 43 G1
Irstead 47 J4
Irthington 64 B1
Irthlingborough 34 C2
Irton 61 H2
Irvine 78 F8
Isauld 110 F2
Isbister, Orkney 112 C4
Isbister, Orkney 112 D5
Isbister, Shetld 115 H2
Isfield 15 H4
Isham 34 B2
Isle Abbotts 10 E3
Isle Brewers 10 E3
Isleham 36 B2
Isle of Whithorn 69 F7
Isleornsay or Eilean Iarmain 92 C4
Islesburgh 113 C3
Isleworth 23 G5
Isley Walton 43 G4
Islington 23 J4
Islip, Northnts 34 C2
Islip, Oxon 21 K1
Islivig 106 D5
Istead Rise 24 C6
Isycoed 40 F1
Itchen Abbas 13 H2
Itchen Stoke 13 H2
Itchingfield 14 E3
Itchington 20 A4
Itteringham 47 G3
Itton 9 G6
Itton Common 19 J3
Ivegill 63 K3
Ivelet 65 G8
Iver 22 F4
Iver Heath 22 F4
Iveston 65 J2
Ivinghoe 22 E1
Ivinghoe Aston 22 E1
Ivington 31 F4
Ivington Green 31 F4
Ivybridge 5 G4
Ivychurch 17 H3
Ivy Hatch 24 B7
Iwade 24 E6
Iwerne Courtney or Shroton 11 K4
Iwerne Minster 12 A4
Ixworth 36 E2
Ixworth Thorpe 36 E2

J

Jack Hill 59 H5
Jackstown 97 G2
Jackton 79 H6
Jacobstow 8 B6
Jacobstowe 9 F5
Jameston 26 E7
Jamestown, Highld 102 C7
Jamestown, Strath 79 F3
Jamestown, D. & G. 73 H5
Jarrow 66 D1
Jawcraig 80 D4
Jayes Park 14 E1
Jaywick 25 H1
Jedburgh 74 C2
Jeffreyston 26 E6
Jemimaville 102 F6
Jevington 16 C5
Johnby 64 B4
John o' Groats 111 K1
Johnshaven 89 K2
Johnston 26 D5
Johnstone 79 G5
Johnstonebridge 73 G5
Jordans 22 E3
Jordanston 26 D3
Jump 53 F3
Juniper Green 81 G5
Jurby East 56 Q2
Jurby West 56 Q2

K

Kaber 64 E6
Kaimes 81 H5
Kalnakill 100 C7
Kames, Strath 72 B2
Kames, Strath 78 B4
Kea 3 G5
Keadby 54 C2
Keal 55 H7
Keal Cotes 55 H7
Kearsley 51 G3
Kearstwick 57 K2
Kearton 65 G8
Keasden 58 C4
Keddington 55 H5
Kedington 36 C5
Kedleston 43 F2
Keelby 55 F3
Keele 41 K2
Keeley Green 34 D5
Keeston 26 D5
Keevil 20 D7
Kegworth 43 G4
Kehelland 2 E5
Keig 96 F4
Keighley 59 F6
Keilarsbrae 80 D2
Keilhill 105 G3
Keillmore 77 F3
Keills 76 D5
Keils 76 E5
Keinton Mandeville 11 G2
Keir Mill 72 D5
Keisby 44 D4
Keiss 111 K2
Keith 104 D3
Keithock 89 J2
Kelbrook 58 E6
Kelby 44 D2
Keld, Cumbr 64 C6
Keld, N. Yks 65 F7
Keldholme 60 E2
Kelfield 60 C7
Kelham 44 A1
Kellan 85 G4
Kellas, Tays 89 G5
Kellas, Grampn 103 K7
Kellaton 5 J6
Kelleth 64 D7
Kelleythorpe 61 H5
Kelling 47 F2
Kellington 53 H1
Kelloe 66 D4
Kelly 4 D1
Kelly Bray 4 D2
Kelmarsh 33 K2
Kelmscott 21 G3
Kelsale 37 J3
Kelsall 50 E7
Kelshall 35 G6
Kelso 74 D1
Kelston 20 B6
Keltneyburn 87 K4
Kelton 65 G5
Kelton Hill or Rhonehouse 69 J5
Kelty 81 G2
Kelvedon 24 E1
Kelvedon Hatch 24 B3
Kelynack 2 B7
Kemacott 9 G1
Kemback 89 G7
Kemberton 41 J6
Kemble 20 D3
Kemerton 32 B6
Kemeys Commander 19 H2
Kemnay 97 G4
Kempley 31 H7
Kempsey 32 A5
Kempsford 21 F3
Kempston 34 D5
Kempston Hardwick 34 D5
Kempton 30 E1
Kemp Town 15 G5
Kemsing 23 L7
Kenardington 17 G2
Kenchester 31 F5
Kencott 21 G2
Kendal 57 J1
Kenfig 18 C4
Kenfig Hill 18 C4
Kenilworth 32 E2
Kenley, Shrops 41 G6
Kenley, G. Lon 23 J7
Kenmore, Highld 100 D7
Kenmore, Tays 87 K4
Kenn, Avon 19 J6
Kenn, Devon 9 K7
Kennacraig 77 H5
Kennerleigh 9 J5
Kennet 80 E2
Kennethmont 96 E3
Kennett 36 C3
Kennford 9 K7
Kenninghall 36 F1
Kennington, Kent 17 H1
Kennington, Oxon 21 K2
Kennoway 81 J1
Kenny Hill 36 B2
Kennythorpe 60 E4
Kenovay 84 A4
Kensaleyre 99 K7
Kensington 23 H5
Kensworth 22 F1
Kentchurch 31 F7
Kentford 36 C3
Kentisbeare 10 B5
Kentisbury 9 G1
Kentmere 64 B7
Kenton, Suff 37 G3
Kenton, G. Lon 23 G4
Kenton, Devon 9 K7
Kentra 85 H2
Kents Bank 57 G3
Kent's Green 31 J7
Kent's Oak 13 F3
Kenwick 41 F3
Kenwyn 3 G5
Kenyon 51 F4
Keoldale 108 E2
Keose 107 H6
Keppoch 93 E3
Kepwick 60 B1
Keresley 33 F1
Kerne Bridge 19 K1
Kerridge 51 J6
Kerris 2 C7
Kerry 40 C7
Kerrycroy 78 D5
Kerrysdale 100 E5
Kerry's Gate 30 E6
Kersall 54 B7
Kersey 36 F5
Kershader 107 H6
Kershopefoot 74 A6
Kersoe 32 B5
Kerswell 10 B5
Kerswell Green 32 A5
Kesgrave 37 H5
Kessingland 37 L1
Kestle Mill 3 G4
Keston 23 K6
Keswick, Cumbr 63 H5
Keswick, Norf 47 H6
Keswick, Norf 47 J3
Kettering 34 B2
Ketteringham 47 G6
Kettins 88 E5
Kettlebaston 36 E4
Kettlebrook 42 E6
Kettleburgh 37 H3
Kettleness 67 J6
Kettleshulme 51 J6
Kettlesing Bottom 59 H5
Kettlestone 46 E3
Kettlethorpe 54 C6
Kettletoft 113 G3
Kettlewell 58 E3
Ketton 44 C6
Kew 23 G5
Kew Bridge 23 G5
Kewstoke 19 H6
Kexbrough 53 F3
Kexby, Lincs 54 C5
Kexby, N. Yks 60 E5
Key Green 51 H7
Keyham 43 J6
Keyhaven 13 F6
Keyingham 55 G1
Keymer 15 G4
Keynsham 20 A6
Keysoe 34 D3
Keysoe Row 34 D3
Keyston 34 D2
Keyworth 43 J3
Kibblesworth 66 C2
Kibworth Beauchamp 43 J7
Kibworth Harcourt 43 J7
Kidbrooke 23 K5
Kiddemore Green 42 A6
Kidderminster 31 K2
Kiddington 33 G7
Kidlington 21 J1
Kidmore End 22 B5
Kidsgrove 41 K1
Kidstones 58 E2
Kidwelly 27 J6
Kielder 74 C5
Kiells 76 D5
Kilbarchan 79 G5
Kilbeg 92 C5
Kilberry 77 G5
Kilbirnie 78 F6
Kilbride, Highld 92 B3
Kilbride, W. Isles 90 C4
Kilbride, Strath 85 K6
Kilburn, N. Yks 60 C3
Kilburn, Derby 43 F2
Kilby 43 J7
Kilchattan 76 C2
Kilchattan Bay 78 D6
Kilchenzie 70 B2
Kilchiaran 76 B5
Kilchoan 85 F2
Kilchoman 76 B5
Kilchrenan 86 C6
Kilconquhar 82 C1
Kilcot 31 H7
Kilcoy 102 D7
Kilcreggan 78 E3
Kildale 67 G7
Kildalloig 70 C3
Kildary 103 F5
Kildonan 70 F2
Kildonnan 92 A7
Kildrummy 96 D4
Kildwick 58 F6
Kilfinan 77 J4
Kilfinnan 93 J6
Kilgetty 26 F6
Kilgwrrwg Common 19 J3
Kilham, Northum 74 E1
Kilham, Humbs 61 H4
Kilkenneth 84 A4
Kilkhampton 8 C4
Killamarsh 53 G5
Killay 27 L7
Killean 77 F7
Killearn 79 H3
Killen 102 E7
Killerby 66 B6
Killichonan 87 H3
Killiechonate 93 J7
Killiechronan 85 G4
Killiecrankie 88 B2
Killiemor 85 F5
Killilan 93 F2
Killimster 111 K3
Killin 87 H5
Killinghall 59 H5
Killingholme 55 F2
Killington 57 K2
Killochyett 82 C7
Killundine 85 G4
Kilmacolm 79 F5
Kilmahumaig 77 G2
Kilmaluag 99 K5
Kilmany 89 F6
Kilmarie 92 B4
Kilmarnock 79 G8
Kilmartin 77 H2
Kilmaurs 79 G7
Kilmelford 85 K7
Kilmeny 76 C5
Kilmersdon 20 A7
Kilmeston 13 H3
Kilmichael Glassary 77 H2
Kilmichael of Inverlussa 77 G3
Kilmington, Devon 10 D6
Kilmington, Wilts 11 J2
Kilmonivaig 93 H7
Kilmorack 102 C8
Kilmore 92 C5
Kilmory, Strath 70 E2
Kilmory, Highld 85 G1
Kilmory, Strath 77 G4
Kilmuir, Highld 102 E8
Kilmuir, Highld 103 F5
Kilmuir, Highld 99 H8
Kilmuir, Highld 99 J5
Kilnave 76 B4
Kilncadzow 80 D7
Kilndown 16 E2
Kilnhurst 53 G4
Kilninian 84 F4
Kilninver 85 K6
Kiln Pit Hill 65 H2
Kilnsea 55 J2
Kilnsey 58 E4
Kilnwick 61 G6
Kiloran 76 C2
Kilpatrick 70 E2
Kilpeck 31 F6
Kilpheder 90 C4
Kilphedir 111 F7
Kilpin 54 B1
Kilrenny 89 H8
Kilsby 33 H2
Kilspindie 88 E6
Kilsyth 80 C4
Kiltarlity 94 D1
Kilton 10 C1
Kilvaxter 99 J6
Kilve 10 C1
Kilvington 44 B2
Kilwinning 78 F7
Kimberley, Norf 46 F6
Kimberley, Notts 43 H2
Kimble 22 D2
Kimblesworth 66 C3
Kimble Wick 22 D2
Kimbolton, Cambs 34 D3
Kimbolton, H. & W. 31 G3
Kimcote 33 H1
Kimmeridge 6 D7
Kimmerston 83 H8
Kimpton, Wilts 12 E1
Kimpton, Herts 23 G1
Kinbrace 110 E5
Kinbuck 87 K8
Kincaple 89 G7
Kincardine, Fife 80 E3
Kincardine, Highld 102 E4
Kincardine O'Neil 96 E6
Kincorth 97 J5
Kincraig 95 G5
Kineton, Glos 32 C7
Kineton, Warw 33 F4
Kinfauns 88 D6
Kingarth 78 C6
Kingcoed 19 J2
Kingforth 54 E2
Kingham 32 E7
Kingholm Quay 72 E7
Kinghorn 81 H3
Kinglassie 81 H2
Kingoodie 89 F6
King's Acre 31 F5
Kingsand 4 E4
Kingsbarns 89 H7
Kingsbridge, Somer 10 A2
Kingsbridge, Devon 5 H5
King's Bromley 42 D5
Kingsburgh 99 J7
Kingsbury, Warw 42 E7
Kingsbury, G. Lon 23 G4
Kingsbury Episcopi 11 F3
King's Caple 31 G7
Kingsclere 21 K7
King's Cliffe 44 D7
Kingscote 20 C3
Kingscott 9 F4
King's Coughton 32 C4
Kingscross 70 F2
Kingsdon 11 G3
Kingsdown 17 L1
Kingseat 81 G2
Kingsey 22 C2
Kingsfold 14 E2
Kingsford 31 K1
Kingshall Street 36 E3
King's Heath 32 C1
Kingskerswell 5 J3
Kingskettle 88 F8
Kingsland 31 F3
Kings Langley 22 F2
Kingsley, Hants 14 A2
Kingsley, Staffs 42 C2
Kingsley, Ches 50 E6
Kingsley Green 14 B2
King's Lynn 45 K5
King's Meaburn 64 D5
Kingsmuir, Tays 89 G4
Kings Muir, Border 81 H8
Kingsnorth, Kent 24 E5
Kingsnorth, Kent 17 H2
King's Norton, W. Mids 32 C2
King's Norton, Leic 43 J6
King's Nympton 9 G4
King's Pyon 31 F4
Kings Ripton 35 F2
King's Somborne 13 F2
King's Stag 11 J4
King's Stanley 20 C2
Kings Sutton 33 G6
Kingstanding 42 C7
Kingsteignton 5 J2
King Sterndale 52 C6
Kings Thorn 31 F6
Kingsthorpe 34 A3
Kingston, Grampn 104 C2
Kingston, Lothn 82 D3
Kingston, Hants 12 D5
Kingston, Dorset 6 D7
Kingston, Cambs 35 G4
Kingston, Devon 5 G5
Kingston, Kent 25 H7
Kingston, Dorset 11 J5
Kingston, I. of W. 7 J6
Kingston Bagpuize 21 J3
Kingston Blount 22 C3
Kingston by Sea 15 F5
Kingston Deverill 11 K2
Kingstone, Staffs 42 C4
Kingstone, Somer 10 E4
Kingstone, H. & W. 31 F6
Kingston Lisle 21 H4
Kingston near Lewes 15 G5
Kingston on Soar 43 H4
Kingston Seymour 19 J6
Kingston St Mary 10 D3
Kingston upon Hull 61 H8
Kingston upon Thames 23 G6
Kingstown 63 J2
King's Walden 34 E7
Kingswear 5 J4
Kingswells 97 H5
Kingswinford 32 A1
Kingswood, Avon 20 A5
Kingswood, Bucks 22 B1
Kingswood, Glos 20 B3
Kingswood, Warw 32 D2
Kingswood, H. & W. 30 D4
Kingswood, Powys 40 D6
Kingswood, Kent 24 E7
Kingswood, Surrey 23 H7
King's Worthy 13 G2
Kington, H. & W. 32 B4
Kington, Powys 30 E4
Kington Langley 20 D5
Kington Magna 11 J3
Kington St Michael 20 D5
Kingussie 94 F5
Kingweston 11 G2
Kinharrachie 97 J2
Kinknockie 97 K1
Kinlet 31 J1
Kinloch, Highld 92 C4
Kinloch, Tays 88 D4
Kinloch, Highld 108 E5
Kinloch, Highld 91 K6
Kinlochard 79 G1
Kinlochbervie 108 D3
Kinlocheil 93 F8
Kinlochewe 101 G6
Kinloch Hourn 93 F5
Kinloch Laggan 94 D7
Kinlochleven 86 D2
Kinlochmore 86 D2
Kinloch Rannoch 87 J3
Kinlochspelve 85 H6
Kinloss 103 J6
Kinmel Bay 49 J2
Kinmuck 97 H4
Kinmundy 97 H4
Kinnadie 105 J4
Kinnaird 88 E6
Kinnell 89 J3
Kinnerley 40 E4
Kinnersley, H. & W. 32 A5
Kinnersley, H. & W. 30 E5
Kinnerton, Clwyd 50 C7
Kinnerton, Powys 30 D3

178 Kinnesswood Lillington

Kinnesswood 81 G1
Kinninvie 65 H5
Kinoulton 43 J3
Kinross 81 G1
Kinrossie 88 D5
Kinsham 30 E3
Kinsley 53 G2
Kintarvie 107 G7
Kintbury 21 H6
Kintessack 103 J6
Kintillo 88 D7
Kintocher 96 E5
Kintore 97 G4
Kintour 76 D6
Kinuachdrachd 77 G2
Kinveachy 95 H4
Kinver 31 K1
Kippax 59 K7
Kippen 79 J2
Kippford or Scaur 69 K5
Kirbister 112 D6
Kirbuster 112 C4
Kirby Bedon 47 H6
Kirby Bellars 43 K5
Kirby Cane 47 J7
Kirby Cross 37 H7
Kirby Grindalythe 61 G4
Kirby Hill, N. Yks 59 J4
Kirby Hill, N. Yks 65 J7
Kirby Knowle 60 B2
Kirby-le-Soken 37 H7
Kirby Mills 60 E2
Kirby Misperton 60 E3
Kirby Muxloe 43 H6
Kirby Row 47 J7
Kirby Sigston 59 K1
Kirby Underdale 60 F5
Kirby Wiske 59 J2
Kirdford 14 D3
Kirivick 107 F4
Kirk 111 J3
Kirkandrews-on-Eden 63 J2
Kirkbampton 63 J2
Kirkbean 62 E1
Kirk Bramwith 53 J2
Kirkbride 63 H2
Kirkbuddo 89 H4
Kirkburn 61 G5
Kirkburton 52 D2
Kirkby, Mers 50 D4
Kirkby, Lincs 54 E4
Kirkby, N. Yks 67 F7
Kirkby Fleetham 59 H1
Kirkby Green 44 D1
Kirkby in Ashfield 43 H1
Kirkby-in-Furness 57 F2
Kirkby la Thorpe 44 D2
Kirkby Lonsdale 57 K3
Kirkby Malham 58 D4
Kirkby Mallory 43 G6
Kirkby Malzeard 59 H3
Kirkby Mills 60 E2
Kirkbymoorside 60 D2
Kirkby on Bain 55 G7
Kirkby Overblow 59 J6
Kirkby Stephen 64 E7
Kirkby Thore 64 D5
Kirkby Underwood 44 D4
Kirkcaldy 81 H2
Kirkcambeck 74 B8
Kirkcarswell 69 J6
Kirkcolm 70 F8
Kirkconnel 72 C3
Kirkcowan 68 E4
Kirkcudbright 69 H5
Kirk Deighton 59 J5
Kirk Ella 61 H8
Kirkfieldbank 80 D7
Kirkgunzeon 72 D8
Kirkham, N. Yks 60 E4
Kirkham, Lancs 57 H7
Kirkhamgate 52 E1
Kirk Hammerton 60 B5
Kirkharle 75 G6
Kirkheaton, W. Yks 52 D2
Kirkheaton, Northum 75 G7
Kirkhill, Highld 102 D8
Kirkhill, Tays 89 J2
Kirkhope 73 J2
Kirkhouse 73 J1
Kirkibost, Highld 92 B4
Kirkibost, W. Isles 107 F5
Kirkinner 68 F5
Kirkintilloch 79 J4
Kirk Ireton 42 E1
Kirkland, D. & G 72 C3
Kirkland, Cumbr 64 D4
Kirkland, D. & G 72 D5
Kirkland, Cumbr 62 F6
Kirk Langley 42 E3
Kirkleatham 67 F5
Kirklevington 66 E7
Kirkley 47 L7
Kirklington, Notts 43 J1
Kirklington, N. Yks 59 J2
Kirklinton 73 K8
Kirkliston 81 G4
Kirkmaiden 68 C7
Kirk Merrington 66 C4
Kirkmichael, Tays 88 C2
Kirkmichael, Strath 71 J4
Kirk Michael, I. of M 56 Q2
Kirkmond le Mire 55 F4
Kirkmuirhill 80 C7
Kirknewton, Northum 74 F1
Kirknewton, Lothn 81 G5
Kirk of Shotts 80 D5
Kirkoswald, Cumbr 64 C3
Kirkoswald, Strath 71 H4
Kirkpatrick Durham 72 C7
Kirkpatrick-Fleming 73 H7
Kirk Sandall 53 J3
Kirksanton 56 E2
Kirk Smeaton 53 H2
Kirkstile 96 E2
Kirkton, Border 74 B3
Kirkton, Strath 72 E2
Kirkton, Highld 92 E3
Kirkton, D. & G 72 E6
Kirkton, Highld 93 F1
Kirkton, Highld 103 F3
Kirkton, Grampn 105 F3
Kirkton, Grampn 97 F3
Kirkton, Fife 89 F6
Kirkton, Tays 89 G4
Kirkton, Grampn 105 J3
Kirkton Manor 81 H8
Kirkton of Auchterhouse 89 F5
Kirkton of Auchterless 97 G1
Kirkton of Barevan 103 G8
Kirkton of Bourtie 97 H3
Kirkton of Collace 88 D5
Kirkton of Craig 89 K3
Kirkton of Culsalmond 97 F2
Kirkton of Durris 97 G6
Kirkton of Glenbuchat 96 C4
Kirkton of Glenisla 88 E2
Kirkton of Kingoldrum 89 F3
Kirkton of Largo 82 C1
Kirkton of Lethendy 88 D4
Kirkton of Logie Buchan 97 J3
Kirkton of Maryculter 97 H6
Kirkton of Menmuir 89 H2
Kirkton of Monikie 89 H5
Kirkton of Rayne 97 F2
Kirkton of Skene 97 H5
Kirkton of Tough 96 F4
Kirktown 105 K3
Kirktown of Alvah 104 F2
Kirktown of Bourtie 97 H3
Kirktown of Deskford 104 E2
Kirktown of Fetteresso 97 H7
Kirkwall 112 E5
Kirkwhelpington 75 F6
Kirk Yetholm 74 E2
Kirmington 54 F2
Kirmond le Mire 55 F4
Kirn 78 D4
Kirriemuir 89 F3
Kirstead Green 47 H7
Kirtlebridge 73 H7
Kirtling 36 B4
Kirtling Green 36 B4
Kirtlington 21 K1
Kirtomy 110 D2
Kirton, Lincs 45 G3
Kirton, Suff 37 H6
Kirton, Notts 53 J7
Kirton End 45 F2
Kirton Holme 45 F2
Kirton in Lindsey 54 D4
Kislingbury 33 J4
Kites Hardwick 33 G3
Kittybrewster 97 J5
Kitwood 13 J2
Kiveton Park 53 G5
Knaith 54 C5
Knaphill 22 E7
Knapp 10 E3
Knapton, N. Yks 60 C5
Knapton, N. Yks 61 F3
Knapton, Norf 47 J3
Knapwell 35 G3
Knaresborough 59 J5
Knarsdale 64 D2
Knaven 105 H4
Knayton 59 K2
Knebworth 35 F7
Kneep 106 E5
Kneesall 53 J7
Kneesworth 35 G5
Kneeton 43 K2
Knelston 27 J8
Knightacott 9 G2
Knightcote 33 F4
Knighton, Powys 30 D2
Knighton, Devon 4 F5
Knighton, Staffs 51 G7
Knighton, Staffs 41 J4
Knighton, Leic 43 J6
Knightwick 31 J4
Knill 30 D3
Knipton 44 B3
Knitsley 65 J3
Kniveton 42 E1
Knochenkelly 70 F2
Knock, Cumbr 64 D5
Knock, Grampn 104 E3
Knock, Strath 85 G5
Knockally 111 H6
Knockan 101 J1
Knockandhu 96 B3
Knockando 95 K1
Knockbain 102 E7
Knockbrex 69 G6
Knock Castle 78 D5
Knockdee 111 H2
Knockenkelly 70 F2
Knockentiber 79 F8
Knockholt 23 K7
Knockholt Pound 23 K7
Knockin 40 E4
Knocknaha 70 B3
Knockrome 76 E4
Knocksharry 56 P3
Knodishall 37 K3
Knolls Green 51 H6
Knolton 40 E3
Knook 12 B1
Knossington 44 B6
Knott End-on-Sea 57 G6
Knotting 34 D3
Knottingley 53 G1
Knotty Green 22 E3
Knowbury 31 G2
Knowehead 72 B5
Knowesgate 75 F6
Knoweside 71 H3
Knowes of Elrick 104 F3
Knowetownhead 74 B3
Knowle, W. Mids 32 D2
Knowle, Devon 8 E2
Knowle, Shrops 31 G2
Knowle, Devon 9 H5
Knowle, Avon 19 L5
Knowle Green 58 B7
Knowl Hill 22 D5
Knowlton 25 J7
Knowsley 50 D4
Knowsley Hall 50 D4
Knowstone 9 J3
Knucklas 30 D2
Knutsford 51 G6
Knypersley 42 A1
Kuggar 2 F8
Kyleakin 92 D3
Kyle of Lochalsh 92 D3
Kylerhea 92 D3
Kylesmorar 92 E6
Kyles Scalpay 99 H3
Kyles Stockinish 99 G3
Kylestrome 108 D5
Kyloe 83 J7
Kynnersley 41 H5
Kyre Park 31 H3

L

Labost 107 G4
Laceby 55 G3
Lacey Green 22 D2
Lach Dennis 51 G6
Lache 50 C7
Lackalee 99 G3
Lackford 36 C2
Lacock 20 D6
Ladbroke 33 G4
Laddingford 16 D1
Lade Bank 45 G1
Ladock 3 G4
Ladybank 88 F8
Ladykirk 83 G7
Ladysford 105 J2
Lagavulin 76 D7
Lagg, Strath 70 E2
Lagg, Strath 76 E4
Laggan, Highld 94 E6
Laggan, Highld 93 J6
Lagganulva 85 F4
Laide 101 F3
Laindon 24 C4
Lair 101 G8
Lairg 102 D2
Lairgmore 94 D2
Lake 12 D2
Lakenham 47 H6
Lakenheath 36 C1
Lakesend 45 J7
Lakeside 57 G2
Laleham 22 F6
Laleston 18 C5
Lamarsh 36 D6
Lamas 47 H4
Lambden 82 F7
Lamberhurst 16 D2
Lamberton 83 H6
Lambeth 23 J5
Lambfell Moar 56 P3
Lambley, Northum 64 D2
Lambley, Notts 43 J2
Lambourn 21 H5
Lambourne End 23 K3
Lambs Green 15 F2
Lambston 26 D5
Lamerton 4 E2
Lamesley 66 C2
Lamington, Strath 72 E1
Lamington, Highld 103 F5
Lamlash 70 F1
Lamonby 63 K4
Lamorna 2 C7
Lamorran 3 G5
Lampeter 27 K2
Lampeter Velfry 26 F5
Lamphey 26 E6
Lamplugh 63 F5
Lamport 34 A2
Lamyatt 11 H2
Lana 8 D6
Lanark 80 D7
Lancaster 57 H4
Lanchester 66 B3
Landbeach 35 H3
Landcross 8 E3
Landerberry 97 G5
Landford 12 E4
Landimore 27 J7
Landkey 9 F2
Landore 27 L7
Landrake 4 D3
Landscove 5 H3
Landshipping 26 E5
Landulph 4 E3
Landwade 35 K3
Landywood 42 B6
Laneast 8 C7
Lane End 22 D3
Lane Green 42 B6
Laneham 54 C6
Laneshaw Bridge 58 E6
Langar 43 K3
Langbank 79 F4
Langbar 59 F5
Langcliffe 58 D4
Langdale End 61 G1
Langdon Beck 65 F4
Langdon Hills 24 C4
Langenhoe 25 G1
Langford, Devon 10 B5
Langford, Notts 54 C8
Langford, Essex 24 E2
Langford, Beds 34 E5
Langford, Oxon 21 G2
Langford Budville 10 C3
Langham, Leic 44 B5
Langham, Suff 36 E3
Langham, Norf 46 F2
Langham, Essex 36 F6
Langho 58 C7
Langholm 73 J6
Langleeford 75 F2
Langley, W. Susx 14 B3
Langley, Warw 32 D3
Langley, Kent 24 E7
Langley, Berks 22 F5
Langley, Herts 35 F7
Langley, Hants 13 G5
Langley, Essex 35 H6
Langley, Ches 51 J6
Langley Burrell 20 D5
Langley Marsh 10 B3
Langley Park 66 C3
Langley Street 47 J6
Langney 16 D5
Langold 53 H5
Langore 8 D7
Langport 11 F3
Langrick 45 F2
Langridge 20 B6
Langrigg 63 G3
Langrish 13 K3
Langsett 52 E3
Langshaw 82 D8
Langstone 13 K5
Langthorne 59 H1
Langthorpe 59 J4
Langthwaite 65 H5
Langtoft, Lincs 44 E5
Langtoft, Humbs 61 H4
Langton, Durham 66 B6
Langton, N. Yks 60 E4
Langton, Lincs 55 G7
Langton, Lincs 55 H6
Langton by Wragby 55 F6
Langton Green 16 C2
Langton Herring 11 H7
Langton Matravers 6 E7
Langtree 8 E4
Langwathby 64 C4
Langwith 53 H7
Langwith Junction 53 H7
Langworth 54 E6
Lanivet 3 J3
Lanlivery 3 J4
Lanner 2 F6
Lanreath 4 B4
Lansallos 4 B4
Lanton, Border 74 C2
Lanton, Northum 74 F1
Lapford 9 H5
Laphroaig 76 C7
Lapley 42 A5
Lapworth 32 D2
Larbert 80 D3
Largie 96 F2
Largoward 89 G8
Largs 78 E6
Largybeg 70 F2
Largymore 70 F2
Larkfield 78 E4
Larkhall 80 C6
Larkhill 12 D1
Larling 46 E8
Larriston 74 B5
Lartington 65 H6
Lary 96 C5
Lasham 13 J1
Laskentyre 99 F3
Lassodie 81 G2
Lastingham 60 E1
Latchingdon 24 E2
Latchley 4 E2
Lately Common 51 F4
Lathbury 34 B5
Latheron 111 J5
Latheronwheel 111 H5
Lathones 89 G8
Latimer 22 F3
Latteridge 20 A4
Lattiford 11 H3
Latton 20 E3
Lauchintilly 97 G4
Lauder 82 D7
Laugharne 27 H5
Laughterton 54 C6
Laughton, Lincs 54 C4
Laughton, E. Susx 15 J4
Laughton, Leic 43 J8
Laughton-en-le-Morthen 53 H5
Launcells 8 C5
Launceston 8 D7
Launde Abbey 44 A6
Launton 33 J7
Laurencekirk 89 K1
Laurieston 69 H4
Lavant 14 B5
Lavendon 34 C4
Lavenham 36 E5
Laverhay 73 G5
Laverstock 12 D2
Laverstoke 13 G1
Laverton, Somer 20 B7
Laverton, Glos 32 C6
Laverton, N. Yks 59 H3
Law 80 D6
Lawers 87 J5
Lawford 37 F6
Lawhitton 8 D7
Lawkland 58 C4
Lawley 41 H6
Lawnhead 41 K4
Lawrenny 26 E6
Lawshall 36 D4
Lawton 31 F4
Laxay 107 H6
Laxdale 107 J5
Laxey 56 R3
Laxfield 37 H2
Laxfirth 115 G4
Laxo 115 G2
Laxton, Humbs 54 B1
Laxton, Notts 54 B7
Laxton, Northnts 44 C7
Laycock 58 F6
Layer Breton 25 F1
Layer de la Haye 36 E7
Layham 36 F5
Laytham 60 E7
Lazenby 67 F6
Lazonby 64 C4
Lea, Lincs 54 C5
Lea, Wilts 20 D4
Lea, Shrops 40 E8
Lea, Derby 43 F1
Lea, Shrops 41 F6
Lea, H. & W 31 H7
Leac Eskadale 99 H3
Leachkin 102 E8
Leadburn 81 H6
Leadenham 44 C1
Leaden Roding 24 B1
Leadgate, Cumbr 64 E3
Leadgate, Durham 65 J2
Leadhills 72 D3
Leafield 21 H1
Leagrave 34 D7
Leake Commonside 45 G1
Leake Hurn's End 45 H2
Lealholm 67 H7
Lealt, Highld 100 B6
Lealt, Strath 77 F2
Lea Marston 42 E7
Leamington Hastings 33 G3
Leamington Spa, Royal 33 F3
Leargybreck 76 E4
Learmouth 83 G8
Leasgill 57 H2
Leasingham 44 D2
Leask 97 K2
Leatherhead 23 G7
Leathley 59 H6
Leaton 41 F5
Lea Town 57 H7
Leaveland 25 G7
Leavenheath 36 E6
Leavening 60 E4
Leaves Green 23 K6
Lebberston 61 H2
Lechlade 21 G3
Leck 58 B3
Leckford 13 F2
Leckfurin 110 D3
Leckhampstead, Berks 21 J5
Leckhampstead, Bucks 33 K6
Leckhampton 20 D1
Leckmelm 101 H3
Leckwith 18 F5
Leconfield 61 H6
Ledaig 86 B5
Ledburn 34 C7
Ledbury 31 J6
Ledgemoor 31 F4
Ledicot 31 F3
Ledmore 108 D7
Lednagullin 110 E2
Ledsham, Ches 50 C6
Ledsham, W. Yks 59 K8
Ledston 59 K8
Ledwell 33 G7
Lee, Devon 8 E1
Lee, Shrops 40 F3
Lee, Hants 13 F4
Lee, Strath 84 F6
Lee, Lancs 57 J5
Leebotten 115 G6
Leebotwood 41 F7
Lee Brockhurst 41 G4
Leece 56 E3
Lee Clump 22 E2
Leeds, Kent 24 E7
Leeds, N. Yks 59 J7
Leedstown 2 E6
Leek 42 B1
Leekhampstead 21 J5
Leek Wootton 32 E3
Lee Mill 5 F4
Leeming 59 H2
Leeming Bar 59 H1
Lee Moor 4 F3
Lee-on-the-Solent 13 H5
Lees, Derby 42 E3
Lees, G. Man 51 J3
Leeswood 50 B7
Lee, The 22 E2
Legbourne 55 H5
Legburthwaite 63 J6
Legerwood 82 D7
Legsby 55 F5
Leicester 43 H6
Leicester Forest East 43 H6
Leigh, Kent 16 C1
Leigh, Wilts 20 E3
Leigh, Shrops 40 E6
Leigh, Surrey 15 F1
Leigh, G. Man 51 F3
Leigh, Dorset 11 H5
Leigh, H. & W 31 J4
Leigh Beck 24 E4
Leigh Delamere 20 C5
Leigh Green 17 G2
Leigh-on-Sea 24 E4
Leigh Sinton 31 J4
Leighterton 20 C3
Leigh, The 32 A7
Leighton, Powys 40 D6
Leighton, Shrops 41 H6
Leighton, Somer 11 J1
Leighton Bromswold 34 E2
Leighton Buzzard 34 C7
Leigh upon Mendip 11 H1
Leigh Woods 19 K5
Leinthall Earls 31 F3
Leinthall Starkes 31 F3
Leintwardine 30 F2
Leire 43 H7
Leirinmore 109 F2
Leiston 37 K3
Leith 81 H4
Leitholm 83 F7
Lelant 2 D6
Lelley 61 K7
Lem Hill 31 J2
Lemmington Hall 75 H3
Lempitlaw 74 D1
Lemreway 107 H7
Lendalfoot 71 G6
Lenham 24 E7
Lenham Heath 17 G1
Lenie 94 D3
Lennel 83 G7
Lennoxtown 79 J4
Lenton 44 D3
Lenwade 47 F5
Lenzie 79 J4
Leochel Cushnie 96 E4
Leominster 31 F4
Leonard Stanley 20 C2
Lepe 13 G6
Lephin 99 G8
Lephinmore 78 B2
Leppington 60 E4
Lepton 52 E2
Lerryn 3 K4
Lerwick 115 G4
Lesbury 75 J3
Leslie, Grampn 96 E3
Leslie, Fife 81 H1
Lesmahagow 80 D8
Lesnewth 8 B6
Lessingham 47 J4
Lessonhall 63 H2
Leswalt 68 B4
Letchmore Heath 23 G3
Letchworth 35 F6
Letcombe Bassett 21 H4
Letcombe Regis 21 H4
Letham, Fife 88 F7
Letham, Tays 89 H4
Lethenty 97 H1
Letheringham 37 H4
Letheringsett 46 F3
Lettaford 9 H7
Letterewe 101 F5
Letterfearn 92 E3
Letterfinlay 93 J6
Letters 101 H4
Letterston 26 D4
Lettoch 95 K2
Letton, H. & W 30 E2
Letton, H. & W 30 E5
Letty Green 23 H1
Letwell 53 H5
Leuchars 89 G6
Leurbost 107 H6
Levedale 42 B5
Leven, Fife 81 J1
Leven, Humbs 61 J6
Levens 57 H2
Levenshulme 51 H4
Levenwick 115 G6
Leverburgh 98 F4
Leverington 45 H5
Leverton 45 G2
Levington 37 H6
Levisham 60 F1
Levishie 94 C4
Lew 21 H2
Lewannick 4 C1
Lewdown 8 E7
Lewes 15 H4
Leweston 26 D4
Lewisham 23 J5
Lewiston 94 D3
Lewknor 22 C3
Leworthy 9 G2
Lewtrenchard 8 E7
Ley 4 B3
Leybourne 24 C7
Leyburn 59 G1
Leycett 41 J2
Leyland 50 E1
Leylodge 97 G4
Leys 105 K3
Leysdown on Sea 25 G5
Leysmill 89 J4
Leys of Cossans 89 F4
Leysters 31 G3
Leyton 23 J4
Lezant 4 D2
Lhanbryde 104 B2
Lhen, The 56 Q1
Libanus 29 G7
Libberton 80 E7
Liberton 81 H4
Lichfield 42 D6
Lickey 32 B2
Lickey End 32 B2
Lickfold 14 C3
Liddington 21 G4
Lidgate 36 C4
Lidlington 34 C6
Lieurary 111 G2
Liff 89 F5
Lifton 8 D7
Lighthorne 33 F4
Lightwater 22 E6
Lightwood 42 B2
Lightwood Green 40 E2
Likisto 99 G3
Lilbourne 33 H2
Lilburn Tower 75 G2
Lilleshall 41 J5
Lilley 34 E7
Lilliesleaf 74 B2
Lillingstone Dayrell 33 K6
Lillingstone Lovell 33 K5
Lillington 11 H4

Lilstock....10 C1
Limbrick....50 F2
Limefield....51 H2
Limekilns....81 F3
Limerigg....80 D4
Limington....11 G3
Limmerhaugh....72 B2
Limpenhoe....47 J6
Limpley Stoke....20 B6
Limpsfield....23 J7
Linby....43 H1
Linchmere....14 B2
Lincoln....54 D6
Lincomb....31 K3
Lindale....57 H2
Lindal in Furness....57 F3
Linden....74 A1
Lindfield....15 G3
Lindford....14 B2
Lindores....88 E7
Lindridge....31 H3
Lindsell....36 B7
Lindsey....36 E5
Linford, Essex....24 C5
Linford, Hants....12 D5
Lingague....56 P4
Lingdale....67 G6
Lingen....30 E3
Lingfield....15 G1
Lingwood....47 J6
Liniclate....98 C8
Linicro....99 J6
Linkenholt....21 H7
Linkinhorne....4 D2
Linklater....112 E8
Linksness....113 F5
Linktown....81 H2
Linley....40 E7
Linley Green....31 H4
Linlithgow....80 F4
Linlithgow Bridge....80 E4
Linshader....107 G5
Linshiels....74 E4
Linsidemore....102 D3
Linslade....34 C7
Linstead Parva....37 J2
Linstock....63 K2
Linthwaite....52 D2
Lintlaw....83 G6
Lintmill....104 E2
Linton, Border....74 D2
Linton, Kent....16 E1
Linton, N. Yks....58 E4
Linton, Derby....42 E5
Linton, H. & W....31 H7
Linton, Cambs....35 J5
Linton-on-Ouse....60 B4
Linwood, Hants....12 D5
Linwood, Lincs....54 F5
Linwood, Strath....79 G5
Lional....107 K2
Liphook....14 B2
Liskeard....4 C3
Liss....14 A3
Lissett....61 J5
Liss Forest....14 A3
Lissington....54 F5
Lisvane....19 F4
Litcham....46 D5
Litchborough....33 J4
Litchfield....21 J7
Litherland....50 C4
Litlington, Cambs....35 G5
Litlington, E. Susx....15 J5
Little Abington....35 J5
Little Addington....34 C2
Little Alne....32 D3
Little Asby....64 D7
Little Aston....42 C6
Little Atherfield....7 J6
Little Ayre....112 D7
Little Ayton....67 F6
Little Baddow....24 D2
Little Badminton....20 C4
Little Bardfield....36 B6
Little Barford....34 E4
Little Barningham....47 G3
Little Barrington....21 G1
Little Barugh....60 E3
Little Bealings....37 H5
Little Bedwyn....21 G6
Little Bentley....37 G7
Little Berkhamsted....23 H2
Little Birch....31 G6
Little Blakenham....37 G5
Littleborough, Notts....54 C5
Littleborough, G. Man....51 J2
Littlebourne....25 J7
Little Bowden....34 A1
Little Bradley....36 B4
Little Brampton....30 E1
Little Brechin....89 H2
Littlebredy....11 G7
Little Brickhill....34 C6
Little Brington....33 J3
Little Bromley....37 F7
Little Budworth....50 E7
Little Burstead....24 C3
Littlebury....35 J6
Littlebury Green....35 H6
Little Bytham....44 D5
Little Carlton....55 J5
Little Casterton....44 D6
Little Cawthorpe....55 H5
Little Chalfont....22 E3
Little Chart....17 G1
Little Chesterford....35 J5
Little Cheverell....20 D7
Little Chishill....35 H6
Little Clacton....25 H1
Little Comberton....32 B5
Little Common....16 E5
Little Compton....32 E6
Little Cowarne....31 H4
Little Coxwell....21 G3

Little Cressingham....46 D6
Little Dalby....44 A5
Littledean....20 A1
Little Dens....105 K4
Little Dewchurch....31 G6
Little Downham....35 J1
Little Driffield....61 H5
Little Dunham....46 D5
Little Dunkeld....88 C4
Little Dunmow....36 B7
Little Easton....35 K7
Little Eaton....43 F2
Little Ellingham....46 F7
Little End....23 L2
Little Eversden....35 G4
Little Fakenham....36 E2
Little Faringdon....21 G2
Little Fenton....60 C7
Littleferry....103 G3
Little Fransham....46 E5
Little Gaddesden....22 E1
Little Gidding....34 E1
Little Glemham....37 J4
Little Gransden....35 F4
Little Gruinard....101 F4
Little Habton....60 E3
Little Hadham....35 H7
Little Hallingbury....23 L1
Littleham, Devon....8 E3
Littleham, Devon....5 L1
Little Hampden....22 D2
Littlehampton....14 D5
Little Harrowden....34 B2
Little Haseley....22 B2
Little Hautbois....47 H4
Little Haven....26 C5
Little Hay....42 D6
Little Haywood....42 C4
Littlehempston....5 J3
Little Hereford....31 G3
Little Horkesley....36 E6
Little Horsted....15 H4
Little Horwood....34 A6
Little Houghton, Northnts....34 B4
Littlehoughton, Northum....75 J3
Little Hucklow....52 D6
Little Hulton....51 G3
Little Kingshill....22 D3
Little Langdale....63 J7
Little Langford....12 C2
Little Laver....23 L2
Little Leigh....50 F6
Little Leighs....24 D1
Little Lever....51 G3
Little London, Hants....22 B7
Little London, E. Susx....16 C4
Little London, Hants....13 F1
Little London, Lincs....45 F4
Little Longstone....52 D6
Little Malvern....31 J5
Little Maplestead....36 D6
Little Marcle....31 H6
Little Marlow....22 D4
Little Massingham....46 C4
Little Melton....47 G6
Little Mill, Gwent....19 H2
Littlemill, Highld....103 H7
Littlemill, Strath....71 K3
Little Milton....22 B2
Little Missenden....22 E3
Littlemore....21 K2
Little Ness....41 F5
Little Newcastle....26 D4
Little Newsham....65 J6
Little Oakley, Northnts....34 B1
Little Oakley, Essex....37 H7
Little Orton....63 J2
Littleover....43 F3
Little Paxton....34 E3
Little Petherick....3 H2
Little Plumstead....47 J5
Littleport....35 J1
Little Raveley....35 F1
Little Ribston....59 J5
Little Rissington....21 F1
Little Ryburgh....46 E4
Little Ryle....75 G3
Little Salkeld....64 C4
Little Sampford....36 B6
Little Saxham....36 C3
Little Scatwell....102 B7
Little Shelford....35 H4
Little Smeaton....53 H2
Little Snoring....46 E3
Little Somerford....20 D4
Little Stainton....66 D5
Little Stanney....50 D6
Little Staughton....35 E3
Little Steeping....55 J7
Littlestone-on-Sea....17 H3
Little Stonham....37 G3
Little Stretton, Shrops....41 F7
Little Stretton, Leic....43 J6
Little Strickland....64 C6
Little Stukeley....35 F2
Little Tew....33 F7
Little Thetford....35 J2
Littlethorpe....59 J4
Little Thurlow....36 B4
Little Thurrock....24 C5
Littleton, Ches....50 D7
Littleton, Somer....11 F2
Littleton, Surrey....22 F6
Littleton, Hants....13 G2
Littleton Drew....20 C4
Littleton Panell....20 E7
Littleton-upon-Severn....19 K3
Little Torrington....8 E4
Littletown, Durham....66 D3
Little Town, Cumbr....63 H6
Little Wakering....25 F4
Little Walden....35 J5
Little Waldingfield....36 E5
Little Walsingham....46 E3

Little Waltham....24 D1
Little Warley....24 C3
Little Weighton....61 G7
Little Welnetham....36 D3
Little Wenlock....41 H6
Little Whittingham Green....37 H2
Littlewick Green....22 D4
Little Wilbraham....35 J4
Little Witley....31 J3
Little Wittenham....21 K3
Little Wolford....32 E6
Littleworth, H. & W....32 A4
Littleworth, Staffs....42 C5
Littleworth, Oxon....21 H3
Little Wymondley....35 F7
Little Wyrley....42 C6
Little Yeldham....36 C6
Litton, Derby....52 D6
Litton, N. Yks....58 E3
Litton Cheney....11 G6
Liverpool....50 C4
Liversedge....52 E1
Liverton....67 H6
Livingston....81 F5
Livingston Village....81 F5
Lixwm....50 A6
Lizard....2 F8
Llanaber....38 F5
Llanaelhaearn....38 C2
Llanafan....28 D2
Llanafan-fawr....29 G4
Llanallgo....48 E2
Llanarmon....38 D3
Llanarmon Dyffryn Ceiriog....40 C3
Llanarmon-yn-Ial....40 C1
Llanarth, Dyfed....28 B4
Llanarth, Gwent....19 H1
Llanarthney....27 K4
Llanasa....49 L2
Llanbadarn Fawr....28 D1
Llanbadarn Fynydd....30 C2
Llanbadarn-y-garreg....30 C5
Llanbadrig....48 C1
Llanbeder....19 H3
Llanbedr, Powys....30 C5
Llanbedr, Powys....30 D7
Llanbedr, Gwyn....38 E4
Llanbedr-Dyffryn-Clwyd....50 A8
Llanbedrgoch....48 E2
Llanbedrog....38 C3
Llanbedr-y-cennin....49 G4
Llanberis....38 E4
Llanbister....30 C2
Llanblethian....18 D5
Llanboidy....27 G4
Llanbradach....18 F3
Llanbrynmair....39 J6
Llancarfan....18 E5
Llancayo....19 H2
Llancynfelyn....39 F7
Llandaff....18 F5
Llandanwg....38 E4
Llandawke....27 G5
Llanddaniel Fab....48 D3
Llanddarog....27 K5
Llanddeiniol....28 C2
Llanddeiniolen....48 E4
Llandderfel....39 J3
Llanddeusant, Gwyn....48 C2
Llanddeusant, Dyfed....28 D6
Llanddew....29 H6
Llanddewi....27 J8
Llanddewi Brefi....28 D4
Llanddewi'r Cwm....29 H5
Llanddewi Rhydderch....19 H1
Llanddewi Velfrey....27 F5
Llanddewi Ystradenni....30 C3
Llanddoged....49 H4
Llanddona....48 E3
Llanddowror....27 G5
Llanddulas....49 J3
Llandefaelog, Powys....29 H6
Llandefaelog, Dyfed....27 J5
Llandefaelog tre'r-graig....30 C6
Llandefalle....30 C6
Llandegai....48 E3
Llandegfan....48 E3
Llandegla....40 C1
Llandegley....30 C3
Llandegveth....19 H3
Llandeilo....27 L4
Llandeilo Graban....29 H5
Llandeilo'r-Fan....29 F6
Llandeloy....26 C4
Llandenny....19 J2
Llandevenny....19 J4
Llandinabo....31 G7
Llandinam....29 H1
Llandissilio....26 F4
Llandogo....19 K2
Llandough, S. Glam....18 D5
Llandough, S. Glam....19 F5
Llandovery....28 E6
Llandow....18 D5
Llandre, Dyfed....28 D1
Llandre, Dyfed....27 L2
Llandrillo....40 B3
Llandrillo-yn-Rhos....49 H2
Llandrindod Wells....29 H3
Llandrinio....40 D5
Llandudno....49 G2
Llandudno Junction....49 H3
Llandudwen....38 B3
Llandwrog....38 D1
Llandybie....27 L5
Llandyfan....27 L5
Llandyfriog....27 H2
Llandyfrydog....48 D2
Llandygwydd....28 D2
Llandyrnog....49 L4
Llandyssil....40 C7
Llandysul....27 J2
Llaneglwys....29 H6

Llanegryn....38 F6
Llanegwad....27 K4
Llanelian-yn-Rhos....49 H3
Llanelidan....40 C1
Llanelieu....30 C6
Llanellen....19 H1
Llanelli....27 K6
Llanelltyd....39 G5
Llanelly....19 G1
Llanelly Hill....19 G1
Llanelwedd....29 H4
Llanelwy or St Asaph....49 K3
Llanenddwyn....38 E4
Llanengan....38 B4
Llanerchymedd....48 D2
Llanerfyl....40 B6
Llanfachraeth....48 C2
Llanfachreth....39 G4
Llanfaelog....48 C3
Llanfaes....48 F3
Llanfaethlu....48 C2
Llanfaglan....48 D4
Llanfair Caereinion....40 C6
Llanfair Clydogau....27 L1
Llanfair Dyffryn Clwyd....40 C1
Llanfairfechan....49 F3
Llanfair Kilgeddin....19 H2
Llanfair-Nant-Gwyn....26 F3
Llanfairpwllgwyngyll....48 E3
Llanfair Talhaiarn....49 J3
Llanfair Waterdine....30 D2
Llanfairyneubwll....48 C3
Llanfairynghornwy....48 C1
Llanfallteg....26 F5
Llanfaredd....29 H4
Llanfarian....28 C2
Llanfechain....40 C4
Llanfechan....29 G4
Llanfechell....48 C1
Llanfendigaid....38 E6
Llanferres....50 A7
Llanfflewyn....48 C2
Llanfihangel-ar-arth....27 J3
Llanfihangel Crucorney....30 E7
Llanfihangel Glyn Myfyr....39 J2
Llanfihangel Nant Bran....29 G6
Llanfihangel-nant-Melan....30 C4
Llanfihangel Rhydithon....30 C3
Llanfihangel Rogiet....19 J4
Llanfihangel Tal-y-llyn....30 C7
Llanfihangel-uwch-Gwili....27 J4
Llanfihangel-y-Creuddyn....28 D2
Llanfihangel-yng-Ngwynfa....40 B5
Llanfihangel yn Nhowyn....48 C3
Llanfihangel-y-pennant, Gwyn....38 E2
Llanfihangel-y-pennant, Gwyn....39 F6
Llanfihangel Ystum Llwern....19 J1
Llanfihangel-y-traethau....38 E3
Llanfilo....30 C6
Llanfoist....19 G1
Llanfor....39 J3
Llanfrechfa....19 H3
Llanfrothen....39 F2
Llanfrynach....29 H7
Llanfwrog, Clwyd....40 C1
Llanfwrog, Gwyn....48 C2
Llanfyllin....40 C5
Llanfynydd, Clwyd....40 D1
Llanfynydd, Dyfed....27 K4
Llanfyrnach....27 G3
Llangadfan....40 B5
Llangadog....28 E7
Llangadwaladr, Clwyd....40 C3
Llangadwaladr, Gwyn....48 C4
Llangaffo....48 D4
Llangain....27 H5
Llangammarch Wells....29 G5
Llangan....18 D5
Llangarron....31 G7
Llangasty-Talyllin....30 C7
Llangathen....27 K4
Llangattock....19 G1
Llangattock Lingoed....30 E7
Llangattock-Vibon-Avel....19 J1
Llangedwyn....40 C4
Llangefni....48 D3
Llangeinor....18 D4
Llangeitho....28 D4
Llangeler....27 H3
Llangelynnin....38 E6
Llangendeirne....27 J5
Llangennech....27 K6
Llangennith....27 J7
Llangenny....19 G1
Llangernyw....49 H4
Llangian....38 B4
Llangiwg....18 B2
Llangloffan....26 F4
Llanglydwen....27 G4
Llangoed....48 F3
Llangoedmor....27 G2
Llangollen....40 D2
Llangolman....26 F4
Llangorse....30 C7
Llangorwen....28 D1
Llangovan....19 J2
Llangower....39 J3
Llangranog....28 A4
Llangristiolus....48 D3
Llangrove....19 K1
Llangua....30 E7
Llangunllo....30 D2
Llangunnor....27 J4
Llangurig....29 G1
Llangwm, Dyfed....26 D6
Llangwm, Clwyd....39 J2
Llangwm, Gwent....19 J2
Llangwnnadl....38 B3
Llangwyllog....48 D3
Llangwyryfon....28 D2
Llangybi, Gwyn....38 D2
Llangybi, Gwent....19 H3
Llangybi, Dyfed....27 L1
Llangyfelach....27 L7

Llangynhafal....50 A7
Llangynidr....18 F1
Llangynin....27 G5
Llangynog, Powys....40 B4
Llangynog, Dyfed....27 H5
Llangynwyd....18 C4
Llanhamlach....29 H7
Llanharan....18 E4
Llanharry....18 E4
Llanhennock....19 H3
Llanhilleth....19 G2
Llanidloes....29 G1
Llaniestyn....38 B3
Llanigon....30 D5
Llanilar....28 D2
Llanilid....18 D4
Llanishen, S. Glam....19 F4
Llanishen, Gwent....19 J2
Llanllechid....49 F4
Llanlleonfel....29 G5
Llanllowell....19 H3
Llanllugan....40 B6
Llanllwch....27 H5
Llanllwchaiarn....40 C7
Llanllwni....27 J2
Llanllyfni....38 D1
Llanmadoc....27 J7
Llanmaes....18 D6
Llanmartin....19 H4
Llanmerewig....40 C7
Llanmihangel....18 D5
Llanmiloe....27 G6
Llanmorlais....27 K7
Llannefydd....49 J3
Llannon....27 K6
Llan-non....28 C3
Llannor....28 C3
Llanover....19 H2
Llanpumsaint....27 J4
Llanrhaeadr....49 K4
Llanrhaeadr-ym-Mochnant....40 C4
Llanrhian....26 C3
Llanrhidian....27 J7
Llanrhos....49 G2
Llanrhyddlad....48 C2
Llanrhystud....28 C3
Llanrothal....19 J1
Llanrug....48 E4
Llanrwst....49 H4
Llansadurnen....27 G5
Llansadwrn, Dyfed....28 D6
Llansadwrn, Gwyn....48 E3
Llansaint....27 H6
Llansamlet....18 A3
Llansannan....49 J4
Llansannor....18 D5
Llansantffraed, Dyfed....28 C3
Llansantffraed, Powys....30 C7
Llansantffraed-Cwmdeuddwr....29 G3
Llansantffraid Glan Conwy....49 H3
Llansantffraid-in-Elwel....29 H4
Llansantffraid-ym-Mechain....40 D4
Llansawel....27 L3
Llansilin....40 D4
Llansoy....19 J2
Llanspyddid....29 H7
Llanstadwell....26 D6
Llansteffan, Dyfed....27 H5
Llanstephan, Powys....30 C5
Llanthony....30 D7
Llantilio Crossenny....19 H1
Llantilio Pertholey....19 H1
Llantrisant, Gwyn....48 C2
Llantrisant, M. Glam....18 E4
Llantrisant, Gwent....19 H3
Llantrithyd....18 E5
Llantwit Fardre....18 E4
Llantwit Major....18 D6
Llanuwchllyn....39 H3
Llanvaches....19 J3
Llanvair Discoed....19 J3
Llanvapley....19 H1
Llanvetherine....19 H1
Llanveynoe....30 E6
Llanvihangel Crucorney....30 E7
Llanvihangel Gobion....19 H2
Llanvihangel-Ystern-Llewern....19 J1
Llanwarne....19 G7
Llanwddyn....40 B5
Llanwenog....27 J2
Llanwern....19 H4
Llanwinio....27 G4
Llanwnda, Dyfed....26 D3
Llanwnda, Gwyn....48 D5
Llanwnnen....27 K2
Llanwnog....40 B7
Llanwrda....28 E6
Llanwrin....39 G6
Llanwrthwl....29 G3
Llanwrtyd....29 F5
Llanwrtyd-Wells....29 F5
Llanwyddelan....40 B6
Llanyblodwel....40 D4
Llanybri....27 H5
Llanybydder....27 K2
Llanycefn....26 E4
Llanychaer....26 D3
Llanycrwys....27 L2
Llanymawddwy....39 J5
Llanymynech, Shrops....40 D4
Llanymynech, Powys....40 D4
Llanynghenedl....48 C2
Llanynys....49 L4
Llan-y-pwll....40 E1
Llanyre....29 H3
Llanystumdwy....38 D3
Llanywern....30 C7
Llawhaden....26 E5
Llawnt....40 D3
Llawr Dref....38 B4
Llawryglyn....39 J7
Llay....40 E1
Llechcynfarwy....48 C2
Llechfaen....29 H7
Llechryd, M. Glam....18 F2

Llechryd, Dyfed....27 G2
Lledrod....28 D2
Llidiad-Nenog....27 K3
Llithfaen....38 C2
Llong....50 B7
Llowes....30 C5
Llwchmynydd....38 A4
Llwyn-y-groes....28 C4
Llwydcoed....18 D2
Llwyn....28 B4
Llwyncelyn....28 B4
Llwyndafydd....28 C2
Llwynderw....40 D6
Llwyndyrys....38 C2
Llwyngwril....38 E6
Llwynhendy....27 K7
Llwynmawr....40 D3
Llwynypia....18 D3
Llwyn-y-fran....26 E4
Llywel....29 F6
Loanend....83 H6
Loanhead....81 H5
Loans....71 J1
Lochaber....93 H6
Lochailort....92 D7
Lochaline....85 H4
Lochans....68 B5
Locharbriggs....72 E6
Lochawe....86 D6
Lochboisdale....90 D4
Lochbuie....85 H6
Lochcarnan....98 D8
Lochcarron....93 E2
Lochdon....85 J5
Lochearnhead....87 H6
Lochee....89 F5
Lochend, Highld....94 D2
Lochend, Highld....111 J2
Locheport....98 D6
Locherben....72 E5
Lochfoot....72 D7
Lochgair....77 J2
Lochganvich....107 G6
Lochgarthside....94 D4
Lochgelly....81 G2
Lochgilphead....77 H3
Lochgoilhead....78 D1
Lochhill....104 B2
Lochinver....108 B6
Lochlane....87 L6
Lochluichart....102 B6
Lochmaben....73 G4
Lochmaddy....98 E6
Lochore....81 G2
Lochranza....77 J6
Lochside....89 K2
Lochskipport....90 D2
Lochslin....103 G4
Lochton....97 G6
Lochwinnoch....79 F6
Lochwood....80 B5
Lockengate....3 J3
Lockerbie....73 G6
Lockeridge....21 F6
Lockerley....13 F3
Locking....19 H7
Lockington, Leic....43 G4
Lockington, Humbs....61 G6
Lockleywood....41 H4
Locks Heath....13 H5
Lockton....60 F2
Loddington, Leic....44 A6
Loddington, Northnts....34 B2
Loddiswell....5 H5
Loddon....47 J7
Lode....35 J3
Loders....11 F6
Lodsworth....14 C3
Lofthouse....59 G3
Lofthouse Gate....53 F1
Loftus....67 H6
Logan....72 A2
Loggerheads....41 J3
Loggie....101 H3
Logie, Fife....89 G7
Logie, Tays....89 J2
Logie Coldstone....96 D5
Logie Hill....103 F5
Logie Newton....97 F2
Logie Pert....89 J2
Logierait....88 B3
Login....26 F4
Lolworth....35 G3
Lonbain....100 C7
Londesborough....60 F6
London....23 J5
London (Gatwick) Airport....15 F1
London (Heathrow) Airport....23 F5
London (Luton) Airport....34 E7
London (Stanstead) Airport....35 J7
London Colney....23 G2
Londonderry....59 J2
Londonthorpe....44 C3
Londubh....100 E4
Lonemore, Highld....100 D5
Lonemore, Highld....103 F4
Long Ashton....19 K5
Long Bennington....44 B2
Longbenton....75 J5
Longborough....32 D7
Longbridge, W. Mids....32 C2
Longbridge, Warw....32 E3
Longbridge Deverill....12 A1
Long Buckby....34 A3
Longburton....11 H4
Long Clawson....43 K4
Longcliffe....42 E1
Long Common....13 H4

Long Compton, Staffs............42 A4
Long Compton, Warw............32 E6
Longcot............21 G3
Long Crendon............22 B2
Long Crichel............12 B4
Longden............41 F6
Long Ditton............23 G6
Longdon, Staffs............42 C5
Longdon, H. & W.............31 K6
Longdon on Tern............41 H5
Longdown............9 J6
Longdowns............2 F6
Long Drax............60 D8
Long Duckmanton............53 G6
Long Eaton............43 G3
Longfield............24 C6
Longford, Derby............42 E3
Longford, W. Mids.............33 F1
Longford, G. Lon.............22 F5
Longford, Shrops.............41 H3
Longford, Shrops.............41 J5
Longford, Glos.............31 K7
Longforgan............88 F5
Longformacus............82 E6
Longframlington............75 H4
Long Gill............58 C5
Longham, Dorset............12 C6
Longham, Norf.............46 E5
Long Hanborough............21 J1
Longhirst............75 J6
Longhope, Glos.............20 A1
Longhope, Orkney............112 D7
Longhorsley............75 H5
Longhoughton............75 J3
Long Itchington............33 G3
Long Lawford............33 G2
Longley Green............31 J4
Long Load............11 F3
Longmanhill............105 G2
Long Marston, N. Yks.............60 C5
Long Marston, Herts.............22 D1
Long Marston, Warw.............32 D5
Long Marton............64 D5
Long Melford............36 D5
Longmoor Camp.............14 A2
Longmorn............104 B3
Long Newnton............20 D3
Longnewton, Border............74 B2
Longnewton, Cleve.............66 D6
Longney............20 B1
Longniddry............82 C4
Longnor, Staffs.............52 C7
Longnor, Shrops.............41 F6
Longparish............13 G1
Long Preston............58 D5
Longridge, Lothn.............80 E5
Longridge, Lancs.............57 K7
Longriggend............80 D4
Long Riston............61 J6
Longsdon............42 B1
Longside............105 K4
Longslow............41 H3
Longstanton............35 G3
Longstock............13 F2
Longstowe............35 G4
Long Stratton............47 G2
Long Street.............34 A5
Long Sutton, Somer.............11 F3
Long Sutton, Lincs.............45 H4
Long Sutton, Hants.............13 K1
Longthorpe............44 E7
Long Thurlow............36 F3
Longton, Staffs.............42 B2
Longton, Lancs.............50 D1
Longtown, H. & W.............30 E7
Longtown, Cumbr.............73 J8
Longville in the Dale............41 G7
Long Whatton............43 G4
Longwick............22 C2
Long Wittenham............21 K3
Longwitton............75 G6
Longworth............21 H3
Longyester............82 D5
Lonmore............99 H8
Looe.............4 C4
Loose............24 D7
Loosley Row............22 D2
Lopcombe Corner............12 E2
Lopen.............11 F4
Loppington............41 F4
Lopwell.............4 E3
Lorbottle............75 G4
Lorton.............63 G5
Loscoe............43 G2
Lossiemouth............104 B1
Lostock Gralam............51 F6
Lostock Junction............51 F3
Lostwithiel.............3 K4
Lothbeg............103 H1
Lothersdale............58 E6
Lothmore............110 F7
Loudwater............22 E3
Loughborough............43 H5
Loughor............27 K7
Loughton, Bucks.............34 B6
Loughton, Shrops.............31 H1
Loughton, Essex............23 K3
Lound, Lincs.............44 D5
Lound, Notts.............53 J5
Lound, Suff.............47 L7
Lount............43 F5
Louth............55 H5
Love Clough............51 H1
Lover............12 E3
Loversall............53 H4
Loves Green............24 C2
Loveston............26 E6
Lovington............11 G2
Low Bentham............58 B4
Low Bradfield............52 E4
Low Bradley............58 F6
Low Braithwaite............63 K3
Low Brunton............74 F7
Low Burnham............54 B3

Lowca.............62 E5
Low Catton............60 E5
Low Coniscliffe............66 C6
Lowdham............43 J2
Low Dinsdale............66 D6
Low Dovengill............64 E8
Low Ellington............59 H2
Lower Aisholt............10 D2
Lower Ashton.............9 J7
Lower Assendon............22 C4
Lower Basildon............22 B5
Lower Beeding............15 F3
Lower Benefield............34 C1
Lower Boddington............33 G4
Lower Breinton............31 F6
Lower Bullingham............31 G6
Lower Cam............20 B2
Lower Chapel............29 H6
Lower Chedworth............20 E1
Lower Chute............21 H7
Lower Darwen.............51 F1
Lower Diabaig............100 D6
Lower Down............30 E1
Lower Dunsforth............59 K4
Lower Farringdon............13 K2
Lower Frankton............40 E3
Lower Froyle............14 A1
Lower Gledfield............102 D3
Lower Green, Norf.............46 E3
Lower Green, Berks.............21 H6
Lower Halstow............24 E6
Lower Hardres............25 H7
Lower Heyford............33 G7
Lower Higham............24 D5
Lower Hordley............40 E4
Lower Killeyan............76 B7
Lower Langford............19 J6
Lower Largo............82 C1
Lower Lemington............32 E6
Lower Lye............30 F3
Lower Machen............19 G4
Lower Maes-coed............30 E6
Lower Moor............32 B5
Lower Nazeing............23 J2
Lower Penarth............19 F5
Lower Penn............42 A7
Lower Pennington............13 F6
Lower Peover............51 G6
Lower Quinton............32 D5
Lower Shelton............34 C5
Lower Shiplake............22 C5
Lower Shuckburgh............33 G3
Lower Slaughter............32 D7
Lower Stanton St Quintin............20 D4
Lower Stoke............24 E5
Lower Stondon............34 E6
Lower Sundon............34 D7
Lower Swanwick............13 H5
Lower Swell............32 D7
Lower Thurlton............47 K7
Lower Tysoe............33 F5
Lower Upham............13 H4
Lower Vexford............10 C2
Lower Weare............19 J7
Lower Welson............30 D5
Lower Wield............13 J1
Lower Winchendon or
  Nether Winchendon............22 C1
Lower Withington............51 H7
Lower Woodend............22 D4
Lower Woodford............12 D2
Lowesby............43 K6
Lowestoft............47 L7
Loweswater............63 G5
Lowford............37 F6
Low Gate............65 G1
Lowgill, Lancs.............58 B4
Lowgill, Cumbr.............64 D8
Low Ham............11 F3
Low Hesket............64 B3
Low Hesleyhurst............75 G5
Low Leighton............52 C5
Low Mill............60 D1
Low Moor............58 C6
Lownie Moor............89 G4
Lowood............82 D8
Low Row, Cumbr.............64 C1
Low Row, N. Yks.............65 G8
Lowsonford............32 D3
Lowther............64 C5
Lowthorpe............61 H4
Lowton............51 F4
Lowton Common............51 F4
Low Torry............80 F3
Low Worsall............66 D7
Loxbeare.............9 K4
Loxhill............14 D2
Loxhore.............9 G2
Loxley............32 E4
Loxton............19 H7
Loxwood............14 D2
Lubenham............33 K1
Luccombe.............9 K1
Luccombe Village.............7 K7
Lucker............75 H1
Luckett.............4 D2
Luckington............20 C4
Lucklawhill............89 G6
Luckwell Bridge.............9 K2
Lucton............31 F3
Ludag............90 C4
Ludborough............55 G6
Ludchurch............26 F5
Luddenden............52 C1
Luddenham............24 C6
Luddesdown............24 C6
Luddington............54 C2
Luddington, Warw.............32 D4
Ludgershall, Bucks.............22 B1
Ludgershall, Wilts.............21 G2
Ludgvan.............2 D6
Ludham............47 J5

Ludlow............31 G2
Ludwell............12 B3
Ludworth............66 D3
Luffincott.............8 D6
Lugar............72 A2
Luggate Burn............82 E4
Luggiebank............80 C4
Lugton............79 G6
Lugwardine............31 G5
Luib............92 B3
Lulham............30 F5
Lullington, Somer.............20 B7
Lullington, Derby............42 E5
Lulsgate Bottom............19 K6
Lulsley............31 J4
Lulworth Camp.............11 K7
Lumb............52 C1
Lumby............60 B7
Lumphanan............96 E5
Lumphinnans............81 G2
Lumsdaine............83 G5
Lumsden............96 D3
Lunan............89 J3
Lunanhead............89 G3
Luncarty............88 C6
Lund, N. Yks.............60 D7
Lund, Humbs.............61 G6
Lundie............88 E5
Lundin Links............82 C1
Lunna............115 G2
Lunning............115 H2
Lunsford's Cross.............16 E4
Lunt............50 C3
Luntley............30 E4
Luppitt............10 C5
Lupton............57 J2
Lurgashall............14 C3
Lusby............55 H7
Luskentyre............98 F3
Luss............79 F2
Lussagiven............77 F3
Lusta............99 H7
Lustleigh.............5 H1
Luston............31 F3
Luthermuir............89 J2
Luthrie............89 F7
Luton, Kent............24 D6
Luton, Beds.............34 D7
Luton, Devon.............5 K2
Lutterworth............33 H1
Lutton, Northnts.............34 E1
Lutton, Devon.............5 F4
Lutton, Lincs.............45 H4
Lutworthy.............9 H4
Luxborough............10 A2
Luxulyan.............3 J4
Lybster............111 J5
Lydbury North............30 E1
Lydd............17 H3
Lydden............17 K1
Lyddington............44 B7
Lydd-on-Sea............17 H3
Lydeard St Lawrence............10 C2
Lydford, Devon.............8 F7
Lydford, Somer.............11 G2
Lydgate............51 J1
Lydham............40 E7
Lydiard Millicent............20 E4
Lydiate............50 C3
Lydlinch............11 J4
Lydney............19 L2
Lydstep............26 K6
Lye............32 B1
Lye Green............22 E2
Lyford............21 H3
Lymbridge Green............17 J1
Lyme Regis............10 E6
Lyminge............17 J1
Lymington............13 F6
Lyminster............14 D5
Lymm............51 F5
Lymore............12 E6
Lympne............17 J2
Lympsham............19 H7
Lympstone............10 A7
Lynaberack............95 F5
Lynchat............95 F5
Lyndhurst............13 F5
Lyndon............44 C6
Lyne............22 F6
Lyneal............41 F3
Lyneham, Wilts.............20 E5
Lyneham, Oxon.............32 E7
Lynemouth............75 J5
Lyne of Gorthleck............94 D3
Lyne of Skene............97 G4
Lyness............112 D7
Lyng, Somer.............10 E3
Lyng, Norf.............46 F5
Lynmouth.............9 H1
Lynsted............25 F6
Lynton.............9 H1
Lyon's Gate............11 H5
Lyonshall............30 E4
Lytchett Matravers............12 B6
Lytchett Minster............12 B6
Lyth............111 J2
Lytham............50 C1
Lytham St Anne's.............57 G8
Lythe............67 J6
Lythes............112 E8

M

Maaruig............99 H2
Mabe Burnthouse.............2 F6
Mabie............72 E7
Mablethorpe............55 K5
Macclesfield............51 J6
Macclesfield Forest............51 J6
Macduff............105 G2
Macharioch............70 C4
Machen............19 G4

Machrihanish............70 B3
Machynlleth............39 G6
Mackworth............43 F3
Macmerry............82 C4
Madderty............88 B6
Maddiston............80 E4
Madehurst............14 C4
Madeley............41 J2
Madeley Heath............41 J2
Madingley............35 G3
Madley............31 F6
Madresfield............31 K5
Madron.............2 C6
Maenaddwyn............48 D2
Maenclochog............26 E4
Maendy............18 E5
Maentwrog............39 F2
Maer............41 J3
Maerdy, Clwyd.............40 B2
Maerdy, M. Glam.............18 D3
Maesbrook............40 E4
Maesbury Marsh............40 E4
Maes-glas............19 H4
Maeshafn............50 B7
Maesllyn............27 H2
Maesmynis............29 H5
Maesteg............18 C3
Maesybont............27 K5
Maesycrugiau............27 J2
Maesycwmmer............18 F3
Magdalen Laver............23 L2
Maggieknockater............104 C4
Magham Down............16 D4
Maghull............50 C3
Magor............19 J4
Maiden Bradley............11 K2
Maidencombe.............5 K3
Maidenhead............22 D4
Maiden Law............66 B3
Maiden Newton............11 G6
Maidenwell.............3 K2
Maidford............33 J4
Maids Moreton............33 K6
Maidstone............24 D7
Maidwell............34 A2
Mail............115 G6
Mains of Clunas............103 G8
Mains of Drum............97 H6
Mains of Loch............104 C2
Mainstone............30 D1
Maisemore............31 K7
Makerstoun............82 C7
Malborough.............5 H6
Malden............24 E2
Malham............58 E4
Mallaig............92 C6
Malltraeth............48 D4
Mallwyd............39 H5
Malmesbury............20 D4
Malmsmead.............9 H1
Malpas, Ches.............41 F2
Malpas, Corn.............3 G5
Malpas, Gwent.............19 H3
Maltby, Cleve.............66 E6
Maltby, S. Yks.............53 H4
Maltby le Marsh............55 J5
Maltman's Hill............17 G1
Malton............60 E3
Malvern Link............31 J5
Malvern Wells............31 J5
Mamble............31 H2
Manaccan.............2 F7
Manafon............40 C6
Manaton.............5 H1
Manby............55 H5
Mancetter............43 F7
Manchester............51 H4
Mancot............50 C7
Mandally............93 J5
Manea............45 H8
Manfield............66 C6
Mangersta............106 E5
Mangotsfield............20 A5
Manish............99 G4
Mankinholes............51 J1
Manley............50 E6
Manmoel............19 F2
Mannal............84 A4
Manningford Bohune............21 F7
Manningford Bruce............21 F7
Mannings Heath............15 F3
Mannington............12 C5
Manningtree............37 G6
Mannofield............97 J5
Manorbier............26 E7
Manordeilo............27 L4
Manorowen............26 D3
Mansell Gamage............30 E5
Mansell Lacy............31 F5
Mansfield, Strath.............72 B3
Mansfield, Notts.............53 H7
Mansfield Woodhouse............53 H7
Manston............11 K4
Manswood............12 B5
Manthorpe............44 D5
Manton, Leic.............44 B6
Manton, Humbs.............54 D3
Manton, Wilts.............21 F6
Manuden............35 H7
Maplebeck............54 B7
Maple Cross............22 F3
Mapledurham............22 B5
Mapledurwell............22 B7
Maplehurst............14 E3
Mapperley............43 G2
Mapperton............11 G6
Mappleborough Green............32 C3
Mappleton, Derby............42 D2
Mappleton............61 K6
Mappowder............11 J5
Marazion.............2 D6
Marbury............41 G2
March............45 H7

Marcham............21 J3
Marchamley............41 G4
Marchington............42 D3
Marchington Woodlands............42 D4
Marchwiel............40 E2
Marchwood............13 F4
Marcross............18 D6
Marden, Kent............16 E1
Marden, Wilts.............20 E7
Marden, H. & W.............31 G5
Mardy............19 H1
Marefield............44 A6
Mareham le Fen............55 G7
Mareham on the Hill............55 G7
Maresfield............15 H3
Marfleet............61 J8
Margaret Marsh............11 K4
Margaret Roding............24 B1
Margaretting............24 C2
Margate............25 K5
Margnaheglish............70 F1
Marham............46 C6
Marhamchurch.............8 C5
Marholm............44 E6
Marian-glas............48 E2
Mariansleigh.............9 H3
Marishader............100 A6
Mark............10 E1
Markbeech............15 H1
Markby............55 J6
Mark Causeway............10 E1
Mark Cross............16 C2
Market Bosworth............43 G6
Market Deeping............44 E5
Market Drayton............41 H3
Market Harborough............33 K1
Markethill............88 E5
Market Lavington............20 E7
Market Overton............44 B5
Market Rasen............54 F5
Market Stainton............55 G6
Market Warsop............53 H7
Market Weighton............61 F6
Market Weston............36 E2
Markfield............43 G5
Markham............19 F2
Markinch............81 H1
Markington............59 H4
Marksbury............20 A6
Marks Tey............36 E7
Markyate............22 F1
Marlborough............21 F6
Marlcliff............32 C4
Marldon.............5 J3
Marlesford............37 J4
Marley Green............41 G2
Marlingford............47 G6
Marloes............26 B6
Marlow............22 D4
Marlow Bottom............22 D4
Marlpit Hill............15 H1
Marnhull............11 J4
Marnoch............104 E3
Marnock............80 C5
Marple............51 J5
Marr............53 H3
Marrick............65 H8
Marros............27 G6
Marsden............52 C2
Marsett............58 E2
Marsh............10 D4
Marshalls Heath............23 G1
Marsham............47 G4
Marshaw............57 J5
Marsh Baldon............21 K3
Marshborough............25 K7
Marshbrook............47 F8
Marshchapel............55 H4
Marshfield, Avon.............20 B5
Marshfield, Gwent.............19 G4
Marshgate.............8 B6
Marsh Gibbon............33 J7
Marsh Green, Devon.............10 B6
Marsh Green, Kent.............15 H1
Marsh Green, Shrops.............41 H5
Marshland St James............45 J6
Marshside, Mers.............50 C2
Marshside, Kent.............25 J6
Marsh, The.............40 E7
Marshwood............10 E6
Marske............65 J7
Marske-by-the-Sea............67 G5
Marston, Lincs.............44 B2
Marston, Staffs.............42 B4
Marston, Wilts.............20 D7
Marston, H. & W.............30 E4
Marston, Warw.............33 F5
Marston, Ches.............51 F6
Marston, Oxon.............21 K2
Marston, Staffs.............41 K5
Marston Green............32 D1
Marston Magna............11 G3
Marston Meysey............20 F3
Marston Montgomery............42 D3
Marston Moretaine............34 C5
Marston on Dove............42 D4
Marston Stannett............31 G4
Marston St Lawrence............33 H5
Marston Trussell............33 J1
Marstow............19 K1
Marsworth............22 E1
Marten............21 G6
Marthall............51 H6
Martham............47 K5
Martin, Hants.............12 C4
Martin, Lincs.............54 F8
Martindale............64 B6
Martin Dales............55 F7
Martin Drove End............12 C3
Martinhoe.............9 G1
Martin Hussingtree............32 K3
Martinscroft............51 F5
Martinstown............11 H7
Martlesham............37 H5

Martlesham Heath............37 H5
Martletwy............26 E5
Martley............31 J3
Martock............11 F4
Marton, Lincs.............54 C5
Marton, Shrops.............40 E6
Marton, N. Yks.............60 E2
Marton, Cleve.............66 F6
Marton, Warw.............33 G3
Marton, Ches.............51 H6
Marton, N. Yks.............59 K4
Marvig............107 J7
Marwick............112 C5
Marwood.............9 F2
Marybank............102 C7
Maryburgh............102 D7
Marygold............83 G5
Marykirk............89 J2
Marylebone, G. Man.............50 E3
Marylebone, G. Lon.............23 H4
Marypark............95 K2
Maryport, D. & G.............68 C7
Maryport, Cumbr.............62 F4
Marystow.............8 E7
Mary Tavy.............4 F2
Maryton............89 J3
Marywell, Grampn.............96 E6
Marywell, Tays.............89 J4
Masham............59 H2
Mashbury............24 C1
Masongill............58 B3
Mastrick............97 J5
Matching............23 L1
Matching Green............23 L1
Matching Tye............23 L1
Matfen............75 G7
Matfield............16 D1
Mathern............19 K3
Mathon............31 J5
Mathry............26 C3
Matlaske............47 G3
Matlock............53 F7
Matlock Bath............52 E8
Matson............20 C1
Matterdale End............63 J5
Mattersey............53 J5
Mattingley............22 C7
Mattishall............46 F5
Mattishall Burgh............46 F5
Mauchline............71 K2
Maud............105 J4
Maugersbury............32 E7
Maughold............56 R2
Maulden............34 D6
Maulds Meaburn............64 D6
Maunby............59 J2
Maund Bryan............31 G4
Mautby............47 K5
Mavesyn Ridware............42 C5
Mavis Enderby............55 H7
Mawbray............62 D2
Mawdesley............50 D2
Mawgan.............2 F7
Mawla.............2 F7
Mawnan.............3 F7
Mawnan Smith.............2 F7
Maxey............44 E6
Maxstoke............32 E1
Maxton............74 C1
Maxwellheugh............74 D1
Maybole............71 H4
Mayfield, E. Susx.............16 C3
Mayfield, Staffs.............42 D2
Mayfield, Surrey............22 F7
Mayfield, Lothn.............81 J5
Mayford............22 E7
Mayland............24 F2
Maypole............19 J1
Maypole Green............47 K7
Maywick............115 G6
Meadle............22 D2
Meadowtown............40 E6
Meal Bank............57 J1
Mealista............106 D6
Mealsgate............63 H3
Meanwood............58 D4
Mearbeck............58 D4
Meare............11 F1
Meare Green............10 E3
Mears Ashby............34 B3
Measham............43 F5
Meathop............57 H2
Meaux............61 H7
Meavag............99 G3
Meavaig............99 F2
Meavy.............4 F3
Medbourne............44 B7
Medmenham............75 H7
Meddon.............8 C4
Meden Vale............53 H7
Medmenham............22 D4
Medstead............13 J2
Medstead............13 J2
Meerbrook............51 J7
Meer End............32 E2
Meesden............35 H6
Meeth.............9 F5
Meggethead............73 G2
Meidrim............27 G4
Meifod............40 C5
Meigle............88 E4
Meikle Earnock............80 C6
Meikle Tarty............97 J2
Meikle Wartle............97 G2
Meinciau............27 J5
Meir............42 B2
Meir Heath............42 B2
Melbost............107 J5
Melbost Borve............107 J3
Melbourn............35 G5
Melbourne, Humbs.............60 E6
Melbourne, Derby............43 F4
Melbury Abbas............12 A3
Melbury Bubb............11 G5
Melbury Osmond............11 G5

Melby Narborough, Leic 181

Melby 114 D3
Melchbourne 34 D3
Melcombe Bingham 11 J5
Meldon, Devon 9 F6
Meldon, Northum 75 H6
Meldreth 35 G5
Melfort 85 K7
Melgarve 94 C6
Meliden 49 K2
Melincourt 18 C2
Melin-y-coed 49 H4
Melin-y-ddol 40 B6
Melin-y-grug 40 B6
Melin-y-Wig 40 B2
Melkinthorpe 64 C5
Melkridge 64 E1
Melksham 20 D6
Melldalloch 77 J4
Melling, Mers 50 C3
Melling, Lancs 57 K3
Mellis 37 G2
Mellon Charles 100 E3
Mellon Udrigle 100 E3
Mellor, Lancs 58 B7
Mellor, G. Man 51 J5
Mellor Brook 58 B7
Mells, Som 11 J1
Mells, Suff 37 K2
Melmerby, Cumbr 64 D4
Melmerby, N. Yks 59 F2
Melmerby, N. Yks 59 J3
Melplash 11 F6
Melrose 74 B1
Melsonby 66 B7
Meltham 52 C2
Melton 37 H4
Meltonby 60 E5
Melton Constable 46 F3
Melton Mowbray 44 A5
Melton Ross 54 E2
Melvaig 100 D4
Melverley 40 E5
Melvich 110 E2
Membury 10 D5
Memsie 105 J2
Menai Bridge 48 E3
Mendham 37 H1
Mendlesham 37 G3
Mendlesham Green 37 F3
Menheniot 4 C3
Mennock 72 D4
Menston 59 G6
Menstrie 80 D2
Mentmore 22 E1
Meole Brace 41 F5
Meonstoke 13 J4
Meopham 24 C6
Meopham Station 24 C6
Mepal 35 H1
Meppershall 34 E6
Merbach 30 E5
Mere, Ches 51 G5
Mere, Wilts 11 K2
Mere Brow 50 D2
Mereclough 58 D7
Mere Green 42 D7
Mereworth 24 C7
Mergie 97 G7
Meriden 32 E1
Merkadale 91 J2
Merley 12 C6
Merlin's Bridge 26 D5
Merrington 41 F4
Merrion 26 D7
Merriott 11 F4
Merrivale 4 F2
Merrymeet 4 C3
Mersham 17 H2
Merstham 23 H7
Merston 14 B5
Merstone 13 H7
Merther 3 G5
Merthyr 27 H4
Merthyr Cynog 29 G6
Merthyr Dyfan 18 F5
Merthyr Mawr 18 C5
Merthyr Tydfil 18 E2
Merthyr Vale 18 E3
Merton, Norf 46 E7
Merton, Devon 9 F4
Merton, G. Lon 23 H6
Merton, Oxon 21 K1
Mervinslaw 74 C3
Meshaw 9 H4
Messing 24 E1
Messingham 54 C3
Metfield 37 H1
Metheringham 54 E7
Methil 81 J2
Methley 53 F1
Methlick 97 H2
Methven 88 C6
Methwold 46 C7
Methwold Hythe 46 C7
Mettingham 47 J8
Mevagissey 3 J5
Mexborough 53 G3
Mey 111 J1
Meysey Hampton 20 F2
Miavaig 106 E5
Michael 56 Q2
Michaelchurch 31 G7
Michaelchurch Escley 30 E6
Michaelchurch-on-Arrow 30 D4
Michaelstone-y-Fedw 19 G4
Michaelston-le-Pit 18 F5
Michaelstow 3 J2
Micheldever 13 H2
Michelmersh 13 F3
Mickfield 37 G3
Mickleby 67 J6
Micklefield 59 K7
Mickleham 23 G7
Mickleover 43 F3
Mickleton, Glos 32 D5
Mickleton, Durham 65 G5
Mickle Trafford 50 D7
Mickley 59 H3
Mickley Square 65 H1
Mid Ardlaw 105 J2
Midbea 112 E2
Mid Beltie 96 F5
Mid Culbeuchly 104 F2
Middle Assendon 22 C4
Middle Aston 33 G7
Middle Barton 33 G7
Middlebie 73 H7
Middle Claydon 33 K7
Middleham 59 G2
Middlehope 31 F1
Middle Littleton 32 C5
Middle Maes-coed 30 E6
Middlemarsh 11 H5
Middle Mill 26 C4
Middle Rasen 54 E5
Middlesbrough 66 E5
Middlesmoor 59 F3
Middleston Moor 66 C4
Middlestown 52 E2
Middleton, Strath 84 A4
Middleton, Norf 46 B5
Middleton, Northnts 44 B7
Middleton, Essex 36 D6
Middleton, Warw 42 D7
Middleton, Shrops 40 D7
Middleton, Derby 52 D7
Middleton, Derby 42 E1
Middleton, N. Yks 60 E2
Middleton, Shrops 40 E4
Middleton, Hants 13 G1
Middleton, Northum 75 G2
Middleton, Shrops 31 G2
Middleton, H. & W 31 G3
Middleton, Northum 75 G6
Middleton, N. Yks 59 G6
Middleton, G. Man 51 H3
Middleton, Lancs 57 H5
Middleton, Lothn 81 J6
Middleton, W. Yks 59 J8
Middleton, Cumbr 57 K2
Middleton, Suff 37 K3
Middleton, Northum 83 K8
Middleton Cheney 33 G5
Middleton Green 42 B3
Middleton Hall 75 F2
Middleton-in-Teesdale 65 G5
Middleton-on-Sea 14 C6
Middleton on the Hill 31 G3
Middleton-on-the-Wolds 61 G6
Middleton Priors 41 H7
Middleton Scriven 31 H1
Middleton St George 66 D6
Middleton Stoney 33 H7
Middleton Tyas 66 C7
Middletown 40 E5
Middle Tysoe 33 F5
Middle Wallop 12 E2
Middlewich 51 G7
Middle Winterslow 12 E2
Middle Woodford 12 D2
Middlewood Green 37 F3
Middlezoy 10 E2
Middridge 66 C5
Midfield 109 G2
Midge Hall 50 E1
Midgeholme 64 D2
Midgham 21 K6
Midgley 52 C1
Midhopestones 52 E4
Midhurst 14 B3
Midlem 74 B2
Midsomer Norton 20 A7
Midtown 100 E4
Midtown of Buchromb 104 C4
Midville 45 G1
Mid Walls 114 E3
Mid Yell 117 G3
Migvie 96 D5
Milborne Port 11 H4
Milborne St Andrew 11 K6
Milborne Wick 11 H3
Milbourne 75 H7
Milburn 64 D5
Milbury Heath 20 A3
Milcombe 33 G6
Milden 36 E5
Mildenhall, Suff 36 C2
Mildenhall, Wilts 21 G6
Milebrooke 30 E2
Milebush 16 E1
Mile Elm 20 D6
Mile End, Essex 36 E7
Mile End, Glos 19 K1
Mileham 46 E5
Milesmark 81 F3
Milfield 75 F1
Milford, Staffs 42 B4
Milford, Surrey 14 C1
Milford, Devon 8 C3
Milford, Derby 43 F2
Milford Haven 26 D6
Milford on Sea 12 E6
Milkwall 19 K2
Milland 14 B3
Mill Bank 52 C1
Millbounds 113 F3
Millbreck 105 K4
Millbrex 105 H4
Millbridge 14 B1
Millbrook, Beds 34 D6
Millbrook, Corn 4 E4
Millbrook, Hants 13 F4
Millburn 71 K2
Mill Corner 16 F3
Mill End, Bucks 22 C4
Mill End, Herts 35 G6
Millerhill 81 J5
Miller's Dale 52 D6
Mill Green, Essex 24 C2
Mill Green, Shrops 41 H4
Millheugh 80 C6
Mill Hill 23 H3
Millholme 57 J1
Millhouse, Strath 77 J4
Millhouse, Cumbr 63 J4
Millikenpark 79 G5
Millington 60 F5
Mill Lane 22 C7
Millmeece 41 K3
Millom 56 E2
Millport 78 D6
Mill Side 57 H2
Mill Street 46 F5
Millthrop 58 B1
Milltimber 97 H5
Millton of Corsindale 97 F5
Millton of Murtle 97 H5
Milltown, Devon 9 F2
Milltown, Derby 53 F7
Milltown, D. & G 73 J7
Milltown of Aberdalgie 88 C6
Milltown of Auchindoun 96 C1
Milltown of Craigston 105 G3
Milltown of Edinvillie 96 B1
Milltown of Rothiemay 104 E4
Milltown of Towie 96 D4
Milnathort 88 D8
Milngavie 79 H4
Milnrow 51 J2
Milnthorpe 57 H2
Milovaig 99 G7
Milson 31 H2
Milstead 24 F7
Milston 12 D1
Milton, Staffs 42 B1
Milton, Cumbr 64 C1
Milton, Highld 94 C2
Milton, D. & G 68 D5
Milton, D. & G 72 D7
Milton, Highld 102 D8
Milton, Grampn 104 E2
Milton, Dyfed 26 E6
Milton, Highld 103 F5
Milton, Strath 79 G4
Milton, Oxon 33 G6
Milton, Central 79 H1
Milton, Cambs 35 H3
Milton, Highld 103 H7
Milton, Oxon 21 J3
Milton, Highld 111 K3
Milton, Highld 101 K7
Milton Abbas 11 K5
Milton Abbot 4 E2
Milton Bridge 81 H5
Milton Bryan 34 C6
Milton Clevedon 11 H2
Milton Coldwells 97 J2
Milton Combe 4 E3
Milton Damerel 8 D4
Miltonduff 103 K6
Milton Ernest 34 D4
Milton Green 50 D8
Milton Hill 21 J3
Milton Keynes 34 B6
Milton Keynes Village 34 B6
Milton Libourne 21 F6
Milton Malsor 33 K4
Milton of Auchinhove 96 E5
Milton of Balgonie 81 J1
Milton of Buchanan 79 G2
Milton of Campfield 97 F5
Milton of Campsie 79 J4
Milton of Corsindae 97 F5
Milton of Cushnie 96 E4
Milton of Lesmore 96 D3
Milton of Murtle 97 H5
Milton of Tullich 96 C6
Milton on Stour 11 K3
Milton Regis 24 F6
Milton-under-Wychwood 21 G1
Milverton 10 C3
Milwich 42 B3
Milwr 50 A6
Minard 78 B2
Minchinhampton 20 C2
Mindrum 74 E1
Minehead 10 A1
Minera 40 D1
Minety 20 E3
Minffordd 38 E3
Mingary 90 C3
Miningsby 55 H7
Minions 4 C2
Minishant 71 J3
Minllyn 39 H5
Minnes 97 J3
Minnigaff 71 K8
Minskip 59 J4
Minstead 12 E4
Minster, Kent 25 F5
Minster, Kent 25 K6
Minsteracres 65 H2
Minsterley 40 E6
Minster Lovell 21 H1
Minsterworth 20 B1
Minterne Magna 11 H5
Minting 55 F6
Mintlaw 105 K4
Minto 74 B2
Minton 41 F7
Minwear 26 E5
Minworth 42 D7
Mirbister 112 D4
Mireland 111 K2
Mirfield 52 E2
Miserden 20 D2
Miskin 18 E4
Misson 53 J4
Misterton, Notts 54 B4
Misterton, Somer 11 F5
Misterton, Leic 33 H1
Mistley 37 G6
Mitcham 23 H6
Mitcheldean 20 A1
Mitchell 3 G4
Mitchel Troy 19 J1
Mitford 75 H6
Mithian 2 F4
Mitton 42 A5
Mixbury 33 J6
Mixon 42 C1
Mobberley 51 G6
Moccas 30 E5
Mochdre, Powys 29 H1
Mochdre, Clwyd 49 H3
Mochrum 68 E6
Mockerkin 63 F5
Modbury 5 G4
Moddershall 42 B3
Moelfre, Clwyd 40 C4
Moelfre, Gwyn 48 E2
Moffat 73 F4
Mogerhanger 34 E5
Moira 43 F5
Molash 25 G7
Mol-chlach 91 K4
Mold 50 B7
Molehill Green 35 J7
Molescroft 61 H6
Molesworth 34 D2
Molland 9 J3
Mollington, Ches 50 C6
Mollington, Oxon 33 G5
Mollinsburn 80 C4
Mondynes 97 G8
Monewden 37 H4
Moniaive 72 C5
Monifieth 89 G5
Monikie 89 G5
Monimail 88 E7
Monington 26 F2
Monken Hadley 23 H3
Monk Fryston 60 C8
Monkhopton 41 H7
Monkland 31 F4
Monkleigh 8 E3
Monknash 18 D5
Monkokehampton 9 F5
Monks Eleigh 36 E5
Monk's Heath 51 H6
Monk Sherborne 21 L7
Monkshill 97 G1
Monksilver 10 B2
Monks Kirby 33 G1
Monk Soham 37 H3
Monks Risborough 22 D2
Monkswood 19 H2
Monkton, Devon 10 C5
Monkton, T. & W 66 D1
Monkton, Strath 71 J2
Monkton, Kent 25 J6
Monkton Combe 20 B6
Monkton Deverill 11 K2
Monkton Farleigh 20 C6
Monkton Heathfield 10 D3
Monkton Up Wimborne 12 C4
Monkwood 13 J2
Monmouth 19 K1
Monnington on Wye 30 E5
Monreith 68 E6
Monreith Mains 68 E6
Montacute 11 F4
Montford 41 F5
Montgarrie 96 E4
Montgomery 40 D7
Montgreenan 79 F7
Montrose 89 K3
Montsale 25 G3
Monxton 13 F1
Monyash 52 D7
Monymusk 97 F4
Monzie 88 A6
Moorby 55 G7
Moorcot 30 E4
Moordown 12 C6
Moore 50 E5
Moorends 53 J2
Moorhall 53 F6
Moorhampton 30 E5
Moorhouse, Notts 54 B7
Moorhouse, Cumbr 63 J2
Moorland or Northmoor Green 10 E2
Moorlinch 10 E2
Moor Monkton 60 C5
Moor of Balvack 97 F4
Moorsholm 67 G6
Moorside 51 J3
Moor, The 16 E3
Moortown, Lincs 54 E4
Moortown, I. of W 13 G7
Morangie 103 F4
Morar 92 C6
Morborne 44 E7
Morchard Bishop 9 H5
Morcombelake 10 F6
Morcott 44 C6
Morda 40 D4
Morden, Dorset 12 B6
Morden, G. Lon 23 H6
Mordiford 31 G6
Mordon 66 D5
More 40 E7
Morebath 9 K3
Morebattle 74 D2
Morecambe 57 H4
More Crichel 12 B5
Morefield 101 H3
Moreleigh 5 H4
Moresby 62 E5
Moresby Parks 62 E6
Morestead 13 H3
Moreton, Oxon 22 B2
Moreton, Mers 50 B4
Moreton, Staffs 41 J5
Moreton, Dorset 11 K7
Moreton, Essex 23 L2
Moreton Corbet 41 G4
Moretonhampstead 9 H7
Moreton-in-Marsh 32 E6
Moreton Jeffries 31 H5
Moreton Morrell 33 F4
Moreton on Lugg 31 G5
Moreton Pinkney 33 H5
Moreton Say 41 H3
Moreton Valence 20 B2
Morfa Bychan 38 E3
Morfa Glas 18 C2
Morfa Nefyn 38 B2
Morgan's Vale 12 D3
Morland 64 C5
Morley, W. Yks 52 E1
Morley, Derby 43 F2
Morley, Durham 65 J5
Morley Green 51 H5
Morley St Botolph 46 F7
Morningside 81 H4
Morningthorpe 47 H7
Morpeth 75 H6
Morrey 42 D5
Morriston 27 L7
Morston 46 F2
Morthoe 8 E1
Mortimer 22 B6
Mortimer's Cross 31 F3
Mortimer West End 22 B6
Mortlake 23 H5
Morton, Lincs 54 C4
Morton, Lincs 44 D4
Morton, Shrops 40 D4
Morton, Norf 47 G5
Morton, Derby 53 G7
Morton, Avon 19 L3
Morton Bagot 32 D3
Morton-on-Swale 59 J1
Morvah 2 C6
Morval 4 C4
Morvich, Highld 103 F2
Morvich, Highld 93 F3
Morville 41 H7
Morwenstow 8 C4
Mosborough 53 G5
Moscow 79 G7
Mosedale 63 J4
Moseley, W. Mids 32 C1
Moseley, H. & W 31 K4
Moss, Strath 84 A4
Moss, Clwyd 40 E1
Moss, S. Yks 53 H2
Mossat 96 D4
Mossbank, Shetld 117 F5
Moss Bank, Mers 50 E4
Mossblown 71 K2
Mossburnford 74 C3
Mossdale 72 B7
Mossend 80 C5
Mossgiel 71 K2
Mossley 51 J3
Moss of Barmuckity 104 B2
Moss Side 57 G7
Mosstodloch 104 C2
Mosterton 11 F5
Mostyn 50 A5
Motcombe 11 K3
Motherby 63 K5
Motherwell 80 C6
Mottingham 23 K5
Mottisfont 13 F3
Mottistone 13 G7
Mottram in Longdendale 51 J4
Mottram St Andrew 51 H6
Mouldsworth 50 E6
Moulin 88 B3
Moulsecoomb 15 G5
Moulsford 21 K4
Moulsoe 34 C5
Moulton, Northnts 34 A3
Moulton, Suff 36 B3
Moulton, N. Yks 66 C7
Moulton, Ches 51 F7
Moulton, Lincs 45 G4
Moulton Chapel 45 F5
Moulton Seas End 45 G4
Mount, Corn 3 F4
Mount, Corn 3 K3
Mountain Ash 18 E3
Mountain Cross 81 G7
Mountbenger 73 J2
Mount Bures 36 E6
Mountfield 16 E3
Mountgerald 102 D6
Mount Hawke 2 F5
Mountjoy 3 G3
Mountnessing 24 C3
Mounton 19 K3
Mountsorrel 43 H5
Mousehole 2 C7
Mousen 75 H1
Mouswald 73 F7
Mow Cop, Staffs 42 A1
Mow Cop, Ches 42 A1
Mowhaugh 74 E2
Mowsley 43 J8
Moy 94 C7
Moyles Court 12 D5
Moylgrove 26 F2
Muasdale 77 F7
Muchalls 97 J6
Much Birch 31 G6
Much Cowarne 31 H5
Much Dewchurch 31 F6
Muchelney 11 F3
Much Hadham 35 H7
Much Hoole 50 D1
Muchlarnick 4 C4
Much Marcle 31 H6
Much Wenlock 41 H7
Mucking 24 C4
Mucklestone 41 J3
Muckleton 41 G4
Muckletown 96 E3
Muckton 55 H5
Mudale 109 G5
Muddiford 9 F2
Mudeford 12 D6
Mudford 11 G4
Mudgley 11 F1
Mugdock 79 H4
Mugeary 91 K2
Mugginton 42 E2
Muggleswick 65 H2
Muie 102 E2
Muir 95 J7
Muirden 105 G3
Muirdrum 89 H5
Muirhead, Strath 80 B5
Muirhead, Tays 89 F5
Muirhouses 80 F3
Muirkirk 72 B2
Muir of Fairburn 102 C7
Muir of Fowlis 96 E4
Muir of Lochs 104 C2
Muir of Ord 102 D7
Muirshearlich 93 H7
Muirtack, Grampn 105 H4
Muirtack, Grampn 97 J2
Muirton, Tays 88 B7
Muirton, Highld 103 F6
Muirton of Ardblair 88 D4
Muirton of Ballochy 89 J2
Muker 65 G8
Mulbarton 47 G6
Mulben 104 C3
Mullion 2 E8
Mullion Cove 2 E8
Mumbles, The 27 L8
Mumby 55 K6
Munderfield Row 31 H4
Munderfield Stocks 31 H4
Mundesley 47 J3
Mundford 46 D7
Mundham, W. Susx 14 B5
Mundham, Norf 47 J7
Mundon 24 E2
Munerigie 93 J5
Mungasdale 101 F3
Mungrisdale 63 J4
Munlochy 102 E7
Munsley 31 H5
Munslow 31 G1
Murch 18 F5
Murcott 21 K1
Murkle 111 H2
Murlaggan, Highld 93 G6
Murlaggan, Highld 93 K7
Murrow 45 G6
Mursley 34 B7
Murthly 88 C5
Murton, Durham 66 D3
Murton, N. Yks 60 D5
Murton, Cumbr 64 E5
Murton, Northum 83 H7
Musbury 10 D6
Muscoates 60 D2
Musdale 86 B6
Musselburgh 81 J4
Muston, Leic 44 B3
Muston, N. Yks 61 H3
Mustow Green 32 A2
Mutford 37 K1
Muthill 88 A7
Mutterton 10 B5
Mybster 111 H3
Myddfai 28 E6
Myddle 41 F4
Mydroilyn 28 B4
Mylor Bridge 3 G6
Mynachlog-ddu 26 F3
Myndtown 40 E8
Mynydd-bach 19 J3
Mynydd Isa 50 B7
Mynydd Llandegai 48 F4
Mynydd Mechell 48 C1
Mynytho 38 C3
Myrebird 97 G6
Mytchett 22 D7
Mytholm 51 J1
Mytholmroyd 52 C1
Myton-on-Swale 59 K4

N

Naast 100 E4
Naburn 60 D6
Nackington 25 H7
Nacton 37 H5
Nafferton 61 H5
Nailsea 19 J5
Nailstone 43 G6
Nailsworth 20 C3
Nairn 103 G7
Nancegollan 2 E6
Nancledra 2 C6
Nanhoron 38 B3
Nannerch 50 A7
Nanpantan 43 H5
Nanpean 3 H4
Nanstallon 3 J3
Nant-ddu 18 E1
Nanternis 28 A4
Nantgaredig 27 J4
Nantgarw 18 F4
Nant Glas 29 G3
Nantglyn 49 K4
Nantlle 38 E1
Nantmawr 40 D4
Nantmel 29 H3
Nantmor 38 F2
Nant Peris 48 F5
Nantwich 41 H1
Nant-y-derry 19 H2
Nantyffyllon 18 C3
Nantyglo 19 F1
Nant-y-moel 18 D3
Naphill 22 D3
Nappa 58 D5
Napton on the Hill 33 G3
Narberth 26 F5
Narborough, Norf 46 C5
Narborough, Leic 43 H7

Nasareth................38 D1
Naseby..................33 J2
Nash, Bucks............34 A6
Nash, H. & W..........30 E3
Nash, Shrops..........31 H2
Nash, Gwent...........19 H4
Nash Lee...............22 D2
Nassington.............44 D7
Nasty...................35 G7
Nateby, Cumbr........64 E7
Nateby, Lancs.........57 H6
Natland................57 J2
Naughton..............36 F5
Naunton, H. & W......32 A6
Naunton, Glos.........32 D7
Naunton Beauchamp....32 B4
Navenby...............44 C1
Navestock Heath.......23 L3
Navestock Side........24 B3
Nawton................60 D2
Nayland................36 E6
Nazeing................23 K2
Neacroft...............12 D6
Neal's Green...........33 F1
Neasham...............66 D6
Neath..................18 B3
Neatishead............47 J4
Nebo, Dyfed...........28 C3
Nebo, Gwyn...........38 D1
Nebo, Gwyn...........39 H1
Necton.................46 D6
Nedd..................108 C5
Nedging Tye...........36 F5
Needham...............37 H1
Needham Market.......37 F4
Needingworth.........35 G2
Neen Savage...........31 H2
Neen Sollars..........31 H2
Neenton...............31 H1
Nefyn..................38 C2
Neilston...............79 G6
Nelson, Lancs.........58 D7
Nelson, M. Glam......18 F3
Nelson Village.........75 J7
Nemphlar.............80 D7
Nempnett Thrubwell...19 K6
Nenthead.............64 E3
Nenthorn..............82 E8
Nerabus...............76 B6
Nercwys...............50 B7
Nerston...............79 J6
Nesbit.................75 F1
Ness, Ches............50 C6
Ness, N. Yks..........60 D3
Nesscliffe............40 E5
Neston, Ches.........50 B6
Neston, Wilts.........20 C6
Nether Alderley.......51 H6
Netheravon............12 D1
Nether Blainslie.......82 D7
Netherbrae...........105 G3
Nether Broughton.....43 J4
Netherburn............80 D7
Nether Burrow.........57 K3
Netherbury............11 F6
Nether Cerne..........11 H6
Nether Compton......11 G4
Nether Dallachy......104 C2
Netherend.............19 K2
Nether Exe.............9 K5
Netherfield...........16 E4
Netherhampton........12 D3
Nether Haugh..........53 G4
Nether Heyford........33 J4
Nether Howcleuch.....73 F3
Nether Kellet..........57 J4
Nether Kinmundy....105 K4
Nether Kirkton.........79 G6
Netherlaw.............69 J6
Netherley..............97 H6
Nethermill.............73 F6
Nether Padley.........52 E6
Netherplace...........79 H6
Nether Poppleton......60 C5
Nether Ringorm.......104 B4
Nether Row............63 J4
Netherseal............42 E5
Nether Silton..........59 K1
Nether Stowey........10 C2
Netherthird...........72 A3
Netherthong..........52 D3
Netherton, H. & W....32 B5
Netherton, Mers......50 C3
Netherton, W. Yks....52 E2
Netherton, Northum...75 F4
Netherton, Tays......89 H3
Netherton, Central....79 H4
Netherton, Devon......5 J2
Nethertown, Cumbr...62 E7
Nethertown, Highld...111 K1
Nether Wallop.........13 F2
Nether Wasdale........63 G2
Nether Whitacre......42 E7
Nether Winchendon or
    Lower Winchendon..22 C1
Netherwitton.........75 G5
Nether Worton.........33 G6
Nethy Bridge..........95 J3
Netley.................13 G5
Netley Marsh..........13 F4
Nettlebed.............22 C4
Nettlebridge..........11 H1
Nettlecombe..........11 G6
Nettleden.............22 F1
Nettleham.............54 E6
Nettlestead...........24 C7
Nettlestead Green....24 C7
Nettlestone...........13 J6
Nettleton, Wilts......20 C5
Nettleton, Lincs......54 F3
Neuk, The.............97 G6
Nevendon.............24 D3
Nevern.................26 E2
New Abbey.............72 E8
New Aberdour........105 H2

New Addington.........23 J6
New Alresford.........13 H2
New Alyth..............88 E4
Newark, Orkney......113 H2
Newark, Cambs........45 F6
Newark-on-Trent......44 A1
Newarthill.............80 C6
New Ash Green.........24 C6
New Barn...............24 C6
New Bewick............75 G2
Newbiggin, Cumbr.....64 B5
Newbiggin, Cumbr.....64 C3
Newbiggin, Cumbr.....64 D5
Newbiggin, N. Yks....58 E1
Newbiggin, N. Yks....58 E2
Newbiggin, Cumbr.....57 F4
Newbiggin, Durham...65 G5
Newbiggin-by-the-Sea..75 K6
Newbigging, Tays......88 E4
Newbigging, Strath....80 F7
Newbigging, Tays......89 G5
Newbigging, Tays......89 G5
Newbiggin-on-Lune....64 E7
Newbold, Derby.......53 F6
Newbold, Leic.........43 G5
Newbold on Avon......33 G2
Newbold-on-Stour.....32 E5
Newbold Pacey.........32 E4
Newbold Verdon.......43 G6
New Bolingbroke......45 G1
Newborough, Staffs....42 D4
Newborough, Cambs....45 F6
Newbottle.............33 H6
Newbourne.............37 H5
New Brancepeth.......66 C3
Newbridge, Corn........2 C6
Newbridge, Clwyd.....40 D2
Newbridge, Hants......12 E4
Newbridge, Gwent.....19 G3
Newbridge, Lothn.....81 G4
Newbridge, I. of W....13 G7
Newbridge-on-Usk.....19 H3
Newbridge-on-Wye....29 H4
New Brighton..........50 C4
New Brinsley..........43 G1
Newbrough............74 E8
New Buckenham........47 F7
Newbuildings...........9 H5
Newburgh, Lancs......50 D2
Newburgh, Fife.......88 E7
Newburgh, Grampn...97 J3
Newburn...............66 B1
Newbury...............21 J6
Newby, N. Yks........58 C3
Newby, Cumbr.........64 C5
Newby, N. Yks........66 F6
Newby Bridge.........57 G2
Newby East............64 B2
New Byth.............105 H3
Newby West...........63 J2
Newby Wiske..........59 J2
Newcastle, Shrops.....30 D1
Newcastle, Gwent......19 J1
Newcastle Emlyn.......27 H2
Newcastleton..........74 A6
Newcastle-under-Lyme..42 A2
Newcastle upon Tyne...66 C1
Newchapel, Staffs.....42 A1
Newchapel, Surrey....15 G1
Newchapel, Dyfed.....27 G3
New Cheriton..........13 H3
Newchurch, Powys.....30 D4
Newchurch, Kent......17 H2
Newchurch, Dyfed.....27 H4
Newchurch, I. of W....13 H7
Newchurch, Gwent.....19 J3
Newchurch in Pendle...58 D7
New Clipstone.........53 H7
New Costessey.........47 G6
Newcott...............10 D5
New Cross.............28 D2
New Cumnock..........72 B3
New Deer.............105 H4
Newdigate.............15 E1
New Duston............33 K3
New Earswick..........60 D5
New Edlington.........53 H4
Newell Green..........22 D5
New Eltham............23 K5
New End...............32 D3
Newenden..............16 F3
Newent.................31 J7
New Farnley...........59 H7
New Ferry.............50 C5
Newfield, Durham......66 C4
Newfield, Highld.....103 F5
New Fryston...........53 G1
Newgale...............26 C4
New Galloway..........72 B7
Newgate...............46 F2
Newgate Street.......23 J2
New Grimsby...........2 N2
Newhall, Derby........42 E4
Newhall, Ches.........41 H2
Newham................75 H2
Newham Hall..........75 H2
New Hartley...........75 K7
Newhaven..............15 H5
New Hedges...........26 F6
Newhey................51 J2
New Holland...........54 E1
Newholm...............67 J6
New Horndean.........83 G7
New Houghton, Norf...46 C4
New Houghton, Derby..53 G7
Newhouse.............80 C5
New Houses............58 D3
New Hutton............57 J1
New Hythe.............24 D7
Newick.................15 H3
Newington, Kent......24 E6
Newington, Kent......17 J2
Newington, Oxon......21 L3
New Inn, Gwent.......19 H3

New Inn, Gwent.......19 J2
New Inn, Dyfed.......27 J3
New Invention.........30 D2
New Kelso...........101 F8
New Lanark............80 D7
Newland, N. Yks......53 J1
Newland, H. & W......31 J5
Newland, Glos.........19 K2
Newlandrig............81 J5
Newlands, Grampn....104 C3
Newlands, Highld....103 F8
Newlands, Northum....65 H2
Newlands of Geise...111 G2
New Lane..............50 D2
New Leake.............45 H1
New Leeds............105 J3
New Longton..........50 E1
New Luce..............68 C4
Newlyn..................2 C7
Newmachar............97 H4
Newmains.............80 D6
New Malden...........23 H6
Newmarket, Suff......36 B3
Newmarket, W. Isles..107 J5
New Marske............67 G5
New Marton............40 E3
Newmill, Border.......74 B3
New Mill, Corn.........2 C6
Newmill, Grampn....104 D3
New Mill, W. Yks.....52 D3
New Mill, Herts.......22 E1
Newmill of Inshewan..89 G2
New Mills, Powys......40 B6
New Mills, Corn........3 H4
New Mills, Derby......51 J5
New Mills, Gwent......19 K2
Newmiln................88 D5
Newmilns..............79 H8
New Milton............12 E6
New Moat..............26 E4
Newnham, Glos.........20 A1
Newnham, Hants......22 C7
Newnham, Herts.......35 F6
Newnham, Kent........25 F7
Newnham, H. & W......31 H3
Newnham, Northnts...33 H4
New Ollerton..........53 J7
New Pitsligo.........105 H3
New Polzeath...........3 H1
Newport, Glos.........20 B3
Newport, Dyfed........26 E3
Newport, Devon.........9 F2
Newport, Humbs.......60 F7
Newport, Gwent.......19 H4
Newport, Highld......111 H6
Newport, I. of W......13 H7
Newport, Shrops......41 J5
Newport, Essex.......35 J6
Newport, Norf........47 L5
Newport-on-Tay.......89 G6
Newport Pagnell.......34 B5
Newpound Common.....14 D3
New Quay, Dyfed......28 A4
Newquay, Corn.........3 G3
New Rackheath........47 H5
New Radnor...........30 D3
New Romney...........17 H3
New Rossington.......53 J4
New Row...............58 B7
New Sauchie...........80 D2
New Scone.............88 D6
Newseat................97 G2
Newsham, N. Yks......65 J6
Newsham, Northum...75 K7
Newsholme, Lancs.....58 D5
Newsholme, Humbs....60 E8
New Silksworth........66 D2
Newstead, Border.....74 B1
Newstead, Notts.......43 H1
Newstead, Northum...75 H2
New Stevenston.......80 C6
Newthorpe............60 B7
Newtoft...............54 E5
New Tolsta...........107 K4
Newton, Northnts.....34 B1
Newton, Border.......74 B2
Newton, Lancs.........58 B5
Newton, Strath........78 C2
Newton, Staffs........42 C4
Newton, M. Glam......18 C5
Newton, Lincs.........44 D3
Newton, W. Isles......98 D5
Newton, Norf..........46 D5
Newton, Strath........72 E1
Newton, Wilts.........12 E3
Newton, Ches..........50 E6
Newton, H. & W.......30 E6
Newton, Ches..........50 E8
Newton, Cumbr........57 F3
Newton, Lothn.........81 F4
Newton, Highld......103 F6
Newton, Highld......103 F8
Newton, H. & W.......31 G4
Newton, S. Glam......19 G5
Newton, D. & G.......73 G5
Newton, Northum......65 H1
Newton, Warw..........33 H2
Newton, Cambs........35 H5
Newton, Cambs........45 H5
Newton, Notts.........43 J2
Newton, Lancs.........57 J3
Newton, Strath........75 J5
Newton, Highld......111 K4
Newton, Grampn....103 K6
Newton, W. Glam......27 L8
Newton Abbot..........5 J2
Newton Arlosh.........63 G2
Newton Aycliffe.......66 C5
Newton Bewley........66 E5
Newton Blossomville..34 C4
Newton Bromswold.....34 C3
Newton Burgoland.....43 F6
Newton by Toft........54 E5

Newton Ferrers........4 F5
Newtonferry...........98 D5
Newton Flotman.......47 H7
Newtongrange.........81 J5
Newton Harcourt......43 J7
Newtonhill............97 J6
Newton Kyme..........60 B6
Newton-le-Willows, Mers..50 E4
Newton-le-Willows, N. Yks..59 H2
Newton Longville......34 B6
Newton Mearns........79 H6
Newtonmore...........94 F6
Newton of Ardtoe.....85 H1
Newton of Balcanquhal..88 D7
Newton-on-Ouse.......60 C5
Newton-on-Rawcliffe...60 F1
Newton on the Moor...75 H4
Newton on Trent......54 C6
Newton Poppleford....10 B7
Newton Purcell........33 J6
Newton Regis.........42 E6
Newton Reigny........64 B4
Newton St Cyres.......9 J6
Newton St Faith......47 H5
Newton St Loe.........20 B6
Newton St Petrock.....8 E4
Newton Solney........42 E4
Newton Stacey........13 G1
Newton Stewart.......68 F4
Newton Tony..........12 E1
Newton Tracey.........9 F3
Newton under Roseberry..67 F6
Newton upon Derwent..60 E6
Newton Valence.......13 K2
Newton with Scales...57 H7
Newtown, Wilts.......12 B3
Newtown, Highld......94 B5
Newtown, Cumbr......64 C1
New Town, Lothn......82 C4
Newtown, Dorset......12 C6
Newtown, Powys......40 C7
Newtown, Hants.......12 E4
Newtown, Northum....75 F1
Newtown, Shrops......41 F3
Newtown, Hants.......13 F3
Newtown, Northum....75 G2
Newtown, Northum....75 G4
Newtown, I. of W.....13 G6
Newtown, Ches........41 H2
Newtown, H. & W.....31 H5
Newtown, Hants.......13 J4
Newtown, Ches........51 J5
Newtown, Derby......51 J5
Newtown, Hants.......21 J6
Newtown, Staffs......51 J7
Newtown, I. of M......56 Q4
Newtown-in St Martin...2 F7
Newtown St Boswells..74 B1
New Tredegar.........18 F2
Newtyle................88 E4
New Waltham.........55 G3
New Wimpole..........35 G5
New Winton...........82 C4
New Yatt..............21 H1
New York, Lincs.......45 F1
New York, T. & W......75 K7
Neyland...............26 D6
Nibley.................20 A4
Nicholashayne........10 C4
Nicholaston...........27 K8
Nidd..................59 J4
Nigg, Highld.........103 G5
Nigg, Grampn.........97 J5
Nine Ashes............24 B2
Ninebanks............64 E2
Ninemile Bar or Crocketford..72 D7
Ninfield..............16 E4
Ningwood.............13 G7
Nisbet................74 C2
Niton..................7 K7
Nitshill...............79 H5
Niwbwrch.............48 D4
Noak Hill.............23 L3
Nobottle...............33 J3
Nocton................54 E7
Noke...................21 K1
Nolton................26 C5
Nolton Haven........26 C5
No Man's Heath, Warw..42 E6
No Man's Heath, Ches..41 G2
Nomansland, Wilts....12 E4
Nomansland, Devon....9 J4
Noneley..............41 F4
Nonington............25 J7
Noonsbrough.........114 C3
Nor...................83 H7
Noranside............89 G2
Norbury, Derby.......42 D2
Norbury, Shrops......40 E7
Norbury, Ches........41 G2
Norbury, Staffs......41 J4
Nordelph.............45 J6
Norden, Dorset......12 B7
Norden, G. Man.......51 H2
Nordley...............41 H7
Norham................83 H7
Norley.................50 E6
Norleywood...........13 F6
Normanby, Humbs....54 C2
Normanby, N. Yks....60 E2
Normanby-by-Spital...54 E5
Normanby le Wold....54 F4
Norman Cross........44 E7
Normandy.............22 E7
Norman's Green.......10 B5
Normanton, Lincs.....44 C1
Normanton, Leic......44 C6
Normanton, W. Yks...53 F1
Normanton, Derby....43 F3
Normanton, Notts.....43 K1
Normanton le Heath...43 F5
Normanton-on-the-Wolds..43 J3
Normanton on Soar....43 H4
Normanton on Trent...54 B5

Normoss...............57 G7
Norrington Common...20 C6
Norris Hill............43 F5
Northallerton.........59 J1
Northam, Devon........8 E3
Northam, Hants........13 G4
Northampton..........34 A3
North Ascot...........22 E6
North Aston...........33 G7
Northaw...............23 H2
North Baddesley......13 F4
North Ballachulish....86 C2
North Barrow..........11 H3
North Barsham........46 E3
North Benfleet........24 D4
North Berwick........82 D3
North Boarhunt........13 J4
Northborough.........44 E6
Northbourne...........25 K7
North Bovey...........9 H7
North Bradley.........20 C7
North Brentor..........4 E1
North Buckland........8 E1
North Burlingham.....47 J5
North Cadbury........11 H3
North Cairn...........70 E7
North Carlton.........54 D6
North Cave............61 F7
North Cerney.........20 E2
Northchapel..........14 C3
North Charford.......12 D4
North Charlton.......75 H2
North Cheriton.......11 H3
North Chideock.......11 F6
Northchurch..........22 E2
North Cliffe..........60 F7
North Clifton.........54 C6
North Cotes...........55 H3
North Cove............47 K8
North Cowton.........62 C3
North Crawley.........34 C5
North Cray............23 K5
North Creake.........46 D3
North Curry...........10 E3
North Dalton.........61 G5
North Deighton.......59 J5
North Duffield.........60 D7
Northdyke............112 C4
North Elkington......55 G4
North Elmham........46 E4
Northend, Avon......20 B6
Northend, Bucks......22 C3
North End, W. Susx...14 E5
North End, Hants.....13 J5
North End, Hants.....21 J6
North End, Avon......19 J4
North Erradale......100 D4
North Fearns.........92 B2
North Ferriby.........54 D1
Northfield, W. Mids...32 C2
Northfield, Border....83 H5
Northfield, Grampn...97 J5
Northfleet............24 C5
North Frodingham.....61 H5
Northgate............45 E4
North Gorley..........12 D4
North Green..........37 H1
North Greetwell.......54 E6
North Grimston.......60 F4
North Hayling.........13 K5
North Heasley..........9 H2
North Heath..........14 D3
North Hill, Corn.......4 C2
North Hill, Cambs.....35 H2
North Hinksey Village..21 J2
North Holmwood......14 E1
North Huish...........5 H4
North Hykeham.......54 D7
Northiam.............16 F3
Northill..............34 E5
Northington..........13 H2
North Kelsey.........54 E3
North Kessock.......102 E8
North Kilvington......59 K2
North Kilworth.......33 J1
North Kyme..........44 E1
North Lancing.........14 E5
Northlands...........45 G1
Northleach...........20 F1
North Lee............22 D2
Northleigh, Devon....10 C6
North Leigh, Oxon....21 H1
North Leverton with
    Habblesthorpe......54 B5
Northlew..............8 F6
North Littleton.......32 C5
North Lopham.........36 F1
North Luffenham......44 C6
North Marden.........14 B4
North Marston.........34 A7
North Middleton......81 J6
North Molton..........9 H3
Northmoor............21 K7
Northmoor Green or Moorland.10 E2
North Moreton........21 K4
Northmuir.............89 F3
North Muskham.......54 B8
North Newbold.......61 G7
North Newington......33 G6
North Newnton........20 E6
North Newton........10 D2
North Nibley..........20 B3
North Oakley..........21 K7
North Ockendon......24 B4
Northolt..............23 J4
Northop..............50 B7
Northop Hall..........50 B7
North Ormsby.........55 G4
Northorpe, Lincs......54 C4
Northorpe, Lincs......44 D5
North Otterington.....59 J2
North Owersby.......54 E4
Northowram..........52 D1

North Perrott..........11 F5
North Petherton.......10 D2
North Petherwin........8 C7
North Pickenham......46 D6
North Piddle...........32 B4
Northpunds..........115 G6
North Queensferry....81 G3
Northrepps............47 H3
North Rigton..........59 H6
North Roe............116 E4
North Runcton.........46 B5
North Sandwick......117 G3
North Scale............56 E3
North Scarle...........54 C7
North Seaton...........75 J6
North Shields.........75 K8
North Shoebury.......25 F4
North Shore...........57 G7
North Side.............45 F7
North Somercotes.....55 J4
North Stainley........59 H3
North Stainmore......65 F6
North Stifford.........24 C4
North Stoke, Oxon....22 B4
North Stoke, Avon....20 B6
North Stoke, W. Susx..14 D4
North Street..........13 J2
North Sunderland.....75 J1
North Tamerton........8 C6
North Tawton..........9 G5
North Thoresby.......55 G4
North Tidworth.......12 E1
North Tolsta.........107 K4
Northton..............98 C3
Northtown..........112 C5
North Tuddenham....46 F5
Northwall............113 E7
North Walsham.......47 H3
North Waltham.......13 H1
North Warnborough...22 C7
North Water Bridge...89 J2
North Watten.........111 J3
Northway.............32 B6
North Weald Bassett..23 K2
North Wheatley......54 B5
North Whilborough....5 J3
Northwich.............51 F6
Northwick, Avon......19 K4
North Wick, Avon.....19 K6
North Widcombe......19 K7
North Willingham.....55 F5
North Wingfield......53 G7
North Witham.........44 C4
Northwold............46 C7
Northwood, Derby....52 E7
Northwood, G. Lon...23 F3
Northwood, Shrops....41 F3
Northwood, I. of W...13 G6
Northwood Green....20 B1
North Wootton, Norf..46 B4
North Wootton, Somer..11 G1
North Wootton, Dorset.11 H4
North Wraxall........20 C5
Norton, H. & W.......32 A4
Norton, Glos.........32 A7
Norton, Wilts.........20 C5
Norton, W. Susx......14 C5
Norton, H. & W.......32 C5
Norton, Suff.........36 E3
Norton, Powys........30 E3
Norton, N. Yks........66 E5
Norton, Cleve.........66 E5
Norton, Ches.........50 E5
Norton, Shrops.......31 F1
Norton, S. Yks........53 F5
Norton, Herts.........35 F6
Norton, I. of W......13 F7
Norton, Shrops.......41 G6
Norton, S. Yks........53 H2
Norton, Notts.........53 H6
Norton, Northnts.....33 J3
Norton, Shrops.......41 J6
Norton Bavant........12 B1
Norton Bridge........42 A3
Norton Canes.........42 C6
Norton Canon.........30 E5
Norton Disney.........54 C8
Norton East...........42 C6
Norton Ferris.........11 J2
Norton Fitzwarren....10 C3
Norton Green.........13 F7
Norton Hawkfield.....19 K6
Norton Heath.........24 C2
Norton in Hales......41 J3
Norton-in-the-Moors...42 A1
Norton-Juxta-Twycross..43 F6
Norton-le-Clay.......59 K3
Norton Lindsey.......32 E3
Norton Malreward....19 L6
Norton Mandeville...24 B2
Norton St Philip......20 B7
Norton Subcourse....47 K7
Norton sub Hamdon...11 F4
Norwell...............54 B7
Norwell Woodhouse...54 B7
Norwich..............47 H6
Norwick.............117 H1
Norwood Green.......23 G5
Norwood Hill.........15 F1
Noseley...............43 K7
Noss Mayo.............5 F5
Nosterfield..........59 H2
Nostie.................92 E3
Notgrove.............32 D7
Nottage...............18 C5
Nottingham...........43 H2
Nottington...........11 H7
Notton, Wilts.........20 D6
Notton, W. Yks.......53 F2
Nounsley.............24 D1
Noutard's Green......31 J3
Nox...................41 F5
Nuffield..............22 B4
Nunburnholme........60 F6

Nuneaton...43 F7
Nuneham Courtenay...21 K3
Nun Monkton...60 C5
Nunney...11 J1
Nunnington...60 D3
Nunnykirk...75 G5
Nunthorpe...67 F6
Nunton, W. Isles...98 C7
Nunton, Wilts...12 D3
Nursling...13 F4
Nursted...14 A3
Nutbourne...14 D4
Nutfield...15 G1
Nuthall...43 H2
Nuthampstead...35 H6
Nuthurst...15 E3
Nutley...15 H3
Nutwell...53 J3
Nybster...111 K2
Nyetimber...14 B6
Nyewood...14 B3
Nymet Rowland...9 H5
Nymet Tracey...9 H5
Nympsfield...20 C2
Nynehead...10 C3
Nyton...14 C5

O

Oadby...43 J6
Oad Street...24 E6
Oakamoor...42 C2
Oakbank...81 F5
Oakdale...19 F3
Oake...10 C3
Oaken...42 A6
Oakenclough...57 J6
Oakengates...41 J5
Oakenshaw, Durham...66 C4
Oakenshaw, W. Yks...52 D1
Oakford, Dyfed...28 B4
Oakford, Devon...9 K3
Oakgrove...51 J7
Oakham...44 B6
Oakhanger...14 A2
Oakhill...11 H1
Oakington...35 H3
Oaklands...23 H1
Oakle Street...20 B1
Oakley, Bucks...22 B1
Oakley, Beds...34 D4
Oakley, Fife...80 F3
Oakley, Suff...37 G2
Oakley, Hants...21 K7
Oakley Green...22 E5
Oakley Park...29 G1
Oakridge...20 D2
Oaks...41 F6
Oaksey...20 D3
Oakthorpe...43 F5
Oakwoodhill...14 E2
Oakworth...58 F7
Oare, Somer...9 J1
Oare, Wilts...21 F6
Oare, Kent...25 G6
Oasby...44 D3
Oathlaw...89 G3
Oban...85 K5
Oborne...11 H4
Occlestone Green...51 F7
Occold...37 G2
Ochiltree...71 L2
Ockbrook...43 G3
Ockham...22 F7
Ockle...85 G1
Ockley...14 E1
Ocle Pychard...31 G5
Odcombe...11 G4
Odd Down...20 B6
Oddendale...64 C6
Oddingley...32 B4
Oddington, Glos...32 E7
Oddington, Oxon...21 K1
Odell...34 C4
Odiham...22 C7
Odstock...12 D3
Odstone...43 F6
Offchurch...33 F3
Offenham...32 C5
Offham, Kent...24 C7
Offham, E. Susx...15 H4
Offord Cluny...35 F3
Offord D'Arcy...35 F3
Offton...36 F5
Offwell...10 C6
Ogbourne Maizey...21 F5
Ogbourne St Andrew...21 F5
Ogbourne St George...21 G5
Ogle...75 H7
Ogmore...18 C5
Ogmore-by-Sea...18 C5
Ogmore Vale...18 D3
Okeford Fitzpaine...11 K4
Okehampton...9 F6
Okehampton Camp...9 F6
Old...34 A2
Old Aberdeen...97 J5
Old Alresford...13 H2
Old Basing...22 B7
Oldberrow...32 D3
Old Bewick...75 G2
Old Bolingbroke...55 H7
Oldborough...9 H5
Old Brampton...53 F6
Old Bridge of Urr...72 C8
Old Buckenham...46 F7
Old Burghclere...21 J7
Oldbury, W. Mids...42 B8
Oldbury, Warw...43 F7
Oldbury, Shrops...41 J7
Oldbury-on-Severn...19 L3
Oldbury on the Hill...20 C4
Old Byland...60 C2

Oldcastle...30 E7
Old Cleeve...10 B1
Old Clipstone...53 J7
Old Colwyn...49 H3
Oldcotes...53 H5
Old Dailly...71 H5
Old Dalby...43 J4
Old Deer...105 J4
Old Denaby...53 G4
Old Ellerby...61 J7
Old Felixstowe...37 J6
Oldfield...31 K3
Oldford...20 B7
Old Hall, The...55 G2
Oldham...51 J3
Oldhamstocks...82 F4
Old Heath...36 F7
Oldhurst...35 G2
Old Hutton...57 J2
Old Kea...3 G5
Old Kilpatrick...79 G4
Old Kinnernie...97 G5
Old Knebworth...35 F7
Oldland...20 A5
Old Leake...45 H1
Old Malton...60 E3
Oldmeldrum...97 H3
Old Milverton...33 F3
Old Monkland...80 C5
Old Newton...36 F3
Old Park...41 H6
Old Philpstoun...81 F4
Old Radnor...30 D4
Old Rayne...97 F3
Old Romney...17 H3
Oldshore Beg...108 C3
Oldshoremore...108 D3
Old Sodbury...20 B4
Old Somerby...44 C3
Oldstead...60 C2
Old Swarland...75 H4
Old Town...57 J2
Old Town Farm...74 E5
Old Warden...34 E5
Oldways End...9 J3
Old Weston...34 E2
Oldwhat...105 H3
Old Windsor...22 E5
Old Wives Lees...25 G7
Olgrinmore...111 G3
Oliver's Battery...13 G3
Ollaberry...116 E4
Ollach...92 B2
Ollerton, Ches...51 G6
Ollerton, Shrops...41 H4
Ollerton, Notts...53 J7
Olney...34 B4
Olton...32 D1
Olveston...19 L4
Ombersley...31 K3
Ompton...53 J7
Onchan...56 R4
Onecote...42 C1
Ongar Hill...45 J4
Ongar Street...30 E3
Onibury...31 F2
Onich...86 C2
Onllwyn...18 C1
Onneley...41 J2
Onslow Village...14 C1
Opinan, Highld...100 D5
Opinan, Highld...100 E3
Orby...55 J7
Orchard...11 K4
Orchard Portman...10 D3
Orcheston...12 C1
Orcop...31 F7
Orcop Hill...31 F7
Ord...92 C4
Ordhead...97 F4
Ordie...96 D5
Ordiquish...104 C3
Ore...16 F4
Oreton...31 H1
Orford, Ches...50 F4
Orford, Suff...37 K4
Orgreave...42 D5
Orinsay...107 H7
Orleton, H. & W...31 F3
Orleton, H. & W...31 H3
Orlingbury...34 B2
Ormesby...67 F6
Ormesby St Margaret...47 K5
Ormesby St Michael...47 K5
Ormiscaig...100 E3
Ormiston...82 C5
Ormsaigmore...85 F2
Ormskirk...50 D3
Orpington...23 K6
Orrell...50 E3
Orroland...69 J6
Orsett...24 C4
Orslow...41 K5
Orston...44 A2
Orton, Northnts...34 B2
Orton, Cumbr...64 D7
Orton Longueville...44 E7
Orton-on-the-Hill...43 F6
Orwell...35 G4
Osbaldeston...58 B7
Osbaldwick...60 D4
Oscroft...50 E7
Ose...91 J1
Osgathorpe...43 G5
Osgodby, N. Yks...60 D7
Osgodby, Lincs...54 E4
Osgodby, N. Yks...61 H2
Oskaig...92 B2
Oskamull...85 F4
Osmaston...42 E2
Osmington...11 J7
Osmington Mills...11 J7
Osmotherley...66 E8

Osnaburgh or Dairsie...89 G7
Ospisdale...102 F4
Ospringe...25 G6
Ossett...52 E1
Ossington...54 B7
Ostend...25 F3
Oswaldkirk...60 D3
Oswaldtwistle...51 G1
Oswestry...40 D4
Otford...23 L7
Otham...24 D7
Othery...10 E2
Otley, Suff...37 H4
Otley, W. Yks...59 H6
Otterburn, N. Yks...58 D5
Otterburn, Northum...74 E5
Otterburn Camp...74 E5
Otterden Place...25 F7
Otter Ferry...77 J3
Otterham...8 B6
Ottershaw...22 F6
Otterswick...117 G4
Otterton...10 B7
Ottery St Mary...10 C6
Ottringham...55 G1
Oughtershaw...58 D2
Oughtibridge...53 F4
Oulston...60 C3
Oulton, Staffs...42 B3
Oulton, Norf...47 G4
Oulton, Cumbr...63 H2
Oulton, W. Yks...59 J8
Oulton, Suff...47 L7
Oulton Broad...47 L7
Oulton Street...47 G4
Oundle...34 D1
Ousby...64 D4
Ousden...36 C4
Ouseburn...59 K4
Ousefleet...54 C1
Ouston...36 C7
Outertown...112 C5
Outgate...63 J8
Outhgill...64 E7
Outlane...52 C2
Out Newton...55 H1
Out Rawcliffe...57 H6
Outwell, Cambs...45 J6
Outwell, Norf...45 J6
Outwood, W. Yks...53 F1
Outwood, Surrey...15 G1
Ovenden...52 C1
Over, Cambs...35 G2
Over, Avon...19 K4
Overbister...113 G2
Overbury...32 B6
Overcombe...11 H7
Over Haddon...52 E7
Over Kellet...57 J4
Over Kiddington...33 G7
Over Norton...33 F7
Over Peover...51 G6
Overseal...42 E5
Over Silton...59 K1
Overstone...34 B3
Overstrand...47 H2
Overton, D. & G...62 E1
Overton, Clwyd...40 E2
Overton, Shrops...31 G2
Overton, Hants...13 H1
Overton, Grampn...97 H4
Overton, Lancs...57 H5
Overtown...80 D6
Over Wallop...12 E2
Over Whitacre...42 E7
Oving, W. Susx...14 C5
Oving, Bucks...33 J7
Ovingdean...15 G5
Ovingham...65 H1
Ovington, Essex...36 C5
Ovington, Norf...46 E6
Ovington, Northum...65 H1
Ovington, Hants...13 H2
Ovington, Durham...65 J6
Ower...13 F4
Owermoigne...11 J7
Owlswick...22 C2
Owmby-by-Spital...54 E5
Owslebury...13 H3
Owston...44 A6
Owston Ferry...54 C3
Owstwick...61 K7
Owthorpe...43 J3
Oxborough...46 C6
Oxcombe...55 J7
Oxenholme...57 J2
Oxenhope...58 F7
Oxen Park...57 G2
Oxenton...32 B6
Oxenwood...21 H7
Oxford...33 F5
Oxhill...33 F5
Oxley...42 B6
Oxley's Green...16 D3
Oxnam...74 C3
Oxshott...23 G6
Oxspring...52 E3
Oxted...23 J7
Oxton, Border...82 C6
Oxton, Notts...43 J1
Oxwich...27 J8
Oxwick...46 E4
Oykel Bridge...102 B2
Oyne...97 F3

P

Pabail Iarach...107 K5
Pabail Varach...107 K5
Packington...43 F5
Padanaram...89 G3
Padbury...33 K6

Paddington...23 H4
Paddlesworth...17 J2
Paddockhaugh...104 B3
Paddock Wood...16 D1
Paddolgreen...41 G3
Padeswood...50 B7
Padiham...58 D7
Padstow...3 H2
Padworth...22 B6
Pagham...14 B6
Paglesham Churchend...24 F3
Paglesham Eastend...25 F3
Paible, W. Isles...98 C6
Paible, W. Isles...98 F3
Paignton...5 J3
Pailton...33 G1
Painscastle...30 C5
Painshawfield...65 H1
Painswick...20 C2
Pakefield...47 L7
Pakenham...36 E3
Pale...39 J3
Palestine...12 E1
Paley Street...22 D5
Palgrave...37 G2
Palmerstown...18 F6
Palnackie...69 K5
Palnure...68 F4
Palterton...53 G7
Pamber End...22 B7
Pamber Green...21 L7
Pamber Heath...22 B6
Pamphill...12 B5
Pampisford...35 H5
Panbride...89 H5
Pancrasweek...8 C5
Pandy, Clwyd...40 C3
Pandy, Gwent...30 E7
Pandy, Powys...39 J6
Pandy Tudur...49 H4
Panfield...36 C7
Pangbourne...22 B5
Pannal...59 J5
Pant...40 D4
Panteg...26 D3
Pant Glas...38 D2
Pantgwyn...27 G2
Pant Mawr...29 F1
Pantperthog...39 G6
Pant-pastynog...49 K4
Pantyffynnon...27 L5
Pant-y-dwr...29 G2
Pant-y-ffridd...40 C6
Panxworth...47 J5
Papcastle...63 G4
Papple...82 D4
Papplewick...43 H1
Papworth Everard...35 F3
Papworth St Agnes...35 F3
Par...3 J4
Parbold...50 D2
Parbrook...11 G2
Parc Seymour...19 J3
Pardshaw...63 F5
Parham...37 J3
Park Corner...22 B4
Park End, Northum...74 E7
Parkend, Glos...19 L2
Parkeston...37 H6
Parkgate, Ches...50 B6
Parkgate, Surrey...15 F1
Parkgate, D. & G...73 F6
Park Gate, Hants...13 H5
Parkham...8 D3
Parkham Ash...8 D3
Parkhouse...19 K2
Parkhurst...13 G6
Parkmill...27 K8
Parkstone...12 C6
Parley Cross...12 C6
Parracombe...9 F1
Parrog...26 E3
Parson Cross...53 F4
Parson Drove...45 G6
Partick...79 H5
Partington...51 G4
Partney...55 J7
Parton, D. & G...72 B7
Parton, Cumbr...62 E5
Partridge Green...15 E4
Parwich...42 D1
Passenham...34 A6
Paston...47 J3
Patcham...15 G5
Patchole...9 G1
Patchway...19 L4
Pateley Bridge...59 G4
Pathfinder Village...9 J6
Pathhead, Strath...72 B3
Pathhead, Fife...81 H2
Pathhead, Lothn...81 J5
Patmore Heath...35 H7
Patna...71 K3
Patney...20 E7
Patrick...56 P3
Patrick Brompton...59 H1
Patrington...55 H1
Patrixbourne...25 J7
Patterdale...63 K4
Pattingham...41 K7
Pattishall...33 J4
Patton Bridge...64 C8
Paul...2 C7
Paulerspury...33 K5
Paull...55 F1
Paulton...20 A7
Pavenham...34 B4
Pawston...74 E1
Paxford...32 D6
Paxton...83 H6
Payhembury...10 B5

Paythorne...58 D5
Pcaston...82 C5
Peacehaven...15 H5
Peak Dale...52 C6
Peak Forest...52 D6
Peakirk...44 E6
Peanmeanach...92 D7
Peasedown St John...20 B7
Peasemore...21 J5
Peasenhall...37 J3
Pease Pottage...15 F2
Peaslake...14 D1
Peasmarsh...17 F3
Peaston Bank...82 C5
Peathill...105 J2
Peatling Magna...43 H7
Peatling Parva...43 H8
Peaton...31 G1
Pebmarsh...36 D6
Pebworth...32 D5
Pecket Well...58 E8
Peckforton...41 G1
Peckleton...43 G6
Pedmore...32 B1
Pedwell...11 F2
Peebles...81 H7
Peel...56 P3
Pegswood...75 J6
Peinchorran...92 B2
Peinlich...99 K7
Pelaw...66 C1
Pelcomb Cross...26 D5
Peldon...25 F1
Pelsall...42 C6
Pelton...66 C2
Peluth...63 G3
Pelynt...4 C4
Pembrey...27 J6
Pembridge...30 E4
Pembroke...26 D6
Pembroke Dock...26 D6
Pembury...16 D1
Penallt...19 K2
Penally...26 F7
Penare...3 H5
Penarth...19 F5
Pen-bont Rhydybeddau...28 D1
Penbryn...27 G1
Pencader...27 J3
Pencaitland...82 C5
Pencarreg...27 K2
Pencelli...29 H7
Pen-Clawdd...27 K7
Pencoed...18 D4
Pencombe...31 H4
Pencoyd...31 G7
Pencraig, Powys...40 B4
Pencraig, H. & W...31 G7
Pendas Fields...59 J7
Pendeen...2 B6
Penderyn...18 D2
Pendine...27 G6
Pendlebury...51 G3
Pendleton...58 C7
Pendock...31 J6
Pendoggett...3 J2
Pendoylan...18 E5
Penegoes...39 G6
Penffordd...26 E4
Penffridd...38 E1
Penge...23 J5
Pengorffwysfa...48 D1
Penhalurick...2 F6
Penhow...19 J3
Penhurst...16 D4
Penicuik...81 H5
Peniel...49 K4
Penifiler...92 A1
Peninver...70 C2
Penisa'r Waun...48 E4
Penistone...52 E3
Penjerrick...2 F6
Penketh...50 E5
Penkridge...42 B5
Penley...41 F2
Penllergaer...27 L7
Penllyn, Gwyn...48 C2
Penllyn, S. Glam...18 D5
Penmachno...39 G1
Penmaen, Gwent...19 F3
Penmaen, W. Glam...27 K8
Penmaenmawr...49 G3
Penmaenpool...39 F5
Penmark...18 E6
Penmon...49 F2
Penmorfa...38 E2
Penmynydd...48 E3
Penn...22 E3
Pennal...39 G6
Pennan...105 H2
Pennant, Dyfed...28 C3
Pennant, Powys...39 H7
Pennant, Clwyd...49 H5
Pennant-Melangell...40 B4
Pennard...27 K8
Pennerley...40 E7
Pennington...57 F3
Penn Street...22 E3
Penny Bridge...57 G2
Pennycross...85 G6
Pennygate...9 J4
Pennymoor...9 J4
Penparc...27 G1
Penparcau...28 C1
Penperlleni...19 H2
Penpillick...33 J4
Penpol...3 G6
Penpoll...3 K4
Penpont, Powys...29 J7
Penpont...72 D5
Penrherber...27 G3

Penrhos, Gwent...19 J1
Penrhyn Bay...49 H2
Penrhyn-coch...28 D1
Penrhyndeudraeth...38 F3
Penrhyn-side...49 H2
Penrice...27 J8
Penrose...3 G2
Penruddock...63 K5
Penryn...3 F6
Pen-sarn, Gwyn...38 D2
Pen-sarn, Gwyn...38 E4
Pensarn, Clwyd...49 J3
Pensax...31 J3
Pensby...50 B5
Penselwood...11 J2
Pensford...19 L6
Penshaw...66 D2
Penshurst...15 J1
Pensilva...4 C3
Pentewan...3 J5
Pentir...48 E4
Pentire...3 F3
Pentney...46 C5
Penton Mewsey...13 F1
Pentraeth...48 E3
Pentre, Clwyd...40 C3
Pentre, Clwyd...40 D2
Pentre, Shrops...40 E5
Pentre, Powys...29 H1
Pentrebach, M. Glam...18 E2
Pentre-bach, Powys...29 G6
Pentre-bach, Dyfed...27 K2
Pentre Berw...48 D3
Pentre-bont...39 G1
Pentre-celyn...40 C1
Pentre-cwrt...27 H3
Pentre Dolau Honddu...29 G5
Pentre-dwr, W. Glam...18 A3
Pentredwr, Clwyd...40 C2
Pentrefelin, Powys...38 E3
Pentrefelin, Gwyn...49 H3
Pentrefoelas...39 H1
Pentregat...27 H1
Pentre-Gwenlais...27 L5
Pentre Halkyn...50 B6
Pentre-LLanrhaeadr...49 K4
Pentre-llyn-cymmer...39 J1
Pentre'r beirdd...40 C5
Pentre'r-felin...29 G6
Pentre-tafarn-y-fedw...49 H4
Pentre-ty-gwyn...28 F6
Pentrich...43 F1
Pentridge...12 C4
Pentyrch...18 E4
Penuwch...28 C3
Penwithick...3 J4
Pen-y-banc...27 L4
Penybont, Powys...30 C3
Pen-y-bont, Clwyd...40 D4
Pen-y-bont, Dyfed...27 H4
Penybontfawr...40 B4
Penybryn, M. Glam...18 F3
Pen-y-bryn, Gwyn...39 F5
Pen-y-cae, Powys...18 C1
Penycae, Clwyd...40 D2
Pen-y-cae-mawr...19 J3
Pen-y-cefn...49 L3
Pen-y-clawdd...19 J2
Pen-y-coedcae...18 E4
Penycwm...26 C4
Pen-y-garn...27 K3
Penygarnedd, Powys...40 C4
Pen-y-garnedd, Gwyn...48 E3
Penygraig...18 D3
Penygroes, Gwyn...38 D1
Pen-y-groes, Dyfed...27 K5
Penysarn...48 D1
Pen-y-stryt...40 C1
Penywaun...18 D2
Penzance...2 C6
Peopleton...32 B4
Peover Heath...51 G6
Peper Harow...14 C1
Peplow...41 H4
Percie...96 E6
Percyhorner...105 J2
Perivale...23 G4
Perlethorpe...53 J6
Perranarworthal...2 F6
Perranporth...2 F4
Perranuthnoe...2 D7
Perranzabuloe...2 F4
Perry Barr...42 C7
Perry Green...23 K1
Pershore...32 B5
Pert...89 J2
Pertenhall...34 D3
Perth...88 D6
Perthy...40 E3
Perton...42 A7
Peterborough...45 E7
Peterburn...100 D4
Peterchurch...30 E6
Peterculter...97 H5
Peterhead...105 L4
Peterlee...66 E3
Petersfield...13 K3
Peter's Green...23 G1
Peters Marland...8 E4
Peterstone Wentlooge...19 G4
Peterston-super-Ely...18 E5
Peterstow...31 G7
Peter Tavy...4 F2
Petertown...112 C6
Petham...25 H7
Petrockstowe...8 F5
Pett...16 F4
Pettaugh...37 G4
Pettinain...80 E7
Pettistree...37 H4
Petton, Devon...10 B3
Petton, Shrops...41 F4

Petty....97 G2
Pettycur....81 H3
Pettymuick....97 J3
Petworth....14 C3
Pevensey Bay....16 D5
Pewsey....21 F6
Philham....8 C3
Philiphaugh....73 K2
Phillack....2 D6
Philleigh....3 G6
Philpstoun....81 F4
Phoenix Green....22 C7
Pica....62 F5
Piccotts End....22 F2
Pickering....60 E2
Picket Piece....13 F1
Pickhill....59 J2
Picklescott....41 F7
Pickmere....51 F6
Pickwell, Leic....44 A5
Pickwell, Devon....8 E1
Pickworth, Leic....44 C5
Pickworth, Lincs....44 D3
Picton, Ches....50 D6
Picton, N. Yks....66 E7
Piddinghoe....15 H5
Piddington, Oxon....22 B1
Piddington, Northnts....34 B4
Piddlehinton....11 J6
Piddletrenthide....11 J6
Pidley....35 G2
Piercebridge....66 C6
Pierowall....112 E2
Pigdon....75 H6
Pikehall....52 D8
Pilgrims Hatch....24 B3
Pilham....54 C4
Pill....19 K5
Pillaton....4 D3
Pillerton Hersey....33 F5
Pillerton Priors....32 E5
Pilleth....30 D3
Pilley....53 F3
Piling....57 H6
Piling Lane....57 G6
Pilning....19 K4
Pilsbury....52 D7
Pilsdon....11 F6
Pilsley, Derby....52 E6
Pilsley, Derby....53 G7
Pilton, Leic....44 C6
Pilton, Northnts....34 D1
Pilton, Somer....11 G1
Pimperne....12 B5
Pinchbeck....45 F4
Pinchbeck West....45 F4
Pinfold....50 C2
Pinhoe....9 K6
Pinmore....71 H5
Pinner....23 G4
Pinvin....32 B5
Pinwherry....71 G6
Pinxton....43 G1
Pipe and Lyde....31 G5
Pipe Gate....51 G7
Piperhill....103 G7
Pipewell....34 B1
Pippacott....9 F2
Pirbright....22 E7
Pirnmill....77 H7
Pirton, H. & W....32 A5
Pirton, Herts....34 E6
Pishill....22 C4
Pistyll....38 C2
Pitblae....105 J2
Pitcairngreen....88 C6
Pitcalnie....103 G5
Pitcaple....97 G3
Pitchcombe....20 C2
Pitchcott....34 A7
Pitchford....41 G6
Pitch Green....22 C2
Pitch Place....22 E7
Pitcombe....11 H2
Pitcox....82 E4
Pitfichie....97 F4
Pitgrudy....103 F3
Pitlessie....89 F8
Pitlochry....88 B3
Pitmedden....97 H3
Pitminster....10 D4
Pitmunie....97 F4
Pitney....11 F3
Pitscottie....89 G7
Pitsea....24 D4
Pitsford....34 A3
Pitstone Green....22 E1
Pittendreich....103 K6
Pittentrail....102 F2
Pittenweem....82 D1
Pittington....66 D3
Pitton....12 E2
Pixey Green....37 H2
Place Newton....61 F3
Plains....80 C5
Plaish....41 G7
Plaistow....14 D2
Plaitford....12 E4
Plas....27 J4
Plas Gogerddan....28 D1
Plas Isaf....40 B2
Plas Llwyngwern....39 G6
Plas Llysyn....39 J7
Plastow Green....21 K6
Platt....24 C7
Plawsworth....66 C3
Plaxtol....24 C7
Playden....17 G3
Playford....37 H5
Playing Place....3 G5
Plealey....41 F6
Plean....80 D3
Pleasington....51 F1
Pleasley....53 H7

Plenmeller....64 E1
Pleshey....24 C1
Plockton....92 E2
Plocrapool....99 G3
Plocrapool Point....99 G3
Plowden....30 E1
Ploxgreen....40 E6
Pluckley....17 G1
Plumbland....63 G4
Plumley....51 G6
Plumpton, Cumbr....64 B4
Plumpton, E. Susx....15 G4
Plumpton, Lancs....57 G7
Plumpton Green....15 G4
Plumpton Head....64 C4
Plumstead....47 G3
Plumtree....43 J3
Plungar....44 A3
Plush....11 J5
Plwmp....27 H1
Plymouth....4 E4
Plympton....4 F4
Plymstock....4 F4
Plymtree....10 B5
Pockley....60 D2
Pocklington....60 F6
Pode Hole....45 F4
Podimore....11 G3
Podington....34 C3
Podmore....41 J3
Point Clear....25 G1
Pointon....44 E3
Pokesdown....12 D6
Polapit Tamar....8 D7
Polbain....101 F1
Polbathic....4 D4
Polbeth....81 F5
Polebrook....34 D1
Polegate....16 C5
Pole of Itlaw, The....104 F3
Polesworth....42 E6
Polglass....101 G2
Polgooth....3 H4
Poling....14 D5
Polkerris....3 J4
Pollington....53 J2
Polloch....85 J2
Pollokshaws....79 H5
Pollokshields....79 H5
Polmassick....3 H5
Polnessan....71 K3
Polperro....4 C4
Polruan....3 K4
Polsham....11 G1
Polstead....36 E6
Poltalloch....77 H2
Poltimore....9 K6
Polwarth....82 F6
Polyphant....4 C1
Polzeath....3 H2
Ponde....30 C6
Pondersbridge....45 F7
Ponders End....23 J3
Ponsanooth....2 F6
Ponsworthy....5 H2
Pontamman....27 L5
Pontantwn....27 J5
Pontardawe....18 B2
Pontardulais....27 K6
Pontarsais....27 J4
Pont Creuddyn....27 K1
Pont Cyfyng....39 G1
Pontefract....53 G1
Ponteland....75 H7
Ponterwyd....28 E1
Pontesbury....40 F6
Pontfadog....40 D3
Pontfaen, Dyfed....26 E3
Pont-faen, Powys....29 G6
Pont Henri....27 J6
Ponthir....19 H3
Ponthirwaun....27 G2
Pontllanfraith....19 F3
Pontlliw....27 L6
Pont Llogel....40 B5
Pontllyfni....38 D1
Pontlottyn....18 F2
Pontneddfechan....18 D2
Pont Pen-y-benglog....49 F4
Pontrhydfendigaid....28 E1
Pont Rhyd-y-cyff....18 C4
Pontrhydyfen....18 B3
Pont-rhyd-y-groes....28 E2
Pontrilas....30 E7
Pontrobert....40 C5
Pont-rug....48 E4
Ponts Green....16 B4
Pontshill....31 H7
Pont-Sian....27 J2
Pontsticill....18 E1
Pontyates....27 J6
Pontyberem....27 K5
Pontybodkin....50 B8
Pontyclun....18 E4
Pontycymer....18 D3
Pont-y-pant....39 G1
Pontypool....19 G2
Pontypridd....18 E3
Pontywaun....19 G3
Pooksgreen....13 F4
Pool....2 E5
Poole....12 C6
Poole Keynes....20 E3
Poolewe....100 E4
Pooley Bridge....64 B5
Poolhill....31 J7
Pool of Muckhart....80 F1
Pool Quay....40 D5
Poorton....11 G6
Popham....13 H1
Poplar....23 J4
Porchfield....13 G6
Poringland....47 H6
Porkellis....2 E6

Porlock....9 J1
Port-an-eorna....92 D2
Port Ann....77 J3
Port Appin....86 B4
Port Askaig....76 D5
Port Bannatyne....78 C5
Portbury....19 K5
Port Carlisle....63 H1
Port Charlotte....76 B6
Portchester....13 J5
Portclair....94 C4
Port Driseach....78 B4
Port Ellen....76 C7
Port Elphinstone....97 G3
Port Erin....56 N5
Portesham....11 H7
Port e Vullen....56 R2
Portfield Gate....26 D5
Portgate....8 E7
Portgaverne....3 J1
Port Glasgow....78 F4
Portgordon....104 C2
Portgower....111 G7
Porth....18 E3
Porthallow....3 F7
Porthcawl....18 C5
Porthcurno....2 B7
Port Henderson....100 D5
Porthgain....26 C3
Porthkerry....18 E6
Porthleven....2 E7
Porthllechog....48 D1
Porthmadog....38 E3
Porthmeor....2 C6
Porth Navas....2 F7
Portholland....3 H5
Porthoustock....3 G7
Porthpean....3 J4
Porthtowan....2 E5
Porthyrhyd, Dyfed....28 E6
Porthyrhyd, Dyfed....27 K5
Portincaple....78 E2
Portington....60 E7
Portinscale....63 H5
Port Isaac....3 H1
Portishead....19 J5
Portknockie....104 D2
Portlethen....97 J6
Portlethen Village....97 J6
Portloe....3 H6
Port Logan....68 B6
Portmahomack....103 H4
Portmeirion....38 E3
Portmellon....3 J5
Port Mholair....107 K5
Port Mor....91 K8
Portmore....13 F6
Port Mulgrave....67 H6
Portnacroish....86 B4
Portnahaven....76 A6
Portnalong....91 J2
Portnaluchaig....92 C7
Portnancon....109 F2
Portobello....81 J4
Port of Menteith....79 H1
Porton....12 D2
Portpatrick....68 B5
Portquin....3 H1
Portreath....2 E5
Portree....99 K8
Portscatho....3 G6
Portsea....13 J5
Portskerra....110 E2
Portskewett....19 K4
Portslade....15 F5
Portslade-by-Sea....15 F5
Portsmouth....13 J5
Portsoy....104 E2
Port St Mary....56 P5
Port Sunlight....50 C5
Portswood....13 G4
Port Talbot....18 B3
Portway....32 C2
Port Wemyss....76 A6
Port William....68 E6
Portwrinkle....4 D4
Poslingford....36 C5
Postbridge....5 G2
Postcombe....22 C3
Postling....17 J2
Postwick....47 H6
Potarch....96 F6
Potsgrove....34 C7
Potten End....22 F2
Potterhanworth....54 E7
Potter Heigham....47 K5
Potteries, The....42 A2
Potterne....20 D7
Potterne Wick....20 E7
Potters Bar....23 H2
Potterspury....34 A5
Potter Street....23 K2
Potterton....97 J4
Potto....66 E7
Potton....35 F5
Pott Row....46 C4
Pott Shrigley....51 J6
Poughill, Corn....8 C5
Poughill, Devon....9 J5
Poulshot....20 D7
Poulton....20 F2
Poulton-le-Fylde....57 G7
Pound Bank....31 J2
Pound Hill....15 F2
Poundon....33 J7
Poundsgate....5 H2
Poundstock....8 C6
Powburn....75 G3
Powderham....9 K7
Powerstock....11 G6
Powfoot....63 G1
Powick....31 K4

Powmill....80 F2
Poxwell....11 J7
Poyle....22 F5
Poynings....15 F4
Poyntington....11 H3
Poynton....51 J5
Poynton Green....41 G5
Poystreet Green....36 E4
Praa Sands....2 D7
Pratt's Bottom....23 K6
Praze-an-Beeble....2 E6
Predannack Wollas....2 E8
Prees....41 G3
Preesall....57 G6
Prees Green....41 G3
Preesgweene....40 D3
Prees Higher Heath....41 G3
Prendwick....75 G3
Pren-gwyn....27 J2
Prenteg....38 E2
Prescot....50 C5
Prescott....41 F4
Pressen....83 G8
Prestatyn....49 K2
Prestbury, Glos....32 B7
Prestbury, Ches....51 J6
Presteigne....30 E3
Presthope....41 G7
Prestleigh....11 H1
Preston, Leic....44 B6
Preston, Lothn....82 D4
Preston, Glos....20 E2
Preston, Wilts....20 E5
Preston, Herts....34 E7
Preston, Border....83 F6
Preston, E. Susx....15 G5
Preston, Northum....75 H4
Preston, Glos....31 H6
Preston, Devon....5 J2
Preston, Kent....25 J6
Preston, Humbs....61 J7
Preston, Dorset....11 J7
Preston, Lancs....57 J8
Preston Bagot....32 D3
Preston Bissett....33 J7
Preston Brockhurst....41 G4
Preston Brook....50 E5
Preston Candover....13 J1
Preston Capes....33 H4
Preston Gubbals....41 F5
Preston on Stour....32 E4
Preston on Wye....30 E5
Prestonpans....81 J4
Preston St Mary....36 E4
Preston-under-Scar....59 F7
Preston upon the
  Weald Moors....41 H5
Preston Wynne....31 G5
Prestwich....51 H3
Prestwick, Northum....75 H7
Prestwick, Strath....71 J2
Prestwood....22 D2
Price Town....18 D3
Prickwillow....35 J1
Priddy....19 K7
Priest Hutton....57 J3
Priest Weston....40 D7
Primrose Green....46 F5
Princes Risborough....22 D2
Princethorpe....33 G2
Princetown....5 F2
Priors Hardwick....33 G4
Priors Marston....33 G4
Priory, The....13 J6
Priory Wood....30 D5
Priston....20 A6
Prittlewell....24 E4
Privett....13 J3
Prixford....9 F2
Probus....3 G5
Proncy....103 F3
Prospect....63 G3
Prudhoe....65 H1
Puckeridge....35 G7
Puckington....10 E4
Pucklechurch....20 B5
Puddington, Ches....50 C6
Puddington, Devon....9 J4
Puddledock....46 F7
Puddletown....11 J6
Pudleston....31 G4
Pudsey....59 H7
Pulborough....14 D4
Puleston....41 J4
Pulford....50 C8
Pulham....11 J5
Pulham Market....37 G1
Pulham St Mary....37 H1
Pulloxhill....34 D6
Pulverbatch....41 F6
Pumsaint....27 L2
Puncheston....26 E4
Puncknowle....11 G7
Punnett's Town....16 D3
Purbrook....13 J5
Purfleet....23 L5
Puriton....10 E1
Purleigh....24 E2
Purley....23 J6
Purley on Thames....22 B5
Purlogue....30 D2
Purls Bridge....35 H1
Purse Caundle....11 H4
Purslow....30 D1
Purston Jaglin....53 G2
Purton, Glos....20 A2
Purton, Glos....20 A2
Purton, Wilts....20 E3
Purton Stoke....20 E3
Pury End....33 K5
Pusey....21 H3
Putley....31 H6
Putney....23 H5
Puttenham, Surrey....14 C1

Puttenham, Herts....22 D1
Puxton....19 J6
Pwll....27 J6
Pwllcrochan....26 D6
Pwllheli....38 C3
Pwllmeyric....19 K3
Pwll-y-glaw....18 B3
Pyecombe....15 F4
Pye Corner....19 H4
Pyle, M. Glam....18 C4
Pyle, I. of W....7 J7
Pylle....11 H2
Pymore....35 H1
Pyrford....22 F7
Pyrton....22 B3
Pytchley....34 B2
Pyworthy....8 D5

Q

Quabbs....30 D1
Quadring....45 F3
Quainton....34 A7
Quarley....12 E1
Quarndon....43 F2
Quarrier's Homes....79 F5
Quarrington....44 D2
Quarrington Hill....66 D4
Quarry Bank....32 B1
Quarry, The....20 B3
Quarrywood....103 K6
Quarter....80 C6
Quatford....41 J7
Quatt....31 J1
Quebec....66 B3
Quedgeley....20 C1
Queen Adelaide....35 J1
Queenborough....24 F5
Queen Camel....11 G3
Queen Charlton....19 L6
Queensbury....59 G7
Queensferry, Clwyd....50 C7
Queensferry, Lothn....81 G4
Queenzieburn....80 B4
Quendale....115 F7
Quendon....35 J6
Queniborough....43 J5
Quenington....21 F2
Quernmore....57 J4
Quethiock....4 D3
Quholm....112 C5
Quidenham....36 F1
Quidhampton, Wilts....12 D2
Quidhampton, Hants....21 K7
Quidnish....99 F4
Quilquox....97 J2
Quindry....112 E7
Quine's Hill....56 O4
Quinton....34 A4
Quoditch....8 E6
Quorndon or Quorn....43 H5
Quorn or Quorndon....43 H5
Quothquan....80 E8
Quoyloo....112 C4
Quoys....117 H1

R

Raby....50 C5
Rachub....49 F4
Rackenford....9 J4
Rackham....14 D4
Rackheath....47 H5
Racks....73 F7
Rackwick, Orkney....112 C7
Rackwick, Orkney....112 E1
Radcliffe, G. Man....51 G3
Radcliffe, Northum....75 J4
Radcliffe on Trent....43 J3
Radclive....33 J6
Radcot....21 G3
Raddery....102 F7
Radernie....89 G8
Radford Semele....32 F3
Radlett....23 G2
Radley....21 K3
Radnage....22 C3
Radstock....20 A7
Radstone....33 H5
Radway....32 E4
Radway Green....41 J1
Radwell....35 F6
Radwinter....35 K6
Radyr....18 F4
Rafford....103 J7
Ragdale....43 J5
Raglan....19 J2
Ragnall....54 C6
Rainford....50 D3
Rainham, Kent....24 E6
Rainham, G. Lon....23 L4
Rainhill....50 D4
Rainow....51 J6
Rainworth....53 H8
Raisbeck....64 D7
Rait....88 E3
Raithby, Lincs....55 H7
Raithby, Lincs....55 H7
Rake....14 B3
Rame, Corn....2 E5
Rame, Corn....4 E5
Ram Lane....24 F1
Rampisham....11 G5
Rampton, Notts....54 B6
Rampton, Cambs....35 G2
Ramsbottom....51 G2
Ramsbury....21 G5

Ramscraigs....111 H6
Ramsdean....13 K3
Ramsdell....21 K7
Ramsden....21 H1
Ramsden Bellhouse....24 D3
Ramsden Heath....24 D3
Ramsey, Cambs....35 F1
Ramsey, Essex....37 H6
Ramsey, I. of M....56 R2
Ramseycleuch....73 H3
Ramsey Forty Foot....35 G1
Ramsey Island....25 F2
Ramsey Mereside....45 F8
Ramsey St Mary's....35 F1
Ramsgate....25 K6
Ramsgill....59 G3
Ramshorn....42 C2
Ranby....53 J5
Rand....54 F6
Randwick....20 C2
Ranfurly....79 F5
Rangemore....42 D4
Rangeworthy....20 A4
Ranish....107 J6
Rankinston....71 K3
Ranskill....53 J5
Ranton....42 A4
Ranworth....47 J5
Rapness....113 F2
Rascarrel....69 J6
Raskelf....60 B3
Rassau....18 F1
Rastrick....52 D1
Ratagan....93 F4
Ratby....43 H6
Ratcliffe Culey....43 F7
Ratcliffe on the Wreake....43 J5
Rathen....105 K2
Rathillet....89 F6
Rathmell....58 D5
Ratho....81 G4
Ratho Station....81 G4
Rathven....104 D2
Ratley....33 F5
Ratlinghope....40 F7
Rattar....111 J1
Ratten Row....57 H6
Rattery....5 H3
Rattlesden....36 E4
Rattray....88 D4
Rauceby....44 D2
Raughton Head....63 J3
Raunds....34 C2
Ravenfield....53 G4
Ravenglass....56 D1
Raveningham....47 J7
Ravensdale....56 Q2
Ravensden....34 D4
Ravenseat....65 F7
Ravenshead....43 H1
Ravensmoor....41 H1
Ravensthorpe, W. Yks....52 E1
Ravensthorpe, Northnts....33 J2
Ravenstone, Bucks....34 B4
Ravenstone, Leic....43 G5
Ravenstonedale....64 E7
Ravenstown....57 G3
Ravenstruther....80 E7
Ravensworth....65 J7
Raw....67 K7
Rawcliffe, N. Yks....60 C5
Rawcliffe, Humbs....53 J1
Rawcliffe Bridge....53 K1
Rawdon....59 H7
Rawmarsh....53 G4
Rawreth....24 D3
Rawridge....10 D5
Rawtenstall....51 H1
Raydon....36 F6
Raylees....74 F5
Rayleigh....24 E3
Rayne....34 C7
Reach....35 J3
Read....58 C7
Reading....22 C5
Reading Street....17 G2
Reagill....64 D6
Rearquhar....103 F3
Rearsby....43 J5
Rease Heath....41 H1
Reaster....111 J2
Reawick....115 F4
Reay....110 F2
Rechullin....100 E7
Reculver....25 J6
Redberth....26 E6
Redbourn....23 G1
Redbourne....54 D3
Redbrook....19 K1
Redburn....103 H8
Redcar....67 G5
Redcastle....102 D8
Redcliff Bay....19 J5
Red Dial....63 H3
Redding....80 E4
Reddingmuirhead....80 E4
Redditch....32 C3
Rede....36 D4
Redenhall....37 H1
Redesdale Camp....74 E5
Redesmouth....74 E6
Redford, Tays....89 G5
Redford, Durham....65 H4
Redfordgreen....73 J3
Redgrave....36 F2
Redhill, Grampn....97 F2
Redhill, Grampn....97 G5
Redhill, Avon....19 J6
Redhill, Surrey....23 H7
Redisham....37 K1
Redland, Orkney....112 D4
Redland, Avon....19 K5
Redlingfield....37 G2

Red Lodge................36 C2
Redlynch, Wilts..........12 E3
Redlynch, Somer..........11 J2
Redmarley D'Abitot.......31 J6
Redmarshall.............66 D5
Redmile.................44 A3
Redmire.................58 F1
Redmoor..................3 J3
Rednal..................40 E4
Redpath.................82 D8
Red Rock................50 E3
Red Roses...............27 G5
Red Row.................75 J5
Redruth..................2 F5
Red Street..............41 K1
Red Wharf Bay...........48 E2
Redwick, Gwent..........19 J4
Redwick, Avon...........19 K4
Redworth................66 C5
Reed....................35 G6
Reedham.................47 K6
Reedness................54 B1
Reef...................106 F5
Reepham, Lincs..........54 E6
Reepham, Norf...........47 G4
Reeth...................65 H8
Regaby..................56 R2
Regil...................19 K6
Regoul.................103 G7
Reiff..................108 A7
Reigate.................23 H7
Reighton................61 J3
Reiss..................111 K3
Rejerrah.................3 G4
Relubbus.................2 D6
Relugas................103 H8
Remenham................22 C4
Remenham Hill...........22 C4
Rempstone...............43 H4
Rendcomb................20 E2
Rendham.................37 J3
Rendlesham..............37 J4
Renfrew.................79 H5
Renhold.................34 D4
Renishaw................53 G6
Rennington..............75 J3
Renton..................79 F4
Renwick.................64 C3
Repps...................47 K5
Repton..................43 F4
Resolis................102 E6
Resolven................18 C2
Reston..................83 G5
Retew....................3 H4
Retford.................53 K5
Rettendon...............24 D3
Rettendon Place.........24 D3
Revesby.................55 G7
Rewe.....................9 K6
Reydon..................37 K2
Reymerston..............46 F6
Reynalton...............26 E6
Reynoldston.............27 J7
Rhadmad.................28 C2
Rhandirmwyn.............28 E5
Rhayader................29 G3
Rhedyn..................38 B3
Rheindown..............102 D8
Rhes-y-cae..............50 A6
Rhewl, Clwyd............40 C2
Rhewl, Clwyd............49 L4
Rhiconich..............108 D3
Rhicullen..............102 E5
Rhigos..................18 D2
Rhilochan..............103 F2
Rhiroy.................101 H4
Rhiw....................38 B4
Rhiwbryfdir.............39 F2
Rhiwderin...............19 G4
Rhiwlas, Clwyd..........40 C3
Rhiwlas, Gwyn...........48 E4
Rhiwlas, Gwyn...........39 J3
Rhodesia................53 H5
Rhodes Minnis...........17 J1
Rhondda.................18 D3
Rhonehouse or Kelton Hill..69 J5
Rhoose..................18 E6
Rhos, W. Glam...........18 B2
Rhos, Dyfed.............27 H3
Rhoscefnhir.............48 E3
Rhoscolyn...............48 B3
Rhoscrowther............26 D6
Rhosesmor...............50 B7
Rhos-fawr...............38 C3
Rhosgadfan..............38 E1
Rhos-goch, Powys........30 C3
Rhosgoch, Gwyn..........48 D2
Rhoshirwaun.............38 A4
Rhoslan.................38 D2
Rhoslefain..............38 E6
Rhosllanerchrugog.......40 D3
Rhosmeirch..............48 C3
Rhosneigr...............48 C3
Rhosnesni...............40 E1
Rhos-on-Sea.............49 H2
Rhossili................27 J8
Rhosson.................26 B4
Rhostrehwfa.............48 D3
Rhostryfan..............38 D1
Rhostyllen..............40 E2
Rhosybol................48 D2
Rhos-y-brithdir.........40 C4
Rhos-y-gwaliau..........39 J3
Rhos-y-llan.............38 B3
Rhu.....................78 E3
Rhualt..................49 K3
Rhuddlan................49 K3
Rhue...................101 G3
Rhulen..................30 C5
Rhunahaorine............77 G2
Rhyd, Gwyn..............39 F2
Rhyd, Powys.............39 J6
Rhydargaeau.............27 J4
Rhydcymerau.............27 K3

Rhydd...................31 K5
Rhyd-Ddu................38 E1
Rhydding................18 B3
Rhyd-foel...............49 J3
Rhydlewis...............27 H2
Rhydlios................38 A3
Rhydlydan...............39 H1
Rhydowen................27 J2
Rhydtalog...............40 D1
Rhydwyn.................48 C2
Rhyd-y-clafdy...........38 C3
Rhydycroesau............40 D3
Rhydyfelin, Dyfed.......28 C2
Rhydyfelin, M. Glam.....18 E4
Rhyd-y-fro..............18 B2
Rhydymain...............39 H4
Rhydymwyn...............50 B7
Rhyd-yr-onen............38 F6
Rhyl....................49 K2
Rhymney.................18 F2
Rhynd...................88 D6
Rhynie..................96 D3
Ribbesford..............31 J2
Ribble Head.............58 C3
Ribbleton...............57 J7
Ribchester..............58 B7
Riby....................55 F3
Riccall.................60 D7
Riccarton...............79 G8
Richards Castle.........31 F3
Richmond, N. Yks........66 B7
Richmond, G. Lon........23 G5
Rickarton...............97 H7
Rickinghall.............36 F2
Rickling................35 H6
Rickmansworth..........22 F3
Riddell.................74 B2
Riddlecombe..............9 G4
Riddlesden..............59 F6
Ridge, Wilts............12 B2
Ridge, Dorset...........12 B7
Ridge, Herts............23 H2
Ridge Lane..............42 E7
Ridgeway Cross..........31 J5
Ridgewell...............36 C5
Ridgewood...............15 H4
Ridgmont................34 C6
Riding Mill.............65 H1
Ridlington, Leic........44 B6
Ridlington, Norf........47 J3
Ridsdale................74 F6
Rienachait.............108 B5
Rievaulx................60 C2
Rigg....................73 H8
Riggend.................80 C4
Rigside.................80 D8
Rileyhill...............42 D5
Rilla Mill...............4 C2
Rillington..............60 F3
Rimington...............58 D6
Rimpton.................11 H3
Rimswell................61 L8
Rinaston................26 D4
Ringasta...............113 C6
Ringford................69 H5
Ringland................47 G5
Ringmer.................15 H4
Ringmore.................5 G5
Ring's End..............45 G6
Ringsfield..............37 K1
Ringshall, Herts........22 E1
Ringshall, Suff.........36 F4
Ringshall Stocks........36 F4
Ringstead, Norf.........46 C2
Ringstead, Northnts.....34 C2
Ringwood................12 D5
Ringwould...............17 L1
Rinmore.................96 D4
Rinnigill..............112 D7
Rinsey...................2 D7
Ripe....................15 J4
Ripley, Hants...........12 D6
Ripley, Surrey..........22 F7
Ripley, Derby...........43 G1
Ripley, N. Yks..........59 H4
Riplingham..............61 G7
Ripon...................59 J3
Rippingale..............44 D4
Ripple, H. & W..........32 A6
Ripple, Kent............25 K7
Ripponden..............52 C2
Rireavach..............101 G3
Risabus.................76 C7
Risbury.................31 G4
Risby, Humbs............54 D2
Risby, Suff.............36 D3
Risca...................19 G3
Rise....................61 J6
Risegate................45 F4
Riseley, Berks..........22 C6
Riseley, Beds...........34 D3
Rishangles..............37 G3
Rishton.................58 C7
Rishworth...............52 C2
Rising Bridge...........51 G1
Risley, Ches............51 F4
Risley, Derby...........43 G3
Risplith................59 H4
Rivar...................21 H6
River Bank..............35 J3
Riverhead...............23 L7
Rivington...............51 F2
Roachill.................9 J3
Roade...................34 A4
Roadmeetings............80 D7
Roadside...............111 H2
Roadside of Catterline..97 H8
Roadside of Kinneff.....97 H8
Roadwater...............10 B2
Roag....................99 H8
Roath...................19 F5
Robbingworth............23 L2
Roberton, Strath........72 E2

Roberton, Border........73 K3
Robertsbridge...........16 E3
Roberttown..............52 D1
Robeston Cross..........26 C6
Robeston Wathen.........26 E5
Robin Hood's Bay........67 K7
Roborough................9 F4
Roby Mill...............50 E3
Rocester................42 D3
Roch....................26 C4
Rochdale................51 H2
Roche....................3 H3
Rochester, Kent.........24 D6
Rochester, Northum......74 E5
Rochford, Essex.........24 E3
Rochford, H. & W........31 H3
Rock, Corn...............3 H2
Rock, Northum...........75 J2
Rock, H. & W............31 J2
Rockbeare...............10 B6
Rockbourne..............12 D4
Rockcliffe, Cumbr.......63 J1
Rockcliffe, D. & G......69 K5
Rock Ferry..............50 C5
Rockfield, Highld......103 H4
Rockfield, Gwent........19 J1
Rockhampton.............20 A3
Rockingham..............44 B7
Rockland All Saints.....46 E7
Rockland St Mary........47 J6
Rockland St Peter.......46 E7
Rockley.................21 F5
Rockwell End............22 C4
Rodbourne...............20 D4
Rodd....................30 E3
Roddam..................75 G2
Rodden..................11 H7
Rode....................20 C7
Rodeheath, Ches.........51 H7
Rode Heath, Ches........41 K1
Rodel...................98 F4
Roden...................41 G5
Rodhuish................10 B2
Rodington...............41 G5
Rodley..................20 B1
Rodmarton...............20 D3
Rodmell.................15 H5
Rodmersham.............24 F6
Rodney Stoke............19 J7
Rodsley.................42 E2
Roecliffe...............59 J4
Roehampton..............23 H5
Roffey..................15 E2
Rogart.................103 F2
Rogate..................14 B3
Rogerstone..............19 G4
Rogerton................79 J6
Rogiet..................19 J4
Roker...................66 E2
Rollesby................47 K5
Rolleston, Notts........44 A1
Rolleston, Staffs.......42 E4
Rolleston, Leic.........43 K6
Rolston.................61 K6
Rolvenden...............16 F2
Rolvenden Layne.........16 F2
Romaldkirk..............65 G5
Romanby.................59 J1
Romannbridge............81 G7
Romansleigh..............9 H3
Romford.................23 L4
Romiley.................51 J4
Romsey..................13 F3
Romsley, H. & W.........32 B1
Romsley, Shrops.........31 J1
Ronague.................56 P4
Rookby..................65 F6
Rookhope................65 G3
Rookley.................13 H7
Rooks Bridge............19 H7
Roos....................61 K7
Roosebeck...............57 F4
Rootpark................80 E6
Ropley..................13 J2
Ropley Deane............13 J2
Ropsley.................44 C3
Rora...................105 K3
Rorrington..............40 E6
Rose.....................2 F4
Roseacre................57 H7
Rose Ash.................9 H3
Rosebank................80 D7
Rosebush................26 E4
Rosedale Abbey..........60 E1
Roseden.................75 G2
Rosehall...............102 C2
Rosehearty.............105 J2
Rosehill................41 H3
Roseisle...............103 K6
Rosemarket..............26 D6
Rosemarkie............103 F7
Rosemary Lane...........10 C4
Rosemount, Tays.........88 D4
Rosemount, Strath.......71 J2
Rosenannon..............3 H3
Rosewell................81 H5
Roseworthy..............2 E6
Rosgill.................64 C6
Roshven.................92 D8
Roskhill................99 H8
Rosley..................63 J3
Roslin..................81 H5
Rosliston...............42 E5
Rosneath................78 E3
Ross, D. & G............69 H6
Ross, Northum...........83 K8
Rossett.................40 E1
Rossington..............53 J4
Rossland................79 G4
Ross-on-Wye.............31 H7
Roster.................111 J5
Rostherne...............51 G5
Rosthwaite..............63 H6
Roston..................42 D2
Rosyth..................81 G2

Rothbury................75 G4
Rotherby................43 J5
Rotherfield.............16 C3
Rotherfield Greys.......22 C4
Rotherfield Peppard.....22 C4
Rotherham...............53 G4
Rothersthorpe...........33 K4
Rotherwick..............22 C7
Rothes.................104 B4
Rothesay................78 C5
Rothiebrisbane..........97 G2
Rothienorman............97 G2
Rothiesholm............113 G4
Rothley.................43 H5
Rothmaise..............97 F2
Rothwell, Northnts......34 B1
Rothwell, Lincs.........55 F4
Rothwell, W. Yks........59 J8
Rotsea..................61 H5
Rottal..................89 F2
Rottingdean.............15 G5
Rottington..............62 E6
Roud....................7 K6
Rougham.................46 D4
Rougham Green...........36 E3
Roughburn...............94 B7
Rough Close.............42 B3
Rough Common............25 H7
Roughlee................58 D6
Roughley................42 D7
Roughsike..............74 B7
Roughton, Lincs.........55 G7
Roughton, Norf..........47 H3
Roughton, Shrops........41 J7
Roundhay................59 J7
Roundstreet Common......14 D3
Roundway................20 E6
Rousdon.................10 D6
Rousham.................21 J6
Rous Lench..............32 C4
Routh...................61 H6
Row, Cumbr..............57 H2
Row, Corn................3 J2
Rowanburn...............73 K7
Rowde...................20 D6
Rowen...................49 G3
Rowfoot.................64 D1
Rowhedge................36 F7
Rowhook.................14 E2
Rowington...............32 E3
Rowland.................52 E6
Rowland's Castle........13 K4
Rowlands Gill...........66 B2
Rowledge................14 B1
Rowlestone..............30 E7
Rowly...................40 E6
Rowney Green............32 C2
Rownhams................13 F4
Rowrah..................62 D1
Rowsham.................22 D1
Rowsley.................52 E7
Rowston.................44 D1
Rowton, Ches............50 D7
Rowton, Shrops..........41 H5
Roxburgh................74 C1
Roxby, Humbs............54 D2
Roxby, N. Yks...........67 H4
Roxton..................34 E4
Roxwell.................24 C2
Royal British Legion Village..24 D7
Royal Leamington Spa....33 F3
Royal Tunbridge Wells...16 C2
Roybridge...............93 J7
Roydon, Norf............46 C4
Roydon, Norf............37 F1
Roydon, Essex...........23 K1
Royston, S. Yks.........53 F2
Royston, Herts..........35 G5
Royton..................51 J3
Ruabon..................40 E2
Ruaig...................84 B4
Ruan Lanihorne..........3 G5
Ruan Minor...............2 F8
Ruardean................19 L1
Ruardean Woodside.......19 L1
Rubery..................32 B2
Rubha Bhocaig...........99 G3
Rubha Cam nan Gall......98 D8
Rubha Crago.............99 H3
Rubh' Aird-mhicheil.....90 C2
Ruckcroft...............64 C3
Ruckinge................17 H2
Ruckland................55 H6
Ruckley.................41 G6
Ruddington..............43 H3
Rudge...................20 C7
Rudgeway................19 L4
Rudgwick................14 D2
Rudhall.................31 H7
Rudloe..................20 C6
Rudry...................18 F4
Rudston.................61 H4
Rudyard.................42 B1
Rufford.................50 D2
Rufforth................60 C5
Rugby...................33 H2
Rugeley.................42 C5
Ruilick................102 D8
Ruisgarry...............98 F2
Ruishton................10 D3
Ruislip.................22 F4
Ruislip Common..........23 F4
Rumbling Bridge.........80 F2
Rumburgh................37 J1
Rumford.................19 G5
Rumney..................19 G5
Runcorn.................50 E5
Runcton.................14 B5
Runcton Holme...........45 K6
Runfold.................14 B1
Runhall.................46 F6
Runham..................47 K5
Runnington..............10 C3
Runswick Bay...........67 J6

Runwell.................24 D3
Ruscombe................22 C5
Rushall, W. Mids........42 C6
Rushall, Wilts..........20 F7
Rushall, Norf...........37 G1
Rushbrooke..............36 D3
Rushbury................41 G7
Rushden, Northnts.......34 C3
Rushden, Herts..........35 G6
Rushford................36 E1
Rush Green..............23 L4
Rushlake Green..........16 D4
Rushmere................37 K1
Rushmere St Andrew......37 H5
Rushmoor................14 B1
Rushock.................32 A2
Rusholme................51 H4
Rushton, Northnts.......34 B1
Rushton, Ches...........50 E7
Rushton, Shrops.........41 H6
Rushton Spencer.........51 J7
Rushwick................31 K4
Rushyford...............66 C5
Ruskie..................79 J1
Ruskington..............44 D1
Rusland.................57 G2
Rusper..................15 F2
Ruspidge................20 A1
Russell's Water.........22 C4
Rustington..............14 D5
Ruston..................61 H4
Ruston Parva............61 H4
Ruswarp.................67 J7
Rutherford..............74 C1
Rutherglen..............79 H5
Ruthernbridge............3 J3
Ruthin..................50 A8
Ruthrieston.............97 J5
Ruthven, Grampn.......104 E4
Ruthven, Tays...........88 E4
Ruthven, Highld.........95 G2
Ruthvoes.................3 H3
Ruthwell................73 G8
Ruyton-XI-Towns.........40 E4
Ryal....................75 G7
Ryal Fold...............51 F1
Ryall...................10 F6
Ryarsh..................24 C7
Rydal...................63 J7
Ryde....................13 H6
Rye.....................17 G3
Rye Foreign.............17 G3
Rye Harbour.............17 G4
Ryhall..................44 D5
Ryhill..................53 F2
Ryhope..................66 E2
Rylstone................58 E5
Ryme Intrinseca.........11 G4
Ryther..................60 C7
Ryton, N. Yks...........60 E3
Ryton, T. & W...........65 J1
Ryton, Shrops...........41 J6
Ryton, Glos.............31 J6
Ryton-on-Dunsmore.......33 F2

S

Saasaig.................92 C5
Sabden..................58 C7
Sacombe.................23 J1
Sacriston...............66 C3
Sadberge................66 D6
Saddell.................70 C1
Saddington..............43 J7
Saddle Bow..............45 K5
Saddlethorpe............60 F8
Sadgill.................64 B7
Saffron Walden..........35 J6
Saham Toney.............46 E6
Saighton................50 D7
St Abbs.................83 H5
St Agnes.................2 F4
St Albans...............23 G2
St Allen.................3 G4
St Andrews..............89 H7
St Andrews Major........18 F5
St Annes................57 G8
St Ann's................73 F5
St Ann's Chapel, Corn....4 E2
St Ann's Chapel, Devon...5 G5
St Anthony-in-Meneage....3 F7
St Arvans...............19 K3
St Asaph or Llanelwy....49 K3
St Athan................18 E6
St Austell...............3 J4
St Bees.................62 E6
St Blazey................3 J4
St Boswells.............74 B1
St Breock................3 H2
St Breward...............3 J2
St Briavels.............19 K2
St Brides...............26 B5
St Bride's Major........18 C5
St Bride's-super-Ely....18 E5
St Brides Wentloog......19 G4
St Budeaux...............4 E4
Saintbury...............32 D6
St Buryan................2 C7
St Catherine............20 B5
St Catherines...........86 D8
St Clears................4 C3
St Cleer.................4 C3
St Clement...............3 G4
St Clether...............8 C7
St Colmac...............78 C5
St Columb Major..........3 H3
St Columb Minor..........3 G3
St Columb Road...........3 H4
St Combs...............105 K2
St Cross South Elmham...37 H1
St Cyrus................89 K2
St David's, Dyfed.......26 B4

St David's, Tays........88 B6
St Day...................2 F5
St Dennis................3 H4
St Dogmaels.............26 F2
St Dominick..............4 E3
St Donat's..............18 D6
St Endellion.............3 H2
St Enoder................3 G4
St Erme..................2 G5
St Erth..................2 D6
St Erth Praze............2 D6
St Ervan.................3 G3
St Eval..................3 G3
St Ewe...................3 H5
St Fagans...............18 F5
St Fergus..............105 K3
St Fillans..............87 J6
St Florence.............26 E6
St Gennys................8 B6
St George...............49 J3
St George's, S. Glam....18 F5
St Georges, Avon........19 H6
St Germans...............4 D4
St Giles in the Wood.....9 F4
St Giles on the Heath....8 D6
St Harmon...............29 G2
St Helen Auckland.......66 B5
St Helens, Mers.........50 E4
St Helens, I. of W......13 J7
St Hilary, Corn..........2 D6
St Hilary, S. Glam......18 E5
Saint Hill..............15 G2
St Illtyd...............19 G2
St Ippollitts...........35 E7
St Ishmael's............26 C6
St Issey.................3 H2
St Ive...................4 D3
St Ives, Corn............2 D5
St Ives, Dorset.........12 D5
St Ives, Cambs..........35 G2
St James South Elmham...37 J1
St John..................4 E4
St Johns, H. & W........31 K4
St John's, I. of M......56 P3
St John's Chapel........65 F4
St John's Fen End.......45 J5
St John's Highway.......45 J5
St John's Town of Dalry..72 K2
St Judes................56 Q2
St Just..................2 B6
St Just in Roseland......3 G5
St Katherines...........97 G2
St Keverne...............3 F7
St Kew...................3 J2
St Kew Highway...........3 J2
St Keyne.................4 C3
St Lawrence, Essex......25 G2
St Lawrence, Corn........3 J3
St Lawrence, I. of W.....7 K7
St Leonards, Dorset.....12 D5
St Leonards, Bucks......22 E2
St Leonards, E. Susx....16 E5
St Levan.................2 B7
St Lythans..............18 F5
St Mabyn.................3 J2
St Madoes...............88 D6
St Margarets............30 E6
St Margaret's at Cliffe..17 L1
St Margaret's Hope.....112 E7
St Margaret South Elmham..37 J1
St Mark's...............56 P4
St Martin, Corn..........4 C4
St Martin, Corn..........2 F7
St Martins, Tays........88 D5
St Martin's, Shrops.....40 E3
St Mary Bourne..........21 J7
St Mary Church..........18 E5
St Mary Cray............23 K6
St Mary Hill............18 D5
St Mary Hoo.............24 E5
St Mary in the Marsh....17 H3
St Mary's..............112 E7
St Mary's Bay...........17 H3
St Mawes.................3 G6
St Mawgan................3 G3
St Mellion...............4 D3
St Mellons..............19 G4
St Merryn................3 G3
St Mewan.................3 H4
St Michael Caerhays......3 H5
St Michael Penkevil......3 G5
St Michaels, Kent.......17 F2
St Michaels, H. & W.....31 G3
St Michael's on Wyre....57 H6
St Michael South Elmham..37 J1
St Minver................3 H2
St Monance..............82 D1
St Neot..................4 B3
St Neots................34 E3
St Newlyn East...........3 G4
St Nicholas, Dyfed......26 D3
St Nicholas, S. Glam....18 E5
St Nicholas at Wade.....25 J6
St Ninians..............80 C2
St Osyth................25 H1
St Owen's Cross.........31 G7
St Paul's Cray..........23 K6
St Paul's Walden........35 E7
St Peter's..............25 K6
St Petrox...............26 D7
St Pinnock...............4 C3
St Quivox...............71 J2
St Stephen...............3 H4
St Stephens, Cornw.......8 D7
St Stephens, Corn........4 E4
St Teath.................3 J1
St Tudy..................3 J2
St Twynnells............26 D7
St Vigeans..............89 J4
St Wenn..................3 H3
St Weonards.............31 F7
St Winnow................3 K4
Salcombe.................5 H6
Salcombe Regis..........10 C7
Salcott.................25 F1

Sale....51 G4
Saleby....55 J6
Sale Green....32 B4
Salehurst....16 E3
Salem, Dyfed....28 D1
Salem, Dyfed....27 L4
Salen, Strath....85 G4
Salen, Highld....85 H2
Salesbury....58 B7
Salford, Beds....34 C6
Salford, Oxon....32 E7
Salford, G. Man....51 H4
Salford Priors....32 C4
Salfords....15 F1
Salhouse....47 H5
Saline....80 F2
Salisbury....12 D3
Sallachy....93 F2
Salle....47 G4
Salmonby....55 H6
Salperton....32 C7
Salph End....34 D4
Salsburgh....80 D5
Salt....42 B4
Saltash....4 E4
Saltburn....102 F6
Saltburn-by-the-Sea....67 G5
Saltby....44 B4
Saltcoats....78 E7
Saltdean....15 G5
Salter....57 K4
Salterforth....58 D6
Salterswall....51 F7
Saltfleet....55 J4
Saltfleetby All Saints....55 J4
Saltfleetby St Clement....55 J4
Saltfleetby St Peter....55 J5
Saltford....20 A6
Salthaugh Grange....55 G1
Salthouse....46 F2
Saltmarshe....54 B1
Salton....60 E2
Saltwood....17 J2
Salum....84 B4
Salwarpe....32 A3
Salwayash....11 F6
Samala....98 C6
Sambourne....32 C3
Sambrook....41 J4
Samlesbury....57 J7
Samlesbury Bottoms....57 K8
Sampford Arundel....10 C4
Sampford Brett....10 B1
Sampford Courtenay....9 G5
Sampford Peverell....10 B4
Sampford Spiney....4 F2
Samuelston....82 C4
Sanachan....92 E1
Sancreed....2 C7
Sand, Shetld....115 F4
Sand, Highld....101 F3
Sandaig....92 D5
Sandbach....51 G7
Sandbank....78 D3
Sandbanks....12 C7
Sandend....104 E2
Sanderstead....23 J6
Sandford, Dorset....12 B7
Sandford, Strath....80 C7
Sandford, Cumbr....64 E6
Sandford, Devon....9 J5
Sandford, Avon....19 J7
Sandfordhill....105 L4
Sandford-on-Thames....21 K2
Sandford Orcas....11 H3
Sandford St Martin....33 G7
Sandgate....17 K2
Sandgreen....69 G5
Sandhaven....105 J2
Sandhead....68 B5
Sandhoe....75 F8
Sandholme, Humbs....60 F7
Sandholme, Lincs....45 G3
Sandhurst, Berks....22 D6
Sandhurst, Kent....16 E3
Sandhurst, Glos....31 K7
Sand Hutton, N. Yks....60 D5
Sandhutton, N. Yks....59 J2
Sandiacre....43 G3
Sandilands....55 K5
Sandiway....50 F6
Sandleheath....12 D4
Sandleigh....21 J2
Sandling....24 D7
Sandness....114 D3
Sandon, Staffs....42 B4
Sandon, Essex....24 D2
Sandon, Herts....35 G6
Sandown....13 H7
Sandplace....4 C4
Sandridge....23 G1
Sandringham....46 B4
Sandsend....67 J6
Sandsound....115 F4
Sandtoft....54 B3
Sandwich....25 K7
Sandwick, Orkney....112 E8
Sandwick, Shetld....115 G6
Sandwick, W. Isles....98 D8
Sandwick, W. Isles....107 J5
Sandwick, Cumbr....63 K6
Sandwith....62 E6
Sandy....34 E5
Sandycroft....50 C7
Sandygate....56 Q2
Sandyhills....69 K5
Sandy Lane....20 D6
Sangobeg....109 F2
Sannox....78 C7
Sanquhar....72 C4
Santon....61 G7
Santon Bridge....63 G2
Santon Downham....36 D1
Sapcote....43 G7
Sapey Common....31 J3

Sapiston....36 E2
Sapperton, Glos....20 D2
Sapperton, Lincs....44 D3
Saracen's Head....45 G4
Sarclet....111 K4
Sarisbury....13 H5
Sarn, M. Glam....18 D4
Sarn, Powys....40 D7
Sarnau, Powys....40 D5
Sarnau, Dyfed....27 H1
Sarnau, Dyfed....27 H5
Sarnau, Gwyn....39 J3
Sarn Bach....38 C4
Sarnesfield....30 E4
Sarn Meyllteyrn....38 B3
Saron, Dyfed....27 H3
Saron, Dyfed....27 L5
Sarratt....22 F3
Sarre....25 J6
Sarsden....32 E7
Satley....65 J3
Satterleigh....9 G3
Satterthwaite....57 G1
Sauchen....97 G4
Saucher....88 D5
Sauchieburn....89 J2
Sauchrie....71 J3
Saughall....50 C6
Saughtree....74 B5
Saul....20 B2
Saundby....54 B5
Saundersfoot....26 F6
Saunderton....22 C2
Saunton....8 E2
Sausthorpe....55 H7
Saval....102 D2
Savon Street....36 B4
Sawbridgeworth....23 K1
Sawdon....61 G2
Sawley, Lancs....58 C6
Sawley, Derby....43 G3
Sawley, N. Yks....59 H4
Sawrey....57 G1
Sawston....35 H5
Sawtry....34 E1
Saxby, Leic....44 B4
Saxby, Lincs....54 E5
Saxby All Saints....54 D2
Saxelbye....43 K4
Saxilby....54 C6
Saxlingham....46 F3
Saxlingham Nethergate....47 H7
Saxmundham....37 J3
Saxondale....43 J3
Saxtead....37 H3
Saxtead Green....37 H3
Saxthorpe....47 G3
Saxton....60 B7
Sayers Common....15 F4
Scackleton....60 D3
Scadabay....99 G3
Scaftworth....53 J4
Scagglethorpe....60 F3
Scalasaig....76 C2
Scalby....61 H1
Scaldwell....34 A2
Scaleby....64 B1
Scaleby Hill....64 B1
Scale Houses....64 C3
Scales, Cumbr....57 F3
Scales, Cumbr....63 J5
Scalford....44 A4
Scaling....67 H6
Scalloway....115 G5
Scamblesby....55 G6
Scampston....60 F3
Scampton....54 D6
Scarastavore....98 F3
Scarborough....61 H2
Scarcliffe....53 G7
Scarcroft....59 J6
Scardroy....101 J7
Scarfskerry....111 J1
Scargill....65 H6
Scarinish....84 B4
Scarisbrick....50 C2
Scarning....46 E5
Scarrington....43 K2
Scarth Hill....50 D3
Scartho....55 G3
Scaur or Kippford....69 K5
Scawby....54 D3
Scawton....60 C2
Scayne's Hill....15 G3
Scethrog....30 C7
Scholar Green....41 K1
Scholes, W. Yks....52 D3
Scholes, W. Yks....59 J7
Schoolhill....97 G5
Scleddau....26 D3
Scole....37 G2
Scolpaig....98 C5
Scolton....26 D4
Sconser....92 B2
Scoor....84 F7
Scopwick....54 E8
Scoraig....101 G3
Scorborough....61 H6
Scorrier....2 F5
Scorton, N. Yks....66 C7
Scorton, Lancs....57 J6
Sco Ruston....47 H4
Scotasay....99 G3
Scotby....64 B2
Scotch Corner....66 C7
Scotforth....57 H5
Scothern....54 E6
Scotland Gate....75 J6
Scotlandwell....81 G1
Scotsburn....102 F5
Scots' Gap....75 G6
Scots Hole....54 F7
Scotston....85 K2
Scottas....92 D5
Scotter....54 C3

Scotterthorpe....54 C3
Scotton, Lincs....54 C4
Scotton, N. Yks....59 G1
Scotton, N. Yks....59 J5
Scottow....47 H4
Scoughall....82 E3
Scoulton....46 E6
Scourie....108 C4
Scousburgh....115 F7
Scrabster....111 G1
Scrainwood....75 F4
Scrane End....45 G2
Scraptoft....43 J6
Scratby....47 L5
Scrayingham....60 E4
Screapadal....100 B8
Scredington....44 D2
Scremby....55 J7
Scremerston....83 J7
Screveton....43 K2
Scriven....59 J5
Scrooby....53 J4
Scropton....42 D3
Scrub Hill....45 F1
Scruton....59 J1
Sculcoates....59 H6
Sculthorpe....46 D3
Scunthorpe....54 C2
Scurlage....27 J8
Seaborough....11 F5
Seacombe....50 C4
Seacroft....55 K7
Seaford....15 H6
Seaforth....50 C4
Seaforth Head....107 G7
Seagrave....43 J5
Seaham....66 E3
Seahouses....75 J1
Seal....23 L7
Sealand....50 C7
Seamer, N. Yks....66 E6
Seamer, N. Yks....61 H2
Seamill....78 E7
Sea Palling....47 K4
Searby....54 E3
Seasalter....25 G6
Seascale....62 F7
Seathorne....55 K7
Seathwaite, Cumbr....57 F1
Seathwaite, Cumbr....63 H6
Seaton, Leic....44 C7
Seaton, Durham....66 D3
Seaton, Corn....4 D4
Seaton, Devon....10 D6
Seaton, Cumbr....62 F4
Seaton, Humbs....61 J6
Seaton, Northum....75 K7
Seaton Burn....75 J7
Seaton Carew....66 F5
Seaton Delaval....75 K7
Seaton Ross....60 E6
Seaton Sluice....75 K7
Seatown....11 F6
Seave Green....67 F7
Seaview....13 J6
Seavington St Mary....10 E4
Seavington St Michael....10 F4
Sebastapol....19 G3
Sebergham....63 J3
Seckington....42 E6
Sedbergh....58 B1
Sedbury....19 K3
Sedbusk....58 D1
Sedgeberrow....32 C6
Sedgebrook....44 B3
Sedgefield....66 D5
Sedgeford....46 C3
Sedgehill....12 A3
Sedgley....42 B7
Sedgwick....57 J2
Sedlescombe....16 E4
Seend....20 D6
Seend Cleeve....20 D6
Seer Green....22 E3
Seething....47 J7
Sefton....50 C3
Seghill....75 J7
Seighford....42 A4
Seilebost....98 F3
Seisdon....41 K7
Seisiadar....107 K5
Selattyn....40 D3
Selborne....13 K2
Selby....60 D7
Selham....14 C3
Selkirk....74 A2
Sellack....31 G7
Sellafirth....117 G3
Sellindge....17 J2
Selling....25 G7
Sells Green....20 D6
Selly Oak....32 C1
Selmeston....15 J5
Selsdon....23 J6
Selsey....14 B6
Selside, N. Yks....58 C3
Selside, Cumbr....64 C8
Selston....43 G1
Selworthy....9 K1
Semer....36 F5
Semington....20 C6
Semley....12 A3
Senghenydd....18 F3
Sennen....2 B7
Sennen Cove....2 B7
Sennybridge....29 G7
Sereveton....43 K2
Sessay....59 K3
Setchey....46 B5
Setley....13 F5
Setter....117 F4
Settiscarth....112 D5
Settle....58 D4

Settrington....60 F3
Sevenhampton, Glos....32 C7
Sevenhampton, Wilts....21 G3
Seven Kings....23 K4
Sevenoaks....23 L7
Sevenoaks Weald....23 L7
Seven Sisters....18 C2
Severn Beach....19 K4
Severn Stoke....32 A5
Sevington....17 H1
Sewards End....35 J6
Sewerby....61 J4
Seworgan....2 F6
Sewstern....44 B4
Sezincote....32 D6
Sgiogarstaigh....107 K2
Shabbington....22 B2
Shackerstone....43 F6
Shackleford....14 C1
Shader....107 H3
Shadforth....66 D3
Shadingfield....37 K1
Shadoxhurst....17 G2
Shaftesbury....12 A3
Shafton....53 F2
Shalbourne....21 H6
Shalcombe....13 F7
Shalden....13 J1
Shaldon....5 K2
Shalfleet....13 G7
Shalford, Essex....36 C7
Shalford, Surrey....14 D1
Shalford Green....36 C7
Shalmsford Street....25 H7
Shalstone....33 J6
Shamley Green....14 D1
Shandon....78 E3
Shandwick....103 G5
Shangton....43 K7
Shanklin....7 K6
Shanquhar....96 E2
Shap....64 C6
Shapwick, Dorset....12 B5
Shapwick, Somer....11 F2
Shardlow....43 G3
Shareshill....42 B6
Sharlston....53 F2
Sharnbrook....34 C4
Sharnford....43 G7
Sharoe Green....57 J7
Sharow....59 J3
Sharpenhoe....34 D6
Sharperton....75 F4
Sharpness....20 A2
Sharpthorne....15 G2
Sharrington....46 F3
Shatterford....31 J1
Shaugh Prior....4 F3
Shavington....41 H1
Shaw, Wilts....20 C6
Shaw, G. Man....51 J3
Shaw, Berks....21 J6
Shawbost....107 G4
Shawbury....41 G4
Shawell....33 H1
Shawford....13 G3
Shawforth....51 H1
Shawhead....72 D7
Shaw Mills....59 H4
Shearsby....43 J7
Shebbear....8 E5
Shebdon....41 J4
Shebster....111 G2
Shedfield....13 H4
Sheen....52 D7
Sheepscombe....20 C1
Sheepstor....4 F3
Sheepwash....8 E5
Sheepy Magna....43 F6
Sheepy Parva....43 F6
Sheering....23 L1
Sheerness....24 F5
Sheet....14 A3
Sheffield....53 F5
Sheffield Bottom....22 B6
Shefford....34 E6
Sheinton....41 H6
Shelderton....30 F2
Sheldon, Devon....10 C5
Sheldon, W. Mids....32 D1
Sheldon, Derby....52 D7
Sheldwich....25 G7
Shelf....59 G8
Shelfanger....37 G1
Shelford....42 C6
Shelford....43 J2
Shelley....52 E2
Shellingford....21 H3
Shellow Bowells....24 C2
Shelsley Beauchamp....31 J3
Shelsley Walsh....31 J3
Shelton, Notts....44 A2
Shelton, Northnts....34 D3
Shelton, Norf....47 H7
Shelton Green....47 H7
Shelve....40 E7
Shelwick....31 G5
Shenfield....24 C3
Shenington....33 F5
Shenley....23 G2
Shenley Brook End....34 B6
Shenleybury....23 G2
Shenley Church End....34 B6
Shenmore....30 E6
Shenstone, H. & W....32 A2
Shenstone, Staffs....42 D6
Shenton....43 F6
Shenval, Grampn....96 B3
Shenval, Highld....94 C3
Shepherd's Green....22 C4
Shepherdswell or Sibertswold....17 K1
Shepley....52 D3
Shepperdine....19 L3
Shepperton....23 G6
Shepreth....35 G5

Shepshed....43 G5
Shepton Beauchamp....10 F4
Shepton Mallet....11 H1
Shepton Montague....11 H2
Shepway....24 D7
Sheraton....66 E4
Sherborne, Glos....21 F1
Sherborne, Dorset....11 H4
Sherborne St John....22 B7
Sherbourne....32 E3
Sherburn, Durham....66 D3
Sherburn, N. Yks....61 G3
Sherburn in Elmet....60 B7
Shere....14 D1
Shereford....46 D4
Sherfield English....12 E3
Sherfield on Loddon....22 B7
Sheriffhales....41 J5
Sheriff Hutton....60 D4
Sheringham....47 G2
Sherington....34 B5
Shernborne....46 C3
Sherrington....12 B2
Sherston....20 C4
Sherwood Green....9 F3
Shettpeston....79 J5
Shevington....50 E3
Shevington Moor....50 E2
Sheviock....4 D4
Shiel Bridge....93 F4
Shieldaig, Highld....100 E5
Shieldaig, Highld....100 E7
Shieldhill....80 D4
Shielfoot....85 H1
Shifnal....41 J6
Shilbottle....75 H4
Shildon....66 C5
Shillingford, Devon....10 A3
Shillingford, Oxon....21 K3
Shillingford St George....9 K7
Shillingstone....11 K4
Shillington....34 E6
Shillmoor....74 E4
Shilton, Warw....33 G1
Shilton, Oxon....21 G2
Shimpling, Suff....36 D4
Shimpling, Norf....37 G1
Shimpling Street....36 D4
Shiney Row....66 D2
Shinfield....22 C6
Shinness....102 D2
Shipbourne....24 B7
Shipdham....46 E6
Shipham....19 J7
Shiphay....5 J3
Shiplake....22 C5
Shipley, W. Susx....14 E3
Shipley, W. Yks....59 G7
Shipley, Shrops....41 K7
Shipmeadow....47 J7
Shippon....21 J3
Shipston-on-Stour....32 E5
Shipton, N. Yks....60 C5
Shipton, Glos....20 E1
Shipton, Shrops....41 G7
Shipton Bellinger....12 E1
Shipton Gorge....11 F6
Shipton Green....14 B6
Shipton Moyne....20 C4
Shipton-on-Cherwell....21 J1
Shiptonthorpe....60 F6
Shipton-under-Wychwood....21 G1
Shirburn....22 B3
Shirdley Hill....50 C2
Shirebrook....53 H7
Shirehampton....19 K5
Shiremoor....75 K7
Shirenewton....19 J3
Shire Oak....42 C6
Shireoaks....53 H5
Shirkoak....17 G2
Shirland....53 F8
Shirley, W. Mids....32 D2
Shirley, Derby....42 E2
Shirley, Hants....13 G4
Shirl Heath....31 F4
Shirrell Heath....13 H4
Shirwell....9 F2
Shiskine....70 E1
Shobdon....30 F3
Shobrooke....9 J5
Shocklach....41 F2
Shoeburyness....25 F4
Sholden....25 K7
Sholing....13 G4
Sholver....51 J3
Shop, Corn....8 C4
Shop, Corn....3 G2
Shoreditch....23 J4
Shoreham....15 L6
Shoreham-by-Sea....15 F5
Shoresdean....83 H7
Shoreswood....83 H7
Shoreton....102 E6
Shorncote....20 E3
Shorne....24 C5
Shortgate....15 H4
Shorthanesend....3 G5
Shortlees....79 G8
Shortley Bridge....65 H2
Shorwell....13 G7
Shoscombe....20 B7
Shotesham....47 H7
Shotgate....24 D3
Shotley....37 H6
Shotley Gate....37 H6
Shottenden....25 G7
Shottermill....14 B2
Shottery....32 D4
Shotteswell....33 G5
Shottisham....37 J5
Shottle....43 F2

Shotton, Clwyd....50 C7
Shotton, Northum....74 E1
Shotton, Durham....66 E4
Shotts....80 D5
Shotwick....50 C6
Shoughlaige-e-Caine....56 Q3
Shouldham....46 B6
Shouldham Thorpe....46 B6
Shoulton....31 K4
Shrawardine....40 F5
Shrawley....31 K3
Shrewley....32 E3
Shrewsbury....41 F5
Shrewton....12 C1
Shripney....14 C5
Shrivenham....21 G4
Shropham....46 E7
Shroton or Iwerne Courtney....11 K4
Shrub End....36 E7
Shucknall....31 G5
Shudy Camps....35 K5
Shulishader....107 K5
Shurdington....20 D1
Shurlock Row....22 D5
Shurrery....111 G3
Shurton....10 D1
Shustoke....42 E7
Shute....10 D6
Shutford....33 F5
Shuthonger....32 A6
Shutlanger....33 K5
Shuttington....42 E6
Shuttlewood....53 G6
Sibbertoft....33 J1
Sibdon Carwood....31 F1
Sibertswold or Shepherdswell....17 K1
Sibford Ferris....33 F6
Sibford Gower....33 F6
Sible Hedingham....36 C6
Sibsey....45 G1
Sibson, Cambs....44 D7
Sibson, Leic....43 F6
Sibthorpe....44 A2
Sibton....37 J3
Sicklesmere....36 D3
Sicklinghall....59 J6
Sidbury, Devon....10 C6
Sidbury, Shrops....31 H1
Sidcup....23 K5
Siddington, Glos....20 E3
Siddington, Ches....51 H6
Sidestrand....47 H3
Sidford....10 C6
Sidinish....98 D6
Sidlesham....14 B6
Sidley....16 E5
Sidmouth....10 C7
Sigford....5 H2
Sigglesthorne....61 J6
Silchester....22 B6
Sileby....43 J5
Silecroft....56 E2
Silian....27 K1
Silkstone....52 E3
Silkstone Common....52 E3
Silk Willoughby....44 D2
Silloth....63 G2
Sillyearn....104 E3
Siloh....28 E6
Silpho....61 G1
Silsden....58 F6
Silsoe....34 D6
Silton....11 J3
Silverburn....81 H5
Silverdale, Cumbr....57 H3
Silverdale, Staffs....41 K2
Silver End....24 E1
Silverford....105 G2
Silverley's Green....37 H2
Silverstone....33 J5
Silverton....9 K5
Silwick....114 E4
Simonburn....74 E7
Simonsbath....9 H2
Simonstone....58 C7
Simprim....83 G7
Simpson....34 B6
Simpson Cross....18 C1
Sinclairston....71 K3
Sinderby....59 J2
Sinderhope....65 F2
Sindlesham....22 C6
Singleton, W. Susx....14 B4
Singleton, Lancs....57 G7
Singlewell....24 C5
Sinnahard....96 D4
Sinnington....60 E2
Sinton Green....31 K3
Sipson....22 F5
Sirhowy....18 F1
Sissinghurst....16 E2
Siston....20 A5
Sithney....2 E7
Sittingbourne....24 F6
Six Ashes....31 J1
Sixhills....55 F5
Sixpenny Handley....12 B4
Sizewell....37 K3
Skares....71 L3
Skateraw....82 F4
Skaw....115 H2
Skeabost....99 K8
Skeabrae....112 C4
Skeffington....44 A6
Skeffling....55 H2
Skegby....53 G7
Skegness....55 K7
Skelberry....115 F7
Skelbo....103 F3
Skeldyke....45 G3
Skellingthorpe....54 D6
Skellister....115 G3
Skellow....53 H2
Skelmanthorpe....52 E2

Skelmersdale........................50 D3
Skelmorlie...........................78 D5
Skelpick.............................110 D3
Skelton, Cumbr.......................64 B4
Skelton, N. Yks......................60 C5
Skelton, Cleve.......................67 G6
Skelton, N. Yks......................65 H7
Skelton on Ure.......................59 J4
Skelwick............................113 E2
Skelwith Bridge......................63 E3
Skendleby...........................55 J7
Skenfrith............................31 F7
Skerne..............................61 H5
Skerray............................109 H2
Sketty...............................27 L7
Skewen...............................18 B3
Skewsby..............................60 D3
Skeyton..............................47 H4
Skidbrooke...........................55 J4
Skidby...............................61 H7
Skilgate.............................10 A3
Skillington..........................44 B4
Skinburness..........................63 G2
Skinflats............................80 E3
Skinidin.............................99 H8
Skinningrove.........................67 H6
Skipness.............................77 J6
Skipsea..............................61 J5
Skipton..............................58 E5
Skipton-on-Swale.....................59 J3
Skipwith.............................60 D7
Skirlaugh............................61 J7
Skirling.............................81 F8
Skirmett.............................22 C3
Skirpenbeck..........................60 E5
Skirwith.............................64 D4
Skirza..............................111 K2
Skulamus.............................92 C3
Skullomie...........................109 H2
Skye of Curr.........................95 H3
Slack................................58 E8
Slackhall............................52 C5
Slackhead...........................104 D2
Slacks of Cairnbanno................105 H4
Slad.................................20 C2
Slade.................................8 F1
Slade Green..........................23 L5
Slaggyford...........................64 D2
Slaidburn............................58 C5
Slaithwaite..........................52 C2
Slaley...............................65 G2
Slamannan............................80 D4
Slapton, Bucks.......................34 C7
Slapton, Devon........................5 J5
Slapton, Northnts....................33 J5
Slaugham.............................15 F3
Slawston.............................44 A7
Sleaford, Hants......................14 B2
Sleaford, Lincs......................44 D2
Sleagill.............................64 C6
Sleapford............................41 H5
Sledge Green.........................31 K6
Sledmere.............................61 G4
Sleightholme.........................65 G6
Sleights.............................67 J7
Slepe................................12 B6
Slickly.............................111 K2
Sliddery.............................70 E2
Slimbridge...........................20 B3
Slindon, W. Susx.....................14 C5
Slindon, Staffs......................41 K3
Slinfold.............................14 E2
Slingsby.............................60 D3
Slip End.............................23 F1
Slipton..............................34 C2
Slochd...............................95 G3
Slockavullin.........................77 H2
Sloley...............................47 H4
Sloothby.............................55 J8
Slough, Powys........................30 E3
Slough, Berks........................22 E4
Slyne................................57 H4
Smailholm............................82 E8
Smallbridge..........................51 J2
Smallburgh...........................47 J4
Smallburn, Strath....................72 B2
Smallburn, Grampn....................97 K1
Small Dole...........................15 F4
Smalley..............................43 G2
Smallfield...........................15 G1
Small Hythe..........................17 F2
Smallridge...........................10 E5
Smardale.............................64 E7
Smarden..............................17 F1
Smeatharpe...........................10 C4
Smeeth...............................17 H2
Smeeton Westerby.....................43 J7
Smerclate............................90 C4
Smerral.............................111 H5
Smethwick............................32 C1
Smirisary............................92 C8
Smisby...............................43 F5
Smithfield...........................64 B1
Smithincott..........................10 B4
Smithton............................102 F8
Smithstown...........................40 E6
Smithy Green.........................36 B3
Snailbeach...........................61 G2
Snainton.............................53 J1
Snaith...............................60 D7
Snape, N. Yks........................59 H2
Snape, Suff..........................37 J4
Snarestone...........................43 F6
Snarford.............................54 E5
Snargate.............................17 G3
Snave................................17 H3
Snead................................40 E7
Sneaton..............................67 J7
Sneatonthorpe........................67 K7
Snelland.............................54 E5
Snelston.............................42 D2
Snettisham...........................46 B3
Snishival............................90 C2
Snitter..............................75 G4
Snitterby............................54 D4
Snitterfield.........................32 E3

Snitton..............................31 G2
Snodhill.............................30 E5
Snodland.............................24 D6
Snowshill............................32 C6
Soberton.............................13 J4
Soberton Heath.......................13 J4
Soham................................35 J2
Soldon Cross..........................8 D4
Soldridge............................13 J2
Sole Street, Kent....................24 C6
Sole Street, Kent....................17 H1
Solihull.............................32 D2
Sollas...............................98 D5
Sollers Dilwyn.......................31 F4
Sollers Hope.........................31 H6
Sollom...............................50 D2
Solva................................26 C4
Somerby..............................44 A5
Somercotes...........................43 G1
Somerford Keynes.....................20 E3
Somerley.............................14 B6
Somerleyton..........................47 K7
Somersal Herbert.....................42 D3
Somersby.............................55 H6
Somersham, Suff......................37 F5
Somersham, Cambs.....................35 G2
Somerton, Somer......................11 F3
Somerton, Oxon.......................33 G7
Somerton, Norf.......................47 K5
Sompting.............................14 E5
Sonning..............................22 C5
Sonning Common.......................22 C4
Sopley...............................12 D6
Sopworth.............................20 C4
Sorbie...............................68 F6
Sordale.............................111 H2
Sorisdale............................84 D2
Sorn.................................72 A2
Sortat..............................111 J2
Sotby................................55 G6
Sots Hole............................54 F7
Sotterley............................37 K1
Soudley..............................41 J4
Soughton or Sychdyn..................50 B7
Soulbury.............................34 B7
Soulby...............................64 E6
Souldern.............................33 H6
Souldrop.............................34 C3
Sound, Shetld.......................115 F3
Sound, Shetld.......................115 G4
Soundwell............................20 A5
Sourhope.............................74 E2
Sourin.............................112 E3
Sourton...............................9 F6
Soutergate...........................57 F2
South Acre...........................46 D5
Southall.............................23 G4
South Allington.......................5 H6
South Alloa..........................80 D2
Southam, Glos........................32 B7
Southam, Warw........................33 G3
South Ambersham.....................14 C3
Southampton..........................13 G4
South Bank...........................67 F5
South Barrow.........................11 H3
South Benfleet.......................24 D4
Southborough.........................16 C1
Southbourne, W. Susx.................14 A5
Southbourne, Dorset..................12 D6
South Brent...........................5 G3
Southburgh...........................46 E6
South Burlingham.....................47 J6
South Cadbury........................11 H3
South Carlton........................54 D6
South Cave...........................61 G7
South Cerney.........................20 E3
South Chard..........................10 E5
South Charlton.......................75 H2
South Cheriton.......................11 H3
Southchurch..........................24 F4
South Cliffe.........................60 F7
South Clifton........................54 C6
South Cove...........................37 K1
South Creake.........................46 D3
South Croxton........................43 J5
South Dalton.........................61 G6
South Darenth........................24 B6
South Duffield.......................60 D7
Southease............................15 H5
South Elkington......................55 G5
South Elmsall........................53 G2
Southend, Strath.....................70 B4
South End, Cumbr.....................56 F4
Southend, Berks......................21 K5
Southend-on-Sea......................24 E4
Southerndown.........................18 C5
Southerness..........................62 E2
South Erradale......................100 D5
Southery.............................45 K7
South Fambridge......................24 E3
South Fawley.........................21 H4
South Ferriby........................54 D1
Southfleet...........................24 C5
South Garvan.........................93 F8
Southgate, Norf......................47 G4
Southgate, G. Lon....................23 J3
Southgate, W. Glam...................27 K8
South Godstone.......................15 G1
South Gorley.........................12 D4
South Green..........................24 C3
South Hanningfield...................24 D3
South Harting........................14 A4
South Hayling........................13 K6
South Heath..........................22 E2
South Heighton.......................15 H5
South Hetton.........................66 D3
South Hiendley.......................53 F2
South Hill............................4 D2
South Hole............................8 C4
South Holmwood.......................14 E1
South Hornchurch.....................23 L4
South Hylton.........................66 D2
Southill.............................34 E5
South Kelsey.........................54 E4
South Kilvington.....................59 K2

South Kilworth.......................33 J1
South Kirkby.........................53 G2
South Kirkton........................97 G5
South Kyme...........................44 E2
South Lancing........................14 E5
Southleigh, Devon....................10 D6
South Leigh, Oxon....................21 H2
South Leverton.......................54 B5
South Littleton......................32 C5
South Lochboisdale...................90 C4
South Lopham.........................36 F1
South Luffenham......................44 C6
South Malling........................15 H4
South Marston........................21 F4
South Milford........................60 B7
South Milton..........................5 G5
South Mimms..........................23 H2
Southminster.........................25 F3
South Molton..........................9 H3
South Moor, Durham...................66 B2
Southmoor, Oxon......................21 J3
South Moreton........................21 K4
South Mundam.........................14 B5
South Muskham........................44 A1
South Newington......................33 G6
South Newton.........................12 C2
South Normanton......................43 G1
South Norwood........................23 J6
South Nuffield.......................15 G1
South Ockendon.......................24 B4
Southoe..............................34 E3
Southolt.............................37 G3
South Ormsby.........................55 H6
Southorpe............................44 D6
South Otterington....................59 J2
Southowram...........................52 D1
South Oxhey..........................23 G3
South Perrott........................11 F5
South Petherton......................11 F4
South Petherwin.......................8 D7
South Pickenham......................46 D6
South Pool............................5 H5
Southport............................50 C2
South Raynham........................46 D4
Southrepps...........................47 H3
South Reston.........................55 J5
Southrey.............................55 F7
Southrop.............................21 G2
Southrope............................13 J1
South Runcton........................46 B6
South Scarle.........................54 C7
Southsea.............................13 J6
South Shields........................75 K8
South Shore..........................57 G7
South Somercotes.....................55 J4
South Stainley.......................59 J4
South Stainmore......................65 F6
Southstoke, Avon.....................20 B6
South Stoke, W. Susx.................14 D4
South Stoke, Oxon....................21 K4
South Street.........................15 G4
South Tawton..........................9 G6
South Thoresby.......................55 J6
South Tidworth.......................12 E1
Southtown, Orkney...................113 E7
South Town, Hants....................13 J2
Southwaite...........................64 B3
South Walsham........................47 J5
South Warnborough...................13 K1
Southwater...........................14 E3
Southway.............................11 G1
South Weald..........................24 B3
Southwell, Dorset.....................6 A7
Southwell, Notts.....................43 K1
South Weston.........................22 C3
South Wheatley........................8 C6
Southwick, Wilts.....................20 C7
Southwick, T. & W....................66 D2
Southwick, Northnts..................44 D7
Southwick, W. Susx...................15 F5
Southwick, Hants.....................13 J5
South Widcombe.......................19 K7
South Wigston........................43 H7
South Willingham.....................55 F5
South Wingfield......................43 F1
South Witham.........................44 C5
Southwold............................37 L2
South Wonston........................13 G2
Southwood............................47 J6
South Woodham Ferrers................24 E3
South Wootton........................46 B4
South Zeal............................9 G6
Soutra Farm..........................82 C6
Sowerby, W. Yks......................52 C1
Sowerby, N. Yks......................59 K2
Sowerby Bridge.......................52 C1
Sowerby Row..........................63 J3
Sowton...............................10 A6
Spa Common...........................47 H3
Spalding.............................45 F4
Spaldington..........................60 E7
Spaldwick............................34 E2
Spalford.............................54 C7
Sparham..............................46 F5
Spark Bridge.........................57 G2
Sparkford............................11 H3
Sparkwell.............................5 F4
Sparrowpit...........................52 C5
Sparsholt, Hants.....................13 G2
Sparsholt, Oxon......................21 H4
Spaunton.............................60 E2
Spaxton..............................10 D2
Spean Bridge.........................93 J7
Speen, Bucks.........................22 D3
Speen, Berks.........................21 J6
Speeton..............................61 J3
Speke................................50 D5
Speldhurst...........................16 C1
Spellbrook...........................23 K1
Spelsbury............................33 F7
Spencers Wood........................22 C6
Spennithorne.........................59 G2
Spennymoor..........................66 C4
Spetchley............................32 A4
Spetisbury...........................12 B5

Spexhall.............................37 J1
Spey Bay............................104 C2
Speybridge...........................95 J3
Spilsby..............................55 J7
Spindlestone.........................75 H1
Spinningdale........................102 E4
Spirthill............................20 D5
Spithurst............................15 H4
Spittal, Lothn.......................82 C4
Spittal, Dyfed.......................26 D3
Spittal, Highld.....................111 H3
Spittal, Northum.....................83 J6
Spittalfield.........................88 D4
Spittal of Glenmuick.................96 C7
Spittal of Glenshee..................88 D1
Spixworth............................47 H5
Spofforth............................59 J5
Spondon..............................43 G3
Spooner Row.........................47 F7
Sporle...............................46 D5
Spott................................82 E4
Spratton.............................33 K2
Spreakley............................14 B1
Spreyton..............................9 G6
Spridlington.........................54 E5
Springburn...........................79 J5
Springcorrie........................107 G5
Springfield, W. Mids.................32 C1
Springfield, Fife....................89 F7
Springfield, Grampn.................103 J6
Springholm...........................72 D8
Springside...........................79 F8
Springthorpe.........................54 C5
Spring Green.........................61 J7
Sproatley............................61 J7
Sproston Green.......................51 G7
Sprotbrough..........................53 H3
Sproughton...........................34 E5
Sprouston............................82 F8
Sproxton, Leic.......................44 B4
Sproxton, N. Yks.....................60 D2
Spurstow.............................41 G1
Square and Compass...................26 C3
Stackhouse...........................58 D4
Stackpole............................26 D7
Stacksteads..........................51 H1
Staddiscombe..........................4 F4
Staddlethorpe........................60 F8
Stadhampton..........................21 L3
Staffield............................64 C3
Staffin..............................99 K6
Stafford.............................42 B5
Stagsden.............................34 C5
Stainacre............................67 K7
Stainburn............................59 H6
Stainby..............................44 C4
Staincross...........................53 F2
Staindrop............................65 J5
Stainfield, Lincs....................44 D4
Stainfield, Lincs....................54 F6
Stainforth, N. Yks...................58 D4
Stainforth, S. Yks...................53 J2
Staining.............................57 G7
Stainland............................52 C2
Stainsacre...........................67 K7
Stainton, Cumbr......................64 B5
Stainton, Cleve......................66 E6
Stainton, N. Yks.....................59 G1
Stainton, S. Yks.....................53 H4
Stainton, Durham.....................65 H6
Stainton, Cumbr......................57 J2
Stainton by Langworth................54 E6
Staintondale.........................67 K8
Stainton le Vale.....................55 F4
Stainton with Adgarley...............57 F3
Stair, Cumbr.........................63 H5
Stair, Strath........................71 K2
Staithes.............................67 H6
Stakeford............................75 J4
Stake Pool...........................57 H6
Stalbridge...........................11 J4
Stalbridge Weston....................11 J4
Stalham..............................47 J4
Stalham Green........................47 J4
Stalisfield Green....................25 F7
Stallingborough......................55 G2
Stalling Busk........................58 E2
Stalmine.............................57 G6
Stalybridge..........................51 J4
Stambourne...........................36 C6
Stambourne Green.....................36 C6
Stamford.............................44 D6
Stamford Bridge......................60 E5
Stamfordham.........................75 G7
Stanborough..........................23 H1
Stanbridge, Dorset...................12 C5
Stanbridge, Beds.....................34 C7
Stand................................80 C5
Standburn............................80 E4
Standeford...........................42 B6
Standen..............................16 F1
Standford............................14 B2
Standish.............................50 E2
Standlake............................21 H2
Standon, Hants.......................13 G3
Standon, Herts.......................35 G7
Standon, Staffs......................41 K3
Stane................................80 D6
Stanfield............................46 E4
Stanford, Beds.......................34 E5
Stanford, Kent.......................17 J2
Stanford Bishop......................31 H4
Stanford Bridge......................31 J3
Stanford Dingley.....................21 K5
Stanford in the Vale.................21 H3
Stanford-le-Hope.....................24 C4
Stanford on Avon.....................33 H2
Stanford on Soar.....................43 H4
Stanford on Teme.....................31 J3
Stanford Rivers......................23 L2
Stanghow.............................67 G6
Stanhoe..............................46 D3
Stanhope, Border.....................73 G2
Stanhope, Durham.....................65 G4

Stanion..............................34 C1
Stanley, Staffs......................42 B1
Stanley, Durham......................66 B2
Stanley, Tays........................88 D5
Stanley, W. Yks......................53 F1
Stanley, Derby.......................43 G2
Stanley Crook........................66 B4
Stanmer..............................15 G5
Stanmore, G. Lon.....................23 G3
Stanmore, Berks......................21 J5
Stannington, S. Yks..................53 F5
Stannington, Northum.................75 J7
Stansbatch...........................30 E3
Stansfield...........................36 C4
Stanstead............................36 D5
Stanstead Abbotts....................23 J1
Stansted.............................24 C6
Stansted Mountfitchet................35 J7
Stanton, Glos........................32 C6
Stanton, Staffs......................42 D2
Stanton, Suff........................36 E2
Stanton, Derby.......................42 E5
Stanton, Gwent.......................30 E7
Stanton by Bridge....................43 F4
Stanton-by-Dale......................43 G3
Stanton Drew.........................19 K6
Stanton Fitzwarren...................21 F3
Stanton Harcourt.....................21 J2
Stanton Hill.........................53 G7
Stanton in Peak......................52 E7
Stanton Lacy.........................31 F2
Stanton Long.........................41 G7
Stanton-on-the-Wolds.................43 J3
Stanton Prior........................20 A6
Stanton St Bernard...................20 E6
Stanton St John......................21 K2
Stanton St Quintin...................20 D4
Stanton Street.......................36 E3
Stanton under Bardon.................43 G5
Stanton upon Hine Heath..............41 G4
Stanton Wick.........................19 L6
Stanwardine in the Fields............41 F4
Stanway, Glos........................32 C6
Stanway, Essex.......................36 E7
Stanwell.............................22 F5
Stanwell Moor........................22 F5
Stanwick.............................34 C2
Stanwick-St-John.....................66 B6
Stanydale...........................114 E3
Stape................................60 E1
Stapehill............................12 C5
Stapeley.............................41 H2
Stapenhill...........................42 E4
Staple...............................25 J7
Staplecross..........................16 E3
Staplefield..........................15 F3
Stapleford, Lincs....................44 B1
Stapleford, Leic.....................44 B5
Stapleford, Wilts....................12 C2
Stapleford, Notts....................43 G3
Stapleford, Cambs....................35 H4
Stapleford, Herts....................23 J1
Stapleford Abbotts...................23 L3
Stapleford Tawney....................23 L3
Staplegrove..........................10 D3
Staplehay............................10 D3
Staplehurst..........................16 E1
Staplers.............................13 H7
Stapleton, Cumbr.....................74 B7
Stapleton, N. Yks....................66 C6
Stapleton, H. & W....................30 E3
Stapleton, Somer.....................11 F3
Stapleton, Shrops....................41 F6
Stapleton, Leic......................43 G7
Stapleton, Avon......................19 L5
Stapley..............................10 C4
Staploe..............................34 E3
Staplow..............................31 H4
Star, Dyfed..........................27 G3
Star, Fife...........................81 J1
Star, Somer..........................19 J7
Starbotton...........................58 E3
Starcross.............................5 K1
Starston.............................37 H1
Startforth...........................65 H6
Startley.............................20 D4
Stathe...............................10 E3
Stathern.............................44 A3
Station Town.........................66 E4
Staughton Highway....................34 E3
Staunton, Glos.......................31 J7
Staunton, Glos.......................31 H6
Staunton on Arrow....................30 E3
Staunton on Wye......................30 E5
Staveley, Cumbr......................64 B8
Staveley, Derby......................53 G6
Staveley, N. Yks.....................59 J4
Staveley-in-Cartmel..................57 G2
Staverton, Glos......................32 A7
Staverton, Wilts.....................20 C6
Staverton, Northnts..................33 H3
Staverton, Devon......................5 H3
Stawell..............................10 E2
Staxigoe............................111 K3
Staxton..............................61 H3
Staylittle...........................39 H7
Staythorpe...........................44 A1
Stean................................59 F3
Stearsby.............................60 D3
Steart...............................10 D1
Stebbing.............................36 B7
Stedham..............................14 B3
Steel Roads..........................74 B5
Steen's Bridge.......................31 G4
Steep................................13 K3
Steep, Dorset........................12 D6
Steeple, Essex.......................25 F2
Steeple Ashton.......................20 D7
Steeple Aston........................33 G7
Steeple Barton.......................33 G7
Steeple Bumpstead....................36 B5
Steeple Claydon......................33 J7
Steeple Gidding......................34 E1
Steeple Langford.....................12 C2

Steeple Morden.......................35 F5
Steeton..............................58 F6
Steinmanhill........................105 G4
Steisay..............................98 D8
Stelling Minnis......................17 J1
Stemster............................111 H1
Stenalees.............................3 J4
Stenhousemuir........................80 D3
Stenton..............................82 E4
Stepney..............................23 J4
Steppingley..........................34 D6
Stepps...............................79 J5
Sternfield...........................37 J3
Stert................................20 E7
Stetchworth..........................36 B4
Stevenage............................35 F7
Stevenston...........................78 E7
Steventon, Hants.....................13 H1
Steventon, Oxon......................21 J3
Stevington...........................34 C4
Stewartby............................34 D5
Stewarton............................79 G7
Stewkley.............................34 B7
Stewton..............................55 H5
Steyning.............................14 E4
Steynton.............................26 D6
Stibb.................................8 C4
Stibbard.............................46 E4
Stibb Cross...........................8 E4
Stibb Green..........................21 G6
Stibbington..........................44 D7
Stichill.............................82 F8
Sticker...............................3 H4
Stickford............................55 H8
Sticklepath...........................9 G6
Stickney.............................45 G1
Stiffkey.............................46 E2
Stifford's Bridge....................31 J5
Stilligarry..........................90 C2
Stillingfleet........................60 C6
Stillington, N. Yks..................60 C4
Stillington, Cleve...................66 D5
Stilton..............................44 E8
Stinchcombe..........................20 B3
Stinsford............................11 J6
Stirchley............................41 J6
Stirling.............................80 C2
Stisted..............................36 D7
Stithians.............................2 F6
Stittenham..........................102 E5
Stivichall...........................33 F2
Stixwould............................55 F7
Stoak................................50 D6
Stobo................................81 G8
Stoborough...........................12 B7
Stoborough Green.....................12 B7
Stock................................24 C3
Stockbridge..........................13 F2
Stockbriggs..........................80 C8
Stockbury............................24 E6
Stockcross...........................21 J6
Stockdalewath........................63 J3
Stockeinteignhead.....................5 K2
Stockerston..........................44 B7
Stock Green..........................32 B4
Stockingford.........................43 F7
Stocking Pelham......................35 H7
Stockinish Island....................99 G3
Stockland............................10 D5
Stockland Bristol....................10 D1
Stockleigh English....................9 J5
Stockleigh Pomeroy....................9 J5
Stockley.............................20 E6
Stockport............................51 H4
Stocksbridge.........................52 E4
Stocksfield..........................65 H1
Stockton, Wilts......................12 B2
Stockton, Warw.......................33 G3
Stockton, H. & W.....................31 G3
Stockton, Norf.......................47 J7
Stockton, Shrops.....................41 J7
Stockton Heath.......................50 F5
Stockton-on-Tees.....................66 E6
Stockton on Teme.....................31 J3
Stockton on the Forest...............60 D5
Stock Wood...........................32 C4
Stodmarsh............................25 J6
Stoer...............................108 B6
Stoford, Wilts.......................12 C2
Stoford, Somer.......................11 G4
Stogumber............................10 B2
Stogursey............................10 D1
Stoke, Devon..........................8 C3
Stoke, Kent..........................24 E5
Stoke, Hants.........................21 J7
Stoke, Hants.........................13 K5
Stoke Abbott.........................11 F5
Stoke Albany.........................34 B1
Stoke Ash............................37 G2
Stoke Bardolph.......................43 J2
Stoke Bliss..........................31 H3
Stoke Bruerne........................34 A5
Stoke by Clare.......................36 C5
Stoke-by-Nayland.....................36 E6
Stoke Canon...........................9 K6
Stoke Charity........................13 G2
Stoke Climsland.......................4 D7
Stoke D'Abernon......................23 G7
Stoke Doyle..........................34 D1
Stoke Dry............................44 B7
Stoke Ferry..........................46 C6
Stoke Fleming.........................5 J5
Stokeford............................12 A7
Stoke Gabriel.........................5 J4
Stoke Gifford........................19 L4
Stoke Golding........................43 F7
Stoke Goldington.....................34 B5
Stokeham.............................54 B6
Stoke Hammond.......................34 B7
Stoke Heath..........................41 H4
Stoke Holy Cross.....................47 H6
Stoke Lacy...........................31 H5
Stoke Lyne...........................33 H7
Stoke Mandeville.....................22 D1
Stokenchurch.........................22 C3

Stoke Newington...23 J4
Stokenham...5 J5
Stoke on Tern...41 H4
Stoke-on-Trent...42 A2
Stoke Orchard...32 B7
Stoke Poges...22 E4
Stoke Prior, H. & W...32 B3
Stoke Prior, H. & W...31 G4
Stoke Rivers...9 G2
Stoke Rochford...44 C4
Stoke Row...22 B4
Stokesay...31 F1
Stokesby...47 K5
Stokesley...66 F7
Stoke St Gregory...10 E3
Stoke St Mary...10 D3
Stoke St Michael...11 H1
Stoke St Milborough...31 G1
Stoke sub Hamdon...11 F4
Stoke Talmage...22 B3
Stoke Trister...11 J3
Stolford...10 D1
Stondon Massey...24 B2
Stone, H. & W...32 A2
Stone, Glos...20 A3
Stone, Staffs...42 B3
Stone, Kent...24 B5
Stone, Bucks...22 C1
Stone Allerton...19 J7
Ston Easton...19 L7
Stonebroom...53 G8
Stone Cross...16 D5
Stonegate...16 D3
Stonegrave...60 D3
Stonehaugh...74 D7
Stonehaven...97 H7
Stonehouse, Glos...20 C2
Stone House, Cumbr...58 C2
Stonehouse, Strath...80 C7
Stonehouse, Northum...64 D2
Stone in Oxney...17 G3
Stoneleigh...33 F2
Stonely...34 E3
Stonesby...44 B4
Stonesfield...21 H1
Stones Green...37 G7
Stoneybridge...90 C2
Stoneyburn...80 E5
Stoney Cross...12 E4
Stoneygate, Leic...43 J6
Stoneygate, Grampn...97 K2
Stoneyhills...25 F3
Stoneykirk...68 B5
Stoney Middleton...52 E6
Stoney Stanton...43 G7
Stoney Stratton...11 H2
Stoney Stretton...40 E6
Stoneywood...97 H4
Stonham Aspal...37 G4
Stonnall...42 C6
Stonor...22 C4
Stonton Wyville...43 K7
Stonybreck...112 N1
Stony Stratford...34 A5
Stoodleigh...9 K4
Stopham...14 D4
Stopsley...34 E7
Storeton...50 C5
Stornoway...107 J5
Storridge...31 J5
Storrington...14 D4
Storrs...57 H1
Storth...57 H3
Stotfold...35 F6
Stottesdon...31 H1
Stoughton, W. Susx...14 B4
Stoughton, Surrey...22 E7
Stoughton, Leic...43 J6
Stoul...92 D6
Stoulton...32 B5
Stourbridge...32 B1
Stourpaine...12 A5
Stourport-on-Severn...31 K2
Stour Provost...11 J3
Stour Row...11 K3
Stourton, Staffs...32 A1
Stourton, Warw...32 E6
Stourton, Wilts...11 J2
Stourton Caundle...11 J4
Stoven...37 K1
Stow, Lincs...54 C5
Stow, Border...82 C7
Stow Bardolph...45 K6
Stow Bedon...46 E7
Stowbridge...45 K6
Stow cum Quy...35 J3
Stowe...30 E2
Stowe-by-Chartley...42 C4
Stowell...11 H3
Stowford...8 E7
Stowlangtoft...36 E3
Stow Longa...34 E2
Stow Maries...24 E3
Stowmarket...36 F4
Stow-on-the-Wold...32 D7
Stowting...17 J1
Stowupland...34 D3
Straad...78 C5
Strachan...97 F6
Strachur...78 C1
Stradbroke...37 H2
Stradishall...36 C4
Stradsett...46 B6
Stragglethorpe...44 C1
Straiton, Lothn...81 H5
Straiton, Strath...71 J4
Straloch...88 C2
Stramshall...42 C3
Stranraer...68 B4
Strata Florida...28 E3
Stratfield Mortimer...22 B6
Stratfield Saye...22 B6
Stratfield Turgis...22 B6
Stratford...23 J4
Stratford St Andrew...37 J3

Stratford St Mary...36 F6
Stratford Tony...12 C3
Stratford-upon-Avon...32 E4
Strath...100 D5
Strathan, Highld...108 B6
Strathan, Highld...93 F6
Strathaven...80 C7
Strathblane...79 H4
Strathdon...96 C4
Strath Kanaird...101 H2
Strathkinness...89 G7
Strathmiglo...88 E7
Strathpeffer...102 C7
Strathrannoch...102 B5
Strathtay...88 B3
Strathwhillan...78 C8
Strathy...110 E2
Strathyre...87 H7
Stratton, Corn...8 C5
Stratton, Glos...20 E2
Stratton, Dorset...11 H6
Stratton Audley...33 J7
Stratton-on-the-Fosse...20 A7
Stratton St Margaret...21 F4
Stratton St Michael...47 H7
Stratton Strawless...47 H4
Streat...15 G4
Streatham...23 H5
Streatley, Beds...34 D7
Streatley, Berks...21 K4
Street, Somer...11 F2
Street, N. Yks...67 H7
Street, Lancs...57 J5
Street End...14 B6
Streethay...42 D5
Streetly...42 C7
Strefford...31 F1
Strensall...60 D4
Strensham...32 B5
Stretcholt...10 D1
Strete...5 J5
Stretford...51 G4
Stretford Court...31 F4
Strethall...35 H6
Stretham...35 J2
Strettington...14 B5
Stretton, Staffs...42 A5
Stretton, Leic...44 C5
Stretton, Staffs...42 E4
Stretton, Ches...41 F1
Stretton, Ches...50 F5
Stretton, Derby...53 F7
Stretton en le Fields...43 F5
Stretton Grandison...31 H5
Stretton Heath...40 E5
Stretton-on-Dunsmore...33 G2
Stretton-on-Fosse...32 E6
Stretton Sugwas...31 F5
Stretton under Fosse...33 G1
Stretton Westwood...41 G7
Strichen...105 J3
Stringston...10 C1
Strixton...34 C3
Stroat...19 K3
Stromeferry...92 E2
Stromemore...92 E2
Stromness...112 C6
Stronachlachar...87 G7
Strond...98 F4
Strone, Strath...78 D3
Strone, Highld...94 D3
Strone, Highld...93 H7
Stronenaba...93 J7
Stronmilchan...86 D6
Strontian...85 K2
Strood...24 D6
Stroud, Glos...20 C2
Stroud, Hants...13 K3
Struan, Highld...91 J2
Struan, Tays...87 L2
Strubby...55 J5
Strumpshaw...47 J6
Strutherhill...80 C7
Struy...94 C2
Stuartfield...105 J4
Stubbington...13 H5
Stubbins...51 G2
Stubhampton...12 B4
Stubton...44 B2
Stuckton...12 D4
Studham...22 F1
Studland...12 C7
Studley, Warw...32 C3
Studley, Wilts...20 D5
Studley Roger...59 H3
Stuntney...35 J2
Sturbridge...41 K3
Sturmer...36 B5
Sturminster Marshall...12 B6
Sturminster Newton...11 J4
Sturry...25 H6
Sturton by Stow...54 C5
Sturton le Steeple...54 B5
Stuston...37 G2
Stutton, N. Yks...60 B6
Stutton, Suff...37 G6
Styal...51 H5
Suainebost...107 K2
Suckley...31 J4
Sudborough...34 C1
Sudbourne...37 K4
Sudbrook, Lincs...54 E6
Sudbrook, Gwent...19 K4
Sudbury, Derby...42 D3
Sudbury, Suff...36 D5
Sudgrove...20 D2
Suffield...47 H3
Sugnall...41 K3
Sulby...56 Q2
Sulgrave...33 H5
Sulham...22 B5
Sulhamstead...22 B6
Sullington...14 D4
Sullom...116 E5
Sully...18 F6

Sumburgh...115 F8
Summerbridge...59 H4
Summercourt...3 G4
Summerleaze...19 J4
Summerseat...51 G2
Summit...51 J2
Sunbiggin...64 D7
Sunbury...22 F6
Sunderland, T. & W...66 D2
Sunderland, Cumbr...63 G4
Sunderland Bridge...66 C4
Sundhope...73 J2
Sundon Park...34 D7
Sundridge...23 K7
Sunk Island...55 G2
Sunningdale...22 E6
Sunninghill...22 E6
Sunningwell...21 J2
Sunniside, T. & W...66 C2
Sunniside, Durham...65 J4
Sunnylaw...80 C2
Sunnyside...15 G2
Surbiton...23 G6
Surfleet...45 F4
Surfleet Seas End...45 F4
Surlingham...47 J6
Sustead...47 G3
Susworth...54 C3
Sutcombe...8 D4
Suton...47 F7
Sutors of Cromarty...103 G6
Sutterton...45 F3
Sutton, Notts...44 A3
Sutton, W. Susx...14 C4
Sutton, Cambs...44 D7
Sutton, Beds...35 F5
Sutton, Shrops...35 H1
Sutton, Cambs...35 H2
Sutton, Shrops...41 H3
Sutton, G. Lon...23 H6
Sutton, Shrops...31 J1
Sutton, Oxon...21 J2
Sutton, Staffs...41 J4
Sutton, Norf...47 J4
Sutton, Suff...37 J5
Sutton, Notts...53 J5
Sutton, Kent...17 L1
Sutton Abinger...14 E1
Sutton at Hone...23 L5
Sutton Bassett...44 A7
Sutton Benger...20 D5
Sutton Bonington...43 H4
Sutton Bridge...45 H4
Sutton Cheney...43 G6
Sutton Coldfield...42 D7
Sutton Courtenay...21 K3
Sutton Crosses...45 H4
Sutton Grange...59 H3
Sutton Hill...41 J6
Sutton Howgrave...59 J3
Sutton in Ashfield...53 G8
Sutton-in-Craven...58 F6
Sutton Lane Ends...51 J6
Sutton Leach...50 E4
Sutton Maddock...41 J6
Sutton Mallet...10 E2
Sutton Mandeville...12 B3
Sutton Montis...11 H3
Sutton-on-Hull...61 J7
Sutton on Sea...55 K5
Sutton-on-the-Forest...60 C4
Sutton on the Hill...42 E3
Sutton on Trent...54 B7
Sutton Scotney...13 G2
Sutton St Edmund...45 G5
Sutton St James...45 G5
Sutton St Nicholas...31 G5
Sutton-under-Brailes...33 F6
Sutton-under-Whitestonecliffe...60 B2
Sutton upon Derwent...60 E6
Sutton Valence...16 F1
Sutton Veny...12 A1
Sutton Waldron...12 A4
Sutton Weaver...50 E6
Swaby...55 H6
Swadlincote...43 F4
Swaffham...46 D6
Swaffham Bulbeck...35 J3
Swaffham Prior...35 J3
Swafield...47 H3
Swainby...66 E7
Swainshill...31 F5
Swainsthorpe...47 H6
Swalcliffe...33 F6
Swalecliffe...25 H6
Swallow...55 F3
Swallowcliffe...12 B3
Swallowfield...22 C6
Swanage...6 E7
Swanbister...112 D6
Swanbourne...34 B7
Swan Green...51 G6
Swanland...54 D1
Swanley...23 L6
Swanmore...13 H4
Swannington, Norf...47 G5
Swannington, Leic...43 G5
Swanscombe...24 C5
Swansea...27 L7
Swanton Abbot...47 H4
Swanton Morley...46 F5
Swanton Novers...46 F3
Swanwick, Derby...43 G1
Swanwick, Hants...13 H5
Swarby...44 D2
Swardeston...47 H6
Swarister...117 G4
Swarkestone...43 F4
Swarland...75 H4
Swarthmoor...57 F3
Swaythling...13 G4

Sweffling...37 J3
Swepstone...43 F5
Swerford...33 F6
Swettenham...51 H7
Swffryd...19 G3
Swilland...37 G4
Swillington...59 J7
Swimbridge...9 G3
Swinbrook...21 G1
Swinderby...54 C7
Swindon, Staffs...42 A7
Swindon, Glos...32 B7
Swindon, Wilts...21 F4
Swine...61 J7
Swinefleet...54 B1
Swineshead, Northnts...34 D3
Swineshead, Lincs...45 F2
Swineshead Bridge...45 F2
Swiney...111 J5
Swinford, Leic...33 H2
Swinford, Oxon...21 J2
Swingfield Minnis...17 K1
Swinhoe...75 J2
Swinhope...55 G4
Swinithwaite...58 F2
Swinscoe...42 D2
Swinside Hall...74 D3
Swinstead...44 D4
Swinton, N. Yks...60 E3
Swinton, G. Man...51 G3
Swinton, S. Yks...53 G4
Swinton, Border...83 G7
Swinton, N. Yks...59 H3
Swintonmill...83 G7
Swithland...43 H5
Swordale...102 D6
Swordland...92 D6
Swordly...110 D2
Sworton Heath...51 F5
Swydd-ffynnon...28 D3
Swynnerton...42 A3
Swyre...11 G7
Sychdyn or Soughton...50 B7
Syde...20 D1
Sydenham, Oxon...22 C2
Sydenham, G. Lon...23 J5
Sydenham Damerel...4 E2
Sydling St Nicholas...11 H6
Sydmonton...21 J7
Syerston...44 A2
Syke...51 H2
Sykehouse...53 J2
Sykes...58 B5
Syleham...37 H2
Sylen...27 K6
Symbister...115 H2
Symington, Strath...80 E8
Symington, Strath...71 J1
Symonds Yat...19 K1
Symondsbury...11 F6
Synod Inn...28 B4
Syre...109 H4
Syreford...32 C7
Syresham...33 J5
Syston, Lincs...44 C2
Syston, Leic...43 J5
Sytchampton...31 K3
Sywell...34 B3

T

Tabost...107 K2
Tackley...33 G7
Tacolneston...47 G7
Tadcaster...60 B6
Tadden...12 B5
Taddington...52 D6
Tadley...21 L6
Tadlow...35 F5
Tadmarton...33 F6
Tadworth...23 H7
Tafarnaubach...18 F1
Tafarn-y-Gelyn...50 A7
Taff's Well...18 F4
Tafolwern...39 H6
Taibach, W. Glam...18 B4
Tai-bach, Clwyd...40 C4
Tain, Highld...103 H4
Tain, Highld...111 J2
Tai'n Lon...38 D1
Takeley...35 J7
Talachddu...29 H6
Talacre...50 A5
Talaton...10 B6
Talbenny...26 C5
Talerddig...39 J6
Talgarreg...27 J1
Talgarth...30 C6
Talisker...91 J2
Talke...41 K1
Talkin...64 C2
Talladale...101 F5
Tallarn Green...41 F2
Tallentire...63 G4
Talley...27 L3
Tallington...44 D6
Talmine...109 G2
Talog...27 H4
Talsarn...28 C4
Talsarnau...38 F3
Talskiddy...3 H3
Talwrn...48 D3
Tal-y-bont, Gwyn...38 E4
Tal-y-bont, Dyfed...38 E8
Tal-y-bont, Gwyn...49 G4
Talybont-on-Usk...30 C7
Tal-y-cafn...49 G3
Talyllyn, Powys...30 C7
Tal-y-llyn, Gwyn...39 G6
Talysarn...38 D1
Tal-y-Wern...39 H6

Tamerton Foliot...4 E3
Tamworth...42 E6
Tandridge...23 J7
Tanfield...66 B2
Tangasdale...90 B5
Tangley...21 H7
Tangmere...14 C5
Tangwick...116 D5
Tankerness...113 F6
Tankersley...53 F4
Tannach...111 K4
Tannadice...89 G3
Tannington...37 H3
Tansley...53 F8
Tansor...44 D7
Tantobie...66 B2
Tanton...66 H6
Tanworth-in-Arden...32 D2
Tan-y-fron...49 J4
Tangyrisiau...39 F2
Tan-y-groes...27 G2
Taplow...22 E4
Tarbert, Strath...76 F3
Tarbert, W. Isles...99 G2
Tarbert, Strath...77 H5
Tarbet, Highld...108 C4
Tarbet, Highld...92 D6
Tarbet, Strath...86 F8
Tarbock Green...50 D5
Tarbolton...71 K2
Tarbrax...80 F6
Tarfside...96 D8
Tarland...96 D5
Tarleton...50 D1
Tarlogie...103 F4
Tarlscough...50 D2
Tarlton...20 D3
Tarnbrook...57 J5
Tarporley...50 F7
Tarr...10 C2
Tarrant Crawford...12 B5
Tarrant Gunville...12 B4
Tarrant Hinton...12 B4
Tarrant Keynston...12 B5
Tarrant Launceston...12 B5
Tarrant Monkton...12 B5
Tarrant Rawston...12 B5
Tarrant Rushton...12 B5
Tarrel...103 G4
Tarring Neville...15 H5
Tarrington...31 H5
Tarskavaig...92 B5
Tarves...97 H2
Tarvie...102 C7
Tarvin...50 D7
Tasburgh...47 H7
Tasley...41 H7
Taston...33 F7
Tatenhill...42 E4
Tatham...57 K4
Tathwell...55 H5
Tatsfield...23 K7
Tattenhall...50 D8
Tatterford...46 D4
Tattersett...46 D4
Tattershall...45 F1
Tattershall Bridge...45 E1
Tattershall Thorpe...55 G8
Tattingstone...37 G6
Tatworth...10 E5
Taunton...10 D3
Taverham...47 G5
Tavernspite...26 F5
Tavistock...4 E2
Taw Green...9 G6
Tawstock...9 F3
Taxal...52 C6
Tayinloan...77 F7
Tayinish...77 G3
Taynton, Oxon...21 G1
Taynton, Glos...31 J7
Taynuilt...86 C5
Tayport...89 G6
Tay Road Bridge...89 G6
Tayvallich...77 G3
Tealby...55 F4
Tealing...89 G4
Teanamachar...98 C6
Teangue...92 C5
Tebay...64 D7
Tebworth...34 C7
Tedburn St Mary...9 J6
Teddington, Glos...32 B6
Teddington, G. Lon...23 G5
Tedstone Delamere...31 H4
Tedstone Wafre...31 H4
Teeton...33 J2
Teffont Evias...12 B2
Teffont Magna...12 B2
Tegryn...27 G3
Teigh...44 B5
Teigngrace...5 J2
Teignmouth...5 K2
Telford...41 H5
Telham...20 C7
Telscombe...15 H5
Templand...73 F6
Temple, Strath...79 H5
Temple, Lothn...81 J6
Temple, Corn...3 K2
Temple Bar...28 C4
Temple Cloud...19 L7
Templecombe...11 J3
Temple Ewell...17 K1
Temple Grafton...32 D4
Temple Guiting...32 C7
Temple Hirst...53 J1
Temple Normanton...53 G7
Temple Sowerby...64 D5
Templeton, Dyfed...26 F5
Templeton, Devon...9 J4
Templeton Bridge...9 J4
Tempsford...34 E4
Tenbury Wells...31 G3
Tenby...26 F6

Tendring...37 G7
Ten Mile Bank...45 K7
Tenston...112 C5
Tenterden...17 F2
Terling...24 D1
Ternhill...41 H3
Terregles...72 E7
Terrington...60 D3
Terrington St Clement...45 J4
Terrington St John...45 J5
Teston...24 D7
Testwood...13 G4
Tetbury...20 C3
Tetbury Upton...20 C3
Tetchill...40 E3
Tetcott...8 D6
Tetford...55 H6
Tetney...55 H3
Tetney Lock...55 H3
Tetsworth...22 B2
Tettenhall...42 A6
Teversal...53 G7
Teversham...35 H4
Teviothead...73 K4
Tewin...23 H1
Tewkesbury...32 A6
Teynham...25 F6
Thainstone...97 F8
Thakeham...14 E4
Thame...22 C2
Thames Ditton...23 G6
Thamesmead...23 K4
Thaneston...97 F8
Thanington...25 H7
Thankerton...80 E8
Tharston...47 G7
Thatcham...21 K6
Thatto Heath...50 E4
Thaxted...35 K6
Theakston...59 J2
Thealby...54 C2
Theale, Berks...22 B5
Theale, Somer...11 F1
Thearne...61 H7
Theberton...37 K3
Thedden Grange...13 J2
Theddingworth...33 J1
Theddlethorpe All Saints...55 J5
Theddlethorpe St Helen...55 J5
Thelbridge Barton...9 H4
Thelnetham...36 F2
Thelwall...51 F5
Themelthorpe...46 F4
Thenford...33 H5
Therfield...35 G2
Thetford...36 D1
Theydon Bois...23 K3
Thickwood...20 C5
Thimbleby, Lincs...55 G7
Thimbleby, N. Yks...59 K1
Thirkleby...60 B3
Thirlby...60 B2
Thirlestane...82 D7
Thirn...59 H2
Thirsk...59 K2
Thistleton...44 C5
Thistley Green...36 B2
Thixendale...60 F4
Tholomas Drove...45 H6
Tholthorpe...60 B4
Thomas Chapel...26 F6
Thomastown...96 E2
Thompson...46 E7
Thomshill...104 B3
Thong...24 C5
Thoralby...58 F2
Thoresway...55 F4
Thorganby, N. Yks...60 D6
Thorganby, Lincs...55 G4
Thorington...37 K2
Thorington Street...36 F6
Thorlby...58 E5
Thorley...23 K1
Thornaby-on-Tees...66 E6
Thornage...46 F3
Thornborough, Bucks...34 A6
Thornborough, N. Yks...59 H3
Thornbury, Devon...8 E5
Thornbury, H. & W...31 H4
Thornbury, Avon...19 L3
Thornby...33 J2
Thorncliffe...52 C8
Thorncombe...10 E5
Thorncombe Street...14 D1
Thorndon...37 G3
Thorndon Cross...9 F6
Thorne...53 J2
Thorner...59 J6
Thorne St Margaret...10 B3
Thorney, Notts...54 C6
Thorney, Cambs...45 F6
Thorney Hill...12 E6
Thornfalcon...10 D3
Thornford...11 H4
Thorngumbald...55 G1
Thornham...46 C2
Thornham Magna...37 G2
Thornham Parva...37 G2
Thornhaugh...44 D6
Thornhill, D. & G...72 G5
Thornhill, Derby...52 D5
Thornhill, M. Glam...18 F4
Thornhill, Hants...13 G4
Thornhill, Central...79 J2
Thornhill Edge...52 E2
Thorncombe...12 A5
Thornley, Durham...66 D4
Thornley, Durham...65 J4
Thornliebank...79 H6
Thorns...36 C4
Thornthwaite, N. Yks...59 G5
Thornthwaite, Cumbr...63 H5
Thornton, Bucks...34 A6
Thornton, Mers...50 C3

Thornton, Humbs.....54 E2
Thornton, Humbs.....60 E6
Thornton, Lancs.....57 G6
Thornton, Lincs.....55 G7
Thornton, W. Yks.....59 G7
Thornton, Fife.....81 H2
Thornton, Northum.....83 H7
Thornton Hough.....79 H6
Thorntonhall.....50 C5
Thornton-in-Craven.....58 E6
Thornton-le-Beans.....59 J1
Thornton-le-Clay.....60 D4
Thornton-le-Dale.....60 F2
Thornton le Moor, Lincs.....54 E4
Thornton-le-Moor, N. Yks.....59 J2
Thornton-le-Moors.....50 D6
Thornton-le-Street.....59 K2
Thorntonloch.....82 F4
Thornton Rust.....58 E2
Thornton Steward.....59 G2
Thornton Watlass.....59 H2
Thornwood Common.....23 K2
Thoroton.....44 A2
Thorp Arch.....59 K6
Thorpe, Notts.....44 A2
Thorpe, Cumbr.....64 B5
Thorpe, Derby.....42 D1
Thorpe, N. Yks.....58 F4
Thorpe, Surrey.....22 F6
Thorpe, Lincs.....55 J5
Thorpe, Norf.....47 K7
Thorpe Abbotts.....37 G2
Thorpe Acre.....43 H4
Thorpe Arnold.....44 A4
Thorpe Audlin.....53 G2
Thorpe Bassett.....60 F3
Thorpe Bay.....24 F4
Thorpe by Water.....44 B7
Thorpe Constantine.....42 E6
Thorpe End.....47 H5
Thorpe Fendykes.....55 J7
Thorpe Green.....36 E4
Thorpe Hesley.....53 F4
Thorpe in Balne.....53 H2
Thorpe Langton.....44 A7
Thorpe Larches.....66 D5
Thorpe le Fallows.....54 D5
Thorpe-le-Soken.....37 G7
Thorpe Malsor.....34 B2
Thorpe Mandeville.....33 H5
Thorpe Market.....47 H3
Thorpe Morieux.....36 E4
Thorpeness.....37 K4
Thorpe on the Hill.....54 D7
Thorpe Salvin.....53 H5
Thorpe Satchville.....43 K5
Thorpe St Andrew.....47 H6
Thorpe Thewles.....66 E5
Thorpe Underwood.....60 B5
Thorpe Waterville.....34 D1
Thorpe Willoughby.....60 C7
Thorp St Peter.....55 J7
Thorrington.....37 F7
Thorverton.....9 K5
Thrandeston.....37 G2
Thrapston.....34 C2
Threapwood.....41 F2
Three Bridges.....15 F2
Three Cocks.....30 C6
Three Crosses.....27 K7
Three Holes.....45 J6
Threekingham.....44 D3
Three Leg Cross.....16 D2
Three Legged Cross.....12 C5
Three Mile Cross.....22 C6
Threemilestone.....3 F7
Threlkeld.....63 J5
Threshfield.....58 E4
Thrigby.....47 K5
Thringarth.....65 G5
Thringstone.....43 G5
Thrintoft.....59 J1
Thriplow.....35 H5
Throcking.....35 G6
Throckley.....75 H8
Throckmorton.....32 B5
Throphill.....75 H6
Thropton.....75 G4
Throwleigh.....9 G6
Throwley.....25 F7
Throwley Forestal.....25 F7
Thrumpton.....43 H3
Thrumster.....111 H4
Thrunton.....75 G3
Thrupp, Glos.....20 C2
Thrupp, Oxon.....21 J1
Thrushelton.....8 D2
Thrushgill.....58 B4
Thrussington.....43 J5
Thruxton, Hants.....12 E1
Thruxton, H. & W.....31 F6
Thrybergh.....53 G4
Thundersley.....24 D4
Thundridge.....23 J1
Thurcaston.....43 H5
Thurcroft.....53 G5
Thurgarton, Norf.....47 G3
Thurgarton, Notts.....43 J2
Thurgoland.....52 E3
Thurlaston, Warw.....33 G2
Thurlaston, Leic.....43 H7
Thurlby, Lincs.....44 D5
Thurlby, Lincs.....55 G6
Thurleigh.....34 D4
Thurlestone.....5 G6
Thurloxton.....10 D2
Thurlstone.....52 E3
Thurlton.....47 K7
Thurmaston.....43 J6
Thurnby.....43 J6
Thurnham, Kent.....24 E7
Thurnham, Lancs.....57 H5
Thurning, Northnts.....34 D1
Thurning, Norf.....47 F4
Thurnscoe.....53 G3

Thursby.....63 J2
Thursford.....46 E3
Thursley.....14 C2
Thurso.....111 H2
Thurstaston.....50 B5
Thurston.....36 E3
Thurstonfield.....63 J2
Thurstonland.....52 D2
Thurton.....47 J6
Thurvaston.....42 E3
Thuxton.....46 F6
Thwaite, N. Yks.....65 F8
Thwaite, Suff.....37 G3
Thwaite St Mary.....47 J7
Thwing.....61 H3
Tibbermore.....88 C6
Tibberton, H. & W.....32 B4
Tibberton, Shrops.....41 H4
Tibberton, Glos.....31 J7
Tibenham.....47 G8
Tibshelf.....53 G7
Tibthorpe.....61 G5
Ticehurst.....16 D2
Tichborne.....13 H2
Tickencote.....44 C6
Tickenham.....19 J5
Tickhill.....53 H4
Ticklerton.....41 F7
Ticknall.....43 F4
Tickton.....61 H6
Tidcombe.....21 G7
Tiddington, Oxon.....22 B2
Tiddington, Warw.....32 E4
Tidebrook.....16 D3
Tideford.....4 D4
Tidenham.....19 K3
Tideswell.....52 D6
Tidmarsh.....22 B5
Tidmington.....32 E6
Tidpit.....12 C4
Tiers Cross.....26 D5
Tiffield.....33 J4
Tifty.....97 G1
Tigerton.....89 H2
Tigharry.....98 C5
Tighnabruaich.....78 B4
Tighnafiline.....100 E4
Tigley.....5 H3
Tilbrook.....34 D3
Tilbury.....24 C5
Tilbury Juxta Clare.....36 C5
Tile Cross.....32 D1
Tile Hill.....32 E2
Tilehurst.....22 B5
Tilford.....14 B1
Tillathrowie.....96 D2
Tillicoultry.....80 E2
Tillingham.....25 F2
Tillington, W. Susx.....14 C3
Tillington, H. & W.....31 F5
Tillington Common.....31 F5
Tillycorthie.....97 J3
Tillydrine.....96 F6
Tillyfourie.....97 F4
Tillygreig.....97 H3
Tilmanstone.....25 K7
Tilney All Saints.....45 J5
Tilney High End.....45 J5
Tilney St Lawrence.....45 J5
Tilshead.....12 C1
Tilstock.....41 G3
Tilston.....41 F1
Tilstone Fearnall.....50 E7
Tilsworth.....34 C7
Tilton on the Hill.....44 A6
Timberland.....54 F8
Timbersbrook.....51 H7
Timberscombe.....9 K1
Timble.....59 G5
Timperley.....51 G5
Timsbury, Avon.....20 A7
Timsbury, Hants.....13 F3
Timsgarry.....106 E5
Timworth Green.....36 D3
Tincleton.....11 J6
Tindale.....64 D2
Tingewick.....33 J6
Tingley.....52 E1
Tingrith.....34 D6
Tinhay.....8 D7
Tinshill.....59 H7
Tinsley.....53 G4
Tintagel.....8 A7
Tintern Parva.....19 K2
Tintinhull.....11 F4
Tintwistle.....52 C4
Tinwald.....73 F6
Tinwell.....44 D6
Tipperty.....97 J3
Tipton.....42 B7
Tipton St John.....10 B6
Tiptree.....24 E1
Tirabad.....29 F5
Tirley.....31 K7
Tirphil.....18 F2
Tirril.....64 C5
Tisbury.....12 B3
Tissington.....42 D1
Titchberry.....8 C3
Titchfield.....13 H5
Titchmarsh.....34 D2
Titchwell.....46 C2
Titley.....30 E3
Titlington.....75 G2
Tittensor.....42 A3
Tittleshall.....46 D4
Tiverton, Ches.....50 E7
Tiverton, Devon.....9 K4
Tivetshall St Margaret.....37 G1
Tivetshall St Mary.....37 G1
Tixall.....42 B4
Tixover.....44 C6
Toab, Orkney.....113 H6
Toab, Shetld.....115 F7
Tobermory.....85 G3

Toberonochy.....85 J8
Tobson.....107 F5
Tocher.....97 F2
Tockenham.....20 E5
Tockenham Wick.....20 E4
Tockholes.....51 F1
Tockington.....19 L4
Tockwith.....60 B5
Todber.....11 J3
Toddington, Glos.....32 C6
Toddington, Beds.....34 D7
Todenham.....32 E6
Todhills, Tays.....89 G5
Todhills, Cumbr.....63 J1
Todmorden.....51 J1
Todwick.....53 G5
Toft, Lincs.....44 D5
Toft, Cambs.....35 G4
Toft Hill.....65 J3
Toft Monks.....47 K7
Toft next Newton.....54 E5
Toftrees.....46 D4
Toftwood.....46 E5
Togston.....75 J4
Tokavaig.....92 C4
Tokers Green.....22 B5
Tolland.....10 C2
Tollard Royal.....12 B4
Toll Bar.....53 H3
Toller Fratrum.....11 G6
Toller Porcorum.....11 G6
Tollerton, N. Yks.....60 C4
Tollerton, Notts.....43 J3
Tollesbury.....25 F1
Tolleshunt D'Arcy.....24 F1
Tolleshunt Major.....24 F1
Tolpuddle.....11 J6
Tolsta Chaolais.....107 F5
Tolworth.....23 G6
Tomatin.....95 G3
Tombreck.....94 E2
Tomchrasky.....93 J4
Tomdoun.....93 H5
Tomich, Highld.....102 F5
Tomich, Highld.....93 K3
Tomintoul, Grampn.....95 K4
Tomintoul, Grampn.....95 K6
Tomnavoulin.....96 B3
Tonbridge.....16 C1
Tondu.....18 C4
Tong.....41 J6
Tonge.....43 G4
Tongham.....14 B1
Tongland.....69 H5
Tongue.....109 G3
Tongwynlais.....18 F4
Tonmawr.....18 C3
Tonna.....18 B3
Ton-teg.....18 E4
Tonwell.....23 J1
Tonypandy.....18 D3
Tonyrefail.....18 E4
Toot Baldon.....21 K2
Toothill, Hants.....13 F4
Toot Hill, Essex.....23 L2
Topcliffe.....59 K3
Topcroft.....47 H7
Topcroft Street.....47 H7
Toppesfield.....36 C6
Toppings.....51 G2
Topsham.....9 K7
Torbay.....5 J3
Torbeg.....70 E2
Torbryan.....5 J3
Torcross.....5 J4
Tore.....102 E7
Torksey.....54 C6
Torlum.....98 C7
Torlundy.....93 H8
Tormarton.....20 B5
Tormitcheli.....71 H5
Tormore.....70 D1
Tornagrain.....103 F8
Tornahaish.....96 B5
Tornaveen.....96 F5
Torness.....94 D3
Torpenhow.....63 H4
Torphichen.....80 E4
Torphins.....96 F5
Torpoint.....4 E4
Torquay.....5 K3
Torquhan.....82 C7
Torran.....100 B8
Torrance.....79 J4
Torridon.....100 E7
Torrin.....92 B3
Torrisdale.....109 H2
Torrisholme.....57 H4
Torroble.....102 D2
Torry, Grampn.....96 D1
Torry, Grampn.....97 J5
Torrylinn.....70 E2
Torterston.....105 K4
Torthorwald.....73 F7
Tortington.....14 D5
Tortworth.....20 B3
Torvaig.....100 A8
Torver.....57 F1
Torwood.....80 D3
Torworth.....53 J5
Toscaig.....92 D2
Toseland.....35 F3
Tosside.....58 C5
Tostock.....36 E3
Totaig.....99 H7
Totarol.....107 F5
Tote, Highld.....100 B7
Tote, Highld.....99 K8
Totegan.....110 E2
Totland.....13 F7
Totley.....53 F6
Totnes.....5 J3
Totronald.....84 B6
Totscore.....99 J6
Tottenham.....23 J3
Tottenhill.....46 B5

Totteridge, Bucks.....22 D3
Totteridge, G. Lon.....23 H3
Totternhoe.....34 C7
Tottington.....51 G2
Totton.....13 F4
Tournaig.....100 E4
Toux, Grampn.....104 E3
Toux, Grampn.....105 J3
Tovil.....24 D7
Toward.....72 B3
Towcester.....33 J5
Towednack.....2 C6
Towersey.....22 C2
Towie.....96 D4
Towiemore.....104 C4
Tow Law.....65 J4
Town End.....45 H7
Townhead, Cumbr.....64 D4
Townhead, D. & G.....69 H6
Townhead of Greenlaw.....69 J4
Townhill.....81 G3
Townshend.....2 D6
Town Yetholm.....74 E2
Towthorpe.....60 D5
Towton.....60 B7
Towyn.....49 J3
Toynton All Saints.....55 H7
Toynton Fen Side.....55 H7
Toynton St Peter.....55 J7
Toy's Hill.....23 K7
Trabboch.....71 K2
Trabbochburn.....71 K2
Traboe.....2 F7
Tradespark, Orkney.....112 E6
Tradespark, Highld.....103 G7
Trafford Park.....51 G4
Trallong.....29 G7
Trallwng or Welshpool.....40 D6
Tranent.....82 C4
Trantlemore.....110 E3
Tranwell.....75 H6
Trapp.....27 L5
Traprain.....82 D4
Traquair.....73 J1
Trawden.....58 E7
Trawsfynydd.....39 G3
Trealaw.....18 E3
Treales.....57 H7
Trearddur.....48 B3
Treaslane.....99 J1
Trebartha.....4 C2
Trebetherick.....3 H2
Treborough.....10 B2
Trebudannon.....3 G3
Treburley.....4 D2
Trecastle.....29 F7
Trecwn.....26 D3
Trecynon.....18 D2
Tredavoe.....2 C7
Tredegar.....18 F2
Tredington.....32 E5
Tredinnick.....3 H2
Tredomen.....30 C6
Tredrizzick.....3 H2
Tredunnock.....19 H3
Treen.....2 B7
Treeton.....53 G5
Trefasser.....26 C4
Trefdraeth.....48 D3
Trefecca.....30 C6
Trefeglwys.....39 J7
Trefenter.....26 D4
Treffgarne.....26 D4
Treffynnon.....26 C4
Trefil.....18 F1
Trefilan.....26 C3
Trefin.....26 C3
Trefnanney.....40 D5
Trefnant.....49 K3
Trefonen.....40 D4
Trefor, Gwyn.....48 C2
Trefor, Gwyn.....38 C2
Treforest.....18 E4
Trefriw.....49 G4
Tregadillett.....8 C7
Tregaian.....48 D3
Tregare.....19 J1
Tregaron.....28 D3
Tregarth.....48 F6
Tregeare.....8 C7
Tregeiriog.....40 C3
Tregele.....48 C1
Tregidden.....2 F7
Treglemais.....26 C4
Tregole.....8 B6
Tregonetha.....3 H3
Tregony.....3 H5
Tregoyd.....30 C6
Tre-groes.....27 J2
Tregurrian.....3 G3
Tregynon.....40 B7
Trehafod.....18 E3
Treharris.....18 E3
Treherbert.....18 D3
Treknow.....8 A7
Trelan.....2 F8
Trelash.....8 B6
Trelassick.....3 G4
Trelawnyd.....49 K3
Trelech.....27 G3
Treleddyd-fawr.....26 B4
Trelewis.....18 F3
Treligga.....8 A7
Trelights.....3 H2
Trelill.....3 J2
Trelissick.....3 G6
Trellech.....19 K2
Trelleck Grange.....19 J2
Trelogan.....49 L2
Tremadog.....38 E2
Tremail.....8 B7
Tremain.....27 G2
Tremaine.....8 C7
Tremar.....4 C3
Trematon.....4 D4
Tremeirchion.....49 K3
Trenance.....3 G3
Trenarren.....3 G1

Trench.....41 H5
Treneglos.....8 C7
Trenewan.....4 B4
Trent.....11 G4
Trentham.....42 A2
Trentishoe.....9 G1
Treoes.....18 D5
Treorchi.....18 D3
Tre'r-ddol.....39 F7
Tresaith.....27 G1
Trescott.....41 K7
Trescowe.....2 C6
Tresham.....20 B3
Tresillian.....3 G6
Tresinwen.....26 D2
Tresmeer.....8 C7
Tressait.....87 L2
Tresta.....115 F3
Treswell.....54 B6
Tre Taliesin.....39 F7
Trethewey.....2 B7
Trethomas.....19 F4
Trethurgy.....3 J4
Tretio.....26 B4
Tretire.....31 G7
Tretower.....30 C7
Treuddyn.....50 B8
Trevalga.....8 A6
Trevanson.....3 H2
Trevarren.....3 H3
Trevarrick.....3 H5
Trevellas.....2 F4
Treverva.....2 F6
Trevethin.....19 G2
Trevigro.....4 D3
Treviscoe.....3 H4
Trevone.....3 G2
Trewarmett.....8 A7
Trewarthenick.....3 H5
Trewassa.....8 B7
Trewellard.....2 B6
Trewen.....8 C7
Trewidland.....4 C4
Trewint.....8 B6
Trewithian.....3 G6
Trewoon.....3 H4
Treyarnon.....3 G2
Treyford.....14 B4
Trickett's Cross.....12 C5
Trimdon.....66 D4
Trimdon Grange.....66 D4
Trimingham.....47 H3
Trimley St Martin.....37 H6
Trimley St Mary.....37 H6
Trimpley.....31 J2
Trimsaran.....27 J6
Trimstone.....8 F1
Trinafour.....19 G2
Tring.....22 E1
Trinity.....89 J2
Trislaig.....93 G8
Trispen.....3 G4
Tritlington.....75 J5
Trochry.....88 B4
Troedyraur.....27 H2
Troedyrhiw.....18 E2
Troon, Corn.....2 E6
Troon, Strath.....71 J1
Troston.....36 D2
Trottiscliffe.....24 C6
Trotton.....14 B3
Troutbeck, Cumbr.....63 J5
Troutbeck, Cumbr.....63 K7
Troutbeck Bridge.....63 K7
Trowbridge.....20 C7
Trow Green.....19 K2
Trowle Common.....20 C7
Trows.....74 C1
Trowse Newton.....47 H6
Trudoxhill.....11 J1
Trull.....10 D3
Trumisgarry.....98 D5
Trumpan.....99 H6
Trumpet.....31 H6
Trumpington.....35 H4
Trunch.....47 H3
Truro.....3 G5
Trusham.....9 J7
Trusley.....42 E3
Trusthorpe.....55 K5
Trysull.....42 A7
Tubney.....21 J3
Tuckenhay.....5 J4
Tuckhill.....31 J1
Tuddenham, Suff.....36 C2
Tuddenham, Suff.....37 G5
Tudeley.....16 D1
Tudhoe.....66 C4
Tudweiliog.....38 B3
Tuffley.....20 C1
Tufton.....18 D3
Tugby.....44 A6
Tugford.....31 G1
Tullibody.....80 B5
Tullich.....86 C7
Tullich Muir.....103 F5
Tulloch.....89 K1
Tullochgorm.....96 B4
Tullynessle.....96 E4
Tumble.....27 K5
Tumby Woodside.....45 F1
Tummel Bridge.....87 K3
Tunbridge Wells, Royal.....16 C2
Tunga.....107 J5
Tunstall, Staffs.....42 A1
Tunstall, Kent.....24 E6
Tunstall, N. Yks.....59 H1
Tunstall, Suff.....37 J4
Tunstall, Lancs.....57 K3
Tunstall, Norf.....47 K6
Tunstall, Humbs.....61 L7
Tunstead.....47 H4
Tunworth.....13 J1
Tupsley.....31 G5
Tupton.....53 F7

U

Uachdar.....98 D7
Uags.....92 D2
Ubbeston Green.....37 J2
Ubley.....19 K7
Uckerby.....66 C7
Uckfield.....15 H3
Uckington.....32 B7
Uddingston.....80 B5
Uddington.....72 D1
Udimore.....16 F4
Udny Green.....97 H3
Udny Station.....97 J3
Uffcott.....20 F5
Uffculme.....10 B4
Uffington, Lincs.....44 D6
Uffington, Shrops.....41 G5
Uffington, Oxon.....21 H4
Ufford, Cambs.....44 D6
Ufford, Suff.....37 H4
Ufton.....33 F3
Ufton Nervet.....22 B6
Ugadale.....70 C2
Ugborough.....5 G4
Uggeshall.....37 K1
Ugglebarnby.....67 J7
Ugley.....35 J7

Ugley Green	35	J7
Ugthorpe	67	H6
Uig, Highld	99	G7
Uig, Highld	99	J6
Uigshader	99	K8
Uisken	84	E7
Ulbster	111	K4
Ulceby, Humbs	54	F2
Ulceby, Lincs	55	J6
Ulcombe	16	F1
Uldale	63	H4
Uley	20	B3
Ulgham	75	J5
Ullapool	101	H3
Ullenhall	32	D3
Ullenwood	20	D1
Ulleskelf	60	C6
Ullesthorpe	33	H1
Ulley	53	G5
Ullingswick	31	G4
Ullinish	91	J2
Ullock	62	F5
Ulpha	56	E1
Ulrome	61	J5
Ulsta	117	F4
Ulverston	57	F3
Ulzieside	72	C4
Umberleigh	9	G3
Unapool	108	D5
Underbarrow	57	H1
Underriver	23	L7
Underwood, Notts	43	G1
Underwood, Gwent	19	H4
Undy	19	J4
Unifirth	114	E3
Union Mills	56	O4
Unstone	53	F6
Unthank	64	B4
Upavon	21	F7
Up Cerne	11	H5
Upchurch	24	E6
Upcott	30	E4
Upend	36	C4
Up Exe	9	K5
Uphall	81	F4
Uphall Station	81	F4
Upham, Hants	13	H3
Upham, Devon	9	J5
Up Hatherley	32	B7
Uphill	19	H7
Up Holland	50	E3
Uplawmoor	79	G6
Upleadon	31	J7
Upleatham	67	G6
Uploders	11	G6
Uplowman	10	B4
Uplyme	10	E6
Upminster	24	B4
Up Nately	22	B7
Upnor	24	D5
Upottery	10	D5
Upper Affcot	31	F1
Upper Ardchronie	102	E4
Upper Arley	31	J1
Upper Astrop	33	H6
Upper Basildon	21	K5
Upper Beeding	15	F4
Upper Benefield	44	C8
Upper Boddington	33	G4
Upper Borth	28	D1
Upper Breinton	31	F5
Upper Broughton	43	J4
Upper Bucklebury	21	K6
Upper Caldecote	34	E5
Upper Chapel	29	H5
Upper Chute	21	G7
Upper Clatford	13	F1
Upper Dallachy	104	C2
Upper Dean	34	D3
Upper Denby	52	E3
Upper Derraid	95	J2
Upper Dicker	16	C4
Upper Dunsforth	59	K4
Upper Eathie	103	F6
Upper Elkstone	52	C8
Upper End	52	C6
Upper Farringdon	13	K2
Upper Framilode	20	B1
Upper Froyle	14	A1
Upper Gravenhurst	34	E6
Upper Green	21	H6
Upper Hackney	52	E7
Upper Hale	14	B1
Upper Hambleton	44	C6
Upper Hardres Court	25	H7
Upper Hartfield	15	H2
Upper Heath	31	G1
Upper Helmsley	60	D5
Upper Heyford, Oxon	33	G7
Upper Heyford, Northnts	33	J4
Upper Hill	31	F4
Upper Hopton	52	D2
Upper Hulme	52	C7
Upper Inglesham	21	G3
Upper Killay	27	K7
Upper Knockando	103	K8
Upper Lambourne	21	H4
Upper Lochton	97	F6
Upper Longdon	42	C5
Upper Longwood	41	H6
Upper Lydbrook	19	L1
Upper Maes-coed	30	E6
Uppermill	51	J3
Upper Minety	20	E3
Upper North Dean	22	D3
Upper Poppleton	60	C5
Upper Quinton	32	D5
Upper Sanday	113	F6
Upper Sapey	31	H3
Upper Seagry	20	D4
Upper Shelton	34	C5
Upper Sheringham	47	G2
Upper Skelmorlie	78	D5
Upper Slaughter	32	D7
Upper Soudley	20	A1
Upper Stondon	34	E6
Upper Stowe	33	J4
Upper Street, Hants	12	C4
Upper Street, Norf	47	J5
Upper Sundon	34	D7
Upper Swainswick	20	B6
Upper Swell	32	D7
Upper Tean	42	C3
Upperthong	52	D3
Upper Tillyrie	88	D8
Upperton	14	C3
Upper Tooting	23	H5
Uppertown	111	K1
Upper Tysoe	33	F5
Upper Upham	21	G5
Upper Wardington	33	G5
Upper Weald	34	B6
Upper Weedon	33	J4
Upper Wield	13	J2
Upper Winchendon	22	C1
Upper Woodford	12	D2
Uppingham	44	B7
Uppington	41	G6
Upsall	59	K2
Upshire	23	K2
Up Somborne	13	F2
Upstreet	25	J6
Up Sydling	11	H5
Upton, Somer	10	A3
Upton, Mers	50	B5
Upton, Dorset	12	B6
Upton, Notts	54	B6
Upton, Bucks	22	C1
Upton, Lincs	54	C5
Upton, Ches	50	D7
Upton, Cambs	34	E2
Upton, Berks	22	E5
Upton, Cambs	44	E6
Upton, Hants	13	F4
Upton, Leic	43	F7
Upton, W. Yks	53	G2
Upton, Hants	21	H7
Upton, Norf	47	J5
Upton, Notts	43	K1
Upton, Northnts	33	K3
Upton, Oxon	21	K4
Upton Bishop	31	H7
Upton Cheyney	20	A6
Upton Cressett	41	H7
Upton Cross	4	C2
Upton Grey	13	J1
Upton Hellions	9	J5
Upton Lovell	12	B1
Upton Magna	41	G5
Upton Noble	11	J2
Upton Pyne	9	K6
Upton Scudamore	12	A1
Upton Snodsbury	32	B4
Upton St Leonards	20	C1
Upton upon Severn	32	A5
Upton Warren	32	B3
Upwaltham	14	C4
Upware	35	J2
Upwell, Cambs	45	J6
Upwell, Norf	45	J6
Upwey	11	H7
Upwood	35	F1
Urafirth	116	E5
Urchfont	20	E7
Urdimarsh	31	G5
Urgha	99	G3
Urlay Nook	66	E6
Urmston	51	G4
Urquhart	104	B2
Urra	67	F7
Urray	102	D7
Urswick	57	F3
Usan	89	K3
Ushaw Moor	66	C3
Usk	19	H2
Usselby	54	E4
Utkinton	50	E7
Utley	59	F6
Uton	9	J6
Utterby	55	H4
Uttoxeter	42	C3
Uwchmynydd	38	A4
Uxbridge	22	F4
Uyeasound	117	G2
Uzmaston	26	D5

V

Valleyfield	80	F3
Valsgarth	117	H1
Valtos, Highld	100	B6
Valtos, W. Isles	106	E5
Vange	24	D4
Varteg	19	G2
Vatersay	90	B6
Vatten	99	H8
Vauld, The	31	G5
Vaynor	18	E1
Vaynor Park	40	C6
Veensgarth	115	G4
Velindre	30	C6
Veness	113	F4
Vennington	40	E6
Venn Ottery	10	B6
Ventnor	7	K7
Vernham Dean	21	H7
Vernham Street	21	H7
Vernolds Common	31	F1
Verran Island	90	C2
Verwood	12	C5
Veryan	3	H6
Vicarage	10	D7
Vickerstown	56	E4
Victoria	3	H3
Vidlin	115	G2
Viewpark	80	C5
Village Abberley, The	31	J3
Village, The	42	A8
Vinehall Street	16	E3
Vines Cross	16	C4
Virginia Water	22	E6
Virginstow	8	D6
Vobster	11	J1
Voe	115	G2
Vowchurch	30	E6

W

Waberthwaite	56	E1
Wackerfield	65	J5
Wacton	47	G7
Wadborough	32	B5
Waddesdon	22	C1
Waddingham	54	D4
Waddington, Lancs	58	C6
Waddington, Lincs	54	D7
Wadebridge	3	H2
Wadeford	10	E4
Wadenhoe	34	D1
Wadesmill	23	J1
Wadhurst	16	D2
Wadshelf	53	F6
Wadworth	53	H4
Waen-fach	40	D5
Wainfleet All Saints	55	J8
Wainfleet Bank	55	J8
Wainhouse Corner	8	B6
Wainscott	24	D5
Wainstalls	58	F8
Waitby	64	E7
Wakefield	53	F1
Wakerley	44	C7
Wakes Colne	36	D7
Walberswick	37	K2
Walberton	14	C5
Walcot, Lincs	44	D3
Walcot, Warw	32	D4
Walcot, Shrops	30	E1
Walcot, Shrops	41	G5
Walcote	33	H1
Walcott, Lincs	44	E1
Walcott, Norf	47	J3
Walden	58	F2
Walden Head	58	E2
Walden Stubbs	53	H2
Walderslade	66	D6
Walderton	14	A4
Walditch	11	F6
Waldridge	66	C2
Waldringfield	37	H5
Waldron	16	C4
Wales	53	G5
Walesby, Lincs	55	F4
Walesby, Notts	53	J6
Walford, H. & W	30	E2
Walford, Shrops	41	F4
Walford, H. & W	31	G7
Walgherton	41	H2
Walgrave	34	B2
Walkden	51	G3
Walker	66	C1
Walkerburn	81	J8
Walker Fold	58	B6
Walkeringham	54	B4
Walkerith	54	B4
Walkern	35	F7
Walker's Green	31	G5
Walkhampton	4	F3
Walkington	61	G7
Walk Mill	58	D7
Wall, Staffs	42	D6
Wall, Northum	74	F8
Wallacetown	71	J2
Wallasey	50	B4
Wallingford	21	L4
Wallington, Herts	35	F6
Wallington, Hants	13	H5
Wallington, G. Lon	23	H6
Wallis	26	E4
Walliswood	14	E2
Wallis	114	E4
Wallsend	75	J8
Wall under Heywood	41	G7
Wallyford	81	J4
Walmer	25	K7
Walmer Bridge	50	D1
Walmersley	51	H2
Walmley	42	D7
Walpole	37	J2
Walpole Highway	45	J5
Walpole St Andrew	45	J5
Walpole St Peter	45	J5
Walsall	42	C7
Walsall Wood	42	C6
Walsden	51	J1
Walsgrave on Sowe	33	F1
Walsham le Willows	36	F2
Walsoken	45	H5
Walston	81	F7
Walter's Ash	22	D3
Walterstone	30	E7
Waltham, Humbs	55	G3
Waltham, Kent	17	J1
Waltham Abbey	23	J2
Waltham Chase	13	H4
Waltham Cross	23	J2
Waltham on the Wolds	44	B4
Waltham St Lawrence	22	D5
Walthamstow	23	J4
Walton, Bucks	34	B6
Walton, Cumbr	64	C1
Walton, Powys	30	D4
Walton, Warw	32	E4
Walton, Somer	11	F2
Walton, W. Yks	53	F2
Walton, Derby	53	F7
Walton, Shrops	41	G5
Walton, Leic	33	H1
Walton, Suff	37	H6
Walton, W. Yks	59	K6
Walton Cardiff	32	B6
Walton East	26	E4
Walton Highway	45	H5
Walton-in-Gordano	19	J5
Walton-le-Dale	50	E1
Walton-on-Thames	23	G6
Walton, Dorset	12	C6
Walton-on-the-Hill, Staffs	42	B4
Walton on the Hill, Surrey	23	H7
Walton-on-the-Naze	37	H7
Walton-on-Trent	42	E5
Walton West	26	C5
Walworth	66	C6
Walwyn's Castle	26	C5
Wambrook	10	D5
Wanborough	21	G4
Wandsworth	23	H5
Wangford	37	K2
Wanlip	43	H5
Wanlockhead	72	D3
Wansford, Cambs	44	D7
Wansford, Humbs	61	H5
Wanstead	23	K4
Wanstrow	11	J1
Wanswell	20	A2
Wantage	21	J4
Wapley	20	B5
Wappenbury	33	F3
Wappenham	33	J5
Warbleton	16	D4
Warborough	21	K3
Warboys	35	G1
Warbstow	8	C6
Warburton	51	G5
Warcop	64	E6
Warden	25	G5
Ward Green	36	F3
Wardington	33	G5
Wardle, Ches	41	H1
Wardle, G. Man	51	J2
Wardley	44	B6
Wardlow	52	D6
Wardy Hill	35	H1
Ware	23	J1
Wareham	12	B7
Warehorne	17	G2
Wareside	23	J1
Waresley	35	F4
Warfield	22	D5
Warford	51	J1
Wargrave	22	C5
Warham	46	E2
Wark, Northum	74	E7
Wark, Northum	83	G8
Warkleigh	9	G3
Warkton	34	B2
Warkworth	75	J4
Warlaby	59	J1
Warland	51	J1
Warleggan	3	K3
Warlingham	23	J7
Warmfield	53	F1
Warmingham	51	G7
Warmington, Northnts	44	D7
Warmington, Warw	33	G5
Warminster	12	A1
Warmsworth	53	H3
Warmwell	11	J7
Warndon	32	A4
Warnford	13	J3
Warnham	14	E2
Warninglid	15	F3
Warren, Dyfed	26	D7
Warren, Ches	51	H6
Warren Row	22	D4
Warren Street	24	F7
Warrington, Bucks	34	B4
Warrington, Ches	50	F5
Warsash	13	G5
Warslow	52	C8
Warter	60	F5
Warthill	60	D5
Wartling	16	D5
Wartnaby	43	K4
Warton, Warw	42	E6
Warton, Northum	75	G4
Warton, Lancs	57	H8
Warton, Lancs	57	J3
Warwick, Warw	32	E3
Warwick Bridge	64	B2
Warwick-on-Eden	64	B2
Wasbister	112	D3
Wasdale Head	63	G7
Washaway	3	J3
Washbourne	5	H4
Washfield	9	K4
Washford	10	B1
Washford Pyne	9	J4
Washingborough	54	E6
Washington, T. & W	66	D2
Washington, W. Susx	14	E4
Wasing	21	K6
Waskerley	66	A3
Wasperton	32	E4
Wass	60	C3
Watchet	10	B1
Watchfield, Somer	10	E1
Watchfield, Oxon	21	G3
Watchgate	64	C8
Watendlath	63	H6
Water	35	H1
Waterbeach	35	J2
Waterbeck	73	H7
Waterden	46	D3
Water End, Herts	22	F1
Water End, Herts	23	H2
Waterfall	42	C1
Waterfoot, Lancs	51	H1
Waterfoot, Strath	79	H6
Waterhead, Strath	72	A3
Waterhead	66	E6
Waterhouses, Durham	66	B3
Waterhouses, Staffs	42	C1
Wateringbury	24	C7
Waterlip	11	H1
Waterloo, Mers	50	C4
Waterloo, Tays	88	C5
Waterloo, Dorset	12	C6
Waterloo-on-the-Hill	42	B4
Waterloo, Strath	80	D6
Waterloo, Norf	47	H5
Waterlooville	13	J5
Watermeetings	72	E3
Watermillock	64	B5
Water Newton	44	E7
Water Orton	42	D7
Waterperry	22	B2
Waterrow	10	B3
Watersfield	14	D4
Waterside, Strath	79	G2
Waterside, Strath	79	H5
Waterside, Strath	79	J4
Waterside, Strath	71	K4
Waterstock	22	B2
Waterston	26	D6
Water Stratford	33	J6
Waters Upton	41	H5
Waterthorpe	53	G5
Water Yeat	57	F2
Watford, Herts	23	G3
Watford, Northnts	33	J3
Wath, N. Yks	59	G4
Wath, N. Yks	59	J3
Wath upon Dearne	53	G3
Watlington, Oxon	22	B3
Watlington, Norf	45	K5
Watnall	43	H2
Watten	111	J3
Watterow	10	B3
Wattisfield	36	F2
Wattisham	36	F4
Watton, Norf	46	E6
Watton, Humbs	61	H5
Watton at Stone	23	J1
Wattston	80	C5
Wattstown	18	E3
Wattsville	19	G3
Waunarlwydd	27	L7
Waunfawr	48	E5
Wavendon	34	C6
Waverton, Ches	50	D7
Waverton, Cumbr	63	H3
Wawne	61	H7
Waxham	47	K4
Waxholme	61	L8
Wayford	10	F5
Way Village	9	J4
Weachyburn	104	F2
Wealdstone	23	G4
Weare	19	J7
Weare Giffard	8	C3
Wearhead	65	F4
Weasdale	64	D7
Weasenham All Saints	46	D4
Weasenham St Peter	46	D4
Weaverham	50	F6
Weaverthorpe	61	G3
Webheath	32	C3
Wedderlairs	97	H2
Weddington	43	F7
Wedhampton	20	E7
Wedmore	11	F1
Wednesbury	42	B7
Wednesfield	42	B6
Weedon	34	D1
Weedon Bec	33	J4
Weedon Lois	33	J5
Weeford	42	D6
Week	9	H4
Weekley	34	B1
Week St Mary	8	C6
Weeley	37	G7
Weeley Heath	37	G7
Weem	87	L4
Weeping Cross	42	B4
Weeting	36	C1
Weeton, Lancs	57	G7
Weeton, N. Yks	59	H6
Weir	51	H1
Welbeck Abbey	53	H6
Welborne	46	F6
Welbourn	54	D7
Welburn	60	E4
Welburn	66	D7
Welby	44	C4
Welches Dam	35	H1
Welcombe	8	C4
Welford, Northnts	33	J1
Welford, Berks	21	J5
Welford-on-Avon	32	D4
Welham	44	A7
Welham Green	23	H2
Well, Hants	14	A1
Well, N. Yks	59	H2
Well, Lincs	55	J6
Welland	31	J5
Wellbank	89	G5
Wellesbourne	32	E4
Well Hill	23	K5
Welling	23	K5
Wellingborough	34	B3
Wellingham	46	D4
Wellingore	44	C1
Wellington, Somer	10	C3
Wellington, H. & W	31	F5
Wellington, Shrops	41	H5
Wellington Heath	31	J5
Wellow, Avon	20	B7
Wellow, I. of W	13	F7
Wellow, Notts	53	J7
Wells	11	G1
Wellsborough	43	F6
Wells-next-the-Sea	46	E2
Wellwood	81	F3
Welney	45	J7
Welshampton	41	F3
Welsh Bicknor	19	K1
Welsh End	41	G3
Welsh Frankton	40	E3
Welsh Hook	26	D4
Welsh Newton	19	K1
Welshpool or Trallwng	40	D6
Welsh St Donats	18	E5
Welton, Humbs	54	D1
Welton, Lincs	54	E6
Welton, Northnts	33	H3
Welton, Cumbr	63	J3
Welton le Marsh	55	J7
Welton le Wold	55	G5
Welwick	55	H1
Welwyn	23	H1
Welwyn Garden City	23	H1
Wem	41	G4
Wembdon	10	D2
Wembley	23	G4
Wembury	4	F5
Wembworthy	9	G5
Wemyss Bay	78	D5
Wendens Ambo	35	J6
Wendlebury	21	K1
Wendling	46	E5
Wendover	22	D2
Wendron	2	E4
Wendy	35	G5
Wenhaston	37	K2
Wennington, Cambs	35	F2
Wennington, Lancs	57	K3
Wennington, G. Lon	23	L4
Wensley, Derby	52	E7
Wensley, N. Yks	59	F2
Wentbridge	53	G2
Wentnor	40	E7
Wentworth, S. Yks	53	F4
Wentworth, Cambs	35	H2
Wenvoe	18	F5
Weobley	30	F4
Weobley Marsh	31	F4
Wereham	46	B6
Wergs	46	A6
Wernrheolydd	19	H1
Werrington, Staffs	42	B1
Werrington, Corn	8	D7
Werrington, Cambs	44	E6
Wervin	50	D6
Wesham	57	H7
Wessington	43	F1
West Acre	46	C5
West Allerdean	83	H7
West Alvington	5	H5
West Anstey	9	J3
West Ashby	55	G6
West Ashling	14	B5
West Ashton	20	C7
West Auckland	66	B5
West Bagborough	10	C2
West Barns	82	E4
West Barsham	46	E3
West Bay	11	F6
West Beckham	47	G3
Westbere	25	H6
West Bergholt	36	D6
West Bexington	11	G7
West Bilney	46	C5
West Blatchington	15	F5
Westborough	44	B2
Westbourne, W. Susx	14	A5
Westbourne, Dorset	12	C6
West Bradford	58	C6
West Bradley	11	G2
West Bretton	52	E2
West Bridgford	43	H3
West Bromwich	42	C7
West Buckland, Somer	10	C3
West Buckland, Devon	9	G2
West Burrafirth	114	E3
West Burton, W. Susx	14	C4
West Burton, Lancs	58	E4
West Burton, N. Yks	58	F2
Westbury, Wilts	20	C7
Westbury, Shrops	40	E6
Westbury, Bucks	33	J6
Westbury Leigh	20	C7
Westbury-on-Severn	20	B1
Westbury-sub-Mendip	11	G1
Westby	57	G7
West Caister	47	L5
West Calder	80	F5
West Camel	11	G3
West Challow	21	H4
West Charleton	5	H5
West Chelborough	11	G5
West Chevington	75	J5
West Chiltington	14	D4
West Chinnock	11	F4
West Clandon	22	F7
West Cliffe	17	L1
Westcliff-on-Sea	24	E4
West Clyne	103	G2
West Coker	11	G4
Westcombe	11	H2
West Compton, Somer	11	G1
West Compton, Dorset	11	G6
Westcote	32	D7
Westcott, Devon	10	B5
Westcott, Bucks	22	C1
Westcott, Surrey	14	E1
Westcott Barton	33	G7
West Cross	27	L8
West Curthwaite	63	J3
West Dean, W. Susx	14	B4
West Dean, Hants	12	E3
Westdean, E. Susx	15	J6
West Deeping	44	E6
West Derby	50	C4
West Dereham	46	B6
West Ditchburn	75	H2
West Down	9	F1
West Drayton, G. Lon	22	F5
West Drayton, Notts	53	K6
West End, Beds	34	C4
West End, Surrey	22	E6
West End, Hants	13	G4
West End, N. Yks	59	G5
West End, Humbs	61	G7
West End, Oxon	21	J2

West End, Avon.....19 J6
West End, Norf.....47 K5
West End Green.....22 B6
Westerdale, N. Yks.....67 G7
Westerdale, Highld.....111 H3
Westerfield, Shetld.....115 F3
Westerfield, Suff.....37 G5
Wester Fintray.....97 H4
Westergate.....14 C5
Wester Gruinards.....102 D3
Westerham.....23 K7
Westerleigh.....20 B5
Wester Quarff.....115 G5
Wester Skeld.....114 E4
Westerton.....89 J3
Westerwick.....114 E4
West Farleigh.....24 D7
West Felton.....40 E4
Westfield, Lothn.....80 E4
Westfield, Norf.....46 E6
Westfield, E. Susx.....16 F4
Westfield, Highld.....111 G2
West Firle.....15 H5
West Fleetham.....75 H2
Westgate, Humbs.....54 B3
Westgate, Norf.....46 E2
Westgate, Durham.....65 G4
Westgate on Sea.....25 K5
West Gerinish.....90 C1
West Ginge.....21 J4
West Grafton.....21 G6
West Green.....22 C7
West Grimstead.....12 E3
West Grinstead.....14 E3
West Haddlesey.....53 H1
West Haddon.....33 J2
West Hagbourne.....21 K4
West Hall, Cumbr.....74 B8
Westhall, Suff.....37 K1
West Hallam.....43 G2
West Halton.....54 D1
Westham, E. Susx.....16 D5
Westham, Somer.....10 F1
West Ham, G. Lon.....23 K4
Westhampnett.....14 B5
West Handley.....53 F6
West Hanney.....21 J3
West Hanningfield.....24 D3
West Hardwick.....53 G2
West Harptree.....19 K7
West Hatch.....10 D3
Westhay.....11 F1
Westhead.....50 D3
West Heath.....22 D7
West Helmsdale.....111 G7
West Hendred.....21 J4
West Heslerton.....61 G3
Westhide.....31 G5
West Hill, Devon.....10 B6
Westhill, Highld.....102 F8
Westhill, Grampn.....97 H5
West Hoathly.....15 G2
West Holme.....12 A7
Westhope, Shrops.....31 H1
Westhope, H. & W.....31 F4
West Horndon.....24 C4
Westhorpe, Suff.....36 F3
Westhorpe, Lincs.....45 F3
West Horrington.....11 G1
West Horsley.....22 F7
West Hougham.....17 K1
Westhoughton.....51 F3
Westhouse.....58 B3
Westhouses.....53 G8
Westhumble.....23 G7
West Hyde.....22 F3
West Ilsley.....21 J4
Westing.....117 G2
West Itchenor.....14 A5
West Kennett.....20 F6
West Kilbride.....78 E7
West Kingsdown.....24 B6
West Kington.....20 C5
West Kirby.....50 B5
West Knighton.....11 J7
West Knoyle.....11 K2
Westlake.....5 G4
West Langdon.....17 L1
West Langwell.....102 E2
West Lavington, W. Susx.....14 B3
West Lavington, Wilts.....20 E7
West Layton.....65 J7
West Leake.....43 H4
Westleigh, Devon.....10 B4
Westleigh, Devon.....8 E3
Westleton.....37 K3
West Lexham.....46 D5
Westley, Suff.....36 D3
Westley, Shrops.....40 E6
Westley Waterless.....35 K4
West Lilling.....60 D4
Westlington.....22 C1
West Linton, Border.....81 G6
Westlinton, Cumbr.....63 J1
West Littleton.....20 B5
West Lulworth.....11 K7
West Lutton.....61 G4
West Malling.....24 C7
West Malvern.....31 J5
West Marden.....14 A4
West Markham.....54 B6
Westmarsh.....25 J6
West Marton.....58 D5
West Meon.....13 J3
West Mersea.....25 G1
Westmeston.....15 G4
Westmill.....35 G7
West Milton.....11 G6
Westminster.....23 H5
West Monkton.....10 D3
West Moors.....12 C5
Westmuir, Tays.....89 F3
West Muir, Tays.....89 H2
West Newton, Norf.....46 B4
Westnewton, Cumbr.....63 G3

West Newton, Humbs.....61 J7
West Norwood.....23 J5
West Ogwell.....5 J2
Weston, Dorset.....6 A7
Weston, Staffs.....42 B4
Weston, Avon.....20 B6
Weston, Notts.....54 B7
Weston, N. Yks.....60 E4
Weston, Ches.....50 E5
Weston, Lincs.....45 F4
Weston, Herts.....35 F6
Weston, Shrops.....41 G4
Weston, N. Yks.....59 G6
Weston, Shrops.....41 G7
Weston, Northnts.....33 H5
Weston, Ches.....41 J1
Weston, Berks.....21 J5
Weston, Hants.....13 K3
Weston Bampfylde.....11 H3
Weston Beggard.....31 G5
Westonbirt.....20 C4
Weston by Welland.....44 A7
Weston Colville.....35 K4
Weston Green.....35 K4
Weston Heath.....41 J5
Weston Hills.....45 F4
Westoning.....34 D6
Weston in Gordano.....19 J5
Weston Jones.....41 J4
Weston Longville.....47 G5
Weston Lullingfields.....41 F4
Weston-on-the-Green.....21 K1
Weston-on-Trent.....43 G4
Weston Patrick.....13 J1
Weston Rhyn.....40 D3
Weston-sub-Edge.....32 D5
Weston-super-Mare.....19 H6
Weston Turville.....22 D1
Weston-under-Lizard.....41 K5
Weston under Penyard.....31 H7
Weston under Wetherley.....33 F3
Weston Underwood, Bucks.....34 B4
Weston Underwood, Derby.....42 E2
Westonzoyland.....10 E2
West Overton.....21 F6
West Parley.....12 C6
West Peckham.....24 C7
West Pennard.....11 G2
West Pentire.....2 F3
West Perry.....34 E3
Westport.....10 E3
West Putford.....8 D4
West Quantoxhead.....10 C1
West Rainton.....66 D3
West Rasen.....54 E5
West Raynham.....46 D4
Westrigg.....80 E5
West Row.....36 B2
West Rudham.....46 D4
West Runton.....47 G2
Westruther.....82 E6
Westry.....45 G7
West Saltoun.....82 C5
West Sandwick.....117 F4
West Scrafton.....59 F2
West Stafford.....11 J7
West Stockwith.....54 B4
West Stoke.....14 B5
West Stonesdale.....65 F7
West Stoughton.....11 F1
West Stour.....11 J3
West Stourmouth.....25 J6
West Stow.....36 D2
West Stowell.....21 F6
West Street.....24 F7
West Tanfield.....59 H3
West Tarbert.....77 H5
West Thorney.....14 A5
West Thurrock.....24 B5
West Tilbury.....24 C5
West Tisted.....13 J3
West Tofts.....88 D5
West Torrington.....55 F5
West Town.....19 J6
West Tytherley.....12 E3
West Walton.....45 H5
Westward.....63 H3
Westward Ho!.....8 E3
Westwell, Oxon.....21 G1
Westwell, Kent.....17 G1
Westwell Leacon.....17 G1
West Wellow.....12 E4
West Wemyss.....81 J2
Westwick, Cambs.....35 H3
Westwick, Norf.....47 H4
West Wick, Avon.....19 H6
West Wickham, G. Lon.....23 J6
West Wickham, Cambs.....35 K5
West Winch.....46 B5
West Winterslow.....12 E2
West Wittering.....14 A6
West Witton.....59 F2
Westwood, Devon.....10 B6
Westwood, Wilts.....20 C7
West Woodburn.....74 E6
West Woodhay.....21 H6
West Woodlands.....11 J1
Westwoodside.....54 B4
West Worldham.....13 K2
West Wratting.....35 K4
West Wycombe.....22 D3
West Yell.....117 F4
Wetheral.....64 B2
Wetherby.....59 K6
Wetherden.....36 F3
Wetheringsett.....37 G3
Wethersfield.....36 C6
Wethersta.....115 F2
Wetherup Street.....37 G3
Wetley Rocks.....42 B2
Wettenhall.....51 F7
Wetton.....42 D1
Wetwang.....61 G5
Wetwood.....41 J3
Wexcombe.....21 G7

Weybourne.....47 G2
Weybread.....37 H1
Weybridge.....22 F6
Weydale.....111 H2
Weyhill.....13 F1
Weymouth.....11 H8
Whaddon, Bucks.....34 B6
Whaddon, Glos.....20 C1
Whaddon, Wilts.....12 D3
Whaddon, Cambs.....35 G5
Whale.....64 C5
Whaley.....53 H6
Whaley Bridge.....52 C5
Whaley Thorns.....53 H6
Whalley.....58 C7
Whalton.....75 H6
Wham.....58 C4
Whaplode.....45 G4
Whaplode Drove.....45 G5
Wharfe.....58 C4
Wharles.....57 H7
Wharncliffe Side.....52 E4
Wharram le Street.....60 F4
Wharton, Ches.....51 F7
Wharton, H. & W.....31 G4
Washton.....65 J7
Whatcombe.....11 K5
Whatcote.....33 F5
Whatfield.....36 F5
Whatley.....11 J1
Whatlington.....16 E4
Whatstandwell.....43 F1
Whatton.....44 A3
Whauphill.....68 F6
Wheatacre.....47 K7
Wheathampstead.....23 G1
Wheathill.....31 H1
Wheatley, Hants.....14 A1
Wheatley, Oxon.....21 K2
Wheatley Hill.....66 D4
Wheatley Lane.....58 D7
Wheaton Aston.....42 A5
Wheddon Cross.....9 K2
Wheedlemont.....96 D3
Wheelerstreet.....14 C1
Wheelock.....51 G8
Wheelton.....50 F1
Wheldrake.....60 D6
Whelford.....21 F3
Whelpley Hill.....22 E2
Whenby.....60 D4
Whepstead.....36 D4
Wherstead.....37 G5
Wherwell.....13 F1
Wheston.....52 D6
Whetsted.....16 D1
Whetstone.....43 H7
Whicham.....56 E2
Whichford.....33 F6
Whickham.....66 C1
Whiddon Down.....9 G6
Whigstreet.....89 G4
Whilton.....33 J3
Whimple.....10 B6
Whimpwell Green.....47 J4
Whinburgh.....46 F6
Whinnyfold.....97 K2
Whippingham.....13 H6
Whipsnade.....22 F1
Whipton.....9 K6
Whissendine.....44 B5
Whissonsett.....46 E4
Whistley Green.....22 C5
Whiston, Staffs.....42 A5
Whiston, Northnts.....34 B3
Whiston, Staffs.....42 C2
Whiston, Mers.....50 D4
Whiston, S. Yks.....53 G4
Whitbeck.....56 E2
Whitbourne.....31 J4
Whitburn, T. & W.....66 E1
Whitburn, Lothn.....80 E5
Whitby, Ches.....50 C6
Whitby, N. Yks.....67 J6
Whitchurch, Bucks.....34 B7
Whitchurch, Dyfed.....26 C4
Whitchurch, Devon.....4 E2
Whitchurch, S. Glam.....18 F4
Whitchurch, Hants.....13 G1
Whitchurch, Shrops.....41 G2
Whitchurch, H. & W.....31 K1
Whitchurch, Avon.....19 L6
Whitchurch Canonicorum.....10 E6
Whitchurch Hill.....22 B5
Whitchurch-on-Thames.....22 B5
Whitcott Keysett.....30 D1
Whitebridge.....97 C4
Whitebrook.....19 K2
Whitecairns.....97 J4
Whitechapel.....57 J6
White Coppice.....50 F2
Whitecraig.....81 J4
Whitecroft.....19 L2
Whiteface.....102 F4
Whitefield.....51 H3
Whiteford.....97 G3
Whitegate.....51 F7
Whitehall.....112 D3
Whitehaven.....62 E6
Whitehill.....14 A2
Whitehills.....104 F2
Whitehouse, Grampn.....96 F4
Whitehouse, Strath.....77 H5
Whitekirk.....82 D3
White Kirkley.....65 H4
White Lackington.....11 J6
White Ladies Aston.....32 B4
Whiteley Village.....23 F6
Whitemans Green.....15 G3
Whitemire.....103 H7
Whitemoor.....3 H4
White Notley.....24 D1
Whiteparish.....12 E3
Whiterashes.....97 H3
White Rocks.....31 F7

White Roding or
  White Roothing.....24 B1
White Roothing or
  White Roding.....24 B1
Whiterow.....111 K4
Whiteshill.....20 C2
Whiteside.....80 E5
Whitesmith.....15 J4
Whitestaunton.....10 D4
Whitestone.....9 J6
White Waltham.....22 D5
Whiteway.....20 D1
Whitewell.....58 B6
Whitewreath.....104 B3
Whitfield, Avon.....20 A3
Whitfield, Northum.....64 E2
Whitfield, Bucks.....33 J6
Whitfield, Northnts.....33 J6
Whitfield, Kent.....17 L1
Whitford, Clwyd.....50 A6
Whitford, Devon.....10 D6
Whitgift.....54 C1
Whitgreave.....42 A4
Whithorn.....68 F6
Whiting Bay.....70 F2
Whitland.....27 G5
Whitletts.....71 J2
Whitley, Berks.....22 C5
Whitley, Wilts.....20 C6
Whitley, Ches.....50 F6
Whitley, N. Yks.....53 H1
Whitley Bay.....75 K7
Whitley Chapel.....65 G2
Whitley Row.....23 K7
Whitlock's End.....32 D2
Whitminster.....20 B2
Whitmore.....41 K2
Whitnage.....10 B4
Whitnash.....33 F3
Whitney-on-Wye, H. & W.....30 D5
Whitrigg.....63 H4
Whitsbury.....12 D4
Whitsome.....83 G6
Whitson.....19 H4
Whitstable.....25 H6
Whitstone.....8 C6
Whittingham.....75 G3
Whittingslow.....41 F8
Whittington, Staffs.....32 A1
Whittington, H. & W.....32 A4
Whittington, Norf.....46 C7
Whittington, Glos.....32 C7
Whittington, Staffs.....42 D6
Whittington, Shrops.....40 E3
Whittington, Derby.....53 F6
Whittington, Lancs.....57 K3
Whittlebury.....33 J5
Whittle-le-Woods.....50 E1
Whittlesey.....45 F7
Whittlesford.....35 H5
Whitton, Humbs.....54 D1
Whitton, Border.....74 D2
Whitton, Powys.....30 D3
Whitton, Cleve.....66 D5
Whitton, Shrops.....31 G2
Whitton, Northum.....75 G4
Whitton, Suff.....37 G5
Whittonditch.....21 G5
Whittonstall.....65 H2
Whitwell, Leic.....44 C6
Whitwell, N. Yks.....66 C8
Whitwell, Herts.....34 E7
Whitwell, Derby.....53 H6
Whitwell, I. of W.....7 K7
Whitwell-on-the-Hill.....60 E4
Whitwick.....43 G5
Whitwood.....53 G1
Whitworth.....51 H2
Whixall.....41 G3
Whixley.....59 K5
Whorlton, N. Yks.....66 E7
Whorlton, Durham.....65 J6
Whyle.....31 G3
Whyteleafe.....23 J7
Wibdon.....19 K3
Wibtoft.....33 G1
Wichenford.....31 J3
Wichling.....24 F7
Wick, Avon.....20 B5
Wick, H. & W.....32 B5
Wick, Highld.....111 K3
Wick, M. Glam.....18 D5
Wick, W. Susx.....14 D5
Wick, Dorset.....12 D6
Wick, Highld.....111 K3
Wickam Street.....36 C4
Wicken, Northnts.....34 A6
Wicken, Cambs.....35 J2
Wicken Bonhunt.....35 J6
Wickenby.....54 E5
Wickersley.....53 G4
Wickford.....24 D3
Wickham, Hants.....13 H4
Wickham, Berks.....21 H5
Wickham Bishops.....24 E1
Wickhambreaux.....25 J7
Wickhambrook.....36 C4
Wickhamford.....32 C5
Wickham Market.....37 J4
Wickhampton.....47 K6
Wickham Skeith.....37 F3
Wickham St Paul.....36 D6
Wickham Street.....37 G3
Wicklewood.....46 F6
Wickmere.....47 G3
Wick St Lawrence.....19 H6
Wickwar.....20 B4
Widcombe in the Moor.....5 H7
Widegates.....4 C4
Widemouth Bay.....8 C5
Wide Open.....75 J7
Widewall.....112 E7
Widford, Essex.....24 C2

Widford, Herts.....23 K1
Widmerpool.....43 J4
Widnes.....50 E5
Wigan.....50 E3
Wiggaton.....10 C6
Wiggenhall St Germans.....45 J5
Wiggenhall St Mary
  Magdalen.....45 J5
Wiggenhall St Mary
  the Virgin.....45 J5
Wigginton, Oxon.....60 C5
Wigginton, Herts.....22 E1
Wigginton, Staffs.....42 E6
Wigginton, Oxon.....33 F6
Wigglesworth.....58 D5
Wiggonby.....63 J2
Wighill.....60 B6
Wighton.....46 E3
Wigley.....54 C6
Wigmore, Kent.....24 E6
Wigmore, H. & W.....31 F3
Wigsley.....54 C6
Wigsthorpe.....34 D1
Wigston.....43 J7
Wigtoft.....45 F3
Wigton.....63 H3
Wigtown.....68 F5
Wilbarston.....34 B1
Wilberfoss.....60 E5
Wilburton.....35 H2
Wilby, Northnts.....34 B3
Wilby, Norf.....46 F8
Wilby, Suff.....37 H2
Wilcot.....21 F6
Wilcott.....40 E4
Wildboarclough.....51 J7
Wilden, Beds.....34 D4
Wilden, H. & W.....31 K2
Wildhern.....21 H7
Wildsworth.....54 C4
Wilford.....43 H3
Wilkesley.....41 H2
Wilkhaven.....103 H4
Wilkieston.....81 G5
Willand.....10 B4
Willaston, Ches.....50 C6
Willaston, Ches.....41 H1
Willen.....34 B5
Willenhall, W. Mids.....42 B7
Willenhall, W. Mids.....33 F2
Willerby, N. Yks.....61 H3
Willerby, Humbs.....61 H7
Willersey.....32 D6
Willersley.....30 E5
Willesborough Lees.....17 H1
Willesden.....23 H4
Willett.....10 C2
Willey, Warw.....33 G1
Willey, Shrops.....41 H7
Williamscot.....33 G5
Willian.....35 F6
Willingale.....24 B2
Willingdon.....16 C5
Willingham.....35 H2
Willingham by Stow.....54 C5
Willington, Durham.....66 B4
Willington, Derby.....42 E4
Willington, Beds.....34 E5
Willington, Warw.....32 E6
Willington, T. & W.....75 K8
Willington Corner.....50 E7
Willitoft.....60 E1
Williton.....10 B1
Willoughby, Warw.....33 H3
Willoughby, Lincs.....55 J6
Willoughby-on-the-Wolds.....43 J4
Willoughby Waterleys.....43 H7
Willoughton.....54 D4
Wilmcote.....32 D4
Wilmington, E. Susx.....16 C5
Wilmington, Devon.....10 D6
Wilmington, Kent.....23 L5
Wilmslow.....51 H5
Wilnecote.....42 E6
Wilpshire.....58 B7
Wilsden.....59 F7
Wilsford, Lincs.....44 D2
Wilsford, Wilts.....12 D2
Wilsford, Wilts.....20 F7
Wilsill.....59 G4
Wilson.....43 G4
Wilstead.....34 D5
Wilsthorpe.....44 D3
Wilstone.....22 E1
Wilton, Wilts.....12 C2
Wilton, N. Yks.....60 F2
Wilton, Cleve.....67 F6
Wilton, Wilts.....21 G6
Wilton Dean.....74 A3
Wimbish.....35 J6
Wimbish Green.....35 K6
Wimbledon.....23 H5
Wimblington.....45 H7
Wimborne Minster.....12 C5
Wimbotsham.....45 K6
Wimpstone.....32 E5
Wincanton.....11 J3
Wincham.....51 F6
Winchburgh.....81 F4
Winchcombe.....32 C7
Winchelsea.....17 G4
Winchelsea Beach.....17 G4
Winchester.....13 G3
Winchet Hill.....16 D1
Winchfield.....22 C7
Winchmore Hill, Bucks.....22 E3
Winchmore Hill, G. Lon.....23 J3
Wincle.....51 J7
Windermere.....63 K6
Winderton.....33 F5
Windlesham.....22 E6
Windley.....43 F2
Windmill Hill, E. Susx.....16 D4
Windmill Hill, Somer.....10 E4
Windrush.....21 F1
Windsor.....22 E5
Windygates.....81 J1
Wineham.....15 F3

Winestead.....55 H1
Winfarthing.....37 G1
Winford.....19 K6
Winforton.....30 D5
Winfrith Newburgh.....11 K7
Wing, Leic.....44 B6
Wing, Bucks.....34 B7
Wingate.....66 E4
Wingates, G. Man.....51 F3
Wingates, Northum.....75 G5
Wingerworth.....53 F7
Wingfield, Wilts.....20 C7
Wingfield, Beds.....34 D7
Wingfield, Suff.....37 H2
Wingham.....25 J7
Wingrave.....22 D1
Winkburn.....54 B8
Winkfield.....22 E5
Winkfield Row.....22 D5
Winkhill.....42 C1
Winkleigh.....9 G5
Winksley.....59 H3
Winless.....111 K3
Winmarleigh.....57 H6
Winnersh.....22 C5
Winscales.....62 E5
Winscombe.....19 J7
Winsford, Ches.....51 F7
Winsford, Somer.....9 K2
Winsham.....10 E5
Winshill.....42 E4
Winskill.....64 C4
Winslade.....13 J1
Winsley.....20 C6
Winslow.....34 A7
Winson.....20 E2
Winster, Derby.....52 E7
Winster, Cumbr.....57 H1
Winston, Suff.....37 G3
Winston, Durham.....65 J6
Winstone.....20 D2
Winswell.....8 E4
Winterborne Clenston.....11 K5
Winterborne Herringston.....11 H7
Winterborne Houghton.....11 K5
Winterborne Kingston.....12 A6
Winterborne Monkton.....11 K5
Winterborne Stickland.....11 K5
Winterborne Whitechurch.....11 K5
Winterborne Zelston.....12 A6
Winterbourne, Avon.....20 A4
Winterbourne, Berks.....21 J5
Winterbourne Abbas.....11 H6
Winterbourne Bassett.....20 F5
Winterbourne Dauntsey.....12 D2
Winterbourne Earls.....12 D2
Winterbourne Gunner.....12 D2
Winterbourne Monkton.....20 F5
Winterbourne Steepleton.....11 H7
Winterbourne Stoke.....12 C1
Winterburn.....58 E5
Winteringham.....54 D1
Winterley.....41 J1
Wintersett.....53 F2
Wintershill.....13 H4
Winterton.....54 D2
Winterton-on-Sea.....47 K5
Winthorpe, Notts.....44 B1
Winthorpe, Lincs.....55 K7
Winton, Dorset.....12 C6
Winton, Cumbr.....64 E6
Wintringham.....61 F3
Winwick, Cambs.....34 E1
Winwick, Northnts.....33 J2
Winyates.....32 C3
Wirksworth.....42 E1
Wirswall.....41 G2
Wisbech.....45 H6
Wisbech St Mary.....45 H6
Wisborough Green.....14 D3
Wiseton.....54 B5
Wishaw, Strath.....80 C6
Wishaw, Warw.....32 D7
Wisley.....22 F7
Wispington.....55 G8
Wissett.....37 J2
Wistanstow.....31 F1
Wistanswick.....41 H4
Wistaston.....41 H1
Wiston, Strath.....72 C1
Wiston, W. Susx.....14 E4
Wiston, Dyfed.....26 E5
Wistow, N. Yks.....60 C7
Wistow, Cambs.....35 F1
Wiswell.....58 C7
Witcham.....35 H2
Witchampton.....12 B5
Witchford.....35 J2
Witham.....24 E1
Witham Friary.....11 J1
Witham on the Hill.....44 D5
Witherenden Hill.....16 D3
Witheridge.....9 J4
Witherley.....43 F7
Withern.....55 H1
Withernsea.....55 H1
Withernwick.....61 H6
Withersdale Street.....37 H1
Withersfield.....36 B5
Witherslack.....57 H2
Withiel.....3 H3
Withiel Florey.....10 A2
Withington, Glos.....20 E1
Withington, Shrops.....41 G5
Withington, H. & W.....31 G5
Withington, G. Man.....51 H4
Withington Green.....51 H6
Withleigh.....9 K4
Withnell.....51 F1
Withybrook.....33 G1
Withycombe.....10 B1
Withyham.....15 H2
Withypool.....9 J2
Witley.....14 C1
Witnesham.....37 G4

Witney...................................21 H2
Wittering...............................44 D6
Wittersham...........................17 F3
Witton Bridge........................47 J3
Witton Gilbert........................66 C3
Witton-le-Wear.......................65 J4
Witton Park...........................66 B4
Wiveliscombe........................10 B3
Wivelsfield............................15 G3
Wivelsfield Green...................15 G4
Wivenhoe.............................36 F7
Wiveton...............................46 F2
Wix......................................37 G7
Wixford................................32 C4
Wixoe..................................36 C5
Woburn................................34 C6
Woburn Sands.......................34 C6
Wokefield Park.......................22 B6
Woking................................22 F7
Wokingham...........................22 D6
Woldingham..........................23 J7
Wold Newton, Humbs............55 G4
Wold Newton, Humbs............61 H3
Wolferlow.............................31 H3
Wolferton.............................46 B4
Wolfhill................................88 D5
Wolf's Castle.........................26 D4
Wolfsdale.............................26 D4
Woll....................................73 K2
Wollaston, Northnts...............34 C3
Wollaston, Shrops..................40 E5
Wollerton.............................41 H3
Wolsingham..........................65 H4
Wolston...............................33 G2
Wolvercote...........................21 J2
Wolverhampton.....................42 B7
Wolverley, Shrops..................41 F3
Wolverley, H. & W..................31 K2
Wolverton, Bucks...................34 B5
Wolverton, Warw...................32 E3
Wolvesnewton........................19 J3
Wolvey................................21 K7
Wolviston.............................66 E5
Wombleton............................60 D2
Wombourne...........................42 A7
Wombwell.............................53 F3
Womenswold.........................25 J7
Wonastow.............................19 J1
Wonersh..............................14 D1
Wonson................................9 G7
Wonston, Hants.....................13 G2
Wonston, Dorset....................11 J5
Wooburn...............................22 E4
Wooburn Green......................22 E4
Woodale..............................58 F3
Woodbastwick........................47 J5
Woodbeck.............................54 B6
Woodborough, Wilts...............20 F7
Woodborough, Notts...............43 J2
Woodbridge...........................37 H5
Woodbury.............................10 B7
Woodbury Salterton...............10 B7
Woodchester.........................20 C2
Woodchurch..........................17 G2
Woodcote.............................22 B4
Woodcroft.............................19 K3
Wood Dalling.........................47 F4
Woodditton...........................36 B4
Woodeaton...........................21 K1
Wood End, Warw....................32 D2
Woodend, Cumbr....................56 E1
Wood End, Warw....................42 E7
Wood End, Herts....................35 G7
Woodend, Northnts.................33 J5
Wood Enderby.......................55 G7
Woodfalls.............................12 D3

Woodford, Northnts................34 C2
Woodford, Corn.......................8 C4
Woodford, Devon.....................5 H4
Woodford, G. Man..................51 H5
Woodford, G. Lon...................23 K3
Woodford Bridge.....................23 K3
Woodford Green......................23 K3
Woodford Halse......................33 H4
Woodgate, W. Mids................32 B1
Woodgate, H. & W..................32 B3
Woodgate, W. Susx................14 C5
Woodgate, Norf......................46 F5
Wood Green, G. Lon...............23 J3
Woodhall..............................58 E1
Woodhall Spa........................55 F7
Woodham..............................22 F6
Woodham Ferrers...................24 D3
Woodham Mortimer................24 E2
Woodham Walter.....................24 E2
Woodhaven...........................89 G6
Woodhead.............................97 G2
Woodhill...............................31 J1
Woodhorn.............................75 J6
Woodhouse, S. Yks................53 G5
Woodhouse, Leic....................43 H5
Woodhouse Eaves...................43 H5
Woodhouselee.......................81 H5
Woodhurst.............................35 G2
Woodingdean.........................15 G5
Woodland, Devon.....................5 H3
Woodland, Durham..................65 H5
Woodlands, Dorset..................12 C5
Woodlands, Hants...................13 F4
Woodlands, Grampn................97 G6
Woodlands Park.....................22 D5
Woodlands St Mary.................21 H5
Wood Lanes..........................51 J5
Woodleigh..............................5 H5
Woodlesford..........................59 J8
Woodley................................22 C5
Woodmancote, W. Susx..........14 A5
Woodmancote, Glos................32 B7
Woodmancote, Glos................20 E2
Woodmancote, W. Susx..........15 F4
Woodmancott........................13 H1
Woodmansey.........................61 H7
Woodmansterne.....................23 H6
Woodminton...........................12 C3
Woodnesborough...................25 K7
Woodnewton..........................44 D7
Wood Norton.........................46 F4
Woodplumpton.......................57 J7
Woodrising...........................46 E6
Woodseaves, Shrops..............41 H3
Woodseaves, Staffs...............41 K4
Woodsend.............................21 G5
Woodsetts............................53 H5
Woodsford.............................11 J6
Woodside, Berks....................22 E5
Woodside, Tays.....................88 E5
Woodside, Herts....................23 H2
Woodstock............................21 J1
Wood Street..........................22 E7
Woodthorpe, Derby.................53 G6
Woodthorpe, Leic...................43 H5
Woodton...............................47 H7
Woodtown..............................8 E3
Woodville.............................43 F5
Woodwalton..........................35 F1
Woodyates............................12 C4
Woofferton...........................31 G3
Wookey................................11 G1
Wookey Hole.........................11 G1
Wool....................................11 K7
Woolacombe...........................8 E1
Woolage Green.......................17 K1

Woolaston.............................19 K3
Woolavington........................10 E1
Woolbeding...........................14 B3
Wooler.................................75 F2
Woolfardisworthy, Devon..........8 D3
Woolfardisworthy, Devon..........9 J5
Woolfords Cottages................80 F6
Woolhampton........................21 K6
Woolhope..............................31 H6
Woolland..............................11 J5
Woolley, Cambs.....................34 E2
Woolley, W. Yks....................53 F2
Woolmer Green......................23 H1
Woolpit................................36 E3
Woolscott.............................33 G3
Woolsington..........................75 H7
Woolstaston..........................41 F7
Woolsthorpe Belvoir...............44 B3
Woolston, Shrops...................40 E4
Woolston, Shrops...................31 F1
Woolston, Ches......................51 F5
Woolston, Hants....................13 G4
Woolston, Devon.....................5 H5
Woolstone, Bucks...................34 B6
Woolstone, Oxon....................21 G4
Woolston Green........................5 H3
Woolton................................50 D5
Woolton Hill.........................21 J6
Woolverstone.........................37 G6
Woolverton............................20 B7
Woolwich..............................23 K5
Woolwich Ferry......................23 K5
Woore..................................41 J2
Wooton, Staffs......................42 D2
Wootton, Northnts.................34 A4
Wootton, Beds.......................34 D5
Wootton, Humbs.....................54 E2
Wootton, Hants.....................12 E6
Wootton, Oxon......................21 J1
Wootton, Oxon......................21 J2
Wootton, Kent.......................17 K1
Wootton, Staffs.....................41 K4
Wootton Bassett....................20 E4
Wootton Bridge.....................13 H6
Wootton Common...................13 H6
Wootton Courtenay..................9 K1
Wootton Fitzpaine..................10 E6
Wootton Rivers......................21 F6
Wootton St Lawrence.............21 K7
Wootton Wawen.....................32 D3
Worcester............................32 A4
Worcester Park......................23 H6
Wordsley..............................32 A1
Worfield...............................41 J7
Workington............................62 E5
Worksop................................53 H6
Worlaby...............................54 E2
World's End...........................21 J5
Worle..................................19 H6
Worleston.............................41 H1
Worlingham..........................47 K8
Worlington, Cambs.................36 B2
Worlington, Devon....................9 H4
Worlingworth.........................37 H3
Wormbridge...........................31 F6
Wormegay.............................46 B5
Wormelow Tump....................31 F6
Wormersley...........................53 H2
Wormhill...............................52 D6
Wormiehills...........................89 J5
Wormingford.........................36 E6
Worminghall.........................22 B2
Wormington...........................32 C6
Worminster...........................11 G1
Wormit.................................89 F6
Wormleighton........................33 G4
Wormley...............................23 J2

Wormley West End................23 J2
Wormshill..............................24 E7
Wormsley.............................31 F5
Worplesdon...........................22 E7
Worrall................................53 F4
Worsbrough...........................53 F3
Worsley...............................51 G3
Worstead.............................47 J4
Worsthorne...........................58 D7
Worston...............................58 C6
Worth, W. Susx.....................15 F2
Worth, Kent..........................25 K7
Wortham..............................37 F2
Worthen...............................40 E6
Worthenbury..........................41 F2
Worthing, Norf......................46 E5
Worthing, W. Susx.................14 E5
Worthington...........................43 G4
Worth Matravers......................6 D7
Wortley.................................53 F4
Worton.................................20 D7
Wortwell..............................37 H1
Wotherton.............................40 D6
Wotter...................................4 F3
Wotton................................14 E1
Wotton-under-Edge................20 B3
Wotton Underwood.................22 B1
Woughton on the Green..........34 B6
Wouldham.............................24 D6
Wrabness.............................37 G6
Wrafton.................................8 E2
Wragby................................55 F6
Wramplingham......................47 G6
Wrangham.............................97 F2
Wrangle...............................45 H1
Wrangway.............................10 C4
Wrantage.............................10 E3
Wrawby.................................54 E3
Wraxall, Wilts.......................20 C6
Wraxall, Somer......................11 H2
Wraxall, Avon........................19 J5
Wray...................................57 K4
Wraysbury............................22 F5
Wrea Green...........................57 G7
Wreay, Cumbr........................64 B3
Wreay, Cumbr........................64 B5
Wrekenton.............................66 C2
Wrelton................................60 E2
Wrenbury.............................41 G2
Wreningham..........................47 G7
Wrentham.............................37 K1
Wressle................................60 E7
Wrestlingworth......................35 F5
Wretham...............................46 E7
Wretton................................46 B7
Wrexham...............................40 E1
Wribbenhall..........................31 J2
Wrightington Bar...................50 E2
Wrinehill...............................41 J2
Wrington................................19 J6
Writtle..................................24 C2
Wrockwardine.......................41 H5
Wroot.................................54 B3
Wrotham...............................24 C6
Wrotham Heath.....................24 C7
Wroughton............................21 F4
Wroxall, Warw......................32 E2
Wroxall, I. of W......................7 K7
Wroxeter..............................41 G6
Wroxham..............................47 J5
Wroxton...............................33 G5
Wyaston..............................42 D2
Wyberton.............................45 G2
Wyboston.............................34 E4
Wybunbury...........................41 H2
Wychbold.............................32 B3
Wych Cross..........................15 H2

Wyche.................................31 J5
Wyck..................................14 A2
Wyck Rissington....................32 D7
Wycombe Marsh....................22 D3
Wyddial...............................35 G6
Wye.....................................17 H1
Wyke, W. Yks.......................52 D1
Wyke, Shrops........................41 H6
Wyke, Dorset........................11 J3
Wykeham, N. Yks..................60 F3
Wykeham, N. Yks..................61 G2
Wyke Regis............................6 A7
Wyke, The...........................41 J6
Wykey.................................40 E4
Wylam.................................65 J1
Wylde Green.........................42 D7
Wylye..................................12 C2
Wymering.............................13 J5
Wymeswold..........................43 J4
Wymington...........................34 C3
Wymondham, Leic.................44 B5
Wymondham, Norf.................47 G6
Wyndham..............................18 D3
Wynford Eagle......................11 G6
Wyre Piddle..........................32 B5
Wysall................................43 J4
Wythall................................32 C2
Wytham...............................21 J2
Wyverstone...........................36 F3
Wyverstone Street.................36 F3

Y

Yaddlethorpe.........................54 C3
Yafford..................................7 J6
Yafforth................................59 J1
Yalding................................24 D7
Yanworth..............................20 E1
Yapham................................60 E5
Yapton.................................14 C5
Yarburgh..............................55 H4
Yarcombe.............................10 D5
Yardley................................32 D1
Yardley Gobion......................34 A5
Yardley Hastings....................34 B4
Yardro.................................30 D4
Yarkhill................................31 H5
Yarlet..................................42 B4
Yarlington............................11 H3
Yarm...................................66 E6
Yarmouth..............................13 F7
Yarnfield..............................42 A3
Yarnscombe............................9 F3
Yarnton................................21 J1
Yarpole................................31 F3
Yarrow................................73 J2
Yarrow Feus.........................73 J2
Yarsop.................................31 F5
Yarwell................................44 D7
Yate.....................................20 B4
Yateley.................................22 D6
Yatesbury.............................20 E5
Yattendon.............................21 K5
Yatton, H. & W......................31 F3
Yatton, Avon.........................19 J6
Yatton Keynell......................20 C5
Yaverland..............................13 J7
Yaxham................................46 F5
Yaxley, Cambs......................44 E7
Yaxley, Suff..........................37 G2
Yazor...................................30 F5
Yeading................................23 G4
Yeadon................................59 H6
Yealand Conyers....................57 J3
Yealand Redmayne................57 J3

Yealmpton..............................4 F4
Yearsley...............................60 C3
Yeaton.................................41 F5
Yeaveley..............................42 D2
Yedingham............................61 F3
Yelden.................................34 D3
Yelford.................................21 H2
Yelland..................................8 E2
Yelling.................................35 F3
Yelvertoft.............................33 H2
Yelverton, Devon.....................4 F3
Yelverton, Norf......................47 H6
Yenston...............................11 J3
Yeoford..................................9 H6
Yeolmbridge...........................8 D7
Yeo Mill.................................9 J3
Yeovil..................................11 G4
Yeovil Marsh.........................11 G4
Yeovilton.............................11 G3
Yerbeston............................26 E6
Yesnaby..............................112 C5
Yetlington............................75 G4
Yetminster...........................11 G4
Yettington............................10 B7
Yetts o' Muckhart..................80 F1
Y Fan...................................29 G1
Y Felinheli............................48 E4
Y Ffor..................................38 C3
Yieldshields..........................80 D6
Yiewsley...............................22 F4
Ynysboeth.............................18 E3
Ynysddu...............................19 F3
Ynyshir................................18 E3
Ynyslas................................38 F7
Ynysybwl.............................18 E3
Yockenthwaite.......................58 E3
Yockleton.............................40 F5
Yokefleet..............................54 C1
Yoker..................................79 H5
Yonder Bognie......................104 F4
York....................................60 D5
Yorkletts..............................25 G6
Yorkley................................19 L2
Yorton..................................41 G4
Youlgreave............................52 E7
Youlstone...............................8 C4
Youlthorpe.............................60 E5
Youlton................................60 B4
Young's End..........................24 D1
Yoxall.................................42 D1
Yoxford................................37 J3
Ysbyty Ifan...........................39 H2
Ysbyty Ystwyth.....................28 E2
Ysceifiog..............................50 A6
Ystalyfera.............................18 B2
Ystrad.................................18 D3
Ystrad Aeron.........................28 C4
Ystradfellte...........................18 D1
Ystradffin.............................28 E2
Ystradgynlais.........................18 B2
Ystradmeurig........................28 E3
Ystrad Mynach.......................18 F3
Ystradowen, Dyfed................18 B1
Ystradowen, S. Glam.............18 E5
Ythanbank............................97 J2
Ythanwells...........................97 F2
Ythsie.................................97 H2

Z

Zeal Monachorum.....................9 H5
Zeals..................................11 J2
Zelah....................................3 G4
Zennor...................................2 C6

M25 AND ROUTES INTO LONDON

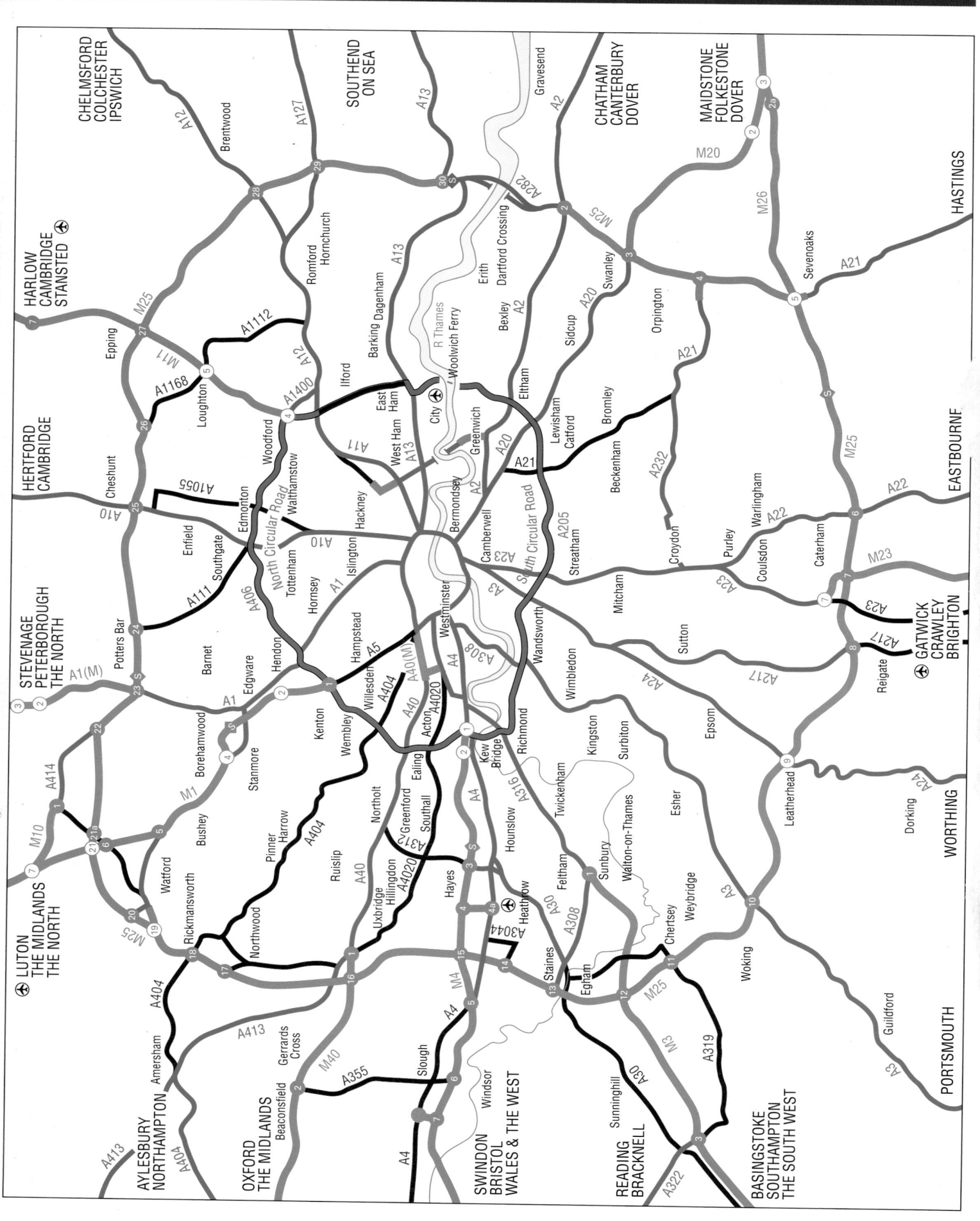